PENGUIN BOOKS

EQUIANO, THE AFRICAN

Vincent Carretta is a professor of English at the University
of Maryland. His books include scholarly editions of the
works of Equiano and of Equiano's contemporaries Ignatius
Sancho, Ottobah Cugoano, and Phillis Wheatley.

EQUIANO
THE AFRICAN

Biography of a Self-Made Man

VINCENT CARRETTA

PENGUIN BOOKS

PENGUIN BOOKS
Published by the Penguin Group
Penguin Group (USA) Inc., 375 Hudson Street, New York, New York 10014, U.S.A.
Penguin Group (Canada), 90 Eglinton Avenue East, Suite 700, Toronto,
Ontario, Canada M4P 2Y3 (a division of Pearson Penguin Canada Inc.)
Penguin Books Ltd, 80 Strand, London WC2R 0RL, England
Penguin Ireland, 25 St Stephen's Green, Dublin 2, Ireland (a division of Penguin Books Ltd)
Penguin Group (Australia), 250 Camberwell Road, Camberwell,
Victoria 3124, Australia (a division of Pearson Australia Group Pty Ltd)
Penguin Books India Pvt Ltd, 11 Community Centre, Panchsheel Park, New Delhi – 110 017, India
Penguin Group (NZ), cnr Airborne and Rosedale Roads, Albany,
Auckland 1310, New Zealand (a division of Pearson New Zealand Ltd)
Penguin Books (South Africa) (Pty) Ltd, 24 Sturdee Avenue,
Rosebank, Johannesburg 2196, South Africa

Penguin Books Ltd, Registered Offices:
80 Strand, London WC2R 0RL, England

First published in the United States of America by the University of Georgia Press 2005
Published in Penguin Books 2006

1 3 5 7 9 10 8 6 4 2

Map design by Deborah Reade

THE LIBRARY OF CONGRESS HAS CATALOGED THE HARDCOVER EDITION AS FOLLOWS:
Carretta, Vincent.
Equiano, the African : biography of a self-made man / Vincent Carretta.
p.   cm.
Includes bibliographical references and index.
ISBN 0-8203-2571-6 (hc.)
ISBN 978-0-14-303842-9 (pbk.)
1. Equiano, Olaudah, b. 1745.   2. Slaves–Great Britain–Biography.
3. Slaves–United States–Biography.   I. Title.
HT869.E6C37 2005
306.3'62'092–dc22   2005011989

Printed in the United States of America
Designed by Kathi Dailey Morgan
Set in Berthold Baskerville, Trajan, and Bickham Script

Frontispiece: Detail of the frontispiece from the first edition of volume 1 of Olaudah Equiano's
Interesting Narrative (London, 1789) (The John Carter Brown Library at Brown University)

PUBLICATION OF THIS BOOK WAS MADE POSSIBLE,

IN PART, BY A GENEROUS GIFT FROM

Anna, Adam, Lynne, and Steve Wrigley

Contents

Illustrations

FIGURES

MAPS

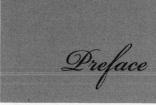

Preface

No one has a greater claim to being called a self-made man than the writer now best known as Olaudah Equiano. According to his autobiography, *The Interesting Narrative of the Life of Olaudah Equiano, or Gustavus Vassa, the African. Written by Himself* (London, 1789), Equiano was born in 1745 in what is now southeastern Nigeria. There, he says, he was enslaved at the age of eleven and sold to English slave traders, who took him on the Middle Passage to the West Indies. Within a few days, he tells us, he was taken to Virginia and sold to a local planter. After about a month in Virginia he was purchased by Michael Henry Pascal, an officer in the British Royal Navy who renamed him Gustavus Vassa and brought him to London. With Pascal, Equiano saw military action on both sides of the Atlantic Ocean during the Seven Years' War. In 1762, at the end of the conflict, Pascal shocked Equiano by refusing to free him, selling him instead to the West Indies. Escaping the horrors of slavery in the sugar islands, Equiano managed to save enough money to buy his own freedom in 1766. In Central America he helped purchase and supervised slaves on a plantation. Equiano set off on voyages of commerce and adventure to North America, the Mediterranean, the West Indies, and the North Pole. Equiano was now a man of the Atlantic. A close encounter with death during his Arctic voyage forced him to recognize that he might be doomed to eternal damnation. He resolved his spiritual crisis by embracing Methodism in 1774. Later he became an outspoken opponent of the slave trade, first in his letters to newspapers and then in his autobiography. In 1792 he married an Englishwoman, with whom he had two daughters. Thanks largely to profits from his publications, when Equiano died on 31 March 1797 he was probably the wealthiest and certainly the most famous person of African descent in the Atlantic world.

Over the past thirty-five years historians, literary critics, and the general public have come to recognize the author of *The Interesting Narrative* as one of the most accomplished English-speaking writers of his age and unquestionably the most accomplished author of African descent. Several modern editions of his autobiography are now available. The literary status of *The Interesting Narrative* has been acknowledged by its inclusion in the Penguin Classics series. It is universally accepted as the fundamental text in the genre of the slave narrative. Excerpts from the book appear in every anthology and on any Web site covering American, African American, British, and Caribbean history and literature of the eighteenth century. The most frequently excerpted sections are the early chapters on his life in Africa and his experience on the Middle Passage crossing the Atlantic to America. Indeed, it is difficult to think of any historical account of the Middle Passage that does not quote his eyewitness description of its horrors as primary evidence. Interest in Equiano has not been restricted to academia. He has been the subject of television shows, films, comic books, and books written for children. The story of Equiano's life is part of African, African American, Anglo-American, African British, and African Caribbean popular culture. Equiano is also the subject of a biography published in 1998 by James Walvin, an eminent historian of slavery and the slave trade.

These last thirty-five years have witnessed a renaissance of interest in Equiano's autobiography and its author. During Equiano's own lifetime *The Interesting Narrative* went through an impressive nine editions. Most books published during the eighteenth century never saw a second edition. A few more editions of his book appeared, in altered and often abridged form, during the twenty years after his death in 1797. Thereafter, he was briefly cited and sometimes quoted by British and American opponents of slavery throughout the first half of the nineteenth century. He was still well enough known publicly that he was identified in 1857 as "Gustavus Vassa the African" on the newly discovered gravestone of his only child who survived to adulthood. But after 1857 Equiano and his *Interesting Narrative* seem to have been forgotten on both sides of the Atlantic for more than a century. The declining interest in the author and his book is probably explained by the shift in emphasis from the abolition of the British-dominated transatlantic slave trade to the abolition of slavery, particularly in the United States, following the outlawing of the transatlantic trade in 1807.

The twentieth-century recovery of the man and his work began with the publication in 1969 by Paul Edwards of a facsimile edition of *The Interesting Narrative*. I have been teaching and researching Equiano since the early 1990s. I first saw his autobiography in a bookstore near the University of Maryland when I came across a copy of Henry Louis Gates Jr.'s then recently published anthology entitled *The Classic Slave Narratives*. It includes an 1814 edition of *The Interesting Narrative*. Although I had heard of Equiano before then, I had never seen a copy of his work, and from what I had read about it I assumed that it was a text more appropriate for American literature courses than for the British courses I was teaching at the time. Placing Equiano in the tradition of American autobiographical writing exemplified by Benjamin Franklin went unchallenged. They were both seen as self-made men who raised themselves by their own exertions from obscurity and poverty. No one thought to point out that since the publication in London of Equiano's autobiography preceded by decades that of Franklin's in the United States, rather than considering Equiano an African American Franklin we would more accurately call Franklin an Anglo-American Equiano.

Attempts to pin Equiano down to either an American or a British identity are doomed to failure. Once he was free, Equiano judged parts of North America reasonably nice places to visit, but he never revealed any interest in voluntarily living there. By Equiano's account, the amount of time he spent in North America during his life could be measured in months, not years. Whether he spent a few months, as he claims, or several years, as other evidence suggests, living in mainland North America, he spent far more time at sea. He spent at least ten years on the Atlantic Ocean and Mediterranean Sea during periods of war and peace between 1754 and 1785. The places he considered for a permanent home were Britain, Turkey, and Africa. Ultimately, he chose Britain, in part because Africa was denied him, despite his several attempts to get there. Truly a "citizen of the world" (337),[1] as he once called himself, Equiano was the epitome of what the historian Ira Berlin has called an "Atlantic creole":

> Along the periphery of the Atlantic – first in Africa, then in Europe, and finally in the Americas – [Anglophone African] society was a product of the momentous meeting of Africans and Europeans and of their equally fateful encounter with the peoples of the Americas. Although the countenances

of these new people of the Atlantic – Atlantic creoles – might bear the features of Africa, Europe, or the Americas in whole or in part, their beginnings, strictly speaking, were in none of those places. Instead, by their experiences and sometimes by their persons, they were part of the three worlds that came together along the Atlantic littoral. Familiar with the commerce of the Atlantic, fluent in its new languages, and intimate with its trade and cultures, they were cosmopolitan in the fullest sense.[2]

Preparing to teach *The Interesting Narrative* and later editing the text for Penguin Putnam, I began a series of discoveries that led to my decision to write a biography of its author. Like everyone else, I had assumed that only eight editions of *The Interesting Narrative* had appeared during the author's lifetime, the last in 1794. But I found that a ninth edition had also appeared in 1794 and, even more unexpectedly, that the University of Maryland owned one of only three copies of it then known to exist. (Another has subsequently turned up in Germany.) Many of those discoveries were ones I never expected, indeed, never wanted to make because they so profoundly challenged my sense of who Olaudah Equiano, or Gustavus Vassa, the African, was.

Recent biographical discoveries have cast doubt on Equiano's story of his birth and early years. The available evidence suggests that the author of *The Interesting Narrative* may have invented rather than reclaimed an African identity. If so, Equiano's literary achievements have been vastly underestimated. Baptismal and naval records say that he was born in South Carolina around 1747. If they are accurate, he invented his African childhood and his much-quoted account of the Middle Passage on a slave ship.[3] Other newly found evidence proves that Equiano first came to England years earlier than he says. He was clearly willing to manipulate at least some of the details of his life. Problematic as such evidence may be, any would-be biographer must now take it into account. Walvin observes that historians have a "predominant tendency . . . to quote Equiano as unproblematic."[4] But in his own biography of Equiano, which very usefully places *The Interesting Narrative* in its historical context, Walvin accepts the veracity of Equiano's own account of his life. Evidence not available to Walvin supplements as well as challenges Equiano's version of his own story.

Reasonable doubt raised by the recent biographical discoveries inclines me to believe that the accounts of Africa and the Middle Passage in *The Interesting Narrative* were constructed – and carefully so – rather than actually experienced and that the author probably invented an African identity. But we must remember that reasonable doubt is not the same as conviction. We will probably never know the truth about the author's birth and upbringing. The burden of proof, however, is now on those who believe that *The Interesting Narrative* is a historically accurate piece of nonfiction. Anyone who still contends that Equiano's account of the early years of his life is authentic is obligated to account for the powerful conflicting evidence.

Some of that evidence derives from Equiano's writings other than his autobiography. Commentators have largely overlooked his shorter published and unpublished works, many of which have only very recently been recovered. I have tried to take these writings into account wherever possible. I have also tried to deal with published and unpublished writings that were attributed to Equiano during his lifetime as well as writings that may have been his. One does not need to subject these writings to a computerized stylistic analysis to conclude that many of them differ substantially in content, style, syntax, vocabulary, and voice from *The Interesting Narrative.* If any of these other writings are indeed by Equiano, the differences between them and his known works may be explained by the widespread eighteenth-century assumption that a skillful rhetorician could speak or write in many voices and in various styles appropriate to different occasions and audiences. None of these other works differs as much from *The Interesting Narrative* as his autobiography differs from unpublished letters we know to be his. As far as I know, no one during Equiano's lifetime charged that the writer of his unpublished letters could not have written his autobiography, though some commentators suggested that others probably helped him polish its prose. And although the truthfulness of his account of his life was challenged, no one questioned whether he was the author of *The Interesting Narrative.* If nothing else, I hope that *Equiano, the African: Biography of a Self-Made Man* demonstrates how skillful a writer Equiano was.

Equiano's biographer faces many problems. First of all, by what name should he or she refer to the subject? The author of *The Interesting Narrative* was known by many names during his lifetime, two of which he includes in the title of his autobiography. I considered referring to him as Olaudah Equiano before he became the slave of Michael Henry Pascal in 1754; as Gustavus Vassa, the slave name Pascal gave him, from 1754 to 1788; and again as Olaudah Equiano from 1788 until his death in 1797, the period during which he publicly either reclaimed or assumed the identity of a native-born African. I decided against doing so to avoid confusing the reader. I also decided not to refer to him consistently by his less familiar name of Vassa, though that is the one he most often used. Outside of his autobiography, the author of *The Interesting Narrative* almost never called himself Equiano. He retained Gustavus Vassa as his legal name, and it appears on his baptismal, naval, and marriage records as well as in his will. In all his writings other than *The Interesting Narrative* he used Vassa in public and private. For the sake of simplicity I have chosen to call him Equiano throughout the following pages, using the name he is now best known by, much as a biographer of Samuel Langhorne Clemens might consistently refer to him by his pen name, Mark Twain.

The second major problem Equiano's biographer faces relates closely to the first: how to deal with Equiano's own, probably fictitious, accounts of his early years in Africa and his experience of the Middle Passage. Since Equiano's is the only story available for this period of his life, I have chosen to treat it in the following pages as if it were true, expecting readers to keep in mind that this part of his account of his life may be historical fiction rather than autobiography. Unlike the biographer of Franklin or Twain, the biographer of Equiano cannot check much of the information Equiano records about his early life against the historical record or external sources. Whether Equiano was born and raised in Africa, as he says, or in South Carolina, as other evidence suggests, he spent the first years of his life in a nonliterate society. On the other hand, once Equiano entered the literate society of the Royal Navy his account of his subsequent life is remarkably consistent with the historical record.

Equiano was certainly African by descent. The circumstantial evidence that Equiano was also African American by birth and African British by choice is compelling but not absolutely conclusive. Although the circumstantial evidence is not equivalent to proof, anyone dealing with Equiano's life and art must consider it. Supporting Equiano's claim of an African birth, Adam Hochschild argues, is "the long and fascinating history of autobiographies that distort or exaggerate the truth. . . . But in each of these cases, the lies and inventions pervade the entire book. Seldom is one crucial portion of a memoir totally fabricated and the remainder scrupulously accurate; among autobiographers, as with other writers, both dissemblers and truth-tellers tend to be consistent."[5] A writer as skillful and careful as Equiano, however, could have been one of the rare exceptions that Hochschild acknowledges exist. Equiano certainly knew that to do well financially by doing good for the abolitionist cause he needed to establish and maintain his credibility as an eyewitness to the evils of the transatlantic slave trade and slavery in its various eighteenth-century forms. He also knew what parts of his story could be corroborated by others and, more important if he was combining fiction with fact, what parts could not easily be contradicted.

Equiano's biographer has relatively little information about his personal life beyond what is found in *The Interesting Narrative*. Whether we believe Equiano's own account of his early years or the contradictory historical records, before the 1780s he was living in conditions that did not prompt others to record for posterity their interactions with him. Before the last decade of his life he lived in relative obscurity, whether enslaved or free. Even after 1787, when he became a public figure, his known correspondence consisted mostly of open letters and advertisements published in the London and provincial press. His very few remaining private letters are all quite brief and mainly deal with business matters.

In the sense of raising himself from poverty and obscurity, Equiano was a more self-made man than Franklin, and he was as successful during his lifetime as Franklin in marketing that image of himself. Through a combination of talent, opportunity, and determination Equiano became the first successful professional black writer. Franklin rose from poverty to prosperity; Equiano rose from being property in the eyes of the law to being the wealthiest person of African descent in Britain. Like Franklin, Equiano offered his own life as a model for others to follow. Equiano's personal conversions and transformations from enslaved to free, pagan to Christian, and proslavery to abolitionist anticipated the changes he hoped to make in his readers as well as the transformation he called for in the relationship between Britain and Africa.

The author of *The Interesting Narrative* was an even more profoundly self-made man than Franklin if he invented an identity to suit the times. Why might Equiano have created an African nativity and disguised an American birth? Before 1789 the abundant evidence and many arguments against the transatlantic slave trade came from white voices alone. Initially, opponents of the trade did not recognize the rhetorical power an authentic African voice could wield in the struggle. Equiano appreciated that "only something so particular as a single life . . . could capture the multiplicity of . . . lives" in the eighteenth-century Atlantic world.[6] Equiano knew that to continue its increasing momentum the anti-slave-trade movement needed precisely the kind of account of Africa and the Middle Passage that he, and perhaps only he, could supply. An African, not an African American, voice was what the abolitionist cause required. He gave a voice to the millions of people forcibly taken from Africa and brought to the Americas as slaves. Equiano recognized a way to do very well financially by doing a great deal of good in supplying that much-needed voice.

Equiano may have forged a part of his personal identity and created an Igbo national identity *avant la lettre* in order to enable himself to become an effective spokesman for his fellow diasporan Africans. As the Nigerian author Chinua Achebe has observed, the consciousness of the Igbo identity that Equiano asserts is a far more recent phenomenon:

> The duration of awareness, of consciousness of an identity, has really very little to do with how deep it is. You can suddenly become aware of an identity which you have been suffering from for a long time without knowing. For instance, take the Igbo people. In my area, historically, they did not see themselves as Igbo. They saw themselves as people from this village or that village. In fact in some places "Igbo" was a word of abuse; they were the "other" people, down in the bush. And yet, after the experience of the Biafran War, during a period of two [*sic*] years [1967–70], it became a very powerful consciousness. But it was *real* all the time. They all spoke the same language, called "Igbo," even though they were not using that identity in any way. But the moment came when this identity became very very powerful . . . and over a very short period.[7]

If Equiano forged both his personal and national African identities, he risked being exposed as an imposter, thus discrediting the abolitionist cause, but the financial and rhetorical success of his book demonstrated that it was a risk well worth taking.

Every autobiography is an act of re-creation, and autobiographers are not under oath when they are reconstructing their lives. Furthermore, an autobiography is an act of rhetoric. That is, any autobiography is designed to influence the reader's impression of its author and often, as in the case of *The Interesting Narrative*, to affect the reader's beliefs or actions as well. Looking backward, do autobiographers perceive or impose the order they shape and fashion from the mass of data available to them alone? Only in retrospect could Equiano say, "I regard myself as a *particular favourite of Heaven*, and acknowledge the mercies of Providence in every occurrence of my life" (31). Like any autobiographer, Equiano selected, emphasized, arranged, and deleted details of his life to present his readers with a flatteringly accurate *character* of himself: an integrated, essential *self* abstracted from the disparate and sometimes conflicting particular details. Whenever we say that someone "has character," is "acting out of character," or can offer a "character reference," we assume that people indeed have such essential *selves*. The biographer, too, must identify and represent his or her subject's *character*, which may or may not be consistent with an autobiographer's self-representation. The most constant quality of Equiano's *self* was his ability to transform himself, to redefine and refashion his identity in response to changing circumstances.

No autobiographer has faced a greater opportunity for redefinition than has a manumitted (freed) slave. Manumission necessitated redefinition. The profoundest possible transformation was the one any slave underwent when freed, moving from the legal status of property to that of person, from commodity to human being. Former slaves were also immediately compelled to redefine themselves by choosing a name. Even retention of a slave name was a choice. Choosing not to choose was not an option. With freedom came the obligation to forge a new identity, whether by creating one out of the personal qualities and opportunities at hand or by counterfeiting one. Equiano may have done both. In one sense, the world lay all before the former slave, who as property had been a person without a country or a legal personal identity. Equiano's restlessness and apparent wanderlust once he was free may have been the result of his quest for an identity and a place in the world.

As an "Atlantic creole" Equiano was ideally positioned to construct an identity for himself. He defined himself as much by movement as by place. Indeed, he spent as much of his life on the water as in any place on land. Even while he was a slave, the education and skills he acquired with the Royal Navy rendered him too valuable to be used for the dangerous and backbreaking labor most slaves endured. Service at sea on royal naval and commercial vessels gave him an extraordinary vantage point from which to observe the world around him. His social and geographical mobility exposed him to all kinds of people and levels of Atlantic society. The convincing account of Africa he offered to his readers may have been derived from the experiences of others he tells us he listened to during his many travels in the Caribbean, North America, and Britain. His genius lay in his ability to create and market a voice that for over two centuries has spoken for millions of his fellow diasporan Africans.

Equiano's voice is so distinctive that wherever possible in the following pages I have let him tell his own story of his "life and fortune" (236). Created or revealed, the various overlapping identities the author displays in *The Interesting Narrative* should warn us not to try to limit him to one nationality. A self-described "citizen of the world," Equiano was an "Atlantic creole" who throughout his life maintained an allegiance to the Africa of his ancestors. He speaks as powerfully now as he first did more than two centuries ago.

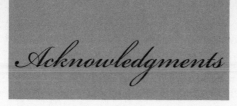

Acknowledgments

I am greatly indebted to the staffs and collections of the following institutions: the McKeldin Library of the University of Maryland; the John Carter Brown Library; the Folger Shakespeare Library; the Howard University Library; the Widener and Houghton Libraries at Harvard University; the British Library; the British Museum; the Public Record Offices (PRO) in Kew and London; Dr. Williams's Library, London; the Library of the Society of Friends House, London; the Family Records Centre, London; the Greater London Record Office; the Goldsmiths' Library of the University of London Library; the City of Westminster Libraries; the Guildhall Library of the City of London; the London Metropolitan Archives; the Rhodes House Library, Oxford; the Cambridgeshire County Record Office; the University of Glasgow Library; the Gloucestershire County Record Office; the Hornby Collection of the Liverpool Libraries and Information Services; the Shropshire County Record Office; the Worcestershire County Record Office; the Norfolk Record Office; the trustees of the Wedgwood Museum, Barlaston, Staffordshire; the Wisbech and Fenland Museum, Cambridgeshire; the Banks Archive Project (the Natural History Museum, London); the Church of Latter Day Saints' Family History Centers in Annandale and Falls Church, Virginia, and Princeton, New Jersey; the Van Pelt Library of the University of Pennsylvania; Princeton University Library; and the Library of Congress.

For advice, encouragement, and assistance in my research and writing

I thank William L. Andrews, John Barrell, Michael Benjamin, Ira Berlin, Christopher L. Brown, Alexander X. Byrd, Patricia Carretta, Neil Chambers, Malcolm Dick, Kenneth Donovan, Susan Essman, Henry Louis Gates Jr., Adam Hochschild, Derek Hyra, Mark Jones, Anthonia Kalu, George Karlsson, Reyahn King, Irving Lavin, Paul Magnuson, Joseph F. Marcey, Jr., Lynn Miller, Michael Millman, Philip D. Morgan, Ruth Paley, Stephen Price, N. A. M. Rodger, Nini Rodgers, Erin Sadlack, Philip Saunders, David Shields, J. V. Thorpe, Arthur Torrington, Pam and Joe Trickey, James Walvin, Iain Whyte, and David Worrall. Adam Hochschild very generously read and commented on an earlier version of my manuscript. I am also grateful to the anonymous readers for the University of Georgia Press for their comments and suggestions.

For generous financial support for the research and writing of this book I am very grateful to the University of Maryland; the National Endowment for the Humanities; the School of Historical Studies, Institute for Advanced Study, Princeton, New Jersey; and the W. E. B. Du Bois Institute for African and African American Research, Harvard University. I thank my dean, James Harris, and my department chair, Charles Caramello, for granting me leave to accept fellowships at the Institute for Advanced Study and the Du Bois Institute. One could not ask for better places to work.

My greatest debt is to Pat, my partner in life and research.

Note on Money

Before 1971, when the British monetary system was decimalized, British money was counted in pounds sterling (£), shillings (s.), pence or pennies (d.), and farthings. One pound sterling = 20 shillings; 5 shillings = 1 crown; 1 shilling = 12 pennies; 1 farthing = $^1/_4$ pence. One guinea = 21 shillings. (The coin was so named because the gold from which it was made came from the Guinea coast of Africa and because the coin was first struck to celebrate the founding in 1663 of the slave-trading monopoly known as the Royal Adventurers into Africa.)

Each British colony issued its own local paper currency. A colonial pound was worth less than a pound sterling, with the conversion rates for the currencies of the various colonies fluctuating throughout the century. Because of restrictions on the export of coins from England, the colonies relied on foreign coins, particularly Spanish, for local transactions. The basic Spanish denomination for silver coinage was the real ("royal"), with the peso (piece of 8 reales, or pieces of eight) known in British America as the dollar. Hence, 2 reales, or bits, became known as a quarter. Spanish reales were preferred as specie because their face value was equivalent to their intrinsic silver value. The Spanish pistareen, on the other hand, had a face value of 2 reales but an intrinsic value of only one fifth of a Spanish dollar. The Spanish doubloon was an 8-escudo gold coin worth, in 1759 pounds sterling, £3 6s. At the same time, a Spanish dollar was worth, in local currency, 7s. 6d. in Philadelphia and 8 shillings in New York. Conversion charts showing the value of foreign money in colonial currency and pounds sterling were frequently published through-out the eighteenth century. Also in circulation were coins like the copper ones paid to Equiano that lacked either face or intrinsic value.

To arrive at a rough modern equivalent of eighteenth-century money, multiply by about 80. In mid-eighteenth-century urban England a family of four could live modestly on £40 sterling a year, and a gentleman could support his standard of living on £300 sterling a year. A maid might be paid (in addition to room, board, cast-off clothes, and tips) around 6 guineas per year; a manservant, around £10 per year; and an able seaman, after deductions, received £14 12s. 6d. per year in addition to room and board. The price of a 4-pound loaf of bread ranged from 5.1 pence to 6.6 pence between 1750 and 1794, when Equiano was charging 5 shillings for a copy of *The Interesting Narrative*. Samuel Johnson left his black servant, Francis Barber, an annuity of £70 sterling a year; the Duchess of Montagu left her black butler, Ignatius Sancho, a sum of £70 sterling plus £30 sterling a year; Sancho's widow received more than £500 sterling from the sale of his *Letters*; and Equiano's daughter inherited £950 sterling from her father's estate.

BRITISH COINAGE

Guinea		Sterling (£)		Crown		Shilling (s.)		Pence/Pennies (d.)		Farthing		Modern Rough Equivalent
1	=					21						
$^{20}/_{21}$	=	1	=	4	=	20	=	240	=	960	=	£80
		$^1/_4$	=	1	=	5	=	60	=	240	=	£20
		$^1/_{20}$	=	$^1/_5$	=	1	=	12	=	48	=	£ 4
		$^1/_{240}$	=	$^1/_{60}$	=	$^1/_{12}$	=	1	=	4	=	£ $^1/_3$
		$^1/_{960}$	=	$^1/_{240}$	=	$^1/_{48}$	=	$^1/_4$	=	1	=	£ $^1/_{12}$

SPANISH COINAGE

Peso (Spanish dollar)		Pistareen (face value)		Pistareen (intrinsic value)		Real
1	=	4	=	5	=	8
$^1/_4$	=	1	=	$1^1/_4$	=	2
$^1/_5$	=	$^4/_5$	=	1	=	$1^3/_5$
$^1/_8$	=	$^1/_2$	=	$^5/_8$	=	1

The Atlantic Ocean (1766), by Thomas Jefferys. (Library of Congress)

EQUIANO
THE AFRICAN

Chapter One

EQUIANO'S AFRICA

In the spring of 1789 millions of enslaved Africans and their descendants were given a face, a name, and, most important, a voice. Until *The Interesting Narrative of the Life of Olaudah Equiano, or Gustavus Vassa, the African. Written by Himself* appeared three months before the beginning of the French Revolution, its author had publicly used only his legal name, Gustavus Vassa, the slave name he had been given thirty-five years earlier. He had, ironically, been named after Gustavus Vasa, the sixteenth-century Swedish monarch who had liberated his people from Danish tyranny. Readers familiar with Vassa from his publications in the *Public Advertiser*, the *Morning Chronicle*, and other newspapers during 1787 and 1788 knew him as a controversialist who firmly defended his personal reputation while opposing the transatlantic trade in enslaved Africans and the institution of slavery. Publishing his autobiography allowed him to address these issues with more subtlety and more authority and at greater length.[1] He could also reach a much wider audience than he could through newspapers and correspondence alone. Vassa had identified himself at various times in earlier writings as a "son of Africa," an "Ethiopian," and an "African." By the end of the eighteenth century, however, all those terms included people of African descent born outside of Africa as well as native-born Africans. Readers surprised to learn that Gustavus Vassa was also Olaudah Equiano, the African, would have been interested to know that his baptismal record in February 1759 as well as naval records in 1773 say that he was born in South Carolina.

The timing of the publication of *The Interesting Narrative* was no accident. Abolition of the slave trade had become a truly popular cause only since the mid-1780s, especially after the founding in London in 1787 of the Society for Effecting the Abolition of the Slave Trade. During the eighteenth century *abolition* almost always referred to eradication of the trade. The term rarely included the much smaller number of people openly calling for *emancipation*, eradication of the institution of slavery. Opponents of slavery became generally known as abolitionists only after the transatlantic slave trade became illegal in 1807. Responding to the growing public interest in abolition, in February 1788 King George III ordered the Privy Council Committee for Trade and Plantations to investigate British commercial relations with Africa and the nature of the slave trade. That summer Parliament passed, and the king gave the royal assent to, a law Sir William Dolben had proposed to regulate some of the conditions on overcrowded slave ships. During the following session of Parliament the House of Commons began to hear testimony on the slave trade. Much of the evidence dealt with conditions in Africa and during the Middle Passage, the trip across the Atlantic to the Americas endured by the enslaved Africans.

Arguments about the slave trade depended on or at least reflected arguments about Africa and Africans. Prior to the abolitionist debate over the slave trade, accounts of Africa often attempted to represent the complexity and variety of its peoples and societies. The earlier accounts cannot be called disinterested: the writers assumed that their readers shared their acceptance of the slave trade and slavery as economic necessities. But one rarely senses defensiveness in their descriptions, many of which are still relied on, although cautiously, by contemporary anthropologists and ethnographers. Once the slave-trade debate began in the 1780s, however, new descriptions of Africa and Africans were usually recognizably propagandistic and highly selective in the evidence they presented, with works opposing the trade outnumbering those supporting it.

Mainly through the efforts of the philanthropist Thomas Clarkson, the organized opposition to the African slave trade gathered and published evidence against the infamous practice from 1787 on. Before 1789, however, the evidence and arguments against the slave trade came from white voices alone. The only published black witnesses were clearly fictitious, found, for example, in the poems of Hannah More and William Cowper.[2] In *An Essay on the Slavery and Commerce of the Human Species* (London, 1786), Equiano's future subscriber Thomas Clarkson acknowledged the desirability of dramatizing the transatlantic slave trade by placing the trade in "the clearest, and most conspicuous point of view," the victim's. Employing the virtual reality of fiction to convey factual experience, he imagined himself interviewing a "melancholy African." "We shall," he wrote, "throw a considerable part of our information on this head into the form of a narrative: we shall suppose ourselves, in short, on the continent of Africa, and relate a scene, which, from its agreement with unquestionable facts, might not unreasonably be presumed to have been presented to our view, had we really been there."[3] Initially, not even black opponents of the trade recognized the rhetorical power an authentic African voice could wield in the struggle. When Equiano's friend, collaborator, and future subscriber Quobna Ottobah Cugoano published *Thoughts and Sentiments on the Evil and Wicked Traffic of the Slavery and Commerce of the Human Species* in London in 1787 he chose not to describe Africa or the Middle Passage in much detail. A member of the Fante people from the area of present-day Ghana who had been kidnapped into slavery around 1770, Cugoano believed that "it would be needless to give a description of all the horrible scenes which we saw, and the base treatment which we met with in this dreadful captive situation, as the similar cases of thousands, which suffer by this infernal traffic, are well known."[4]

Shortly after Gustavus Vassa started publishing letters in the London newspapers, he began to see the need for his autobiography as Olaudah Equiano. He had in the past occasionally been identified as having been born in Africa. In 1779 he described himself as "a native of Africa" in a letter he wrote to the bishop of London, and on 29 December 1786 the *Morning Herald* reported that he was "from Guinea." But the revelation that Gustavus Vassa was a native-born Igbo ("Eboe") originally named Olaudah Equiano appears to have evolved during 1788 in response to the needs of the abolitionist movement. In a book review in the *Public Advertiser* in February 1788 he noted that "were I to enumerate even my own sufferings in the West Indies, which perhaps I may one day offer to the public, the disgusting catalogue would be almost too great for belief" (331–32). Although he was clearly contemplating writing the story of his life to serve the abolitionist cause in 1788,

his testimony would be based on his experience in the West Indies. No mention was made of Africa. The next month he offered to testify before the
committee investigating the African slave trade, but when his offer was
not accepted, he submitted a written statement, dated 13 March, to Lord
Hawkesbury, president of the Board of Trade.[5] He also had it printed in the
Public Advertiser on 31 March. Neither time did he invoke personal experience to support his argument that "a commercial Intercourse with Africa
opens an inexhaustible Source of Wealth to the manufacturing Interest of
Great Britain; and to all which the Slave Trade is a physical Obstruction"
(335–36). Three months later he published an open letter addressed to the
members of the House of Commons, whose recent debate on the slave trade
he had attended. In the letter he expresses regret that he had not been given
"an opportunity of recounting to you not only my own sufferings, which,
though numerous, have been nearly forgotten, but those of which I have been
a witness for many years, that they might have influenced your decision." He
invokes, for the first time, a memory of Africa, but a memory very different in
detail and tone from what appears later in his *Interesting Narrative*. He tells the
legislators that "if it should please Providence to enable me to return to my estate in Elese, in Africa, and to be happy enough to see any of these worthy sen-
ators there . . . we will have such a libation of pure virgin palm-wine, as shall
make their hearts glad!!!" (339, 340). Equiano's 1788 image of Africa is quite
generalized, the only specific detail being an "estate in Elese" never mentioned in his subsequent autobiography.

Equiano knew that what the anti-slave-trade movement needed most in
1789 to continue increasing its momentum was precisely the kind of account
he supplied, a story that corroborated and even explicitly drew on earlier reports of Africa and the trade by some white observers and challenged those
of others. He also knew that two years earlier Cugoano had missed his
chance to give such an account. On 25 April 1789 Prime Minister William
Pitt presented before the House of Commons the published version of all the
testimony on the slave trade taken the preceding year, including Equiano's letter to Hawkesbury. Also on 25 April, just days before the publication of his *Interesting Narrative*, Equiano, along with Cugoano and several other people of
African descent, published a letter in the newspaper the *Diary; or Woodfall's
Register* thanking William Dickson for having just attacked the slave trade in
his *Letters on Slavery*. In the letter Vassa used the name Olaudah Equiano for
the first time in print. He and the distributor he shared with Dickson must
have been delighted with Dickson's observation that "no literary perform-

ance would be better received by the humane and liberal people of England, than a vindication of African capacity by the pen of an African." The stage was set for the story of Olaudah Equiano in his own words.

All that we know of Olaudah Equiano's existence in Africa comes from his own account, and that account was clearly intended to be part of the dialogue about the African slave trade. His representation of Igboland challenged images of Africa as a land of savagery, idolatry, cannibalism, indolence, and social disorder. Proponents of the slave trade argued that enslavement by Europeans saved Africans from such evils and introduced them to civilization, culture, industry, and Christianity. Climate, disease, population density, the relative lack of navigable harbors and rivers, native military and political power, and the absence of desired products other than slaves seemed to conspire to keep Europeans from penetrating the African hinterland. The number of books and periodical publications that treated Africa during the eighteenth century indicates a growing interest in the accounts of travelers to the continent, most of whom were associated with the slave trade.[6] But the rapidly increasing number of discussions of Africa, especially West Africa and its peoples, did not reflect an equivalent number of new sources. Later accounts copied, abridged, or otherwise adapted much of their material from the relatively few earlier narratives by individual travelers. These later versions appeared in expensive collections that were republished in enlarged editions throughout the century.[7] More modest collections of travelers' accounts and geographical surveys published from midcentury on reflected the widening audience for information on Africa.

Eighteenth-century Britons received very conflicting images of Africa. Philip Dormer Stanhope, fourth Earl of Chesterfield, conveyed a common negative view to his son in a geography lesson: "Africa is, as you know, divided into nine [sic] principal parts, which are Egypt, Barbary, Biledulgerid, Zaara, Nigritia, Guinea, Nubia, and Ethiopia. The Africans are the most ignorant and unpolished people in the world, little better than the lions, tigers and leopards and other wild beasts, which that country produces in great numbers. . . . The Africans that lie near the Mediterranean Sea sell their children for slaves to go to the West Indies; and likewise sell all those prisoners that they take in war. We buy a great many of them to sell again to advantage in the West Indies."[8] As sophisticated and well educated as Chesterfield was, he clearly felt no compunction about conflating vastly different sections of a large continent to discuss an imaginary "country" called Africa. Another teacher might have chosen the positive image of Africa that Michel Adanson offers in his *Voyage*

to Senegal: "Which way soever I turned my eyes on this pleasant spot, I beheld a perfect image of pure nature: an agreeable solitude, bounded on every side by a charming landskip."[9] Adanson's passage was frequently used in anti-slave-trade writings such as Thomas Day and John Bicknell's *The Dying Negro* (London, 1773), a poem Equiano quotes at length in his *Interesting Narrative*. Anthony Benezet, a Philadelphia Quaker, gave readers on both sides of the Atlantic affordable access to excerpts and abridgements of favorable comments on Africa and Africans by the many writers collected in his works.[10] Benezet's *Some Historical Account of Guinea* supplied Clarkson with much of the information in his *Essay*, and Equiano cites and quotes Benezet in his autobiography.

Although Africa was one of the "Old World" continents known to Europeans for centuries, the parts they were most familiar with were the countries of northern Africa. Sub-Saharan Africa remained almost as unexplored by Europeans in the eighteenth century as the recently discovered continent of

Australia. The slave-trade debate reminded the public how little they understood about much of Africa and its peoples. Motivated by a desire to collect
unbiased information about the flora, fauna, and cultures of the continent, on
9 June 1788 Sir Joseph Banks and others who shared his interests in science
formed the Association for Promoting the Discovery of the Interior Parts of
Africa, commonly known as the African Association. Equiano and Cugoano
were among the earliest men to volunteer to be sent to Africa under the aus-
pices of the association. The British public were clearly hungry for news about
the "dark" continent.

Equiano's "imperfect sketch my memory has furnished me with of the
manners and customs of a people among whom I first drew my breath" (43)
combines personal recollection, cited authorities, unacknowledged accounts
by others, and information gained from some of the "numbers of the natives
of Eboe" (38) he encountered in London. Given the number and variety of his
sources, we may reasonably ask whether Equiano was experiencing recovered memory or the power of suggestion as he constructed his autobiography.
A combination of personal experience, conflated sources, recovered memory,
and the power of suggestion should not be surprising in a work that may be as
much the biography of a people as it is the autobiography of an individual.
Even the strongest believers in the truthfulness of Equiano's account of Africa
acknowledge that "it is impossible to locate Equiano's birthplace, Essaka, with
any great precision, and suggestions have been made placing it to both east
and west of the Niger."[11] Referring to Equiano's "half-remembered African
childhood," the Nobel prize–winning novelist and critic Chinua Achebe admits that by the time Equiano wrote his *Interesting Narrative* "his ancestral Igboland had become a fragmented memory."[12]

Most of the "sketch" of life in Africa occurs in the first chapter of Equiano's
Interesting Narrative, which includes by far more footnotes than any other chapter in his autobiography. Some of the notes provide sources for information unavailable to any individual in Africa such as the extent of the kingdom of
Benin; others corroborate or illustrate evidence found elsewhere; and others
give sources for information unknowable by a child, such as customs only
adults would have practiced. Since, he tells us, he lived in Africa only until he
"turned the age of eleven," Equiano was well aware that his readers might need
some reassurance about the accuracy of his account:

> I hope the reader will not think I have trespassed on his patience in
> introducing myself to him with some account of the manners and customs
> of my country. They had been implanted in me with great care, and made

an impression on my mind, which time could not erase, and which all the adversity and variety of fortune I have since experienced served only to rivet and record: for, whether the love of one's country be real or imaginary, or a lesson of reason, or an instinct of nature, I still look back with pleasure on the first scenes of my life, though that pleasure has been for the most part mingled with sorrow. (46)

Equiano's more skeptical readers would have felt an even greater need for reassurance had they known that external evidence in baptismal and naval records indicates that he was born in America rather than Africa and that meteorological, naval, and newspaper records show he could not have been eleven years old, as he says, when he claims to have been kidnapped in Africa. He first reached England in mid-December 1754, not, as he says, "about the beginning of the spring 1757" (67).[13] Taking into consideration the approximately fourteen months that he tells us passed between the time he was kidnapped in Africa and when he was brought to England, he would have been only about seven or eight years old when he was first abducted. He certainly sounds younger than eleven years old when we first encounter him in Africa.

Whether we consider Equiano's account of Africa as historical fiction or as straightforward autobiography, much of its power derives from the innocent child's voice heard by the reader. Equiano assumed that his readers would make allowances for the romanticized recollection of childhood he offered them. He also knew that his readers would be repelled by the violent disruption of that innocent past. And whether his tale was fiction or truth, it is easy to imagine why emotionally he may have needed to tell such a story. Enslavement, whether initially in Africa or South Carolina, had severed his African roots, effectively denying him a past outside of slavery. Creating or re-creating an African past allowed him to forge a personal and national identity other than the one imposed on him by Europeans. Writing his autobiography gave him the chance to publicly remake himself. One of Equiano's goals in his *Interesting Narrative* was to demonstrate that his success was deserved and achieved.

Equiano describes himself as an exceptional child, destined for greatness in the paradise that was about to be lost to him. Equiano's "father, besides many slaves, had a numerous family, of which seven lived to grow up, including myself and a sister, who was the only daughter. As I was the youngest of the sons, I became, of course, the greatest favourite with my mother, and was always with her; and she used to take particular pains to form my mind. I was trained up from my earliest years in the arts of agriculture and war: my daily exercise was shooting and throwing javelins; and my mother adorned me with emblems, after the manner of our greatest warriors" (46). Like the enslaved African royalty who appear so often in fictional accounts of the slave trade, Equiano represents himself as having had an exalted status in "Eboe": "Those children whom our wise men foretell will be fortunate are then presented to different people. I remember many used to come to see me, and I was carried about to others for that purpose. . . . Our children were named from some event, some circumstance, or fancied foreboding at the time of their birth. I was named *Olaudah*, which, in our language, signifies vicissitude, or fortunate also; one favoured, and having a loud voice and well spoken" (41). He says nothing about the significance of the name Equiano, which modern scholars have very plausibly suggested may be a version of Ekwuno, Ekwuano, or Ekweano.[14]

"As far as [Equiano's] slender memory extended," in the quasi autonomy that was typical of Igbo villages in Benin, "every transaction of the government . . . was conducted by the chiefs or elders of the place" (32). Equiano's unnamed father "was one of those elders or chiefs . . . styled Embrenché; a term . . . importing the highest distinction, and signifying in our language a mark of grandeur" (32). As one of the "Embrenché," or Mgburichi ("men who bear such marks"), who "decided disputes and punished crimes" (33), he had undergone facial cicatrisation or scarification "conferred on the person entitled to it, by cutting the skin across at the top of the forehead, and drawing it down to the eye-brows; and, while it is in this situation, applying a warm hand, and rubbing it until it shrinks up into a thick *weal* across the lower part of the forehead" (32–33). Equiano was "*destined* to receive [the same mark]" (33). The Embrenché administered "the law of retaliation" as swiftly as Old Testament patriarchs, and justice was fair, without preferential treatment for rank or status: "I remember a man was brought before my father, and the other judges, for kidnapping a boy; and, although he was the son of a chief or senator, he was condemned to make recompense by a man or woman slave" (33). For more than one modern critic, "the few words of his native language recorded in the *Narrative* leave no doubt that Equiano was an Ibo. . . . The word 'Embrenché' . . . is the modern *mgburichi*, the name given to those who either receive or make the *ichi* facial scars, the mark of a titled man. The word is recorded by other early writers."[15] One could argue, however, that the possible Igbo words Equiano uses are so few (fewer than ten) that he could easily have learned them outside of Africa.

Though destined for distinction in Africa, the child Equiano shows us was unusually sensitive and vulnerable so much so, in fact, that were he

actually as old as eleven he would probably strike most readers as quite im-
mature. He tells us that he was "always" with his mother, even when he
should not have been: "Every woman too, at certain times [during menstru-
ation], was forbidden to come into a dwelling-house, or touch any person, or
any thing we ate. I was so fond of my mother I could not keep from her, or
avoid touching her at some of those periods, in consequence of which I was
obliged to be kept out with her, in a little house made for that purpose, till offering was made, and then we were purified" (42). The African boy was father to the author Equiano in that both were exceptional individuals ideally
located emotionally, intellectually, and socially to observe and judge the societies in which they found themselves. Like the man, the boy was extraordinary by nature and situation.

Equiano's description of his African life offers us a fascinating ethnographic record of eighteenth-century Igbo culture. He tells us that he was
born in 1745 in "that part of Africa, known by the name of Guinea, to which
the trade for slaves is carried on." His certainty about the date of his birth un-
dermines rather than inspires confidence in his account because no record of
his birth would have existed. Of the many kingdoms between Senegal and
Angola, "the most considerable is the kingdom of Benin, both as to extent
and wealth, the richness and cultivation of the soil, the power of its king, and
the number and warlike disposition of the inhabitants." Benin "extends along
the coast about 170 miles, but runs back into the interior part of Africa to a
distance hitherto I believe unexplored by any traveller; and seems only terminated at length by the empire of Abyssinia, near 1500 miles from its beginning." Of the "many provinces or districts" Benin comprises, Equiano's
homeland is "one of the most remote and fertile . . . called Eboe . . . in a
charming fruitful vale, named Essaka." "Eboe" is so far inland that Equiano
"had never heard of white men or Europeans, nor of the sea," and it was
typical of the loosely organized confederation of quasi-autonomous political
units that constituted the eighteenth-century empire of Benin: its "subjection
to the king of Benin was little more than nominal" (32).

In Igbo society wives convicted of adultery were punished with "slavery
or death" (33). Justice, however, could be tempered with mercy: "A woman
was convicted before the judges of adultery, and delivered over, as the custom
was, to her husband to be punished. Accordingly he determined to put her to
death: but it being found, just before her execution, that she had an infant at
her breast; and no woman being prevailed on to perform the part of a nurse,
she was spared on account of the child." Husbands, however, "do not preserve

the same constancy to their wives, which they expect from them; for they indulge in a plurality, though seldom in more than two." Couples are usually betrothed as children by their parents, though males can betroth themselves. The betrothal is announced publicly at a feast so that no one else will court the girl. Later, at another feast at the home of the groom, the bride's parents "deliver her to the bridegroom" (33) and "tie round her waist a cotton string of the thickness of a goose-quill, which none but married women are permitted to wear." The couple's friends give them a dowry, "which generally consists of portions of land, slaves, and cattle, household goods, and implements of husbandry." The husband's dominant role is not surprising, given that "the parents of the bridegroom present gifts to those of the bride, whose property she is looked upon before marriage; but after it she is esteemed the sole property of her husband" (34). As "head of the family" the husband "usually eats alone," the women, children, and slaves sitting apart (35).

Like other public events, marriages were celebrated with music and dancing. "Eboe" is "almost a nation of dancers, musicians, and poets" (34), a characterization surprising only because of the addition of "poets," an addition that challenged Equiano's readers' belief that only preliterate Homeric Greece and Celtic Britain had been nations of poets. In Equiano's description, the poetry of "Eboe" consists of theatrical dances accompanied by a variety of instruments:

> Every great event, such as a triumphant return from battle, or other cause of public rejoicing, is celebrated in public dances, which are accompanied with songs and music suited to the occasion. The assembly is separated into four divisions, which dance either apart or in succession, and each with a character peculiar to itself. The first division contains the married men, who in their dances frequently exhibit feats of arms, and the representation of a battle. To these succeed the married women, who dance in the second division. The young men occupy the third; and the maidens the fourth. Each represents some interesting scene of real life, such as a great achievement, domestic employment, a pathetic story, or some rural sport; and as the subject is generally founded on some recent event, it is therefore ever new. This gives our dances a spirit and variety which I have scarcely seen elsewhere. (34)[16]

The people of "Eboe," Equiano recalls, are monotheists who have an underdeveloped conception of spirituality and eternity:

The natives believe that there is one Creator of all things, and that he lives
in the sun, and is girded round with a belt, that he may never eat or drink;
but, according to some, he smokes a pipe, which is our own favourite luxury. They believe he governs events, especially our deaths or captivity;
but, as for the doctrine of eternity, I do not remember to have ever heard
of it: some however believe in the transmigration of souls in a certain degree. Those spirits, which are not transmigrated, such as our dear friends
or relations, they believe always attend them, and guard them from the
bad spirits of their foes. (40)

Although there were no "places of public worship, we had priests and
magicians, or wise men," who "were also our doctors or physicians." The
people revered them because they "had . . . some extraordinary method of
discovering jealousy, theft, and poisoning." They also "calculated our time,
and foretold events, as their name imported, for we called them Ah-affoe-
way-cah, which signifies calculators, or yearly men, our year being called Ah-
affoe" (42).[17]

Many of the religious practices and beliefs in "Eboe" were similar to
those found in the Old Testament: "We practised circumcision like the Jews,
and made offering and feasts on that occasion in the same manner as
they did." Cleanliness was "a part of religion, and therefore we had many pu-
rifications and washings; indeed almost as many, and used on the same occasions, if my recollection does not fail me, as the Jews." And an equivalent of
the commandment against using the Lord's name in vain was observed: "I
remember we never polluted the name of the object of our adoration; on the
contrary, it was always mentioned with the greatest reverence; and we were
totally unacquainted with swearing, and all those terms of abuse and reproach which find the way so readily and copiously into the languages of
more civilized people" (41).

Because the economy of "Eboe" is agricultural and largely self-sufficient
rather than commercial and dependent on trade with outsiders, Equiano's
village is a microcosm of the whole kingdom: "The manners and government of a people who have little commerce with other countries are generally very simple; and the history of what passes in one family or village may
serve as a specimen of the whole nation" (32). "Uncommonly rich and
fruitful," his "Eboe" produces "all kinds of vegetables in great abundance."
There is "plenty of Indian corn, and vast quantities of cotton and tobacco" as
well as "honey in abundance" and "a variety of delicious fruits . . . never seen
in Europe; together with gums of various kinds." Since "agriculture is our

chief employment" and "all our industry is exerted to improve those blessings of nature . . . , we are all habituated to labour from our earliest years"
(37). Consequently, "as our manners are simple, our luxuries are few," and
"our manner of living is entirely plain; for as yet the natives are unacquainted
with those refinements in cookery which debauch the taste" (34, 35). Their
food consists of bullocks, goats, and poultry, seasoned with "pepper, and
other spices" as well as "salt made from wood ashes." Their principal vegetables are "plantains, eadas [an edible tuberous plant], yams, beans, and Indian
corn." Livestock "constitute likewise the principal wealth of the country, and
the chief articles of its commerce." Equiano comes from an abstemious culture in which "cleanliness on all occasions is extreme" and that is "totally unacquainted with strong or spirituous liquors," with the exception of palm
wine. Their "principal luxury" is perfume (35). Everyone "contributes something to the common stock; and as we are unacquainted with idleness, we
have no beggars" (38).

The benefits of such a combination of temperate living and healthy exercise are obvious:

> The West-India planters prefer the slaves of Benin or Eboe to those of any
> other part of Guinea, for their hardiness, intelligence, integrity, and zeal.
> Those benefits are felt by us in the general healthiness of the people, and
> in their vigour and activity; I might have added too in their comeliness.
> Deformity is indeed unknown amongst us, I mean that of shape. . . . Our
> women too were, in my eyes at least, uncommonly graceful, alert, and
> modest to a degree of bashfulness; nor do I remember to have ever heard
> of an instance of incontinence amongst them before marriage. They are
> also remarkably cheerful. Indeed cheerfulness and affability are two of
> the leading characteristics of our nation. (38)

In its simplicity, "Eboe" architecture reflects the people's basic values of
hospitality and independence: "In our buildings we study convenience
rather than ornaments" for both the owners and "to accommodate strangers"
(36). Their houses, which "never exceed one story," are "so constructed and
furnished" that they "require but little skill to erect them." Independence is
tempered by communal cooperation: "Every man is a sufficient architect for
the purpose. The whole neighbourhood afford their unanimous assistance
in building them, and, in return, receive and expect no other recompense
than a feast." If a man's family members and slaves are sufficiently numerous, his dwellings "present the appearance of a village" (36). All adults

share responsibility for defending the village they have built together: "All are taught the use of the weapons. Even our women are warriors, and march boldly out to fight along with the men. Our whole district is a kind of militia" (39). The image of a militia as the first line of domestic defense was reassuring to Equiano's readers who shared the widespread British distrust of a professional standing army.

Equiano's depiction of his "uncommonly rich and fruitful" "Essaka" in "Eboe" is reminiscent of the nostalgic image of a romanticized rural English village offered by Oliver Goldsmith in his poem *The Deserted Village* (1770). Unlike Goldsmith's formerly self-sufficient village, now depopulated and destroyed by the evils of commerce and luxury, however, Equiano's "Essaka" remains largely unaffected by contact with the outside world (37). Hence, at least in Equiano's memory, "Essaka" continues to exist in the present tense, unchanged by commercial development. "In such a state money is of little use," though some coins are in circulation. The Igbo manufacture a few goods, but only for domestic consumption: "calicoes, earthen ware, ornaments, and instruments of war and husbandry." Agricultural products are exchanged at markets for "fire-arms, gun-powder, hats, beads, and dried fish" brought by "stout [strong, powerful], mahogany-coloured men from the south west of us: we call them *Oye-Eboe*, which term signifies red men living at a distance." Although "*Oye-Eboe*" may be a version of the Igbo word *oyibo* used in the nineteenth century to mean "white man," Equiano clearly uses it to refer to other Africans, perhaps the Aro slave traders. At this point in his life, he tells us, he had not yet seen or even heard of a European.[18]

What little commerce "Eboe" has with the outside world comes with a significant price, however. The "*Oye-Eboe*" linked "Eboe" and the transatlantic slave trade:

They always carry slaves through our land; but the strictest account is exacted of their manner of procuring them before they are suffered to pass. Sometimes indeed we sold slaves to them, but they were only prisoners of war, or such among us as had been convicted of kidnapping, or adultery, and some other crimes which we esteemed heinous. This practice of kidnapping induces me to think, that, notwithstanding all our strictness, their principal business among us was to trepan [ensnare, trap] our people. I remember too they carried great sacks along with them, which, not long after, I had an opportunity of fatally seeing applied to that infamous purpose. (37)

Equiano certainly does not avoid the problem of African complicity in the transatlantic slave trade, but he distinguishes carefully between the causes and consequences of domestic African slavery and the chattel slavery Europeans practiced. The transatlantic trader – Equiano's ironic "enlightened merchant" – exploits the military expertise of African men and women:

> From what I can recollect of these battles, they appear to have been irruptions of one little state or district on the other, to obtain prisoners or booty. Perhaps they were incited to this by those traders who brought the European goods I mentioned amongst us. Such mode of obtaining slaves in Africa is common; and I believe more are procured this way, and by kidnapping, than any other.[19] When a trader wants slaves, he applies to a chief for them, and tempts him with his wares. It is not extraordinary, if on this occasion he yields to the temptation with as little firmness, and accepts the price of his fellow creature's liberty with as little reluctance, as the enlightened merchant. (38–39)

Within "Eboe" society itself slaves are virtually part of the family:

> Those prisoners which were not sold or redeemed we kept as slaves: but how different was their condition from that of the slaves in the West-Indies! With us they do no more work than other members of the community, even their master. Their food, cloathing, and lodging were nearly the same as theirs, except that they were not permitted to eat with those who were free born and there was scarce any other difference between them, than a superior degree of importance which the head of a family possesses in our state, and that authority which, as such, he exercises over every part of his household. Some of these slaves have even slaves under them, as their own property, and for their own use. (39–40)

Equiano's readers recognized the significance of his account of an African birth and the emotional appeal of his reported kidnapping. In the third stanza of his poem "On the African Slave-Trade" the provincial English preacher Joshua Peel appended the footnote "See the Life of Olaudah Equiano (afterwards called *Gustavus Vassa*), written by himself" to the lines

> Infants are stole, and from their parents torn,
> As if for wo[e] the innocent was born:

> Young boys and girls, when at their homes at play,
> Are also caught, and kidnapp'd far away.[20]

The transatlantic slave trade introduced young Equiano to a very different system of slavery, rendering his account of an idyllic Igbo life at best a memory retrievable only with the help of others.

Chapter Two

THE MIDDLE PASSAGE

According to *The Interesting Narrative*, Equiano's world came to an abrupt end around 1753. He would have been about seven or eight years old. Equiano knew that African slave dealers took "opportunities of our parents' absence, to attack and carry off as many as they could seize" (47). He once saved some of his comrades from enslavement by sounding the alarm when he saw from his perch in a tree a man attempt to kidnap them. But soon thereafter, when his unnamed "dear sister" and he "were left to mind the house, two men and a woman got over our walls, and in a moment seized us both" (47). He explains neither why he was not working with the other boys and men if he was indeed "turned the age of eleven" (46), as he claims, nor why he and his sister were unattended if he was several years younger. This was to be the first of a series of separations Equiano and his sister were to suffer. The two small children had begun the first stage of the forced journey on land and sea that constituted what, in 1784, Equiano's friend James Ramsay called the "Middle Passage" from freedom in Africa to enslavement in the Americas.[1] Others have used the phrase to refer to the slave trade as the second of three passages in the triangular trade linking Europe, Africa, and the Americas. The first passage brought textiles, alcohol, manufactured goods, firearms and gunpowder, tobacco, and metal to Africa; the second, or middle, brought enslaved Africans across the Atlantic; and the third passage returned to Europe bearing colonial agricultural products. Recent research, however, questions the economic significance of the third passage in the triangle. Most of the vessels used in the slave trade were smaller than those used to bring commodities directly from America to Europe, and slave ships often returned to Europe without cargoes.[2] Although the phrase *Middle Passage* conventionally refers only to the Atlantic crossing from Africa to the Americas, I use the phrase to comprise the whole period from initial enslavement in Africa to the period of so-called seasoning in the Americas.[3]

Equiano and his sister were about to become victims of the largest forced migration in history – the African diaspora of the transatlantic slave trade. To most Europeans and Euro-Americans the slave trade was a necessary part of the economic system that provided pleasures of life such as sugar and tobacco. Sugar in particular was difficult, dangerous, and expensive to grow, harvest, and process, making coerced labor economically more attractive to planters than paid labor. Throughout the eighteenth century slaves were imported directly to the colonies from Africa. Between 1492 and around 1870 Christian traders enslaved more than twelve million Africans to be sent to the Americas. About eleven million actually departed. Between the Middle Ages and the end of the twentieth century Islamic traders enslaved approximately another twelve million Africans, sending them across the Sahara Desert, Red Sea, and Pacific Ocean to eastern markets.[4] Over six million enslaved Africans arrived in the Americas between 1700 and the legal suppression of the transatlantic slave trade in 1808. Most of the Africans were taken to the European colonies in the Caribbean and South America. About 29 percent of the total number brought to the Americas went to the British colonies. Before 1808 perhaps fewer than four hundred thousand enslaved Africans were brought to British North America, where they maintained a positive rate of growth from the eighteenth century on. The vast majority of Britain's slaves, more than four out of five, were destined for the West Indies.[5]

In terms of both the African slave trade and economic value, compared to the West Indian plantations the North American colonies were of relatively marginal significance to Britain during the eighteenth century. On the eve of the American Revolution, of the total population of five hundred thousand people throughout the British West Indies, more than 90 percent were of African descent. Jamaica was by far the most populous, with about three hundred thousand people; Barbados had one hundred thousand. By comparison, at midcentury, of the approximately two million people in the North American colonies that would become the United States, overall about 20 percent were of African descent, but within those colonies the rate ranged from 2 percent in Massachusetts to 60 percent in South Carolina. Blacks composed 44 percent of the population of Virginia, 20 percent of Georgia, and 2.4 percent of Pennsylvania. In England, with around 6.5 million people in 1771, the five to twenty thousand blacks made up less than 0.2 percent of the total population and were concentrated in the slave-trading ports of Bristol, Liverpool, and especially London.

The number of Africans annually forced across the Atlantic reached around sixty thousand between 1740 and 1760 and peaked during the 1780s at about eighty thousand, more than half of them on British ships based in Bristol, Liverpool, and London. Enslaved Africans outnumbered European immigrants to the Americas by a ratio of more than three to one before the nineteenth century.[6] But because of the brutal working conditions in the most valuable British colonial possessions, enslaved Africans had a much higher mortality rate than European immigrants. The high death rate, combined with the age and gender imbalance of the overwhelmingly male imported slaves, led to the negative growth rate of the overall West Indian slave population. Without the continuous importation of enslaved Africans, the Caribbean slave population would have declined by between 2 and 4 percent annually.

Extraordinarily high mortality rates affected the European slave traders as well as the African slaves. Diseases like malaria and yellow fever and the existence of powerful African political and military coastal states restricted Europeans to factories (trading posts) on the coast of Africa or to their slave ships "coasting" offshore, dependent on Africans for the maintenance of the slave trade. Nearly half of the deaths of crew members of slave ships occurred while they waited offshore in the hostile disease environment to collect their human cargoes. Approximately 50 percent of the Europeans who went ashore in Africa died from disease. Perhaps a million of the enslaved people died before they left Africa. They perished from abuse, disease, exhaustion, and depression on their way from the African interior to the Atlantic coast or while waiting aboard ships as the European slave traders completed their human cargoes. About an equal number died from the same causes as well as from suicide, rebellions, and shipwreck during the portion of the Middle Passage between the African and American coasts. And as many as one third of the imported slaves may have died during seasoning, the period of a few months after arriving in the New World during which the enslaved Africans were supposed to become acclimated to the alien diseases and harsh social environments of the Americas.[7]

Without the complicity of other Africans, very few black slaves could have been exported to the Americas. Traditionally, societies that practice slavery enslave outsiders. For example, ancient Hebrews and eighteenth-century Muslims reserved the condition of chattel slavery for unbelievers. Defenders of slavery could cite, for example, Leviticus 25:39–46 to justify their enslavement of outsiders. Europeans were able to exploit this tradition of enslaving those perceived as outsiders, aliens, or strangers in Africa because the concept of *Africa* was mainly geographic, not also social, political, and religious to the extent that the concept of *Europe* had become by the eighteenth century. Nor was the notion of *nation* or *state* equivalent in the two continents. The indigenous peoples of Africa did not think of themselves as *African*: they were Ashanti, Fante, Yoruba, or any one of a number of other ethnic groups with differing languages, religions, and political systems. Tending to see themselves as more dissimilar than alike, the various African peoples were willing to enslave and sell to Europeans those outside their own group because they did not identify with them. Only toward the end of the eighteenth century did some of the people removed from Africa as slaves begin to embrace a diasporan public social and political identity of *African*, calling themselves "Sons of Africa" in both Britain and America, for example. In a sense, *Africa* did not exist as an idea as well as a place until after the anti-slave-trade and antislavery movements began.

Before the last quarter of the eighteenth century most Britons accepted slavery as one of the long-familiar statuses of the social and economic structure that formed the hierarchies of most societies. All recorded history, including the Bible, recognized the existence of slavery. Although some people called for ameliorating the conditions of the enslaved, very few people imagined that slavery could or perhaps even should be eradicated. An idealized vision of a perfect society, like that found in Thomas More's *Utopia* (1516), could even include slavery. Eighteenth-century slavery was not strictly defined by white ownership of black workers. Throughout the century writers noted the existence of white slaves, especially in eastern Europe, and the word *slave* itself comes from the word *Slav*. Slavery was not abolished in Muscovy (Russia) until 1723. The enslavement of Christian Europeans by Muslim Africans on the Barbary Coast or by Muslim Ottoman Turks in Asia was a major concern during the period, getting more treatment in print before 1770 than the condition of black African slaves. As the performance and publication of Susanna Haswell Rowson's play *Slaves in Algiers; or, A Struggle for Freedom* (Philadelphia, 1794) indicate, the subject remained topical throughout the century. Indeed, Britain was not able to force North African Muslims to abolish the enslavement of Christians until 1816, nearly a decade after it had abolished its own trade in black Africans. As a free adult Equiano observed the brutal treatment of white galley slaves in Italy. From the perspective of history we are living in an unusually slave-free time. Slavery ended in Brazil barely one hundred years ago, and slavery was outlawed in Saudi Arabia only in 1970. But the evil has not yet been completely eradicated: antislavery societies still exist because of the hundreds of thousands of slaves (mainly women and children) remaining in the world.

Various forms of bondage and involuntary servitude other than slavery existed in Europe, the Mediterranean, and the Americas during the eighteenth century. Serfdom replaced slavery in Russia. Serfs were bound directly to the land and thus only indirectly to the land's current owner. Though they were obligated to work for the landowner and were treated contemptuously by their social superiors, serfs did have the rights to have some personal property and land, to marry, and to attend church. Frederick the Great did not outlaw serfdom in Prussia until 1773; it continued in Austrian Poland until Emperor Joseph II banned it in 1782. Throughout Europe the dominant gentry and nobility justified their rule over social inferiors with the claim that their underlings were inherently radically different from themselves. In Poland, for example, members of the gentry promoted the myth that they belonged to a race (bloodline or family of descent) different from that of the peasants below them. Ruling classes saw the lower social orders as naturally lazy, bestial, irrational, and incapable of self-rule. They needed to be coerced into productivity.

Coerced labor took various forms in Britain. Since the sixteenth century people convicted of petty crimes such as vagrancy were sentenced to involuntary servitude in workhouses called bridewells. Scots miners, although they were not chattels (personal possessions of an owner), belonged, like feudal serfs, to the mine in which they worked. This labor system did not legally end until the middle of the eighteenth century. Coerced labor of whites in Britain and its colonies included indentured servants (and even apprentices), who signed away their freedom for a specified amount of time in exchange for room and board and a guaranteed job (or job training). In effect, they became voluntary slaves. White indentured servants were the primary source of labor in the British Caribbean and North American colonies during the first decades of settlement. After the Transportation Act of 1718 at least fifty thousand convicts were transported at the government's expense from Britain to the colonies to be sold as servants to work out their sentences. Before 1718 convicts like Benjamin Banneker's English grandmother, Molly Welsh, who arrived in Maryland around 1683, frequently received pardons on the condition that they would either pay for their own passage to America or go at the expense of merchants, who then sold them as indentured servants in the colonies. Even the legal enslavement of poor white Britons not convicted of crimes was still imaginable during the first half of the eighteenth century.[8]

Britons did not believe that being of African descent necessarily meant that one was suited for slavery. Social status could supersede race as a defining category, as it does in Aphra Behn's novel *Oroonoko, or the History of the Royal Slave* (ca. 1678) and in Thomas Southerne's 1696 play based on Behn's novel, or in the historical cases of Ayuba Suleiman Diallo and Prince William Ansah Sessarakoo that found their way into print in the 1730s and 1740s.[9] One of the cruel ironies of the "democratic" revolution in the thirteen North American colonies was that it also "democratized" slavery, making all people of African descent equally eligible for enslavement. Throughout the eighteenth century the more hierarchical Britons recognized slavery as an inappropriate status for at least some Africans. But those fortunate Africans were a precious few. Sub-Saharan Africa became first the primary and then the exclusive source of slave labor for the labor-intensive European colonies in the Americas largely because no alternative source was available. The Ottoman Empire closed the eastern and southern shores of the Mediterranean as sources. Not enough Europeans were available for indentured servitude to meet the American demand for labor. The Native American populations, ravaged by the introduction of new diseases from the Old World, were either too sparse and mobile to recruit for gang labor or so numerous and stationary that using them as semifree labor was economically and politically more efficient.

Even though Europeans brought a particularly virulent form of slavery – large scale, hereditary, and race restricted – they did not introduce the concept of slavery itself to the Americas, where small-scale, domestic slavery already existed. Despite the longevity of slavery as an institution and the persistence of many forms of unfree labor, however, New World slavery was significantly different from classical types of slavery. As other peoples became unavailable for enslavement by Europeans, the standard justifications for slavery were increasingly applied only to people of African descent: economic necessity, the alleged poor work ethic, and the supposed irrationality and bestiality of the enslaved. During the last quarter of the century, when the slave trade came under sustained religious, moral, and economic attack, supporters of slavery began to develop the racist defense that in the next century would become the now all-too-familiar justification of the institution. The traditional definition of *race* as *bloodline* was increasingly replaced by the notion of *race* as *species* that became dominant in the nineteenth century. This "modern" concept of race, which was secondary during the early colonial American period, became primary.[10] Former differences in degree between equally human masters and slaves became differences in kind between white humans and black nonhumans. This new type of slavery was ethnic at its core. All slaves were now of African descent (though not all persons of African descent were slaves). And this type of slavery was hereditary, with no statute of limitation. Enslaved human beings were legally defined as chattel, capital, or property whose labor was at their owner's command. They could not marry or practice their religion without permission. Their bodies and hence their sexuality and reproductive capacities belonged to their masters. They lacked any legal standing in the eyes of the law except as property and so could be bought and sold at their owner's whim. Stripped of their personal identities and history, enslaved Africans and their descendants were forced to suffer what has been aptly called "social death."[11]

Equiano and his sister, of course, had no idea what the world of chattel slavery they were being forced into would be like. They left a society with slaves, in which those slaves constituted a relatively small percentage of the total population and accounted for a relatively minor percentage of the society's economic productivity. They were forced across the Atlantic to enter a slave society, whose economy depended on the productivity of numerous enslaved workers. Bound and gagged, the children were hustled away from their village as quickly as possible by their "robbers." Their attempts to cry out to passersby were suppressed, and within days they found themselves in unfamiliar territory. Refusing to eat, "the only comfort we had was in being in one another's arms all that night, and bathing each other with our tears" (47). But even that small comfort was taken from them when they were separated. The

small boy "was left in a state of distraction not to be described. I cried and
grieved continually; and for several days I did not eat any thing but what
they forced into my mouth. At length, after many days travelling, during
which I had often changed masters, I got into the hands of a chieftain, in a
very pleasant country. This man had two wives and some children, and they
all used me extremely well, and did all they could to comfort me; particularly
the first wife, who was something like my mother." Equiano's "first master . . . , as I may call him, was a smith," who, he says, worked gold, though it
was more likely brass.[12] His new life seemed not so different from his past:
his first mistress was like a foster mother, and despite having traveled "a great
many days journey" from home, "these people spoke exactly the same language" as his own (48).

Equiano was far from content, however. After about a month he began
to be given enough freedom that he was able to ask people the way back
home. He knew from his own observations that he had been taken westward
from his home, though at the time he was unfamiliar with the concepts of
east, west, north, and south: "My father's house was towards the rising of
the sun" (48). His motives for wanting "to seize the first opportunity of making my escape" were mixed: grief over separation from his "mother and
friends," his "love of liberty, ever great," and his mortification at "not daring
to eat with the free-born children, although I was mostly their companion"
(48–49). Equiano represents himself, even as a child, as aware that slavery
was inappropriate for someone of his social status.

Before he could form a plan of escape, an accident forced him to act prematurely. While feeding some chickens he foolishly killed one with "a small
pebble." When asked by an old slave woman what had happened, Equiano,
like a precursor of the mythical George Washington, was unable to prevari-
cate: "I told her the truth, because my mother would never suffer me to tell a
lie." When she "flew into a violent passion" and went to tell their mistress, the
little boy fled to the woods to avoid "an instant correction, which to me was
uncommonly dreadful; for I had seldom been beaten at home" (49). Hiding
in the bushes, he overheard people looking for him mention that he could not
make his way back home because it was so far away: "When I heard this I
was seized with a violent panic, and abandoned myself to despair. Night too
began to approach, and aggravated all my fears. I had before entertained
hopes of getting home, and I had determined when it should be dark to make
the attempt; but I was now convinced it was fruitless, and I began to consider
that, if possibly I could escape all other animals, I could not those of the hu-

man kind; and that, not knowing the way, I must perish in the woods"
(49–50). The sounds in the night and his fear of snakes quickly rendered "the
horror" of his "situation . . . quite insupportable," leaving him "with an anxious wish for death to relieve me from all my pains." Terrified, the little boy
crept back to the security of his master's fireplace, where the old slave found
him the next morning. Rather than receiving the punishment he had feared,
he was only "slightly reprimanded" before being welcomed back (50).

His sense of security was short lived. His master, heartbroken over the
death of his only daughter, soon sold the young boy again: "I was now carried to the left of the sun's rising, through many dreary wastes and dismal
woods, amidst the hideous roarings of wild beasts. – The people I was sold to
used to carry me very often, when I was tired, either on their shoulders or on
their backs" (50). He eventually

> came to a town called Tinmah, in the most beautiful country I had yet
> seen in Africa. It was extremely rich, and there were many rivulets which
> flowed through it; and supplied a large pond in the center of the town,
> where the people washed. Here I first saw and tasted cocoa nuts, which I
> thought superior to any nuts I had ever tasted before; and the trees, which
> were loaded, were also interspersed amongst the houses, which had com-
> modious shades adjoining, and were in the same manner as ours, the in-
> sides being neatly plastered and whitewashed. Here I also saw and tasted
> for the first time sugar-cane. Their money consisted of little white shells,
> the size of the finger nail: they are known in this country by the name of
> *core.* I was sold here for one hundred and seventy-two of them by a mer-
> chant who lived and brought me there. (52)

By mentioning "sugar-cane" Equiano subtly reminds his readers of the
common abolitionist argument that the most important product of the West
Indies could be profitably cultivated in Africa by free native labor. As part of
the global economy in the eighteenth century European slave traders and
their African suppliers used "core," cowry shells from the Maldive Islands in
the Indian Ocean, as currency in West Africa, particularly in the Bight (bay)
of Benin. Equiano must mean 172 pounds of cowry shells, because the price
of slaves during the century ranged between 100 and 300 pounds apiece.

Equiano seemed to have entered as happy a valley as the one he had
been violently taken from in "Eboe." The merchant sold him to a wealthy
widow, who bought Equiano to be a companion to her son and who, to his
surprise, treated him as her son's equal:

The next day I was washed and perfumed, and when meal-time came, I was led into the presence of my mistress, and ate and drank before her with her son. This filled me with astonishment: and I could scarce help expressing my surprise that the young gentleman should suffer [allow] me, who was bound [enslaved], to eat with him who was free; and not only so, but that he would not at any time either eat or drink till I had taken first, because I was the eldest, which was agreeable to our custom. Indeed every thing here, and all their treatment of me, made me forget that I was a slave. The language of these people resembled ours so nearly, that we understood each other perfectly. They had also the very same customs as we. There were likewise slaves daily to attend us, while my young master and I, with other boys, sported with our darts and bows and arrows, as I had been used to do at home. In this resemblance to my former happy state I passed about two months, and I now began to think I was to be adopted into the family. (52–53)

The African domestic slavery he shows us was quite benign, but it was still slavery – one's own life could change unexpectedly at the whim of another. Equiano's delusion of having found security and equality within the institution of slavery ended abruptly: "Without the least previous knowledge, one morning early, while my dear master and companion was still asleep, I was awakened out of my reverie to fresh sorrow, and hurried away even amongst the uncircumcised" (53).

Equiano's reference to uncircumcised Africans is odd, since ethnographers believe that probably all peoples in what is now southern Nigeria practiced circumcision.[13] His rhetorical intention seems clear, however. Like the Jews, Equiano uses this contemptuous label to distinguish other races from his own. The closer he came to the Atlantic coast the more alien the Africans he encountered appeared to him and the more obviously corrupted morally by contact with Europeans:

All the nations and people I had hitherto passed through resembled our own in their manners, customs and language: but I came at length to a country, the inhabitants of which differed from us in all those particulars. I was very much struck with this difference, especially when I came among a people who did not circumcise, and eat [ate] without washing their hands. They cooked also in iron pots, and had European cutlasses and cross bows, which were unknown to us, and fought with their fists amongst themselves. Their women were not so modest as ours, for they ate, and drank, and slept, with their men. (53–54)

Equiano offers evidence to support the argument frequently made by white abolitionists that the Africans who had direct contact with Europeans were consequently the most morally corrupted. John Wesley, for example, says, "The Negroes who inhabit the coast of *Africa* . . . are represented by them who have no motive to flatter them, as remarkably sensible, . . . as industrious, . . . [a]s fair, just, and honest in all their dealings, unless where Whitemen have taught them otherwise, . . . [a]nd as far more mild, friendly and kind to Strangers, than any of our Forefathers were."[14]

What strikes Equiano most about the coastal Africans would have sounded like barbarism to his British readers: "But, above all, I was amazed to see no sacrifices or offerings among them. In some of those places the people ornamented themselves with scars, and likewise filed their teeth very sharp. They wanted sometimes to ornament me in the same manner, but I would not suffer them; hoping that I might some time be among a people who did not thus disfigure themselves, as I thought they did" (54). Equiano's successful refusal to be scarified by his latest owners is remarkable to the point of incredibility. Like many of the details in his account of his forced journey from "Eboe" to the sea, if not simply unbelievable, his ability to resist his masters is unrepresentative of the experiences of the vast majority of enslaved Africans destined for the Americas. Perhaps he was not originally intended for the transatlantic slave trade. That might help explain why he "continued to travel, sometimes by land, sometimes by water, through different countries, and various nations, till, at the end of six or seven months after I had been kidnapped, I arrived at the sea coast" (54). His journey to the coast may have been more circular than linear, or he may have been abducted from nearer present-day Cameroon, southeast of Igboland, than from the Niger River region on the western edge of Igboland. From speaking to Vassa around 1788 James Ramsay had the impression that he had been kidnapped "perhaps above 1000 miles in land," which is consistent with Equiano's statement that his people "had never heard of white men or Europeans, nor of the sea" (32).[15]

Equiano writes that he was initially taken west, away from "the rising of the sun," but he says that he was later taken north, "carried to the left of the sun's rising" and thus away from the coast (48, 50). About half the time between his initial abduction and reaching the coast he was stationary, staying in one place for a month, in another for two months. At least three months of movement passed before, he says, he reached a river as large as the Niger or the Cross. The gradual progress he describes toward the coast, with frequent stops, may have been more representative of the movement of slaves brought from the Biafran hinterland than the popular image of supply-laden slaves forced to march in coffles – chained together in column-caravans – to the coast as quickly as possible.[16] Few slaves, though, would have received the consideration he says he was shown: "The people I was sold to used to carry me very often, when I was tired, either on their shoulder or on their backs" (50). Perhaps because his own journey was so leisurely and he seems never to have been one of a group of slaves, Equiano mentions none of the deaths that typically occurred during the march to the coast.

Whether true or not, his account appears clearly designed to further the cause of those opposed to the transatlantic slave trade. Most enslaved Africans had been taken as prisoners of war or convicted of crimes, and European defenders of slavery frequently argued that enslavement saved the lives of those who would otherwise have been executed. Although kidnapping was indeed one of the ways Africans were enslaved and children were certainly enslaved during the eighteenth century, kidnapping accounted for only a small percentage of the Africans brought to the Americas, and children, especially ones as young as Equiano, were not very marketable overseas. The kidnapping of children was, however, more common in the Biafran hinterland, and women and children composed a higher percentage of slaves taken from the Bight of Biafra than from other ports.[17] None of Equiano's readers could fairly argue that a seven- or eight-year-old boy might willingly and knowingly engage in military or criminal activities that might justifiably lead to either capital punishment or involuntary servitude.

An innocent little boy violently seized with his sister was an object of emotional pathos and pity, not the subject of rational argument. The never-named sister is the last link between Equiano and the mother to whom he was extraordinarily attached. Even though he tells us an Igbo man slept "with his male children" (36), Equiano, presumably because he was so young, "always lay" with his mother in her "night-house" (43). He "was very fond of [his] mother, and almost constantly with her." He accompanied her even when doing so frightened him: "When she went to make these oblations at her mother's tomb, which was a kind of small solitary thatched house, I sometimes attended her. There she made her libations, and spent most of the night in cries and lamentations. I have been often extremely terrified on these occasions. The loneliness of the place, the darkness of the night, and the ceremony of libation, naturally awful and gloomy, were heightened by my mother's lamentations; and these, concurring with the doleful cries of birds, by which these places were frequented, gave an inexpressible terror to the scene" (40).

Equiano represents the trauma of enslavement as a domestic tragedy of separation, heightened in his case by multiplying the act of separation, initially from his mother and then twice from his sister. Unlike the tearful scenes of reunion common in eighteenth-century novels and sentimental comedies, however, Equiano's reencounter with his sister leads to even greater, not less, grief:

> In this manner I had been travelling for a considerable time, when one evening, to my great surprise, whom should I see brought to the house where I was but my dear sister. As soon as she saw me she gave a loud shriek, and ran into my arms. – I was quite overpowered; neither of us could speak, but, for a considerable time, clung to each other in mutual embraces, unable to do any thing but weep. Our meeting affected all who saw us; and indeed I must acknowledge, in honour of those sable destroyers of human rights, that I never met with any ill treatment, or saw any offered to their slaves, except tying them, when necessary, to keep them from running away. When these people knew we were brother and sister they indulged us to be together; and the man, to whom I supposed we belonged, lay with us, he in the middle, while she and I held one another by the hands across his breast all night; and thus for a while we forgot our misfortunes in the joy of being together: but even this small comfort was soon to have an end; for scarcely had the fatal morning appeared, when she was again torn from me for ever! I was now more miserable, if possible, than before. The small relief which her presence gave me from pain was gone, and the wretchedness of my situation was redoubled by my anxiety after her fate, and my apprehensions lest her sufferings should be greater than mine, when I could not be with her to alleviate them. (51)

The temporary reunion with his sister allows Equiano to draw an implicit contrast between the "sable destroyers of human rights" and the depictions of heartless European slave owners more familiar to his readers through abolitionist writings. His African enslavers never mistreated him or, as far as he witnessed, any other slave in Africa. Unlike European slave traders,

Africans were affected by the sight of the reunion of the siblings. Further-more, the scene enables Equiano to show himself, even as a child, more con-cerned with the welfare and feelings of another than with his own.

Equiano's Africans are far more culturally coherent than the chaotic col-lection of warring ethnicities described by proponents of the slave trade: "All the nations and people I had hitherto passed through resembled our own in their manners, customs and language" (53). But he never contends that any African nation was as developed as those in Europe, especially England: "From the time I left my own nation I always found somebody that under-stood me till I came to the sea coast. The languages of different nations did not totally differ, nor were they so copious as those of the Europeans, partic-ularly the English. They were therefore easily learned; and, while I was jour-neying thus through Africa, I acquired two or three different tongues" (51). The use of language was considered a uniquely human achievement, separat-ing humans from animals; hence, the more civilized the people, the more de-veloped, or "copious," the language was thought to be. More complex ideas required more words. As a small child Equiano may well have picked up a working knowledge of new languages quite rapidly, especially if he refers to different dialects of Igbo, but his claim is improbable that all the African lan-guages he encountered were alike during a months-long journey that must have covered many miles.

An Africa that was relatively unified by culture and language was far more attractive to potential European investors than a continent containing a myriad of mutually unintelligible and difficult tongues. Such a uniform Africa would be particularly attractive if it also had untapped desirable natu-ral resources like cotton, gums, and mahogany that could be safely, easily, and profitably extracted: "In all the places where I was, the soil was exceed-ingly rich; the pomkins [pumpkins], eadas, plantains, yams, &c. &c. were in great abundance, and of incredible size. There were also vast quantities of different gums, though not used for any purpose; and every where a great deal of tobacco. The cotton even grew quite wild; and there was plenty of red wood" (54).

As Equiano's audience well knew, the major export from Africa was hu-man, a fact that confronted Equiano when he reached the Atlantic coast: "The first object which saluted my eyes when I arrived on the coast was the sea, and a slave-ship, which was then riding at anchor, and waiting for its cargo." As a slave brought from the hinterland of Biafra, he would most likely have been brought to the port of Bonny on the Bight of Biafra. The slave ship facing him may have been the newly built *Ogden*, a snow, or small two-masted vessel, owned by Thomas Stevenson & Company in Liverpool, England. It cleared Liverpool on 5 June 1753 under the command of William Cooper to begin the ten- to twelve-week voyage to Bonny for a cargo of four hundred slaves.[18] Hoping to make at least the 10 percent profit that was the average profit a slave ship realized within a few years of its voyage, the eight-gun, 110-ton *Ogden* left England with a crew of thirty-two men, more than double the number on an equivalent commercial vessel not engaged in the deadly slave trade. Its cargo of trade goods was worth more than the vessel itself, its crew's wages, and their provisions combined. African slaves were expensive commodities. They were also dangerous cargoes, requiring an enlarged crew to maintain security. The *Ogden* arrived at Bonny when the yam harvest was in, the optimum time for slave traders. Yams, the principal food of Igboland, were available then for the trade, as were more slaves.[19] To protect their investment, British slavers fed their purchases twice a day. For Biafran slaves the first meal would be yams and the second a combination of grains and biscuits.

Equiano's immediate reaction to "the African snow" (63) and its human cargo was inexpressible and emotional: "These filled me with astonishment, which was soon converted into terror, which I am yet at a loss to describe, nor the then feelings of my mind. . . . [Q]uite overpowered with horror and anguish, I fell motionless on the deck and fainted." He was horror stricken by the sight of the "white men with horrible looks, red faces, and long hair," the first Europeans he had ever seen: "I was now persuaded that I had gotten into a world of bad spirits, and that they were going to kill me. Their complexions too differing so much from ours, their long hair, and the language they spoke, which was very different from any I had ever heard, united to confirm me in this belief." Equiano instinctively recognized that he was facing an unfamiliar form of servitude: "[I] would have . . . exchanged my condition with that of the meanest slave in my own country" (55).

From Equiano's perspective, the roles of civilized and savage as Europeans saw them were reversed. The sight of the "large furnace of copper boiling" used for cooking the yams and other provisions for cargo and crew made him think that he and "the multitude of black people of every description chained together" had fallen into the hands of cannibals (55). The women would have been wearing small pieces of cloth given them; the men and boys were most likely naked. The widely reported African belief that the slave traders ate the people they took away is not so implausible when we consider that the enslaved almost never returned to their places of origin.[20] Equiano's account provided support for the common abolitionist argument that the slave trade brutalized the enslavers as well as the enslaved: "The white people looked and acted, as I thought, in so savage a manner; for I had never seen among any people such instances of brutal cruelty; and this not only shewn towards us blacks, but also to some of the whites themselves. One white man in particular I saw, when we were permitted to be on deck, flogged so unmercifully with a large rope near the foremast,[21] that he died in consequence of it; and they tossed him over the side as they would have done a brute" (56–57). The tyrannical captain became almost a stock figure in abolitionist literature. The apologists for slavery, on the other hand, argued that the slave trade served as a nursery, or training ground, for seamen. Evidence confirms the abolitionists' claims that the trade was even more lethal, on an average percentage basis, for the crews than for the slaves.

Equiano says that he experienced the brutality of the Middle Passage firsthand. To try to revive him when he fainted, a member of the crew forced him to swallow his first taste of alcohol, and when, out of despair, he refused to eat, he was flogged. Manifesting the stereotypical traits of "melancholy reflections," "depression of spirits," and "constitutional timidity" Bryan Edwards attributed to the Igbo, more than once the little boy "wished for the last friend, Death" (56).[22] Had he been able to he would have climbed over the rope nettings placed along the sides of the ship to form a caged enclosure that prevented the slaves from jumping overboard to escape or commit suicide. Where he failed, others succeeded: "Two of my wearied countrymen, who were chained together (I was near them at the time), preferring death to such a life of misery, somehow made it through the nettings, and jumped into the sea: immediately another quite dejected fellow, who, on account of his illness, was suffered to be out of irons, also followed their example; and I believe many more would very soon have done the same, if they had not been prevented by the ship's crew, who were instantly alarmed" (59). The slaves were flogged for trying to commit suicide passively by not eating or actively by jumping overboard.

Because he was "reduced so low" from having been put briefly below deck, and given his "extreme youth," Equiano was not fettered like the older boys and men, who were chained to each other in pairs to keep them from attempting to escape or rebel. Nor was he, as they were, kept below deck for most of the voyage to the West Indies. From his privileged vantage point he could see more of the workings of the trade than most slaves were able to observe, and he could indulge his curiosity. After he found some of his "own nation," who told him they were all being taken to work, he "was a little revived, and thought, if it were no worse than working, my situation was not so desperate" (56). But his "countrymen" could not satisfy his curiosity about where these white men came from, where their women were, or how they made the vessel move and stop.

The *Ogden* waited offshore for an unusually long time collecting its human cargo, double the four-month average for slave ships in the Bight of Biafra. Slave vessels "coasted" for so long because they typically took on at most a few slaves a day. Facilities for bulking (warehousing) slaves onshore in order to board them in large groups would have been prohibitively expensive. The longer a slave ship stayed near the coast of Africa, the greater the risk of disease for its crew and human cargo. The Bight of Biafra in particular was "remarkable for great Mortality in Slaves."[23] Although the rate of course varied widely from individual ship to ship, the overall mortality rate for slaves departing from the Bight of Biafra was "more than 50 percent greater than the mean for the whole of sub-Saharan Africa."[24] In the slave trade as a whole, the 20 percent mortality rate for European crew members was even greater than the average rate that decimated the slaves. The *Ogden* finally set sail to cross the Atlantic around the beginning of March 1754 with about three hundred slaves, headed for the sugar colonies of the West Indies, the destination for 80 percent of enslaved Africans.

By 1789 the horrors of the coerced Atlantic crossing had already been widely reported, as Equiano knew, in publications like Alexander Falconbridge's *An Account of the Slave Trade on the Coast of Africa*, Thomas Clarkson's *An Essay on the Slavery and Commerce of the Human Species*, and John Newton's *Thoughts on the African Slave Trade*, all published or reprinted in London in 1788, as well as in testimony Equiano had heard in the House of Commons that year. Many of these earlier accounts were fuller and more graphic than his own. His description of the preparation for departure from Africa, however, is the most frequently quoted record of the Middle Passage because he gives a voice to the inarticulate millions who suffered it:

> At last, when the ship we were in had got in all her cargo, they made ready with many fearful noises, and we were all put under deck, so that we could not see how they managed the vessel. But this disappointment was the least of my sorrow. The stench of the hold while we were on the coast was so intolerably loathsome, that it was dangerous to remain there

for any time, and some of us had been permitted to stay on the deck for
the fresh air; but now that the whole ship's cargo were confined together,
it became absolutely pestilential. The closeness of the place, and the heat
of the climate, added to the number in the ship, which was so crowded
that each had scarcely room to turn himself, almost suffocated us. This
produced copious perspirations, so that the air soon became unfit for res-
piration, from a variety of loathsome smells, and brought on a sickness
among the slaves, of which many died, thus falling victims to the improv-
ident avarice, as I may call it, of their purchasers. This wretched situation
was again aggravated by the galling of the chains, now become insupportable; and the filth of the necessary tubs [latrines], into which the children
often fell, and were almost suffocated. The shrieks of the women, and the
groans of the dying, rendered the whole a scene of horror almost incon-
ceiveable. (58)

To the great joy of its crew, under the command of James Walker the *Ogden* arrived at Barbados on 9 May 1754, delivering a cargo of 243 enslaved
Africans after a voyage that normally took about two months. The original
captain, William Cooper, may have been one of the many European slave
traders to die either on the coast of Africa or during the Middle Passage. The
number of crew members who died during the voyage is not known, but we
can estimate the losses using surviving data from the voyage the *Ogden* made
the following year.[25] On a longer voyage from Liverpool to Bonny to Jamaica, the vessel traveled farther in less time than during the 1754 trip. Perhaps most significantly, the second voyage spent less time off the African
coast than had the first. On the 1755 voyage, of the 343 enslaved Africans
who departed from Bonny, 280 survived the trip to Kingston. Only 23 of the
original 32 crew members reached Jamaica.

In the great arc formed by the islands in the Caribbean, Barbados is the
closest to Africa. Although Barbados had been surpassed in the eighteenth
century by Jamaica as a producer of sugar and the final destination for imported slaves, its location as the first Caribbean landfall made it the major
transshipment point of slaves between Africa and the British West Indian and
North American colonies. Slave ships anchored off the harbor of Bridgetown,
the capital of Barbados, so that slave dealers could inspect their cargoes before bringing them ashore, where they sold, on average, for three times their
purchase price in Africa. The *Ogden* reached Barbados just as the November
to May sugar season, when slaves were most in demand, was coming to an

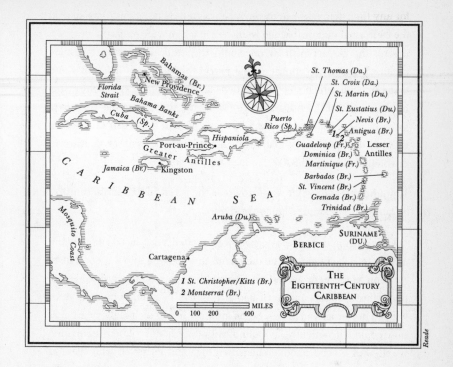

The Eighteenth-Century Caribbean

end. Equiano and his fellow slaves endured the humiliation of being divided into "parcels" and made to "jump" to display their health and strength to the dealers, who frightened them so much that they needed to be reassured about their future: "We thought by this we should be eaten by these ugly men, as they appeared to us; and, when soon after we were all put down under the deck again, there was much dread and trembling among us, and nothing but bitter cries to be heard all the night from these apprehensions, insomuch that at last the white people got some old slaves from the land to pacify us. They told us we were not to be eaten, but to work, and were soon to go on land, where we should see many of our country people" (60).

Onshore they met "Africans of all languages" before being "conducted immediately to the merchant's yard, where we were all pent up together like so many sheep in a fold, without regard to sex or age." The young slave was initially more intrigued by his first exposure to horses than by what might be about to happen to him or his "fellow prisoners," whom he could understand, "though they were from a distant part of Africa" (60). But inevitably the reality of his condition dominated his mind:

We were not many days in the merchant's custody before we were sold after their usual manner, which is this: – On a signal given (as the beat of a
drum), the buyers rush at once into the yard where the slaves are
confined, and make choice of that parcel they like best. The noise and
clamour with which this is attended, and the eagerness visible in the
countenances of the buyers, serve not a little to increase the apprehensions of the terrified Africans, who may well be supposed to consider
them as the ministers of that destruction to which they think themselves
devoted [doomed]. (60–61)

Equiano refers to what was known as the scramble, described more fully
by the surgeon Alexander Falconbridge:

On a day appointed, the negroes were landed, and placed altogether in
a large yard, belonging to the merchants to whom the ship was consigned.
As soon as the hour agreed on arrived, the doors of the yard were suddenly thrown open, and in rushed a considerable number of purchasers,
with all the ferocity of brutes. Some instantly seized such of the negroes as
they could conveniently lay hold of with their hands. Others, being prepared with several handkerchiefs tied together, encircled with these as
many as they were able. While others, by means of a rope, effected the
same purpose. It is scarcely possible to describe the confusion of which
this mode of selling is productive. It likewise causes much animosity
among the purchasers, who, not unfrequently upon these occasions, fall
out and quarrel with each other. The poor astonished negroes were so
much terrified by these proceedings, that several of them, through fear,
climbed over the walls of the court yard, and ran wild about the town; but
were soon hunted down and retaken.[26]

The "scramble" in Barbados was simply the latest, but far from the last,
of the serial separations that Equiano experienced since his kidnapping in
Africa: "In this manner, without scruple, are relations and friends separated,
most of them never to see each other again. . . . [S]everal brothers . . . were
sold in different lots; and it was very moving on this occasion to see and hear
their cries at parting." "Not saleable among the rest," Equiano, too, felt the
pain of separation: "I now totally lost the small remains of comfort I had enjoyed in conversing with my countrymen; the women too, who used to wash
and take care of me, were all gone different ways, and I never saw one of
them afterwards." He became one of the approximately 5–10 percent of en-

slaved Africans transshipped to North America, in his case as what was called a "refuse" slave, because West Indian buyers had rejected him.

On 21 May the sloop *Nancy*, owned by Alexander Watson of Virginia and commanded by Richard Wallis, left Barbados with thirty-one slaves and brought them up the York River in Virginia on 13 June 1754.[27] Equiano landed in Virginia less than two weeks after he had arrived in Barbados. En route he was fed "plenty of rice and fat pork," no doubt in an attempt to make him more attractive for the next market. He arrived in the Chesapeake region during the May to August period of highest demand for enslaved Africans. By 1750 nearly 60 percent of the slaves in the thirteen North American colonies were concentrated in the tobacco-producing farms of Maryland and Virginia. Approximately 70 percent of slaves brought from Africa to the Chesapeake area arrived in the summertime. Demand was so high then that even the less desirable Biafran slaves could be sold.[28]

Almost 40 percent of the Africans imported by Virginia planters from 1710 to 1760 originated from the Bight of Biafra.[29] Surprisingly, however, for the first time since his initial capture, Equiano "saw few or none of our native Africans, and not one soul who could talk to" him. He found himself the refuse of the refuse, eventually purchased by a planter named Mr. Campbell. Assigned the least skilled labor of "weeding grass, and gathering stones" for his new master, little Equiano watched each of his companions be sold until "only myself was left." No one remained who could understand him, leaving him "grieving and pining, and wishing for death" (62).

The few weeks he spent weeding and gathering stones were the only time in his life he worked in the fields where the overwhelming majority of slaves lived out their lives. His fortunes took a turn for the better when he was brought to his ailing master's house to fan Campbell. The sight of the cook forced to wear an iron muzzle, which kept her from tasting the food she was preparing, startled him. Even more astonishing were the technological marvels he observed while his master slept: he thought the watch hanging on the chimney and the portrait on the wall were both devices designed to monitor his movements. The painting, moreover, he thought "might be some way the whites had to keep their great men when they died." Under Campbell, Equiano suffered a form of control common to all slaves, the imposition of a new identity through renaming: "In this place I was called Jacob; but on board the African snow I was called Michael" (63).

But moving from the fields to Campbell's house led to one of the greatest changes in the little boy's life. In the summer of 1754 he met one of

Campbell's business associates. Michael Henry Pascal, a lieutenant on extended leave from the British Royal Navy, took such an immediate liking to the child that he bought him from Campbell for "thirty or forty pounds sterling," a rather high price for such a young refuse slave (63–64). One of the happiest periods of the eight- or nine-year-old slave's life was about to begin.

Chapter Three

AT SEA

Of French Protestant extraction, Michael Henry Pascal had received his commission as a lieutenant in the Royal Navy in 1745 during the War of Jenkins' Ear. That conflict between Britain and Spain lasted from 23 October 1739 until 17 October 1749. Its odd popular name came from its ostensible cause, Spain's mistreatment of British seamen. Around 1730 Spain began to stop and search foreign vessels it suspected of trading illegally with its American colonies. In 1738 a smuggler named Capt. Robert Jenkins displayed his mangled ear in the House of Commons to support his testimony that a Spanish coast guard had boarded his ship in 1731 and mutilated him. British commercial interests, which had been promoting a more aggressive posture toward Spain, successfully seized on the image of Jenkins to justify a war to defend Britain's honor and the freedom of the seas. France officially entered the war as Spain's ally on 31 March 1744, fighting Britain in what was called in North America King George's War and in Europe the War of the Austrian Succession. Like the other wars between France and Britain fought since the late seventeenth century, the War of the Austrian Succession was more dynastic than territorial, more about the control of thrones than land. And like the earlier wars, after the waste of much blood and treasure, the conflict pitting roughly equivalent British superiority at sea against French superiority on land ended in an inconclusive and unstable restoration of the status quo before the war. The Treaty of Aix-la-Chapelle in 1748 required Britain to return its only significant conquest, the strategic fort of Louisbourg guarding the entrance to France's colony Canada, in exchange for France's agreeing not to destroy the British troops left at its mercy in Europe.

Following the end of the war, like many of his fellow officers, Pascal had been on extended leave at half pay since mid-1751.[1] And like many other officers on leave during one of the brief intervals of peace between France and Britain in the eighteenth century, Pascal successfully solicited permission from the Admiralty Board to extend his leave so that he could accept employment commanding a commercial vessel. On 4 February 1752 the Admiralty Board "resolved that Lt. Michael Henry Pascal have leave to go to Virginia in the Merchant's Service, for ten Months."[2] Pascal's naval records demonstrate the common eighteenth-century practice of spelling words in various ways, including even proper names, and especially foreign-sounding ones. The board extended the leave of "Pascall," "Pascoll," "Pascott," and "Pascal" in February 1753 and 1754 and again in January 1755, a further twelve months each time. By the latter date, however, Pascal had already returned to England.

Since by convention anyone in command of a merchant vessel was called captain, on the *Industrious Bee* Lieutenant Pascal temporarily became Captain Pascal. The small ship and its crew reflected the transatlantic nature of the eighteenth-century British imperial economy. Built in New England but based at the island of Guernsey in the English Channel, the *Industrious Bee* was a snow with six guns, and a burthen, or interior carrying capacity, of only about 120 tons. The eighteenth-century antecedent of gross tonnage, burthen was estimated by using the dimensions of a ship to derive an unreliable measurement of capacity that underestimated its real displacement. The *Industrious Bee* was certified in late January 1752 as bound from the mouth of the Thames River to Virginia, a voyage that normally took seven or eight weeks in the mid-eighteenth century. The ship's ten-man crew included two non-British sailors.[3] Four members of the crew apparently saw arriving in America as the chance to make their own fortunes: on 5 June 1752 Pascal advertised in the *Virginia Gazette* a reward for their return after they jumped ship. For the next two years Pascal engaged in colonial trade, returning to

England with a cargo of tobacco and other colonial goods in December 1754. Among Pascal's goods was Equiano, now approximately nine or ten years old, "meant" as "a present to some of his friends in England" (64).

The young boy was easily misled into thinking that his suffering lay all behind him:

> I had sails to lie on, and plenty of good victuals to eat; and every body on board used me very kindly, quite contrary to what I had seen of any white people before; I therefore began to think that they were not all of the same disposition. A few days after I was on board we sailed for England. I was still at a loss to conjecture my destiny. By this time, however, I could smatter a little imperfect English; and I wanted to know as well as I could where we were going. Some of the people of the ship used to tell me they were going to carry me back to my own country, and this made me very happy. I was quite rejoiced at the idea of going back; and thought if I should get home what wonders I should have to tell. (64)

At this point in his life Equiano was, of course, being deceived by those who told him he was returning to his country, but they were also ironically prophetic, because after he had first experienced life in England he always saw it rather than North America, the West Indies, or even Africa as his home. Physical and psychological abuse soon undeceived him, however. During the voyage "my captain and master named me *Gustavus Vasa*. I at that time began to understand him a little, and refused to be called so, and told him as well as I could that I would be called Jacob; but he said I should not, and still called me Gustavus; and when I refused to answer to my new name, which at first I did, it gained me many a cuff; so at length I submitted, and by which I have been known ever since" (64). Slaves were often given ironically inappropriate names of powerful historical figures like Caesar and Pompey to emphasize their subjugation to their masters' wills.

British audiences associated the name Gustavus Vasa with eighteenth-century arguments over political freedom in Britain. In 1738 the government led by the dominant, or "prime," minister Sir Robert Walpole had used the Licensing Act of 1737 to block the performance of Henry Brooke's transparently anti-Walpole play, *Gustavus Vasa, the Deliverer of His Country*. Despite being published in 1739, the play was not staged in England until 1805, when it was performed at the Covent Garden theater in London. (Retitled *The Patriot*, the play had been performed in 1742 in Dublin.) Republication of *Gustavus Vasa* in 1761, 1778, 1796, and 1797 kept the play and its discourse of political

slavery before the British public. Although Equiano had been unaware of the significance of the name he had been forced to accept in 1754, as a free man in 1789 he no doubt expected his readers to recognize the irony of his initial resistance to his new name. Like his royal Swedish namesake he had become a freedom fighter in leading his people's struggle against the slave trade.[4]

Pascal physically forced the child Equiano to accept an imposed identity. Pascal and others also mentally abused him by playing on the young boy's fears. As one would expect of a child among strangers in an unfamiliar setting, Equiano often hid and watched his shipmates, not understanding these "white people [who] did not make any offerings at any time." When a man was lost overboard, the young slave "began, as usual, to be very much afraid, and to think they were going to make an offering with me, and perform some magic; which I still believed they dealt in." At another time, believing that killer whales had caused the winds to die, "I hid myself in the fore-part of the ship, through fear of being offered up to appease them" (66), rendering Equiano "ludicrous enough in my crying and trembling" to his master, Pascal (67).

One of his greatest fears was that of becoming the victim of cannibalism during the long voyage, with its consequent "short allowance of provisions":

> In our extremities the captain and people told me in jest they would kill and eat me, but I thought them in earnest, and was depressed beyond measure, expecting every moment to be my last. While I was in this situation one evening they caught, with a good deal of trouble, a large shark, and got it on board. This gladdened my poor heart exceedingly, as I thought it would serve the people to eat instead of their eating me; but very soon, to my astonishment, they cut off a small part of the tail, and tossed the rest over the side. This renewed my consternation; and I did not know what to think of these white people; I very much feared they would kill and eat me. (64–65)

As Equiano discovered, the English considered sharks inedible. Sharks frequently followed slave ships, drawn to them by the bodies of dead slaves thrown overboard in the course of the Middle Passage. One of the greatest terrors of the sea, the shark was often brutally treated when caught. Returning the finless shark to the ocean doomed it to a lingering and painful death.

Equiano mistakenly says in his autobiography that "it was about the beginning of the year 1757 when I arrived in England, and I was near twelve years of age at that time." Commercial, meteorological, and naval records enable us to correct his misdating of when the *Industrious Bee*, "after a passage of thirteen weeks," arrived at Falmouth, where he first encountered snow (67). Pascal must have sailed from Virginia with his newly purchased slave in early September 1754, because on 14 December 1754, about thirteen weeks later, the London newspaper the *Public Advertiser* reported the arrival at Falmouth, England, of the "Industrious Bee, [commanded by] Pascall, from [Newfoundland, Canada]." Seamen generally avoided transatlantic voyages to and from the lower North American and all the Caribbean colonies during the hurricane season in late summer and fall, as well as during the dead of winter. Going north to Newfoundland from Virginia and then across the Atlantic greatly reduced the risk of encountering deadly storms. A Newfoundland to England crossing also accounts for the extraordinary length of the voyage.

After such "a very long voyage" (64) Pascal understandably brought the *Industrious Bee* to the nearest English port, Falmouth, on the English Channel side of the southwestern county of Cornwall. Influenced by the Gulf Stream, the weather in Cornwall, particularly on its Atlantic coast, is uncharacteristically warm for Britain, so warm in fact that imported palm trees thrive in the mild climate. The Cornish climate makes all the more remarkable one of Equiano's first experiences in the new world of England:

> One morning, when I got upon deck, I saw it covered all over with the snow that fell over-night: as I had never seen any thing of the kind before, I thought it was salt; so I immediately ran down to the mate, and desired him, as well as I could, to come and see how somebody in the night had thrown salt all over the deck. He, knowing what it was, desired me to bring some of it down to him: accordingly I took up a handful of it, which I found very cold indeed; and when I brought it to him he desired me to taste it. I did so, and I was surprised beyond measure. I then asked him what it was? he told me it was snow: but I could not in any wise understand him. (67)

Equiano first reached England during the unusually cold Cornish winter of 1754–55. Before the time when the government began gathering official meteorological information, what evidence we have about local English weather conditions comes from amateur observers. One such was William Borlase, rector of Ludgvan, a small village approximately 25 miles west of Falmouth, whose records reveal that the winter of 1754–55 was one of the two snowiest seasons in southern Cornwall between 1753 and 1772.[5]

Despite the mental and physical abuse Equiano endured on his initial voyage to England and his notably cold reception there, his trip on the *Industrious Bee* marked the beginning of one of the happiest stages of his life. The unpredictable disruptions of his life during the past few years seemed at an end. The authority and order of the Royal Navy replaced the arbitrary tyranny of enslavers, who had held the power of life and death over him. The navy's rules applied to his superiors as well as to himself. He was still a slave, but because of his youth and status as an officer's servant his was a relatively privileged position. He had lost one family but found another, he thought, in his fellow seamen. Most important, he once again appeared to be in a stable relationship with an adult male figure of authority. The orphaned little boy quickly attached himself emotionally to the man who had bought him and who, Equiano assumed, reciprocated that emotional attachment. In Equiano's eyes Pascal filled the role not only of adult, master, and superior officer but, more significantly, of substitute father. Moreover, Equiano's relationship with Pascal and the navy placed him in the position he sought throughout his life – a vantage point from which to observe and comment on the actions of others. Like most children his age, Equiano was not mature enough to be terrified by the thrilling action he saw while serving Pascal.

Equiano spent most of the period between August 1755 and December 1762 aboard various Royal Navy vessels before and during the Seven Years' War (better known to North Americans as the French and Indian War). The first truly worldwide conflict, the Seven Years' War rendered Britain an undisputed imperial superpower. Equiano's autobiography is the most extended and detailed account of naval experience left by any eighteenth-century writer of African descent. Although war between Britain and France was not officially declared until 17 May 1756, tensions between the two countries had been rising since at least May 1754, when a series of seemingly minor and apparently inconsequential military skirmishes began along the ill-defined border between British and French colonial claims in North America. Commercial interests probably prompted Pascal's decision to return to England in 1754. He and his young slave arrived there just as the British government was preparing uncertainly for the impending conflict.

Equiano began one of the happiest periods of his life accompanied by his first non-African friend, Richard Baker, a boy four or five years his elder. A "native of America" with "an excellent education" and "a most amiable temper," Dick Baker "had never been at sea before." Pascal brought Baker, the slave-owning son of his landlady in Virginia, to Britain as his servant. All officers in the Royal Navy were permitted to have servants aboard ship, the number depending upon each officer's rank and the size of the vessel. For the next three years Pascal's slave and servant were inseparable companions. For

the young slave Dick Baker was the first of a series of older male figures he
sought to please and emulate: "a kind interpreter, an agreeable companion,
and a faithful friend; who, at the age of fifteen, discovered [revealed] a mind
superior to prejudice; and who was not ashamed to notice, to associate with,
and to be the friend and instructor of one who was ignorant, a stranger, of a
different complexion, and a slave!" (65). Through Baker, Equiano's attitude
toward whites began to evolve, though he still maintained a critical distance:

> My little friend Dick used to be my best interpreter; for I could make free
> with him, and he always instructed me with pleasure: . . . in seeing these
> white people did not sell one another, as we did, I was much pleased; and
> in this I thought they were much happier than we Africans. I was aston-
> ished at the wisdom of the white people in all things I saw; but was
> amazed at their not sacrificing, or making any offerings, and eating with
> unwashed hands, and touching the dead. I likewise could not help re-
> marking the particular slenderness of their women, which I did not at first
> like; and I thought they were not so modest and shamefaced as the
> African women. (68)

The bond between the young slave and the older boy grew stronger during
the months Pascal left them together on the island of Guernsey while he
sailed to London to sell his cargo of tobacco. Equiano would not see his master, Pascal, again until he joined him aboard the *Roebuck* in August 1755,
nearly a month after Pascal had been appointed the ship's first lieutenant.

Only commissioned and warrant officers can be said to have joined the
navy in the sense we now use the phrase "joining the navy" to mean enlisting in the military service as a career for an extended or permanent period
and being assigned by the Admiralty to a ship's company.[6] Commissioned
officers (lieutenants and post captains), after having served six years at sea, at
least two of which had to be as a midshipman or master's mate, were exam-
ined orally on their knowledge of seamanship. Consequently, all commissioned officers on the quarterdeck began as ratings, or enlisted men, working
below decks. The famous explorer Capt. James Cook, the son of a farm-
worker, was one example of a man who rose from being a seaman to become
a post captain in the Royal Navy. A naval commission conveyed the status of
gentleman on the recipient based on his knowledge, skill, and experience, regardless of his prior social status. The navy was the only eighteenth-century
profession open to talent, with little consideration of monetary, social, or political influence. The commissioned officers were the executive officers com-

manding the ship and its crew. Warrant officers, which included the boatswain, carpenter, cook, master (navigator), purser, and surgeon, were certified specialists and craftsmen with defined duties.

Despite his title the purser bore no responsibility for paying the officers and crew. His primary duty was accounting for the supply and disbursement of the ship's victuals (the standard rations of food and drink issued by the navy's Victualling Board) and "slops" (clothes bought before 1758 from a private contractor and after from the Navy Board). He also, at his own expense, provided the ship and its personnel with prescribed amounts of consumable "necessaries" such as candles and bedding. The navy reimbursed him for the ship's necessaries. Necessaries distributed to officers and crew were charged against their wages in the ship's paybook. In his private capacity as a merchant, the purser sold tobacco, which was also charged against wages. The purser maintained the ship's muster, the list of all people actually on the ship, most of whom were ratings. The captain, master, boatswain, and purser signed the muster. The captain rated each member of the crew according to his skills and duties. In descending order of abilities and responsibilities these ratings were able seaman, ordinary seaman, landsman, and boy. The muster list included not only the vessel's complement of officers, crew, and marines but also "supernumeraries" – anyone aboard ship not part of its designated complement such as passengers, prisoners of war, and people rescued at sea. Because the purser had to pay for any difference between the victuals, slops, and necessaries supplied and those dispersed and because he sold tobacco privately, the muster lists and paybooks tend to be very reliable records of everyone aboard any vessel in the navy, whether a member of its company or not.

As one of the boys or servants on a naval ship, Equiano would have hung his hammock in the lower deck of the ship's stern, and he would have eaten better than he had for many months:

> Every man and boy borne on the books of any of his Majesty's ships, are
> allowed as follows[:] . . . a pound of biscuit-bread and a gallon of beer per
> day; on Tuesday and Saturday 2 lb. of beef, or else 1 lb. of beef and 1 lb.
> of flour with plums for a pudding; . . . on Thursdays and Sundays, every
> two has a 3 lb. piece of pork and each a pint of pease to boil into soup; the
> other three days are called banian days, in allusion to a people in Asia
> who always abstain from the use of animal food, and are known by the
> name of Banians; on each of these days we have 2 oz. of butter and ¼ lb.

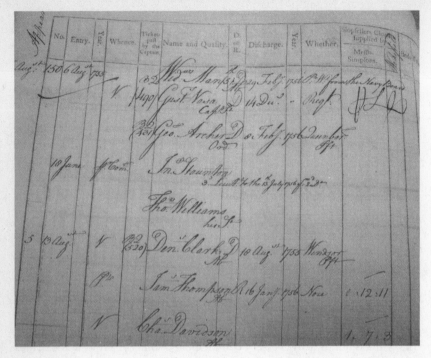

Roebuck muster list, 6 August 1755. Gustavus Vassa's name appears on the second line.
(Public Records Office, Kew, England.)

of Cheshire cheese; and on Wednesdays, $1/2$ pint of gort or ground oat-meal boiled into burgoo for breakfast, and a pint of pease to make soup for dinner; on Monday we have no pease, but have our burgoo for dinner. When ships are abroad they cannot get beer, but have an allowance of that sort of liquor which the country produces in lieu thereof. . . . [I]f they are on a long cruise in the home seas and their beer is expended, they have $1/2$ a pint of brandy and $1^1/_2$ pints of water mixed into grog . . . [I]n the Mediterranean seas . . . the daily allowance is a pint of white wine mixed with another of water, and served out twice, either at breakfast and dinner or dinner and 4 o'clock in the afternoon.[7]

Whenever possible, the victuals supplied by either the Navy Board or private contractors were supplemented by fresh water, meat, vegetables, and fruit, the latter protecting the men from scurvy. At midcentury, however, avoiding scurvy by consuming vitamin C was accidental rather than intentional, since the cause of the disease was not known. During the War of the

Austrian Succession the British navy lost more men to scurvy than to their
French and Spanish enemies. And during Lord Anson's circumnavigation of
the globe in 1740–44, three quarters of his crews on five ships succumbed to
scurvy. The Royal Navy did not require distribution of lemon juice to its
seamen until 1795.[8]

Landings to resupply also gave Equiano a chance to sample local
culture:

> We came to Barcelona, a Spanish sea-port, remarkable for its silk manu-
> factories. Here the ships were all to be watered [took on fresh water for
> drinking]; and my master, who spoke different languages, and used often
> to interpret for the admiral, superintended the watering of ours. For that
> purpose he and the officers of the other ships, who were on the same ser-
> vice, had tents pitched in the bay; and the Spanish soldiers were stationed
> along the shore, I suppose to see that no depredations were committed by
> our men.
>
> I used constantly to attend my master, and I was charmed with this
> place. All the time of our stay it was like a fair with the natives, who
> brought us fruits of all kinds, and sold them to us much cheaper than I
> had got them in England. They used also to bring wine down to us in hog
> and sheep skins, which diverted me very much. (80–81)

A seaman joined a ship's company, not the Royal Navy itself, and his
service obligation lasted until he was discharged from that ship or paid off. A
person inexperienced and unskilled in seamanship usually entered the
muster list as a servant, volunteer, or landsman (think of him as an apprentice seaman) who participated in much of the heaviest labor aboard ship such
as pulling and hauling. Commonly, at the discretion of the commissioned officers, after a year at sea a landsman became an ordinary seaman and after
two years an able seaman. An ordinary seaman was generally expected to be
able to identify the parts of the ship, its rigging, and sails as well as be profi-
cient in rowing, in the use of weapons large and small, and in the making of
rope and knots. The typical able seaman, in addition to the duties of a landsman and ordinary seaman, knew how to take the helm to steer, heave a lead
to take soundings to measure the depth of water, and sew and work the vessel's sails and rigging.

Up to a third of the ratings in wartime were landsmen who had volunteered to serve. During peacetime the navy usually had no problem enlisting
voluntary ratings, but, as Equiano discovered even before he joined Pascal

aboard the *Roebuck*, during times of war the navy had to resort to a coercive, controversial, and unpopular method of finding qualified seamen to man its ships – impressment. The Royal Navy gave post captains the authority to forcibly draft experienced seamen into service by boarding incoming merchant vessels or sending press-gangs ashore to impress, or press, any seamen they wanted. From 1754 on the navy's press-gangs were very active. Most men were pressed at sea from merchant vessels, often as their ships approached England, because the press-gang could reasonably assume that those aboard were qualified seamen. Led by a ship's captain or lieutenant, a press-gang operating on land was usually based at a rendezvous-house, a place, most commonly an inn near the Thames, where the commanding officer of a press-gang lodged his gang, received volunteers, and gathered information. The rendezvous-house was also the base of operations for impressing seamen from local taverns.

No one wanted to be forced unexpectedly and without notice into the navy, and individuals as well as some local governments often resisted press-gangs. Illegal and violent impressments were frequent subjects in literature, and many people noted the paradox of depending on some Englishmen (allegedly) deprived of their rights to protect the rights of other Englishmen. Some commentators went so far as to compare the practice to chattel slavery. For example, the anonymously published pamphlet *The Sailors Advocate* describes impressments as an unqualified evil: "Oppression certainly debases the mind, and what can be a greater Oppression than forcing Men as prisoners on board a Man of war without necessaries, without allowing them time to order their affairs, or to take leave of their families. How can it be expected that a man should fight for the Liberty of others, whilst he himself feels the pangs of Slavery."[9] The antipressing sentiment was obviously popular: *The Sailors Advocate* had gone through seven editions by 1777. But popularity does not guarantee accuracy. To compare impressments, which compelled men to work for pay for a limited period, to chattel slavery trivializes the latter. And many examples exist of men who, though initially forced against their will to join naval ships, came to love a life at sea. Equiano was one of them, though he entered a ship as chattel.

As Equiano, Baker, and a former mate of Pascal sailed from Guernsey to join Pascal at the Nore, an area near the mouth of the Thames where naval fleets assembled,

> a man of war's boat came along-side to press our people; on which each
> man ran to hide himself. I was very much frightened at this, though I did

not know what it meant, or what to think or do. However, I went and hid myself also under a hencoop. Immediately the press-gang came on board with their swords drawn, and searched all about, pulled the people out by force, and put them into the boat. At last I was found out also; the man that found me held me up by the heels while they all made their sport of me, I roaring and crying out all the time most lustily; but at last the mate, who was my conductor, seeing this, came to my assistance, and did all he could to pacify me; but all to very little purpose, till I had seen the boat go off. Soon afterwards we came to the Nore, where the Roebuck lay; and, to our great joy, my master came on board to us, and brought us to the ship. (69)

By describing the threat of impressment from the perspective of himself as a child, the adult narrator Equiano renders the action more comic than dangerous and thus prepares the reader to hear at the end of the same chapter that a now more experienced Equiano joined his master over three years later in "a press-gang, as we wanted some hands to complete our complement" (76). Pascal may have been a particularly aggressive commander of press-gangs that included Equiano. In 1760 Pascal faced the prospect of legal prosecution for pressing men he wrongly thought had deserted from the navy. In a letter to the Admiralty Board dated 5 May 1760 Francis Holburne, the King's Harbourmaster at Plymouth, supported Pascal. The board followed Holburne's recommendation that His Majesty's solicitor be ordered to defend Pascal, should he be prosecuted.[10]

As a boy at most ten years of age in 1755 and small enough to be held up in the air by his heels, Equiano was not cowardly in "roaring and crying out all the time most lustily" at the prospect of what must have appeared to him to be a kidnapping attempt. Given Equiano's "extreme youth," one can understand why, when Pascal had several months earlier joked about leaving him behind in Falmouth betrothed to a little girl, Equiano had "cried immediately, and said I would not leave him" (68). Whether training a small child or a puppy, the threat of abandonment is a powerful means of enforcing loyalty and proximity. Richard Baker, Equiano, and the unnamed mate together constituted a retinue whose primary allegiance was to the man they followed, Pascal. We mistakenly tend to assume that the relatively horizontal structure of society familiar since the end of the eighteenth century, when Equiano wrote his autobiography, in which people identified themselves with others of an equivalent economic and social class, also characterized earlier periods. But Equiano's naval experience occurred when "vertical bonds of patronage and protection were still far stronger and more important than the nascent interests of class."[11] As a seaman Equiano's first allegiance would naturally be to his patron and protector, the naval officer Pascal; as a small boy his first allegiance was to the only family he felt he now had, Dick Baker, and the authority figure, Pascal, he feared so much to lose. Once aboard ship Equiano's professional and personal allegiances became mutually reinforcing.

A sense of wonder at the brave new wooden world that lay before him soon supplanted Equiano's fear of the unknown: "I was amazed indeed to see the quantity of men and the guns. However my surprise began to diminish, as my knowledge increased; and I ceased to feel those apprehensions and alarms which had taken such strong possession of me when I first came among the Europeans, and for some time after. . . . My griefs too, which in young minds are not perpetual, were now wearing away; and I soon enjoyed myself pretty well, and felt tolerably easy in my present situation" (69–70). With the livestock it also carried to supply the crew with fresh food, the *Roebuck* must have seemed like a floating village to the boy. Equiano's sense of amazement and surprise reflected his youth and inexperience with a life at sea more than his status as a slave. A white boy expressed the same sense of wonder at entering the maritime world with customs, dress, and language so different from those familiar on land: "Nor could I think what world I was in, weather among Spirits or Devills. All seemed strange; different languidge, and strange exprefhions of tonge, that I thought myself always asleep or in a dream, and never properly awake."[12]

The largest ships of war were divided into six classes, or rates, depending on the number of artillery pieces carried: a first rate had 100 guns, a second 90, a third 64–80, a fourth 50–60, a fifth 30–44, and a sixth 20–28. Normally, only the first four rates were considered ships of the line, battleships designed to line up lengthwise to fire broadsides at an opposing line of enemy ships in what was essentially a duel of floating artillery batteries. Equiano described the *Roebuck* as a "5th rate 40"; in other words, it was a two-deck fifth rate man-of-war, carrying about 40 guns (it actually carried 44) and an authorized complement of 240 to 280 men. Fifth and sixth rates during the 1750s were early versions of frigates, often used as cruisers deployed separately or with one or two other ships. Below the rates in size and firepower were a variety of auxiliary military vessels, including bomb ketches – strongly reinforced ships built to carry and transport heavy mortars – and fireships – vessels filled with combustible materials and designed to be attached to or aimed at enemy ships and set afire.

The larger rates included in their complements upward of fifty boys between six and eighteen years old. The exact number of boys on any ship is impossible to know before 1764, when the Admiralty first required that the ages (and birthplaces) of the ship's company be recorded. Most of the boys intended to qualify to become warrant and commissioned officers through on-the-job training. Many began as officers' servants, though very few of them had exclusively domestic duties. Even a smaller rate like the *Roebuck* carried "a number of boys on board" (70). Pascal's name first appears on the *Roebuck's* 18 June 1755 muster list, joined by his servant, Richard Baker, on 28 June. A lieutenant was permitted only one servant. Probably for that reason as well as because naval slave owners felt obligated to hide the social condition of their slaves, Equiano's name first appeared on the muster list on 6 August as a "Volunteer." "Gust. Vasa Capt. St." was identified as one of the eight servants permitted to Matthew Whitwell, the *Roebuck's* captain. The relationship between an officer and his servant was similar to that between a master and his apprentice. Like apprentices, officer's servants were unpaid, though the officers were given an allowance for them. Officers' servants generally had high social status aboard ship because they were often officers in the making. Hence, in effect, though a slave, as a captain's servant Equiano probably shared the status at sea of his social superiors on land.

Equiano and the other boys spent "a great part of our time . . . in play." What he remembers most vividly was being encouraged by the captain and crew to box other boys on the quarterdeck, a "sport" that earned him five to nine shillings for each fight and the opportunity to experience a new form of equality: "the first time I ever fought with a white boy." He "never knew what it was to have a bloody nose before" (70). He also learned "many of the manoeuvres of the ship during our cruise; and I was several times made to fire the guns" while the ship traveled twice across the North Sea to Holland and sailed to Scotland to pick up soldiers to bring back to England. Cruising off the coast of France, the *Roebuck* captured seventeen prizes, enemy ships whose contents would be sold, the value to be divided among the officers and crew as prize money, by far the greater proportion of which went to the captain. The ships they captured were probably commercial rather than military vessels. Like most boys Equiano grew increasingly keen to savor victory over a worthier foe than a merchantman. When the *Roebuck* encountered "a fine large French-built frigate" one evening off the coast of France at Havre de Grâce, the crew "got all things ready for fighting; and I now expected I should be gratified in seeing an engagement, which I had so long wished for in vain." The nationality of ships was very difficult to identify in darkness, and commanders often kept their identities hidden as long as possible either because they did not know whom they were facing or because they wanted to maintain the element of surprise. To the boy's "no small disappointment," however, just as the *Roebuck* commenced firing the other ship "hoisted English colours," proving "to be the Ambuscade man of war" (71). The *Embuscade*, which had been captured from the French by the British during the previous war on 21 April 1746, was indeed "French-built": it had been converted from the *Amuscade*, a fifth rate 40.

The *Roebuck*'s prizes were among some three hundred French merchant vessels the British seized on the high seas and in English ports before declaring war against France on 18 May 1756, followed by France's declaration against Britain on 9 June. Although hostilities between the two countries had been growing more widespread, intense, and significant, neither country wanted to declare war prematurely. Britain and France still saw the North American stage as a sideshow to the main theater of military events in Europe. The prime minister, the constitutionally indecisive Duke of Newcastle, had hoped to avoid war in Europe by a combination of military success in America and diplomacy. Popular sentiment and some of his own cabinet members, most notably his secretary at war, Henry Fox, pressured Newcastle to be more aggressive toward France, especially along the North American colonial border. Fox's position was strongly supported by William Augustus, the Duke of Cumberland, captain-general of the British army, and King George II's favorite son (though not his heir apparent). The royal favor and his reputation as a commander of the ruthless suppression of the Jacobite rebellion in the Scottish Highlands, which earned him the nickname the Butcher of Culloden, made Cumberland a formidable political force. Newcastle, Fox, and Cumberland formed an uneasy political alliance. As a nobleman Newcastle sat in the House of Lords, whose members were normally compliant supporters of measures favored by the monarch. With Fox managing the far less reliable House of Commons, whose members had to vote for the funding to support the Newcastle-Fox-Cumberland strategy, the British government acted as if it were preparing for war, seeking Continental allies to supplement its relatively weak ground forces. In response, France heavily reinforced its position in Canada and increased the size of its navy.

As a result, full-scale war between France and Britain was virtually inevitable by the end of 1755.[13] After suffering a series of defeats in North America during the preceding year, Britain saw its worst defeat yet in 1756, and it came at sea. Through 1755 France had been assembling in its channel ports a massive invasion force of one hundred thousand troops destined, the British assumed, for either Canada or England itself. At Toulon France was also creating a naval fleet that clearly threatened Britain's strategic Mediterranean naval base on Minorca. In March Newcastle ordered a small fleet of undermanned ships in need of repairs commanded by Adm. John Byng, a man of unproven courage, to sail to the British base at Gibraltar and, depending on the French fleet's actions, either follow it to Canada or protect Minorca's fortress, St. Philip's Castle, from attack. When Byng reached Gibraltar in early May he learned that the French had already landed on Minorca and were besieging the fortress. Without stopping to refit and make the repairs he needed he hastened to the island, prompted no doubt by the knowledge that without external aid in siege warfare the besieged always ultimately had to surrender. After the American defeats, Newcastle and his fellow ministers knew that their government could not survive a British naval defeat in European waters. Even before news of the outcome in the Mediterranean, the politicians at home were preparing to find someone to blame for any defeat. Byng engaged the French fleet off of Minorca on 20 May 1756, only two days after Britain had declared war. Facing a better-supplied and better-manned fleet commanded by the marquis de La Galissoniäre, half of Byng's ships were heavily damaged while having little effect on the enemy ships during the four-hour action. Fortunately for Byng, La Galissoniäre disengaged so that he could protect the troops on the island. Rather than waiting for reinforcements, four days later Byng decided to return to Gibraltar, thereby sealing the fate of the besieged British garrison, which eventually surrendered with honor. The person to blame was obvious.

While news of the disgrace of Byng and, consequently, the Newcastle ministry was spreading in Britain, Pascal's career was advancing. On 13 July 1756 he was promoted to first lieutenant on the *Roebuck*. On 6 December he left the *Roebuck* to join the fourth rate *Preston* on 7 January 1757 as its first lieutenant. A fourth rate 50 with a complement of 300 to 350 men, the *Preston* was commanded by Capt. John Evans. Equiano left the *Roebuck* on 14 December 1756 "at his own request." He and Baker went to Plymouth to serve from 12–21 January 1757 under Cdr. Joseph Peyton on the *Savage*, an eight-gun sloop with a complement of eighty men. Equiano was entered as "Gusta Worcester." Seamen were often lent for brief periods of time from one ship to another. Equiano reached Plymouth "just at the trial of Admiral Byng (whom I saw several times during it)" (71), which lasted from 27 December 1756 to 27 January 1757. Brought back to England under arrest for cowardice, disaffection, and neglect of duty, Byng was found guilty only of the latter. When

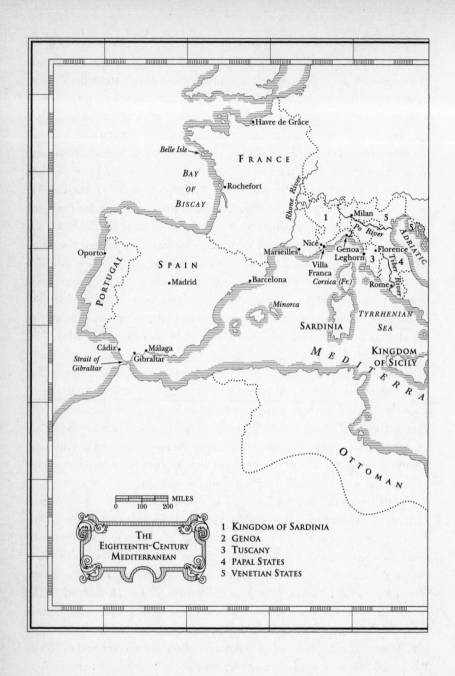

Havre de Grâce

FRANCE

Belle Isle

BAY
OF
BISCAY

Rochefort

Rhône River

1 Milan 5

Po River 5

Nicé 2

Marseilles Genoa Florence

Leghorn 3 4

Villa ADRIATIC

Franca Tiber River

Corsica (Fr.) Rome

Oporto

PORTUGAL

SPAIN

Madrid

Barcelona

Minorca

TYRRHENIAN
SEA

SARDINIA

Cádiz Málaga

Strait of Gibraltar

Gibraltar

MEDITERRA

KINGDOM
OF SICILY

OTTOMAN

MILES

0 100 200

THE
EIGHTEENTH-CENTURY
MEDITERRANEAN

1 KINGDOM OF SARDINIA
2 GENOA
3 TUSCANY
4 PAPAL STATES
5 VENETIAN STATES

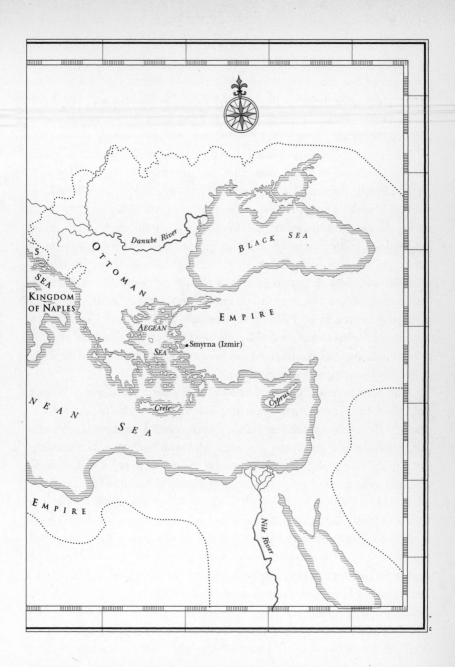

BLACK SEA

Danube River

OTTOMAN

EMPIRE

SEA

KINGDOM
OF NAPLES

AEGEAN

SEA

Smyrna (Izmir)

Cyprus

NEAN

SEA

Crete

EMPIRE

Nile River

George II refused to pardon him, he was executed by firing squad on the quarterdeck of the third rate 74 *Monarch* (the former French *Monarque*, captured in the previous war) at Portsmouth on 14 March 1757. Much of the British public was furious with both Byng and the government, which was widely thought to have prosecuted him as a scapegoat for the ministry's own failure to wage war vigorously.

As expected, the Byng affair led to the dismissal of Newcastle as prime minister, even before Byng's execution, and ultimately to a political realignment of British domestic politics that would greatly affect Equiano's naval experience and the course of the war. The monarchy was still powerful enough during the eighteenth century that no political administration could survive long without full regal support. Although under the unwritten British constitution the office of prime minister did not officially exist, in practice the strongest and most successful ministries were those headed by a dominant figure who pursued a strategy favored by the monarch and who had enough political influence to get Parliament, especially the House of Commons, to implement the measures needed to pursue that strategy. The most effective prime ministers were members of the House of Commons, unlike the Duke of Newcastle, and great orators, unlike Henry Fox.

The man preeminently qualified on both counts in 1756 was William Pitt, "the Great Commoner," a decisive man of great ambition and extraordinary self-confidence. His son William, known as the Younger Pitt, was the prime minister when Equiano was writing his autobiography. Two obstacles stood in the way of the Great Commoner: he refused to serve with Newcastle, and the king could not stand him. For years Pitt had been the great outsider, leading the opposition in criticizing the Newcastle ministry's men and measures. The king disliked Pitt because his supporters included the Leicester House faction, a group of MPs protecting the interests of George's grandson and teenaged heir apparent, the future George III, who lived with his mother in Leicester House. Before the end of the year Newcastle's position was no longer tenable. He resigned office on 11 November 1756. With little choice, the king reluctantly asked Pitt to form a ministry in which Pitt took the office of Southern secretary. Pitt promised to pursue more vigorously the development of the army and navy and to make North America the main theater of warfare. Despite having castigated Newcastle's policy of subsidizing foreign troops, Pitt promised to have subsidized allied forces protect British interests in Europe, particularly the king's beloved homeland, the electorate of Hanover. To defend the British homeland he proposed to create a militia of thirty-two thousand men raised and based in the counties. Pitt had barely had a chance to start trying to implement his measures when he made a mistake that gave George II the excuse he had been looking for to dismiss him. Pitt asked for clemency for Byng. In April 1757 the king told Pitt and the other members of his ministry to leave.

After three months of confusion during which politicians jockeyed for power while a war was going on, George II could not find an alternative to a ministry led by Pitt. Acknowledging begrudgingly that the political crisis was more about men than measures, the king, Newcastle, and Pitt agreed at the end of June to the formation of the Pitt-Newcastle ministry, with Pitt directing policy and measures as Southern secretary and Newcastle responsible for patronage and finances in his former position as first lord of the treasury. The result would become the most successful wartime ministry in British history and one of the happiest periods in Equiano's life.

But in late 1757 the war was still going very badly for the British. Accompanied by his servant, Baker, and the captain's servant "Gustavus Vavasa," Pascal served on the *Preston* as its first lieutenant from 7 January 1757 to 10 November 1757.[14] Pascal was discharged to serve under Capt. William Paston on the *Jason*, an undermanned fifth rate 44 carrying only about eighty of its full complement of two hundred men from 10 November 1757 to 27 December 1757.[15] The *Preston*'s most significant mission had been to bring the disgraced Duke of Cumberland back to England from Holland. In July 1757 George II had sent his son to command the Hanoverian army in defense of the electorate. He was soon attacked by a superior French force, which trapped his army with no chance of escape near Hastenbeck, between the Aller and Elbe rivers, unable to reach the sea and any possibility of support from the British navy. On 8 September Cumberland surrendered to the French commander, Louis-François-Armand de Plessis, who had conquered Minorca the year before. By the terms of the Convention of Kloster-Zeven German troops were withdrawn from Hanover, replaced by a French occupation force. Publicly denounced for his actions by the king upon his return to London, the humiliated Cumberland felt obligated to resign from the army on 15 October.

Like Cumberland facing disaster at Hastenbeck, the new Pitt-Newcastle ministry looked to the sea for a reversal of Britain's military fortunes. The pride of Pitt's growing navy was the *Royal George*, a first rate 100, ten years in the making at the Woolwich royal dockyard and launched on 18 February 1756. On 27 December 1757 Pascal appeared on the *Royal George* as its sixth lieutenant. As his servant, "Gustavus Vasser" entered its muster list on 12 January 1758. Pascal was not being demoted from first to sixth lieutenant; he was being promoted from the senior lieutenant on a much smaller ship to the lieutenant with the least seniority on the largest ship in the Royal Navy.[16] Each first and second rate ship had six lieutenants. The difference in size between the ship he had left and the one he was joining dazzled Equiano: "The Royal George was the largest ship I had ever seen; so that when I came on board of her I was surprised at the number of people, men, women, and children, of every denomination; and the largeness of the guns, many of them also of brass, which I had never seen before. Here were also shops or stalls of every kind of goods, and people crying their different commodities about the ship as in a town. To me it appeared a little world." With an authorized complement of 880 men, the Royal George often had on board well over 1,100 people, including dependents and purveyors of goods, when in a home port. In addition, ships usually carried livestock to supply fresh food while in port and at sea. When the Royal George sank while under repair at Spithead in August 1782, more than 800 of the 1,100 onboard drowned, including Rear Adm. Richard Kempenfelt. Approximately half of the victims were women and children visiting the ship. During the eighteenth century most people, including Equiano and most other seamen, did not know how to swim.

Equiano almost did not join Pascal on the Royal George. Pascal had wanted him to remain on the Preston with Baker, where he would learn to play the French horn, "but the ship being ordered for Turkey, I could not think of leaving my master, to whom I was very warmly attached; and I told him, if he left me behind it would break my heart." Equiano's pleasure at the sight of the "little world" of the Royal George was diminished by a sense of loss: "I was again . . . without a friend, for I had no longer my dear companion Dick" (72).

Thoughts of Dick Baker were very quickly superseded by renewed "hopes soon to have an opportunity of being gratified with a sea-fight" (73) in what would be Britain's first major victory and the turning point in the war. On 27 January 1758 Pascal, his servant "Gustavus Vasser," and the rest of the crew of the Royal George were transferred to the Namur, a second rate 90 with a complement of 750 to 780 men. The Namur was fitting up at Spithead as the flagship for Vice Adm. Edward Boscawen.[17] Nicknamed Old Dreadnought, Boscawen was one of the most distinguished commanders in the navy because of his conduct in the West Indies at the taking of Porto Bello (1739) and at the siege of Cartagena (1741) during the last war. The Namur led a fleet of twenty-three men-of-war and sixteen smaller vessels, carrying crews, marines, and soldiers totaling fourteen thousand men and nearly two thousand guns. The men and their equipment had been assembled to lay siege to the city and fortress of Louisbourg, which guarded the mouth of the St. Lawrence River and thus the approach by water to Quebec and Montreal in the French colony of Canada. Complementing Boscawen's naval forces were some thirteen thousand British and Colonial soldiers commanded by Maj. Gen. Jeffrey Amherst and Brig. Gen. James Wolfe. Louisbourg had psychological as well as strategic value: the British had failed to subdue the fortress the previous year. In 1758 almost six thousand men as well as eleven French warships in its sheltered harbor, five of them ships of the line, defended the entrance to Canada. The British military advantage was even greater than the numbers suggest. Because of a recent crop failure, the defenders were less well supplied than in the earlier siege, and since then the French government had decided to concentrate its forces in Europe. No help would be sent to relieve the besieged.

Setting forth from England before the end of February, accompanied by another fleet commanded by Adm. Sir Samuel Cornish in the *Lenox* destined for India, Boscawen's armada did not reach Halifax, Nova Scotia, until the second week of May. Contrary winds had driven it to Tenerife, the largest of the Canary Islands, where Equiano was "struck with its noted peak. Its prodigious height, and its form, resembling a sugar loaf, filled me with wonder" (73). Having refitted, resupplied, and linked up with the Colonial troops in Halifax, Boscawen's fleet reached Louisbourg on 2 June to begin the combined land and sea assault.

As one might expect of a boy on the edge of adolescence, Equiano seems to have been more impressed by the spectacle of the battle than its significance, by the bizarre as much as the noteworthy. Since "my master had some part in superintending the landing . . . I was in a small measure gratified in seeing an encounter between our men and the enemy. The French were posted on the shore to receive us, and disputed our landing for a long time: but at last they were driven from their trenches, and a complete landing was effected. Our troops pursued them as far as the town of Louisbourgh. In this action many were killed on both sides" (73). Equiano was struck by the sight of a lieutenant being shot through the cheek as he gave a command. He also found "remarkable" the death and disfigurement of one of the Mi'kmaq allies of the French: "I had that day in my hand the scalp of an Indian king, who was killed in the engagement: the scalp had been taken off by a Highlander. I saw this king's ornaments too, which were very curious, and made of feathers" (73–74).[18] Perhaps in retelling his story in 1789 Equiano assumed that his readers did not need to have spelled out for them the barbaric implications of the act he had noted so matter-of-factly as a boy in 1758.

Although the French defenders valiantly resisted the landing and the siege for six weeks, they must have known from the beginning that they were doomed to defeat. The siege conventionally began as soon as the British landed on 8 June. The British dug a trench parallel to the wall of the fortress, then another trench called a sap directly toward the wall, then another trench, another sap, another trench, moving men and artillery through the trenches and saps until they were in range of the wall. British bombs and carcasses (mortar and incendiary shells) were soon exploding within the walls of the city. Meanwhile, artillery and mortars brought ashore were trained on the French ships in the harbor, now caught in a cross fire because of the British ships outside the harbor. On the night of 25 July, under the cover of heavy fog, "about fifty boats belonging to the English men of war, commanded by Captain George Balfour of the Aetna fireship, and Mr. Laforey, another junior captain, attacked and boarded the only remaining French men of war in the harbour. They also set fire to a seventy-gun ship, but they brought off a sixty-four, called the Bienfaisant" (74). (Balfour and Laforey each had the rank of commander, not post-captain; Equiano here follows the custom of calling anyone in charge of a vessel of whatever size "captain.") The *Bienfaisant* was the flagship of the French squadron. On 26 July Louisbourg's governor, Augustin, chevalier de Drucour, gave up the fight:

> At last Louisbourgh was taken, and the English men of war came into the harbour before it, to my very great joy; for I had now more liberty of indulging myself, and I went often on shore. When the ships were in the harbour, we had the most beautiful procession on the water I ever saw. All the admirals and captains of the men of war, full dressed, and in their barges, well ornamented with pendants, came alongside of the Namur. The Vice-admiral then went on shore in his barge, followed by the other officers in order of seniority, to take possession, as I suppose, of the town and fort. Some time after this the French governor and his lady, and other persons of note, came on board our ship to dine. On this occasion our ships were dressed with colours of all kinds, from the topgallant-mast head to the deck; and this, with the firing of guns, formed a most grand and magnificent spectacle. (74)

Equiano's account of the great victory, completely consistent with the historical record of events, though viewed from the bottom up, reads like a historical novel in which famous people have walk-on roles in the story of the life of a common man. On the transatlantic voyage, for example, "the good and gallant General Wolfe on board our ship . . . often honoured me, as well as other boys, with marks of his notice; and saved me once a flogging for fighting with a young gentleman." Equiano confirms the popular conception of Wolfe as someone "whose affability made him highly esteemed and beloved by all the men" (73). Equiano humanizes the man familiar to his readers in 1789 as the heroic figure depicted in Benjamin West's 1770 painting of his death on 13 September 1759 at the battle of the Heights of Abraham during the final successful assault on Quebec. In the process Equiano praises himself indirectly. During the eighteenth century fighting across the lines of social status was considered improper behavior. A gentleman would not challenge a laborer to a duel because to do so would be contemptible. Similarly, punishments were intended to be appropriate to one's status. A common criminal was flogged, but a gentleman was not. Wolfe's saving Equiano from being flogged indicates not only Wolfe's humanity but Equiano's implicit status as well. Similarly, Equiano's retelling of his encounter with George Balfour, a retired admiral in 1789 and one of the naval heroes of the Louisbourg victory, renders him more significant than Balfour, "who was pleased to notice me, and liked me so much that he often asked my master to let him have me, but he would not part with me; and no consideration would have induced me to leave him" (74).

Equiano would not see major combat again until August 1759. The voyage back across the Atlantic during the winter of 1758–59 was uneventful until the night the ship neared the English coast, when it encountered "seven sail of large men of war," at first mistakenly taken for British ships (75). In the darkness and confusion the *Namur*'s crew managed to prepare it to fight – most of its guns had been "housed in, so that not a single gun on board was ready to be fired at any of the French ships" (75). Luckily, the French failed to take advantage of the situation, and the only loss by either side in the encounter was the recapture from the French of a merchant ship trading with Asia, an "English East-Indiaman" they had taken. Equiano learned only later that the French fleet was commanded by Adm. Hubert de Conflans, who would be defeated decisively by Adm. Sir Edward Hawke on 20–22 November 1759 at Quiberon Bay at the mouth of the Loire River in northwestern France.

Equiano went to sea again aboard the *Namur* in spring 1759, sailing to

Gibraltar to patrol the Mediterranean and keep the French fleet based at Toulon from passing through the Straits and joining the French fleet at Brest on the Atlantic coast to invade England. The Mediterranean French fleet nearly escaped being detected by Boscawen one August evening, slipping by while the British

fleet was watering and doing other necessary things. While we were in this situation, one day the admiral, with most of the principal officers, and many people of all stations, being on shore, about seven o'clock in the evening we were alarmed by signals from the frigates stationed for that purpose; and in an instant there was a general cry that the French fleet was out, and just passing through the streights. The admiral immediately came on board with some other officers; and it is impossible to describe the noise, hurry, and confusion, throughout the whole fleet, in bending their sails, and slipping their cables [releasing the ropes that held them]; many people and ship's boats were left on shore in the bustle. We had two captains on board of our ship, who came away in the hurry and left their ships to follow. We shewed lights from the gun-wales to the main-top-mast-head; and all our lieutenants were employed amongst the fleet to tell the ships not to wait for their captains, but to put the sails to the yards, slip their cables and follow us; and in this confusion of making ready for fighting, we set out for sea in the dark after the French fleet. . . . They had got the start of us so far that we were not able to come up with them during the night; but at day-light we saw seven sail of ships of the line some miles a-head. We immediately chased them till about four o'clock in the evening, when our ships came up with them; and though we were about fifteen large ships, our gallant admiral only fought them with his own division, which consisted of seven; so that we were just ship for ship. We passed by the whole of the enemy's fleet in order to come at their commander, Mons. La Clue, who was in the Ocean, an eighty-four gun ship: as we passed they all fired on us; and at one time three of them fired together, continuing to do so for some time. Notwithstanding which our admiral would not suffer a gun to be fired at any of them, to my astonishment; but made us lie on our bellies on the deck till we came quite close to the Ocean, who was a-head of them all; when we had orders to pour the whole three tiers into her at once.

The engagement now commenced with great fury on both sides: the Ocean immediately returned our fire, and we continued engaged with each other for some time; during which I was frequently stunned with the thundering of the great guns, whose dreadful contents hurried many of my companions into awful eternity. At last the French line was entirely broken, and we obtained the victory, which was immediately proclaimed with loud huzzas and acclamations. We took three prizes, La Modeste, of sixty-four guns, and Le Temeraire and Centaur, of seventy-four guns each. The rest of the French ships took to flight with all the sail they could crowd. Our ship being very much damaged, and quite disabled from pursuing the enemy, the admiral immediately quitted her, and went in the broken, and only boat we had left, on board the Newark [a second rate 80], with which, and some other ships, he went after the French. The Ocean, and another large French ship, called the Redoutable, endeavouring to escape, ran ashore at Cape Logas, on the coast of Portugal; and the French admiral and some of the crew got ashore; but we, finding it impossible to get the ships off, set fire to them both. About midnight I saw the Ocean blow up, with a most dreadful explosion. I never beheld a more awful scene. About the space of a minute, the midnight seemed turned into day by the blaze, which was attended with a noise louder and more terrible than thunder, that seemed to rend every element around us. (81–83)

Boscawen's 17–19 August 1759 victory over Admiral de La Clue Sabran at Lagos Bay destroyed France's hopes of merging its Atlantic fleet based at Brest with its Mediterranean fleet at Toulon in preparation for the planned invasion of Scotland by Maurice of Saxony, marshal general of France. Together with Admiral Hawke's victory at Quiberon Bay several months later, Lagos Bay effectively ended France's ability to invade Britain or to protect Canada. Lagos Bay and Quiberon Bay were the greatest naval successes during Britain's annus mirabilis, 1759, in which victory followed victory. Equiano's description of the pursuit from Gibraltar and the running engagement off the Bay of Lagos (which he consistently misspells) is probably so full because it recalls Britain's greatest triumphs and because it appears to have been the first one in which he participated:

My station during the engagement was on the middle deck, where I was quartered with another boy, to bring powder to the aftermost gun; and here I was a witness of the dreadful fate of many of my companions, who, in the twinkling of an eye, were dashed in pieces, and launched into eternity. Happily I escaped unhurt, though the shot and splinters flew thick about me during the whole fight. Towards the latter part of it my master was wounded, and I saw him carried down to the surgeon; but, though I was much alarmed for him, and wished to assist him, I dared not leave my post. At this station my gun-mate (a partner in bringing powder for the same gun) and I ran a very great risk for more than half an hour of blowing up the ship. For, when we had taken the cartridges out of the boxes, the bottoms of many of them proving rotten, the powder ran all about the deck, near the match-tub: we scarcely had water enough at the last to throw on it. We were also, from our employment, very much exposed to the enemy's shots; for we had to go through nearly the whole length of the ship to bring the powder. I expected therefore every minute to be my last; especially when I saw our men fall so thick about me; but, wishing to guard as much against the dangers as possible, at first I thought it would be safest not to go for the powder till the Frenchmen had fired their broadside; and then, while they were charging, I could go and come with my powder: but immediately afterwards I thought this caution was fruitless. (83–84)

In the typical six-man gun crew, boys worked as "powder monkeys," bringing up to the three-gun decks of a large man-of-war the gunpowder stored deep in the ship's hull to reduce the chances of its being ignited by enemy fire. For the same reason, only as much powder as could be used quickly was brought up at a time. In the age of sail fire was always a threat in the wooden ships. Accidents were as dangerous as enemy action and probably destroyed as many ships. British naval superiority may have been due primarily to the greater speed with which the crew fired the ship's guns. During combat gun crews had to rapidly load, aim, and fire the guns. At the same time they had to protect themselves from incoming fire and the deadly shrapnel-like splinters of wood it caused when it hit the gun deck. They also had to anticipate the possible consequences of their own actions. Each time a gun was fired its fuse had to be lit from the nearby match-tub, which contained smoldering combustible material. The threat of accidental explosions from loose gunpowder near the constant ignition source was ever present in the confusion of battle.

After making extensive needed repairs and being refitted the victorious *Namur* returned to England, bringing its captured prizes. As Pascal recovered from his wounds, Boscawen promoted him on 21 August to the rank of commander and "appointed him captain of the Aetna fire-ship, on which he and I left the Namur, and went on board of her at sea." "Fire-ships," reported a contemporary of Equiano, are for the purpose of burning a ship or ships in the enemy's line, &c. and mount 8 guns, and carry 45 men; they have several ports on each side, which are made to fall down instead of hauling up, and are provided with grapplings or hooks at their lower yard arms; and being well stored with combustibles of various kinds, to which a train is laid, if a fleet has the weather-gage, the Commander makes a signal for a fire-ship to bear down, and for a line of battle-ships to cover her, i.e. keep between her and her object; also in the mean time to take out the men except the Captain and a boat's crew, with one to steer, who should be a good swimmer: When she has gained a proper distance, the covering ship shoots a-head, then backs his main top-sail and lays to, when the man at the helm gives the ship a yaw, and jumping overboard, is taken up by the boat; and the Captain having put the match to the train as he quitted the ship, she then begins to burn; and falling along side the enemy, and hooking to his rigging, sets him on fire; and when her port ropes are burnt to let the ports fall, the fire issues from each of them in a stream; and the covering ship having taken up the boat, falls again into her station. – If one of these be taken when her train is laid, the men are mostly hanged at the yard-arms by the enemy.[19]

Converted to a fireship from the former commercial vessel *Charlotte*, the *Aetna* was larger than the standard purpose-built fireship William Spavens describes. When Pascal took charge of the same eight-gun fireship Balfour had commanded at the siege of Louisbourg the year before, it carried 55 men. Under Balfour its complement had ranged from 80 to 120 men between March 1757 and January 1758. "Gustavus Vassan" was one of Pascal's two servants on the *Aetna*, the other being James Williams.[20] In effect, however, Equiano "became the captain's steward, in which situation I was very happy, for I was extremely well treated by all on board" (84). Since pursers did not serve on naval vessels as small as the *Aetna*, Pascal acted in that capacity. As Pascal's unofficial steward, in addition to whatever domestic duties Equiano may have done for Pascal personally, Equiano probably also performed the ship's duties of a purser's steward on a larger vessel: assisting in distributing the victuals and maintaining the equivalent of a purser's rough mess book, the monthly account of the victuals consumed by the members of the crew, who ate in groups of four or six called messes. "The Steward," Spavens noted, "makes a fresh mess-book every month, so that the men can change their mess-mates as often as they please; and when he serves their beef or pork, he calls forward one day and backward the next, to give them an equal chance of time to eat it."[21] No wonder that, as the *Aetna*'s steward, Equiano was so "well treated by all."

Equiano spent the fall and winter of 1760–61 back in England. After re-fitting at Portsmouth the *Aetna* was stationed at Spithead, rumored to become part of a large fleet "intended against the Havannah," capital of the Spanish colony of Cuba, though Britain and Spain would not go to war with each other until the following year (85). Like other vessels in His Majesty's navy, the *Aetna* spent less than half its time at sea. A ship spent a relatively brief amount of time in a harbor such as Portsmouth being refitted, cleaned, and resupplied. Most of the time a vessel was said to be "in port" it was actually just offshore in a road, or sheltered place where it could safely anchor near a major harbor: Spithead near Portsmouth or the Nore near the mouth of the Thames, for example. Whatever the fleet's actual intended destination, its mission was suspended by the death of George II on 25 October 1760 and the coming to the throne of his very inexperienced grandson, twenty-two-year-old George III. George III's father, Frederick Lewis, Prince of Wales, had died in 1751. Influenced by the Earl of Bute, his former tutor, the new king had grave reservations about continuing the war, reservations shared by Newcastle. While the British waited to see how the change at the top might affect the composition of the ministry and the course of the war, the *Aetna* was stationed at Cowes, the Isle of Wight, awaiting orders.

The orders came in March, when the *Aetna* joined the fleet directed to attack the heavily fortified island of Belle-Île-en-Mer at the entrance to Quiberon Bay. Pitt had overcome the resistance of the king, Bute, and New-castle to his strategy of taking the island so that the British could easily raid the French coast, thereby forcing France to divert part of its army from fight-ing Britain's Continental allies. Belle-Île-en-Mer was also seen as an impor-tant bargaining chip for the inevitable peace negotiations France had been seeking since the beginning of the year. The naval forces were commanded by Capt. Augustus Keppel, who bore the temporary title of commodore given to a post captain who had the responsibilities of a rear admiral – command of a division of the squadron – but not the rank because of lack of seniority. Gen. Studholme Hodgson led the British ground forces. The siege of the citadel on Belle-Île-en-Mer, defended by General Chevalier de Saint Croix, lasted from 7 April to 8 June. Pascal shared the command of the ini-tial landing attempt on 8 April, which failed in the face of very strong resist-ance, during which his lieutenant, Isaac Lewis, was killed.[22] Two weeks later the British were able to drive the French out of their shore batteries and into the citadel. When the siege began "my master was ordered on shore to superintend the landing of all materials necessary for carrying on the siege; in this service I mostly attended him" (88).

Once the siege commenced and the British batteries had silenced the citadel's cannon, the seamen had only to wait for the inevitable outcome. Equiano now had the opportunity to resume the role of observer he seems to have played more often than actor during the Seven Years' War, only this time his curiosity almost cost him his life. Wanting

to see the mode of charging the mortars, and letting off the shells . . . I went to an English battery that was but a very few yards from the walls of the citadel. There indeed I had an opportunity of completely gratifying myself in seeing the whole operation, and that not without running a very great risk, both from the English shells that burst while I was there, but likewise from those of the French. One of the largest of their shells bursted within nine or ten yards of me: there was a single rock close by . . . and I got instant shelter under it in time to avoid the fury of the shell. . . . When I saw what perilous circumstances I was in, I attempted to return the nearest way I could find, and thereby I got between the English and the French centinels. . . . While I was in this situation I observed at a little distance a French horse belonging to some islanders, which I thought I would now mount, for the greater expedition of getting off. Accordingly, I took some cord which I had about me, and making a kind of bridle of it, I put it round the horse's head, and the tame beast very quietly suffered [allowed] me to tie him thus and mount him. As soon as I was on the horse's back I began to kick and beat him, and try every means to make him go quick, but all to very little purpose: I could not drive him out of a slow pace. While I was creeping along, still within reach of the enemy's shot, I met with a servant well mounted on an English horse. I immediately stopped; and, crying, told him my case; and begged of him to help me, and this he effectually did; for, having a fine large whip, he began to lash my horse with it so severely, that he set off full speed with me towards the sea, while I was quite unable to hold or manage him. In this manner I went along till I came to a craggy precipice. I now could not stop my horse; and my mind was filled with apprehensions of my deplorable fate, should he go down the precipice, which he appeared fully disposed to do: I therefore thought I had better

throw myself off him at once, which I did immediately with a great deal
of dexterity, and fortunately escaped unhurt. As soon as I found myself at
liberty, I made the best of my way for the ship, determined I would not
be so fool-hardy again in a hurry. (89–90)

Even before the defenders of Belle-Île-en-Mer had capitulated, the struggle for control of the Atlantic and thus the North American colonies was already effectively over. French freedom of action at sea was severely restricted
by British blockades of French naval ports. From June 1761 to February 1762
the *Aetna* took part in patrolling the Basque Road lying between the Île de Ré
and the Île d'Oleron at the entrance to the French naval base of Rochefort in
order to contain a French fleet. The only actions Equiano witnessed were in-
effective attacks on the British by French bomb-vessels and fireships. With
Pitt out of office since October 1761, the advocates for peace in the ministry,
now headed by Bute, were clearly in charge and in negotiations with France.
Although the Treaty of Paris, which recognized most of Britain's great territorial gains at the expense of the French, was not signed until 10 February
1763, by late fall 1762 the end of the Seven Years' War was obviously at hand.
Everyone had begun to think of the future:

> Our ship having arrived at Portsmouth, we went into the harbour, and re-
> mained there till the end of November, when we heard great talk about
> peace; and, to our very great joy, in the beginning of December we had
> orders to go up to London with our ship, to be paid off. We received this
> news with loud huzzas, and every other demonstration of gladness; and
> nothing but mirth was to be seen through every part of the ship. I too was
> not without my share of the general joy on this occasion. I thought now
> of nothing but being freed, and working for myself . . . and my heart
> burned within me, while I thought the time long till I obtained my free-
> dom: for though my master had not promised it to me, yet, besides the as-
> surances I had received that he had no right to detain me, he always
> treated me with the greatest kindness, and reposed in me an unbounded
> confidence; he even paid attention to my morals; and would never suffer
> me to deceive him, or tell lies, of which he used to tell me the conse-
> quences; and that if I did so, God would not love me; so that, from all this
> tenderness, I had never once supposed, in all my dreams of freedom, that
> he would think of detaining me any longer than I wished. (91–92)

Pascal, however, had other plans.

Chapter Four

FREEDOM DENIED

Equiano's high expectations at the close of the Seven Years' War were not un-warranted. By the end of 1762 he had spent nearly half of his life aboard royal naval vessels, where his status as Pascal's slave had been effectively hidden. One can understand why Equiano might have thought of his enslaved condition as merely nominal. His freedom of movement appears to have been no more limited than that of other officers' servants who were legal minors though not chattel slaves. Unlike most slaves, Equiano was out of his owner's sight for months at a time on Guernsey, for weeks on loan to other vessels, and for days and hours during military engagements. Pascal had even been prepared to send Equiano off to the Mediterranean with Richard Baker on the *Preston* for more than a year. Equiano always remained tied to Pascal, however, by a quasi-familial relationship based on loyalty and affection toward Pascal, Baker, and their shipmates. As a slave Equiano was not paid for his services to Pascal, but he would not have been paid as a servant to a naval officer either. Naval officers were given an allowance for their servants, the money being paid to the officer, not the servant. No distinction is made between Equiano and Baker in the ships' paybooks, though aboard ships where Baker was a lieutenant's servant and Equiano a captain's servant, Equiano arguably held the higher social status. By the end of 1762 he had achieved a higher rating – able seaman – than Baker, still a captain's servant, had when he died at a comparable age several years earlier.

Equiano's relationship with Baker anticipated the relationships he generally had with others during his life aboard royal naval vessels. His life in the "little world" (72) of the navy was one in which the content of his character mattered more than the color of his complexion, to paraphrase Martin Luther King Jr. Not once in his detailed account of his naval experience did he see himself as a victim of what we recognize today as racial prejudice. He offers us in the little wooden worlds of the ships of the British Royal Navy and the merchant marine a vision of an almost utopian, microcosmic alternative to the slavery-infested greater world. His memory of events and details of thirty years earlier may be so remarkably precise and accurate because he saw his naval experience as a model for the relationship between Europeans and Africans. The demands of the seafaring life permitted him to transcend the barriers imposed by what we call race.

Equiano was rarely compelled during his years with Pascal to remember his complexion and past, each time with a decreasing sense of discomfort and alienation. He very quickly began to adopt English standards of appearance and conduct in early 1755:

As I was now amongst a people who had not their faces scarred, like some of the African nations where I had been, I was very glad I did not let them ornament me in that manner when I was with them. When we arrived at Guernsey, my master placed me to board and lodge with one of his mates, who had a wife and family there; and some months afterwards he went to England, and left me in the care of this mate, together with my friend Dick. This mate had a little daughter aged about five or six years, with whom I used to be much delighted. I had often observed, that when her mother washed her face it looked very rosy; but when she washed mine it did not look so; I therefore tried oftentimes myself if I could not by washing make my face of the same colour as my little playmate (Mary), but it was all in vain; and I now began to be mortified at the difference in our complexions. This woman behaved to me with great kindness and attention; and taught me every thing in the same manner as

FREEDOM DENIED ■ 73

she did her own child, and indeed in every respect treated me as such. (68–69)

Foster parental and sibling figures rapidly replaced the family Equiano tells us he had been torn from in Africa. Within a few years Equiano "began to consider myself as happily situated; for my master treated me always extremely well; and my attachment and gratitude to him were very great. From the various scenes I had beheld on ship-board, I soon grew a stranger to terror of every kind, and was, in that respect at least, almost an Englishman" (77). Having embraced a substitute family, he was not overwhelmed by grief when his hopes of being reunited with his sister were disappointed in 1759:

> I had frequently told several people, in my excursions on shore, the story of my being kidnapped with my sister, and of our being separated, as I have related before; and I had as often expressed my anxiety for her fate, and my sorrow at having never met her again. One day, when I was on shore, and mentioning these circumstances to some persons, one of them told me he knew where my sister was, and if I would accompany him, he would bring me to her. Improbable as this story was, I believed it immediately, and agreed to go with him, while my heart leaped for joy; and, indeed, he conducted me to a black young woman, who was so like my sister that, at first sight, I really thought it was she; but I was quickly undeceived; and, on talking to her, I found her to be of another nation. (79–80)

In the very next paragraph Equiano recalls having reacted far less dispassionately to the loss of his "dear companion Dick":

> While we lay here the Preston came in from the Levant [the eastern shore of the Mediterranean between Greece and Egypt]. As soon as she arrived, my master told me I should now see my old companion Dick, who was gone in her when she sailed for Turkey. I was much rejoiced at this information, and expected every minute to embrace him; and when the captain came on board of our ship, which he did immediately after, I ran to enquire about my friend; but, with inexpressible sorrow, I learned from the boat's crew that the dear youth was dead! and that they had brought his chest, and all his other things to my master: these he afterwards gave to me, and I regarded them as a memorial of my friend, whom I loved and grieved for as a brother. (80)

Two years later, on the Isle of Wight, Equiano experienced "a trifling incident" that seems to have startled him with its reminder of his complexion and ethnicity:

> While I was here, I met with a trifling incident which surprised me agreeably. I was one day in a field belonging to a gentleman who had a black boy about my own size; this boy having observed me from his master's house, was transported at the sight of one of his own countrymen, and ran to meet me with the utmost haste. I not knowing what he was about, turned a little out of his way at first, but to no purpose; he soon came close to me, and caught hold of me in his arms as if I had been his brother, though we had never seen each other before. After we had talked together for some time, he took me to his master's house, where I was treated very kindly. This benevolent boy and I were very happy in frequently seeing each other, till about the month of March 1761, when our ship had orders to fit out again for another expedition. (85)

In his memory at least the reminders of the difference in complexion between the child Equiano and the Europeans with whom he found himself were isolated events that happened only onshore. At sea, artificially imposed racial limitations would have destroyed everyone, white and black. In many ways Equiano's experience exemplifies the opportunities a person of African descent found in the Royal Navy, where color was not a matter of record. For example, the muster lists recording the rating, or rank and job, of each member of the crew do not identify members of the crew by what we call race or ethnicity or by free or slave status. Nor do the paybooks, perhaps because, as one historian observes, "naval opinion in general and the Admiralty's in particular inclined to regard a man-of-war as a little piece of British territory in which slavery was improper."[1] The Admiralty's position on slavery in England and by extension on its ships anticipated by decades the ruling in 1772 by the Earl of Mansfield, chief justice of the King's Bench, which held that slaves brought to England could not legally be forced to return to the colonies. Naval practice was ahead of eighteenth-century law. Equiano's case was typical in that, if we did not know from external sources that he was of African descent, we could not have deduced that fact from his naval records. Equiano's association with the Royal Navy from 1755 to 1762 was also representative of the experiences of many other seamen, white and black, who first went to sea as boys or landsmen. A landsman could gain the experience to eventually deserve the designation of able seaman. A boy would strive to

Grog on Board a Ship (1785), by Thomas Rowlandson. Note the black and white boys on the left looking at a book together. At sea, sailors lived in relative equanimity regardless of race. (Mary Evans Picture Library)

achieve the status of officer by commission or warrant among the more than eighty-five thousand men in "the largest industrial unit of its day in the western world."[2] Within the ratings black sailors ate the same food as their white counterparts, wore the same clothes, shared the same quarters, received the same pay, benefits, and health care, undertook the same duties, and had the same opportunities for advancement.

Equiano's time with Pascal was not idyllic. He observed or experienced the good as well as the bad aspects of naval life. In 1759 "while we were at Gibraltar I saw a soldier hanging by the heels at one of the moles.[3] I thought this a strange sight, as I had seen a man hanged in London by his neck. At another time I saw the master of a frigate towed to shore on a grating [platform], by several of the men of war's boats, and discharged [from] the fleet, which I understood was a mark of disgrace for cowardice. On board the same ship a sailor was also hung up at the main-yard-arm" (80). In each case Equiano saw how the British army and navy enforced discipline through the use of public shaming. Equiano comments in a footnote that the soldier hanged by his heels "had drowned himself in endeavouring to desert" (262).

In early 1757 Equiano suffered the occupational hazard of contracting chilblains, an inflammation of the skin on the hands or feet caused by the damp cold endemic to ships during the winter. He was annoyed that the chilblains delayed for so long his chance to visit "London, the place I had long desired to see" (71). His desire was understandable. Greater London was by far the largest and most important city in the Western Hemisphere. It was the cultural and economic as well as political capital of the transatlantic British Empire. Although Anglo-American populations can only be roughly estimated before the official decennial censuses began, respectively, in the United States in 1790 and in Britain in 1801, the relative size of London was undeniable. Its mid-eighteenth-century population of around 675,000 grew to approximately 900,000 by the first census. The next-largest European city, Paris, had about five hundred thousand people in 1750. The next-largest English towns of Manchester, Liverpool, and Birmingham each had less than 10 percent of London's population. For generations observers had likened the relationship of London to England to an oversized head on the national body. Between 1750 and 1801 London was home to over 10 percent of the total population of England and Wales, which grew from nearly six to almost nine million. By one authoritative calculation more than one in six eighteenth-century English people lived at least part of their lives in London.[4] Most of the population lived and worked in Greater, or outer, London. The City of London, the "city within the walls," had a population in the late eighteenth century of around seventy thousand relatively wealthy residents living in an area of 1 square mile. "The City" still refers to the small area bounded by the Thames River on the south, the Tower of London on the east, the Inns of Court on the west, and the London Wall (roughly the present-day Barbican) on the north. Most of Greater London was in the county of Middlesex, which surrounded the City of London. With its own Lord Mayor and local government, the City was the financial and commercial center of Greater London; Westminster was the administrative center of Great Britain. Samuel Johnson was not the only Englishman who believed that "when a man is tired of London, he is tired of life; for there is in London all that life can afford."[5]

In his first attempt to get to London, because of illness Equiano reached only as far as Hyde Park Corner, in the village of Knightsbridge on the western outskirts of Westminster. He spent most of the period between the end of January and the beginning of November 1757 hospitalized first for chilblains and then for smallpox: "I had at this time the chilblains to such a degree that

I could not stand for several months, and I was obliged to be sent to St. George's Hospital. There I grew so ill, that the doctors wanted to cut my left leg off at different times, apprehending a mortification [gangrene]; but I always said I would rather die than suffer it; and happily (I thank God) I recovered without the operation. After being there several weeks, and just as I had recovered, the small-pox broke out on me, so that I was again confined; and I thought myself now particularly unfortunate. However, I soon recovered again" (71).

One of the opportunities the navy offered Equiano and anyone else in the service was education, both formal and experiential. For Equiano, almost every experience, no matter how dangerous or disheartening, was an opportunity for learning. In recounting his life he marks his progress from a world of magic to one of science. From the time he tells us he was kidnapped into slavery, the European world in which he became immersed left him "amazed," "beyond measure astonished," "often very much astonished," "persuaded that I had gotten into a world of bad spirits, and that they were going to kill me," "exceedingly amazed," "lost in astonishment," "convinced it was done by magic," and "still more astonished" (54–61). Even in the midst of his account of the horrors of the Middle Passage, he digresses quite startlingly from mentioning latrines to record moments of wonder prompted by his curiosity about nature and an instrument used to determine latitude by measuring the altitude of the sun or stars:

> Many a time we were near suffocation, from the want of fresh air, which we were often without for whole days together. This, and the stench of the necessary tubs, carried off many. During our passage I first saw flying fishes, which surprised me very much: they used frequently to fly across the ship, and many of them fell on the deck. I also now first saw the use of the quadrant. I had often with astonishment seen the mariners make observations with it, and I could not think what it meant. They at last took notice of my surprise; and one of them, willing to increase it, as well as to gratify my curiosity, made me one day look through it. The clouds appeared to me to be land, which disappeared as they passed along. This heightened my wonder: and I was now more persuaded than ever that I was in another world, and that every thing about me was magic. (59)

His "surprise began to diminish, as [his] knowledge increased" (71), and he quickly sought to supplement his experiences with education, "as well as I was

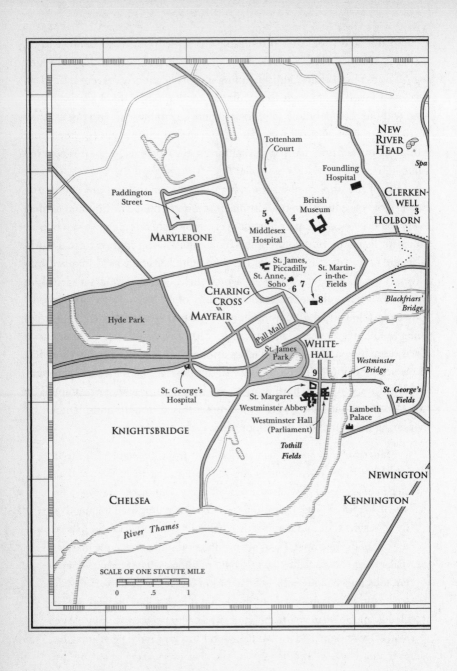

NEW
RIVER
HEAD

Spa

CLERKEN-
WELL
HOLBORN

3

Tottenham
Court

Foundling
Hospital

British
Museum

Blackfriars'
Bridge

Paddington
Street

MARYLEBONE

5

Middlesex
Hospital

4

St. James,
Piccadilly
St. Anne,
Soho

St. Martin-
in-the-
Fields

6 7

CHARING
CROSS
MAYFAIR

Pall Mall

8

WHITE-
HALL

Westminster
Bridge

Hyde Park

St. James
Park

9

St. George's
Fields

St. George's
Hospital

St. Margaret
Westminster Abbey
Westminster Hall
(Parliament)

Lambeth
Palace

KNIGHTSBRIDGE

Tothill
Fields

NEWINGTON

KENNINGTON

CHELSEA

River Thames

SCALE OF ONE STATUTE MILE

0   .5   1

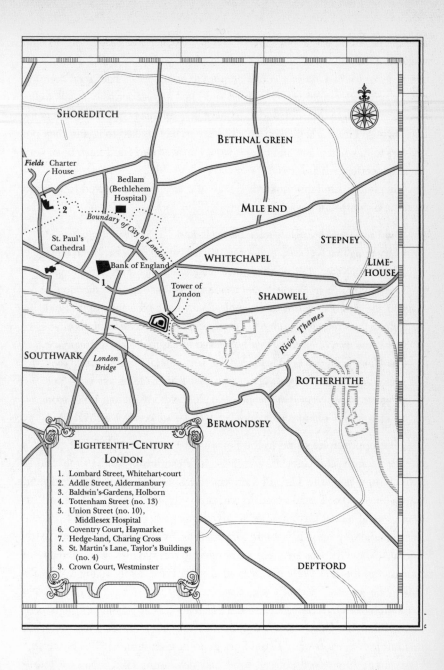

SHOREDITCH

BETHNAL GREEN

Fields Charter House

Bedlam (Bethlehem Hospital)

MILE END

Boundary of City of London

STEPNEY

St. Paul's Cathedral

LIME-HOUSE

Bank of England

WHITECHAPEL

Tower of London

SHADWELL

River Thames

SOUTHWARK

London Bridge

ROTHERHITHE

BERMONDSEY

EIGHTEENTH-CENTURY LONDON

1. Lombard Street, Whitehart-court
2. Addle Street, Aldermanbury
3. Baldwin's-Gardens, Holborn
4. Tottenham Street (no. 13)
5. Union Street (no. 10), Middlesex Hospital
6. Coventry Court, Haymarket
7. Hedge-land, Charing Cross
8. St. Martin's Lane, Taylor's Buildings (no. 4)
9. Crown Court, Westminster

DEPTFORD

able to speak and ask about things." His first teacher was Baker, "for I could make free with him, and he always instructed me with pleasure." Equiano's desire to learn to read led to a comic attempt at imitation: "I had often seen my master and Dick employed in reading; and I had a great curiosity to talk to the books, as I thought they did; and so to learn how all things had a beginning: for that purpose I have often taken up a book, and have talked to it, and then put my ears to it, when alone, in hopes it would answer me; and I have been very much concerned when I found it remained silent" (68).[6]

Thereafter, Equiano took advantage of every chance he had to learn to read the old-fashioned way. By the end of 1757 he

> could now speak English tolerably well, and . . . perfectly understood every thing that was said. I now not only felt myself quite easy with these new countrymen, but relished their society and manners. I no longer looked upon them as spirits, but as men superior to us; and therefore I had the stronger desire to resemble them; to imbibe their spirit, and imitate their manners; I therefore embraced every occasion of improvement; and every new thing that I observed I treasured up in my memory. I had long wished to be able to read and write; and for this purpose I took every opportunity to gain instruction, but had made as yet very little progress. However, when I went to London with my master, I had soon an opportunity of improving myself, which I gladly embraced. (77–78)

That opportunity came in the persons of Pascal's and hence Equiano's extended family, the Guerins, who lived in Westminster, at the time a fairly distinct suburb of the City of London. Elizabeth Martha, Maynard, and Mary Guerin were Pascal's cousins and probably the "friends in England" to whom Pascal had at first intended to give Equiano as "a present" (64). As the oldest daughter, only Elizabeth Martha was by convention called "Miss Guerin." Maynard was an agent authorized to receive in London the pay of seamen and marines while they served abroad. Presumably acting as Pascal's banker, he was sent Pascal's wages while Pascal served on the *Roebuck*. No doubt motivated by a desire to introduce Equiano to Christianity through reading the Bible, the Guerin sisters sent the boy to school. He soon learned from the Guerins' servants that "I could not go to heaven, unless I was baptized," which made him "very uneasy; for I had now some faint idea of a future state." When Miss Guerin asked Pascal's permission to have Equiano baptized, Pascal at first refused, perhaps out of fear that baptism would jeopardize his claim to Equiano as chattel because of the still widespread belief that Christians could not legally enslave fellow Christians. But because she insisted and

because Pascal was "under some obligation" to Maynard Guerin (78), probably financial, he ultimately complied. On 9 February 1759, in St. Margaret's,
Westminster (the parish church of the House of Commons), "Gustavus Vassa
a Black born in Carolina 12 years old" was baptized. Miss Guerin and her
brother stood as his godparents. Ignatius Sancho, the most famous African
British author before Equiano, had been married in St. Margaret's two months
earlier. Sancho and Equiano must have known each other at least by sight.
Sancho lived only a few blocks away from the Guerins in Westminster. Whenever Equiano stayed with the Guerins, he and Sancho undoubtedly noticed
each other among their mostly white fellow worshipers at St. Margaret's.

The clergyman who baptized Equiano gave him his first book, Thomas
Wilson's *An Essay towards an Instruction for the Indians* (1740). Wilson was the
bishop of Sodor and Man. By giving Equiano the book the minister authorized Equiano's access to literacy, an access he fully exploited. He learned
not only from his "school-master, whom I liked very much," but also from
his "kind patronesses, the Miss Guerins," who "often used to teach me to
read, and took great pains to instruct me in the principles of religion, and the
knowledge of God" (79).

Equiano's education continued at sea as he moved from one teacher to
another. After leaving the Guerins he continued his formal education aboard
the *Namur,* which like all the larger ships included a schoolmaster, whose primary role was to prepare the young boys to become officers. His qualifications and duties are spelled out in the navy's official *Regulations and Instructions
Relating to His Majesty's Service at Sea*:

> No person shall be warranted to serve as schoolmaster in any of His
> Majesty's ships who have not been first examined before the Master,
> Wardens and Assistants of the Trinity House of Deptford Strond and pro-
> duced a certificate under their hands of his being well skilled in the the-
> ory and practice of the art of navigation and qualified to teach youth
> therein, and another under the hand of persons of known credit testifying
> the sobriety of his life and conversation. . . . He is to employ his time on
> board in instructing the volunteers in writing, arithmetic and the study of
> navigation and in whatsoever may contribute to render them artists in
> that science. . . . He is likewise to teach the other youths of the ship ac-
> cording to such orders as he shall receive from the Captain and with re-
> gard to their several capacities, whether in reading, writing or otherwise.[7]

The education needed to make the precise mathematical calculations and to
write the detailed records required of officers was far from rudimentary.

Equiano's schoolmasters on land and sea enabled him to continue learning on his own: "While on shipboard I . . . endeavoured to improve myself" (91). Hence, he enjoyed his later position as steward on the *Aetna* in part because it granted him the "leisure to improve myself in reading and writing" (84–85).

He found the opportunity for more formal instruction even on a ship of war as small as the *Aetna*, which lacked a warranted schoolmaster. Pascal's clerk, Patrick Hill, taught Equiano to write and introduced him to the rule of three, a rule in mathematics whereby the fourth proportional number can be calculated from three given numbers. More important, Equiano's messmate Daniel Queen (or Quin, according to the paybook), "about forty years of age, a man very well educated, who . . . dressed and attended the captain, . . . soon became very much attached to me, and took very great pains to instruct me in many things. He taught me to shave and dress hair a little, and also to read in the Bible, explaining many passages to me, which I did not comprehend." Queen played a crucial role in Equiano's later reconstruction of an African past: "I was wonderfully surprised to see the laws and rules of my country written almost exactly here [in the Bible]; a circumstance which I believe tended to impress our manners and customs more deeply on my memory. I used to tell him of this resemblance; and many a time we have sat up the whole night together at this employment." Queen soon became yet another father figure to Equiano, whose personal identification with Queen was even stronger than that with Pascal:

> In short he was like a father to me; and some even used to call me after
> his name; they also styled me the black Christian. Indeed I almost loved
> him with the affection of a son. Many things I have denied myself that he
> might have them; and when I used to play at marbles, or any other game,
> and won a few halfpence, or got any little money, which I did sometimes,
> for shaving any one, I used to buy him a little sugar or tobacco, as far as
> my stock of money would go. He used to say, that he and I never should
> part; and that when our ship was paid off, as I was as free as himself or
> any other man on board, he would instruct me in his business, by which
> I might gain a good livelihood. (91–92)

In December 1762 the *Aetna* approached Deptford, on the Thames be-low London. Equiano apparently had every reason to be optimistic about his future. His years in the navy had given him a new sense of family and ren-dered him literate, acculturated to English society, and trained to make a liv-ing as a domestic servant, a hairdresser, or a professional seaman. On 29 September 1762 Pascal had promoted him to the rating of able seaman, though if Pascal planned to try to continue pocketing Equiano's salary, his motivation for the promotion combined self-interest with recognition of his slave's naval skills.[8] Although Equiano never mentions his promotion in his autobiography, as the *Aetna*'s steward he was very likely aware of Pascal's action. As someone who had led a "long sea-faring life" (94), Equiano certainly knew that an able seaman could not be a slave, because he was entitled to be paid. Assuming that he knew of his promotion, he had every reason to expect to be manumitted when the *Aetna* reached England and its crew was paid off. Pascal may have originally intended the promotion as a sign to Equiano that his freedom was almost at hand and that it was to be given at Pascal's discretion alone.

Equiano's naval experience like that of many others offers a powerful corrective to common misconceptions about life at sea during the eighteenth century. On 10 April 1778, using language more commonly found in descriptions of the Middle Passage of enslaved Africans being brought to the Americas, Samuel Johnson remarked to his future biographer, James Boswell, that "as to the sailor, when you look down from the quarter deck to the space below, you see the utmost extremity of human misery; such crouding, such filth, such stench!" To Boswell's rejoinder, "Yet sailors are happy," Johnson replied, "They are happy as brutes are happy, with a piece of fresh meat, – with the grossest sensuality." On 18 March 1776 Boswell recorded perhaps Johnson's best-known words on the subject of a naval career: "[Johnson] took occasion to enlarge, as he often did, upon the wretchedness of a sea-life. 'A ship is worse than a gaol. There is, in a gaol, better air, better company, better conveniency of every kind; and a ship has the additional disadvantage of being in danger. When men come to like a sea-life, they are not fit to live on land.'" Boswell responded, "Then . . . it would be cruel in a father to breed his son to the sea." Johnson replied, "'It would be cruel in a father who thinks as I do. Men go to sea before they know the unhappiness of that way of life; and when they have come to know it, they cannot escape from it, because it is then too late to choose another profession; as indeed is generally the case with men, when they have engaged in any particular way of life.'"[9] Given Johnson's experience with the naval service of Francis Barber, his own black servant and eventual heir, Johnson should have known better.

Richard Bathurst, the father of Johnson's good friend Dr. Richard Bathurst, had brought Francis Barber to England from Jamaica in 1750. Barber entered Johnson's domestic service in 1752, shortly after the death of Johnson's wife, when Barber was about seven years old. Starting in October 1756 Barber worked for an apothecary named Farren in Cheapside but returned to Johnson's employ about two years later. To Johnson's dismay young Barber soon grew restless, and by autumn 1758 he had run away, eventually entering as one of 220 men on the H.M.S. *Stag*, a new fifth rate 32, no doubt attracted by the same possibility of adventure that so invigorated his contemporary Equiano. The muster list of the *Stag* records Barber's entry on 17 December 1758 with the rating of "Landman," indicating that he had volunteered rather than been forcibly impressed to serve on the ship. Johnson seems to have known that only experienced seamen were eligible for impressment. When Johnson sought, for the second time, the aid of George Hay, M.P., in November 1759 to get Barber released from service, Johnson noted that "if the Lords of the Admiralty would be pleased to discharge him, which as he is no seaman, [it] may be done with little injury to the King's Service." Barber was not officially discharged from the *Stag* until 8 October 1760, though his name appears on the muster lists as late as the 1 November–31 December 1760 muster, suggesting that he chose to remain on board for months longer than necessary.[10] Though Barber was indeed "no seaman" in terms of his rating, his loss would have been more than a "little injury to the King's Service" because even the most unskilled seaman contributed to the running of a ship. After two years of service Barber must have become a significant asset to the navy. Many years later Barber told Boswell that he was discharged "without any wish of his own."[11]

Unlike Barber, however, Equiano was ready in December 1762 to be discharged from the navy and try his hand at something new as a free man. He was prepared to take his books, chest of clothes, and the nearly nine guineas he had saved from tips and small investments and start a new life with the help of Daniel Queen. Equiano never imagined that the man who had been like a father to him for almost half his life would object.

Before Equiano could even tell Pascal of his "dreams of freedom," Pascal stopped him from trying to realize those dreams: "The ship was up about half an hour, when my master ordered the barge to be manned; and all in an instant, without having before given me the least reason to suspect any thing of the matter, he forced me into the barge, saying, I was going to leave him, but he would take care I should not. I was so struck with the unexpectedness of this proceeding, that for some time I did not make a reply, only I made an offer to go for my books and chest of clothes, but he swore I should not move out of his sight; and if I did he would cut my throat, at the same time taking his hanger [a short, curved broadsword that hangs from the belt]" (92–93). Equiano was momentarily dumbfounded. While discussing his hopes and plans with Queen he had forgotten how difficult it was to keep secrets aboard ship. As one admiral later noted, "Men are nowhere crowded in so small a space as in a ship of war. The individuals of which the company is composed may literally be said to live in public. Actions can never be concealed; even whispers may be heard. . . . Nothing private can be transacted in such a community; even a gust of passion is incapable of being concealed."[12]

Recovering from his shock and "plucking up courage," Equiano told Pascal, "I was free, and he could not by law serve me so. But this only enraged him the more." Equiano and Pascal both recognized that the legality of slavery was usually not recognized de facto (in practice) in either England or the Royal Navy. The status of slavery in England de jure (by law), however, was not clear because Parliament had not passed a "positive" law either way on the issue. That is, Parliament had created no written law addressing the issue of slavery in England. Consequently, to justify their respective positions, proponents and opponents of slavery were all forced to appeal to the tradition of common law practice and the concept of natural rights. The status of slavery was left for the courts rather than the legislature to determine. Many people believed that the legality of slavery had been established in 1729, when attorney general Sir Philip Yorke and solicitor general Charles Talbot unofficially offered their opinion that slavery was legal in England, that a slave's status was not affected by baptism, and that "the master may legally compel him to return again to the plantations."[13] But the authority of the Yorke-Talbot opinion as legal precedent was disputed and challenged by other rulings. In 1569 the ruling in the Cartwright case, which involved a Russian slave brought to England, declared slavery illegal on English soil. Lord Chancellor Robert Henley held that slaves became free as soon as they set foot in England. But these were isolated and unpublicized cases whose legal implications were not widely recognized. Jane Collier, for example, confidently asserted in 1753 that "purchased slaves are not allowed" in Britain.[14] Although the great jurist Sir William Blackstone later qualified his statement, the first edition of his *Commentaries on the Laws of England* (London, 1765) declared that "a slave or negro, the instant he lands in England, becomes a freeman."[15]

Equiano's sympathetic crewmates passively resisted their captain's commands and offered their colleague words of encouragement: "[Pascal] was resolved to put me on board the first vessel he could get to receive me. The boat's crew, who pulled against their will, became quite faint at different times, and would have gone ashore; but he would not let them. Some of them strove then to cheer me, and told me he could not sell me, and that they would stand by me, which revived me a little, and encouraged my hopes; for as they pulled along he asked some vessels to receive me, and they would not." Downriver, Pascal at last found James Doran, captain of the merchant ship *Charming Sally*, who was willing to buy Equiano and take him to Montserrat once Doran's ship had joined a convoy forming at Portsmouth to sail under armed escort to the West Indies.

Doran quickly asserted his authority over his new slave:

> Captain Doran asked me if I knew him. I answered that I did not; "Then," said he "you are now my slave." I told him my master could not sell me to him, nor to any one else. "Why," said he, "did not your master buy you?" I confessed he did. But I have served him, said I, many years, and he has taken all my wages and prize-money, for I only got one sixpence during the war; besides this I have been baptized; and by the laws of the land no man has a right to sell me: and I added, that I had heard a lawyer, and others at different times, tell my master so. They both then said that those people who told me so were not my friends: but I replied – It was very extraordinary that other people did not know the law as well as they. (93–94)

Doran told Equiano that he "talked too much English," acknowledging that Equiano knew his legal precedents better than either Doran or Pascal had expected. Doran had no recourse but to resort to threats of physical harm: "If I did not behave myself well, and be quiet, he had a method on board to make me" (93–94). Pascal and Doran clearly had might on their side and were willing to use it against Equiano. But Equiano arguably had right on his, and they probably knew it. Their use of stealth and threats to resort to force certainly suggested so.

Almost exactly four years earlier the Admiralty Board had established a precedent obviously applicable to Equiano's situation. The complex case began in mid-December 1758, when William Castillo addressed his "Humbly Pettison" to William Pitt, the prime minister.[16] According to Castillo, he had been born in Barbados and "Brought over to England By James Jones Master of his Majestys Ship the Northumberland in the Year 1752." He had been baptized in Plymouth, "which I most humbly Conceive intitles me to the previllege of a free Subject." But Jones had ordered him "put a Board the Hunter Tender, at the Tower, and Sent from thence In a Post Chaise in Irons to Portsmouth." He was "Now on Board his Majestys ship the Neptune at Spithead, with a Collar on my Neck in Day and in Irons att night in Order to Be sent on Board the first Ship Bound to Barbadoes to Be Sold." Claiming "the Previllege of a free Subject which I Most humbly Conceive I am in Titled to By the Laws of this Land" and "Being Willing to Serve on Board his Majestys Ship, Which I am a Board of Now," Castillo sought protection from being sent back into slavery. Pitt forwarded Castillo's petition to the Admiralty Board, which ordered the Portsmouth harbormaster, Adm. Francis Holburne, to investigate the situation.

Responding to Holburne's inquiry, Jones submitted his own statement of the case, which differed significantly from Castillo's. According to Jones, the former "Castalio Smith" had renamed himself "William Castalio" in an apparent act of independence common among manumitted or self-emancipated slaves. As if to deny the validity of Castillo's new identity, Jones consistently refers to him as "Castalio." Jones and Castillo had met while working on the same commercial vessel in the Boston, Massachusetts, harbor in 1751. Only after Castillo's repeated requests and his shedding of many tears did Jones agree to buy Castillo for £70 so that he would not be sold onshore. Castillo agreed to sign indentures committing him to serve Jones for seven years or until he had paid Jones his purchase price. Besides the purchase price Jones "was at Ten or Twelve Pounds expence in getting him instructed to Play on the Violin in London as He had always an inclination to play on that Instrument." Jones accuses Castillo of ingratitude: "To requite me for all my kindnesses this very Negro Man left me secretly the 16 May 1756 about the Middle of his Aprenticeship whereby I have suffered greatly in my property that He carried with him." By chance, one of Jones's lieutenants came upon Castillo while impressing men in London and had him sent, as Castillo described, to Portsmouth, where Jones had him "confined so as to prevent him from making his Escape, but had not the least thought of sending him to be sold at Barbados as represented by him which is an absolute falsehood for I only thought as He had been some time in his Majestys Service to keep him still in it as being an able Man and very fit to serve his Majesty." Jones seems aware that he was vulnerable to the charge of false imprisonment and that his right to reclaim Castillo as a runaway slave rather than a runaway apprentice would be indefensible to the Admiralty: "Neither had I the least design to do any unlawful act by bringing him thus down to this place which I thought I had a right to do being an Aprentice who had deserted from my Service, and God forbid it should be taken amiss as I had no other View than to oblige him to return to his Duty, and would not on any Consideration transgress the Laws on this or any other Occasion."

Despite Jones's attempt to represent Castillo as disloyal to both his benefactor and his country, Holburne and the Lords of the Admiralty agreed with Castillo that the issue was slavery, not disloyalty, and they took particular offense at Jones's use of a collar frequently imposed on slaves. The Admiralty's judgment, rendered on Christmas Day 1758, was quick, short, and unequivocal: "Acquaint Admiral Holburne that the Laws of this Country admit of no Badges of Slavery, therefore the Lords hope and expect whenever he discovers any attempt of this kind he should prevent it; and that the Lords desire to be informed how Castillo is rated on the Ship's Books." Holburne wrote the Admiralty two days later: "Their Lordships may be assured that had I known any thing of him, or having a Collar being put on, I should have prevented it, but I was a Stranger both to the man & the manner of his Confinement." The Lords of the Admiralty were concerned about Castillo's rating because they knew, as well as Pascal and Equiano later should have known, that if a crew member was listed as an able seaman, he was receiving his pay and thus was not being kept on board as an unacknowledged slave.

Castillo and Equiano were expressing an assertiveness Sir John Fielding would warn slave owners about ten years later. A magistrate in the London suburb of Middlesex and half-brother of the novelist Henry Fielding, Sir John warned slave owners not to bring their slaves from America "to *England* as cheap Servants."

Both Jones and Pascal lacked the wisdom or generosity to let Castillo and Equiano simply go "about their Business." For Castillo justice came quickly; Equiano had to wait years. Forced to leave his most valued possessions, "my Bible, and the Guide to the Indians, the two books I loved above all others" (119), stripped of his only coat, and denied any right to prize money or salary by Pascal, Equiano still maintained some hope of deliverance. He hid from Pascal and Doran the money he had saved, "still hoping that by some means or other I should make my escape to the shore, and indeed some of my old shipmates told me not to despair, for they would get me back again; and that, as soon as they could get their pay, they would immediately come to Portsmouth to me" (94). Unfortunately, they reached Portsmouth just as the *Charming Sally* was about to set sail for the West Indies. They were only able to send him "some oranges, and other tokens of their regard." Nor was Pascal's former mistress, who lived in nearby Gosport, able to help Equiano, who "used to sell and take care of a great deal of property for her in different ships," because "she was succeeded in my master's good graces by another lady" (97).

Equiano's disappointment at having his hopes dashed and his shock at being betrayed by someone he had assumed reciprocated his love are understandable. But why did Pascal react so angrily to Equiano's aspirations? Pas-

Parish register of St. Margaret's, Westminster, London, 1759. The baptism of "Gustavus Vassa a Black born in Carolina 12 years old" is recorded on 9 February 1759. (Copyright Dean and Chapter of Westminster)

cal was about to leave England to help develop the naval capabilities of Portugal, Britain's most dependable and dependent ally. Taking Equiano, now with the rating of an able seaman, with him would be difficult because Equiano would have an unquestioned right to his own pay. Many masters in Pascal's situation would have manumitted their slaves as a reward for years of faithful service, and manumission may have been Pascal's original intention. The boy who had served him for seven years was now a man. In many ways it would have been easier for Pascal just to let Equiano go with Pascal's blessing. Although we can only speculate about Pascal's possible motives, the causes of his seemingly irrational behavior toward Equiano may have been both personal and professional. Pascal may have perceived Equiano's desire for freedom as an act of betrayal against Pascal, especially if he was jealous of the familial relationship Equiano tells us he had developed with Queen. Pascal must have seen how emotionally close his slave and steward had become with his hairdresser and personal attendant, since Pascal spent a great deal of time with them together as well as separately. He may also have felt that Equiano was ungrateful for the promotion he had so recently given him.

Professionally, Pascal may have perceived Equiano's unilateral decision to leave him and the navy as something akin to an act of mutiny. As commander of the *Aetna* Pascal exercised power and authority that could not easily be checked by the Admiralty, especially at sea. His behavior toward Equiano may have been a demonstration of the truth of the adage that power corrupts and absolute power corrupts absolutely:

> The extent of a sea officer's command . . . is truly peculiar to him. He has the power in his own person to impose very serious hardships, from the nature of the imprisonment customary in the Navy as well as by the severity of the punishment he can inflict; nor is this imprisonment or punishment subject to any review or control. Tyranny has been and may be carried to the most alarming height by men in this situation and it is very favourable to every selfish and interested passion. Sea officers, by not having been aware of the various temptations to which they are exposed by the possession of arbitrary power, deviate from the paths of justice and moderation in common with the rest of mankind and consequently may have sometimes incurred the imputation of an inclination to despotism in their general characters. The same possession of absolute power will also account for the frequent instances which occur in the Navy, of men whose conduct has been unexceptionable in subordinate situations, upon being advanced to the command of ships becoming capricious and tyrannical in a high degree, neglecting even the common rules of justice and the rights of humanity, which are concealed from themselves under the mistaken idea of a rigid discipline.[17]

Pascal may have seen Equiano's assumption that he would be freed as a usurpation of Pascal's authority to manumit him.

Perhaps emotionally unwilling or unable to hold Pascal alone responsible for betraying him, even nearly thirty years after the event, Equiano looked for someone else to blame for his sudden reversal of fortune. His "conscience smote" him when he "recollected that on the morning of our arrival at Deptford I had rashly sworn that as soon as we reached London I would spend the day in rambling and sport. . . . I felt that the Lord was able to disappoint me in all things, and immediately considered my present situation as a judgment of Heaven on account of my presumption in swearing" (95). Today we tend to underestimate the religious significance of swearing, which we usually associate with the use of four-letter words. In earlier periods, however, swearing was generally viewed as an infraction of the third commandment, which forbids taking the name of the Lord in vain. Seamen were notorious for swearing and foul language (they still are), and the navy sought to regulate such irreligious behavior. The official *Regulations and Instructions* contains many admonitions to officers, chaplains, and schoolmasters to control their own language as well as that of their subordinates and charges. The navy's official concern with swearing was also reflected in popular works such as Dr. Josiah Woodward's *The Seaman's Monitor, or Advice to Sea-Faring Men*, first published in London in 1700 and frequently reprinted, and Jonas Hanway's *The Seaman's Faithful Companion* (London, 1763). From a theological perspective, Equiano correctly saw that his swearing to spend his time in London "in rambling and sport" asserted his own self-sufficiency to freely will his actions, thus implicitly denying God's power to control the events of his life. Quickly repenting, he asked God "not to abandon me in my distress." Once his "grief, spent with its own violence, began to subside" he became more philosophical, recognizing that "God might perhaps have permitted this [enslavement] in order to teach me wisdom and resignation" (95).

Equiano was not emotionally satisfied with this theological justification of the "horrors" he now faced (95). He needed a human agent to blame. He found one in Pascal's current mistress, motivated by jealousy of her predecessor and envy at the prospect of her employing a free Equiano as an eighteenth-century mark of conspicuous consumption and status. Given the male-centered "little world" in which Equiano had spent half his life, with its clearly demarcated chain of proper command, it may have been inevitable that he ultimately blamed his misfortune on the disruptive figure of the "lady, who appeared sole mistress of the Aetna, and mostly lodged on board," thus usurping the authority of his father figure, Pascal. Equiano tells us he was "not so great a favourite with this lady as with the former; she had conceived a pique against me on some occasion when she was on board, and she did not fail to instigate my master to treat me in the manner he did" (97). In a footnote found in every edition of his *Interesting Narrative*, Equiano elaborates: "Thus was I sacrificed to the envy and resentment of this woman, for knowing that the lady whom she had succeeded in my master's good graces designed to take me into her service; which, had I once got on shore, she would not have been able to prevent. She felt her pride alarmed at the superiority of her rival in being attended by a black servant; it was not the less to prevent this than to be revenged on me, that she caused the captain to treat me thus cruelly" (267).

Chapter Five

BEARING WITNESS

Having mistakenly expected all his "toils to end," Equiano faced the prospect of "a new slavery" in the West Indies (95). The difference between the "little world" he was leaving, in which he had been largely immune from the realities of chattel slavery, and the larger world he was about to enter, in which most slaves suffered and died, was anticipated by the contrast between the behavior of his former shipmates and that of his new ones. He misguidedly placed his confidence in one of Captain Doran's crew members whose morals had been corrupted by participation in the slave trade: "A sailor on board took a guinea from me on pretence of getting me a boat; and promised me, time after time, that it was hourly to come off. When he had the watch upon deck I watched also; and looked long enough, but all in vain; I could never see either the boat or my guinea again. And what I thought was still the worst of all, the fellow gave information, as I afterwards found, all the while to the mates of my intention to go off, if I could in any way do it; but, rogue-like, he never told them he had got a guinea from me to procure my escape." Though Equiano soon found "some satisfaction in seeing him detested and despised" by the rest of the ship's crew for his behavior to Equiano, the treacherous sailor was the first of many whites who cheated and deceived Equiano in the Americas (96). At one point in his account Equiano is more explicit about the corrupting influence West Indian slavery had on whites: "One of these depredators once, in St. Eustatia, came on board of our vessel, and bought some fowls and pigs of me; and a whole day after his departure with the things, he returned again and wanted his money back: I refused to give it, and, not seeing my captain on board, he began the common pranks with me; and swore he would even break open my chest and take my money. I therefore expected, as my captain was absent, that he would be as good as his word; and he was just proceeding to strike me, when fortunately a British seaman on board, whose heart had not been debauched by a West India climate, interposed and prevented him" (108–9).

Before any of Equiano's friends could come to his aid, the *Charming Sally* set sail from England on 30 December 1762. Because Britain was still technically at war with France and Spain, the H.M.S. *Aeolus*, under the command of Capt. William Hotham, escorted the convoy destined for the West Indies. His hopes of deliverance completely frustrated, Equiano saw himself as "a prisoner on board, now without hope," and was once again overwhelmed by despair: "In one day's time I lost sight of the wished-for land. In the first expressions of my grief I reproached my fate, and wished I had never been born. I was ready to curse the tide that bore us, the gale that wafted my prison, and even the ship that conducted us; and I called on death to relieve me from the horrors I felt and dreaded" (97). Once under sail he became more resigned to his fate, but the sight of "our destined island Montserrat" on 13 February 1763 again reduced him to despair: "At the sight of this land of bondage, a fresh horror ran through all my frame, and chilled me to the heart. My former slavery now rose in dreadful review to my mind, and displayed nothing but misery, stripes, and chains; and, in the first paroxysm of my grief, I called upon God's thunder, and his avenging power, to direct the stroke of death to me, rather than permit me to become a slave, and to be sold from lord to lord" (98). Sardonically looking backward from the vantage point of freedom in 1789, Equiano saw himself distracted from despair in 1763 by the hard labor of loading and unloading the ship and the ironic "comfort" two deserters from the *Charming Sally* gave him: "To comfort me in my distress . . . two of the sailors robbed me of all my money, and ran away from the ship." Even the climate and shore appeared hostile: "I had been so long used to an European climate that at first I felt the scorching West-India sun very painful, while the dashing surf would toss the boat and the people in it frequently above high-water mark. Sometimes our limbs were broken with this, or even attended with instant death, and I was day by day mangled and torn" (99).

For the next three and a half years Montserrat would be Equiano's home base. It is a tiny tear-shaped island of about 39 square miles, just over half the size of Washington, D.C. At the outbreak of the Seven Years' War Montserrat had a population of 10,283, of whom 8,853 were of African descent and only 1,430 of European descent. Many of the latter comprised an Irish underclass of indentured servants, convicts, and their offspring the colonial government had feared would collaborate with French invaders. Colonial governments in the West Indies always feared uprisings by the numerically vastly superior slaves, especially during the unstable times of war. During the recent war Montserrat had been the base of privateers, maritime mercenaries hired by the British government to complement the overextended Royal Navy in the Caribbean. A letter of marque and reprisal authorized them to prey on enemy commercial and military vessels. By the end of the war Montserrat's sugar industry was producing at full capacity, with virtually every acre of arable land cleared and planted, making it in 1763 the sixth most productive British colony in sugar, sixth in rum, and third in cacao. One of the many unanticipated consequences of Britain's overwhelming victory in the war was France's cession of its West Indian colonies of Dominica, Grenada, Saint Vincent, and Tobago, each of which produced sugar more inexpensively than Montserrat, making Montserrat relatively less significant in the British Empire than it had been. With the former French islands came seventy thousand slaves.

Equiano at first desperately hoped that his stay in the West Indies would be brief. When the *Charming Sally* was ready in mid-May 1763 to sail for England with its produce from Montserrat, he begged Captain Doran to take him along. Well aware of the odds that once back in England Equiano would simply emancipate himself by absconding to the welcoming arms of his many former comrades, Doran declined: "If he were to stay in the West Indies he would be glad to keep me himself; but he would not venture to take me to London, for he was very sure that when I came there I would leave him." Less than five months spent with Equiano had transformed Doran's initial hostility toward him into concern for his welfare. Doran assured his slave that Pascal had sent him to the West Indies to be sold, "but that he had desired him to get me the best master he could, as he told him I was a very deserving boy." Consequently, Doran told him, "he had got me the very best master in the whole island, with whom I should be as happy as if I were in England." Rather than letting "his own brother-in-law" buy Equiano "for a great deal more money," Doran sold him to "Robert King, a quaker and the first merchant in the place." King "bought me . . . on account of my good character; and, as he had not the least doubt of my good behaviour, I should be very well off with him" (99).

Once more Equiano suffered the pain of forced separation. As the *Charming Sally* was preparing to depart, "I went on board again, and took my leave of all my shipmates; and the next day the ship sailed. When she weighed anchor I went to the waterside and looked at her with a very wishful and aching heart, and followed her with my eyes until she was totally out of sight. I was so bowed down with grief that I could not hold up my head for many months; and if my new master had not been kind to me, I believe I should have died under it at last." Robert King proved to be a man of his word, making Equiano "very thankful to Captain Doran, and even to my old master, for the character they had given me; a character which I afterwards found of infinite service" (100).

The relationship between King and his new slave reflected the complexity of the eighteenth-century system of slavery and the compromises and contradictions it caused. King was a Quaker, that is, a member of the Society of Friends, which traced its origin to the moment in England in 1647 when George Fox felt inspired to declare that every man and woman contained the inward light of salvation. Those who shared his belief he called the "Friends of Truth." During the period of Puritan rule during the mid-seventeenth century, when many Protestant sects were allowed to flourish in England, the number of Friends grew rapidly. Within a few years meetings of Friends were taking place on both sides of the Atlantic and the Channel. But when the monarchy was restored and the Church of England reestablished in 1660, the Friends were persecuted because they were pacifists and because of their opposition to paying tithes, to the priesthood, and to formal worship. They also refused to remove their hats or bow to mere mortals, no matter how high their social or political stations. From the beginning their detractors called them "Quakers" because they were often physically moved by the Holy Spirit. In response to their oppression they established the annual Meeting for Sufferings in London to deal with their persecution and agree on policies. As if turning the other cheek, they also accepted being called Quakers. By 1689, when the Toleration Act reduced the degree of their oppression, Quakers numbered around sixty thousand, despite lacking a formal creed. By the end of the eighteenth century their membership had dropped to between twenty and thirty-two thousand in Britain, with probably at least the same numbers in North America.[1] But Quaker economic and eventually moral and political influence was out of all proportion to their numbers. Their disproportionate influence was due to their reputation as honest businessmen who sold high-quality goods, their strong ties of social and economic intermarriage that protected their investments from the vagaries of the market, their interest in education and publishing, their national and transatlantic organizational structure that maintained a network of communication and distribution centered in London, and their record of defending the high ground on controversial moral issues.

The moral issue that became increasingly associated with the Quakers during the eighteenth century was slavery. The central Meeting in London put increasing pressure on Friends throughout Britain and its colonies to renounce slavery as a moral evil, eventually threatening slave dealers or owners with expulsion from the society. The threat needed to be repeated because Robert King was not the only Quaker to ignore the society's strictures, which became much more severe after the period when he owned Equiano.[2] To place King's behavior in perspective we should remember that in slave-based societies like Montserrat, where slaves were a substantial proportion of the total population and the principal source of labor, most white or black freemen believed they had virtually no choice but to use slave labor in order to be economically competitive. In a society with slaves like Philadelphia, where slaves were a relatively small percentage of the population and constituted one among several competing sources of labor, employers were well aware that they had other options.

The backbreaking labor most slaves endured on Montserrat's sugar plantations was not to be Equiano's fate because of the talents and skills he had developed and learned while in the navy. As he quickly discovered, even slave-based societies like those in the West Indies and the southern British colonies in North America were economically far more complicated than one might assume. Not all slaves worked without pay; not all slaves were geographically restricted; and not all slaves were unskilled field hands. "It is a common practice in the West Indies," Equiano observed, "for men to purchase slaves, though they have not plantations themselves, in order to let them out to planters and merchants, at so much a-piece by the day, and they give what allowances they choose out of this produce of their daily work to their slaves for subsistence" (101). King did not buy Equiano simply because

he came with a good character reference. King "dealt in all manner of merchandize," including "rum, sugar, and other goods," throughout the Caribbean,
employing up to six clerks at a time and a small fleet of vessels. King told his
new slave that when they reached Philadelphia, "as I understood something of
the rules of arithmetic, . . . he would put me to school and fit me for a clerk."
Since slave societies could not prosper without the contributions of educated
and skilled slaves as well as the labor of agricultural workers, "Mr. King soon
asked me what I could do; and at the same time said he did not mean to treat
me as a common slave. I told him I knew something of seamanship, and
could shave and dress hair pretty well; and I could refine [purify or clarify]
wines, which I had learned on shipboard, where I had often done it; and that
I could write, and understood arithmetic tolerably well as far as the Rule of
Three. He then asked me if I knew any thing of gauging [determining the capacity of a ship]; and, on my answering that I did not, he said one of his
clerks should teach me to gauge" (99–100).

> [Before long] there was scarcely any part of his business, or household af-
> fairs, in which I was not occasionally engaged. I often supplied the place
> of a clerk, in receiving and delivering cargoes to the ships, in tending
> stores, and delivering goods; and, besides this, I used to shave and dress
> my master when convenient, and take care of his horse; and when it was
> necessary, which was very often, I worked likewise on board of different
> vessels of his. By these means I became very useful to my master, and
> saved him, as he used to acknowledge, above a hundred pounds a year.
> Nor did he scruple to say I was of more advantage to him than any of his
> clerks; though their usual wages in the West Indies are from sixty to a
> hundred pounds current a year. (103)

Equiano's own experience disproved the assertion sometimes heard from defenders of slavery that the value of a slave's labor never equaled the price the
owner initially paid for the slave, an assertion also disproved when those
who made it "exclaim[ed] the most loudly against the abolition of the slave
trade" (103).

By Equiano's account King was a model slave owner, exemplary in being "very charitable and humane" (100). At a time when the abolition of slavery as an institution in the West Indies seemed economically impractical,
King embodied the ameliorationist position advocated by many opponents
of the transatlantic slave trade. Assuming that immediate and unilateral abolition of slavery by Britain would be commercially disastrous and that the

trade continued because the West Indian slave population failed to be self-sustaining due to brutal conditions, opponents of the trade argued that were owners to ameliorate those conditions, slaves would be more productive, demographic longevity and fertility would increase, and consequently the transatlantic trade would no longer be necessary. Without a constant supply of relatively cheap enslaved Africans, the argument went, owners would be compelled to treat their slaves more humanely. Many of the opponents of the trade hoped that eventually slave labor would be replaced by wage labor as the demand for labor became better balanced in relation to its supply.

Like many other opponents of the trade, Equiano attributed much of the brutal treatment meted out to slaves and the consequent decline in population to the use of "overseers," who did not share the owners' vested interest in the well-being of the slaves. Such overseers "are indeed for the most part persons of the worst character of any denomination of men in the West Indies. Unfortunately, many humane gentlemen, by not residing on their estates, are obliged to leave the management of them in the hands of these human butchers" (105). To support his argument about the effects of the declining slave population in the West Indies, Equiano relied on the comments of Edmund Burke, a member of Parliament, and William Burke, whom Edmund referred to as his cousin. The Burkes contended that the high death rate in the Caribbean necessitated the transatlantic slave trade. Equiano cited the Quaker abolitionist Anthony Benezet as his source for the information in the Burkes' *An Account of the European Settlements in America* (1758).

Equiano determined from his own observations that the solution was amelioration:

> I can quote many instances of gentlemen who reside on their estates in the West Indies, and then the scene is quite changed; the negroes are treated with lenity and proper care, by which their lives are prolonged, and their masters are profited. To the honour of humanity, I knew several gentlemen who managed their estates in this manner; and they found that benevolence was their true interest. And, among many I could mention in several of the islands, I knew one in Montserrat[3] whose slaves looked remarkably well, and never needed any fresh supplies of negroes; and there are many other estates, especially in Barbadoes, which, from such judicious treatment, need no fresh stock of negroes at any time. (105)

Enlightened self-interest motivated Robert King's treatment of his own slaves, despite the objections of other owners to his "feeding his slaves so well." He did so, he advised them, "because the slaves thereby looked better

and did more work" (104). If any of them "behaved amiss, he did not beat or
use them ill, but parted with them. This made them afraid of disobliging him;
and as he treated his slaves better than any other man on the island, so he
was better and more faithfully served by them in return" (100). King was a
"man of feeling" (101), someone who could sympathize and even empathize
with others because he exemplified the belief of philosophers like Francis
Hutcheson, David Hume, and Adam Smith that we all have an innate sentimental sensibility, or moral sense, that enables us to respond emotionally –
sentimentally – to the suffering of others and to distinguish good from evil.
Many supporters of slavery argued that an African was less human than a European because, supposedly lacking such moral sensibility, he "is incapable
of moral sensations, or perceives them only as beasts do simple ideas, without the power of combination, in order to use; it is a mark that distinguishes
him from the man who feels, and is capable of these moral sensations, who
knows their application, and the purposes of them, as sufficiently, as he himself is distinguished from the highest species of brute."[4]

Recognizing King as a "man of feeling," slaves "were always glad to work
for him in preference to any other gentlemen." Although many other masters
were penny-wise and pound-foolish in their allowances to their slaves, King's
generosity approached the line between slave and wage labor: "I have rowed
the boat, and slaved at the oars, from one hour to sixteen in the twenty-four;
during which I had fifteen pence sterling per day to live on, though sometimes
only ten pence. However, this was considerably more than was allowed to
other slaves that used to work often with me, and belonged to other gentlemen
on the island: these poor souls had never more than nine-pence a day, and seldom more than six-pence, from their masters or owners, though they earned
them three or four pisterines[5] a day" (101). King was a man of so much feeling that he often supplied slaves directly with food and drink lest they be
shortchanged by their owners. He also interceded on behalf of the slaves of
others when employers threatened to flog them for seeking the money they
owed them. Equiano expected his readers to respond to his story as persons
of feeling as well, "for where the conduct of men is so manifestly impious,
there can be no need, either of a single argument or a reflection; as every
reader of sensibility will anticipate them in his own feelings."[6]

Equiano soon appreciated his good fortune in having King as his owner:

> Once, for a few days, I was let out to fit a vessel, and I had no victuals
> allowed me by either party; at last I told my master of this treatment, and
> he took me away from him. In many of the estates, on the different is-

lands where I used to be sent for rum or sugar, they would not deliver it to me, or to any other negro; he was therefore obliged to send a white man along with me to those places; and then he used to pay him from six to ten pisterines a day. From being thus employed, during the time I served Mr. King, in going about the different estates on the island, I had all the opportunity I could wish for, to see the dreadful usage of the poor men; usage that reconciled me to my situation, and made me bless God for the hands into which I had fallen. (102–3)

Equiano's service on King's various vessels indeed gave him all the opportunity he could wish for to hear and see evidence of the abuses of slavery and against the slave trade. He frequently observed one "unfeeling owner" (108) or another cheat his slaves out of money owed them or what little property they were able to acquire. For example, Montserrat's governor appropriated the hard-earned boat of a slave without any compensation; other whites took from slaves the bits of grass they had collected to sell in the market. While transporting slaves for sale among the islands and between the Caribbean and North America Equiano "was often a witness to cruelties of every kind, which were exercised on my unhappy fellow slaves. . . . [I]t was almost a constant practice with our clerks, and other whites, to commit violent depredations on the chastity of the female slaves; and these I was, though with reluctance, obliged to submit to at all times, being unable to help them. When we have had some of these slaves on board my master's vessels to carry them to other islands, or to America, I have known our mates to commit these acts most shamefully, to the disgrace, not of Christians only, but of men. I have even known them gratify their brutal passion with females not ten years old" (104). Equiano noted the hypocrisy of whites who implicitly condoned the white rape of black children while condemning to castration and torture a black man who had intercourse with a white prostitute.

Equiano's attempts to make morally obtuse slave owners aware of their own hypocrisy were doomed to failure: "One Mr. Drummond told me that he had sold 41,000 negroes, and that he once cut off a negro-man's leg for running away. – I asked him, if the man had died in the operation? How he, as a Christian, could answer for the horrid act before God? And he told me, answering was a thing of another world; but what he thought and did were policy. I told him that the Christian doctrine taught us to do unto others as we would that others should do unto us. He then said that his scheme had the desired effect – it cured that man and some others of running away" (104–5).

Slave owners used psychological as well as physical punishments to break the spirits and bodies of their slaves:

It was very common in several of the islands, particularly in St. Kitt's, for the slaves to be branded with the initial letters of their master's name, and a load of heavy iron hooks hung about their necks. Indeed, on the most trifling occasions they were loaded with chains, and often other instruments of torture were added. The iron muzzle, thumb-screws, &c. are so well known, as not to need a description, and were sometimes applied for the slightest faults. I have seen a negro beaten till some of his bones were broken, for only letting a pot boil over. It is not uncommon, after a flogging, to make slaves go on their knees, and thank their owners, and pray, or rather say, God bless them. I have often asked many of the men slaves (who used to go several miles to their wives, and late in the night, after having been wearied with a hard day's labour) why they went so far for wives, and why they did not take them of their own master's negro women, and particularly those who lived together as household slaves? Their answers have ever been – "Because when the master or mistress choose to punish the women, they make the husbands flog their own wives, and that they could not bear to do." Is it surprising that usage like this should drive the poor creatures to despair, and make them seek a refuge in death from those evils which render their lives intolerable[?] (107)

Under the dehumanizing conditions of chattel slavery suicide was not a choice of action restricted to Igbos; it was an understandable option in a world where "meager" slaves were "put into scales and weighed . . . to sell by the lump" (110) and where resistance seemed futile: "Another negro man was half hanged, and then burnt, for attempting to poison a cruel overseer. Thus by repeated cruelties are the wretched first urged to despair, and then murdered, because they still retain so much of human nature about them as to wish to put an end to their misery, and retaliate on their tyrants!" (105).

By the end of 1763 Equiano's life in the West Indies had begun to improve considerably. One of King's best employees was Capt. Thomas Farmer, an Englishman who commanded "a Bermudas sloop, about sixty tons burthen." Equiano soon discovered that Farmer was another "man of feeling." Like Equiano "a very alert and active man," Farmer brought King much profit "by his good management in carrying passengers from one island to another." But his sailors often got drunk and ran "away with the vessel's boat, which hindered him in his business very much" (114). Having taken a liking to

11

Equiano and because "sailors were generally very scarce in the island," especially responsible seamen, Farmer repeatedly implored King to let Equiano serve on his crew, which consisted of whites and both free and enslaved blacks. Concerned that Equiano would run away if allowed the mobility and lack of direct supervision service at sea would entail, King resisted Farmer's pleas as long as he could, until "at last, from necessity, or force, my master was prevailed on, though very reluctantly, to let me go with this captain." King agreed on the conditions that Equiano be employed only for day trips, that he be watched very carefully whenever the vessel was at anchor, and that Farmer would pay King for Equiano if he ran off.

Equiano soon became as indispensable to Farmer as he was to King: "Thus was I slaving, as it were for life, sometimes at one thing, and sometimes at another; so that the captain and I were nearly the most useful men in my master's employment. I also became so useful to the captain on ship board, that many times" he would "tell my master that I was better to him on board than any three white men he had." Equiano observed that his indispensability could be used for leverage in bargaining for better conditions. By refusing to undertake voyages for King without Equiano, Farmer eventually forced King to admit that Equiano had passed his period of day-trip probation and to allow him to serve on longer voyages, where the risk of escape was much greater. Equiano immediately saw that Farmer's successful negotiations with King gave him the opportunity to increase his own options: "I immediately thought I might in time stand a chance by being on board to get a little money, or possibly make my escape if I should be used ill: I also expected to get better food, and in greater abundance" (115). Although joining Farmer's crew did not lessen Equiano's workload, it did allow him to manipulate both King and Farmer and improve his own living conditions about as much as the system of chattel slavery permitted: "Between the vessel and the shore, when she was in port, I had little or no rest, as my master always wished to have me along with him. Indeed he was a very pleasant gentleman, and but for my expectations on shipboard I should not have thought of leaving him. But the captain liked me also very much, and I was entirely his right-hand man. I did all I could to deserve his favour, and in return I received better treatment from him than any other I believe ever met with in the West-Indies in my situation" (116).

Equiano took advantage of his new position and the mobility returning to the sea gave him. He became a venture capitalist, though at first "one single half bit, which is equal to three pence in England, made up my whole stock" (116). Selling tumblers, glasses, and gin in Montserrat that he had bought cheaply at the Dutch island of Saint Eustatius, "a general mart for the West Indies," in a few weeks he doubled and tripled his capital. Within months he "became master of a few pounds" (119) and was soon able to buy luxuries, enabling him to reconstruct in part the life in the navy he had lost: "At one of our trips to St. Kitt's, I had eleven bits of my own; and my friendly captain lent me five bits more, with which I bought a Bible. I was very glad to get this book, which I scarcely could meet with any where. I think there was none sold in Montserrat; and, much to my grief, from being forced out of the Aetna in the manner I have related, my Bible, and the Guide to the Indians, the two books I loved above all others, were left behind" (118–19).

By lending Equiano the money he needed to buy the Bible, Farmer was not only being "friendly." He was also helping Equiano subvert slavery by owning property and using his literacy. Moreover, Farmer was giving Equiano direct access to the knowledge of Christianity, with its doctrine of the equality of souls, which many owners believed posed a revolutionary threat to the institution of slavery. True friendship can only be between equals, and within the confines of slavery the increasingly complex relationship between Equiano and Farmer evolved toward, without ever being able to completely reach, equality. Although still a slave, Equiano's indispensability gave him some degree of power in relation to his captain. Whenever Farmer tried to "take liberties" with him because of the money he had saved or "treated me waspishly, I used plainly to tell him my mind, and that I would die before I would be imposed upon as other negroes were, and that to me life had lost its relish when liberty was gone. This I said, although I foresaw my then well-being or future hopes of freedom (humanly speaking) depended on this man. However, as he could not bear the thoughts of my not sailing with him, he always became mild on my threats" (120).

Unfortunately, whatever leverage Equiano achieved over Farmer and King did not apply to other whites: "I have experienced many instances of ill usage, and have seen many injuries done to other negroes in our dealings with whites; and, amidst our recreations, when we have been dancing and merry-making, they, without cause, have molested and insulted us" (116–17). Equiano's entrepreneurial endeavors were always at the mercy of the unchecked power any white had over any slave. When he and a much older slave tried to sell some fruit on the Danish island of Santa Cruz, whites quickly took advantage of them. His comrade had combined "six bits worth of limes and oranges in a bag; I had also my whole stock; which was about twelve bits' worth of the same kind of goods, separate in two bags." As soon as they landed, two white men, noting they were strangers as well as slaves, immediately seized their fruit and threatened to beat them if they did not leave. Their appeal to "the commanding officer of the fort" gained them only "a volley of imprecations against us" and the threat of being whipped (117). Momentarily refusing to turn the other cheek, Equiano "in the agony of distress and indignation, wished that the ire of God, in his forked lightning, might transfix these cruel oppressors among the dead" (118). But recognizing that action was not a realistic option for a slave, he and his companion again begged the thieves to give back the fruit. They had little choice but to accept the compromise some bystanders offered – to let the thieves keep one of the three stolen bags. To the great distress of the old slave, they chose his bag of mixed fruit, "which so moved me with pity for him, that I gave him nearly one third of my fruits." Notwithstanding all they had suffered, he and the old man sold their remaining fruit at a great profit. Equiano reaffirmed his faith in God, who, with the aid of some timely human agency, would turn evil into good: "Such a surprising reverse of fortune in so short a space of time seemed like a dream to me, and proved no small encouragement for me to trust the Lord in any situation. My captain afterwards frequently used to take my part, and get me my right when I have been plundered or used ill by these tender Christian depredators; among whom I have shuddered to observe the unceasing blasphemous execrations which are wantonly thrown out by persons of all ages and conditions; not only without occasion, but even as if they were indulgencies and pleasures" (118).

Equiano was not content to rely solely on the kindness of strangers, the friendship of Captain Farmer, or the grace of God for his freedom:

The reader cannot but judge of the irksomeness of this situation to a mind like mine, in being daily exposed to new hardships and impositions, after having seen many better days, and been, as it were, in a state of freedom and plenty; added to which, every part of the world in which I had hitherto been in seemed to me a paradise in comparison of the West-Indies. My mind was therefore hourly replete with inventions and thoughts of being freed, and, if possible, by honest and honourable means; for I always remembered the old adage, and I trust that it has ever been my ruling principle, "that Honesty is the best policy"; and likewise that other golden precept – "To do unto all men as I would they should do unto me." (119)

Equiano probably sounds keener to play by the rules than he actually was. Although he does not say so, he had a very good pragmatic reason for preferring to accept his freedom rather than seize it. If he was "freed . . . by honest and honourable means," his legal status in the West Indies would be clear, although, as he was well aware, his actual status there would remain precarious. Legally free, he could choose to risk staying in a slave society. After all, the world he now knew best was the colonies of British America. Or he could go anywhere he wanted to legally because he would now own himself. If he seized his freedom, however, he would have to make his way to England, where he would be relatively but not completely safe. Before the Mansfield decision of 1772 ruled otherwise, slave owners could legally force their slaves to return from England back into American slavery. If Equiano freed himself, his status would always be open to legal challenge, and he would be liable to be reappropriated by King.

Despite Equiano's claim that he "was from early years a predestinarian" who "thought whatever fate had determined must ever come to pass," he repeatedly acted very differently from someone who believes that external forces, not his own choices, determine, or predestine, the events and direction of his life. His God was clearly one who helped those who helped themselves: "I therefore looked up with prayers anxiously to God for my liberty; and at the same time used every honest means, and did all that was possible on my part to obtain it" (119). Determined to gain his freedom and "return to Old England" as soon as possible, Equiano began to make his plans to buy his freedom if he could but to escape if necessary: "I thought a knowledge of navigation might be of use to me; for, though I did not intend to run away unless I should be ill used, yet, in such a case, if I understood navigation, I might attempt my escape in our sloop, which was one of the swiftest sailing vessels in the West Indies, and I could be at no loss for hands to join me: and, if I should make this attempt, I had intended to have gone for England" (122). To that end he paid the mate of "our vessel" to teach him navigation. Rebuking the mate for charging Equiano for the lessons, Captain Farmer began teaching Equiano himself but desisted when "some of our passengers, and others, seeing this, found much fault with him for it, saying, it was a very dangerous thing to let a negro know navigation" (123).

Frustrated in his attempt to learn how to escape on his own to England, Equiano still took the calculated risk to resist the temptation to run away. He had many chances to escape, as, for example, when a fleet of French merchant ships assembled at the island of Guadeloupe. Bound for "old France" and in need of seamen, the fleet advertised "from fifteen to twenty pounds a man for the run." Though Equiano had formed a bond with his fellow crewmen like that he had developed with his shipmates in the navy and was tempted to run away with them, he still hoped that his opportunity to buy his freedom outright was not far off: "Our mate, and all the white sailors, left our vessel on this account, and went aboard of the French ships. They would have had me also gone with them, for they regarded me, and swore to protect me, if I would go; and, as the fleet was to sail the next day, I really believe I could have got safe to Europe at that time. However, as my master was kind, I would not attempt to leave him; still remembering the old maxim, that 'honesty is the best policy,' I suffered them to go without me" (123).

Equiano's opportunities to save money toward the purchase of his freedom multiplied considerably near the end of 1764, when King put Farmer in command of the *Prudence*, "about seventy or eighty tons," a sloop large enough to trade between the Caribbean and British North America. Given his desire "to lose sight of the West Indies," Equiano was delighted at the prospect of making more money and visiting new places, although he discovered, since the ship carried "live cargo (as we call a cargo of slaves)" from the islands to the colonies of Georgia and South Carolina (133), that slave societies were fundamentally alike, no matter where they were located: "I got ready all the little venture I could; and, when the vessel was ready, we sailed to my great joy. When we got to our destined places, Georgia and Charles Town, I expected I should have an opportunity of selling my little property to advantage; but here, particularly in Charles Town, I met with buyers, white men, who imposed on me as in other places" (124). By 1750 forty thousand slaves were laboring in the Georgia–South Carolina area, cultivating rice near the coast and indigo in the backcountry. Equiano's experience in Charles Town (renamed Charleston after the American Revolution), a city of almost eight thousand people, would not have surprised him had he known the colony's history. Carolina (through the eighteenth century Carolina, South Carolina, and North Carolina were often used interchangeably) was initially settled in the 1660s by planters from Barbados who brought their slaves and their slave culture from the West Indies to the mainland, and in the 1690s the Carolina Assembly modeled their slave laws closely on the Barbadian code. Carolina was, in effect, an extension of the West Indies.

Ironically, Equiano reached Charles Town in May 1766, where he "saw the town illuminated; the guns were fired, and bonfires and other demonstrations of joy shewn, on account of the repeal of the stamp-act." Parliament repealed the Stamp Act in London on 18 March 1766, and news of its repeal

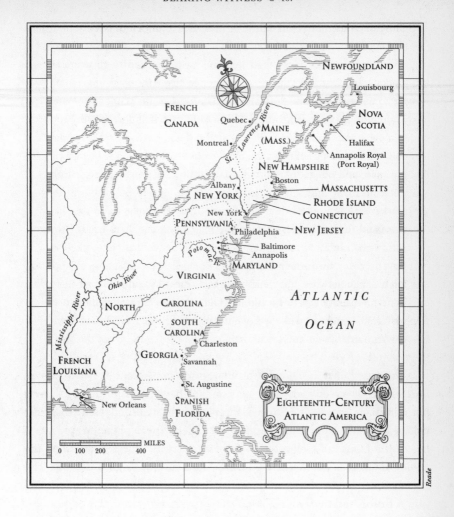

reached America about two months later. The repeal was widely viewed at the time as a restoration of American liberty. Subsequently, it was seen as one of the early events of the American Revolution. For a slave, the repeal of the Stamp Act was essentially meaningless:

> Here I disposed of some goods on my own account; the white men buying them with smooth promises and fair words, giving me, however, but very indifferent payment. There was one gentleman particularly who bought a puncheon of rum of me, which gave me a great deal of trouble; and although I used the interest of my friendly captain, I could not obtain any thing for it; for, being a negro man, I could not oblige him to pay me.

This vexed me much, not knowing how to act; and I lost some time in seeking after this Christian; and though, when the sabbath came (which the negroes usually make their holiday) I was inclined to go to public worship, but, instead of that, I was obliged to hire some black men to help me to pull a boat across the water to go in quest of this gentleman. When I found him, after much entreaty, both from myself and my worthy captain, he at last paid me in dollars, some of them, however, were copper, and of consequence of no value; but he took advantage of my being a negro man, and obliged me to put up with those or none, although I objected to them. Immediately after, as I was trying to pass them in the market amongst other white men, I was abused for offering to pass bad coin; and though I shewed them the man I had got them from, I was within one minute of being tied up and flogged without either judge or jury; however, by the help of a good pair of heels, I ran off and so escaped the bastinadoes [a beating with a cudgel or stick] I should have received. I got on board as fast as I could, but still continued in fear of them until we sailed, which, I thank God, we did, not long after; and I have never been amongst them since. (128–29)

The time Equiano spent in Carolina was so unpleasant he never wanted to return to the colony where he may, in fact, have been born. But a "worse fate than ever" awaited him in Georgia, the most recently settled British colony in North America. James Edward Oglethorpe, a philanthropic member of the House of Commons and a former army officer, established the colony in 1733 as an alternative to imprisonment for English debtors. The British government also saw the new colony as a military buffer zone between British and Spanish colonies. Initially, slavery was outlawed both for philanthropic motives and out of concern that slaves might make common cause with the Spanish against the colonists. In 1749 the spread of rice cultivation from South Carolina to the new colony made demands by planters for the legalization of slavery irresistible. Georgia rapidly became as thoroughly a slave society as South Carolina. For Equiano Georgia was inextricably associated with sickness and abuse. On his first visit he grew so ill from overwork in his desire "to make our voyage as short as possible" that he "caught a fever and ague [a recurrent chill]" (127). Fear of dying made him promise God he would reform if he recovered. He did, with the aid of "an eminent doctor." On his return to Montserrat, however, "in spite of all I could do, as we drew nearer and nearer to the islands, my resolutions more and more declined, as if the very air of that country or climate seemed fatal to piety. When we were safe arrived at Montserrat, and I had got ashore, I forgot my former resolutions" (128).

His second trip to Georgia brought Equiano even closer to death. One Sunday night he visited some slaves in Savannah. They belonged to a Dr. Perkins, who lived next door to where Farmer was lodging. Enraged to see "strange Negroes in his yard," the drunken Perkins, with one of his white servants, assaulted Equiano. Equiano identified himself and begged for mercy. Although Perkins knew Farmer, he and his man beat Equiano senseless, dragging his bloody body off to jail the next morning. When Farmer discovered what had happened, he immediately came to Equiano's aid. Equiano's condition appeared hopeless: "As soon as the good man saw me so cut and mangled, he could not forbear weeping; he soon got me out of jail to his lodgings, and immediately sent for the best doctors in the place, who at first declared it as their opinion that I could not recover" (129). Several lawyers told Farmer that "they could do nothing for me as I was a negro." Farmer did not even get the satisfaction of being able to take the law into his own hands. He "went to Dr. Perkins, the hero who had vanquished me, and menaced him, swearing he would be revenged of him, and challenged him to fight. But cowardice is ever the companion of cruelty – and the Doctor refused." Only the skill of "one Doctor Brady" and the care of Farmer enabled Equiano to recover. As a true "man of feeling" Equiano suffered more from the anguish of the "worthy" captain than from his own physical wounds: "Yet I was in more pain on account of the captain's uneasiness about me than I otherwise should have been." More than two weeks passed before he could get out of bed and another two before he could return to the ship, where he "was very much wanted on board," having long since become the most useful member of the crew (130).

Hope that he could save enough money to buy his freedom and return to England enabled Equiano to endure the hardships he faced in the West Indies, South Carolina, and Georgia and motivated him to work "with double alacrity." As he had at the close of the Seven Years' War, Equiano expected his master to be willing to free him at the appropriate time. But, as then, he was banking on his faith in his master's benevolence rather than an explicit promise. In 1765 King almost made Equiano feel as disappointed and betrayed as Pascal had three years earlier. Having spent the better part of the last year making and saving money, Equiano was looking forward to his first voyage with Farmer "to see the city of Philadelphia, which I had heard a great deal about for some years past" (124). Philadelphia was the most populous city in British North America, with about twenty thousand people at mid-century. Philadelphia also was, Equiano imagined, a beacon of freedom in a society with slaves. Just as he had collected his merchandise for sale and the ship was preparing to sail, Equiano was called before King and Farmer. He was stunned to learn that King intended to sell him because he had "heard that I meant to run away from him when I got to Philadelphia." King had bought him for forty pounds sterling, but he could get a hundred guineas for him from "Captain Doran's brother-in-law, a severe master," who still wanted to employ Equiano as an overseer. He could get even more for him if he sold him "in Carolina," where one man wanted to make him "a captain of one of his rice vessels," though he quickly lost interest in buying Equiano when Farmer told him he "knew something of navigation" (125).

His "mind . . . big with inventions, and full of schemes to escape" as he listened to King's threats to sell him, Equiano still had the presence of mind to try to convince his master and captain that he never planned to run away in Philadelphia. He reminded them that he had never failed to return to the ship and that he had not seized the obvious opportunity to follow his fellow crew members in joining the French fleet: "To my no small surprise, and very great joy, the captain confirmed every syllable I said, and even more; for he said he had tried different times to see if I would make any attempt of this kind, both at St. Eustatia and in America, and he never found that I made the smallest; but, on the contrary, I always came on board according to his orders; and he did really believe, if ever I meant to run away, that, as I could never have had a better opportunity, I would have done it the night the mate and all the people left our vessel at Guadaloupe" (123). Convinced of Equiano's fidelity, Farmer told him and King that his supposed plan to escape had been reported by the vessel's mate, whom Equiano had rightly accused of misusing the vessel's provisions.

What had begun as a seemingly terrible repetition of his last meeting with Pascal had a distinctly different ending. The perverse effect the institution of slavery had on human relationships probably accounts for the difficulty King and Farmer had in making the transition from considering Equiano as a piece of property to treating him as a man. Even acts of kindness were expressions of power and reflections of inequality. After firing the mate who had informed against him, King and Farmer felt compelled to prove their faith in Equiano and their respect for him. King now assured him that "he never did intend to use me as a common slave," as shown by his will-

ingness to let him be so mobile. Furthermore, he gave Equiano the promise
he had expected but never received from Pascal:

> He also intended to encourage me . . . by crediting me with half a pun-
> cheon of rum and half a hogshead of sugar at a time; so that, from being
> careful, I might have money enough, in some time, to purchase my free-
> dom: and, when that was the case, I might depend upon it he would let me
> have it for forty pounds sterling money, which was only the same price he
> gave for me. . . . He then gave me a large piece of silver coin, such as I had
> never seen or had before, and told me to get ready for the voyage, and he
> would credit me with a tierce [42 gallons] of sugar and another of rum; he
> also said that he had two amiable sisters in Philadelphia, from whom I
> might get some necessary things.

The men who, minutes before, Equiano had thought were about to betray his
faith in them were now "noble," and he "could have kissed both of their feet"
(126). He may have felt so grateful because his own sense of fairness had also
become distorted by the perversity of slavery. But his gamble in playing by
the rules was about to pay off.

The "elegant town of Philadelphia" turned out to be all he had hoped.
He found it a "charming town," where everything was "plentiful and cheap"
and where he sold his goods "pretty well, . . . chiefly to the Quakers," who
"always appeared to be a very honest discreet sort of people, and never attempted to impose on" him. He "therefore liked them, and ever after chose
to deal with them in preference to any others" (131–32). He even indulged
himself in having his fortune told by "a *wise* woman, a Mrs. Davis," despite
his conviction that no "mortal could forsee the future disposals of Providence" and his disbelief "in any other revelation than that of the holy Scriptures." As one might expect, she delighted him by telling him exactly what
he wanted to hear. With the prediction of his desired manumission no doubt
echoing in his head, Equiano "sailed from this agreeable spot for Montserrat,
once more to encounter the raging surfs" (127).

He returned to Montserrat more impatient than ever for "an opportunity
of getting a sum large enough to purchase" his freedom. To Equiano's de-
light, King bought a much larger sloop, the *Nancy*, at the beginning of 1766,
which meant that Equiano "had more room, and could carry a larger quantity of goods" to sell for his personal profit. Since he had recently "made near
three hundred per cent. by four barrels of pork I brought from Charlestown,
I laid in as large a cargo as I could, trusting to God's Providence to prosper

my undertaking." The nearly three-week-long voyage was a pleasant one, allowing him the chance to observe some "large sea monsters," whales with their young, along the way (134). Once their business in the "fruitful land" of Philadelphia was done they set sail for Montserrat, where he expected to sell his goods for enough money to cover the cost of his freedom. His opportunity was deferred, however, when King ordered Farmer to go first to Saint Eustatius to pick up a "live cargo" of slaves to sell in Georgia, where Equiano had a chance to thank Dr. Brady again for his care in Savannah (133).

King's unexpected order to go to Georgia before returning to Montserrat made Equiano all the more impatient to be able to buy his freedom. Because of his desire to get as much money as quickly as possible, Equiano, along with Captain Farmer, became the victim of a confidence man. In retrospect, Equiano saw the humor in his mishap. While in Savannah he and Farmer encountered a silversmith they had brought there from the West Indies on an earlier voyage. He booked passage with them to return to the West Indies, promising "to give the captain a great deal of money, having pretended to take a liking to him, and being as we thought very rich." Like many con men, the silversmith depended for his success on the greed of his victims and their confidence in his word. As Farmer and his crew were loading the ship the silversmith took ill. He promised Farmer not only the money for the passage but also, since he had no family, to make him his heir if he would care for him in his illness. As the silversmith's condition worsened, Farmer grew increasingly convinced that he was about to become rich and offered Equiano ten pounds "when he should get the man's property" if Equiano would help Farmer attend the dying man. In anticipation of his own windfall from the silversmith's anticipated death Equiano "laid out above eight pounds . . . for a suit of superfine cloathes to dance in at my freedom, which I hoped was then at hand." When Farmer woke Equiano a few nights later with news of the silversmith's death and asked him to go with him to get the expected money as soon as possible, Equiano at first responded rather callously: "I told him I was very sleepy, and wished he would take somebody else with him; or else, as the man was dead, and could want no farther attendance, to let all things remain as they were till the next morning." But Farmer convinced him, and they soon "saw the man as dead as we could wish." Delighted by the prospect of wealth, Farmer promised to give him "a grand burial." But when they went through his possessions, they found in the smallest of "a nest of trunks" not even enough money to pay for the silversmith's coffin: "Our sudden and exquisite joy was now succeeded by as sudden and exquisite pain; and my captain and I exhibited, for some time, most ridiculous figures – pictures of chagrin and disappointment! We went away greatly mortified, and left the deceased to do as well as he could for himself, as we had taken so good care of him when alive for nothing" (134–35).

"Much out of humour with our friend the silversmith" they returned to Montserrat, where Equiano found himself "master of about forty-seven pounds" after selling his "venture." Following the advice he sought from his "true friend," the captain, Equiano met with him and King a few days later when they were breakfasting together and reminded his master of the promise he had made. Equiano's recollection of the exchange that followed reads like a lighthearted reversal of the tone and substance of his earlier discussion of freedom with Pascal:

> When I went in I made my obeisance to my master, and with my money in my hand, and many fears in my heart, I prayed him to be as good as his offer to me, when he was pleased to promise me my freedom as soon as I could purchase it. This speech seemed to confound him; he began to recoil; and my heart that instant sunk within me. "What!" said he, "give you your freedom? Why, where did you get the money; Have you got forty pounds sterling?" "Yes, sir," I answered. "How did you get it"; replied he; I told him, "Very honestly." The captain then said he knew I got the money very honestly, and with much industry, and that I was particularly careful. On which my master replied, I got money much faster than he did; and said he would not have made me the promise he did if he had thought I should have got money so soon. "Come, come," said my worthy captain, clapping my master on the back, "Come, Robert, (which was his name), I think you must let him have his freedom; – you have laid your money out very well; you have received good interest for it all this time, and here is now the principal at last. I know Gustavus has earned you more than an hundred a-year, and he will still save you money, as he will not leave you: Come, Robert, take the money." My master then said, he would not be worse than his promise; and, taking the money, told me to go to the Secretary at the Register Office, and get my manumission drawn up. These words of my master were like a voice from heaven to me; in an instant all my trepidation was turned into unutterable bliss; and I most reverently bowed myself with gratitude, unable to express my feelings, but by the overflowing of my eyes, and a heart replete with thanks to God; while my true and worthy friend the captain congratulated us both with a peculiar degree of heartfelt pleasure. (135–36)

Feeling like the apostle Peter released from prison and with wings on his feet "like Elijah, as he rose to Heaven," Equiano flew to the Register Office, "blaz[ing] about the virtue of my amiable master and captain" on the way. He recalled the words from Psalm 126 in which he had put his faith ever since Pascal's betrayal at Deptford: "I glorified God in my heart, in whom I trusted." Even the registrar seemed to be inspired by charity – he drew up the manumission papers for half the usual price of a guinea:

> Montserrat. – To all men unto whom these presents shall come: I Robert King, of the parish of St. Anthony, in the said island, merchant, send greeting: Know ye, that I the aforesaid Robert King, for, and in consideration of the sum of seventy pounds current money of the said island, [local money was normally inflated in relation to pounds sterling] to me in hand paid, and to the intent that a negro man slave, named Gustavus Vasa, shall and may become free, have manumitted, emancipated, enfranchised, and set free, and by these presents do manumit, emancipate, enfranchise, and set free, the aforesaid negro man-slave, named Gustavus Vasa, for ever; hereby giving, granting, and releasing unto him, the said Gustavus Vasa, all right, title, dominion, sovereignty, and property, which, as lord and master over the aforesaid Gustavus Vasa, I have had, or which I now have, or by any means whatsoever I may or can hereafter possibly have over him the aforesaid Negro, for ever. In witness whereof, I the abovesaid Robert King, have unto these presents set my hand and seal, this tenth day of July, in the year of our Lord one thousand seven hundred and sixty-six.

> ROBERT KING
> Signed, sealed, and delivered in the presence of Terry Legay.
> Montserrat,
> Registered the within manumission, at full length, this eleventh day of July, 1766, in liber D.[7]
> TERRY LEGAY, Register

Equiano, "who had been a slave in the morning, trembling at the will of another," had become his "own master, and completely free" (137). But that freedom was also granted only "at the will of another." Equiano's inclusion of his manumission, or freedom, paper in his autobiography suggests that he kept a copy with him at all times, because the liberty of a free black man was always open to challenge wherever race-based slavery existed.

Equiano's enslavement in the Americas was extraordinarily unrepresentative of the lives suffered by the vast majority of people of African descent doomed to work in the fields. But it was unrepresentative in ways that enabled him to acquire a perspective on slavery in the Americas unavailable to any one individual slave. The mobility of his occupation in the Americas, his literacy, and his good fortune in the masters he had gave him access to information about the range of slave conditions throughout the British American colonies that enabled him in 1789 to bear witness against slavery as a spokesman for the millions of his voiceless fellow slaves. He was able to transcend the limits of merely personal experiences to identify general truths about the evil institution: "In all the different islands in which I have been (and I have visited no less than fifteen) the treatment of the slaves was nearly the same; so nearly indeed, that the history of an island, or even a plantation, with a few . . . exceptions . . . might serve for a history of the whole" (111).

At one point after he had been freed, Equiano noted what he saw as a significant distinction between the treatment of slaves in the British West Indies and their treatment in the French Caribbean. Speaking of Martinique, he observed, "While I was on this island I went about a good deal, and found it very pleasant: in particular, I admired the town of St. Pierre, which is the principal one in the island, and built more like an European town than any I had seen in the West Indies. In general also, slaves were better treated, had more holidays, and looked better than those in the English islands" (161). There was much contemporaneous debate in 1789 about whether slaves were relatively worse off in the British West Indies than in the French, where the *Code noir* of 1685 regulated their treatment, at least in theory but not always in practice. Underlying the debate was the dispute over whether slavery was best regulated by the metropolitan European government in Paris or London or by the local Caribbean governments. Equiano's account of his life in the West Indies combines recollection of personal experience, personal observations, testimony from others, references to printed sources, and his own editorial comments. Like his account of his life in Africa, his recollection of the West Indies conflates the personal with the communal experience and autobiography with history.

As related in 1789, Equiano's experiences of West Indian slavery confirmed the testimony and arguments white opponents to the slave trade had recently been making in print and Parliament. The difference between a "man of feeling" like Robert King and "an unfeeling owner" like Mr. Drummond lay in the nature of the trade itself, which brutalized both master and slave: "But is not the slave trade entirely at war with the heart of man? And surely that which is begun, by breaking down the barriers of virtue, involves in its continuance destruction to every principle, and buries all sentiments in ruin!" (110). Only the burial of all sentiments could account for the passage on 8 August 1688 of the notorious 329th Act of the Assembly of Barbados, cited by Equiano as "universally known" because so often quoted by Benezet and others in the debate over the trade. Equiano quotes the passage punishing whites who willfully kill a slave with a fine of only fifteen pounds sterling because it was the precedent for similar laws in subsequently settled colonies: "And it is the same in most, if not all, of the West India islands. Is not this one of the many acts of the islands which call loudly for redress? And do not the assembly which enacted it, deserve the appellation of savages and brutes rather than of Christians and men? It is an act at once unmerciful, unjust, and unwise; which for cruelty would disgrace an assembly of those who are called barbarians; and for its injustice and *insanity* would shock the morality and common sense of a Samaide or a Hottentot."[8] And only the burial of all sentiments could explain the French planter who bragged that he had fathered many of his own slaves: "Pray, reader, are these sons and daughters of the French planter less his children by being begotten on black women! And what must be the virtue of those legislators, and the feelings of those fathers, who estimate the lives of their sons, however begotten, at no more than fifteen pounds, though they should be murdered, as the act says, *out of wantonness and bloody-mindedness*?" (109–10).

As does his chapter on Africa, Equiano's initial chapter on the West Indies closes with a passage of heightened rhetoric and controlled rage. Momentarily, Equiano reveals that his true goal may be more radical than he has been claiming. He does so by conflating abolition of the slave trade, amelioration of slavery, and eradication of slavery in his verbal outburst. In effect, the author's rage at the evils of slavery erupts through the narrative as his voice changes from that of autobiographer to that of preacher. The result is one of the most direct assaults of the institution of slavery found anywhere in Equiano's writings. He calls on slave owners to become men of feeling like Robert King, Thomas Farmer, and himself. He begins by identifying the causes and consequences of burying all sentiments:

> Such a tendency has the slave-trade to debauch men's minds, and harden them to every feeling of humanity! For I will not suppose that the dealers in slaves are born worse than other men – No! it is the fatality of this mistaken avarice, that it corrupts the milk of human kindness, and turns it

into gall. And, had the pursuits of those men been different, they might have been as generous, as tender-hearted, and just, as they are unfeeling, rapacious, and cruel. Surely this traffic cannot be good, which spreads like a pestilence, and taints what it touches! Which violates that first natural right of mankind, equality and independency, and gives one man a dominion over his fellows which God could never intend! For it raises the owner to a state as far above man as it depresses the slave below it; and, with all the presumption of human pride, sets a distinction between them, immeasurable in extent, and endless in duration! Yet how mistaken is the avarice even of the planters. Are slaves more useful by being thus humbled to the condition of brutes, than they would be if suffered to enjoy the privileges of men? The freedom which diffuses health and prosperity throughout Britain answers you – No. (111)

From cause Equiano moves to the likely consequences of continuing the slave trade. He quotes Beelzebub, "the prince of the devils," from John Milton's *Paradise Lost* to underscore the risk slave owners take in refusing to reform. Milton's expressed purpose in *Paradise Lost* is to "justifie the wayes of God to men."[9] Equiano justifies the ways of men to God by expressing through the voice of one of Milton's demons the sufferings of slaves and their urge to rebel.[10] Because Satan and his followers were doomed to failure, by quoting Beelzebub Equiano manages to convey the danger slave owners face if they do not change their ways, and yet he does not quite condone the violence threatened:

When you make men slaves, you deprive them of half their virtue, you set them, in your own conduct, an example of fraud, rapine, and cruelty, and compel them to live with you in a state of war; and yet you complain that they are not honest or faithful! You stupify them with stripes, and think it necessary to keep them in a state of ignorance; and yet you assert that they are incapable of learning; that their minds are such a barren soil or moor, that culture would be lost on them; and that they came from a climate, where nature (though prodigal of her bounties in a degree unknown to yourselves) has left man alone scant and unfinished, and incapable of enjoying the treasures she has poured out for him! An assertion at once impious and absurd.[11] Why do you use those instruments of torture? Are they fit to be applied by one rational being to another? And are ye not struck with shame and mortification, to see the partakers of your nature reduced so low? But, above all, are there no dangers attending this mode of treatment? Are you not hourly in dread of an insurrection? Nor would it be surprising; for when

> . . . No peace is given
> To us enslav'd, but custody severe;
> And stripes and arbitrary punishment
> Inflicted – What peace can we return?
> But to our power, hostility and hate;
> Untam'd reluctance, and revenge, tho' slow,
> Yet ever plotting how the conqueror least
> May reap his conquest, and may least rejoice
> In doing what we most in suff'ring feel.[12] (111–12)

The causes and consequences of burying one's sentiments are many and complex, but amelioration is simple: "By changing your conduct, and treating your slaves as men, every cause of fear would be banished. They would be faithful, honest, intelligent and vigorous; and peace, prosperity, and happiness would attend you" (112). The words of Equiano's solution sound far more dispassionate than the voice we hear behind them. The calm language only underscores the righteous anger beneath.

Chapter Six

FREEDOM OF A SORT

From the observations he made as a slave, Equiano knew that freedom in the West Indies was not sufficient to guarantee true liberty. Freedom from the West Indies was necessary as well. Wherever race-based slavery existed, people of African descent were victimized by the institution, regardless of their wealth or social status. On Saint Kitts Equiano witnessed "a very curious imposition on human nature. . . . A white man wanted to marry in the church a free black woman that had land and slaves at Montserrat: but the clergyman told him it was against the law of the place to marry a white and a black in the church. The man then asked to be married on the water, to which the parson consented, and the two lovers went in one boat, and the parson and clerk in another, and thus the ceremony was performed. After this the loving pair came on board our vessel, and my captain treated them extremely well, and brought them safe to Montserrat" (119).

In slave societies like the European colonies in the West Indies and the British colonies in southern North America free blacks were always vulnerable to claims of ownership, and their power to protect their freedom was very limited. One of Equiano's fellow crew members, "a very clever and decent free young mulatto-man" named Joseph Clipson, "had a free woman for his wife, by whom he had a child; and she was then living on shore, and all very happy." The captain, mate, and other crew members "knew [that] this young man from a child . . . was always free," that he had been trained as a boat builder, and that "no one had ever claimed him as their property." But not even the "certificate of his being born free in St. Kitt's," which Clipson always carried with him, protected him from the claim by a Bermuda-based captain that he was a runaway slave. The captain promised to take Clipson ashore, as he requested, "before the secretary or magistrate," but "these infernal invaders of human rights," kidnapped him instead, never to see his family again (121). Subsequently, Equiano saw "in Jamaica, and other islands," many instances of "free men, whom I have known in America, thus villainously trepanned [entrapped] and held in bondage. I have heard of two similar practices even in Philadelphia: and were it not for the benevolence of the quakers in that city, many of the sable race, who now breathe the air of liberty, would, I believe, be groaning under some planter's chains" (122).

Equiano also recognized that legal enslavement might even be psychologically preferable to precarious freedom in a slave society:

> These things opened my mind to a new scene of horror, to which I had been before a stranger. Hitherto I had thought only slavery dreadful; but the state of a free negro appeared to me now equally so at least, and in some respects even worse, for they live in constant alarm for their liberty, which is but nominal, for they are universally insulted and plundered without the possibility of redress; for such is the equity of the West Indian laws, that no free negro's evidence will be admitted in their courts of justice. In this situation, is it surprising that slaves, when mildly treated, should prefer even the misery of slavery to such a mockery of freedom? (122)

Despite all he had seen of the limitations free blacks faced, in a triumph of hope over experience Equiano embraced the news of his own freedom with an almost inexpressible and incomparable exuberance: "Heavens! who could do justice to my feelings at this moment? Not conquering heroes themselves, in the midst of a triumph – Not the tender mother who has just regained her long-lost infant, and presses it to her heart – Not the weary hungry mariner, at the sight of the desired friendly port – Not the lover, when he once more embraces his beloved mistress, after she had been ravished from his arms! – All within my breast was tumult, wildness, and delirium!" (136). Feeling restored to his "original free African state" (138), he welcomed the "blessings and prayers of the sable race, particularly the aged, to whom my heart had ever been attached with reverence" (137). Everyone, whites "as well as black people[,] immediately styled" him "by a new appellation[,] . . . the most desirable in the world, which was freeman." To celebrate he sponsored several dances, where he wore his "Georgia super-fine blue cloathes," making "no indifferent appearance," if he did say so himself, in the suit made of the best material he had bought in Georgia in anticipation of his manumission. The combination of his new status, dashing appearance, and generosity had its desired effect: "Some of the sable females, who formerly stood aloof, now began to relax, and appear less coy" (138).

Equiano was able to resist temptation, however, because he had other plans, as King and Farmer soon discovered. He was determined to return to London. But he found he could not say no to the request of his "worthy captain, and his owner my late master" that he continue to work on King's vessels: "Gratitude bowed me down; and none but the generous mind can judge of my feelings, struggling between inclination and duty." Duty won. King had freed him as promised. The transition from a master-slave relationship to an employer-employee contract must have been difficult to make on both sides. Like Pascal before them, both King and Farmer had often alternated between treating the enslaved Equiano kindly and callously, even threatening that the promise of freedom might be withdrawn. Could Equiano trust them to deal with him as fairly as they would with any employee over whom they had never had absolute power? Would Farmer, whom Equiano had come to see as another father figure, be able to accept him as an independent adult? Equiano agreed to serve his "benefactors" no longer as a slave but now "as an able-bodied sailor, at thirty – six shillings per month, besides what perquisites I could make" selling "ventures." He intended to "make a voyage or two, entirely to please my honoured patrons," before crossing the Atlantic again. As "an able-bodied sailor" in 1766 he assumed the commercial equivalent of the military status of "able seaman" Pascal had given him in 1762.

Equiano may have noted the equivalency because thoughts of Pascal and restoration were very much on his mind in July 1766. Like an alienated child anxious to win back the affection of his parent, Equiano had great hopes for his return to England: "I determined that the year following, if it pleased God, I would see Old England once more, and surprise my old master, Capt. Pascal, who was hourly in my mind; for I still loved him, notwithstanding his usage of me, and I pleased myself with thinking of what he would say when he saw what the Lord had done for me in so short a time, instead of being, as he might perhaps suppose, under the cruel yoke of some planter. With these kind of reveries I often used to entertain myself, and shorten the time till my return" (138).

The harsh realities a free black man faced in the slave societies of the West Indies and Georgia quickly woke him from those reveries. The month after being manumitted, August 1766, he sailed aboard the *Nancy* in a "state of serenity" over "smooth seas" with "pleasant weather" to Saint Eustatius for cargo and then on to Savannah (138). Fending off alligators as he brought agricultural products downriver to the *Nancy* was the least of the dangers he experienced there. One evening a slave belonging to a Savannah merchant named Read began to verbally abuse Equiano without provocation. Knowing that "there was little or no law for a free negro," Equiano patiently tried to diffuse the situation, but the slave only grew more intemperate. He became so overwrought that he hit Equiano, who then "lost all temper, and fell on him and beat him soundly." Fearing the possible repercussions, the next morning Equiano told Captain Farmer of the incident and asked him to go with him to talk to Read. Farmer thought Equiano was exaggerating the significance of the fight, assuring him that he would mollify Read if necessary. Later that morning Equiano discovered he had reason for concern. Read came to the wharf where the *Nancy* was docked and demanded that Equiano come ashore to be "flogged all round the town, for beating his negro slave." Ignoring Equiano's claim that he acted only in self-defense, Read told Farmer to turn him over. Farmer's response astounded his crew member: "He said he knew nothing of the matter, I was a free man." "Astonished and frightened" by Farmer's statement, Equiano realized that in some ways black freemen were virtually slaves without masters, more vulnerable to abuse than chattel slaves protected by owners guarding their property. Farmer's response reminded Equiano that, with neither law to protect him nor apparently anyone in power with a vested interest in his well-being, "might too often overcomes right" in slave societies.

Recognizing that his was a case where discretion was the better part of valor, he refused to go ashore to be flogged "without judge or jury." Seething with anger, Read swore he would return with all the town's constables to remove Equiano from the vessel. Equiano had seen enough instances of the abuse of black freemen not to doubt Read's word. For example, a carpenter he knew was thrown into jail merely for requesting the money he had earned from a white man who later had him removed from Georgia, falsely accused of having planned "to set the gentleman's house on fire" and of having "run away with his slaves" (139).

Equiano was less upset about the possibility of physical injury than by the threat Read posed to his sense of honor as a free man: "I dreaded, of all things, the thoughts of being stripped, as I never in my life had the marks of any violence of that kind. At that instant a rage seized my soul, and for a while I determined to resist the first man that should attempt to lay violent hands on me, or basely use me without a trial; for I would sooner die like a free man, than suffer myself to be scourged by the hands of ruffians, and my blood drawn like a slave." The captain and others eventually convinced him, however, that Read was such a spiteful man that resistance would be futile. Equiano agreed to take refuge in a house their landlord owned outside of town. Just after he left town, Read returned with his constables, swearing to take Equiano "dead or alive." Five days passed before Farmer took any action on Equiano's behalf, and only then in response to the threats some of Equiano's friends made to put him on another vessel. Farmer begged Read to forgive Equiano, who was a man of good character with a flawless reputation and who was an essential crew member. Read begrudgingly gave in, saying Equiano "might go to hell" for all he cared (140). Thinking he had succeeded in his mission, Farmer had to be reminded that he needed to retrieve the constables' warrant before the affair was legally ended and Equiano was safe from his "hunters." At last, he could safely return to the *Nancy*, though he was stuck with paying all the legal expenses.

Plenty of work on board awaited him. After thanking his friends onshore for all their aid he helped load the *Nancy* for its return voyage to the West Indies with a cargo of twenty cattle and other livestock much in demand in the islands. To compensate Equiano for time he had lost and to encourage him to work as hard as usual, Farmer promised him that he could bring two head of cattle of his own for sale. But when the time came to put them on board, he told Equiano there was no room for even one of them. Equiano, "a good deal mortified at this usage, . . . told him I had no notion that he intended thus to impose on me: nor could I think well of any man that was so much worse than his word. On this we had some disagreement, and I gave him to understand that I intended to leave the vessel." Once again fearful that he would lose Equiano and at the prompting of the ailing mate, whose duties Equiano had already taken on, Farmer apologized, promised to make it up to

Equiano when they reached the Caribbean, and appealed to his sense of duty because "the mate was so sickly, he could not do without me . . . and the safety of the vessel and cargo depended greatly upon me." Equiano reluctantly "consented to slave on as before" (141).

To make amends for having denied him space for his cattle Farmer encouraged him to bring turkeys and other fowl on board to sell in the islands. Never having dealt with turkeys before and convinced that they were too tender to survive the voyage, Equiano resisted. The more he resisted, the more Farmer insisted. The captain ultimately prevailed by offering to insure Equiano against all losses on the only goods he found he could buy with his colonial paper money. Unhappy about having to take the turkeys and displeased as well as disappointed by Captain Farmer's recent treatment of him, Equiano "determined to make no more voyages to this quarter, nor with this captain" (142).

He would indeed make no more trips under Farmer's command. On the voyage to Montserrat in November the mate grew increasingly ill. Captain Farmer also complained of feeling sick after one of the bullocks butted him in the chest. The rough seas they encountered made their conditions worse, rendering them unable to help the other seven men forced to continuously pump water out of the *Nancy*. Not a very tight vessel to begin with, in the stormy weather and high seas she was taking in so much water that in about a week several of the bullocks drowned and the others were in danger of doing so. Neither the mate nor the captain was well enough to come on deck "to make observations above four or five times the whole passage. The whole care of the vessel rested therefore upon me; and I was obliged to direct her by mere dint of reason, not being able to work a traverse" (142). Farmer now regretted that he had not taught Equiano how to use trigonometry to calculate distances and locations by noting latitudes and the angles of departure from the meridian. Nor had he taught him to use a traverse board, "a thin piece of board, marked with all the points of the compass, and having eight holes bored in each, and eight small pegs hanging from the center of the board, . . . to determine the different courses run by a ship during the period of the watch; and to ascertain the distance of each course."[1]

Farmer did not live long enough to fulfill his promise to rectify his mistake. In a little over two weeks Farmer became bedridden, though he continued to keep Robert King's "interest at heart; for this just and benevolent man ever appeared much concerned about the welfare of what he was intrusted with." As a true "man of feeling," he died more concerned about another

Frontispiece from the first edition of volume 2 of Olaudah Equiano's *Interesting Narrative*
(London, 1789). The drawing, titled *Bahamas Banks, 1767*, depicts the wreck of the
Nancy, which Equiano took command of. The frontispiece's accompanying caption was
from Job 33: "Thus God speaketh once, yea, twice, yet Man perceiveth it not.
In a Dream, in a Vision, of the Night, when deep sleep falleth upon Men in slumberings
upon the Bed; Then he openeth the Ears of Men, & sealeth their instruction."
(The John Carter Brown Library at Brown University)

than himself: "When this dear friend found the symptoms of death approaching, he called me by my name; and, when I came to him, he asked (with almost his last breath) if he had ever done me any harm? 'God forbid I should think so,' I replied, 'I should then be the most ungrateful of wretches to the best of benefactors.' While I was thus expressing my affection and sorrow by his bed-side, he expired without saying another word, and the day following we committed his body to the deep." Loved by all his comrades, Farmer's loss was much regretted. But only Farmer's death made Equiano recognize how much Farmer had meant to him and the extent to which Farmer had replaced Pascal in his affections: "I did not know, till he was gone, the strength of my regard for him. Indeed I had every reason in the world to be attached to him; for, besides that he was in general mild, affable, generous, faithful, benevolent, and just, he was to me a friend and father; and had it pleased Providence that he had died but five months before, I verily believe I should not have obtained my freedom when I did; and it is not improbable that I might not have been able to get it at any rate afterwards" (143).

After Farmer died, his duties and responsibilities fell upon the mate, who "made such observations as he was able, but to no purpose" because he was as untrained as Equiano in navigation. More important, he lacked the compensating reason Equiano could apply to the task. Consequently, Equiano took command, rightly confident now that since the winds had diminished, he could steer the leaky vessel to Antigua and from there on to Montserrat. In about ten days they were home. By the end of the voyage all the bullocks had drowned below deck, but Equiano's turkeys, "though on the deck, and exposed to so much wet and bad weather, did well." They did so well, in fact, that he made a nearly 300 percent profit on them, despite his initial misgivings.

The joy he took in his unexpected profit was far surpassed by the pride he felt at the recognition the voyage brought him. Perhaps only someone with naval experience could fully appreciate the satisfaction he took in succeeding his acknowledged foster father as the vessel's commander. For a moment he seemed to find himself once again in a world where merit mattered more than complexion: "Many were surprised when they heard of my conducting the sloop into the port, and I now obtained a new appellation, and was called captain. This elated me not a little, and it was quite flattering to my vanity to be thus styled by as high a title as any sable freeman in this place possessed. When the death of the captain became known, he was much regretted by all who knew him; for he was a man universally respected. At the same time the sable captain lost no fame; for the success I had met with increased the affection of my friends in no small measure." In later editions of his *Interesting Narrative* Equiano further emphasized and embellished the significance of this passage, which ends chapter 7, by making it a separate paragraph and by concluding it with the words, "and I was offered, by a gentleman of the place, the command of his sloop to go amongst the islands, but I refused" (144).

The moment passed. As a free black man Equiano was not permitted to command a merchant vessel officially, despite his demonstrated qualifications. With Farmer dead nothing more could keep him in the West Indies besides his gratitude to his former master, Robert King. Equiano wanted more than ever to return "to England, where my heart had always been." King, however, successfully implored him to undertake "another voyage to Georgia, as the mate from his ill state of health, was quite useless in the vessel."

King hired as captain an old acquaintance of Equiano named William Phillips, a Welshman. After refitting the *Nancy* and taking on a live cargo of about twenty slaves, they sailed first to Saint Eustatius and then, on 29 January 1767, toward Georgia. The new captain's behavior quickly raised concerns about his competency: "Our new captain boasted strangely of his skill in navigating and conducting a vessel; and, in consequence of this, he steered a new course, several points more to the westward than we ever did before; this appeared to me very extraordinary" (147).

No doubt subconsciously influenced by his worry over the competency of Phillips, Equiano began to have a series of dreams that "the ship was wrecked amidst the surfs and rocks, and that I was the means of saving every one on board." He paid the dream no notice the first two times he had it. One night, weary from his turn at pumping water out of the vessel's leaky hull, he "uttered with an oath, 'Damn the vessel's bottom out.' But my conscience instantly smote me for the expression. When I left the deck I went to bed, and had scarcely fallen asleep when I dreamed the same dream again about the ship that I had dreamt the two preceding nights." Later that night the helmsman called Equiano's attention to what he said was a large sea animal of some sort in the vessel's path, but Equiano soon recognized that it was not a moving animal but a stationary rock.

He immediately went below to warn Captain Phillips of the danger and told him he needed to come on deck to assess the situation. The captain failed to come as promised. He again failed to come when Equiano returned below to warn him that the current was pushing the vessel toward the rock. A third time, having heard the sound of the breakers against the rock they were rapidly approaching, Equiano "lost all patience; and, growing quite enraged, . . . ran down to him again, and asked him, why he did not come up, and what he could mean by all this?" (148–49). At last the feckless captain responded and called all hands on deck. But just as they released the anchor to try to hold the vessel in its present position, "with one single heave of the swells, the sloop was pierced and transfixed among the rocks." Equiano considered himself responsible for the disaster because he had cursed the vessel earlier that night, and he "determined[,] if I should still be saved, that I would never swear again." Though temporarily dispirited by their predicament, he soon "began to think how we might be saved; and, I believe no mind was ever like mine so replete with inventions and confused with schemes, though how to escape death I knew not." Relying on the captain's judgment was certainly not the answer. His first command was to nail down the hatches with the slaves still in the hold. Equiano momentarily fainted at the shocking idea that his sin of swearing would cause God "to charge me with these people's blood" (149). He tried to convince the captain not to doom the slaves to death, but Phillips was convinced that if they were not imprisoned in the sinking vessel, they would try to get into its boat, which could not carry them as well as the crew to safety.

For a man who had proudly served with the Royal Navy, Equiano's response and reaction to his commanding officer were stunning. Insubordinate in word and deed, he publicly reprimanded Phillips, in effect leading the crew to mutiny against his orders and authority: "I could no longer restrain my emotion, and I told him he deserved drowning for not knowing how to navigate the vessel; and I believe the people would have tossed him overboard if I had given them the least hint of it. However, the hatches were not nailed down." From that point on Equiano took unchallenged command of the situation. The crew agreed with Equiano that, rather than having a few men abandon the *Nancy* during the night to try to reach an unknown destination in a damaged boat that probably "could not survive the surfs," the safer course of action was to trust in God, repair the boat as he suggested, and stay on the dry part of the vessel until morning. Daylight brought mixed relief. The swells subsided somewhat, and now they could see "a small key, or desolate island, about five or six miles off; but a barrier soon presented itself; for there was not water enough for our boat to go over the reefs, and this threw us again into a sad consternation" (150). To get everyone to safety Equiano had no choice but to take the few men he could count on to drag and carry the boat over the reefs several times, cutting themselves on the rocks each time:

> There were only four people that would work with me at the oars; and they consisted of three black men and a Dutch creole sailor;[2] and, though we went with the boat five times that day, we had no others to assist us. But, had we not worked in this manner, I really believe the people could not have been saved; for not one of the white men did any thing to preserve their lives; and indeed they soon got so drunk that they were not able, but lay about the deck like swine, so that we were at last obliged to lift them into the boat, and carry them on shore by force. This want of assistance made our labour intolerably severe. . . . [But] out of thirty-two people we lost not one. (150–51)

The success of Equiano's leadership reminded him of his three dreams, "for our danger was the same I had dreamt of; and I could not help looking on myself as the principal instrument in effecting our deliverance." Had he not forcibly moved the drunken whites when he did, while the leather patch he had made to repair the boat still held, they would inevitably have drowned. They, too, came to see him as the man in charge of their salvation: "Though I warned the people who were drinking, and entreated them to embrace the moment of deliverance, nevertheless they persisted, as if not possessed of the least spark of reason. I could not help thinking, that if any of these people had been lost, God would charge me with their lives, which, perhaps, was one cause of my labouring so hard for their preservation, and indeed every one of them afterwards seemed so sensible of the service I had rendered them, that while we were on the key, I was a kind of chieftain amongst them" (151). As if laying a claim to the small desert isle, one of the Bahama keys, as its discoverer and owner, Equiano planted some limes, oranges, and lemons "as a token to any one that might be cast away hereafter" (151–52).

Equiano and his crewmates soon discovered that the island, only about a mile in circumference, was apparently not deserted after all. At a distance they saw a group of figures, "as large as men," walking backward and forward. The captain immediately identified them as cannibals. Having "created a great panic among us," Phillips "wanted to go to a key that was within sight, but a great way off; but I was against it, as in so doing we should not be able to save all the people." Again countermanding their captain, Equiano decided that rather than fleeing from his cannibals they should approach them to see if they could chase them off the island. Doing so, they found the captain's cannibals to be flamingoes.

Turtles and fish in the waters around the island gave them welcome relief from the heavily salted meat they had. Collected rainwater satisfied their thirst, and sails taken from the vessel provided housing. It took eleven days to render the boat seaworthy again. Once more Equiano and his captain jockeyed for command: "The captain wanted me to stay on shore, while he went to sea in quest of a vessel to take all the people off the key; but this I refused; and the captain and myself, with five more, set off in the boat towards New Providence," the capital of the British colony of the Bahamas (152–53). With what few provisions they could carry they set off, reaching a deserted and wooded part of the island of Obbico, modern-day Abaco, in two days. There they searched desperately for freshwater, without which their salted beef was inedible, all the while fearing attacks from wild beasts. Just as they were all about to abandon themselves to despair, the captain, finally almost getting something right, spotted a sail on the horizon.

Dismissing the captain's conviction that the sail belonged to a pirate ship and that they would all be killed if they approached it, the crew followed Equiano's judgment that "be that as it might, we must board her if we were to die for it; and, if they should not receive us kindly, we must oppose them as well as we could: for there was no alternative between their perishing and ours. This counsel was immediately taken; and I really believe that the captain, myself, and the Dutchman, would then have faced twenty men" (154).

The captain's pirate ship turned out to be a local wrecker, a small vessel whose crew looked for wrecks to salvage what they could from them and to save survivors in exchange for the ships' cargo. Most of the forty-some people aboard the wrecker were crew members of a whaling schooner who, like Equiano and his men, had set out in boats to try to reach New Providence to engage a vessel to rescue the majority of their crew left stranded on a small island. Equiano and his comrades convinced the wrecker's crew to rescue the survivors from the *Nancy* first because they were in imminent danger of dying of thirst. Because there were so many men from the whaler aboard the wrecker, they were left, with the *Nancy*'s boat, to salvage what they could from the *Nancy*, while the wrecker set out with Equiano and his crewmates toward New Providence, which was much farther away than they could have traveled in their own boat.

On the voyage to New Providence the wrecker was caught in a wind storm so violent that the crew "were obliged to cut away the mast" (155) to reduce the amount of the vessel's surface exposed to the wind and thus to try to keep it from being forced to heel, or lean over, so far that it would founder, or sink. Separated by the wind from its anchors, the wrecker was repeatedly driven into the shallows. The situation appeared so hopeless that "my old captain and sickly useless mate, and several others, fainted; and death stared us in the face on every side. All the swearers on board now began to call on the God of Heaven to assist them." Only a miracle could save them, Equiano thought. It came in the form of "two intrepid water heroes," expert swimmers who, with "the prayers of all that remained in their senses," risked their lives to paddle out to the buoy marking the position of the detached anchor. They connected a hawser from the wrecker in the shallows to the cable of the anchor in the deeper water so that the crew could haul the vessel out of danger. As soon as they reached safer waters, the useless captain and mate, "whose strength and senses were gone, came to themselves, and were now as elated as they were before depressed" (156). After the crew came ashore, where they found, mended, and refitted their mast, they proceeded on to

New Providence, finally bringing their three-week-long ordeal to an end among hospitable and friendly people.

Had his heart not still been set on returning to England, Equiano would have been happy to have remained in New Providence. He "liked the place extremely, and there were some free black people here who were very happy, and we passed our time pleasantly together, with the melodious sound of the catguts [i.e., stringed instruments] under the lime and lemon trees." He turned down a chance to get to Georgia on a merchant sloop, exchanging his labor for passage, because the owner told him, only after having had him help load the vessel, that they must first stop in Jamaica. After a little more than two weeks on the island Equiano agreed to go with Captain Phillips to Georgia in a schooner he had hired to transport the slaves he failed to sell in the Bahamas. Regretfully, Equiano took his leave of New Providence, only to have the vessel forced back to port the next day by heavy seas. Equiano was one of the few crew members who kept his head and his faith: "Some of the people swore that we had spells set upon us, by somebody in Montserrat; and others said that we had witches and wizzards amongst the poor helpless slaves; and that we never should arrive safe at Georgia. But these things did not deter me; I said, 'Let us again face the winds and seas, and swear not, but trust to God, and he will deliver us'" (158). Seven days later they were in Savannah.

Returning to Georgia brought Equiano back to the harsh realities of slavery and the limitations it placed on his freedom. He spent his first evening in Savannah with his enslaved friend Mosa, talking past nine o'clock. The light in the house drew the attention of the watchmen, who decided to investigate it. Invited in by Mosa and offered punch, they asked Equiano for some of his limes, which he readily gave them. After accepting Mosa's hospitality they suddenly announced that Equiano must go to the watch house with them because "all negroes, who had a light in their houses after nine o'clock were to be taken into custody, and either pay some dollars or be flogged. Some of these people knew that I was a free man; but, as the man of the house was not free, and had his master to protect him, they did not take the same liberty with him they did with me" (158). Ignoring Equiano's protests that he was a free man, newly arrived from the Bahamas and well known in Savannah, the watchmen forced him to come with them. He could not help but think he was about to experience the same sort of robbery he had suffered at Santa Cruz. But the watchmen had something worse in mind. The next morning they "flogged a negro man and woman that they had in the watch-house, and then they told me that I must be flogged too." Equiano's challenge to their right to do so "only exasperated them the more, and they instantly swore they would serve me as Doctor Perkins had done." Fortunately for Equiano, one of them had second thoughts about the legality of such abuse, giving him the chance to call once again on Dr. Brady, who gained his release.

At times Equiano was more active in his resistance to abuse. Just outside of Savannah he "was beset by two white men, who meant to play their usual tricks with me in the way of kidnapping." When one of them, claiming Equiano as his runaway slave, was about to lay his hands on him, Equiano "told them to be still and keep off, for I had seen those tricks played upon other free blacks, and they must not think to serve me so." One of the whites initially responded to Equiano's threats much as Captain Doran had to his claim to legal rights four years earlier, but this time the now-free Equiano was ready to act as well as speak to defend his rights: "They paused a little, and one said to the other – it will not do; and the other answered that I talked too good English. I replied, I believed I did; and I had also with me a revengeful stick equal to the occasion; and my mind was likewise good. Happily, however, it was not used; and, after we had talked together a little in this manner, the rogues left me" (159).

In order to get back to Montserrat so that he could bid farewell to Robert King before returning to "Old England," in late spring 1767 Equiano booked passage from Savannah on the *Speedwell*, a Grenada-based sloop commanded by John Bunton, bound first to Martinique with a cargo of rice. A far more competent captain than Phillips, Bunton reached the French colony after a pleasantly uneventful voyage in May. From there he went to the Grenadines. Equiano had little choice but to stay with the vessel, even though he was growing increasingly anxious to get to Montserrat in time to get passage with the transatlantic fleet, which had to sail by 26 July to avoid the dangers of the hurricane season. He had made the mistake of lending Captain Bunton some money, which Equiano now needed to pay his way. Since by law as a black man he could not take Bunton to court to recover his loan, he had to hope the captain would honor his obligation to repay the loan and give Equiano his wages. When Bunton finally paid him, he had already missed an opportunity for a free passage to Montserrat and barely had time to catch a vessel to Saint Eustatius and from there another to Saint Kitts.

With Montserrat almost in sight Equiano suffered his last indignity as a free black in the West Indies. He found a vessel bound for Montserrat, but the captain refused to allow him on board until he had first advertised himself, giving public notice that he was planning to leave the island in case anyone had a claim on him as a fugitive slave. Risking having to delay his departure to England until the following year, Equiano frantically sought some local character references because he refused to "be compelled to submit to this degrading necessity, which every black freeman is under, of advertising himself like a slave, when he leaves an island, and which I thought a gross imposition upon any freedom" (162). Luckily, some white acquaintances from Montserrat vouched for him to the captain.

Equiano's Montserrat friends and Robert King in particular were overjoyed to see him after his six-month absence, even though Equiano's news of the wreck of the *Nancy* compounded the losses King had suffered while Equiano was gone. A flood had destroyed his house, much of his property, and nearly his life. King "warmly advised me to stay there; insisting, as I was much respected by all the gentlemen in the place, that I might do very well, and in a short time have land and slaves of my own" (164). This time, however, Equiano was not to be deflected from his plan to return to England, as soon as he held some "free dances, as they are called, with some of my friends and countrymen."

On 26 July 1767, for a salary of seven guineas, Equiano set off to London aboard the *Andromache*, commanded by John Hamer. He had successfully bargained for a relatively large lump sum payment rather than the monthly peacetime salary of twenty-five to thirty shillings more normally paid for transatlantic voyages.[3] The character reference he had requested from King was in his pocket:

> *Montserrat, 26th of July*, 1767.
>
> The bearer hereof, Gustavus Vasa, was my slave for upwards of three years, during which he has always behaved himself well, and discharged his duty with honesty and assiduity.
>
> ROBERT KING.
>
> To all whom this may concern.

Equiano was "exceedingly glad to see" himself "once more on board of a ship, and still more so, in steering the course" he "had long wished for": "With a light heart I bade Montserrat farewell, and never had my feet on it since; and with it I bade adieu to the sound of the cruel whip, and all other dreadful instruments of torture! adieu to the offensive sight of the violated chastity of the sable females, which has too often accosted my eyes! adieu to oppressions (although to me less severe than to most of my countrymen!) and adieu to the angry howling dashing surfs! I wished for a grateful and thankful heart to praise the Lord God on high for all his mercies! in this extacy I steered the ship all night" (164).

Fittingly, in the image he gives us of himself as he left the West Indies he is in command of the ship and director of his own destiny. As soon as he set sail for England he felt truly free. His experiences in British North America and the Caribbean had been ones of chattel slavery and greatly restricted freedom in the slave societies. Only at sea in the Americas, out of necessity, was his merit acknowledged despite his complexion or condition, as it had been during his years with the Royal Navy. His assumption of command during the wreck of the *Nancy* and thereafter was such a significant defining moment in the development of his sense of self-worth that he chose a depiction of the wreck as the subject for the frontispiece of volume 2 of his autobiography. In so doing, he implies that his handling of the wreck is as much a key to his character as the portrait of himself he commissioned to be the frontispiece of volume 1 of his *Interesting Narrative*.

TOWARD THE NORTH POLE

After "a most prosperous" seven-week voyage, in September 1767 the *Andro-mache* arrived at Cherry-Garden Stairs, a landing place on the south bank of the Thames about 4 miles downriver from Westminster Palace. Equiano's "longing eyes" were "once more gratified with a sight of London." "Full of hope," he sought to reestablish his former relationships now that he was a free man barely in his twenties with thirty-seven guineas in his pocket. He had some difficulty finding the Guerin sisters because they had moved from the more fashionable Westminster to May's Hill, Greenwich, probably to economize following the death of their brother in 1760. Surprised and delighted to see Equiano again, they were shocked to learn of their cousin's treatment of him, behavior they thought did "Capt. Pascal no honour" (164). Since Pascal and Equiano were now both frequent visitors to the Guerins, the paths of the former slave and his former master inevitably crossed in nearby Greenwich Park. Unfortunately, with a combination of sarcasm, recrimination, and denial, their relationship, too, picked up just where it had left off:

> When [Pascal] saw me, he appeared a good deal surprised, and asked me how I came back? I answered, "In a ship." To which he replied dryly, "I suppose you did not walk back to London on the water." As I saw, by his manner, that he did not seem to be sorry for his behaviour to me, and that I had not much reason to expect any favour from him, I told him that he had used me very ill, after I had been such a faithful servant to him for so many years; on which, without saying any more, he turned about and went away. A few days after this I met Capt. Pascal at Miss Guerin's house, and asked him for my prize-money. He said there was none due to me; for, if my prize-money had been £10,000, he had a right to it all. I told him I was informed otherwise, on which he bade me defiance, and, in a bantering tone, desired me to commence a law-suit against him for it: "There are lawyers enough," said he, "that will take the cause in hand, and you had better try it." I told him then that I would try it, which enraged him very much. (165)

Out of consideration for Pascal's cousins, however, Equiano decided not to pursue the matter. He believed that he had enough money to tide him over until he settled on a new career or to support him while he trained under a master – an employer, not an owner – in a skilled occupation. His first choice was to go into service, that is, to become a domestic servant, preferably in the Guerin household. Domestic service was the most common occupation for young men and women of low social status and few marketable skills, regardless of their color. But people of color were often hired as fashionable status symbols of their employers' wealth and imperial connections. Probably because of their straitened financial situation, the Guerins politely told Equiano that they could not hire him, but they did the next best thing. They helped him find a master who could train him in his chosen line of work – hairdressing.

From September 1767 to February 1768 Equiano trained under a hairdresser in Coventry Court, Haymarket. Since he "did not like to be idle," to fill up his "vacant hours innocently" Equiano paid a neighbor to teach him to play the French horn Pascal had wanted him to learn ten years earlier. Was he subconsciously still trying to please Pascal, despite the numerous rejections he had suffered? From another neighbor "who kept an academy and an evening school" Equiano sought to improve himself in arithmetic by learning barter and alligation, computational skills any man of business needed to calculate, respectively, the equivalent quantities and values of different commodities (166).

Equiano learned enough in just five months to find employment as a hairdresser for "Dr. Charles Irving, in Pall-mall, so celebrated for his successful experiments in making sea-water fresh" (166). Although the principle of distilling freshwater from seawater had long been known, earlier attempts to produce potable water at sea involved bulky equipment, great amounts of fuel, and chemical additives that left nasty aftertastes. Irving's method basically relied on a "simple addition to the common ship's kettles" used for cooking so that only one source of heat was needed to both boil provisions and distill seawater to produce freshwater through collected condensation.[1] Irving, whose name was variously reported as Erwin, Irvin, Irvine, Irwin, and Christopher Irwin, had been a celebrity since 1759, when newspapers and magazines announced his invention of the marine chair, a device designed to compensate for the motion of a ship so that telescopes could be used on the most turbulent seas to calculate celestial measurements. When Equiano entered his employ in February 1768, Irving was on the verge of great fame and reward. The Royal Navy began using his desalination process in 1770. In 1772 Parliament awarded Irving the princely sum of five thousand pounds–equivalent today to about three hundred thousand pounds, or nearly six hundred thousand dollars – for "his discovery of making salt-water fresh and wholesome at sea."[2] Equiano found Irving to be a "gentleman . . . an excellent master . . . exceedingly kind and good-tempered" who "allowed me in the evenings to attend my schools" (166). Unfortunately, Equiano found that he could not make ends meet on his annual salary of twelve pounds. The costs of his schools had already exhausted all but one of the thirty-seven pounds he had brought to England.

In May 1768 Equiano decided that to repair his fortunes he should "try the sea again in quest of more money, as I had been bred to it, and hitherto found the profession of it successful." Besides, he wanted to gratify his "very great desire to see Turkey." What might account for Equiano's "roving disposition"? As he notes, necessity played a part, but necessity alone would not explain his actions. Although he says that he loved England, he spent much of the next decade at sea or in other lands, including some slave societies. Part of the answer no doubt lay in his temperament. As far back as he could remember he had been an avid observer of everyone and everything around him. He had always seen himself as exceptional. As a black man in England he was more exceptional than ever. As an extraordinarily perceptive and adaptable outsider he was unusually skilled at objectively assessing alien societies in which he found himself without fully becoming a part of those societies.

Surely much of the reason for his desire to rove lay in his personal history. Enslavement had rendered him a man without a country, someone who seemed to define himself as much by movement as by staying in any one place for long. Slavery had controlled his mobility. Freedom meant that he could choose where and when to travel. "Bred to" the sea by his experience with the Royal Navy, he was drawn to the opportunity to relive his happy shipboard life. To experience freedom, he seemed to feel, he had to roam, and nothing would test the limits of his new freedom more than risking a return to the belly of the beast of slavery – the West Indies. Having crossed economic, geographical, legal, political, religious, and social boundaries since childhood, Equiano was already well on his way to becoming the "citizen of the world" he later called himself.

He had no trouble finding the master of a ship "fitted up with great taste" bound for the Mediterranean in July 1768. In peacetime, when the wages of merchant seamen averaged barely half those in wartime, an experienced sailor like Equiano could expect to make between twenty-five and thirty shillings per month – between fifteen and eighteen pounds per year – plus victuals.[3] Equiano presumably made even more because in addition to being an able seaman he could dress hair and perform the duties of a steward. By going back to sea he saved the expense of his school fees. After testing Equiano's skill as a hairdresser, "John Jolly, a neat, smart, good-humoured man, just such a one as I wished to serve," hired Equiano aboard the *Delaware* (166). Equiano seized every opportunity to continue his education. On the voyage Equiano "learned navigation of the mate." The *Delaware* took him first to the south of France and Italy, where he "was charmed with the richness and beauty of the countries, and struck with the elegant buildings with which they abound." He visited the French ports of Villefranche-sur-Mer and Nice and the Tuscan port of Livorno (Leghorn) on the Italian coast. The "extraordinary good wines and rich fruits" allowed Equiano to satisfy his taste as well as his curiosity (167). He had ample opportunity to be a tourist because Captain Jolly always lodged onshore.

In effect, Equiano found himself between 1768 and 1772 on the working man's version of the grand tours taken by the sons of the wealthy to finish their educations by traveling around Europe. But unlike those tourists, whose goal was to observe the grandeur of the past in Continental Europe, Equiano's tour included a comparative study of modern systems of slavery in the Mediterranean and West Indies. From Italy the *Delaware* sailed to Smyrna, modern-day İzmir, the third largest city in Turkey and the largest natural harbor in western Turkey. Located in the middle of Turkey's Mediterranean coast, with its large Greek population and the site of a Greek Orthodox see, Smyrna had been a center of Greek culture before coming under Ottoman Turkish rule in 1424. It was also a major center for trade between India and Europe before the Suez Canal was completed in 1869. Equiano saw "many caravans from India, with some hundreds of camels, laden with different goods," and he was impressed that the "people of these caravans [were] quite brown" (169). Equiano "liked the place and the Turks extremely well" during his first five-month stay in Smyrna (168). He was enchanted by the city's architecture, agriculture, and prices: "This is a very ancient city; the houses are built of stone, and most of them have graves adjoining to them; so that they sometimes present the appearance of church-yards. Provisions are very plentiful in this city, and good wine less than a penny a pint. The grapes, pomegranates, and many other fruits, were also the richest and largest I ever saw or tasted" (167). The size and shape of the tails of sheep, too, were noteworthy. Even more intriguing were the reception he received and the customs he observed: "The natives are well-looking and strong made, and treated me always with great civility. In general I believe they are fond of black people; and several of them gave me pressing invitations to stay amongst them, although they keep the Franks, or Christians,[4] separate, and do not suffer them to dwell immediately amongst them. I was astonished in not seeing women in any of their shops, and very rarely any in the streets; and whenever I did they were covered with a veil from head to foot, so that I could not see their faces, except when any of them, out of curiosity, uncovered them to look at me, which they sometimes did" (167). On his second visit to Smyrna, in December 1769, "a seraskier, or officer, took a liking to me here, and wanted me to stay, and offered me two wives; however I refused the temptation, thinking one was as much as some could manage, and more than others would venture on" (169). Although Equiano noted the oppression of the Greeks by the Turks, he did not directly condemn it: "I was surprised to see how the Greeks are, in some measure, kept under by the Turks, as the negroes are in the West-Indies by the white people" (167–68). Modern readers may see Equiano's comments on the Turks as, perhaps unintentionally, ironic.

Equiano was pleased to be the object of attention and to be so easily accepted, but he seems naively unaware that the attention and acceptance imply that his degree of Christian faith in 1769 was perceived as little threat to believers in Islam. Infidel Christians were segregated from the Muslim population to keep them from corrupting true believers. And though Equiano says little about slavery in the Middle East, Islamic slave traders took as many as seven million enslaved people from Africa before and during the period of the European transatlantic slave trade.

The innocent eye Equiano cast on the Greeks and Turks in Asia Minor contrasts sharply with the more experienced eye he cast on Europeans in the Mediterranean. The only slavery he observed during his commercial voyages in Europe involved Europeans as both the enslavers and the enslaved. In Oporto, Portugal, which he visited during carnival in May 1769, anyone "in whose custody a bible was found concealed, was to be imprisoned and flogged, and sent into slavery for ten years" (168). And the beauty and grandeur of Genoa, seen in September 1769, were, "in my eyes, disgraced by the galley-slaves, whose condition, both there and in other parts of Italy, is truly piteous and wretched" (169). To Equiano the Turks, commonly represented in eighteenth-century popular literature as brutal unbelievers and tyrants, were more humane than many professed Christians.

To observe the worst possible form of slavery one needed to go to the West Indies. There one could see chattel slavery, in which groups of human beings and their descendants were legally defined as property. European slavery was judicial: individuals were sentenced to limited terms of involuntary servitude as punishment for specific crimes. Having returned to England in March 1770, Equiano did not ship out again until April 1771, when Capt. William Robertson hired him as steward on the *Grenada Planter*, bound for Madeira, Barbados, and Grenada. Equiano wanted "once more to try my fortune in the West-Indies." West Indian whites were as "honest" in their dealings with him as they had ever been (170). When one threatened him and a fellow black for trying to get him to pay them, they sought with the usual success to get a justice of the peace to make him pay. Only when they were able to team up with three white sailors to whom he also owed money were they together able to frighten him enough with threats of violence to be able to collect some of what they were due. "Being still of a roving disposition, and desirous of seeing as many parts of the world as I could," Equiano returned to the West Indies early in 1772 as steward on Capt. David Watt's ship, the *Jamaica*, bound for Nevis and Jamaica.

The great differences among the various colonies in the percentages of the enslaved population that had recently been brought from Africa led to vast ethnic, cultural, economic, and political differences among them as well. Because many slaves, and most in the West Indies, knew from their own African experiences that being black was not equivalent to being enslaved, non-Creole black Africans often led the fairly frequent West Indian slave revolts. Freedom for them was a memory of the recent past rather than at best a dream of the distant future. In general, the higher the percentage of the population that was enslaved, the more dependent the slave owners were on external European military and naval forces to enforce the status quo, and consequently the more loyal the white planters tended to be to the metropolitan European powers. African customs, religious beliefs, languages, and other types of cultural survival tended to be strong during the eighteenth century in areas with high percentages of slaves such as the West Indies and South Carolina, especially areas with concentrations of particular ethnic groups and continuous imports of people from Africa.

Jamaica was Britain's most valuable colony, with an annual revenue of £1.6 million from sugar.[5] In the 1770s the average Jamaican plantation had 204 slaves on more than 1,000 acres. With a total slave population of around 300,000, some 150,000 of them African born, Jamaica was also Britain's largest market for enslaved Africans. Approximately 30 percent of all the people of African descent in the British Empire were living in Jamaica when Equiano was there. Because of the brutal working conditions, malnutrition, and disease, the death rate exceeded the birth rate, and female fertility was very low throughout the eighteenth century. As a result, Jamaican planters had to import slaves just to maintain the population. During the century 575,000 enslaved Africans were needed to raise the population to about 250,000 by the end of the period, and after 1750 the Bight of Biafra was the principal source of Africans.[6] The continuous importation of so many enslaved Africans enabled native African customs to survive: "When I came to Kingston, I was surprised to see the number of Africans, who were assembled together on Sundays; particularly at a large commodious place called Spring Path. Here each different nation of Africa meet and dance, after the manner of their own country. They still retain most of their native customs: they bury their dead, and put victuals, pipes, and tobacco, and other things in the grave with the corpse, in the same manner as in Africa" (172).

Jamaica was also the colony where the horrors of slavery perpetrated by white slave owners and their black drivers, or overseers, were "perfected":

> There are negroes whose business it is to flog slaves; they go about to different people for employment, and the usual pay is from one to four bits. I saw many cruel punishments inflicted on the slaves in the short time I staid here. In particular I was present when a poor fellow was tied up and kept hanging by the wrists at some distance from the ground, and then some half hundred weights were fixed to his ancles, in which posture he was flogged most unmercifully. There were also, as I heard, two different masters noted for cruelty on the island, who had staked up two negroes naked, and in two hours the vermin stung them to death. I heard a gentleman, I well knew, tell my captain, that he passed sentence on a negro man to be burnt alive for attempting to poison an overseer. (171–72)

His grand tours of the Mediterranean and the West Indies over, Equiano returned to London in August 1772. "Tired of the sea," he approached his "old and good master, Dr. Irving," who quickly rehired him. Living with Irving, he was "daily employed in reducing old Neptune's dominions by purifying the briny element, and making it fresh" (172). His "roving disposition" soon reasserted itself.

"Roused by the sound of fame to seek new adventures, and to find, towards the North Pole . . . a passage to India," Equiano embarked with Irving in May 1773 on his greatest adventure yet, participation in the expedition led by Constantine John Phipps (172). The possibility of finding a way from the Atlantic Ocean to the Pacific to reach the East Indies by sailing north and west rather than south and east had intrigued Europeans since the beginning of the sixteenth century. Such a route would cut months off the nearly two-year-long voyage from Europe to Asia via the Cape of Good Hope at the southern tip of Africa. Besides the commercial motive for seeking an Arctic passage to Asia, individuals were inspired by a desire for glory, scientific organizations by a quest for knowledge, and governments by the hope of gaining military dominance or national prestige. Numerous attempts had been made before 1773 to find either a northwest passage through or around Canada, a northeast passage along the northern coast of Russia, or a passage through the ice across the North Pole, located at latitude 90° north. At least three whalers had sailed beyond 80° north: Thomas Robinson in the *St. George* (81°16'), John Clarke in the *Sea Horse* (81°30'), and Captain Bateson in the *Whale* (82°15').[7] For a sense of how far north they had reached, keep in mind that New York City is located just above 40° north, London just over 50°, and the Shetland Islands at 60°. The northern coast of Iceland borders the Arctic Circle at 66°32', northernmost Norway is just above 70°, and Svalbard (also known in the eighteenth century as New Greenland), a group of mountainous islands, the largest of which is Spitsbergen, lies about 370 miles north of Norway, on the edge of latitude 80° north.

Publication of Samuel Engel's *Mémoires et Observations Géographiques et Critiques sur la Situation des Pays Septentrionaux de l'Asie et l'Amérique* in 1765 greatly increased interest in the possibility of discovering a polar passage.[8] A Swiss geographer whose theory was uncontaminated by Arctic experience, Engel claimed that polar and northeast passages existed because the Arctic Sea was ice free once mariners sailed far enough from coastal waters, where the ice was the result of freshwater from rivers. Constant sunlight, the churning of the sea, and the fact that saltwater could not freeze meant that the Arctic was an open sea, or so the theory went. One of Engel's foreign correspondents was Daines Barrington, an antiquarian, lawyer, and naturalist and a member of the Council of the Royal Society in London. Barrington needed little convincing. He quickly began indiscriminately collecting every rumor and report of a polar passage he could find to support Engel's theory and discussed the idea of a government-sponsored scientific exploration with his friend, John Montagu, fourth Earl of Sandwich and First Lord of the Admiralty. Barrington subsequently raised the issue at a council meeting in January 1773, telling his fellow members that he had already discussed it with Lord Sandwich. Given Barrington's report, the secretary of the Royal Society optimistically wrote to Lord Sandwich proposing that an expedition be mounted to find a polar passage to the East Indies. His optimism was justified.[9]

In early February 1773 Lord Sandwich presented a proposal to King George III "for an expedition to try how far navigation was practicable towards the North Pole." The king warmly endorsed the project.[10] We are fortunate to have three accounts of the expedition, two of which were published in 1774, that we can compare to Equiano's. Constantine John Phipps's *A Voyage towards the North Pole* is the official, illustrated story of the voyage, complete with numerous appendixes covering scientific experiments and measurements. Equiano obviously read Phipps's book, probably to refresh his memory when he was writing his autobiography a quarter century after the event. He borrows some passages directly from Phipps. *The Journal of a*

Voyage Undertaken by Order of His Present Majesty was published anonymously
by someone on the *Carcass*. Internal evidence – references to himself as "our
journalist" and to the crew working while he was taking notes as well as detailed descriptions of victuals – suggests that the author was one of the ship's
"idlers," perhaps the purser or steward. As one of the nonseaman specialists,
which included the purser, steward, carpenter, and surgeon, an idler did
not have to stand watches. The third account is the incomplete journal of
Thomas Floyd, one of Equiano's crewmates on the *Racehorse*. Floyd was
about nineteen years old during the expedition. His manuscript remained
unpublished until 1879.[11] Floyd's journal and Equiano's few published pages
on the expedition represent the below-the-deck views of able seamen.

Phipps, later Lord Mulgrave, volunteered to command the expedition as
soon as he learned of the project. Only a year or so older than Equiano,
Phipps had been in the Royal Navy since 1760. During the Seven Years' War
he had fought the French in the West Indies. In 1763 he was promoted to
commander and in 1765 to post captain. In 1768 he entered Parliament as the
member for Lincoln. He was also a member of the Council of the Royal Society and a boyhood friend of Sir Joseph Banks. Banks, the preeminent naturalist of the age, had been a friend and the scientific advisor of the king since
1772. Phipps's naval, personal, and political connections made him an ideal
choice to be commodore of the fleet of two vessels, the *Racehorse*, under his
command, and the *Carcass*, under Capt. Skeffington Lutwidge. The ships
were bombs or bomb ketches, relatively small ships used as platforms for the
naval bombardment of targets on land. Bomb ketches carried heavy mortars
on deck that could fire at more elevated targets than could the guns belowdecks on ships of the line. Because the mortars were very heavy and the re-
coil from firing them had to be absorbed by the deck, bomb ketches were
structurally strongly reinforced vessels. The *Racehorse* had a burthen of 350
tons and carried eight six-pounders and fourteen swivel guns, more for communication with the *Carcass* than for defense during peacetime. The *Carcass*
had a burthen of 300 tons and an equivalent number of guns.

The First Lord of the Admiralty did what he could, given eighteenth-
century naval technology, to convert the *Racehorse* and the *Carcass* into
icebreakers for the Phipps expedition:

> The vessels that were made choice of were the properest that could be
> devised. Bomb ketches are in the first instance stoutly built, and not being
> over large, are best adapted for navigating seas that are known to abound

with shoals and covered rocks: these vessels, besides their natural strength, were sheathed with plank of seasoned oak three inches thick, to fortify them against the shocks and pressure of the ice, that, in their progress, they must infallibly encounter. They were, besides, furnished with a double set of ice poles, anchors, cables, sails and rigging, to provide against the terrible effects of the severe and tempestuous weather, that frequently happens in high latitudes, even in the middle of the most temperate seasons.[12]

The First Lord of the Admiralty also tried to make sure that the crew's provisions were adequate for the unprecedented expedition:

His first care was, to issue orders for killing and curing a sufficient quantity of beef and pork in the best manner possible, that their provisions might be good and fresh; and his next, to cause one hundred butts of porter to be brewed with the best malt and hops, that they might have proper drink to fortify them against the rigour of the climate they were about to pass. Their pease, oatmeal, rice and molossus, were all provided with equal care, and when all things were in readiness, the beer was stowed in the holds, and the vacancies filled up with coals, which served as ballast, that firing might not be wanting to warm and dry them when cold, or wet with labour, or with watching. Add to this, that a double quantity of spirits were put on board, with a large proportion of wine, vinegar, mustard, &c. &c. and what, we believe, was never thought of in the fitting out of any King's ships, a considerable quantity of tea and sugar for the sick . . . and should [tea] fail to answer the purposes of nourishment, a quantity of portable soup was likewise provided. And to compleat the whole, a stock of warm cloathing was laid in, consisting of six fearnought jackets for each man, two milled caps, two pair of fearnought trowsers, four pair of milled stockings, and an excellent pair of boots, with a dozen pair of milled mitts, two cotton shirts, and two handkerchiefs.[13]

Phipps received his commission on 19 April 1773, and the vessels were fitted and manned at the Nore, just off the mouth of the Thames, by 21 May. Sometime in April Banks wrote a letter to Phipps detailing the observations and collections he wished him to make, even though "a voyage so short as the intended one is not likely to furnish many objects of Natural history." One of the specimens he hoped Phipps would bring back was a live polar bear cub. For information on Arctic wildlife Banks counted on Irving, who "is so well acquainted with the desiderata of Zoology." Banks relied on Israel Lyons, who is identified on the muster list of the *Racehorse* as a supernumerary astronomer, for botanical observations.[14] The Royal Society's great expectations of the expedition were matched by the Admiralty's: Lord Sandwich inspected the ships before they set sail on 4 June. Phipps's orders were clear: "to make the best of my way to the Northward, and proceed up to the North Pole, or as far towards it as possible, and as nearly upon a meridian as the ice or other obstructions might admit; and, during the course of the voyage, to make such observations of every kind as might be useful to navigation, or tend to the promotion of natural knowledge: in case of arriving at the Pole, and even finding free navigation on the opposite meridian, not to proceed any farther; and at all events to secure my return to the Nore before the winter should set in."[15]

Each ship was originally to have a complement of ninety men, of whom fifty were seamen, but at Lutwidge's request that of the *Carcass* was reduced to eighty: with its full complement of men and their provisions the vessel was deemed "too deep in the water to proceed to sea with safety."[16] In addition to their complements, to compensate for the naval officers' inexperience in Arctic waters each ship carried two Greenland pilots, so-called because, though based in England, they hunted the Greenland right whale during its April–July feeding season. Because of the hazardous duty they all faced, the Admiralty permitted Phipps and Lutwidge to choose a higher than usual number of officers, and the crews were to consist only of "effective men" and exclude "the usual number of boys."[17] An exception was made, however, for fourteen-year-old midshipman Horatio Nelson, the future naval hero whose desire for fame and adventure was as great as Equiano's. Nelson later recounted that "though no boys were allowed to go in the ships (as of no use), yet nothing could prevent my using every interest to go with Captain Lutwidge in the Carcass; and, as I fancied I was to fill a man's place, I begged I might be his coxswain: which, finding my ardent desire to go with him, Captain Lutwidge complied with."[18] Nelson used family connections to help convince Lutwidge that his prior experience as a pilot in coastal waters qualified him to be the coxswain in charge of one of the *Carcass*'s boats. Nelson was the youngest person on the expedition by several years, so young, in fact, that his age was increased by two years on the muster list, probably to avoid having his inclusion questioned.[19] Besides Nelson, the ships' complements included officers, the necessary idlers, and able seamen. With experienced seamen more available during peacetime than during war, when the Admiralty had to compete very actively with merchant ships for them, the navy could muster all-volunteer complements of the best men available. The offer of a signing bonus of "bounty-money of three pounds per man," paid before the voyage began, virtually guaranteed that the best possible crews would be assembled.[20]

The crew members came from around the world. Since 1764 the Admiralty had expected muster lists to record the age and "Place and Country where born" of everyone in the ship's complement as well as the information required before 1764. Compliance with the new expectation was somewhat erratic for the first few decades. Muster lists did not record race, complexion, or social status. The ninety men on the *Racehorse* included six from Sweden, three of whom were from Göteborg, three from Philadelphia, and one each from Amsterdam, Leghorn, Naples, South Carolina, and Virginia in addition to those born in England, Ireland, and Scotland. The two oldest men in the crew were thirty-seven. Besides men from Europe and British America, the complement included at least two able seamen born in Africa: twenty-two-year-old Jonathan Syfax, born in Madagascar, and thirty-year-old Richard Yorke, born in Guinea. The crew of the *Carcass* included the twenty-three-year-old able seaman Joseph Brown, born in Madagascar. Neither Syfax, Yorke, nor Brown saw any reason to conceal an African birth.

During the first two musters no "Place and Country where born" is given for Equiano, who entered the *Racehorse* on 17 May as an able seaman, the same rating Pascal had given him. He was entered on the first muster list as "Gustavus Weston" and on the second as "Gustavus Feston." As unlikely as those names may seem, they are no greater misunderstandings of "Gustavus Vassa" than the "Gusta Worcester" he was listed as on the *Savage* back in 1757. Even more familiar names were apt to be misspelled. Nelson's first name was recorded as "Horation" on one muster entry for the *Carcass*. The absence of a place of birth for Equiano in the early muster lists is not very remarkable. He was one of twenty-four men not so identified on the first list and one of twenty-nine on the second. The purser, Jonathan Strong, either did not have or did not take time to gather the information from all the men. Even on the last muster five men were still lacking entries under "Place and Country where born." In some cases places were included for men in early lists but omitted in one or more of the later lists. For example, Richard Yorke was listed in the third muster as having been born in Guinea but was included in the next two musters without a place of birth. Had Equiano wanted to, he apparently could have remained silent about where he was born, or, as the examples of Brown, Syfax, and Yorke demonstrate, he could have named someplace in Africa. In fact, since there was no way of verifying his claim, he could have given anywhere he had ever been as his birthplace. From the third muster, 31 May, on Equiano is listed as "Gust[avu]s Weston," an able seaman, age twenty-eight. "So. Carolina" is listed as his "Place and Country where born," a birthplace consistent with his baptismal record fourteen years earlier.

None of the accounts of the expedition, including Equiano's, mentions anything about discrimination on the basis of complexion or place of origin. In fact, none says anything at all about the ethnic or national composition of the crew, besides Floyd's reference to the death of "one Swin Christian, a Dane, though one of our seamen."[21] Racial prejudice was apparently not one of the hardships Equiano and his crewmates suffered. Nor did the Admiralty discriminate against Equiano in his pay. The paybook for the *Racehorse*, which tells us for the first time what salary Equiano received from the navy, enables us to compare his pay with that of other able seamen of similar age.[22] At the end of the voyage Equiano was paid £6 7d., Jonathan Syfax received £6, and Richard Yorke received £4 7s. 10p. Edward Stubbons, a twenty-nine-year-old able seaman born in London, received £5, and David Lowall, a twenty-seven-year-old able seaman born in Derry, Ireland, was paid £5 4s. 4p. Equiano's relatively high pay for an able seaman can no doubt be attributed to his greater maritime experience and superior skills. In addition to his naval pay, Equiano no doubt also received a salary from Irving for his personal services such as hairdressing. Equiano's statement that he "attended [Irving] on board the Race Horse, the 24th day of May 1773" (172) may be a bit misleading. Irving entered as the vessel's surgeon, and his surgeon's mate was Alexander Mair. Mair assisted Irving in his official naval duties as surgeon to the officers and crew. Equiano assisted Irving as a member of the crew, and he "attended" him as his personal servant.

Equiano probably helped Irving collect zoological specimens as well as record water temperatures and specific gravity during the voyage. Equiano certainly aided him in desalinating seawater for the crew members: "On the 20th of June we began to use Dr. Irving's apparatus for making salt water fresh; I used to attend the distillery; I frequently purified from twenty-six to forty gallons a day. The water thus distilled was perfectly pure, well tasted, and free from salt; and was used on various occasions on board the ship," mainly for boiling provisions (173–74).[23] Although the Royal Navy had been

Racehorse muster list, 17 May 1773. Equiano's name appears as the third entry, "Gustavus Weston," with his birthplace listed as "South Carolina."
(Public Records Office, Kew, England.)

using Irving's process since 1770, it was still considered experimental in 1773. Part of Equiano's attendance on the distillery no doubt involved continuously mopping Irving's condensation tube with cold water to keep it cool enough to promote condensation. Not all of Irving's experiments were successful: "The gentleman had formed a project for preserving flesh meat fresh and sweet in long voyages, but it did not answer in this."[24]

The *Racehorse* and the *Carcass* sailed through the North Sea, up the east coast of England and Scotland, reaching the Shetland Islands by 11 June. They bought fresh fish and other provisions whenever they could before they entered the Norwegian Sea. The *Racehorse* was a floating laboratory for testing various inventions and instruments and for taking official astronomical and marine measurements. For example, Phipps used the thermometer invented by Lord Charles Cavendish to take water temperatures at various depths, a megameter to calculate longitude from the position of the stars, and several other competing methods to find longitude, including John Harrison's chronometer. In June 1773, during the Phipps expedition, Parliament recognized Harrison's achievement in having produced a timepiece accurate enough to enable mariners to calculate longitude at sea, day or night and in any kind of weather. He was awarded £8,750. Ironically, Phipps decided that, based on his tests, preference should be given to the watch designed by one of Harrison's competitors, John Arnold.[25] Arnold's contribution to solving the problem of calculating longitude was finally recognized and rewarded by the Board of Longitude in 1805, six years after his death. His son received a three-thousand-pound award. Irving no doubt followed the experiments with great interest. His invention of the marine chair was an earlier attempt at solving the longitude problem, at least in clear weather.

The *Racehorse* and the *Carcass* passed latitude 60° north on 15 June, having had generally fair weather all the way. For much of the next two weeks, however, heavy fogs forced the ships to separate repeatedly and to lose sight of each other. They had to use their guns to maintain contact and to avoid crashing into each other. Once the skies cleared, Phipps thought that "the mildness of the weather, the smooth water, bright sunshine, and constant day-light" gave "a chearfulness and novelty to the whole of this striking and romantick scene."[26] On 30 June the ships were just off the southern coast of Spitsbergen, at latitude 78° north, where Equiano "was surprised to see the sun did not set" (174).[27] That day they received their first warnings of the dangers ahead. A passing captain of a Greenland whaler told Phipps that three ships, two English and one Dutch, had already been lost that year. Several days later another whaler told him that "the ice was within ten leagues of Hacluyt's Head, to the North West."[28] Phipps headed straight for it, encountering it on 5 July like a gathering storm coming suddenly over the horizon:

At noon I steered North, seeing nothing of the land; soon after I was told that they saw the ice: I went upon deck, and perceived something white upon the bow, and heard a noise like the surf upon the shore; I hauled down the scudding sails, and hailed the Carcass to let them know that I should stand for it to make what it was, having all hands upon deck ready to haul up at a moment's warning: I desired that they would keep close to us, the fog being so thick, and have every body up ready to follow our motions instantaneously, determining to stand on under such sail as should enable us to keep the ships under command, and not risk parting company. Soon after two small pieces of ice not above three feet square passed us, which we supposed to have floated from the shore. It was not long before we saw something on the bow, part black and part covered with snow, which from the appearance we took to be islands, and thought that we had not stood far enough out; I hauled up immediately to the N N W and was soon undeceived, finding it to be ice which we could not clear upon that tack; we tacked immediately, but the wind and sea both setting directly upon it, we neared it very fast, and were within little more than a cable's length of the ice, whilst in stays. The wind blowing fresh, the ships would have been in danger on the lee ice, had not the officers and men been very alert in working the ship. The ice, as far as we could then see, lay nearly E b[y] N and W b[y] S. At half past seven in the evening, the ship running entirely to the Southward, and the weather clearing a little, I tacked, and stood for the ice. When I saw it, I bore down to make it plain; at ten the ice lay from N W to east, and no opening. Very foggy, and little wind, all day; but not cold. At eleven came on a thick fog. At half past midnight, heard the surge of the ice, and hauled to the East-ward.[29]

The weather soon turned so cold that "the people had an additional quantity of porter and brandy delivered to them; two quarts of porter and a pint of brandy now every man's daily allowance," and "several of the men were confined with colds, which affected them with pains in their bones."[30] Despite the oncoming ice the ships managed to reach a bit farther north, to 80°37', before recognizing that "one compact impenetrable body of ice" blocked their progress.[31] Trying to find their way around it, the men had time to observe and hunt whales and other marine mammals, especially "sea horses," or Arctic walruses.

The indiscriminate killing of wildlife was one of the few diversions the crew members had. "We killed many different animals at this time, and, among the rest, nine bears," Equiano recalls (174). The most famous bear encountered on the expedition, however, was the one that got away from Horatio Nelson. Lutwidge's nineteenth-century account of the incident and the illustrations it inspired quickly became part of the Nelson legend. Very late one night Nelson convinced a companion to sneak off the *Carcass* with him to find a polar bear on the ice so that he "might carry his skin to [Nelson's] father." When Lutwidge discovered the men's absence, he sent a signal up to order them to return. Nelson's companion was unable to convince him to return, in part because Nelson was face-to-face with a bear, separated from him only by a chasm in the ice. When Nelson's "rusty musket" misfired, he decided to try to subdue the beast with the butt of his gun. Seeing the danger Nelson was in, Lutwidge had a gun fired to frighten the bear off. Disappointed in his quest, Nelson was "reprimanded . . . rather sternly for such rashness, and for conduct so unworthy of the situation he occupied."[32]

Nelson was not the only member of the expedition whose desire to kill almost cost him his own life. After having accompanied Irving in his investigation of the flora and fauna on an island, Equiano writes, "Some of our people once, in a boat, fired at and wounded a sea-horse, which dived immediately; and in a little time after brought up with it a number of others. They all joined in an attack upon the boat, and were with difficulty prevented from staving or oversetting her; but a boat from the Carcass having come to assist ours, & joined it, they dispersed, after having wrested an oar from one of the men. One of the ship's boats had before been attacked in the same manner, but happily no harm was done" (174–75). Nelson's nineteenth-century biographers claim that the future hero of Trafalgar led the rescuers in the "boat from the Carcass."[33]

For part of the voyage Equiano had the leisure to appreciate the beauty of the Arctic: "On the 29th and 30th of July we saw one continued plain of smooth unbroken ice, bounded only by the horizon, and we fastened to a piece of ice that was eight yards eleven inches thick. We had generally sunshine, and constant day-light; which gave cheerfulness and novelty to the whole of this striking, grand, and uncommon scene;[34] and, to heighten it still more, the reflection of the sun from the ice gave the clouds a most beautiful appearance" (174). At the beginning of August the Arctic beauty turned deadly when, Equiano recalls,

the two ships got completely fastened in the ice, occasioned by the loose ice that set in from the sea. This made our situation very dreadful and alarming; so that on the 7th day we were in very great apprehension of having the ships squeezed to pieces. The officers now held a council to know what was best for us to do in order to save our lives; and it was determined that we should endeavour to escape by dragging our boats along the ice towards the sea; which, however, was farther off than any of us thought. This determination filled us with extreme dejection, and confounded us with despair; for we had very little prospect of escaping with life. However, we sawed some of the ice about the ships, to keep it from hurting them; and thus kept them in a kind of pond. We then began to drag the boats as well as we could towards the sea; but, after two or three days labour, we made very little progress; so that some of our hearts totally failed us, and I really began to give up myself for lost, when I saw our surrounding calamities. (175)

Phipps had made the mistake of grappling the ships to the ice bordering the land so that he could explore an island, but the loose ice in the sea approached so rapidly that what had been an open waterway became embayed before they could move the ships. At first Phipps tried to cut the ships free, but, finding the ice to be as much as twelve feet thick, the men quickly tired. And it was dangerous work, as Equiano discovered: "I once fell into a pond we had made amongst some loose ice, and was very near being drowned; but providentially some people were near, who gave me immediate assistance, and thereby I escaped drowning" (175). Remaining with the ships was not truly an option because, even if the ice did not crush them, the crew was not prepared to overwinter in the Arctic. Floyd did what he could to try to get ready for what lay ahead: "I therefore went down and put on me, two shirts, two waistcoats, two pairs of breeches, four pairs of stockings, a large pair of boots, a good hat, and stuck a pistol which I had into a canvas belt, which latter at the same time served to keep from falling the few sheets of my journal I had written on the progress of our voyage. The belt was to fasten to a rope to assist in dragging a boat."[35] Nelson saw the predicament as an opportunity: "When the boats were fitting out to quit the two ships blocked up in the ice, I exerted myself to have the command of a four-oared cutter . . . which was given me, with twelve men; and I prided myself in fancying I could navigate her better than any other boat in the ship."[36] Commodore Phipps led part of the crew trying to haul the boats across miles of ice to the open sea, leaving Captain Lutwidge in charge of the ships with the remainder of the men in case an opening in the sea appeared. From the "journalist's" perspective the crew members competed for the honor of hauling the boats. From Phipps's perspective they made good progress in dragging them across the ice, but to Equiano the challenge was simply "hard labour" (175).

Just when their situation seemed most dire, the ice separated enough that they could get the ships to the open sea:

I had no hopes of my life being prolonged for any time; for we saw that our existence could not be long on the ice after leaving the ships, which

View of the Racehorse *and* Carcass, *7 August 1773*. This drawing from Constantine John Phipps's official account of his expedition, *A Voyage towards the North Pole: Undertaken by His Majesty's Command, 1773*, depicts crew members trying to free the two ships from the Arctic ice.
(By permission of the Houghton Library, Harvard University)

were now out of sight, and some miles from the boats. Our appearance now became truly lamentable; pale dejection seized every countenance; many, who had been before blasphemers, in this our distress began to call on the good God of heaven for his help; and in the time of our utter need he heard us, and against hope, or human probability, delivered us! It was the eleventh day of the ships being thus fastened, and the fourth of our drawing the boats in this manner, that the wind changed to the E. N. E. The weather immediately became mild and the ice broke towards the sea, which was to the S. W. of us. Many of us on this got on board again, and with all our might we hove the ships into every open water we could find, and made all the sail on them in our power: now, having a prospect of success, we made signals for the boats and the remainder of the people. This seemed to us like a reprieve from death; and happy was the man who could first get on board of any ship, or the first boat he could meet. We then proceeded in this manner till we got into the open water again, which we accomplished in about thirty hours, to our infinite joy and gladness of heart. (175–76)[37]

To Equiano, the reality behind the Arctic's "beautiful appearance" almost erased his memory of the formerly "striking, grand, and uncommon scene": "On the 19th of August we sailed from this uninhabited extremity of the world, where the inhospitable climate affords neither food nor shelter, and not a tree or shrub of any kind grows amongst its barren rocks, but all is one desolate and expanded waste of ice, which even the constant beams of the sun, for six months in the year, cannot penetrate or dissolve" (176).

Escape from the ice did not mean release from exhausting work. "On the 4th of September," Phipps writes, "the water being perfectly smooth with a dead calm," making soundings he "struck ground in six hundred and eighty-three fathoms," where "the bottom was a fine soft blue clay."[38] Phipps notes only the result of his experiment; the "journalist" notes as well the labor that experiment required: "September 5, when, being clear and calm weather, the Commodore sounded, and found ground with seven hundred fathoms, very soft mud. The people were employed eight hours in heaving up the lead with the capstan."[39] Equiano shared the arduous work of helping to raise the cable by winding it around the capstan, a vertical cylinder that was turned on a spindle by crewmen pushing against capstan bars inserted in holes in the cylinder.

Nor did escaping from the ice mean the end of danger. Phipps reports: "From the 7th of September, when we were off Shetland, till the 24th, when we made Orfordness, we had very hard gales of wind with little intermission. . . . In one of these gales, the hardest, I think, I ever was in, and with the greatest sea, we lost three of our boats, and were obliged to heave two of our guns overboard, and bear away for some time, though near a lee shore, to clear the ship of water."[40] For a crewman like Equiano, the labor was as memorable as the storm:

September the 10th, in latitude 58–59, we met a very severe gale of wind and high seas, and shipped a great deal of water in the space of ten hours.

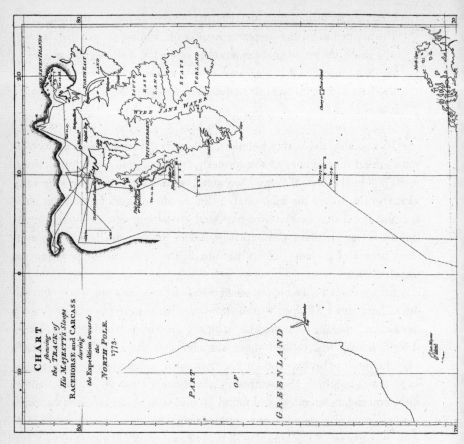

Phipps's expedition to the Arctic (From Phipps, *A Voyage towards the North Pole*;
by permission of the Houghton Library, Harvard University)

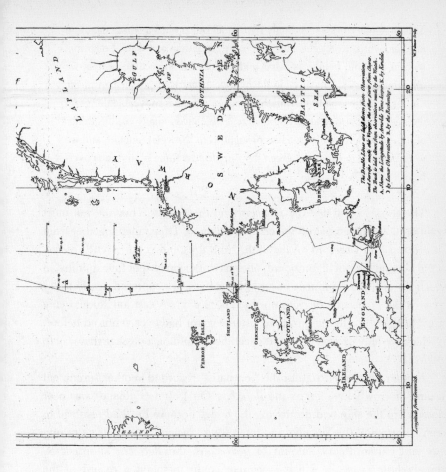

LAPLAND

GULF OF BOTHNIA

SWEDEN

NORWAY

DENMARK

BALTIC SEA

ENGLAND

London

SCOTLAND

IRELAND

ORKNEY I.

SHETLAND

FERROE ISLES

ICELAND

The Double Lines are laid down from Observations and surveys made this Voyage, the other parts from Charts. The Track is laid down from observations made by the Watch. A, where the Longitude by Arnolds Time keeper K. by Kendals ☽ by Lunar Observations R, by the Reckoning.

Longitude from Greenwich

This made us work exceedingly hard at all our pumps a whole day; and one sea, which struck the ship with more force than any thing I ever met with of the kind before, laid her under water for some time, so that we thought she would have gone down. Two boats were washed from the booms, and the long-boat from the chucks;[41] all other moveable things on the deck were also washed away, among which were many curious things of different kinds, which we had brought from [New] Greenland; and we were obliged, in order to lighten the ship, to toss some of our guns over-board. (176–77)

The storms separated the *Racehorse* and the *Carcass.* They did not meet again until 26 September off the coast of England. They sailed together from Orfordness into Deptford on the 30th: "And thus ended our Arctic voyage, to the no small joy of all on board, after having been absent four months; in which time, at the imminent hazard of our lives, we explored nearly as far towards the Pole as 81 degrees north, and 20 degrees east longitude; being much farther, by all accounts, than any navigator had ever ventured before; in which we fully proved the impracticability of finding a passage that way to India" (177).

Neither Phipps, Floyd, nor the "journalist" recorded another "imminent hazard" narrowly avoided by the *Racehorse.* On 15 June Equiano "was near blowing up the ship and destroying the crew" because he "had resolved to keep a journal of this singular and interesting voyage."[42] With its extra officers and extraordinary amount of provisions, the *Racehorse* afforded extremely little space in which a seaman could maintain a record of the expedition in private. Equiano tried to make do by using his sleeping quarters, Irving's storeroom, which "was stuffed with all manner of combustibles, particularly with tow and aquafortis, and many other dangerous things." The hemp strands and corrosive solvent were probably used to remove the salt residue from Irving's distillery. Being belowdecks, the storeroom was perpetually dark. Whether or not "combustibles" were nearby, fire was always a danger on a wooden vessel. The navy's official *Regulations and Instructions Relating to His Majesty's Service at Sea* included many regulations regarding the threat fire posed.[43]

Having served under Pascal, Equiano should have known better than most seamen that one of a naval lieutenant's duties was to make sure that no fires or candles burned between decks and that no one smoked tobacco there either. Equiano, moreover, should have been aware of the danger because of his own recent observations and experience. Returning to England in 1770 on the *Delaware*, he had "met with an accident which was near burning the ship. A black cook, in melting some fat, overset the pan into the fire under the deck, which immediately began to blaze, and the flame went up very high under the foretop. With the fright, the poor cook became almost white, and altogether speechless. Happily, however, we got the fire out without doing much mischief" (170). The following year Equiano himself almost caused disaster on the *Grenada Planter*: "I cannot help remarking here a very narrow escape we had from being blown up, owing to a piece of negligence of mine. Just as our ship was under sail, I went down under the cabin to do some business, and had a lighted candle in my hand, which, in my hurry, without thinking, I held in a barrel of gunpowder. It remained in the powder until it was near catching fire, when fortunately I observed it, and snatched it out in time and providentially no harm happened; but I was so overcome with terror, that I immediately fainted at the deliverance" (171).

Ignoring his own observations, experience, and common sense, Equiano lit a candle onboard the *Racehorse* anyway:

> It happened in the evening, as I was writing my journal, that I had occasion to take the candle out of the lanthorn, and a spark unfortunately having touched a single thread of the tow, all the rest caught the flame, and immediately the whole was in a blaze. I saw nothing but present death before me, and expected to be the first to perish in the flames. In a moment the alarm was spread, and many people who were near ran to assist in putting out the fire. All this time I was in the very midst of the flames; my shirt, and the handkerchief on my neck, were burnt, and I was almost smothered with the smoke. However, through God's mercy, as I was nearly giving up all hopes, some people brought blankets and mattresses, and threw them on the flames, by which means, in a short time, the fire was put out. (173)

"Severely reprimanded and menaced by such of the officers who knew, and strictly charged never more to go there with a light," Equiano was too afraid to risk continuing his journal "for a little time; but at last, not being able to write my journal in any other part of the ship, I was tempted again to venture by stealth with a light in the same cabin, though not without considerable fear and dread on my mind" (173). We do not know how often he gave in to that temptation, but Equiano's journal has not been found. His borrowing verbatim three passages from Phipps's published account suggests that he never finished his own journal.

Assessing the results of the 1773 expedition from the vantage point of 1789, Equiano concluded that "our Creator never intended we should" find an ocean passage to the North Pole (172). The anonymous "journalist" shared Equiano's pessimism about the possibility of finding a northeast passage to India: "Thus ended a voyage, which seems to have determined the question so much agitated concerning the navigation to the north pole, and proved . . . that no passage would ever be found practicable in that direction. . . . [T]hose seas are navigable as far as between the eighty-first and eighty-second degrees of latitude; and it may possibly happen, that in some future years, they may be found navigable a degree or two farther: but it may now with certainty be concluded, that a course under the pole can never be pursued for the purpose of commerce."[44] Phipps, however, remained open to the possibility that a passage might still be found: "There was also most probability, if ever navigation should be practicable to the Pole, of finding the sea open to the Northward after the solstice; the sun having then exerted the full influence of his rays, though there was enough of the summer still remaining for the purpose of exploring the seas to the Northward and Westward of Spitsbergen."[45] The first surface ship to reach the North Pole through the Arctic ice pack was the Soviet nuclear-powered icebreaker *Arktika*, on 16 August 1977.

Chapter Eight

BORN AGAIN

Paid off by the Royal Navy in October 1773, Equiano returned to London with his "master, Doctor Irving, the purifier of waters." He continued to work for Irving through the winter (178), leaving him to become a full-time hairdresser in Coventry Court, Haymarket, in Westminster. But Equiano had returned to London a very different man from the one who had left England the previous May. His desire for fame and "new adventures" had led to a spiritual crisis. Facing seemingly imminent death in the Arctic forced him to recognize that he might be doomed to eternal damnation: "I had the fears of death hourly upon me, and shuddered at the thoughts of meeting the grim king of terrors in the *natural* state I then was in, and was exceedingly doubtful of a happy eternity if I should die in it" (175). He now "began seriously to reflect on the dangers I had escaped, particularly those of my last voyage." Salvation, he hoped, was earned, not given, deserved, not granted. He committed, according to the Church of England, the sin of self-sufficiency by assuming that reliance on his "own strength" alone would bring him spiritual comfort: "I rejoiced greatly;

and heartily thanked the Lord for directing me to London, where I was determined to work out my own salvation, and, in so doing, procure a title to heaven. . . . I was continually oppressed and much concerned about the salvation of my soul, and was determined (in my own strength) to be a first-rate Christian." Equiano's attempt to achieve salvation on his own was doomed to failure, according to the orthodox Protestant belief exemplified in the Thirty-nine Articles of 1571 that loosely constitute the creed of the Church of England. The eleventh article states that believers are justified, or saved, only by faith in Jesus Christ, whose merits compensate for the sinfulness of humanity's natural state, inherited from the original sin of Adam and Eve. Divine grace, or favor, was necessary for salvation. Equiano's dissatisfaction with his spiritual condition in 1773 was inevitable. He recognized only in retrospect that his faith in his own self-sufficiency was "the result of a mind blinded by ignorance and sin" (178).

Searching for salvation, Equiano went shopping for religion. He had earlier observed demonstrations of Christian belief but more as a disinterested window shopper than a determined buyer. In Philadelphia in 1766, for example, he attended a meeting held by the Quakers, who had always treated him well in business dealings:

> One Sunday morning, while I was here, as I was going to church, I chanced to pass a meeting house. The doors being open, and the house full of people, it excited my curiosity to go in. When I entered the house, to my great surprise, I saw a very tall woman standing in the midst of them, speaking in an audible voice something which I could not understand. Having never seen any thing of this kind before, I stood and stared about me for some time, wondering at this odd scene. As soon as it was over, I took an opportunity to make enquiry about the place and people, when I was informed they were called Quakers. I particularly asked what that woman I saw in the midst of them had said, but none of them were pleased to satisfy me; so I quitted them. (132)

James Boswell recorded a similar experience in 1763: "Next day, Sunday, July 31, I told [Samuel Johnson] I had been that morning at a meeting of the people called Quakers, where I had heard a woman preach. JOHNSON. 'Sir, a woman's preaching is like a dog's walking on his hinder legs. It is not done well; but you are surprised to find it done at all.'"[1]

Unlike the established Church of England and Roman Catholicism, with their elaborately structured hierarchies and detailed liturgies and rituals, the

Society of Friends believed that the Bible's teachings were supplemented by individual divine inspiration, the inward light available to both men and women that could be shared in public meetings. These particular messages from God were not always comprehensible by others. During the eighteenth century Protestants who refused Communion in the Church of England were called Dissenters, or Nonconformists. Most of them were Baptists, Congregationalists, or Presbyterians rather than Quakers. The Dissenting sects all rejected the mediating role between believers and God assigned to priests in the Anglican Church and the Church of Rome. Dissenters also rejected the doctrinal status both churches accorded the teachings of medieval theologians (the church fathers) as well as the authority the Roman Catholic Church claimed for the pope. Many of the Dissenting sects shared the Quaker belief in private revelations, and they were often far more evangelical than most Quakers or Anglicans. Evangelicals were committed to zealously preaching and disseminating the Christian Gospel, especially the first four Gospels of the New Testament. They saw themselves as imitators of the first evangelists, the apostles Matthew, Mark, Luke, and John, missionaries spreading the message that salvation is by faith alone and emphasizing the authority of the Bible. Any Dissenter who professed a belief in personal communication with God was liable to be accused of being an "enthusiast," defined by Samuel Johnson as "one who vainly imagines a private revelation; one who has a vain confidence of his intercourse with God." Conservative theologians and politicians saw enthusiastic evangelicals as threats to the stability of the Church of England and the monarch, who was legally its head. In their eyes, emphasizing the authority of the Bible and individual conscience could easily lead to challenges to the authority of the Church and the state it supported.

Equiano had, of course, been a nominal Christian since his baptism in February 1759. Fifteen years later he was seeking to be a Christian in fact as well as name. Not knowing that, according to the church, actions – good works – were simply another form of merely nominal faith, he spent several weeks attending services at his local Anglican church, St. James's, Piccadilly, and others, going sometimes two or three times a day. Not surprisingly, he always "came away dissatisfied: something was wanting that I could not obtain, and I really found more heart-felt relief in reading my bible at home than in attending the church" (178). He tried looking beyond the Church of England: "First I went among the people called Quakers, whose meeting at times was held in silence, and I remained as much in the dark as ever. I then searched into the Roman Catholic principles, but was not in the least edified.

I, at length, had recourse to the Jews, which availed me nothing, as the fear of eternity daily harassed my mind and I knew not where to seek shelter from the wrath to come" (178–79). The egalitarian Quakers did not recognize an authority standing between the believer and God. They did not have a class of clergy (minister, preacher, or priest) separate from a congregation. When no member of a meeting was prompted to speak, public worship was conducted silently, a frequent occurrence. At the other extreme was Roman Catholicism, mockingly called Papism by Protestants who charged that the Church of Rome was a corruption of Christianity that promoted worship of the pope rather than of God. Judaism availed Equiano nothing because it offered him neither salvation through belief in Christ nor the more fully developed concept of an afterlife found in the Christian faiths.

Without a human guide to "the way that leadeth to eternal life" Equiano returned to reading "the Four Evangelists." People he asked for spiritual direction could not agree on "the way," leaving him "much staggered" to discover that he was "more righteous" and more "inclined to devotion" than anyone else he knew: "So righteous was I in my own eyes, that I was convinced I excelled many of them in that point, by keeping eight out of ten [Commandments]; and finding those, who in general termed themselves Christians, not so honest or so good in their morals as the Turks."[2] Self-righteousness led him to misanthropy, and he found pleasure only in playing the French horn. Self-righteousness also led him to theological absurdity. Confusing faith with ethics, he "really thought the Turks were in a safer way of salvation than my neighbours." His delusion that good works were sufficient for salvation became so extreme that he temporarily spoke and acted as if faith in Christ was no longer even necessary. He "determined to go to Turkey . . . never more to return to England" (179). Only intercession by some of his British friends prevented him from going.

Frustrated in his plans, Equiano again sought solace in the Bible, telling himself he was resigned to God's will. His actions said otherwise, however, as he began to reject God and contemplate self-annihilation yet again. But now his despair was more profoundly spiritual than he had ever experienced before: "I continued to travel in much heaviness, and frequently murmured against the Almighty, particularly in his providential dealings; and, awful to think! I began to blaspheme, and wished often to be any thing but a human being" (181). A vision of the Last Judgment began to open his eyes and his understanding, at least enough to make him recognize the perilous state his soul was in: "I would then, if it had been possible, have changed my nature with the meanest worm on the earth, and was ready to say to the mountains and rocks, 'fall on me,' Rev[elation]. vi. 16. but all in vain" (182).

Equiano had to reach the depths of despair – "the greatest agony" – before he finally abandoned his reliance on self-sufficiency and "requested the divine Creator, that he would grant me a small space of time to repent of my follies and vile iniquities, which I felt were grievous." He awoke from his dream vision physically exhausted and weak, but he also felt "the first spiritual mercy" he had ever experienced. No longer self-righteous, he begged God to "never again permit me to blaspheme his most holy name" and admitted his unholiness (182). Hating the house he was lodging in because his fellow lodgers continued to blaspheme, he asked the Lord to direct him to a spiritual guide and to help him love Him more.

His prayer was quickly answered. He met "an old sea-faring man, who experienced much of the love of God shed abroad in the heart," living in Holborn with his wife. They were silk weavers. Never before had Equiano heard "the love of Christ to believers set forth in such a manner, and in so clear a point of view." While they were talking in the man's house, a "Dissenting Minister" joined them. He was a Methodist lay preacher. Equiano probably refers to him as a Dissenter because he was not an ordained Anglican minister.

Methodism, so-called because its adherents sought to methodize the principles and practice of Anglicanism by establishing a routine of personal devotion and charitable acts, was the evangelical reform movement within the Church of England. The brothers Charles and John Wesley, together with George Whitefield, founded Methodism in the 1730s. From the beginning, conservative Anglicans looked with suspicion on the "enthusiastic" Methodists, whom they considered potential Dissenting separatists from the Church. John Wesley and Whitefield were frequently attacked and mocked by their fellow Anglicans for their fervent preaching styles and their itinerant ministering to the lower orders of British society. Methodist preachers were often physically assaulted as well as assailed in print. Methodists frequently brought their extemporaneous preaching outdoors to the people rather than insisting that the people come to church to hear a polished sermon read to them. Such ministry was particularly effective in parts of the country not sufficiently served by existing parish organizations. Whitefield had first taken to preaching in the fields when the churchwardens in Islington, then a suburb of London, refused to allow him to use the pulpit in the parish church.

Equiano heard the celebrated Whitefield preach in Savannah, Georgia, on 11 February 1765 during one of Whitefield's seven missionary tours of North America before his death in 1770:

> I came to a church crowded with people; the church-yard was full like-
> wise, and a number of people were even mounted on ladders, looking in
> at the windows. I thought this a strange sight, as I had never seen
> churches, either in England or the West Indies, crowded in this manner
> before. I therefore made bold to ask some people the meaning of all this,
> and they told me the Rev. George Whitfield was preaching. I had often
> heard of this gentleman, and had wished to see and hear him; but I had
> never before had an opportunity. I now therefore resolved to gratify
> myself with the sight, and pressed in amidst the multitude. When I got
> into the church I saw this pious man exhorting the people with the great-
> est fervour and earnestness, and sweating as much as ever I did while in
> slavery on Montserrat beach. I was very much struck and impressed with
> this; I thought it strange I had never seen divines exert themselves in this
> manner before, and was no longer at a loss to account for the thin
> congregations they preached to. (132)[3]

Eighteenth-century Methodism was not a unified movement. When Equiano heard Whitefield, there were approximately twenty-two thousand British Methodists. A minority of them embraced Whitefield's theology. Whitefield preached the doctrine of the sixteenth-century Protestant theolo-gian John Calvin. Calvinism held that very few Christians were among the elect, that is, those predestined, or elected, by the grace of God to be saved. Grace could only be freely given by God and could not be earned by the good works of professed believers. During the first decades of Methodism Whitefield was more influential than Wesley, primarily because he was con-sidered a more powerful orator. Whitefield also benefited from the organiza-tional skills of his authoritarian patron, Selina Hastings, the Countess of Huntingdon, who established Calvinist Methodist chapels throughout Britain. In 1779 she was compelled to register these chapels, which became known as the Countess of Huntingdon's Connexion, as Dissenting meeting-houses. Increasingly, Huntingdonian Methodists felt obligated to choose be-tween the Connexion and the Anglican Church.

 The Wesley brothers embraced a more liberal, or Arminian, interpreta-tion of the requirements for salvation. Named after Jacobus Arminius (the Latinized form of the Dutch name Jacob Harmensen), one of Calvin's earliest theological opponents, Arminianism held that all who believed and repented of their sins could be saved. Being omniscient, God of course knew who would be saved but had not arbitrarily predetermined and restricted their number. Besides being a gifted speaker, John Wesley was a superb organizer and publicist. Like Whitefield, Wesley published his own sermons, but he also published the works of others, both indirectly through plagiarism and openly in abridged versions of classic religious texts. In 1778 he began the *Arminian Magazine*, renamed the *Methodist Magazine* after his death in 1791. Arminians and Calvinists agreed that personal salvation required recognition that one was a sinner undeserving of redemption. A believer might be granted grace if he or she submitted completely to God. If grace was granted, the believer experienced the joy of the new birth through the assurance, or revelation, of his or her personal salvation.

Like the Quakers, Methodists wielded a moral influence far greater than their actual numbers would suggest. Although the Wesleyan Methodist movement grew throughout the eighteenth century, at the time of John Wesley's death in 1791 Methodists numbered only about sixty thousand. In 1795 Wesleyan Methodists separated from the Church of England. By the time of Equiano's death in 1797 Wesleyan Methodists numbered nearly eighty thousand. Despite rapid growth, Wesleyan Methodists did not constitute as much as 2 percent of the adult English population until the second decade of the nineteenth century.

Although Wesley and Whitefield were concerned with saving souls, not reforming society, eighteenth-century Methodism was perceived as far more subversive than the socially conservative Methodism of the following centuries. The early Methodists were accused of being levelers because they preached against desiring riches of this world and because their sermons were offered to all, regardless of social status or economic class. Opponents of Methodism were especially dismayed by the emotional appeal of Methodist sermons, bothered by how suddenly conversions took place, and concerned about the use of Methodist lay ministers. Methodists were condemned for addressing the poor, who were often ignored by more conservative and less evangelical Anglican ministers.

William Hogarth satirized the Methodist style of preaching and the audiences it attracted in his print *Credulity, Superstition and Fanaticism: A Medley* (1762). The setting of the print appears to be Moorfields Tabernacle in Tottenham Court Road. The preacher is so excited by the inspiration of "St. Money-trap" that his wig falls off to reveal the tonsure of a Jesuit, reminding viewers of the common accusation that Methodists were secret Papists and thus enemies of the established church and state. The clerk below the preacher bears the cross-eyed likeness of Whitefield, identified by the copy of "Whitefield's Journal" in the basket below him and the Whitefield hymn on his lectern. Methodism is represented as a confidence game as fraudulent as the contemporaneous deceits of the woman who claimed to give birth to rabbits and the boy who spewed nails. The images of witches recall Wesley's oft-repeated belief in witchcraft, evidence, his opponents claimed, of the irrationality and superstition that underlay the enthusiasm of Methodism. The thermometer on the viewer's right measures the degree of lunacy in the tabernacle. The chandelier, entitled "A New and Correct Globe of Hell by Romaine," appears to preside over the scene as a malign deity with wide-open eyes and a toothy scowl. Its creator is identified as William Romaine, a very popular fiery Calvinist Anglican clergyman. The members of the congregation below are barely human in appearance. Hogarth represents ironically people of African descent among those attracted to Methodism. A sleeping black man directly below the pulpit appears immune to the fervor of the preacher, but the image of the tiny demon whispering in his ear suggests that passivity is no protection from the dangers of Methodism.

The evangelical Methodists saw all levels of society, including slaves, as potentially sharing in salvation. When physical liberation from enslavement in the present seemed impossible, spiritual freedom and equality in the afterlife offered some solace. And a faith that depended on predestination for salvation rather than on spiritual rewards for good works such as charitable contributions or attendance at church may have been especially attractive to those whose ability to perform good works was severely limited by their social condition. The use of lay ministers by Methodists and other Dissenting sects gave black authors like Equiano, Jupiter Hammon, John Marrant, George Liele, David George, and Boston King the opportunity and authority to exercise agency and influence in person and print.[4]

Whitefield's American preaching tours exposed several members of the first generation of black authors to Methodism. Through Whitefield, James Albert Ukawsaw Gronniosaw, Phillis Wheatley, and Marrant gained access to the Countess of Huntingdon's literary patronage. Blacks were not drawn to Whitefield because of any antislavery beliefs on his part. When Whitefield considered owning slaves in Georgia during the 1740s, he saw the subject not as a moral issue but as an economic necessity. Slaves produced the rice that supported his Orphan House in Bethesda, Georgia. When the countess inherited Whitefield's Georgia holdings in 1770, she, too, became a slave owner.

Credulity, Superstition and Fanaticism: A Medley (1762), by William Hogarth.
Note the sleeping black man in the foreground, below the Methodist preacher.
The presentation of exotic peoples to comment on the foibles of English culture – in this case,
the apparent dangers of Methodism – was a typical tool of eighteenth-century satirists.

Like most evangelicals during the period, neither Whitefield nor the countess saw slavery and Christianity as incompatible. Nowhere in the New Testament is slavery explicitly prohibited.

Unlike Whitefield and the countess, John Wesley opposed the institution of slavery. In *Thoughts upon Slavery* Wesley drew on accounts of Africa by Michel Adanson, Hans Sloane, and others he had read in Benezet's works to derive a very favorable image of Africans: "Our Forefathers! Where shall we find at this day, among the fair-faced natives of *Europe*, a nation generally practising the Justice, Mercy, and Truth, which are found among these poor black *Africans*? Suppose the preceding accounts are true . . . , and we may leave *England* and *France*, to seek genuine Honesty in *Benin*, *Congo*, or *Angola*." Europeans "first taught Africans drunkenness and avarice, and then hired them to sell one another. . . . When did a Turk or Heathen find it necessary to use a fellow-creature thus?" Slavery, Wesley argues, is inconsistent with "even natural justice." The immorality of slavery makes economic arguments for it irrelevant. Wesley proclaims, "It were better that all those [West Indian] Islands should remain uncultivated for ever, yea, it were more desirable that they were all together sunk in the depth of the sea, than that they should be cultivated at so high a price, as the violation of Justice, Mercy and Truth."[5] "Such slavery as [West Indian slavery] is not found among the Turks at *Algiers*, no, nor among the Heathens in *America*." Addressing slave owners directly, Wesley admonishes them: "Compare, (setting prejudice aside) the *Samoeids* and the *Angolans*. And on which side does the advantage lie, in point of understanding? Certainly the *African* is in no respect inferior to the *European*. Their stupidity therefore in our plantations is not natural; otherwise than it is the natural effect of their Condition. Consequently it is not their fault, but *Yours*." Planters have only themselves to blame for the risk of insurrections they face: "What wonder, if they should cut your throat? And if they did, whom could you thank for it but yourself? You first acted the villain in making them slaves, (whether you stole them or bought them). You kept them stupid and wicked, by cutting them off from all opportunities of improving either in Knowledge or Virtue: and now you assign their want of Wisdom and Goodness as the reason for using them worse than brute beasts!"[6]

To those who believed that the afterlife was far more important than temporal existence, what mattered most was that pagan Africans be exposed to the truth of Christianity and be humanely treated in whatever social condition they were placed. Thus, slavery could even be seen as a kind of fortunate fall, whereby the discomfort of the slaves' present life was overcompensated by the chance given them of achieving eternal salvation. Enslavement of their bodies introduced pagans to the means to freedom for their souls. Jacobus Elisa Johannes Capitein, a native African, defends this notion of a fortunate fall in his Latin thesis. Capitein justifies slavery as having biblical precedent in the past and serving evangelical ends in the present and future. One of the most celebrated and learned eighteenth-century blacks, Capitein had been brought from present-day Ghana, where the Dutch had a slave-trading factory at Elmina, to Holland. There he studied theology from 1726 to 1742, when he was ordained. He was returned to Elmina as a missionary. The fortunate fall into slavery is also the subject of Phillis Wheatley's well-known short poem "On Being Brought from Africa to America."

From a spiritual perspective, Equiano's *Interesting Narrative* can also be read as an account of a fortunate fall. When the "Dissenting Minister" learned that Equiano had attended the local Anglican churches, he invited him "to a love feast at his chapel that evening." The conversation and some reading Equiano had just shared with the "old sea-faring man" and the minister left him feeling more spiritually satisfied than he had been for many months. He readily accepted the minister's invitation to a free "banquet" (183). He was a bit surprised that he, a stranger, would be asked to a feast and thought it odd that it would be served in a chapel. When he got there he was understandably "much astonished to see the place filled with people, and no signs of eating and drinking." After hymn singing and prayers led by the many ministers in the gathering, "some of the guests began to speak their experience, agreeable to what I read in the Scriptures: much was said by every speaker of the providence of God, and his unspeakable mercies to each of them. This I knew in a great measure, and could most heartily join them. But when they spoke of a future state, they seemed to be altogether certain of their calling and election of God; and that no one could ever separate them from the love of Christ, or pluck them out of his hands" (183–84). Equiano was filled "with utter consternation, intermingled with admiration" by their expression of the Calvinistic belief that divine grace, or salvation, was freely given to those God chose, not earned by humans through their actions, or good works. God predestined those He called and elected to be saved. Consequently, their faith was sufficient for salvation; their good works might be a sign but not a cause of salvation. Equiano's reaction was emotional, not rational. Amazed at what he saw, he felt his heart "attracted" and his "affections" enlarged. "Entirely overcome," he "wished to live and die thus." He had been invited not to a feast for his stomach – the food and drink consisted only of bread and water – but to his "first soul-feast" (184), which lasted about four hours. They worshiped in "Christian fellowship," he thought, like "the primitive Christians" who lived in the early days of the faith before the establishment of churches and the rise of doctrinal disputes.

Having seen the true happiness of God-fearing people, Equiano could return to his lodgings only with great difficulty. He gave up "card-playing and vain-jesting, &c.," lest he be unprepared should God, like a thief in the night, come for him at "midnight-call." He saw more of the pious old couple in Holborn, who not only gave him edifying conversation but also lent him a copy of Laurence Harlow's *The Conversion of an Indian* (1774), the story of a poor man who, like himself, came from overseas to seek the Christian God.

Through God's direction and the old couple's associations, Equiano was "weaned" from his "former carnal acquaintances" and "soon connected with those whom the Scripture calls the excellent of the earth." At last he "heard the gospel preached, and the thoughts of [his] heart and actions were laid open . . . and the way of salvation by Christ alone was evidently set forth" (185). For nearly two months he was happy.

When he heard a Mr. Green "speak of a man who had departed this life in full assurance of his going to glory," he suddenly realized that a higher level of spiritual consciousness was unknown to him. He knew that he had faith and that he still "kept eight commandments out of ten," but he did not have the conviction of his own salvation. Green and others told him that no one could keep all ten commandments on his own and that if he "did not experience the new birth, and the pardon of [his] sins, thro' the blood of Christ, before he died, [he] could not enter the kingdom of heaven." When Equiano asked a cleric in a chapel, "if *he* was to die that moment, whether he was sure to enter the kingdom of God; and added, 'Do you *know* that your sins are forgiven you?' he answered in the affirmative. Then confusion, anger, and discontent seized me, and I staggered much at this sort of doctrine; it brought me to a stand, not knowing which to believe, whether salvation by works, or by faith only in Christ" (186). Though no one told Equiano the name of this "mysterious" doctrine at the time, they all were talking about the experience of *justification*, a believer's sudden awareness that God, because of Christ's righteousness, has pardoned his or her past sins. Seeking further guidance, Equiano went to hear the Reverend Henry Peckwell, a Huntingdonian Methodist minister, preach at the Chapel, in the New Way, Westminster. Encouraged by Peckwell's sermon on the fairness of God's justice, Equiano asked his permission to receive the sacrament of Holy Communion. Upon examination, however, Peckwell determined that Equiano was not yet ready to be admitted as a communicant. To qualify for Communion Equiano needed to continue reading the Bible, hearing sermons, and praying for justification.

Equiano's faith was soon tested again. Lacking sufficient employment in London, he once more went to sea. Capt. Richard Strange hired him as steward on the *Hope*, bound for Cádiz, Spain, in September 1774. Upset by his crewmates' blasphemy, which he feared might be contagious, he "murmured much at God's providential dealings with me, and was discontented with the commandments, that I could not be saved by what I had done; I hated all things, and wished I had never been born; confusion seized me, and I wished to be annihilated. One day I was standing on the very edge of the stern of the ship, thinking to drown myself." Recollection of the words from 1 John 3:15 – "That no murderer hath eternal life abiding in him" – was all that saved him (188). But physical salvation brought him no spiritual comfort. He was now so fearful of dying in his present spiritual state that his incessant fretting, mourning, and praying annoyed everyone around him. When he returned to London he told his "religious friends" that he had decided to beg for survival onshore rather than ever go to sea again among the ungodly. His friends admonished him that the sea was his "lawful calling," and "God was not confined to place."

One friend in particular, George Smith, came to his aid. Like many eighteenth-century evangelicals, Smith was also a social reformer. John Howard, the most famous eighteenth-century proponent of prison reform, and others praised Smith for his management of the Tothill Fields, or Westminster, Bridewell. A bridewell was a house of correction in which prisoners were forced to work. One contemporary said of Smith's governorship of Tothill Fields: "The present keeper is a sober, careful, pious man; reads prayers and exhorts the prisoners every day, and sometimes oftener; by such a conduct he tames the fierce and abandoned savage, and makes those hardened wretches preserve a decent deportment, which is a very rare thing in most of the other gaols, where they appear like so many disorderly fiends, cloathed with wickedness, and steeled with daring effrontery."[7] Through Smith, Equiano "found a heartfelt resignation to the will of God" that enabled him to get back on board the appropriately named *Hope* for the three-week "delightful voyage" to Cádiz (189). With him he took gifts from Smith: a pocket Bible and Joseph Alleine's *An Alarme to Unconverted Sinners* (1673), which was frequently republished in the eighteenth century.

Equiano divided his time in Cádiz between admiring the wealth and beauty of the town and, like Jacob in the Old Testament, wrestling with God through prayers and reading the scriptures. He woke on the morning of 6 October feeling "a secret impulse" that he was about to "see or hear something supernatural," and he felt driven "to a throne of grace." What he had been hoping for happened later that day:

> As I was reading and meditating on the fourth chapter of the Acts, twelfth verse ["Neither is there salvation in any other: for there is none other name under heaven given among men, whereby we must be saved"], under the solemn apprehensions of eternity, and reflecting on my past ac-

tions, I began to think I had lived a moral life, and that I had a proper ground to believe I had an interest in the divine favour; but still meditating on the subject, not knowing whether salvation was to be had partly for our own good deeds, or solely as the sovereign gift of God: – in this deep consternation the Lord was pleased to break in upon my soul with his bright beams of heavenly light; and in an instant, as it were, removing the veil, and letting light into a dark place, Isa[iah]. xxv. 7. I saw clearly, with the eye of faith, the crucified Saviour bleeding on the cross on Mount Calvary: the Scriptures became an unsealed book, I saw myself a condemned criminal under the law, which came with its full force to my conscience, and when "the commandment came sin revived, and I died" [Romans 7:9]. I saw the Lord Jesus Christ in his humiliation, loaded and bearing my reproach, sin, and shame. I then clearly perceived, that by the deed of the law no flesh living could be justified. I was then convinced, that by the first Adam sin came, and by the second Adam (the Lord Jesus Christ) all that are saved must be made alive. It was given me at that time to know what it was to be born again, John iii. 5 ["Jesus answered, 'Verily, verily, I say unto thee, Except a man be born of water and of the Spirit, he cannot enter into the kingdom of God'"]. (189–90)

Justified at last, Equiano now fully apprehended that "self was obnoxious, and good works he had none." He recognized for the first time that everything that had happened to him was part of a providential plan. Providence was God acting as the designer, caretaker, and superintendent of the world and its inhabitants, especially humankind. As the derivation of the term from the Latin *pro-video* (to look forward) implies, events in God's creation happen by plan, not chance. And because God is benevolent, all events, no matter how apparently evil, are part of the grand design whose outline has been revealed to humans in the Bible. As though he were able to step outside of time, "Now every leading providential circumstance that happened to me, from the day I was taken from my parents to that hour, was then, in my view, as if it had but just then occurred. I was sensible of the invisible hand of God, which guided and protected me, when in truth I knew it not." Equiano understood that even slavery, from the perspective of Providence, was a fortunate fall: "Now the Ethiopian was willing to be saved by Jesus Christ" (190). Through "joy in the Holy Ghost" he "felt an astonishing change; the burden of sin, the gaping jaws of hell, and the fears of death, that weighed me down before, now lost their horror; indeed I thought death would now be the best earthly friend I ever had" (190–91). When he came out of his cabin and tried to share his joy with his crewmates, he sounded like an incomprehensible "barbarian" to them. His only companion in the midst of the unjustified was his Bible. "Enlightened with the 'light of the living,'" he understood that through "free grace" he "had a part and lot in the first resurrection," the Crucifixion and Resurrection of Christ (191–92).

He returned to London in December, where a sermon by William Romaine delivered at Blackfriars Church cleared up the last bit of confusion Equiano had about the relationship between good works and "free election" (192). He rushed back to the Chapel, in the New Way, Westminster, where George Smith and his other friends recognized the signs of his rebirth immediately. Reexamined, Equiano was now "received into church-fellowship amongst them," his previous despairing desire for immediate self-annihilation supplanted by the hopeful wish for a timely union with his Savior: "Now my whole wish was to be dissolved, and to be with Christ – but, alas! I must wait my appointed time" (193).

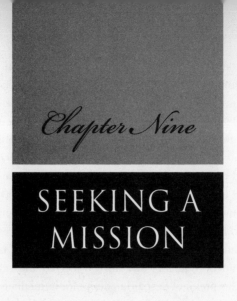

Chapter Nine

SEEKING A MISSION

Spiritually reborn, Equiano spent the following winter in London, "as happy as [he] could wish to be in this life" (198). He had no desire to change his situation in any way. When Captain Strange was ready to return to the Mediterranean in early 1775, Equiano at first refused to rejoin the crew of the *Hope*, but his friends soon again convinced him to go. The *Hope* sailed in March, reaching the Bay of Cádiz, Spain, a month later. Equiano's faith was quickly tested once more. As the *Hope* entered the harbor one Sunday, it struck "a single rock, called the Porpus" (199), which tore through the garboard plank, located at the very bottom of the vessel. Despite his lifelong fear of drowning, Equiano reacted to the accident with joyful resignation: "Although I could not swim, and saw no way of escaping death, I felt no dread in my then situation, having no desire to live. I even rejoiced in spirit, thinking this death would be sudden glory" (198). Those around him were amazed at his calm resignation in the face of the danger that left everyone else confused and begging for God's mercy. Telling "them of the peace of God, which, through sovereign grace, I enjoyed," he silently took comfort in the marine metaphors of a popular hymn:

Christ is my pilot wise, my compass is his word;
My soul each storm defies, while I have such a Lord.
I trust his faithfulness and power,
To save me in the trying hour.

Though rocks and quicksands deep through all my passage lie,
Yet Christ shall safely keep and guide me with his eye.
How can I sink with such a prop,
That bears the world and all things up?"[1]

To Equiano, Providence caused the accident to happen when the harbor was full of vessels and at high tide. With all the extra help from the nearby crews and the *Hope*'s three pumps, the ship was unloaded as quickly as possible and taken ashore to be repaired while its crew conducted their business in Cádiz.

The *Hope* sailed from Cádiz to the British colony of Gibraltar and then on to Málaga to purchase bullion, fruit, and wine. Equiano was impressed by the "pleasant and rich city" on Spain's Mediterranean Costa del Sol. He marveled at the cathedral, which had been under construction since 1528. It "was not then quite finished" when he saw it and has remained in the same condition since 1782. Because it lacks an east tower, the cathedral is nicknamed "La Manquita," the one-armed lady. Most of the cathedral's interior, on the other hand, "was completed, and highly decorated with the richest marble columns, and many superb paintings; it was lighted occasionally by an amazing number of wax tapers of different sizes, some of which were as thick as a man's thigh; these, however, were only used on some of their grand festivals" (199).

its contents as a work of art but not as a place of worship. Much about Málaga struck him as irreligious and immoral, especially "the custom of bull-baiting, and other diversions which prevailed here on Sunday evenings" (199). He complained about what he saw as the unchristian environment to Father Vincent, a priest with whom he "had frequent contests about religion." Father Vincent "took great pains to make a proselyte" of Equiano "to his church." Equiano returned the favor, producing his Bible to show Father Vincent "in what points his church erred." The priest objected, saying that when "he had been in England . . . every person there read the bible, which was very wrong." Father Vincent was simply reflecting the same objections to Bible reading Equiano had seen enforced by the Inquisition in May 1769 in Oporto, Portugal. Equiano countered, "Christ desired us to search the scriptures." Among the major disagreements between the Roman Catholic

Church and Protestantism are those over the relationship between the Bible and divine truth and the way to salvation. For most Protestants, including Methodist Anglicans like Equiano, the Bible is the sufficient source for the tenets of Christianity, containing all that a believer needs to know and directly accessible to the individual believer. Roman Catholic doctrine maintains that the Bible is necessary but not sufficient, needing to be supplemented by the teachings of the church fathers, who wrote after the composition of the Bible. Consequently, the Bible should be mediated to laypeople through the church's priests, who are properly trained to read it. Some Protestant sects, notably the Quakers, rejected the doctrine of mediation by a church but believed that postbiblical personal revelations and visitations by the Holy Spirit supplement the Bible. Roman Catholics and Protestants also disagree about which books of the Bible are canonical. Hence, Roman Catholic authorities perceived the importation of translated Bibles, particularly Protestant ones, as undermining the authority of the church and spreading heresy. In the thirteenth century the Roman Catholic Church established the Holy Office, an ecclesiastical tribunal more commonly known as the Inquisition, to identify and prosecute heretics. The Spanish Inquisition was not abolished until 1834.

Fortunately for Equiano, his debate with Father Vincent was kept between themselves and not brought to the attention of the authorities. The priest tried to convince him to attend one of the Spanish universities "and declared that I should have my education free." Equiano was told that "if I got myself made a priest, I might in time become even Pope; and he said that Pope Benedict was a black man" (200). Father Vincent may have been making a joke, or Equiano may have misremembered their conversation, confusing a pope with a saint. The leader of the Jesuits was called the Black Pope (a reference to the color of the Jesuit habit), and Benedict XIV, the pope from 1740 to 1758, was generally considered to be anti-Jesuit. Benedict the Black was the son of African slaves who had been taken to Messina, Sicily, where he was born in 1526. He was freed at the age of eighteen but continued to work for his former owner. Mistreated by his social peers because of his origin and complexion, he nonetheless remained cheerful and humble. He joined the order of Franciscan friars, reluctantly accepting his appointment as their superior in Palermo. When he died in 1589, King Philip III of Spain had a special tomb constructed for his body. Pope Benedict XIV beatified him in 1743, and Pope Pius VIII canonized him in 1807.

"Ever desirous of learning," Equiano was tempted by Father Vincent's offer. He thought he "might catch some with guile" – that is, trick some Spaniards into Protestantism – while getting a free education. But his conscience reminded him that accepting the offer would be hypocritical in light of his beliefs. Recalling Saint Paul's admonition to the Corinthians to avoid unbelievers, he declined the priest's offer. Having both failed as proselytizers, Equiano and Father Vincent "parted without conviction on either side" (200).

The *Hope* stopped at Cádiz again to pick up two more tons of bullion before sailing for England in June. Off the northwestern coast of the Iberian Peninsula Captain Strange encountered such strong headwinds that the ship could not advance more than six or seven miles over several days. Out of frustration Strange blasphemed the Lord's name, which prompted "a young gentleman on board" to reprimand him for his sin and to remind him that "though the wind was contrary for us, yet it was fair for some others." "With some boldness," Equiano quickly seconded him, adding that "the Lord was better to us than we deserved, and that he had done all things well" (200–201). He and the young gentleman had clearly gotten the captain's attention, for though Equiano expected him to be angry for being reprimanded, Strange "replied not a word" (201).

The next day, 21 June, Equiano saw evidence of "the providential hand of our benign Creator" behind the doldrums. He had dreamed the night before that he "saw a boat immediately off the starboard main shrouds; and exactly at half past one o'clock the following day at noon, while I was below, just as we had dined in the cabin, the man at the helm cried out, A boat! which brought my dream that instant into my mind. I was the first man that jumped on the deck; and looking from the shrouds onward, according to my dream, I descried a little boat at some distance." The tiny boat contained "eleven miserable men," survivors of a ship that had sunk earlier that day when its load of grain shifted (201). Lacking food, water, and a compass, the Portuguese sailors had only part of an oar with which to try to get through the turbulent sea, and they looked as if they could not have lived an hour longer when they were taken aboard the *Hope*. Their rescue reminded Equiano of Psalm 107, which contains the thanksgiving for those who "go down to the sea in ships" (verse 23). Their rescue also led the "poor distressed captain" to acknowledge to Equiano "'that the Lord is good; for, seeing that I am not fit to die, he therefore gave me a space of time to repent.'" Equiano responded by "talking to him on the providence of God" (202).

Returning to London with the rescued seamen, Equiano was glad to be reunited with his friends and fellow believers. In early November 1775 his "old friend, the celebrated Dr. Irving," engaged him in "a new adventure, in cultivating a plantation at Jamaica and the Musquito Shore" in Central America. Irving assured Equiano that he would trust him with the management of the planned "estate in preference to any one" (202). Encouraged by the government, Irving and his partner, Alexander Blair, were setting out to cultivate vegetables to produce oil "used chiefly for oiling wool for the wool-combers."[2] In August 1775 William Legge, second Earl of Dartmouth, secretary of state for the North American colonies, and president of the Board of Trade and Foreign Plantations, had instructed the governor of Jamaica, who had authority over the British settlers on the Mosquito Coast, to establish a legislative council there chosen by the settlers. Equiano's motives for joining the project, he tells us, were more evangelical than materialistic. After getting the advice of his friends he "accepted of the offer, knowing that the harvest was fully ripe in those parts, and I hoped to be an instrument, under God, of bringing some poor sinner to my well-beloved master, Jesus Christ." On 13 November they set sail from Gravesend, downriver from London, for Jamaica on the *Morning Star*, a 150-ton sloop co-owned by Blair and Irving and under the command of David Miller.

They took with them "four Musquito Indians, who were chiefs in their own country, and were brought here by some English traders for some selfish ends." The "selfish ends" were those of settlers upset by the attempts of the superintendent of the shore, Robert Hodgson, to regulate and control the sale of lands. Ironically, the Mosquito, who were heavily involved in enslaving other Indians, had been sent to London to complain that Hodgson was enslaving and selling the native people. Their petition was successful, nonetheless. In August 1775 Lord Dartmouth removed Hodgson from his post. At the British government's expense the Mosquito were returning home, "having been in England about twelve months, during which they learned to speak pretty good English" (202–3).

The Mosquito Coast extended some 550 miles along the Caribbean Sea east along the coast of modern Honduras to Cape Gracias a Dios (Thanks to God), at the northeastern tip of present-day Nicaragua, and south to what is now northeastern Costa Rica. During the eighteenth century the English called the indigenous people on the Mosquito Coast as well as part of the coast of modern Honduras Mosquito, Musqueto, or Musquito. Modern anthropologists and historians refer to them as Miskito, Miskitu, or Mosquito.[3] The combination of hostile terrain, inhospitable climate, voracious insects, and native resistance rendered the Mosquito Coast almost as impenetrable to

Europeans as Africa. From the European perspective the coast was an example of a "marchland," or borderland, in which "violence was a way of life" because imperial control was disputed between Britain and Spain until near the end of the eighteenth century.[4] Lord Dartmouth's August 1775 instructions were intended to strengthen Britain's territorial claim to the region beyond the main settlement at Black River in present-day Honduras: "In 1770, there were, exclusive of the natives, about 1400 inhabitants, subjects of Great Britain, of whom 206 were whites, about as many more of mixed blood, and about 900 slaves. Of these, 136 whites, 112 mixtures, and about 600 slaves, were at, or within a few miles of, Black River."[5] The Peace of Paris in 1763 left European sovereignty over the coast ambiguous. Spain granted Britain the right to harvest logwood, used in making dyes, in exchange for Britain's promise to remove its fortifications along the Bay of Honduras. Although the Mosquito Coast was nominally under Spanish rule, neither Britain nor Spain was willing or able to commit enough settlers or military force to the region to establish uncontested sovereignty despite both countries' economic interest in the coast's natural resources. Consequently, since the seventeenth century the coast had been an unofficial sanctuary for pirates, buccaneers, privateers, and runaway slaves from the Caribbean colonies. The Mosquito Coast was still newsworthy when Equiano published his autobiography. Britain had agreed by treaty in 1786 to remove its settlers from the area in exchange for Spain's continued recognition of Britain's right to harvest logwood and mahogany in Belize.

The Mosquito took full advantage of the power vacuum that existed before the convention of 1786, playing one European power off against the other: "The implacable hatred they bear to the Spaniards, by whom their ancestors were driven from the fertile plains they enjoyed near Lake Nicaragua, goes almost as far back as the discovery of America, and their friendship for the English is as old as the expeditions of the Buccaniers against their common enemy."[6] The English were more than willing to supply the Mosquito with guns, ammunition, and other supplies in exchange for access to raw materials and their continued resistance to Spanish domination. Scores of Mosquito had fought with the British against rebellious slaves in Jamaica before Equiano's trip to the coast, and hundreds more fought with them against the Spanish in 1780. To strengthen British-Mosquito relations, since the seventeenth century the sons of influential Mosquito had been brought to England to be educated. Part of the trade between the English and the Mosquito consisted of slaves. Until the Jamaica Assembly outlawed Indian enslavement in

1741, the Mosquito sold their neighboring Amerindians to the British. To escape slave raids by the Mosquito, other indigenous peoples such as the
Woolwa fled to the hinterland.

By the 1770s the Mosquito Coast had become an ethnically, linguisti-
cally, and culturally hybrid amalgamation of peoples. The natives had inter-
bred with escaped slaves of African descent for more than a century. In 1773
Bryan Edwards reported from Jamaica that the "Musquito Indians . . . were
formerly very numerous; but they were much reduced some years ago by the
small-pox. Their present number is from seven to ten thousand fighting men,
formed into different tribes, both by nature and policy; by nature, from the
general distinction of pure Indians and Samboes [Indian Africans]; by policy,
as living and acting under several chieftains, called king, governor, general
and admiral, each of whom has a different territory, and nearly independent
jurisdiction, though the king has an imperfectly defined supremacy both in
power and dominion."[7] Local Mosquito leaders called themselves "king,"
"governor," "general," and "admiral" in imitation of their British allies. The
cultural influence on the Mosquito of their contact with Europeans was probably superficial, however. The titles they adopted from the English seem not
to have represented any desire to imitate the centralized political authority
found in Britain.[8] And, as Equiano soon discovered, European dress was reserved for special occasions.

One of the "four Musquito Indians" aboard the *Morning Star* "was the
Musquito king's son, a youth of about eighteen years of age" and heir to the
Mosquito throne. He had been baptized while in London. Even before
the vessel left England, Equiano recognized that the Indian passengers, especially Prince George, were worthy objects of his missionary zeal: "When I
came to talk to them, about eight days before we sailed, I was very much
mortified in finding that they had not frequented any churches since they
were here, and were baptized,[9] nor was any attention paid to their morals. I
was very sorry for this mock Christianity, and had just an opportunity to take
some of them once to church before we sailed" (203).

Prince George probably felt as if he were still in church during the
voyage. For most of the trip Equiano found him an apt pupil keen to be instructed "in the doctrines of Christianity, of which he was entirely ignorant."
He learned the alphabet in only eleven days, to the point of making words of
two and three letters. What most interested him were the sensationalistic pictures in Equiano's copy of John Fox's *The Acts and Monuments of the Church, or
Book of Martyrs* (1563), an anti–Roman Catholic work often reprinted during

the eighteenth century in abridged editions with "cuts," or woodcut illustrations: "He used to be very fond of looking into it, and would ask many questions about the papal cruelties he saw depicted there, which I explained to him." George would come to pray with Equiano before retiring for the night, wearing only his shirt, and he would also pray with him before meals. Delighted by George's spiritual progress, Equiano "used much supplication to God for his conversion. I was in full hope of seeing daily every appearance of that change which I could wish. . . . Thus we went on nearly four-fifths of our passage" (203).

But "Satan at last got the upper hand. Some of his messengers, seeing this poor heathen much advanced in piety, began to ask him whether I had converted him to Christianity, laughed and made their jest at him, for which I rebuked them as much as I could; but this treatment caused the prince to halt between two opinions" (203–4). These "true sons of Belial" (a demonic personification mentioned in 2 Corinthians 6:15) told the prince that neither the devil nor an afterlife existed. He became so confused by their teasing and taunting that he "would not drink nor carouse with these ungodly actors, nor would he be with me even at prayers." After Equiano's repeated queries about the cause of his withdrawal from their prayer sessions, George finally responded with a question of his own: "'How comes it that all the white men on board, who can read and write, observe the sun, and know all things, yet swear, lie, and get drunk, only excepting yourself?'" (204).

Although we are startled to hear Equiano called white, he apparently did not even notice. The terms *white* and *black* were used much more flexibly during the eighteenth century than they tend to be today. Britons sometimes referred to Native Americans and often to all Asians as black or Negro (which literally means black) simply because they were darker than most northern Europeans. But English men and women were also called black if they had dark complexions or hair. Hence, one of the characters in Henry Fielding's novel *Tom Jones* (1749) is named "Black George" because of his appearance, though he is not of African descent. Even odder sounding to modern ears is Richard Steele's reference in the *Spectator* 274 (14 January 1711) to "as pretty a black gentlewoman as ever you saw; a little woman, which I know your lordship likes; well shaped, and as fine a complexion for red and white as ever I saw." Steele is talking about a woman with black hair, not an African with a peaches-and-cream complexion. The Indian prince included Equiano among the "white men" because he shared their culture, education, and religion. To the Mosquito, *whiteness* described belief and behavior rather than physical appearance. Wherever and whenever the vast majority of non-Europeans were non-Christian, calling someone a Christian was simply another way of saying that he or she was of European descent, and vice versa.

Equiano tried to convince Prince George that the other whites sinned because they did not fear God. If they continued in their evil ways, they would die in a state of sin and "could not go to, or be happy with God." George responded that he would rather go to hell with his friend than leave him behind. Equiano's censorious reaction "depressed [George's] spirits much; and he became ever after, during the passage, fond of being alone." Although Equiano was more successful at depressing George than converting him, he kept trying until they finally parted. In Jamaica he took George "to church, where he saw the sacrament administered. When we came out we saw all kinds of people, almost from the church door for the space of half a mile down to the water-side, buying and selling all kinds of commodities: and these acts afforded me great matter of exhortation to this youth, who was much astonished" (204–5). George was probably as "astonished" by Equiano's continued exhortations as he was by seeing people breaking the Sabbath.

The *Morning Star* reached Jamaica in mid-January 1776. When the crew had resupplied and was ready to sail on to the Mosquito Coast in February, Equiano "went with the Doctor on board a Guinea-man, to purchase some slaves to carry with us, and cultivate a plantation; and I chose them all of my own countrymen." A Guineaman was any vessel bringing enslaved Africans directly to the Americas from any place along the coast of West Africa, from Senegal to the Bight of Biafra. In the editions of his autobiography published from 1792 on Equiano added the phrase "some of whom came from Lybia" to follow "my own countrymen" and a footnote to emphasize that he was identifying with all Africans, not just Igbo speakers. The footnote directs his readers to Anthony Purver's *A New and Literal Translation of All the Books of the Old and New Testaments; with Notes Explanatory* . . . (1764): "Alexander Polyhistor & Cleodemus Malchus, who both wrote the History of the Barbarians in Greek, say that Apher, one of Abraham's Offspring, led an Army against Libya, and getting the Victory, settled there; from whom his Posterity were called Africans."[10]

Equiano's unquestioning willingness to participate in a project based on slave labor and to condone the slave trade as well as the pride he took in selecting the slaves for the plantation should not surprise us. In 1776 he had not yet turned against the slave trade, let alone against slavery. When Equiano agreed to manage the planned estate, he no doubt assumed that slaves would be used. Operating a plantation in the West Indies without slaves was inconceivable to most people at the time. What alternative labor force was available to do the very arduous work of clearing tropical forest for planting? The indigenous people were not inclined to accept the regimentation required for success, and they were too powerful to be coerced. European workers, if they could be found, would have to be paid. How could planters make a profit if their paid labor had to compete against slave labor? Equiano was convinced that his own experiences and observations as a slave enabled him to be a humane overseer of slaves. Nearly a decade would pass before Equiano recognized that humane slavery was a contradiction in terms.

Equiano and Irving brought their human and other cargo to the Mosquito Coast on 18 February "at a place called Dupeupy" on the coast of present-day Honduras, where "all our Indian guests now, after I had admonished them, and a few cases of liquor given them by the Doctor, took an affectionate leave of us, and went ashore, where they were met by the Musquito king, and we never saw one of them afterwards." From Dupeupy the *Morning Star* sailed south to Cape Gracias a Dios, where the crew found a natural harbor and welcoming natives. The doctor, Equiano, and several others chose a spot with rich soil near a riverbank to establish their plantation. After off-loading their sloop they cleared the land and planted their vegetables, which grew even faster than anticipated. Nightly fires kept the wild animals away while they slept, and the doctor's concoction of strong rum and cayenne pepper cured their slaves and the natives of poisonous snakebites. The only bad news was the seizure on 30 April of the *Morning Star* by two Spanish *guardacostas*, vessels of the colonial coast guard, when the ship went north to trade at Black River (205). The loss of the ship and its contents cost Blair and Irving more than thirty-seven hundred pounds.[11] Under the command of Captain Gastelu, the Spanish had also hoped to capture the Mosquito Indians being returned to the coast.

Irving's fame as a healer spread quickly among the Amerindians, attracting to the plantation even some of the Woolwa, or "flat-headed Indians," who had moved many miles inland to avoid contact with Mosquito enslavers. Called "flat-headed" because they shaped the pliant skulls of their infants by tightly binding them, the Woolwa brought silver to exchange for European goods. The local Indians had only "turtle oil, and shells, little silk grass, and some provisions" to trade. Beyond helping to build houses for the settlers, "which they did exactly like the Africans, by the joint labour of men, women, and children[,] . . . they would not work at anything" for Irving "except fishing." Contact with the natives gave Equiano the opportunity for the ethnographic and moral observations that he loved to make and that he knew his audience loved to read.

He found the Mosquito to be a remarkable people, in many ways morally superior to the Europeans. The women always accompanied their husbands to the plantation. Equiano never saw a man with more than two wives, though numerous wives were a sign of prestige in Mosquito culture. The men and women ate apart, and Equiano never noticed "the least sign of incontinence amongst them." Both men and women painted their faces and bodies. The women also ornamented themselves with beads. Labor was divided: "The women generally cultivate the ground, and the men are all fishermen and canoe-makers." Their only moral flaws appeared to be mild swearing, which they had adopted from the English, and failure to observe the Sabbath:

> Upon the whole, I never met any nation that were so simple in their manners as these people, or had so little ornament in their houses. Neither had they, as I ever could learn, one word expressive of an oath. The worst word I ever heard amongst them when they were quarreling, was one that they had got from the English, which was, "you rascal." I never saw any mode of worship among them; but in this they were not worse than their European brethren or neighbours, for I am sorry to say that there was not one white person in our dwelling, nor any where else, that I saw in different places I was at on the shore, that was better or more pious than those unenlightened Indians; but they either worked or slept on Sundays.

Since the Mosquito were "unenlightened" by Christianity, for them breaking the Sabbath was an innocent mistake. For Equiano's fellow settlers, however, it was a sin: "To my sorrow, working was too much Sunday's employment with ourselves; so much so, that in some length of time we really did not know one day from another" (206–7). Mosquito men were robust warriors who were particularly proud of "having never been conquered by the Spaniards." Despite being "great drinkers of strong liquors," the Mosquito were the most honest people any of the settlers had ever seen: "The country being hot, we lived under an open shed, where we had all kinds of goods, without a door or a lock to any one article; yet we slept in safety, and never lost any thing, or were disturbed. This surprised us a good deal; and the Doctor, myself, and others, used to say, if we were to lie in that manner in Europe we should have our throats cut the first night" (207).

Like a circuit judge with an entourage, the "Indian governor" periodi-

cally traveled around "the province or district" to collect tribute and settle local disputes. The settlers willingly sent this much-respected figure the gunpowder, rum, and sugar he demanded, and they looked forward to his visit.
But instead of the "grave reverend judge, solid and sagacious" they expected,
he turned out to be an intoxicated lout accompanied by a "gang" who plundered the people under his authority. The settlers, who "would gladly have
dispensed with the honour of their company, . . . feasted them plentifully all
the day till the evening; when the Governor, getting quite drunk, grew very
unruly, and struck one of our most friendly chiefs," Captain Plasmyah, "who
was our nearest neighbour, and also took his gold-laced hat from him" (207).
The ensuing uproar grew so great that Irving was unable to still it. Fearing
that he might only make matters worse by continuing to try to intervene, he
left the settlement, leaving Equiano to deal with the problem. Enraged by the
governor's behavior, Equiano would have had him tied to a tree and flogged
were his own men not outnumbered by the governor's. Instead of force he
had to rely on his wits to take command of the situation. Fortunately, he remembered "a passage [he] had read in the life of Columbus, when he was
amongst the Indians in Jamaica." On his fourth voyage to the New World, in
order to frighten the Jamaican natives into supplying his men with provisions, Christopher Columbus used his knowledge of an impending lunar
eclipse to convince them that his God could punish them with a famine if
they continued to refuse his requests. Inspired by Columbus's example,
Equiano grabbed the governor and "pointed up to the heavens. I menaced
him and the rest: I told them God lived there, and that he was angry with
them, and they must not quarrel so; that they were all brothers, and if they
did not leave off, and go away quietly, I would take the book (pointing to the
bible), read, and *tell* God to make them dead. This was something like
magic." The raucous Indians immediately calmed down, and after receiving
some rum and other gifts, they went peaceably on their way. When Irving returned he was delighted by Equiano's success "in thus getting rid of our troublesome guests" (208). Eventually, the governor even restored the stolen hat
to its owner.

The entertainments offered by the "Musquito people in our own vicinity,
out of respect to the Doctor, myself, and his people," were very different from
the governor's reception. Called a "*tourrie* or *drykbot*," which Equiano considered "a corruption of language" for "a feast of drinking about," this grand entertainment centered around drinking an intoxicating mixture of fermented
cassavas that had been "chewed or beaten in mortars" and roasted pineapples

(208). Equiano was "not a little disgusted at the preparations" because the ingredients were "squeezed, dirt and all, into a canoe," to be accompanied by unappetizing but fragrant alligator meat, which he found too "rich" for his taste. The drink was so thick that it was more solid than liquid. None of the settlers could drink it. Fortunately, they had brought rum, which the Mosquito were happy to share. Nor did Equiano find the entertainment any more appealing: "The mirth had begun before we came; and they were dancing with music: and the musical instruments were nearly the same as those of any other sable people; but, as I thought, much less melodious than any other nation I ever knew. They had many curious gestures in dancing, and a variety of motions and postures of their bodies, which to me were in no wise attracting." Irving tried in vain to get the men and women to follow his example and dance together rather than separately. The dress and behavior of their hosts struck Equiano as rather bizarre: "One Owden, the oldest father in the vicinity, was drest in a strange and terrifying form. Around his body were skins adorned with different kinds of feathers, and he had on his head a very large and high head-piece, in the form of a grenadier's cap, with prickles like a porcupine; and he made a certain noise which resembled the cry of an alligator" (209). But despite his reservations about the food and entertainment, Equiano was pleased to observe that the "merry-making at last ended without the least discord in any person in the company, although it was made up of different nations and complexions" (210).

His mission to the Mosquito Coast did not turn out as he had hoped. His one attempt at converting an Indian, which had begun so promisingly, had ended in total failure. The irreligious behavior of his fellow settlers rendered observation of the Sabbath impossible. Feeling that the quest for material gain was forcing him to sin, he recalled the warning from Matthew 16:26: "'What does it avail a man if he gain the whole world, and lose his own soul?'" When the rainy season, which commenced in May, washed away the future provisions they had planted, he saw their loss as "in some measure a judgment upon us for working on Sundays." The use of slave labor on the plantation was not a problem for him in 1776. In fact, he took pride in his conduct as an overseer. He saw himself as a model manager: "All my poor countrymen, the slaves, when they heard of my leaving them, were very sorry, as I had always treated them with care and affection, and did every thing I could to comfort the poor creatures, and render their condition easy" (211). All he wanted to do was to escape from his sinful comrades and return to England. He finally got up his courage to tell Irving so in mid-June. After much opposition the doctor agreed to let him leave, taking with him a "certificate of [his] behavior" he would need to prove that he was a free man and to find any other employment:

> The bearer, Gustavus Vassa, has served me several years with strict honesty, sobriety, and fidelity. I can, therefore, with justice recommend him for these qualifications; and indeed in every respect I consider him as an excellent servant. I do hereby certify that he always behaved well, and that he is perfectly trust-worthy.
> CHARLES IRVING.

Irving accompanied Equiano downriver, where he booked passage on a Jamaica-bound sloop with its captain and one of its two owners. Soon after the doctor and Equiano parted tearfully, Hughes, the other co-owner of the sloop, asked Equiano to work for wages on one of their schooners rather than pay for his passage to Jamaica. When he politely declined, Hughes "immediately changed his tone, and swore, and abused me very much, and asked how I came to be freed! I told him, and said that I came into that vicinity with Dr. Irving, whom he had seen that day. This account was of no use; he still swore exceedingly at me, and cursed the master for a fool that sold me my freedom, and the Doctor for another in letting me go from him." Hughes refused to let Equiano off the vessel. Equiano's response only made Hughes angrier: "I said I had been twice amongst the Turks, yet had never seen any such usage with them, and much less could I have expected any thing of this kind among the Christians" (211). Hughes swore he would sell Equiano to the Spaniards in Cartagena, on the Caribbean coast of present-day Colombia. Equiano disputed Hughes's right to sell a freeman, but "without another word, he made some of his people tie ropes round each of my ancles, and also to each wrist, and another rope round my body, and hoisted me up without letting my feet touch or rest upon any thing." Once again, Equiano was reminded of the precarious state of a free black in the West Indies. Although he repeatedly "cried and begged very hard for some mercy," Hughes would not relent. Only after his "cruel abuser" went to bed several hours later was Equiano able to get some of Hughes's slaves to loosen the ropes, at great personal risk to themselves, since Hughes had already beaten them for not having tied Equiano up quickly enough. Equiano spent the rest of the night praying "to God to forgive this blasphemer" (212). Hughes was still enraged the next morning, but Equiano had to be taken down so the sails could be hoisted. A sympathetic carpenter who knew both Equiano and Irving interceded on Equiano's behalf to the captain, who agreed to let him be taken ashore in a canoe while Hughes was belowdecks. But before Equiano could reach land, Hughes saw him trying to escape and forced him to come back on board or be shot. Fortunately, Hughes and the captain became so embroiled in mutual abuse that Equiano was able to sneak back into the canoe and get out of range before Hughes realized what he had done.

Once ashore, Equiano went to the co-owner of the sloop and complained of Hughes's behavior toward him. The other owner, shocked by what he heard, treated Equiano kindly, giving him some refreshment and provisions. He advised him to travel south to the Mosquito admiral, who would help him get to Jamaica. The trip was painful because of the injuries Equiano had suffered at Hughes's hands, but his welcome by the admiral, whom he had met before, was warm. The Indians "acted towards [him] more like Christians than those whites [he] was amongst the last night" (213–14). The Mosquito helped him make the arduous fifty-mile journey by sea and land through mosquito-infested swamps south to the next port. There he found "a sloop commanded by one captain Jenning," who agreed to let him work in exchange for his passage to Jamaica (214). Deceived again, Equiano discovered that Jenning was headed south along the coast rather than east to Jamaica, and Equiano did not labor on board but at the much harder work of cutting and loading mahogany. After working for Jenning for few victuals and no pay, the crew encountered "a smaller sloop called the Indian Queen, commanded by one John Baker . . . an Englishman . . . trading for turtle shells and silver" (214–15). Short of hands, Baker offered Equiano "forty-five shillings sterling a month" and passage to Jamaica. With the help of "a north pole shipmate" who was working with him for Jenning, Equiano snuck on board the *Indian Queen* on 10 July.

Equiano found he had gone from bad to worse in leaving Jenning and joining Baker. Rather than going to Jamaica, Baker headed south toward Cartagena, but, "what was worst of all, he was a very cruel and bloody-minded man, and was a horrid blasphemer." He physically abused his white pilot, Stoker, as well as some of the blacks on board. On one occasion he beat Stoker severely and then ordered, at gunpoint, two blacks to leave him on a deserted island. Risking their lives, while Baker slept the blacks returned to the island to bring Stoker a blanket, which Equiano believed "was the means of saving his life from the annoyance of insects." The next morning Baker was persuaded to allow Stoker back aboard, but he never recovered from his injuries and subsequent illness and drowned shortly thereafter. Baker was so avaricious that the crew members had to find their own food. Providentially, Equiano believed, God had a large fish jump on deck just when he was most hungry, and, even more amazingly, Baker let him keep it.

But Baker quickly reverted to form. He often beat Equiano out of frustration when the rest of the crew did not return from shore as quickly as he wished:

> One day especially, in this wild, wicked, and mad career, after striking me several times with different things, and once across my mouth, even with a red burning stick out of the fire, he got a barrel of gunpowder on the deck, and swore that he would blow up the vessel. I was then at my wit's end, and earnestly prayed to God to direct me. The head [flat end] was out of the barrel; and the captain took a lighted stick out of the fire to blow himself and me up, because there was a vessel then in sight coming in, which he supposed was a Spanish Guarda Costa, and he was afraid of falling into their hands. Seeing this, I got an axe, unnoticed by him, and placed myself between him and the powder, having resolved in myself, as soon as he attempted to put the fire in the barrel, to chop him down that instant. I was more than an hour in this situation; during which he struck me often, still keeping the fire in his hand for this wicked purpose. (216–17)

Equiano had come close enough to blowing up ships himself in the past to recognize the danger he was in. The stalemate lasted into the night.

The next morning they discovered that the vessel Baker feared so much was an English sloop bound for Jamaica, and on it was Irving. Because his "old master and friend" Irving was only a passenger, he was not able to help Equiano get away from Baker, though he managed to send him some rum and sugar. Equiano learned from Irving that "after I had left the estate which I managed for this gentleman on the Musquito shore, during which the slaves were well fed and comfortable, a white overseer had supplied my place: this man, through inhumanity and ill-judged avarice, beat and cut the poor slaves most unmercifully; and the consequence was, that every one got into a large Puriogua canoe, and endeavoured to escape; but, not knowing where to go, or how to manage the canoe, they were all drowned; in consequence of which the Doctor's plantation was left uncultivated, and he was now returning to Jamaica to purchase more slaves and stock it again" (217–18).

Their paths crossed once more when Baker finally reached Jamaica on 14 October. After the *Indian Queen* was unloaded, he refused to pay Equiano the "eight pounds five shillings sterling" he owed him. Irving tried to help Equiano get the money, going with him to each of Jamaica's nine magistrates, but none would admit the oath of a black man against a white. Baker would have beaten Equiano for demanding his money had he not "got, by means of Dr. Irving, under the protection of Capt. [Stair] Douglas[s], of the Squirrel man of war [a sixth rate 20]." He was no doubt delighted to find serving with Douglass on the *Squirrel* his former shipmate and fellow black on the Arctic expedition, Richard Yorke.[12] Equiano declined Irving's invitation to stay with him, "employed in refining sugars." It was to be the last time they would meet. Several months later Equiano "learned, with much sorrow, that this my amiable friend was dead, owing to his having eaten some poisoned fish" (218). The report of Irving's death was incorrect.

Following a stormy passage across the Atlantic in a convoy led by Douglass in the *Squirrel*, during which they captured and destroyed an American privateer, Equiano reached Plymouth, England, on 7 January 1777. Having spent "some little time at Plymouth and Exeter among some pious friends," he proceeded "to London, with a heart replete with thanks to God for all past mercies" (219). "Disgusted with the seafaring life" after his experiences trying to get out of the West Indies, Equiano spent much of the next seven years working in London as a domestic servant (220). He tells us nothing, however, of what he was doing between the beginning of 1777 and the beginning of 1779. And, except for the mention of the American privateer captured by Captain Douglass as they returned to England, as far as one could tell from *The Interesting Narrative*, the American Revolution never happened. Some published correspondence may help fill in the gaps.

Ten letters signed "Gustavus Vassa" appeared between 24 July 1777 and 10 July 1778 in the London newspaper the *Morning Post, and Daily Advertiser*.[13] We cannot be certain that Equiano was the correspondent in the *Morning Post*. During the 1770s someone other than the author of *The Interesting Narrative* may have assumed the name of Gustavus I or Gustavus Vassa. The first letter in the *Morning Post* closes with the author's hope that his comments will be so well received that he may "think [him]self entitled to the name of GUSTAVUS VASA." Such a hope would be appropriate to anyone sending public advice to the ministry. But for the future author of *The Interesting Narrative* to hope to deserve his slave name would be ironic in a way unavailable to others. The absence in the 1770s of the epithets "the African" or "the Ethiopian," which that author added to "Gustavus Vassa" in his letters published in 1788 and 1789, does not in itself rule him out as the Vassa of the

Morning Post series. He signed all his known pre-1788 letters simply as Gustavus Vassa, without the epithets. I know of no one else who was publishing under the pseudonym Gustavus Vassa during the last quarter of the eighteenth century.

The *Morning Post* letters appeared during a period when we know that Equiano was in London. They would fill a gap between his arrival there in 1777 and his employment in early 1779 by Matthias Macnamara, the former governor of the British province of Senegambia in West Africa. Equiano tells us that after spending "some little time at Plymouth and Exeter" following his arrival at Plymouth on 7 January 1777, he went to London (219). A letter he includes in his *Interesting Narrative* shows that he was in Macnamara's employ by 11 March 1779 and living on Hedge Lane, Charing Cross, in Westminster. The *Morning Post* letters are sent from various locations, moving from east to west in greater London: Anderton's Coffee House, Fleet Street; Peel's Coffee House, Fleet Street; and Hungerford Coffee House, Strand (near St. Martin in the Fields Church and Charing Cross). These sites are consistent with the westward movement from the City of London to Westminster that *The Interesting Narrative* indicates Equiano made between 1777 and 1779.

The *Morning Post* letters would also fill the gap of the American Revolution, a subject almost completely untouched in Equiano's *Interesting Narrative*, perhaps because the humiliating defeat Britain suffered was still a very controversial subject in 1789, when he was trying to appeal to as wide an audience as possible on the issue of the slave trade.[14] (One might note that the American Revolution is untreated as well in Benjamin Franklin's contemporaneously written though much later published *Autobiography*.) The first *Morning Post* letter argues that had the British capitalized on their victories under the leadership of William Pitt the Elder during the Seven Years' War by retaining their conquests in the West Indies, Britain "would for all ages to come have remained the *metropole* of the commercial world, and *mart* of general trade for all Europe, Asia, Africa, and America; as well as the most formidable naval power on earth." The author implies that "the inadequateness of the peace" established by the Treaty of Paris in 1763 laid the groundwork for the present war with the American colonies and the threat of military intervention by France and Spain on behalf of the rebels.

The *Morning Post* writer is a royalist who supports the cause against the American rebels, like the African-born former servant Ignatius Sancho. Sancho published similar newly discovered letters under the pseudonym "Africanus" and his own name, respectively, in the *Morning Post* on 28 August

1778 and 29 December 1779. In his 1 January 1778 letter addressed to the prime minister, Lord North (Frederick North, second Earl of Guilford), "Gustavus Vassa," however, is much harsher than Sancho ever is in his criticism of Lord North's conduct of the war.[15] But even Sancho, who through his former employer, the Duke of Montagu, had connections to Lord North and his family, acknowledged that he "is a good husband! father, friend, and master – a real *good man* – but I fear a bad *m[iniste]r*."[16] The harsh comments in the *Morning Post* were prompted by the defeat at the battle of Saratoga, New York, on 17 October 1777 of the British forces under Gen. John Burgoyne by the American general Horatio Gates. Having marched south from Canada and taken the American fort at Ticonderoga on the route to Saratoga, the overextended Burgoyne was defeated when Sir Henry Clinton failed to reach him with British troops brought up the Hudson River from New York City. "Vassa" and many others faulted Clinton and fellow British general Sir William Howe for failing to prosecute the war vigorously. The defeat at Saratoga was the military turning point of the war, convincing France and Spain to join forces with the Americans early in 1778 and leading to increased political pressure for a negotiated end to the rebellion.

"Gustavus Vassa," like Sancho, opposed Lord North's Reconciliation Bill for offering what he considered overly generous peace terms to the American rebels. The letters of 4 and 10 March 1778 express "Vassa's" growing anger as the original bill became increasingly conciliatory. On 4 March he welcomed the bill, but on 10 March he withdrew his previous support for the rapidly changing proposal. Sancho's letter of 28 August 1778, on the other hand, expresses his relief at the Americans' apparent rejection of the ultimate offer: "I am very glad to see by the newspapers the American rebels have thought fit to reject the much too favourable terms, that, it is said, have been offered to them."[17] The stance of "Gustavus Vassa" in the newspaper letters is consistent with the patriotic pro-British position maintained by Equiano in *The Interesting Narrative* and by Sancho in his *Letters.*

The *Morning Post* letters reveal a familiarity with French and Latin and classical history not found elsewhere in Equiano's work. But the quite limited level of familiarity displayed is less impressive than that found in the posthumously published letters of the self-educated Sancho. It could easily have been achieved by an autodidact like Equiano through reading translations. Some of his learning is clearly a bit uncertain. His 10 March 1778 letter opens with an invocation of Galgacus (Calgacus), who rallied Britons to stop the advance of Julius Agricola, the Roman governor of Britain, into the Scottish

Highlands (Caledonia) in A.D. 83. He probably expected his readers to remember that Galgacus motivated his followers by exhorting them to resist enslavement by the Romans. Tacitus, Agricola's son-in-law, records in *Agricola* that although Agricola won the battle at Mons Graupius because of superior weapons and tactics, the courage and ferocity of the Caledonians led by Galgacus ultimately compelled the Romans to withdraw. His Galgacus seems to speak directly to Caesar, but in Tacitus's *Annals* Caratacus (Caractacus), not Galgacus, is the defeated Briton who addresses Claudius Caesar in Rome in A.D. 51. The speech Tacitus gives Caratacus does not include the sentiments cited by "Gustavus Vassa," though those sentiments are similar to some voiced by Galgacus in *Agricola.* Neither Galgacus nor Caratacus would have spoken the eighteenth-century Irish used by "Vassa" as an epigraph. And the inaccuracy of that anachronistic Irish indicates that he was neither a fluent nor a native speaker.[18] In several of the other *Morning Post* letters "Vassa" is more obviously engaged in fiction writing. For example, the 23 June 1778 letter is historical fiction, and that of 2 July 1778 is an Oriental tale.

Missing in the newspaper essays are the subjects of religion and slavery as well as the use of Biblical quotations so frequently found elsewhere in Equiano's writings, but the same may be said of Sancho's *Morning Post* letters as compared to his other writings. The absence of references to slavery in the *Morning Post* letters should not be surprising: they are not found in Sancho's newspaper letters either. Slavery was much more frequently discussed in print in England after the mid-1780s than before.

If the author of *The Interesting Narrative* is the same "Gustavus Vassa" who wrote the *Morning Post* letters, he clearly fictionalizes his identity – virtually no attempt was made to create a Swedish persona. He offers little autobiographical information. The emphasis on military affairs and the references to the martial experience of the speaker are reminiscent of the way Equiano recounts his experiences of the Seven Years' War in his *Interesting Narrative.* Rhetorical inflation enhances his credibility as a military advisor: "To tell you, that I have been a *Soldier*, would be of no consequence, unless I told you, that I have been a commander of men. Battles and sieges I have frequently been in; and sometimes I have been eminently successful, Mr. Editor. I never quitted the field unsuccessfully but once – that fatal day ended all my hopes of glory!" (23 June 1778).

As Equiano does in his *Interesting Narrative* and as Sancho does in his posthumously published correspondence, "Vassa" rhetorically positions himself in his *Morning Post* letters as the stranger in a strange land. As an outsider he observes the events around him: "The discourse turned upon the antiquity, and origin of the inhabitants of their different countries [England, Scotland, Wales, and Ireland]. Woes me! quoth I, who am not a native of either of the happier isles, but a continental spawn of accident; I can only be an humble hearer in this grand dispute" (11 June 1778). "Vassa," like Equiano, presents himself as a citizen of the world, a man without a country, and at one point tells of a man who appears to have much in common with the Equiano of *The Interesting Narrative*:

> An illustrious person, whose early misfortunes, from the mistaken zeal, and principle of his predecessors, obliged him to become a man of the world, and to endeavour the acquirement of such treasure, as no mortal power could deprive him of, while life remained, travelled Europe, Asia, Africa, and America, as a merchant, and philosopher; both honourable characters, and both of infinite advantage to society!
>
> In his youth he was bred to arms, and bore a distinguished rank before he was twenty years old. A series of misfortunes changed his turn of mind, and he felt a secret pleasure in pursuing, unknown, a scheme of life becoming a private gentleman. (2 July 1778)[19]

Furthermore, Equiano, Sancho, and the "Vassa" of the *Morning Post* share a belief in the civilizing and pacifying powers of international commerce, an interest in peoples at the social and geographical margins of English society and the British Empire, a fascination with the unusual, a recognition that a person may have more than one identity, and the possession of a sardonic sense of humor. The 9 November 1777 essay on the notorious Chevalier d'Eon, with its sociopolitical comments on hermaphroditism and cross-dressing and its anti-Gallicism, demonstrates a satiric side only occasionally and briefly displayed in *The Interesting Narrative*. Like his knowledge of events in America, his information about d'Eon could easily have been gleaned from the daily press, including the *Morning Post*, which extensively covered the dispute over the chevalier's sexual identity, especially when a jury in July 1777 ruled that a bet on d'Eon's gender was legal and in so doing recognized the chevalier as a woman. (D'Eon's death in 1810 revealed that he was a male.)

Although definite attribution of the "Gustavus Vassa" letters in the *Morning Post* to Equiano may never be possible, if they are his they would tell us much about his literary, political, and social interests, and they would explain his silence in *The Interesting Narrative* about the American Revolution.

During 1779 Equiano worked as a servant for Matthias Macnamara. While in his service Equiano frequently tried to get his fellow servants to join

him in prayer, an invitation that merely "excited their mockery." But his behavior made Macnamara recognize that Equiano "was of a religious turn"
(220). When asked what his religion was, Equiano "told [Macnamara] I was
a protestant of the church of England, agreeable to the thirty-nine articles of
that church; and that whomsoever I found to preach according to that doctrine, those I would hear" (220–21). Knowing that Equiano was a professed
Anglican, Macnamara told him that "he would, if I chose, as he thought I
might be of service in converting my countrymen to the Gospel-faith, get me
sent out as a missionary to Africa." Equiano was hesitant to embrace the idea
because of his missionary experience with the Mosquito prince, but Macnamara assured him that "he would apply to the Bishop of London to get me
ordained" (221).

With great expectations Equiano sent a "memorial," or written petition
and statement of facts, to Robert Lowth, the bishop of London until 1787. For
what may have been the first time in England, Equiano publicly claimed an
African birth and identity. But the identity he claimed was very much that of
an African as seen from a European perspective. He writes as if Africa were
one country, with a uniform language and culture:

To The Right Reverend Father in God, ROBERT, *Lord Bishop of London.*

THE MEMORIAL OF GUSTAVUS VASSA,
SHEWETH,

THAT your memorialist is a native of Africa, and has a knowledge of
the manners and customs of the inhabitants of that country.

That your memorialist has resided in different parts of Europe for
twenty-two years last past, and embraced the Christian faith in the year
1759.

That your memorialist is desirous of returning to Africa as a missionary, if encouraged by your Lordship, in hopes of being able to prevail
upon his countrymen to become Christians; and your memorialist is the
more induced to undertake the same, from the success that has attended
the like undertakings when encouraged by the Portuguese through their
different settlements on the coast of Africa, and also by the Dutch; both
governments encouraged the blacks, who by their education are qualified
to undertake the same, and are found more proper than European clergymen, unacquainted with the language and customs of the country.

Your memorialist's only motive for soliciting the office of a missionary
is, that he may be a means, under God, of reforming his countrymen
and persuading them to embrace the Christian religion. Therefore your

memorialist humbly prays your Lordship's encouragement and support
in the undertaking.

GUSTAVUS VASSA.

At Mr. Guthrie's, Tailor,
No. 17, Hedge-lane.

Macnamara wrote a letter in support of Equiano's application:

MY LORD, I have resided near seven years on the coast of Africa, for
most part of the time as commanding officer. From the knowledge I have
of the country and its inhabitants, I am inclined to think that the within
plan will be attended with great success, if countenanced by your Lordship. I beg further to represent to your Lordship, that the like attempts,
when encouraged by other governments, have met with uncommon success; and at this very time I know a very respectable character, a black
priest, at Cape Coast Castle. I know the within-named Gustavus Vassa,
and believe him a moral good man. I have the honour to be,

My Lord,
Your Lordship's
Humble and obedient Servant,
Grove, 11th March, 1779.
MATT. MACNAMARA. (221–22)

Equiano brought these letters as well as one written on his behalf by
Thomas Wallace, "who had resided in Africa for many years," to the bishop
of London. He was received "with much condescension and politeness; but
from some certain scruples of delicacy, and saying the Bishops were not of
opinion in sending a new missionary to Africa, he declined to ordain" him
(222, 223). The reasons the bishop rejected Equiano's petition are not difficult to imagine, and they probably had nothing to do with him personally.
The "certain scruples of delicacy" Equiano so circumspectly mentions most
likely refer to his choice of character references. Macnamara had been appointed lieutenant governor of Senegambia in 1774 and governor in November 1775, but he was not a well-liked man, and as an administrator he was
arrogant, self-important, impolitic, and deceitful. Edward Morse, chief justice
of Senegambia, described him as "a man without education, extremely brutal, vulgar, and avaricious, but possessed of an uncommon share of natural
parts [abilities]."[20] Charges of assault, subornation of perjury, and illegal trad-

ing with the French were brought against him in 1777. Thomas Wallace, his follower, was also accused of subornation of perjury. In June 1777 a jury in Africa found sufficient cause to have the cases resolved in London by the Board of Trade. In March 1778 the council informed King George III that it had determined the charges to be true and recommended that the men be relieved of their duties. Macnamara's appeal to the Privy Council was dismissed, and he was formally notified on 28 August 1778 that he was relieved. Equiano should have picked his character references with more care.

The bishop was also understandably reluctant to send another missionary to Africa, especially during the war that Equiano neglects to mention. The example of Philip Quaque, the "very respectable character, a black priest, at Cape Coast Castle," was not a wise one to invoke. He was the second missionary the Society for the Propagation of the Gospel in Foreign Parts had sent to Cape Coast Castle, the British administrative trading factory on the Gold Coast in what is now Ghana. The first was the Reverend Mr. Thomas Thomson, who went in 1751. Thomson's four-year-long mission was marked by illness and a complete lack of success in converting the native Africans. Before he gave up and returned to England, he proposed that several native youths "of good Families" be sent to England "to be educated in Literature and the Principles of the Christian Religion" and then brought back to Africa "to propagate it in their own Country."[21] As a result, in 1754 Quaque, at about thirteen years of age, was brought to England along with two other African youths. The society and the Company of Merchants Trading to Africa were their sponsors. The company conducted the slave trade and managed the coastal factories related to it. Two of the boys died in London, one after being inoculated against smallpox and the other in a madhouse. In 1765 the bishop of London ordained Quaque a priest. With his English wife Quaque returned the following year to the Gold Coast as a missionary. He was no more successful than Equiano had been among the Mosquito Indians, as his letters sent back to England over the next fifty years attest. He was constantly pleading for support from the society that was not forthcoming. In 1788 the society complained publicly about Quaque's failed ministry: "He has had no Success at all with the Native Blacks; and the Whole of his Mission seems to have been comprized in baptizing a few Mulattoes and Children of the Garrison. . . . [H]e has of late quite deviated from the Intentions of the Society, and his proper Line of Duty, by paying more attention to the Purposes of Trade than of Religion."[22] And although Quaque did not leave Africa until he was an adolescent, and he returned to his place of origin, he felt almost completely alienated culturally from his homeland and its people. It is difficult to imagine how much more alienated Equiano would have felt had the present bishop of London taken him up on his offer, even in the very unlikely event that he had been sent as a missionary to Igboland.

Having failed again in an attempt to become a missionary, Equiano spent the next few years seemingly looking for a calling. Between the time Equiano left Macnamara later in 1779 and "the spring of 1784," when he "thought of visiting [the] old ocean again," he spent several months between 1780 and 1782 as the servant of George Pitt, Baron Rivers. Rivers was commander of the eight-company regiment of the Dorsetshire militia, stationed during that period at Coxheath, near Maidstone, Kent, in southeastern England. Coxheath was the largest of the military camps established in early 1778 throughout southern England in anticipation of an invasion by combined French and Spanish forces. The danger Britain faced at home and Lord North's responsibility for it were subjects of some of the "Gustavus Vassa" letters in the *Morning Post*.[23] Following the British defeat at the battle of Saratoga, on 6 February 1778 France formed a military alliance with the American colonies rebelling against British rule. Spain came into the war on the side of the Americans in June 1778. Augustus Keppel, first Viscount Keppel, accepted command of the British home fleet on 29 March 1778, even though he was an outspoken opponent of the war with the colonists. Keppel was not prepared to stop the French from uniting their Mediterranean and Atlantic fleets in May 1778, withdrawing instead to Spithead to await reinforcements. Enraged at his implicit criticism of the government's naval policy, Lord North replaced him as commander of the Channel fleet with Sir Charles Hardy. Hardy had some forty ships of the line at his command, but in the face of the sixty ships in the combined French and Spanish fleet assembled to convey thirty thousand French and Spanish troops across the English Channel he, too, decided to withdraw to Portsmouth. As Ignatius Sancho wrote to a friend on 7 September 1779, Hardy was forced "to give up the sovereignty of the channel to the enemy – [First Lord of the Admiralty] L[or]d S[andwic]h is gone to Portsmouth, to be a witness of England's disgrace – and his own shame."[24] Sancho was far from the only one to "awake to fears of invasion, to noise, faction, drums, soldiers, and care: – the whole town [London] has now but two employments – the learning of French – and the exercise of arms."[25] Only the ineptitude of the French kept Britain from being invaded.

Once the war ended Equiano was again in search of a calling. In 1783 he toured "eight counties in Wales" out of curiosity. His curiosity almost cost him his life when a coal mine in Shropshire partially collapsed around him, burying one of his companions. The next year he signed on "as steward on board a fine new ship called the London, commanded by Martin Hopkins, and sailed for New York," a city of about thirty thousand people. Equiano "admired this city very much" because he found it "large and well-built, and abounds with provisions of all kinds" (223). The *London* returned to England in January 1785. Equiano thought Hopkins so "agreeable" an employer that he went with him on another voyage, this time to Philadelphia, whose population had doubled since he had first gone there twenty years earlier. Equiano left London in March and returned in August 1785. He was not so fortunate in what turned out to be his last voyage. He "shipped as a steward in an American ship called the Harmony, Captain John Willett, and left London in March 1786, bound to Philadelphia." Because they lost their foremast after only eleven days at sea they "had a nine weeks passage, which caused our trip not to succeed well, the market for our goods proving bad; and, to make it worse, my commander began to play me the like tricks as others too often practise on free negroes in the West Indies." Luckily, Equiano "found many friends" in Philadelphia "who in some measure prevented" Willett from doing so (226). Equiano returned to London in the first week of August 1786 to find a calling and a mission waiting for him.[26]

Chapter Ten

THE BLACK POOR

When he returned to London at the beginning of August 1786, Equiano "was very agreeably surprised to find, that the benevolence of government adopted the plan of some philanthropic individuals, to send the Africans from [England] to their native quarter, and that some vessels were then engaged to carry them to Sierra Leona; an act which redounded to the honour of all concerned in its promotion." The news "filled [him] with prayers and much rejoicing" (226). The "plan of some philanthropic individuals" was the direct result of the war Equiano neglects to mention in his autobiography.[1] Two days before Equiano returned to England, the philanthropist Granville Sharp wrote to the archbishop of Canterbury: "The present set of unfortunate Negroes that are starving in our streets, were brought here on very different occasions. Some, indeed, have been brought as servants, but chiefly by officers; others were Royalists from America; but most are seamen, who have navigated the King's ships from the East and West Indies, or have served in the war, and are thereby entitled to ample protection, and a generous requital."[2]

Although major hostilities on land and sea had effectively ceased with the victory by George Washington's army and his French naval allies over Charles Cornwallis at the battle of Yorktown, Virginia, on 19 October 1781, the Peace of Paris officially ending the American Revolution was not signed until 3 September 1783. The British retained control of Charleston, South Carolina, Savannah, Georgia, and New York City until the peace was signed. Under their control were thousands of former slaves who had fled to them in response to offers of freedom to any slaves of rebels who joined the British and who were evacuated by them at the end of the war, mainly to Canada and England. Of the approximately five hundred thousand slaves in British North America at the beginning of the civil war now known as the American Revolution, perhaps as many as one hundred thousand ended up behind the British lines. Although the majority of them were slaves of loyalist owners who removed them to the West Indies at the end of the war, approximately twenty-five thousand had emancipated themselves by fleeing to the British.[3] Under article 7 of the provisional peace treaty signed in Paris on 30 November 1782, Britain was obliged to withdraw its military forces "with all convenient Speed, and without causing any *Destruction*, or carrying away any *Negroes* or other *Property* of the American Inhabitants." The article was not altered in the final treaty. Despite the strong objections of George Washington and others whose slaves Britain had freed, the British insisted that article 7 did not apply to blacks who had sought refuge behind British lines before the treaty was signed. The British believed they were honor-bound not to return these slaves to their former owners. Hundreds of these former slaves eventually made their way to London after the war officially ended in 1783.

Paradoxically, although Britain had become the most significant participant in the transatlantic slave trade by the 1780s, for years it had also been the promised land of freedom to slaves in British colonies, particularly those in North America. As Equiano's experiences on ships of the Royal Navy and in England demonstrated, the legal status of slavery in Britain was contested long before the American Revolution. Pascal would not have sneaked Equiano out of England in 1762 had he believed he had an unquestioned right to sell him. And Equiano would not have threatened to take Pascal to court in London had he not believed he had legal standing there he knew he lacked in the British colonies.

With the de jure status of slavery so uncertain in England, not surprisingly its de facto status remained unclear in the eighteenth century. The magistrate Sir John Fielding complained in 1768 that slaves brought to London from the West Indies no sooner arrive here, than they put themselves on a Footing with other Servants, become intoxicated with Liberty, grow refractory, and either by Persuasion of others, or from their own Inclinations, begin to expect Wages according to their own Opinion of their Merits. . . . [T]here are already a great Number of black Men and Women who have made themselves so troublesome and dangerous to the Families who brought them over as to get themselves discharged; they enter into Societies, and make it their Business to corrupt and dissatisfy the Mind of every fresh black Servant that comes to *England*; first, by getting them christened or married, which they inform them makes them free (tho' it has been adjudged by our most able Lawyers, that neither of these Circumstances alter the Master's Property in a Slave). However it so far answers their Purpose, that it gets the Mob on their Side, and makes it not only difficult but dangerous to the Proprietor of these Slaves to recover the Possession of them, when once they are spirited away.[4]

Granville Sharp led the campaign to have the courts overturn the Yorke-Talbot opinion and thus declare the de facto illegal status of slavery in England de jure as well. Born in Durham on 19 November 1735 as the youngest son of the archdeacon of Northumberland and the grandson of the archbishop of York, Sharp received only a grammar-school education and was destined for a trade. While apprenticed to a Quaker linen draper in London Sharp taught himself Greek and Hebrew to better understand the Bible. His first publications were on biblical scholarship and linguistics. In 1758 he obtained a position in the Ordnance Department that he felt compelled to resign in 1776 because of his opposition to war with the rebellious American colonies.

Sharp's introduction to the question of the legality of slavery came in 1765 in the person of Jonathan Strong, a sixteen- or seventeen-year-old slave. Strong's master, a lawyer and planter named David Lisle, had brought him to London from Barbados. A brutal owner, Lisle had thrown Strong out into the street after having nearly fatally pistol-whipped him. Sharp met Strong outside the door of Sharp's brother William, who gave free medical help to the poor. Two years later Lisle ran into Strong, now fully recovered with the medical and financial aid of the Sharps. Lisle then sold Strong to James Kerr, a Jamaica planter, for thirty pounds, to be paid when Lisle delivered Strong to a ship bound for Jamaica. Lisle hired two slave catchers, who seized Strong and put him in jail. Strong sent word of his situation to Granville

Granville Sharp, by George Dance. As a leader of the struggle in the British courts to end slavery, Sharp achieved his most significant victory with the Mansfield ruling of 1772, which declared that slaves brought to England could not be forced to return to enslavement in the colonies. Known by Equiano since the late 1770s, Sharp subscribed for two copies of *The Interesting Narrative*. (National Portrait Gallery, London)

Sharp, who gained his release through the intervention of the Lord Mayor of London. Kerr sued Sharp for loss of property, and Lisle challenged him to a duel. When Sharp's own solicitors advised him that Strong was legally a slave and thus a piece of property, Sharp bought a complete law library to prepare himself to argue the law. The results of Sharp's legal research intimidated the plaintiff's lawyers so much that they declined to pursue the case.

Sharp won by default, but the experience determined him to gain a definitive legal ruling that would overturn the 1729 opinion of Yorke and Talbot. While waiting for a suitable case Sharp published his refutation of Yorke and Talbot. *A Representation of the Injustice and Dangerous Tendency of Tolerating Slavery; or of Admitting the Least Claim of Private Property in the Persons of Men, in England* (1769) also includes a denunciation of the hypocrisy of the American colonists who practiced slavery while objecting to political oppression. Sharp's intervention on Strong's behalf quickly became well known in London's African British community, and he was appealed to in the cases of the kidnapped former slaves Mary Hylas in 1766 and Thomas Lewis in 1770, both of whom were physically and legally rescued through Sharp's efforts. But neither case resulted in the definitive ruling against the institution of slavery he sought. He did not have to wait long for the case he wanted.

In 1771 in London the slave James Somerset ran away from his master,

Charles Stewart, a Boston customs official. Stewart had brought Somerset from Massachusetts to England in 1769. Stewart recaptured Somerset on 26 November 1771 and intended to send him out of the country on a ship bound for Jamaica under the command of Capt. John Knowles. When word of Somerset's situation reached Sharp through the black community, he immediately took action. Sharp and several others successfully urged William Murray, first Earl of Mansfield and Lord Chief Justice of the King's Bench, the highest common-law court in England, to issue a writ of habeas corpus ordering the captain to bring Somerset before the court two days after he had been recaptured. Sharp convinced several lawyers to argue Somerset's case free of charge. The inexperienced Francis Hargrave, who wrote an influential account of his defense and went on to establish a distinguished legal career, also volunteered his legal services on behalf of Somerset.

Anticipating possible defeat, the proslavery lobby predicted dire consequences before Lord Mansfield announced the court's decision. In his *Considerations on the Negroe Cause Commonly So Called, Addressed to the Right Honourable Lord Mansfield . . . By a West Indian* (1772) Samuel Estwick observes that were "the decision [to] be in favour of the Negroe . . . the knowledge of their being free might spirit them up to insurrections in America, yet it would put a stop to their importation [into England] by their owners, and they should be more usefully kept and employed in the colonies to which they belonged."[5] At the time, Estwick was living in England as the assistant agent for Barbados representing the interests of the colony's slave-owning planter class.

Not all opponents of slavery saw the Mansfield ruling as an unqualified victory. Posing as a Quaker, Benjamin Franklin pointed out anonymously in the *London Chronicle* on 20 June 1772 that Britain's expected self-congratulatory response to a decision in Somerset's favor would not be fully justified. Americans did not have a monopoly on hypocrisy when the subject was slavery: "*Pharisaical Britain!* To pride thyself in setting free *a single Slave* that happens to land on thy coasts, while thy Merchants in all thy ports are encouraged by thy laws to continue a commerce whereby so many *hundreds of thousands* are dragged into a slavery that can scarce be said to end with their lives, since it is entailed on their posterity!"

Having failed in his attempts to get the opposing parties to settle the case out of court, Mansfield was finally forced to render his decision on 22 June 1772 as Equiano was returning from the West Indies. The court ruled that an owner could not legally force a slave in England back to the colonies.[6] Because the practice of officially recording the oral opinions delivered from the King's Bench did not begin until the nineteenth century, various accounts of Mansfield's words exist. The most authoritative account is probably that of Capel Lofft, a student of law at Lincoln's Inn at the time of the ruling. Called to the bar in 1775, the following year Lofft published a collection of reports of cases in King's Bench. According to Lofft, Mansfield remarked that "the state of slavery is of such a nature, that it is incapable of being introduced on any reasons, moral or political: but only positive law, which preserves its force long after the reasons, occasion, and time itself from whence it was created, is erased from memory: It's so odious, that nothing can be suffered to support it but positive law."[7]

With the Mansfield ruling Sharp appeared to have moved from winning battles to winning the war against slavery in England. Although Mansfield's ruling technically established only that a slave could not be seized by his master and forced against his will to leave England and that a slave could get a writ of habeas corpus to prevent his master's action, the judgment was widely considered then and since as the moment slavery was abolished in England. The Mansfield ruling did not abolish slavery in England de jure, but it certainly undermined it de facto by indisputably denying slave masters the legal coercive power of removal to the colonies. Lacking that power, slave owners could no longer enforce their claims of possession because slaves on English soil could legally emancipate themselves by flight. Sharp made sure through his publications that the ruling's implications would not be ignored.

The popular and pamphlet press quickly announced the ruling and discussed its possible significance. Supporters of slavery recognized that they could no longer assume that the British courts and public would continue to passively accept slavery as an institution. Edward Long, a proslavery former planter, judge, and government official in Jamaica, warned that the decision meant that "the laws of *Great Britain* do not authorize a master to reclaim his fugitive slave, confine or transport him out of the kingdom. In other words; that a Negroe slave, coming from the colonies into *Great Britain*, becomes, *ipso facto*, Free."[8]

London's African British community greeted the Mansfield decision euphorically. The *Gentleman's Magazine* reported in its June 1772 issue:

June 22. The Court of the King's Bench gave judgment in the case of Somerset the slave, viz. that Mr. Stuart his master had no power to compel him on board a ship, or to send him back to the plantations. Lord

Mansfield stated the matter thus: The only question before us is, Is the cause returned sufficient for remanding the slave? If not, he must be discharged. The cause returned is, the slave absented himself, and departed from his master's service, and refused to return and serve him during his stay in England; whereupon, by his master's orders, he was put on board the ship by force, and there detained in secure custody, to be carried out of the kingdom, and sold. So high an act of dominion was never in use here; no master was ever allowed to take a slave by force to be sold abroad, because he had deserted from his service, or for any other reason whatever. We cannot say the cause set forth by this return is allowed or approved of by the laws of this kingdom: therefore, the man must be discharged.

On 23 June the *Morning Chronicle* noted that Mansfield's speech was "as guarded, cautious, and concise, as it could possibly [be] drawn up." The newspaper went on to describe the reaction of the blacks in the audience to the ruling:

> Several Negroes were in court yesterday, to hear the event of a cause so interesting to their tribe, and after the judgment of the court was known, bowed with profound respect to the Judges, and shaking each other by the hand, congratulated themselves upon the recovery of the rights of human nature, and their happy lot that permitted them to breathe the free air of England. – No sight upon earth could be more pleasingly affecting to the feeling mind, than the joy which shone at that instant in these poor men's sable countenances.

The *Public Advertiser* reported on 25 June that black Britons expressed their gratitude more materially: "A Subscription is now raising among a great Number of Negroes, in and about this Metropolis, for the purpose of presenting Somerset with a handsome Gratuity, for having so nobly stood up in Defence of the natural Rights of the sable Part of the human Creation."

In the wake of the ruling, advertisements for sales of slaves, notices of runaway slaves, and attempts to enforce colonial slave laws in Britain – all already rare in England – disappeared.[9] In 1777 Edmund Burke understood the Mansfield judgment to mean that "every man putting his foot on English ground, every stranger owing only a local and temporary allegiance, even a negro slave, who had been sold in the colonies and under an act of parliament, became as free as every other man who breathed the same air with him."[10] Building on the precedent Mansfield set, in 1778 the Scottish court declared slavery illegal in Scotland. Thomas Hutchinson had been governor of Massachusetts at the time of the Mansfield ruling but fled to England after hostilities broke out. On 29 August 1779, during dinner at the home of the Lord Chief Justice, Hutchinson, now an exiled loyalist, told Mansfield that "all Americans who had brought Blacks [to England after the ruling] had, as far as I knew, relinquished their property in them, and rather agreed to give them wages, or suffered [allowed] them to go free." "His Ldship" responded that "there had been no determination that they were free, the judgment (meaning the case of Somerset) went no further than to determine the Master had no right to compel the slave to go into a foreign country, &c."[11] Many contemporaneous observers on both sides of the Atlantic, however, understandably construed the Mansfield ruling as the practical implementation of the constitutional proscription of slavery Sir William Blackstone had described in his extremely influential *Commentaries on the Laws of England* (1765–69). The first Vinerian Professor of Law at Oxford University, Blackstone had delivered the substance of the *Commentaries* as lectures several years earlier. Blackstone's *Commentaries* remains the standard legal reference source on English common law and the U.S. legal system that has developed from it.

Many Britons, especially the thousands of African descent, considered the Mansfield decision an emancipation proclamation. Granville Sharp's heroic status in the black community was undisputed. On 3 August 1779 Ignatius Sancho sent a copy of "Mr. Sharpe's strictures upon slavery" to a friend, telling him, "I think [it] of consequence to every one of humane feelings."[12] In an undated letter of thanks to Sharp ten blacks described themselves to him as "those who were considered as slaves, even in England itself, till your aid and exertions set us free."[13] Quobna Ottobah Cugoano, the most radical African British voice in the eighteenth century, celebrated the ruling in a later version of his *Thoughts and Sentiments on the Evil of Slavery* (1791):

For so it was considered as criminal, by the laws of Englishmen, when the tyrannical paw and the monster of slavery took the man [Somerset] by the neck, in the centre of the British freedom, and thought henceforth to compel him to his involuntary subjection of slavery and oppression; it was wisely determined by some of the most eminent and learned counsellors in the land. The whole of that affair rested solely upon that humane and indefatigable friend of mankind, GRENVILLE SHARP esq. whose name we should always mention with the greatest reverence and honor. The noble decision, thereby, before the Right Hon. Lord Chief Justice MANSFIELD, and the parts taken by the learned Counsellor HAR-GRAVE, are the surest proofs of the most amiable disposition of the laws of Englishmen.[14]

Not surprisingly, by the 1770s Equiano was also aware of the role Sharp had played in the Mansfield decision and of his consequent reputation as a "well-known philanthropist" to blacks. Years before Equiano turned against the institution of slavery, he attempted to save a fellow black from being illegally forced from England into West Indian slavery. In early 1774, disillusioned by the behavior of "those, who in general termed themselves Christians," Equiano "determined at last to set out for Turkey, and there to end my days." He "sought for a master, and found a Captain John Hughes, commander of a ship called Anglicania, fitting out in the river Thames, and bound to Smyrna in Turkey. I shipped myself with him as a steward; at the same time I recommended to him a very clever black man, John Annis, as a cook." Annis had spent many years on the Caribbean island of Saint Kitts as the slave of William Kirkpatrick, "from whom he parted by consent," before Annis went to England (179). Unfortunately, like many other West Indian whites in Equiano's experience, Kirkpatrick was not a man of his word. On his frequent trips to England he had paid a number of captains trading to Saint Kitts to kidnap Annis and bring him back to the Caribbean. "[W]hen all their attempts and schemes of kidnapping proved abortive, Mr. Kirkpatrick came to our ship at Union-stairs [a landing place on the north bank of the Thames about 3.5 miles downriver from Westminster Abbey], on Easter Monday, April the 4th, with two wherry-boats and six men, having learned that the man was on board; and tied, and forcibly took him away from the ship, in the presence of the crew and the chief mate, who had detained him after he had information to come away." Equiano reasonably suspected that Captain Hughes and his mate conspired with Kirkpatrick in the kidnapping. They made no attempt to regain Annis's freedom, nor did the captain agree to give Equiano the nearly five pounds in wages he owed Annis. Equiano "proved the only friend he had, who attempted to regain him his liberty, if possible, having known the want of liberty myself." As soon as he could, Equiano discovered the name of the ship his friend had been taken to downriver, but he learned that it had already sailed.

Having failed to save Annis, Equiano sought a legal judgment against

Kirkpatrick to stop him from going from England to Scotland. With a writ of habeas corpus and a bailiff Equiano staked out Kirkpatrick's residence near Saint Paul's Cathedral. Thinking that Equiano might do so, Kirkpatrick posted a guard and had someone impersonate him in his house. But Equiano out-smarted Kirkpatrick by whitening his face so he wouldn't be recognized and contriving "a well-plotted stratagem" to enable the bailiff to arrest Kirk-patrick and bring him to a judge the following morning. Kirkpatrick, how-ever, was released on bail because he pled that "he had not the body [of Annis] in custody." Frustrated in his own attempt to rescue his friend Annis, Equiano sought the advice of the man who had saved James Somerset two years earlier: "I proceeded immediately to that well-known philanthropist, Granville Sharp, Esq. who received me with the utmost kindness, and gave me every instruction that was needful on the occasion" (180). This may have been the first time the two met. Sharp later told his niece Jemima Sharp that Gen. James Edward Oglethorpe, the philanthropic founder of the originally slave-free colony of Georgia, had recommended Equiano to him.[15] If it was their first meeting, it certainly was not their last. Several years later Sharp gave Equiano a copy of one of his books, but we cannot identify which one because all that remains is its flyleaf. Equiano expressed his personal opinion of Sharp on the blank page:

> Gustavus V.
> His Book.
>   Given to him
> By that Truly Pious,
> And Benevolent man
> Mr. Granville Sharp.
>   April the 13th 1779.
>   London.

Equiano came away from his 1774 meeting with Sharp "in full hopes that I should gain the unhappy man his liberty, with the warmest sense of grati-tude towards Mr. Sharp for his kindness" (180). Unfortunately, the attorney Equiano engaged on behalf of Annis "proved unfaithful," taking his money but doing nothing for months, while Annis was taken back to Saint Kitts. Equiano "made attempts to go after him at a great hazard, but was sadly disappointed." From "two very moving letters" by Annis and from reports he later received "by some very respectable families, now in London," Equiano learned that "when the poor man arrived at St. Kitt's, he was, according to custom, staked to the ground with four pins through a cord, two on his wrists, and two on his ancles, was cut and flogged most unmercifully, and afterwards loaded cruelly with irons about his neck." Annis remained a slave "till kind death released him out of the hands of his tyrants" (181). The Annis affair was newsworthy because Kirkpatrick's actions were clearly illegal in light of the recent Mansfield decision. According to an account in the 27 April 1774 issue of the *London Chronicle*, legal action was under way "to proceed against the Master; and also on the Captain's return to proceed against him for violently and by force taking a man out of the kingdom." But such actions could no longer help Annis. Despite the Mansfield decision, blacks remained in jeopardy as long as slavery was legal in any of the British colonies and as long as an owner was willing to risk arrest for illegally taking a black from England to the Americas.

Colonial newspapers were reporting and discussing the possible significance of the Mansfield decision by the end of the summer of 1772. On Monday, 21 September 1772, the *Boston Gazette* pointed out the perceived implications of the Mansfield decision for any slave owner contemplating taking a slave to England: "*June* 22. A Correspondent observes, that as Blacks are free now in this country [England], Gentlemen will not be so fond of bringing them here as they used to be, it being computed that there are about 14000 blacks in this country." The *Virginia Gazette* (Williamsburg, Virginia), which had published on 27 August 1772 a full account of the Mansfield decision taken, without acknowledgment, from the June 1772 issue of the *Scots Magazine* (Edinburgh), reported several cases of slaves seeking the promised land of England. By 1773 even illiterate rural slaves were aware of England as a sanctuary. On 30 September 1773 slave owner John Austin Finnie advertised in the *Virginia Gazette* for two runaway slaves, "a Wench, named AMY, of a very black Complexion, about 27 Years old," and "a Fellow, *African* born, named BACCHUS, about 19 Years of Age, [who] speaks somewhat broken [English]." Finnie noted that he had "some Reason to believe they will endeavour to get out of the Colony, particularly to *Britain*, where they imagine they will be free (a Notion now too prevalent among the Negroes, greatly to the Vexation and Prejudice of their Masters)." On 30 June 1774 Gabriel Jones of Augusta, Georgia, advertised for another runaway slave named Bacchus, who, Jones predicted, would "probably endeavour to pass for a Freeman by the Name of *John Christian*, and attempt to get on Board some Vessel bound for *Great Britain*, from the Knowledge he has of the late Determination of *Somerset*'s Case."

Some colonists anticipated the application of the Mansfield judgment to America. For example, on 8 January 1774 the loyalist Richard Wells wrote anonymously in the *Pennsylvania Packet*, "I contend, that by the laws of the English constitution, and by our *own declarations*, the instant a Negro sets his foot in America, he is as free as if he had landed in England." The application of the Mansfield decision to the American colonies was questionable because it had been rendered in the court of common law, based on the unwritten English constitution and historical precedent. Unlike the colonies, England had no positive (explicit) laws regarding the institution of slavery on its soil, though of course the English constitution allowed for the making of such positive laws and applying them at home and in the colonies. Blackstone's distinction between "two species of colonies" explained the differing legal status of slavery in the colonies and in England. In effect, each colony had the authority to write positive law on the subject in the absence of any positive metropolitan law:

> But there is a difference between these two species of colonies, with respect to the laws by which they are bound. For it is held, that if an uninhabited country be discovered and planted by English subjects, all the English laws are immediately there in force. For as the law is the birthright of every subject, so wherever they go they carry their laws with them. But in conquered or ceded countries, that have already laws of their own, the king may indeed alter and change those laws; but, till he does actually change them, the antient laws of the country remain, unless such as are against the law of God, as in the case of an infidel country.
>
> Our American plantations are principally of this latter sort, being obtained in the last century either by right of conquest and driving out the natives (with what natural justice I shall not at present enquire) or by treaties. And therefore the common law of England, as such, has no allowance or authority there; they being no part of the mother country, but distinct (though dependent) dominions.[16]

Blackstone's position was widely known in North America. Burke reported in 1775: "I hear that they have sold nearly as many of Blackstone's Commentaries in America as in England."[17]

Friend and foe of slavery alike recognized that the Mansfield decision of 1772 clearly allowed slaves to emancipate themselves in England. In contrast, the Declaration of Independence, signed four years later in Philadelphia, offered nothing to the nearly five hundred thousand blacks in North America,

20 percent of the total population. (The five hundred thousand blacks in the British West Indies, more than 90 percent of the population, were unaffected by either the Mansfield ruling or the Declaration of Independence.) The Mansfield judgment brought to public attention the legal status of the people of African descent who were British yet not English. Their political status became a subject for public argument in light of the ideological conflict during the American Revolution, and their status as human beings was disputed during the crusade in the 1790s to end British involvement in the slave trade with Africa.

The hypocrisy of the white North Americans who demanded liberty for themselves while they enslaved others underscored the difference between the legal statuses of African Britons in the mother country and the colonies. Their hypocrisy prompted criticism by Granville Sharp and others on both sides of the Atlantic. In 1775 Samuel Johnson asked sarcastically, "How is it we hear the loudest yelps for liberty among the drivers of Negroes?"[18] The white Americans' position gave their English opponents an easy opportunity to demonstrate moral and political superiority. Thus, in a letter written to an American correspondent in 1776, Thomas Day, the author of best-selling anti-slavery poetry and fiction, observes:

Slavery . . . is a crime so monstrous against the human species that all those who practise it deserve to be extirpated from the earth. . . .

If men would be consistent, they must admit all the consequences of their own principles; and you and your countrymen are reduced to the dilemma of either acknowledging the rights of your Negroes, or of surrendering your own. – If there be certain natural and universal rights, as the declarations of your Congress [including the Declaration of Independence] so repeatedly affirm, I wonder how the unfortunate Africans have incurred their forfeiture. – Is it the antiquity, or the virtues, or the great qualities of the English Americans, which constitutes the difference, and entitles them to rights from which they totally exclude more than a fourth part of the species? – Or do you choose to make use of that argument, which the great Montesquieu has thrown out as the severest ridicule, that they are black, and you white; that you have lank, long hair, while theirs is short and woolly?[19]

Given African Britons' association of England with potential liberation, slaves understandably saw King George III as a potential savior, not the tyrant depicted in the Declaration of Independence. Under common law the monarch was the legal guardian of the rights of his subjects, particularly those who were unable to defend themselves. On 7 November 1775 the royal governor of Virginia, John Murray, fourth Earl of Dunmore, issued a proclamation promising freedom to all rebel-owned slaves and indentured servants who joined the British forces. Five hundred of the former slaves were organized into the Ethiopian Regiment. George Washington warned Col. Richard Henry Lee of Lord Dunmore's "diabolical schemes": "If that man . . . is not crushed before spring he will become the most formidable enemy America has; his strength will increase as a snowball by rolling; and faster if some expedient cannot be hit upon to convince the slaves and servants of the impotency of his designs."[20] In 1779 British general Henry Clinton issued the Phillipsburg Proclamation in New York offering freedom of employment to any slave deserting an enemy owner and forbidding the sale or restitution to owners of former slaves. Not surprisingly, most of the eighteenth-century blacks whose voices we can recover, either directly or through intermediaries, chose a British rather than an American identity, taking advantage of the British promises of emancipation for refugee slaves of the colonial rebels (but not for refugees from loyalist masters).

Not all eighteenth-century black writers, of course, chose to retain a British identity. As Phillis Wheatley's poem "To His Excellency General Washington" (1775) demonstrates, some free blacks chose the new African American identity now available.[21] In the aftermath of the Revolution, during the period known as the "first emancipation," the antislavery movement grew, especially in the North. The petition of the ex-slave Belinda to the Massachusetts legislature and Benjamin Banneker's letter to Thomas Jefferson indicate how optimistic some African Americans were about the possibility of achieving universal freedom and justice based on principles established during the Revolution. For every Crispus Attucks who identified with the rebel cause, many more blacks chose the other side. After the war Britain and not the new United States continued to serve as the promised land of freedom for present and former slaves in the British Empire such as Equiano, who had spent about five years of his life as a slave in the West Indies as well as about a month in Virginia. Not surprisingly, in his posthumously published *Letters* (1782) Ignatius Sancho never questions the validity of the British cause in the war he supported against the Americans led by the man he mockingly calls "Washintub." In 1789 Equiano referred to "England, where my heart had always been," and in 1793, writing from the Sierra

Leone settlement in Africa, David George, who had been born and raised a slave in South Carolina, considered England to be "home" after finding refuge with the British army during the American Revolution.[22]

The black loyalists arriving from America at the end of the American Revolution joined the thousands of blacks already resident in England. Estimates of the total number of blacks in England in the last quarter of the eighteenth century range between five and twenty thousand.[23] The exact number will never be known because ethnicity was not systematically recorded during the period. Records of infant baptisms rarely indicated color or ethnic origins, though records of noninfant baptisms often did. Eighteenth-century marriage records frequently are silent on ethnicity. If, for example, we did not know from external sources that Ignatius Sancho and his wife, Anne, were both of African descent, we could not derive that fact from their marriage record. Nor could we tell Sancho's ethnicity from the votes he cast as a property owner in two Westminster elections for members of Parliament. Eighteenth-century terminology further complicates any attempt at precision. Since *black* referred to complexion and hair color as well as to geographical origin, people from the Indian subcontinent as well as North American Indians were often called black. The social and legal status of many of the various peoples called black in eighteenth-century England was also murky. Domestic workers were referred to as servants, whether paid or not, so identifying the slaves among them is often impossible. The condition of many blacks was somewhere between enslaved and free, earning them "neither wages nor the whip," as one historian puts it.[24] Another classifies them as "slave-servants" to reflect their ambiguous status.[25]

Many of the blacks in England before the 1780s had arrived there from the Americas either as domestic servants or as seamen. During the seventeenth century black servants became relatively expensive signs of conspicuous consumption and imperial connections, exotic products from the colonies affordable at first only by the wealthy. Black boys and men were especially desired as servants in wealthy and socially pretentious households, particularly in the roles of butler and valet, which brought them into frequent contact with the public. Black servants retained their appeal as status symbols through the eighteenth century: Sancho was the butler of the Duke of Montagu; Cugoano was the servant of Richard Cosway, principal painter to the Prince of Wales. In 1772 Edward Long charged that black servants in Britain were "more for ostentation than any *laudable* use."[26] But, like other originally luxurious colonial products such as coffee, tea, and tobacco, by the end of the eighteenth century black servants were found in much humbler situations as well. Pascal bought Equiano as a present for his cousins. The prints of William Hogarth show that by the middle third of the century blacks were found at all levels of society, including among the poor. But at whatever level of society, blacks were conspicuous because of the color of their skin. The far greater demand for black male servants than for black female servants led to a gender imbalance in the black slave-servant community in England. Consequently, black male/white female couples were more common than the reverse. Such couples were occasionally noted but only very rarely condemned. No record exists, for example, that Equiano's marriage in 1792 to an Englishwoman led to any discrimination against him, his wife, or their two daughters.

Black seamen were discharged in England along with their white shipmates after service with the Royal Navy or after having worked as sailors on merchant vessels. Equiano and his fellow black writers Briton Hammon, James Albert Ukawsaw Gronniosaw, and John Marrant are the best-known examples of former seamen of African descent.[27] Fewer in number than blacks of African descent were the blacks, or "lascars," from the British and Portuguese East Indies who had usually reached England in vessels of the Royal Navy or the East India Company. An article in the *Public Advertiser* on 7 January 1786 explained that the lascars, many of them "strangers to our language and country," ended up in England because they had been needed "to navigate our ships in the room of our sailors who died in the East Indies." They also replaced British sailors who had left their ships in hopes of making their fortunes in India. In the same issue of the *Public Advertiser* "Veritas" defended the East India Company's treatment of its lascar employees: "Every Black who comes over in the East India Company's service, is found in lodging at Stepney, in habitations appointed for that purpose, and one shilling per day during his stay in this country, and until the Company send them out again. This is absolutely the fact. Those who are unprovided for are brought into England by the men of war, and to the eternal shame of our Government, they are not allowed the common necessaries of life." But another writer pointed out that whatever provision the company may give, the sight of "miserable Lascars . . . still seen begging in our streets" showed it to be insufficient. "Veritas" was correct that the company was obligated to care for its employees while they were in England. In return, the lascars were required to return to India on the first available company ship needing their labor. But since in practice the company contracted with private shippers, disputes over who was responsible for lascar crew members were common. And lascar service on ships going to India was often not needed.[28]

Within just a few years after the American Revolution blacks of both African and East Indian origin and descent found themselves in the same desperate circumstances as many poor whites during the postwar economic slump. Eighteenth-century Britain was not a modern welfare state. The national government did not provide care or employment for the deprived and out-of-work. The destitute depended for sustenance, housing, and employment on poor-law relief administered by local authorities and supplemented by any available private or organized charity. But the relief mandated by the poor law required the recipient to have a "settlement," a parish obligated by law to support its indigent, often through employment in a local poorhouse. Whites and blacks born outside of England and never employed in any one parish for at least a year were legally rootless and thus ineligible for local government help. Since most of the black loyalists had not owned any property to lose during the American Revolution, very few were eligible for compensation from the Commission for American Claims. The lascars had even less hope for legal redress from their distress, which was evident to many. In the *Public Advertiser* of 16 March 1785 "Senex" was "shocked at the number of miserable objects, Lascars, that I see shivering and starving in the streets." Several months later, on 6 December 1785, a correspondent for the *Public Advertiser* lamented that the destitute lascars were "a reproach to us as a civilized country."

The East Indian lascars were originally the primary objects of charity aimed at the black poor during the postwar period. The charitable impulse that developed into the project to settle the black poor in Sierra Leone in 1787 began quite modestly the year before. Resettlement was not even mentioned in the original appeal in the 5 January 1786 issue of the *Public Advertiser* for contributions to allow the privately funded distribution of four-pound loaves of bread to continue:

> Whereas there are now wandering about the Streets, in the greatest Distress, many Asiatic Blacks, who have been brought into this country in the India Ships, being in want of the common Necessaries of Lodging, Cloathes, Fire, and Provisions, during the Severity of the Weather, some of whom have absolutely expired in the Streets, no Provision whatever being made for these unhappy Wretches; it is humbly recommended to the Public, to consider their hard Fate, and to provide for their Relief.

A Gentleman, commiserating these unhappy People, has made a Beginning to this charitable Work, by authorizing Mr. Brown, Baker, in Wigmore-street, Cavendish-square, to give a Quartern Loaf to every Black in Distress, who will apply on Saturday next, between the Hours of Twelve and Two.

Subscriptions for this Purpose are taken in at Mr. Faulder's, Bookseller, in Bond-street.

The size and scope of the charitable project grew rapidly. The response to the initial advertisement was so great that on 10 January the *Public Advertiser* announced the formation of a "Committee of Gentlemen," known officially as the Committee for the Relief of the Black Poor, to deal more comprehensively with the problems of the lascars: "Originally" the charity "was only intended to afford a temporary Relief in the Article of Subsistence; but as the Public seem to enter into the Sufferings of these distressed Foreigners, it is hoped that they will carry this Charity much farther, by not only affording them a present Relief, but preventing them suffering in future." The committee consisted of wealthy Anglican and Quaker businessmen and bankers from the City of London known for their philanthropy. In the 16 January issue the newly formed committee advertised that it was now accepting subscriptions at four locations across greater London and that "a considerable Number of African and West India Blacks, and also Blacks from the East Indies" were destitute. On 27 January the newspaper published the charity's lists of its seventeen-member committee, chaired by Montagu Burgoyne, and its 150 men and women subscribers. Their contributions ranged from the five pounds given by Burgoyne to the one shilling received from "A Servant." By that date the committee had "already discovered about 250 Persons, who are Objects of Charity. Of this Number Thirty-five only, are from the East-Indies. One Hundred affirm, that they came over in his Majesty's Ships, having served in the late War. The greatest Part of the Remainder are such, as by various Accidents have been brought from America, and the West Indies, and are desirous of being employed as Seamen." The committee noted that the charity distributed to private individuals would have public benefits by removing beggars and possibly criminals from the streets, rendering a "considerable Advantage to the Police of this Country."

The scope of the project evolved even further in the 3 February announcement in the *Public Advertiser:* "It is the particular End of the Committee to give a temporary Relief to the Objects of this Charity; and in future to provide them with Cloathes, and a Settlement Abroad." On 13 February the amount subscribed totaled more than £550, including £5 5s. from William Pitt, the prime minister. The number of "Objects of Charity" had grown to 320, and the plan now sought to provide "them with the Means of comfortable Assistance in different Settlements Abroad as Freemen." The amount subscribed rose to nearly £650 on 24 February, and the committee stopped trying to keep count of the needy: "The Committee who are investigating this Object find there are considerable numbers, who might be happy to [be] put in a Condition of getting their Bread, in Climes best suited to their Constitutions. Those who are in extreme Distress [have] been relieved for a Season, and there is a Prospect of making a Beginning in providing for some in a proper Manner Abroad." On 17 March, two days before Equiano sailed from London aboard the *Harmony*, the committee, now chaired by Benjamin Johnson, had collected just over £800, nearly £70,000, or $140,000, in today's money.

When the announcement that the subscription had closed appeared in the *Public Advertiser* on 18 April, the committee had collected £890 from hundreds of contributors, many of them future subscribers to Equiano's *Interesting Narrative*. It had dispersed £793 10s. Since 15 March the committee had spent £69 on patients in its hospital, £135 to feed "above 300 Persons," £55 for clothing, £28 for miscellaneous expenses (outpatient care, a clerk, advertisements, etc.), and £12 9s. 6d. on "six sent abroad." In addition to caring for the needy in England the committee had begun resettling people on its own. Its subscribers included Granville Sharp, the hero of the black community, and William Wilberforce, soon to lead the campaign in the House of Commons to abolish the transatlantic slave trade. The largest single donation – £67 – came from "Several of the Society of the People called Quakers," made through Samuel Hoare, Jr., a Quaker member of the committee. George Rose, one of the two secretaries to the Treasury Board, gave £30. Rose also directed the government's subsidies for proministry newspapers, including the *Public Advertiser*. The committee gave aid "at different Times and on divers occasions" to 460 people, but now "the further Hopes they have of making their Situation more comfortable, and the Means of doing it, have been stated and referred to the Wisdom and Humanity of Government."

The need for more government involvement became obvious once attention shifted from the needs of the lascars to the plight of the far more numerous black loyalists from America. The growing number of subscribers with military backgrounds such as Lord Cornwallis reflected the changing emphasis. "Z," a correspondent writing to the *Public Advertiser* on 19 January 1786, pointed out the government's debt to the loyalists, its moral obligation to help them, and the desirability of resettling them overseas, perhaps with other black loyalists who had been resettled in Birchtown, Nova Scotia:

> I am happy to find that some humane persons have interested them-selves in favour of the poor Blacks, whose wretchedness the streets of London too plainly bring to view. Among these poor sufferers, it should be remarked, that the *Lascars* and other *East-Indian* mendicants demand our pity only; but that the *African* Negroes have an actual claim on our justice: – *They*, or the greater part of them, have served Britain, have fought under her colours, and having quitted the service of their American masters, depending on the promise of protection held out to them by British Governors and Commanders, are now left to perish by famine and cold, in the sight of that people for whom they have hazarded their lives, and even (many of them) spilt their blood. – Britain, though unfortunate in her last contest, has yet preserved her honour inviolate. – Those who quitted estates and offices for her sake, have found her not ungrateful to such steady friends. – And shall these poor humble assertors of her rights be left to the agonies of want and despair, because they are unfriended and un-known? – Forbid it, honour! – Forbid it, justice and gratitude! – There is, I am told, a township in Nova Scotia settled and inhabited by Negroes, in the same predicament with the Blacks who daily perish in our streets. – Would it not be a deed of *real charity*, and of *use to society*, to send these poor creatures to their countrymen at this settlement?[29]

While Equiano was still in Philadelphia, Nova Scotia was one of the places considered for resettling the black poor. Another was the Bahamas. As the possibility of resettlement, which some of the black poor had first sug-gested, became greater, the black poor organized themselves and chose lead-ers to negotiate with the committee and the government. None of the parties involved conceived the idea of resettlement as a "back to Africa" movement: the vast majority of the black loyalists had never been to Africa, and their sense of "home" was in the Americas. Indeed, because of the presence of slave traders and the high incidence of disease, Africa was not initially an at-tractive site for relocation to either the prospective settlers or their sponsors.

The salesmanship and enthusiasm of Henry Smeathman changed the minds of the committee members and most of the black poor about the de-sirability of Africa as a destination. Sponsored by Dr. John Fothergill, a wealthy Quaker physician and scientist, as well as several of Fothergill's scientific friends, Smeathman had spent four years in the Sierra Leone region during the 1770s conducting research for a treatise on termites ("white ants"). The result was *Some Account of the Termites, which are Found in Africa and other hot Climates* (1781).[30] While in Africa Smeathman had married into the families of the local rulers: King Tom and Cleveland, whose father was English. He left Africa convinced that a settlement there would be an economic success. In England he tried to find backers for his plan to establish a colony in what he represented as a land of vast agricultural potential. In February 1786, probably with Sharp acting as intermediary, Smeathman brought his proposal for a multiracial settlement in Africa to the committee. Although Sharp was not a member of the committee, perhaps because he was not a wealthy man of business like the others, he had taken an active interest in its activities since its creation, attended some of its meetings, and was an obvious link between the white and black communities. Sharp had been interested in Smeathman's proposal for a colony in Africa for years, in part because such a settlement would give Sharp an opportunity to implement his own ideas about government. In response to Smeathman's original proposal Sharp wrote a tract entitled *Memorandum on a Late Proposal for a New Settlement to Be Made on the Coast of Africa.*[31] The committee approved a version of Smeathman's plan in May.

After his proposal was accepted, Smeathman published his *Plan of a Settlement to Be Made near Sierra Leona* (1786). His earlier proposal had been redesigned to fit the needs and merits of the black poor: "And whereas many black persons, and people of Colour, Refugees from America, disbanded from his Majesty's Service by sea or land, or otherwise distinguished objects of British humanity, are at this time in the greatest distress, they are invited to avail themselves of the advantages of the plan proposed."[32] The charitable impulse was complemented by the desire to abolish the slave trade and to demonstrate that Africa could generate wealth without being forced to export its human resources. The projected self-governing village that the settlers would name Granville Town in honor of Sharp in the Province of Freedom would be established on land bought from local African authorities. Sharp outlined the political constitution of the projected self-governing democratic community in his *Short Sketch of Temporary Regulations (Until Better Shall Be Proposed) for the Intended Settlement on the Grain Coast of Africa, near Sierra Leona* (1786). Smeathman had so endeared himself and his plan to the black poor that, when he died suddenly on 1 July, their choice for his successor as agent conductor of the resettlement project was his clerk and friend, Joseph Irwin, despite his lack of any African or leadership experience.

From May 1786 on, with the Anglican philanthropist Jonas Hanway now as its chairman, the committee worked closely with the government to implement the plans of Smeathman and Sharp. Working through George Rose and Thomas Steele, the two secretaries of the Treasury Board and both members of the House of Commons, the committee quickly received a promise from the Treasury of up to fourteen pounds per person to support transporting and establishing the settlers. Responsibility for transporting the settlers fell on the Navy Board, which consisted of a varying number of commissioners, directed by the comptroller of the navy, Sir Charles Middleton. A friend of Hanway, Middleton was an evangelical Anglican opposed to the slave trade and a member of the House of Commons. Lady Middleton was one of the earliest original subscribers to the committee, as was Elizabeth Bouverie, another evangelical who lived with the Middletons. In exchange for government support while they remained in England and later transportation to Sierra Leone, the voluntary settlers agreed to leave when required. The original aim was to have the settlers embark on 20 October 1786 in time to get established before the May–November rainy season raised the mortality rate, mainly from malaria.

To care for the settlers' spiritual and physical health the government agreed to pay the salaries of the Reverend Patrick Fraser, who had been recommended by the Society for the Propagation of the Gospel, and a Dr. Currie, as well as two surgeons and two schoolmasters. The government also agreed to pay for several months of supplies to get the settlement under way and to provide military protection for it. To administer the exodus of the black poor during the period between embarkation from England and the establishment of self-government in Sierra Leone, the committee and the government created three positions: the commander of the fleet, the agent or superintendent of the settlement, and the commissary on the part of the government. The first position would require the cooperation of the Admiralty, which would provide the warship and its commanding officer. Joseph Irwin, the settlers' choice, already filled the second position. The third, combining the duties of the purser and steward on a naval ship, would supervise the acquisition and distribution of supplies and victuals, including arms and ammunition. But the commissary would also have the much more significant role of bearing gifts from the British government to the local African rulers to exchange for land. In effect, he would be the government's representative in the settlement project. By the time Equiano returned to London in August 1786, the Sierra Leone resettlement project seemed well under way and on schedule.

The committee interviewed Equiano for the position of commissary because "they seemed to think me qualified to superintend part of the undertaking." Equiano says in his autobiography that he "had the honour of being known" to some of the members of the committee, who sent for him as soon as they heard of his return to London. Granville Sharp certainly knew him, though Sharp was not a member of the committee. Others who probably knew him were Henry Thornton, an evangelical Anglican member of the House of Commons, and George Peters, governor of the Bank of England and chairman of the committee since July. Thornton and Peters subscribed to the first edition of Equiano's *Interesting Narrative* in 1789. Samuel Hoare, who succeeded Peters as chairman, may also have previously known Equiano. Equiano later referred to him in a letter to the *Public Advertiser* of 14 July 1787 as someone "who had before appeared to be Mr. Vasa's friend" (328).

The committee may have interviewed Equiano as well because of his connections to the Quaker community and his recognized position as a spokesman for London's blacks. Quakers had long intrigued Equiano. His most benign master, Robert King, was a Quaker. The only honest white merchants Equiano dealt with in North America were Quakers. He attended Quaker services and a wedding out of curiosity. During his stay in Philadelphia in 1785 he visited a school created by Anthony Benezet: "I was very glad to see this favourite old town once more; and my pleasure was much increased in seeing the worthy Quakers, freeing and easing the burthens of many of my oppressed African brethren. It rejoiced my heart when one of these friendly people took me to see a free-school they had erected for every denomination of black people, whose minds are cultivated here, and forwarded to virtue; and thus they are made useful members of the community" (224).

In October 1785, back in London, "accompanied by some of the Africans," Equiano "presented this address of thanks to the gentlemen called Friends or Quakers, in Whitehart-court,[33] Lombard-street":

GENTLEMEN,

By reading your book, intitled, A Caution to Great Britain and her Colonies, concerning the Calamitous State of the enslaved Negroes,[34] We, part of the poor, oppressed, needy, and much degraded negroes, desire to approach you, with this address of thanks, with our inmost love and warmest acknowledgments; and with the deepest sense of your benevolence, unwearied labour, and kind interposition, towards breaking the yoke of slavery, and to administer a little comfort and ease to thousands and tens of thousands of very grievously afflicted and too heavy burthened negroes.

Gentlemen, could you, by perseverance, at last be enabled, under God, to lighten in any degree the heavy burthen of the afflicted, no doubt it would, in some measure, be the possible means under God of saving the souls of many of the oppressors; and if so, sure we are that the God, whose eyes are ever upon all his creatures, and always rewards every true act of virtue, and regards the prayers of the oppressed, will give to you and yours those blessings which it is not in our power to express or conceive, but which we, as a part of those captivated, oppressed, and afflicted people, most earnestly wish and pray for.[35]

The Quakers promised "to exert themselves on behalf of the oppressed Africans" (225).

Whomever he may have known on the committee, Equiano initially had his doubts about the wisdom of the project: "I pointed out to them many objections to my going; and particularly I expressed some difficulties on the account of the slave-dealers, as I would certainly oppose their traffic in the human species by every means in my power." He was soon persuaded, however: "These objections were over-ruled by the gentlemen of the committee, who prevailed on me to consent to go; and recommended me to the honourable Commissioners of his Majesty's Navy, as a proper person to act as commissary for government in the intended expedition; and they accordingly appointed me, in November 1786, to that office, and gave me sufficient power to act for the government in the capacity of commissary; having received my warrant" (226–27). Equiano probably had no difficulty getting the commissioners' approval because he had a personal connection to Sir Charles Middleton, head of the Navy Board. One of Middleton's closest friends was his spiritual advisor, the Reverend James Ramsay. Ramsay had served under Middleton in the Royal Navy, and he had recently published attacks on the slave trade and West Indian slavery. Ramsay had seen the horrible conditions on a slave ship during his time with the navy. As a clergyman for eighteen years on Saint Kitts, where he first met Equiano, Ramsay had tried to better the conditions for slaves. His efforts earned him the resistance and opposition of the local planters. In 1781 he was forced to return to England, where Middleton made him vicar of Teston and rector of Nettlestead, Kent. Equiano probably first met Ramsay on one of his several visits to Saint

Kitts as a slave. Equiano stated in a letter to the *Public Advertiser* of 5 February 1788 that he had "known him well both here [in England] and in the West Indies for many years" (333).[36]

Equiano was the only person of African descent officially involved with the organization and administration of the project to resettle the black poor in Sierra Leone. He had obvious qualifications for the place offered him. He had had ample experience in and out of the Royal Navy performing the duties of steward as well as holding other positions of responsibility. Equiano's primary reservation – concern about the proximity of the proposed settlement to slave-trading factories – may have been one of the reasons the committee invited him to join the project. As a black man his role in the project might have been intended to reassure some of the settlers who had been skeptical about the motives of an emigration plan conceived and executed by whites. And as a black man he was probably presumed to be a more welcome emissary to African leaders from the British government than a European would-be.

As Equiano's friend Cugoano pointed out, the black poor had reason to be suspicious about the government's motives: "For can it be readily conceived that government would establish a free colony for them nearly on the spot, while it supports its forts and garrisons, to ensnare, merchandize, and to carry others into captivity and slavery."[37] Supporters of the project felt compelled to respond. On 1 January 1787 a commentator in the *Public Advertiser* observed:

They must be enemies to public tranquility, to the police, and also to the Blacks, who studiously endeavour to fill the minds of these poor people with apprehensions of slavery, in the intended settlement on the banks of the Sierra Leona. No Ministry would think of breaking public faith with any body of men, however poor and abject they may be: Faith is kept by a nation, not because the persons to whom it is pledged are considerable and powerful, but because it is dishonourable to a nation to break its faith; and the precedent might be attended with consequences highly injurious to the State. . . . The Blacks may therefore embark with confidence: their liberty, so far from being invaded, will be protected by Government; and if they are not deprived of their reason, they will quickly perceive how much more eligible it will be for them to go to a country where they will have lands assigned to them for their support, and all implements of husbandry supplied to them by the bounty of the nation, than to remain in

James Ramsay, by Carl Frederik von Breda.
Ramsay, an abolitionist Anglican minister who had served in the
Royal Navy, initiated the press war during the 1780s over the treatment
of slaves in the West Indies. A friend of Equiano since the 1760s,
Ramsay subscribed for two copies of *The Interesting Narrative*.
(National Portrait Gallery, London)

indigence and want, strolling, wretched spectacles of distress, through our streets; constantly exposed to the temptation of committing felonies, for which they may be either hanged or transported to Africa, and left defenceless on the coast, where they will perish with hunger, be killed by their savage countrymen, or taken by them and sold as slaves: so that they may at length meet real slavery, in consequence of their ill-grounded apprehension of an imaginary one.

Concern among the black poor about the motivation and destination of the project, present from the beginning, grew rapidly during the last months of 1786 as talk and press coverage of the plan to transport convicts to Botany Bay in Australia coincided with news about the Sierra Leone project. The American Revolution had eliminated the thirteen colonies as destinations for convicts, forcing the British government to look elsewhere to dispose of its social undesirables. Before Australia was finally chosen as the site of a penal colony, one of those destinations was the west coast of Africa, where some convicts had already been sent in the 1770s and 1780s. Many of the black poor understandably feared that they would be deportees rather than emigrants. Because of such suspicions and concerns, during the last months of 1786 the gap widened substantially between the number of the poor who accepted the government "bounty" and the number who agreed to board the *Atlantic, Belisarius,* and *Vernon* transport ships. In January 1787 the *Atlantic* and *Belisarius* sailed to Spithead, off Portsmouth. The *Vernon* had joined them there by 8 February.

So few people had boarded the ships by the time Equiano became involved with the project in October 1786 that the date of departure had to be postponed and surplus provisions needed to be sold. When the commissioners of the Navy Board ordered Equiano in January 1787 to "dispose of such surplus to the best advantage you can for the benefit of government, keeping and rendering to us a faithful account of what you do therein," he discovered that Irwin was dishonest. "During my continuance in the employment of government," he later wrote, "I was struck with the flagrant abuses committed by the agent, and endeavoured to remedy them, but without effect. One instance, among many which I could produce, may serve as a specimen. Government had ordered to be provided all necessaries (slops [ready-made clothes], as they are called, included) for 750 persons; however, not being able to muster more than 426,[38] I was ordered to send the superfluous slops, &c. to the king's stores [the Royal Navy storehouses] at Portsmouth; but, when I demanded them for that purpose from the agent, it appeared they had never been bought, though paid for by government" (327–28). Worse yet, he said, was Irwin's treatment of the poor: "But that was not all, government were not the only objects of peculation [embezzlement]; these poor people suffered infinitely more; their accommodations were most wretched; many of them wanted beds, and many more clothing and other necessaries" (328).

Equiano took his charge as the government's representative very seriously – perhaps too seriously. He objected that Irwin had purchased, at the settlers' request, "Tea and Sugar and other Necessaries allowed for the use of the women and children" and that "unauthorized" passengers had been taken on board, even though they were probably white artisans whose skills would be needed in the settlement.[39] Unhappy with Irwin's response to his and the settlers' complaints, Equiano "applied in February 1787 for a remedy" to Thomas Boulden Thompson, commander of the *Nautilus*, a sixteen-gun sloop the navy had assigned the month before to convoy the settlers to Africa. Equiano "even brought him to be a witness of the injustice and oppression" he complained of. He also "informed the Commissioners of the Navy of the agent's proceeding" as well as the chairman of the committee, Samuel Hoare (228, 328). His complaints only contributed to his own dismissal on 24 March.

One of the reasons for Equiano's dismissal was Thompson's letter of 21 March 1787 lamenting to the Navy Board "the conduct of Mr Gustavus Vasa, which has been, since he held the situation of Commissary, turbulent and discontented, taking every means to actuate the minds of the Blacks to discord: and I am convinced that unless some means are taken to quell his spirit of sedition, it will be fatal to the peace of the settlement and dangerous to those intrusted with the guiding [of] it." Thompson complained of Irwin's conduct as well in the same letter.[40] Similar complaints about Equiano had appeared in the *Morning Herald* on 29 December 1786. In a 23 June 1787 letter to his brother, Sharp, too, expressed disapproval of the disruptive behavior of "Mr. Vasa and two or three other discontented persons."[41]

Equiano and Irwin were both at fault. Their overlapping administrative responsibilities probably made conflict between them inevitable.[42] The organizational weakness was exacerbated by their apparent personality clash. At one point they got into a petty competition over who would get more canvas for his tent. Both men had to be ordered to carry out their duties more expeditiously. Equiano made some serious mistakes: his muster lists were inaccurate, he sent them to the wrong department, and he failed to have the arms and ammunition loaded on one of the ships before it left the Thames for Spithead. His errors were probably sufficient to justify his dismissal, which became necessary when his inability to work with Irwin became undeniable and public. The historian of the black poor resettlement project plausibly suggests that Irwin was retained, despite his faults, rather than Equiano, because while the commissary had been selected by Lord Middleton and the navy commissioners, the superintendent was the settlers' own choice.[43] Equiano did not go quietly.

Despite the opinion of some historians, little evidence supports the contention that Equiano's dismissal was racially motivated.[44] Equiano, in a letter to the *Public Advertiser* on 28 June 1788, initially blamed Irwin, Dr. Currie, Reverend Fraser, and Hoare for his firing. He later suggested that Hoare and Irwin acted together to defraud the government and have him dismissed: "My dismission was soon . . . procured by means of [Irwin's] friend, a Banker in the City, possibly his partner in the contract" (342). In a 24 March 1787 letter from Equiano to Cugoano published in the *Public Advertiser* on 4 April, Equiano sounds nearly as intemperate as the "Gustavus Vassa" who wrote to the *Morning Post* almost ten years earlier. "I am sure," he writes, "Irwin, and Fraser the Parson, are great villains, and Dr. Currie. I am exceeding much aggrieved at the conduct of those who call themselves gentlemen. They now mean to serve (or use) the blacks the same as they do in the West Indies." Until now, he says, he had innocently suffered in silence: "For the good of the settlement I have borne every affront that could be given, believe me, without giving the least occasion, or ever yet resenting any." He was speaking out now because he had learned from Middleton that "Irwin and Fraser have wrote to the Committee and Treasury, that I use the white people with arrogance, and the blacks with civility, and stir them up to mutiny: which is not true, for I am the greatest peace-maker that goes out." They lied about him because he reported "their roguery" to Captain Thompson. He was proven right when Thompson, after seeing for himself "the wrongs done to me and the people[,] . . . ordered the things to be given according to contract." Equiano does "not know how this undertaking will end," and indeed now wishes he "had never been involved in it." Perhaps "the Lord will make me very useful at last," he concludes, signing off with the title of "The Commissary for the Black Poor" he lost that day.

Equiano was not left to defend himself alone publicly. On 6 April 1787 the *Public Advertiser* published an anonymous correspondent:

We find his Majesty's servants have taken away the Commissary's commission from Vasa. He came up from Plymouth to complain, and is now gone back again to take his effects on shore. The memorials [written petitions and/or statements of facts] of all the Black people, which they have sent up from Plymouth, represent that they are much wronged, injured, and oppressed natives of Africa, and under various pretences and different manners, have been dragged away from London, and carried captives to Plymouth, where they have nothing but slavery before their eyes, should they proceed to Africa or the West-Indies under the command of the persons who have the charge of them – That many of them served under Lord Dunmore, and other officers in America, in the British army – Also on board the British Fleet in the West-Indies – That the contract, on Mr. Smeathman's plan to settle them in Africa, has not been fulfilled in their favour, but a Mr. Irwin has contrived to monopolize the benefit to himself – That they fear a right plan has not been formed to settle them in Africa with any prospect of happiness to themselves, or any hope of future advantage to Great-Britain. – They cannot conceive, say they, that Government would establish a free colony for them, whilst it supports its forts and factories to wrong and ensnare, and to carry others of their colour and country into slavery and bondage – They are afraid that their doom would be to drink of the bitter water, and observe that it would be their prudence and safety to take warning from the cautions in Scripture: – "Doth a fountain send forth at the same place sweet water and bitter?" – That they say the design of some in sending them away, is only to get rid of them at all events, come of them afterwards what will. – In that perilous situation they see themselves surrounded with difficulties and danger; and what gives them the most dreadful presage of their fate is that the white men set over them have shewn them no humanity or good-will, but have conspired to use them unjustly before they quitted the English coast – And that they had better swim to shore, if they can, to preserve their lives and liberties in Britain, than to hazard themselves at Sea with such enemies to their welfare, and the peril of settling at Sierra Leona under their government.

Although the letter was reproduced without attribution, its content, tone, diction, and style suggest that Cugoano was its author.[45]

After five months of delay due to a combination of reluctant settlers, the premature deaths of some of the organizers, administrative foul-ups, and bad weather, the little fleet of three vessels convoyed by the *Nautilus* finally set sail on 9 April 1787, reaching Sierra Leone a month later as the deadly rainy season was beginning. Because the Province of Freedom was conceived as a self-governing, free settlement, not a British colony, the roles of the Committee for the Relief of the Black Poor and the Treasury ended as the ships set off. The government had spent more than fifteen thousand pounds on the project, not including the "bounty" paid to at least 979 people.[46] In retrospect, Equiano considered the Sierra Leone project "an expedition, which,

232 ■ CHAPTER TEN

however unfortunate in the event, was humane and politic in its design, nor was its failure owing to government; every thing was done on their part; but there was evidently sufficient mismanagement attending the conduct and execution of it to defeat its success" (229). Of the approximately four hundred men, women, and children who set out, including dozens of whites and about fifty lascars, fifteen died of fever on the voyage. By 24 July, 52 of the settlers had died, with another 150 on the sick list. The new environment was particularly deadly for the lascars, most of whom died within a year. The survivors were dispersed in December 1789, when King Jimmy, a local African leader, destroyed Granville Town in retaliation for the hostile actions of a British warship. Cugoano's dire predictions had come true.

Some scholars have argued that the resettlement project was, in effect, an eighteenth-century version of ethnic cleansing motivated by racism and designed to rid London of unwanted blacks.[47] Others have more convincingly argued that while one can find isolated comments of a racist nature in the eighteenth-century discussion of the project, the overwhelming preponderance of evidence indicates that the committee and government were motivated by a sincere desire to help those in need, particularly those who had served their country in a lost cause. The objects of the committee's charity represented a very small percentage of the blacks in England, and they participated voluntarily in a project they had played a large role in defining.[48] The ethnic composition of the settlers who finally left for Sierra Leone in April 1787, a significant percentage of whom were white, challenges any claim that proponents of the resettlement sought to separate the races.

As the fleet was under way, the controversy over Equiano's dismissal continued in the *Public Advertiser*. On 11 April correspondent "X" significantly lowered the tone of the debate by demonizing Equiano and patronizing the settlers:

> The Public will naturally suspend their belief as to the improbable tales propagated concerning the Blacks, especially as the cloven hoof of the author of those reports is perfectly manifest. That one of the persons employed in conducting those poor people is discharged, is certainly true, his own misconduct having given too good reason for his dismission. The Blacks have never refused to proceed on the voyage, but the ships have been delayed at Plymouth by an accidental damage which one of them received in a gale of wind. To sum up all, should the expedition prove unsuccessful, it can only be owing to the over-care of the committee, who, to avoid the most distant idea of compulsion, did not even subject the

Blacks to *any* government, except such as they might chuse for themselves. And among such ill-informed people, this delicacy may have fatal
consequences.

Three days later another correspondent lowered the tone even further
by making Equiano's complexion an issue:

> The expedition of the Blacks to Sierra Leone is not in the least retarded
> by the dismission of V – the Black who was appointed to superintend the
> Blacks.
>
> The assertions made by that man that the Blacks were to be treated as
> badly as West-India negroes, and that he was discharged to make room
> for the appointment of a man who would exercise tyranny to those unfor-
> tunate men, shew him to be capable of advancing falsehoods as deeply
> black as his jetty face. The true reason for his being discharged, was gross
> misbehaviour, which had not only rendered him disagreeable to the offi-
> cers and crew, but had likewise drawn on him the dislike of those over
> whom he had been appointed. . . .
>
> The cloven foot, as observed by a judicious correspondent *X* in
> Wednesday's paper, is perfectly manifest in the improbable tales propa-
> gated on account of the above discharge. . . .
>
> . . . Let us hear no more of those *black* reports which have been so in-
> dustriously propagated; for if they are continued, it is rather more than
> probable that most of the *dark* transactions of a *Black* will be brought to
> *light.*

Equiano maintained his public silence for months in the face of the published attacks. He did not, however, passively accept his dismissal. On 12
May he "humbly" sent "To The Right Honourable the Lords Commissioners
of his Majesty's Treasury. The Memorial and Petition of GUSTAVUS
VASSA, a black man, late Commissary to the Black Poor, going to AFRICA,"
in which he justifies his actions and asks for restitution of his salary and expenses. He represents himself as the helpless victim of powerful enemies:
"By opposing measures of others concerned in the same expedition, which
tended to defeat your Lordships' humane intention, and to put the government to a very considerable additional expence, he created a number of enemies, whose misrepresentations, he has too much reason to believe, laid the
foundation of his dismission. Unsupported by friends, and unaided by the
advantages of a liberal education, he can only hope for redress from the justice of his cause" (229–30).[49]

Before he received a response from the Treasury, in July 1787 Equiano again felt compelled to defend himself publicly. On 2 and 3 July the *London Chronicle* and the *Morning Chronicle* each published the "Extract of a Letter from a Gentleman [the Reverend Patrick Fraser] on board the Ship Atlantic, off Santa Cruz, Teneriffe":

> I take this opportunity of informing you, that we arrived here on Satur-day last, after a most pleasant passage of 13 days from Plymouth. I have the pleasure to inform you, that we are all well, and that the poor blacks are in a much more healthy state than when we left England. Vasa's dis-charge and the dismission of [William] Green and [Lewis] Rose [two of the black settlers], are attended with the happiest effects. Instead of that general misunderstanding under which we groaned through their means, we now enjoy all the sweets of peace, lenity, and almost uninterrupted harmony. The odious distinction of colours is no longer remembered, and all seem to conspire to promote the general good. The people are now regular in their attendance upon divine service on the Sundays, and on public prayers during the week; they do not, as formerly, absent them-selves purposely on such occasions, for no other reasons whatever than that I am white. . . . In short, Sir, our affairs upon the whole are so much changed for the better, that I flatter myself with the pleasing hope that we may still do well, and enjoy the blessing of Providence in the intended set-tlement.

Perhaps Fraser's accusation against Equiano of antiwhite racism prompted him to respond in the 14 July issue of the *Public Advertiser* to Fraser's "injurious reflexions, prejudicial to the character of Vasa." To his pre-vious defenses of his own actions and his claim that he had been the victim of misrepresentation, Equiano added, "The same representation [of Irwin's behavior] was made by Mr. Vasa to Mr. Hoare, which induced the latter, who had before appeared to be Vasa's friend, to go to the Secretary of the Trea-sury, and procure his dismission. The above Gentleman impowered the Agent to take many passengers in, contrary to the orders given to the Commissary" (328). Fraser's comments are interesting in part because they anticipate the more overt charge Equiano's friend Ramsay made privately the following year. The dispute, Ramsay said, was about power: "Those to whom the management of the expedition was committed, dreaded so much his influence over his countrymen, that they contrived to procure an order for his being sent ashore."[50]

Literally and metaphorically, Equiano had the last word in the dispute over his role in the Sierra Leone resettlement project. No more charges and countercharges appeared in print after July 1787 until the publication nearly two years later of his *Interesting Narrative*, in which he reproduced his letter to the Treasury. He exulted that the Treasury had paid him the full fifty pounds sterling he had petitioned for without questioning his claim: "Certainly the sum is more than a free Negro would have had in the western colonies!!!" (231). He was probably unaware that on 26 April 1787, before he submitted his "memorial and petition," the commissioners of the Navy Board had budgeted sixty pounds for him.[51] Equiano did not need to point out to his readers that the presence of the names George Peters, Sir Charles and Lady Middleton, George Rose, and Thomas Steele among his many other subscribers indicated that, at least to some of the most significant members of the committee and government involved in the project to resettle the black poor, he had been vindicated.

Chapter Eleven

TURNING AGAINST THE SLAVE TRADE

The two years between Equiano's dismissal from the Sierra Leone resettlement project and the publication of his autobiography "passed in an even tenor." He devoted his "study and attention" to "the cause of my much injured countrymen" (231). The transition from his significant role in the project to his playing a major part in the movement to abolish the slave trade came easily. Many of the people supporting the Sierra Leone project were motivated by a desire to demonstrate that free Africans could be more economically productive than enslaved Africans. Even though Equiano had failed in his second attempt to be sent to Africa, he felt personally vindicated, and he had become connected to a network of contacts that would serve him for the rest of his life. With the abolitionist cause Equiano finally found a mission that would enable him to do very well by doing good.

Equiano's embrace of the abolitionist cause in the late 1780s was a secular conversion as significant as his spiritual conversion on 6 October 1774 had been. His religious rebirth had happened suddenly, but, like most of his fellow Britons, he only gradually came to oppose the slave trade and slavery. He does not tell us when precisely he made the transition from accepting slavery and the slave trade to condemning them. He had seen and experienced slavery in Africa, the West Indies, the Royal Navy, England, North America, and the Mediterranean. As a result he had become something of an expert on comparative slavery, recognizing that some systems, particularly the slave societies of the West Indies and the Deep South of North America, were worse than others. He also came to recognize that as long as slavery existed anywhere, a free black person could not be completely secure. Indeed, he discovered that slavery threatened everyone. At one point during the Seven Years' War his ship was involved in an exchange of prisoners: "Among others whom we brought from Bayonne, were two gentlemen, who had been in the West Indies, where they sold slaves; and they confessed they had made at one time a false bill of sale, and sold two Portuguese white men among a lot of slaves" (266). In Italy and Turkey he encountered whites treated as slaves. At times before the 1780s Equiano expressed a concern with ameliorating the conditions of the transatlantic slave trade or the institution of slavery, but he had not advocated either abolition or emancipation.

Equiano's contact with Granville Sharp no doubt influenced his views on slavery, which clearly evolved over the years of their interaction. Equiano had sought Sharp's help in trying to save John Annis from being illegally returned to the West Indies in 1774. But Equiano responded to Annis's situation as if it were an isolated event. Slavery was unjust for Annis; Equiano did not yet perceive slavery to be unjust for everyone. In 1776 he was still more than willing to participate in Irving's plantation experiment based on slave labor. He even took pride in what he considered his own benevolent selection and supervision of the slaves. He left his position as overseer because he was dissatisfied with his fellow free employees, not because he had developed reservations about slavery or the slave trade. His memorial to the bishop of London in 1779 asking to be sent to Africa as a missionary mentions nothing about abolition as a motive.

The first time Equiano demonstrated opposition to the slave trade goes unmentioned in his *Interesting Narrative*. On 19 March 1783 Sharp recorded in his journal that "Gustavus Vassa, a negro, called on me, with an account of 130 negroes being thrown alive into the sea."[1] Equiano probably brought

Sharp the report in the *Morning Chronicle, and London Advertiser* (18 March 1783) of the recent court hearing on one of the most notorious atrocities of the slave trade.[2] Commanded by Luke Collingwood, the slave ship *Zong* sailed from the coast of present-day Gabon on 6 September 1781 with a crew of 17 and a cargo of approximately 470 enslaved Africans. When seven of his crew and more than sixty of the Africans had died by 29 November, with many others in failing health, Collingwood explained to his officers that if the Africans died of natural causes the owners of the *Zong* (and Collingwood) would have to absorb the cost, but if they had to be thrown overboard to save the ship and its crew, the insurance underwriters would be obligated to cover the loss. Over the objection of his first mate, James Kelsal, who testified against him, Collingwood ordered that 133 of the sickest Africans be divided into groups and thrown alive into the ocean on the pretext that the ship lacked sufficient drinking water. The ship's records showed, however, that it had 200 unrationed gallons of water on 29 November and 420 gallons when it arrived in Jamaica on 22 December. Kelsal testified that even after a heavy rain Africans continued to be thrown overboard.

When the insurers challenged the claim made by the *Zong*'s owners, the Liverpool banker William Gregson and his associates, the court decided in favor of the owners, awarding them thirty pounds for each murder victim. When the insurers still refused to pay the £3,990, the owners were granted a new trial before the Court of King's Bench, but its outcome is not recorded, and whether the owners received payment is unknown. Although Collingwood died during the proceedings, Granville Sharp sought to prosecute the remaining murderers in the Admiralty Court, but no action was ever taken against them.

The *Zong* atrocity was largely ignored when it happened in 1781 and little remarked upon when the press reported it early in 1783. In 1783 slavery and the slave trade were only just beginning to become dominant national issues. Before the 1760s published opposition to slavery or the slave trade was occasional rather than consistent, with brief periods of activity such as the early 1730s. Sporadic attacks on the trade or institution appeared in print from the late seventeenth century on, but they were apparently discrete comments unconnected to each other. Only slowly did later attacks on the trade start to cite earlier writings for support. For example, in London in 1760 the pseudonymous "J. Philmore" published *Two Dialogues on the Man-Trade*, a conversation in which "Philmore" convinces the slave trader "Allcraft" of the evil of slavery. In support of his position, "Philmore" cites "Snelgrave's account of Guinea" on the happiness of Africans in their native land and Sir Hans Sloane's *Voyage to the Islands of Medera, Barbados, Nieves, S. Christopher's and Jamaica* . . . on the punishments inflicted on West Indian slaves.[3] "Philmore" anticipated many of the sources and arguments abolitionists would use and make in the 1780s about monogenism (the belief that all humans shared common ancestors), the equality of blacks and whites, and the consequent immorality of the slave trade. There is no evidence, however, that he found much of an immediate audience.

Two Dialogues on the Man-Trade did find an audience when the Quaker abolitionist Anthony Benezet first included extracts from it in his *Short Account of that Part of Africa, Inhabited by the Negroes,* published in Philadelphia in 1762. Benezet personified the transatlantic nature of eighteenth-century Anglo-American cultural and publishing networks. *Observations on the Inslaving, Importing and Purchasing of Negroes. With some Advice thereon Extracted from the Yearly Meeting Epistles of London for the Present Year,* one of his earliest tracts against the slave trade, was published in Germantown, Pennsylvania, in 1759. As its title indicates, *Observations* was conceived as part of a dialogue with fellow Quakers in London about the slave trade, but it was published too provincially to evoke a response. Benezet did not make that mistake again. Thereafter he published in Philadelphia and London, reaching audiences well beyond the limited circle of provincial Quakers. His subsequent writings anthologized or mentioned earlier antislavery comments by others, making them available on both sides of the Atlantic. Essentially chronologically arranged digests of European comments on Africa and the slave trade, Benezet's books revised the earlier isolated statements into a tradition of opposition conveniently available to any late-eighteenth-century reader. Consequently, because of Benezet's mediation, later opponents of the trade need not have read the original sources they cite or quote, sources that were mentioned so regularly by subsequent authors that they became quite predictable. Invoking Benezet either directly or by using quotations found in his works served as a common way for writers from the 1780s on to indicate their participation in the growing movement to abolish the African slave trade.

Benezet also exemplified the less public ways the abolitionist movement developed as well as the primary role American Quakers played in initiating and encouraging that movement. To be successful, any American opposition to the African slave trade had to enlist the support of people in Britain, the most significant slave-trading nation. On 28 May 1763 Benezet, a stranger in Pennsylvania, wrote to his fellow Quaker in England, Dr. John Fothergill, the future sponsor of John Smeathman. Benezet asked Fothergill to consider a "Matter of deep Concern to many well-minded People in these Parts of the World which if it ever receives a proper check must come from amongst you; I mean the Negro Trade." Ten years later Benezet encouraged Fothergill to aid his American Quaker brethren in "the best endeavours in our power to draw the notice of the government upon the grievous iniquity and great danger attendant on a farther prosecution of the Slave Trade."[4]

A further ten years passed before the abolition movement could gain traction in Britain in the wake of the American Revolution. According to historian Linda Colley, "The lost war in America . . . precipitated not so much a sea-change in British attitudes to the slave trade, as a converting of already existing qualms into positive action."[5] In effect, the postwar abolition movement took up where the arguments prompted by the Mansfield decision in 1772 left off. Had it not been for the outbreak of hostilities between the North American colonies and Britain in the 1770s, the issue of abolishing the slave trade might have been fully engaged then. Both sides of the debate Mansfield started produced more than a dozen publications during 1772 and 1773 addressing the subject.[6] The progress the British abolitionist cause had made before the war began is epitomized in John Wesley's *Thoughts upon Slavery.*

In 1774 Wesley saw no solution to the problem of colonial slavery because events in North America preoccupied the government. He could only regret how "little would it in all probability avail, to apply to the Parliament. So many things, which *seem* of greater importance lie before them that they are not likely to attend to this."[7] But the American Revolution slowed the abolitionist movement only to accelerate it later. In practical terms the massive disruption of the African slave trade caused by the Revolution suggested that the British economy could survive without it. But, more important, the humbling blow of the loss of the colonies led to a sort of national soul-searching to try to account for why Providence had turned against Britain. What national sin might have justified such punishment? Britain's dominant role in the slave trade was an obvious possible answer. Sharp had warned his fellow Britons on the eve of the American Revolution that tolerating slavery "is a shame to this nation, and may in time prove very dangerous to it."[8] The British had long prided themselves on being a liberty-loving people. Britain's military defeat, however, appeared to ratify the rebellious Americans' claim to be the true defenders of liberty, even though they denied equal rights to their black countrymen. In his draft of the Declaration of Independence Thomas Jefferson accused George III of forcing the slave trade on the Americans. Talk in the

North American colonies of outlawing the transatlantic slave trade would soon become realized in the Constitution of the new United States. Southern slave owners agreed with northern abolitionists to end the trade in 1808 only because the birth rate of Creole slaves was self-sustaining and because slave owners believed that imported slaves undercut the price of domestic slaves. Even the radical Cugoano acknowledged in 1787 the steps some of the former colonies were taking to extend liberty to people of African descent. Britain had lost the war, and now the Americans were apparently taking the high moral ground as well.

Prompted in part by Philadelphia Quakers who called on their British coreligionists in 1782 to take action against the trade, the London organization appointed a twenty-three-man committee in June 1783 to consider the issue. Its members included the international bookseller James Phillips and the banker Samuel Hoare, soon to become Equiano's enemy during the project to resettle the black poor. In 1783 Phillips published *Extracts from the Minutes and Advices of the Yearly Meeting of Friends Held in London, from its first Institution*, which included a chronology of the Quakers' evolving formal opposition to slavery. Also in 1783, on orders of the committee, Phillips printed two thousand copies of *The Case of our Fellow Creatures, the Oppressed Africans, Respectfully Recommended to the Serious Consideration of the Legislature of Great Britain by the People Called Quakers*, which two committee members had written. After the parliamentary elections in March 1784 the committee ordered an additional ten thousand copies of *The Case of our Fellow Creatures* to distribute to members of the House of Commons and the House of Lords, the administration, the royal family, and "throughout the nation."[9]

Probably to avoid oversight by the full twenty-three-man committee, in July 1783 Hoare and four other members of the official committee also formed a separate group "to consider what steps could by them be taken for the Relief and Liberation of the Negro Slaves in the West Indies, and the Discouragement of the Slave Trade on the Coast of Africa."[10] Joining the five members from the informal committee was the Quaker merchant Joseph Woods, a future subscriber to Equiano's autobiography. Hoare's brother-in-law, Woods was a purchasing agent for the Library Company of Philadelphia. Woods had also published articles anonymously in the *Gentleman's Magazine*, one of the most widely distributed periodicals in the English-speaking world.

No doubt because of his experience as a writer and distributor of books to both Quaker and non-Quaker readers, Woods was assigned by the informal committee to send articles about and excerpts from antislavery works to a dozen newspapers in London, the rest of England, and Dublin. Many eighteenth-century book publishers published newspapers as well. Most of the newspapers were subsidized by either the government or the political opposition, which controlled their political content and slant. The newspapers frequently changed sides, however, depending upon who was paying the bills. Unlike modern newspapers, where editorial control is pervasive and contributors are paid for their work, subsidized eighteenth-century newspapers were usually fairly desperate to find nonpolitical items to fill their pages. Unsolicited and unpaid contributions such as advertisements, news items, gossip, correspondence, and book reviews frequently appeared alongside generously quoted sections from other publications. Comparing modern newspaper practice to the earlier period, Adam Hochschild aptly observes that "eighteenth-century papers were . . . much more anarchic, almost like an internet bulletin board where anyone could post almost anything."[11]

In addition to taking advantage of the eighteenth-century desire for newspaper copy, Woods also contributed an original thirty-two-page work to the abolitionist cause. He published *Thoughts on the Slavery of the Negroes* anonymously in London in 1784. Aiming at a nonsectarian audience, Woods argues that regulation of the slave trade rather than its abolition is unacceptable. Slavery, he says, is a morally evil perversion of true commerce. Consequently, consumers of unnecessary commodities produced by slave labor sustain West Indian slavery and the African slave trade. Like Benezet and Wesley before him and Equiano as well as many others after, Woods explicitly invoked the tradition of writings against slavery and the trade. Citing Hans Sloane on the use of dismemberment, flagellation, and the spreading of salt and pepper in wounds as punishments in the West Indies, Woods comments, "When this situation is compared with the liberty, the ease, and the independence which the Africans enjoy in their own country, where, according to the relation of travelers there seems a sort of exemption from the general doom of man to perpetual labour, and nature produces the fruits of the earth almost spontaneously, who but must condemn the rough hand of power which forces them, or the arts of treachery which entice them, to leave it!"[12] Woods anticipated most subsequent anti-slave-trade writers in idealizing Africans. Abolitionist descriptions of the continent tended to be as unrealistic as the denigrating images of Africa and its inhabitants promoted by apologists for the trade. Equiano's account of African society was so compelling in part because he offered a more balanced picture, acknowledging, for example, that Africans practiced slavery.

Woods argues that since all Britons are participants in the crime of slavery through their consumption of its products, their representatives are morally obligated first to abolish the slave trade and then to take up the issue of emancipation:

> The alteration and gradual subversion of this system, can only be hoped
> for from the interposition of the British legislature, which would, in this
> instance, be granted with peculiar propriety, because the revenue of the
> government, the profits of the merchants, and the luxury of the people,
> have involved the whole nation as *participes criminis*: and the burthen of
> restoring to the Africans their alienated rights should not press too par-
> tially on the planters, who adopted, not introduced, this iniquitous traf-
> fick, and have pursued it under the patronage of Britain, but should be
> borne by all who have shared in its advantages. The first measure which
> presents itself to the wish of humanity, seems to be the absolute prohibi-
> tion of all importations of slaves into any part of the British dominions.
> The emancipation of those already in slavery, and the means of supply-
> ing freemen, will claim, no doubt, the maturest deliberation of wise and
> experienced men.[13]

In July 1784 the informal committee ordered James Phillips to print two thousand copies of Woods's *Thoughts on the Slavery of the Negroes.* They were distributed throughout England, including the major slave ports of Bristol and Liverpool. Copies were also sent to specific individuals, including three of Equiano's future subscribers, Anglicans who had already published or preached against the trade: Granville Sharp, Beilby Porteus, bishop of Chester and soon to become bishop of London, and the Reverend James Ramsay.[14] The distribution network Equiano would use for his own book was being established.

By reaching out to Sharp, Porteus, and Ramsay in 1784 the Quakers were acknowledging their parallel efforts in the increasingly nonsectarian aboli-tionist cause. Sharp's contributions had been appearing for the last fifteen years. Porteus first spoke out against Britain's leading role in the transatlantic slave trade in *A Sermon Preached before the Incorporated Society for the Propagation of the Gospel in Foreign Parts; at the Anniversary Meeting in the Parish Church of St. Mary-le-bow, on Friday, February 21, 1783.* Having learned of his sermon, the informal group of Quakers authorized Hoare to approach Porteus about the possibility of their reprinting it. Porteus agreed to allow Phillips to print a thousand copies. Through his contact with Porteus, Hoare began a corre-spondence with Equiano's friend Ramsay.[15]

In his sermon to the Society for the Propagation of the Gospel Porteus announced the forthcoming publication by Phillips of Ramsay's 298-page *Essay on the Treatment and Conversion of African Slaves in the British Sugar Colonies.* Ramsay's work was the opening salvo in the print war over abolition of the trade and slavery that lasted for decades. Anticipating the rhetorical strategy used by others who followed his example, including Equiano, Ramsay carefully took an ameliorationist rather than emancipationist position in his essay when it appeared in June 1784. As he remarked in a subsequent publication, "Though I sincerely hope, that *some* plan will be devised for the future gradual abolition of slavery; and though I am convinced that this may, without any prejudice to the planter, or injury to commerce, be brought about by some such progressive method as is pointed out in the Essay; yet this was not the first, or immediate object of that book."[16] "As far back as history carries us," Ramsay acknowledges, "we read of master and slave." But to the extent that "slavery prevails in any community, so far must that community be defective in answering the purposes of society. And this we affirm to be in the highest degree in our colonies. Slavery, indeed, in the manner wherein it is found there, is an unnatural state of oppression on the one side, and of suffering on the other; and needs only to be laid open or exposed in its native colours, to command the abhorrence and opposition of every man of feeling and sentiment."[17]

After a careful study of West Indian legislation, Ramsay discovered that "a horse, a cow, or a sheep, is much better protected with us by the law, than a poor slave." Paradoxically, slaves are treated most harshly in a land of liberty: "Our constitution has such an excessive bias to personal liberty, that in contradiction to the maxims of every well ordered state, it cannot, or will not, meddle with private behavior. . . . Every where, in every age, the chain of slavery has been fashioned, and applied by the hand of liberty."[18] Better treatment, rewards for their labor, and access to religious instruction would render the slaves more productive and eventually turn them into consumers. With a vested interest in the economic welfare of the colonies, slaves would contribute to the defense of those colonies against foreign enemies rather than continue to pose domestic threats themselves.

Ramsay praises "the active zeal of the benevolent Mr. Granville Sharp," contrasting him with writers like Edward Long and David Hume, who "are so fond of [the polygenist] hypothesis, which indulges pride."[19] Although supposing people of African descent to be "a distinct race, will not immediately affect our arguments for their humane treatment and mental improvement . . . the consequences usually drawn from [such a hypothesis] shock humanity, and check every hope of their advancement: for, if allowed to be a *distinct* race, European pride immediately concludes them an *inferior* race, and then it follows, of course, that nature formed them to be slaves to their superiors."[20] Among others, Francis Williams, the free black Jamaican poet, proves the racist hypothesis wrong, Ramsay contends.[21] Going beyond arguing for equality between Europeans and Africans, Ramsay suggests that at least in music blacks could teach whites: "It is surprising, that during the continued rage for Italian singers, it has never entered among the whims of the age, to try if music might not be imported from the Banks of the Niger. It is certain the natural taste of the Africans for music is considerable."[22]

Ramsay's essay initiated a five-year-long transatlantic pamphlet battle between him and proslavery writers. Equiano soon joined the fight. The timing of Ramsay's publication and his qualifications as an authority on West Indian slavery made him impossible to ignore. As Thomas Clarkson noted, Ramsay's essay had "come so home to the planters (being written by a person who has a thorough knowledge of the subject) as to have occasioned a considerable alarm."[23] Unlike Sharp and Porteus, whose expertise on the conditions of slavery came secondhand through research and thus could relatively easily be ignored or dismissed by the proslavery West Indian interest, Ramsay had firsthand experience on a slave ship, as a resident of the West Indies, and as a former slave owner himself. Although Ramsay had anticipated opposition, he could not have imagined the vitriolic ad hominem attacks and threats against his person that his writings would elicit. In the post–American Revolution atmosphere, British periodicals and newspapers reviewed Ramsay's essay positively. Almost immediately, opponents denied his evidence and libeled his character. Ramsay's influence was transatlantic: the first attack, *An Answer to the Reverend James Ramsay's Essay*, was published anonymously in 1784 in the West Indian island of Saint Kitts. Later that year the pamphlet *Remarks on a Pamphlet, Written by the Reverend James Ramsay, M.A.: Under the Title of Thoughts on the Slavery of the Negroes, in the American Colonies* was published anonymously in London. Its author, another Saint Kitts planter, mistakenly assumed that Ramsay had written Woods's *Thoughts on the Slavery of the Negroes* as well as the essay.

Two of Ramsay's antagonists, James Tobin and Gordon Turnbull, subsequently drew fire from both Cugoano and Equiano. Now living in London, Tobin had been a member of His Majesty's Council in the West Indian island of Nevis. Like Turnbull, he still had strong economic and political ties with the West Indies. Tobin began his attack with his 168-page *Cursory Remarks upon the Reverend Mr. Ramsay's Essay*, published in London in 1785. It was the first of his three attempts to assassinate Ramsay's character.[24] Tobin disingenuously claims to "most sincerely join Mr. Ramsay, and every other man of sensibility, in hoping, the blessings of freedom will in due time, be equally diffused over the face of the whole globe," but he soon denounces Ramsay as a hypocrite in his treatment of his own slaves.[25] Referring to him as "this reverend satirist," Tobin says that Ramsay's depiction of West India planters is a "caricature."[26] When he is not libeling Ramsay's character, Tobin denies his evidence. For example, Tobin professes to doubt that the *Zong* incident, which Ramsay brought to wide public attention in his essay, had ever happened.

Apparently motivated by the kind of blatant racism more commonly expressed during the nineteenth century than the eighteenth, Tobin extended Ramsay's account of the condition of blacks in the West Indies to include those in Britain:

> In the year 1773, when the case of Somerset gave occasion for the subject of slavery to be much agitated, it was pretty accurately determined, that there were at that time in England at least fifteen thousand negroes; and that they have greatly increased since is beyond a doubt. A very small proportion of this number are females; it may, therefore, be fairly presumed, that there are ten or twelve thousand able negro men now in England. Out of all this number, I will ask Mr. Ramsay whether he ever saw a single one employed in any laborious task? Did he ever meet with a black ploughman, hedger, ditcher, mower, or reaper, in the country; or a black porter, or chairman, in London? On the contrary, I will be free to affirm, that out of the whole of this number, those who are not in livery are in rags; and such as are not servants, are thieves or mendicants. Even the sentimental Ignatius Sancho himself, the humble friend and imitator of Sterne, continued to prefer the station of a menial servant, till the infirmities of obesity disqualified him. . . . The great number of negroes at present in England, the strange partiality shewn for them by the lower orders of women, and the rapid increase of a dark and contaminated breed, are evils which have long been complained of, and call every day more loudly for enquiry and redress.[27]

By expanding the argument to include free blacks in England, Tobin clearly wanted to undermine any claims for black equality, and he was willing to distort the evidence to support his case. As he knew from Sancho's *Letters*, rather than being "a menial servant" Sancho had been the butler in a noble household, a position of great trust and responsibility. And as Ramsay quickly pointed out in response to Tobin, blacks who had been employed mainly as domestic servants were unlikely competitors for agricultural jobs. One wonders how long Tobin thought it would take to reach the "due time" for people of African descent to merit the "blessings of freedom."

Like Tobin, Gordon Turnbull argued in his sixty-four-page *Apology for Negro Slavery* (1786) that supporters of slavery, not abolitionists, were the true men of feeling and that, rather than being deserving objects of charity, the black poor in London were living proof of the laziness and inferiority of people of African descent.[28] Turnbull, too, defended the "reasonable hypothesis, that Mr. Hume, and some other eminent writers, imagined the Negro-race to be an inferior species of mankind."[29] Even if we concede that "they *are born equal* with white men," Turnbull says, "yet, a minute observation, or thorough knowledge of their character and disposition, seems to evince, that they are not at all fitted to fill the superior stations, or more elevated ranks in civil society."[30] He concludes his consideration of the question of equality with an assertion of specious and profoundly conservative philosophy: "NEGRO slavery appears, then, to be, as far as reason can judge, one of those indispensable and necessary links, in the great chain of causes and events, which cannot, and indeed ought not to be broken; or, in other words, a *part* of the stupendous, admirable, and perfect *whole*, which, if taken away, would leave a chasm, not to be filled up by all the wit or the wisdom of erring and presumptuous man."[31] Without African slavery, Turnbull would have us believe, the universe would collapse.

Turnbull was not only responding to Ramsay's essay. He was trying as well to refute the anti-slave-trade and antislavery arguments Ramsay had made in another pamphlet published in 1784 by James Phillips, *An Inquiry into the Effects of Putting a Stop to the African Slave Trade, and of Granting Liberty to the Slaves in the British Sugar Colonies.* Turnbull mocks as "eccentric and ridiculous" Ramsay's economic argument for transferring sugar production from the West Indies to Africa, replacing slave labor with free. Ramsay's argument, Turnbull claims, is similar to "accounts which Benezet, and some other writers, have given of the slave-trade . . . evidently calculated to mislead the minds of humane people."[32] A few years later Ramsay developed further his argument that free labor was more profitable than slave: "He who procures a freeman to work for him, will never employ a slave; for the first does twice the work of the other, and when he dies, his place is supplied in the natural course of generation, not an enormous expense from the slave-market."[33] Ramsay and others arguing in favor of free labor found their authority in comments Adam Smith had recently made in his widely known and respected *The Wealth of Nations*:

> It appears . . . from the experience of all ages and nations, I believe, that the work done by freemen comes cheaper in the end than that performed by slaves. It is found to do so even at Boston, New York, and Philadelphia, where the wages of the common labour are so very high. . . . The experience of all ages and nations, I believe, demonstrates that the work done by slaves, though it appears to cost only their maintenance, is in the end the dearest of any. A person who can acquire no property, can have no interest but to eat as much, and to labour as little as possible. Whatever work he does beyond what is sufficient to purchase his own maintenance can be squeezed out of him by violence only, and not by any interest of his own.[34]

Despite Smith's and Ramsay's beliefs, Turnbull contends that laborers in Britain are the true "slaves"; slaves in the West Indies are, in effect, "servants": "Compared with the situation of many poor labouring people in this country, who are forced to be the *slaves of necessity*, the condition of the meanest African, who is subject to a good master, may be called, not only comfortable, but happy."[35] Slaves do not run away in the West Indies, Turnbull says, because of "cruel or rigorous treatment." They flee, he asserts, to avoid "that punishment which they know they have deserved by some atrocious crime" committed against the property of "their well-disposed and industrious fellow-servants."[36] In the picture Turnbull draws of the West Indies, most slaves live in conditions that anticipate the modern European welfare state. Hence, concern for enslaved Africans was misdirected: "Philanthropy has no need, then, to visit distant shores, or to explore the sultry regions of the torrid zone, in search of objects for the exercise of her benevolence. – Here, even in this *land of freedom* – there are enough – here, let her drop the tear of generous pity and commiseration; breathe forth the heart-felt sigh of tender sensibility; and, if blessed with affluence, exert her noblest power – the power of doing good!"[37]

In the midst of the press war Ramsay had started, the future historian of the abolitionist movement entered the fray. The son of a clergyman-schoolteacher, Thomas Clarkson was born in Wisbech, Cambridgeshire, in 1760. An outstanding graduate of Cambridge University in 1783, he first learned about the slave trade when in 1785 he entered the competition for the best essay in Latin on the subject of "anne liceat invitos in servitum dare?" – whether enslaving others against their will was ever justified. The Reverend Peter Peckard, vice chancellor of the university, had chosen the topic. Peckard was also one of Equiano's future subscribers. Clarkson later described himself as initially "wholly ignorant" on the subject of slavery and the trade. His reading of Benezet and Ramsay converted him to abolition with an almost religious fervor: "It was but one gloomy subject from morning to night. In the day-time I was uneasy. In the night I had little rest. I sometimes never closed my eyelids for grief. . . . I always slept with a candle in my room, that I might rise out of bed and put down some thoughts as might occur to me in the night, if I judged them valuable, conceiving that no arguments of any moment should be lost in so great a cause."[38]

The writing assignment changed his life. Having won the prize, Clarkson found himself growing obsessed with the mission of ending slavery. His previous calling to become an Anglican clergyman was now superseded by another. Seeking a publisher for an expanded translation of his essay, Clarkson went to London, where a family friend introduced him to James Phillips, who readily agreed to print and distribute the proposed book. Through Phillips, Clarkson soon met Sharp, Ramsay, and the members of the informal group of Quakers publishing against the slave trade. With financial backing from the group, in June 1786 Phillips published Clarkson's *Essay on the Slavery and Commerce of the Human Species, Particularly the African, Translated from a Latin Dissertation, which Was Honoured with the First Prize in the University of Cambridge, for the Year 1785, with Additions*. Clarkson's tripartite essay covers the history of slavery, the slave trade, and the condition of slaves in the West Indies, but he improved upon the earlier efforts of Benezet, Sharp, and Ramsay. He supplemented information gleaned from publications by interviewing "many, both in the naval and military departments, as well as several others, who have been long acquainted with *America* and the *West-Indian* islands."[39]

Clarkson's "additions" to his original Latin treatise include a preface acknowledging his predecessors, criticizing Tobin, "the *Cursory Remarker*," as a libeler of Ramsay, and dismissing Turnbull's *Apology* as "almost too despicable a composition to merit a reply."[40] One of Clarkson's three substantive additions in the body of his text responds directly to Turnbull's specious argument that the great chain of "causes and events" explained the alleged inferiority of other peoples compared to Europeans because Europeans, at

Thomas Clarkson, by Carl Frederik von Breda.
Clarkson, the leading organizer of the abolitionist movement
throughout Great Britain, gathered evidence against the transatlantic
slave trade to be used in publications and debates in Parliament.
Although Clarkson knew Equiano since the mid-1780s and subscribed
for two copies of *The Interesting Narrative*, his *History of the Abolition
of the Slave Trade* (London, 1808), the first published account of
the abolitionist movement, ignores the role played by Equiano,
or any other black, in the abolitionist cause.
(National Portrait Gallery, London)

least in the eyes of the apologists for slavery, were the highest on the ladder.
Africans and their descendants, the apologists insisted, were innately inferior
to Europeans in mental capacities and hence designed for their role as slaves.
The existence of civilizations in Africa was indisputable, Clarkson pointed

out. So, too, was African proficiency in the arts of music and dance. Africans and people of African descent in the colonies are less accomplished in the liberal arts not because of incapacity but due to lack of opportunity for instruction. Phillis Wheatley, several of whose poems Clarkson reproduces, proves the assertors of African inferiority wrong. Clarkson comments that if Wheatley *"was designed for slavery"* because of her intelligence and literary abilities, as people like Tobin and Turnbull would have to argue from their premises, "the greater part of the inhabitants of Britain must lose their claim to freedom." Clarkson adds that as further proof of blacks' abilities he could also quote "the prose compositions of Ignatius Sancho, who received some little education," but "his letters are too well known, to make any extract, or indeed any farther mention of him, necessary."[41]

While staying with Ramsay at Teston during the summer of 1786, soon after his essay appeared, Clarkson decided to devote himself fully to the abolitionist cause. Clarkson and his new friends decided that to promote the cause they should even more aggressively gather information and distribute it to the public at large directly and via the members of Parliament. Probably through Ramsay's patrons, the Middletons, Clarkson met William Wilberforce, who agreed the following May to lead the fight in the House of Commons against the African slave trade. On 22 May 1787 twelve men representing a range of religious and political beliefs formed the London Abolition Committee, with Granville Sharp as its chairman and Samuel Hoare as its treasurer and banker. The committee became the local engine driving the national organization called the Society for Effecting the Abolition of the Slave Trade (SEAST) that grew out of it. Sharp and Clarkson were two of its three Anglican members. The London Abolition Committee's core came from the five surviving members of the informal Quaker group, including Hoare, Phillips, and Woods.

Unlike the earlier group, SEAST was public from the outset, intended "for procuring such Information and Evidence, and for distributing Clarkson's *Essay* and such other Publications, as may tend to the Abolition of the Slave Trade, and for directing the application of such monies as are already, or may hereafter be collected, for the above Purposes." The founders of SEAST made two strategic decisions that Equiano would also embrace when he wrote his *Interesting Narrative* the following year. They opposed the slave trade on both economic and moral grounds, declaring it "impolitick and unjust."[42] And they decided that to avoid the issues of private property rights and the government's disputable legal power to regulate internal colonial trade, as well as to appeal successfully to as large an audience as possible, SEAST members "should define their object to be the abolition of the Slave-Trade, and not of the slavery which sprang from it."[43] Even Sharp and Woods, who had published arguments against both the trade and the institution, agreed that SEAST should not let the pursuit of the excellent – the eradication of slavery – diminish the chances of achieving the good – abolition of the African slave trade – by alienating anyone who might be willing to take one step in the right direction. Besides, "by aiming at the abolition of the Slave Trade, they believed they were laying the axe at the very root" of the institution of slavery.[44] Not even all the founding members were emancipationists. Hoare, for example, never supported freeing the slaves in the West Indies because he considered the government honor-bound to protect property rights.[45] The emancipationists among SEAST's members hoped that the first step of abolition would compel slave owners to treat their slaves better if the supply of relatively inexpensive imports was stopped, raising the slaves' standards of living and eventually increasing their economic bargaining position to the point where they would be competitors with free labor. After abolition, they assumed, emancipation would follow by evolution. Unfortunately, the practical suspension of the trade during the American Revolution showed that the end of the trade need not mean the end of slavery. Furthermore, the situation in the former British colonies in North America demonstrated that self-sustaining slave populations neither necessarily resulted from nor led to improved living conditions.

SEAST quickly went to work. Two days after forming, it ordered Phillips to print two thousand copies of *A Summary View of the Slave Trade* Clarkson had been commissioned to write, the first of several pamphlets by him SEAST sponsored. Phillips was employed to distribute a circular letter to more than one hundred potential supporters throughout Britain. Meanwhile, SEAST sent Clarkson to Bristol, Lancaster, and Liverpool to collect more evidence and enlist supporters. Responses from people like Wesley demonstrated that SEAST was reaching sympathizers well beyond the Quaker network, and donors sent substantial sums to London. In contact with the London Abolition Committee, local abolition committees were forming by the end of 1787. Two more of Equiano's future subscribers, Thomas Walker and Thomas Cooper, political and social reformers who called for expansion of the electorate, established an abolition committee in Manchester. Opposition to the African slave trade was politically nonpartisan and religiously nonsectarian. Conservative Christians opposed it because it was sinful, political reformers because it denied the natural rights of humanity, social reformers because it was oppressive, and economic theorists because it was inefficient. Abolition was quickly becoming a truly national movement. At the same time, through the transatlantic Quaker network and Phillips, the London Abolition Committee established ties with abolition societies in Philadelphia and New York. SEAST suggested to a French correspondent who offered help that he create a similar organization in France.[46]

Both proponents of the slave trade and abolitionists recognized that the subject of abolition was a very marketable commodity. Publications had helped to create the market; the market in turn demanded more publications. In 1788 SEAST had Phillips reissue Clarkson's *Essay on the Slavery and Commerce of the Human Species*, Benezet's *Some Historical Account of Guinea*, and Wesley's *Thoughts upon Slavery*. In 1787 and 1788 Clarkson was commissioned to write several new tracts for the cause. Phillips and other London publishers also produced abolitionist pamphlets by new writers, including *A Letter to the Treasurer of the Society Instituted for the Purpose of Effecting the Abolition of the Slave Trade* in 1787 by Robert Boucher Nichols, an Anglican minister; *An Account of the Slave Trade on the Coast of Africa* in 1788 by Alexander Falconbridge, a former surgeon on slave ships; and *Thoughts on the African Slave Trade*, also in 1788, by the former slave trader turned evangelical minister John Newton. The proslavery West India interest struck back with its own hired writers, including Hector McNeill, *Observations on the Treatment of the Negroes, in the Island of Jamaica*, published in Liverpool in 1788, and Raymund Harris, *Scriptural Researches on the Licitness of the Slave-Trade, Shewing its Conformity with the Principles of Natural and Revealed Religion, Delineated in the Sacred Writings of the Word of God*, published in London in 1788.

SEAST did not restrict its publicity campaign to the written word.[47] In July 1787 it decided that it should have an official seal and created a subcommittee, which included Hoare, Phillips, and Woods, to design one. To produce the design the subcommittee turned to Josiah Wedgwood, soon to be one of Equiano's first subscribers. James Phillips knew Wedgwood, a non-Quaker, through business ties. Because of his aggressive and imaginative use of advertising to sell the classically designed pottery he manufactured to meet the cultural and social aspirations of the "middling sorts," Wedgwood exemplified the production side of the "consumer revolution" in the later eighteenth century.[48] He was also known as a philanthropist and model employer who provided health care, housing, and schooling for his workers and their families in his factory town of Etruria in Staffordshire. In the fall of 1787

Am I Not a Man and a Brother.
This official seal of the Society
for Effecting the Abolition of the
Slave Trade was designed by
William Hackwood for Josiah
Wedgwood in 1787.
(© Copyright The Trustees
of The British Museum)

Wedgwood delivered the prototype of the circular seal for approval. It depicts a nearly naked enchained slave on one knee who looks up and raises his hands imploringly, as if speaking the words engraved around him: "Am I Not a Man and a Brother?"

While both the pro- and anti-slave-trade forces were trying to sway the public, they also sought to influence the members of Parliament. The Quaker abolitionists had unsuccessfully petitioned Parliament in 1783 to outlaw the slave trade. Five years later the Quakers were but a part of a now far larger and therefore potentially more influential lobby against the trade that included independently organized local abolitionist committees as well as the London Abolition Committee. Having received advice from organizers of earlier national petition campaigns for parliamentary reform, the abolitionists discovered that a large part of the British population was turning against the trade. By early 1788, in Manchester alone, more than ten thousand people signed a petition against the slave trade. The House of Commons received fifteen petitions during the first week of February. Eighty-eight more petitions came in during the next six weeks.

In response to the growing abolitionist pressure the transatlantic slave trade came under official scrutiny by both the executive and legislative branches of the government. On 11 February 1788 the king issued a Royal Order to the Privy Council, directing it to start an investigation of the trade. The Privy Council in 1788 had about 125 members, consisting of representatives from the House of Lords and House of Commons as well as courtiers and ministers who advised the king and who directed the major ecclesiastical, executive, and judicial offices. Investigation of the slave trade fell to the approximately twenty-five members of the Privy Council's Committee on Trade and Foreign Plantations (the Board of Trade), whose president was Charles Jenkinson, Baron Hawkesbury. On 16 February Clarkson, Hoare, Phillips, and three other SEAST members began to gather evidence to present before Hawkesbury.

Concerned that Hawkesbury might try to bury the abolitionist cause at the executive level, SEAST pressed forward with its legislative campaign in the House of Commons. By the beginning of April 1788 everything seemed ready for the abolitionists' assault on the trade. Public pressure was being expressed through the petitions that were pouring in. The chancellor of the exchequer and First Lord of the Treasury, William Pitt, like his father before him the de facto prime minister, was known to be sympathetic to the cause. And the abolitionists had a respected leader in the House, Wilberforce, who was prepared to introduce an abolition bill. The plan fell apart when Wilberforce became critically ill in the third week of April. Disappointed but not desperate, the abolitionists redirected their energies. Pitt himself introduced in May a resolution committing the Commons to taking up the issue of abolition during the next session, which would begin in November. Pitt's political opponents, Charles James Fox and Edmund Burke, spoke in support of the resolution, which passed unanimously.

The abolitionists achieved one legislative victory during the 1787–88 session of Parliament. It was a very small, qualified, and completely unanticipated victory but a victory nonetheless. It would turn out to be the only one they would have before the turn of the century. During the debate over Pitt's resolution Sir William Dolben raised the issue of overcrowding on slave ships.[49] Dolben acted completely on his own, without having consulted SEAST. One of the two members representing Oxford in the House of Commons, Dolben would soon join Equiano's list of subscribers. On 21 May Dolben introduced a bill to regulate the amount of space allotted per slave on the Middle Passage. In response, members representing the West India interest submitted petitions from Liverpool slave traders and merchants defending the trade, but they could not withstand the overwhelming bipartisan support for Dolben's argument that the overcrowding on slave ships would "shock the humanity and rouse the indignation of . . . every man of feeling in the country."[50] Dolben's bill passed easily in the Commons and was taken up in the Lords on 25 June. The elected members of the Commons were far more sensitive and responsive to popular opinion than were the hereditary members of the Lords, as the fate of Dolben's bill and subsequent attempts to abolish the slave trade demonstrated. Because of opposition from members like Lord Sidney, the secretary of state for Home Affairs, and the Lord Chancellor, Edward, Lord Thurlow, who presided over the debate, a much-amended version of the bill passed by only two votes on 10 July. With the king's assent the following day it became the Slave Trade Regulation Act.

Equiano followed with great interest the development of the abolitionist cause in the press and Parliament during the late 1780s, intervening whenever he could. As he did so, his public identity evolved to match the temper of the times. Although he always remained Gustavus Vassa in private, even after the publication of his autobiography, he increasingly embraced an African identity in the two years between his dismissal from the black poor resettlement project in March 1787 and his public claim in April 1789 of an African birth. As his public identity evolved, he also increasingly came to be recognized as the spokesman for people of African descent in Britain.

As we all do, Equiano chose from the various subject positions available to him the one or ones most appropriate for the particular audience or audiences he was addressing. Sometimes he spoke or wrote primarily as a native of Africa, sometimes as a diasporan African, sometimes as an African Briton, sometimes as a Briton, sometimes as a Christian, and at other times as more than one of the above. Just as we are at the same time parents to our children and children to our parents, our position as subject can change while we remain the same. Each of us has overlapping identities, one or more of which dominates in different contexts. Skilled rhetoricians know how to shift their positions, that is, how to emphasize different aspects of their identities to best influence and affect their readers or listeners. The private and public letters, book reviews, and petitions Equiano wrote and published in 1787 and 1788 display a masterful rhetorician honing his skills.

On 15 December 1787, using just the name Gustavus Vassa, Equiano, with nine other men, signed a letter entitled "The Address of Thanks of the Sons of Africa to the Honourable Granville Sharp, Esq." Only Cugoano and one other cosigner of the letter these men sent to Sharp identified themselves with both African and slave names in "this memorial of our thanks for your good and faithful services towards us, and for your humane commiseration of our brethren and countrymen unlawfully held in slavery." Telling Sharp that they wish his "valuable treatises" would "be collected and preserved," these self-styled "Sons of Africa" refer to themselves as "we, who are a part, or descendants, of the much-wronged people of Africa" (329, 328). Clearly, Equiano and his colleagues believed that one was as much a "Son of Africa" by descent as by birth. At the end of the eighteenth century one could be African without ever having set foot in Africa. Consequently, a diasporan African identity was as authentic as a native one.

We can see Equiano shaping his public African identity as he engaged in the press war over abolition through the four book reviews he published in the *Public Advertiser* and the *Morning Chronicle, and London Advertiser* during the first half of 1788. By definition, book reviews are intertextual. The text of the review exists because a prior text – the book reviewed – exists. The review must be read in light of the book reviewed, and the ways the book is subsequently read will be affected by the review. The print exchange between Ramsay and Tobin epitomized the intertextuality of the larger dialogue over abolition during the last decades of the eighteenth century.

Equiano entered the debate by taking on both James Tobin and Gordon Turnbull within one week in the pages of the *Public Advertiser*. On 28 January his letter, "To J.T. Esq; Author of the BOOKS called CURSORY REMARKS & REJOINDER" (330–32) appeared in the newspaper. By calling him "Esquire" Equiano acknowledges Tobin's superior social status as a gentleman. But we quickly discover that that acknowledgment of Tobin's social superiority is strictly pro forma, and it soon turns ironic. Equiano immediately assumes the position of moral superiority to Tobin by invoking the Bible against him. "Sir," says Equiano, "that to love mercy and judge rightly of things is an honour to man, nobody I think will deny; but [quoting Psalm 59:20] 'if he understandeth not, nor sheweth compassion to the sufferings of his fellow-creatures, he is like the beasts that perish.'" "Excuse me Sir," Equiano continues, "if I think you in no better predicament than that exhibited in the latter part of the above clause; for can any man less ferocious than a tiger or a wolf attempt to justify the cruelties inflicted on the negroes in the West Indies? You certainly cannot be susceptible of human pity to be so callous to their complicated woes! Who could but the Author of the Cursory Remarks so debase his nature, as not to feel his keenest pangs of heart on reading their deplorable story?" (330).

Equiano turns Tobin's own rhetoric against him. A committed racist, Tobin had contended that blacks are less than fully human because they are incapable of the same degree of feeling as whites. To Equiano, Tobin, not black slaves, demonstrates "unrelenting barbarity." Consequently, Equiano tells him, "for as you are so fond of flogging others, it is no bad proof of your deserving a flagellation yourself. Is it not written in the 15th chapter of Numbers, the 15th and 16th verses, that there is the same law for the stranger as for you?" Equiano then asks,

> Sir, why do you rob him of the common privilege given to all by the Universal and Almighty Legislator? Why exclude him from the enjoyment of benefits which he has equal right to with yourself? Why treat him as if he was not of like feeling? Does civilization warrant these incursions upon natural justice? No. – Does religion? No. – Benevolence to all is its essence, and do unto others as we would others should do unto us, its grand precept – to Blacks as well as Whites, all being the children of the same parent. Those, therefore, who transgress those sacred obligations, and here, Mr. Remarker, I think you are caught, are not superior to brutes which understandeth not, nor to beasts which perish. (330)

In Equiano's review Tobin the gentleman has become Tobin the beast because of his own actions and statements.

But Equiano is far from done with Tobin. He calls him a liar who delights in misrepresentation: "From your having been in the West Indies, you must know that the facts stated by the Rev. Mr. [James] Ramsay are true; and yet regardless of the truth, you controvert them. This surely is supporting a bad cause at all events, and brandishing falsehood to strengthen the hand of the oppressor" (330). Equiano appropriates the voice of God to curse Tobin and his fellow defenders of slavery, and in so cursing them Equiano overturns the current power relationship between whites and blacks:

> Recollect, Sir, that you are told in the 17th verse of the 19th chapter of Leviticus, "You shall not suffer sin upon your neighbour"; and you will not I am sure, escape the upbraidings of your conscience, unless you are fortunate enough to have none; and remember also, that the oppressor and the oppressed are in the hands of the just and awful God, who says, Vengeance is mine and I will repay – repay the oppressor and the justifier of the oppression. How dreadful then will your fate be? The studied and torturing punishments, inhuman, as they are, of a barbarous planter, or a more barbarous overseer, will be tenderness compared to the provoked wrath of an angry but righteous God! who will raise, I have the fullest

confidence, many of the sable race to the joys of Heaven, and cast the oppressive white to that doleful place, where he will cry, but will cry in vain,
for a drop of water! (330–31)

From invoking divine authority to damn Tobin's immorality, Equiano
shifts to using his own personal experience to undermine Tobin's credibility
on the issue of how well West Indian slaves are treated: "The contrary of this
I know is the fact at every one of the islands I have been, and I have been at
no less than fifteen. But who will dispute with such an invective fibber? Why
nobody to be sure; for you'll tell, I wish I could say truths, but you oblige me
to use ill manners, you lie faster than Old Nick can hear them." Cleverly,
Equiano claims his readers as allies in the case against Tobin: "The public
can bear testimony with me that you are a malicious slanderer of an honest,
industrious, injured people!" (331).

Even more cleverly, Equiano closes his review with a response to Tobin's
passionate treatment of the subject of interracial sexuality, implying not only
that Tobin may have hypocritically engaged in the practice himself but may
even be the product of such intercourse: "Now, Sir, would it not be more honour to us to have a few darker visages than perhaps yours among us, than
inundation of such evils? and to provide effectual remedies, by a liberal policy against evils which may be traced to some of our most wealthy Planters
as their fountain, and which may have smeared the purity of even your own
chastity?" Equiano's readers would have recalled that Ramsay had earlier referred to "some very near black and yellow relations" of Tobin.[51] Equiano's
response to Tobin's dismay about racial pollution in England seems calculated to give Tobin apoplexy:

As the ground-work, why not establish intermarriages at home, and in
our Colonies? and encourage open, free, and generous love upon Nature's own wide and extensive plan, subservient only to moral rectitude,
without distinction of the colour of a skin? . . . That ancient, most wise,
and inspired politician, Moses, . . . established marriage with strangers by
his own example – The Lord confirmed them – and punished Aaron and
Miriam for vexing their brother for marrying the Ethiopian – Away then
with your narrow impolitic notion of preventing by law what will be a
national honour, national strength, and productive of national virtue –
Intermarriages! (332)

Equiano assumes the voice of the evangelist John to conclude his book review by threatening Tobin from the position of the highest human authority: "If

I come, I will remember the deeds which he doeth, prating against us with malicious words" (3 John:10). Equiano ironically signs his review of Tobin's books as "Your fervent Servant, GUSTAVUS VASSA, the Ethiopian and the King's late Commissary for the African Settlement" (332). He calls himself an "Ethiopian" no doubt because of the positive biblical associations with that identity. As an "Ethiopian" he is a "stranger" to his readers, but his reference to himself as "the King's late Commissary" reminds them that at the same time he is also a fellow subject of the realm. He is "fervent," indeed, but not in the way Tobin expected his slaves to demonstrate fervor, and he is "fervent" in subject and language rarely found in his later *Interesting Narrative*. Like any great writer Equiano was a great *reader* of his own audiences, knowing when he could afford to take a radical stance and when a more moderate position would gain him an even wider readership.

He was in no mood to be moderate in 1788, however. Still writing as "Vassa, the Ethiopian and the King's late Commissary," a week after he attacked Tobin he turned his attention to Tobin's "friend" Turnbull. In his letter "To MR. GORDON TURNBULL, Author of an 'Apology for NEGRO SLAVERY,'" like Clarkson and Cugoano before him, Equiano refers to Tobin as "the cursory remarker" (330–32). He even appropriates and polishes a passage from Cugoano's *Thoughts and Sentiments* to compare Turnbull and Tobin to the pagan Demetrius in the New Testament: "You and your friend, J. Tobin, the cursory remarker, resemble Demetrius, the silversmith, seeing your craft in danger, a craft, however, not so innocent or justifiable as the making of shrines for Diana, for that though wicked enough, left the persons of men at liberty, but yours enslaves both body and soul – and sacrifices your fellow-creatures on the altar of avarice" (333).[52]

In Equiano's letter to Turnbull, also published in the *Public Advertiser*, he again uses the rhetoric of inversion. In his letter to Tobin he had called him inhuman. In Equiano's second book review Turnbull's apology for slavery becomes an "Apology for oppression" (332). Turnbull and Tobin are benighted, anti-Christian, and un-British: "In this enlightened age, it is scarcely credible that a man should be born and educated, in the British dominions especially, possessed of minds so warped as the author of the Cursory Remarks and yourself. Strange that in a land which boasts of the purest light of the Gospel, and the most perfect freedom, there should be found advocates of oppression – for the most abject and iniquitous kind of slavery" (332–33). Equiano sarcastically notes "the ability and the modesty" Tobin and Turnbull displayed in their treatment of "that friend to the rights of mankind, the Rev. James Ramsay" and his "noble" essay (333). In 1788 the terms *enlightened, lib-*

erty, and *rights of mankind* did not yet have the radical implications they would acquire after the French Revolution the following year. But Equiano was sufficiently immoderate and radical in his review of Turnbull's book to call explicitly for "the abolition of Slavery" itself and not just the slave trade (333).

Equiano offers himself as a "witness" against the abuses of slavery and in defense of Ramsay: "Many of the facts he relates I know to be true, and many others still more shocking, if possible, have fallen within my own observation, within my own feeling; for were I to enumerate even my own sufferings in the West Indies, which perhaps I may one day offer to the public, the disgusting catalogue would be almost too great for belief" (333–34). To refute Turnbull's "hypothesis, that the Negro race is an inferior species of mankind," he simply advises the "fool" Turnbull to read Acts 17:26: "'God hath made of one blood all nations of men, for to dwell on all the face of the earth, &c.'" (334).

Equiano cites Scripture as if the Bible unequivocally supported the abolitionist position. Unfortunately, such was not the case, as the Reverend Raymund Harris demonstrated with great skill and clarity in his 214-page *Scriptural Researches on the Licitness of the Slave-Trade*, published in Liverpool early in 1788. When Equiano published his letter "To the Rev. Mr. RAYMUND HARRIS, the Author of the Book called – 'Scripture Researches on the Licitness of the Slave Trade'" (337–39) in the 28 April 1788 issue of the *Public Advertiser*, he apparently did not know what would soon become public knowledge. Harris was rather a shady character. His real name was Don Raymondo Hormaza, and he was a Jesuit priest who had been expelled from Spain in 1767. After wandering around Europe for several years he moved to Liverpool, where he opened a school. There he soon found himself disagreeing with the Roman Catholic bishop, who relieved him of his priestly duties. If Equiano did not know, he certainly correctly guessed that Harris was a hired pen. The city of Liverpool awarded Harris one hundred pounds for his efforts on behalf of the slave trade and slavery interests.

Although Harris was not the first apologist to argue from biblical precedents, he was the most effective in forcing his many opponents, including Ramsay, either to concede, at least implicitly, that a literal reading of Scripture did not support abolition or to resort to ad hominem attacks on him to divert attention from the logic of his argument.[53] Equiano's review illustrates the difficulties Harris's respondents faced. The closest Equiano comes to an ad hominem comment is calling Harris an "advocate" for "the Worshipful Committee of the Company of Merchants trading to Africa" (337). As Equiano recognized, the stakes in the abolition debate were higher in late

April than they had been when he reviewed Tobin and Turnbull before either the Privy Council or Commons investigations had begun: "The Subject of Slavery is now grown to be a serious one, when we consider the buying and selling of Negroes not as a clandestine or piratical business, but as an open public trade, encouraged and promoted by Acts of Parliament. Being contrary to religion, it must be deemed a national sin, and as such may have a consequence that ought always to be dreaded. – May God give us grace to repent of this abominable crime before it be too late!" (337).

In trying to reclaim Saint Paul from Harris for the abolitionist cause Equiano was forced to defend the kind of loose interpretation of the Bible Protestants normally accused Roman Catholics and especially Jesuits of practicing. Rather than attending to what Saint Paul literally says about slavery, Equiano contends, we should be concerned with "the whole tenor" of his writings and what he "plainly insinuates" and "implied" (338). Equiano has little choice but to argue that Saint Paul allowed political considerations to compromise his moral clarity:

> St. Paul in his epistles enjoins servants to submission, and not to grieve on the account of their temporal estate. For if, instead of this, he had absolutely declared the iniquity of slavery, tho' established and authorised by the laws of a temporal government, he would have occasioned more tumult than reformation: among the multitude of slaves there would have been more striving for temporal than spiritual happiness; yet it plainly appears by the insinuations which immediately follow, that he thought it derogatory to the honour of Christianity, that men who are bought with the inestimable price of Christ's blood, shall be esteemed slaves, and the private property of their fellow-men. (338)

Under different circumstances, Equiano believes, Saint Paul would have denounced slavery unequivocally: "Had Christianity been established by temporal authority in those countries where Paul preached, as it is at present, in this kingdom, we need not doubt but that he would have urged, nay, compelled the masters, as he did Philemon, by the most pressing arguments, to treat their quondam slaves, not now as servants, but above servants – a brother beloved. – May God open your eyes while it is called to-day, to see aright, before you go hence and be no more seen" (338). Equiano's Saint Paul sounds like an earlier version of Equiano himself and others who opposed slavery but for practical reasons chose to emphasize only their opposition to the slave trade.

Not all of Equiano's book reviews were negative, and he was becoming something of a celebrity. He also praised Beilby Porteus in the *Public Advertiser* on 13 February 1788: "May the worthy Lord Bishop of London be blessed for his pathetic and humane sermon on behalf of the Africans" (335). And his letter "To the Author of the POEM ON HUMANITY" (340–41), published in the *Morning Chronicle, and London Advertiser* on 27 June 1788, commended "the spirit of philanthropy" (340) Samuel Jackson Pratt displayed in his *Humanity, or the Rights of Nature, a Poem; in Two Books. By the Author of Sympathy*. The relative brevity of Equiano's positive reviews suggests that he was most at home as a controversialist. On 1 July the *Morning Chronicle, and London Advertiser* assumed that its readers needed and wanted to know more about him:

> *Gustavus Vasa*, who addressed a letter in the name of his oppressed countrymen, to the author of the popular poem on Humanity, which devotes several pages to that now universal subject of discussion, the Slave Trade, is, notwithstanding its romantick sound, the real name of an Ethiopian now resident in this metropolis, a native of Eboe, who was himself twice kidnapped by the English, and twice sold into slavery. He has since been appointed the King's commissary for the African settlement, and besides having an irreproachable moral character, has frequently distinguished himself by occasional essays in the different papers, which manifest a strong and sound understanding.

Equiano did not restrict his interventions in the abolitionist debate to book reviews. Once the Privy Council and Parliament took up the issue of the slave trade, he sought ways to participate. On 13 February 1788, two days after the king issued his Royal Order to the Privy Council, Equiano used the *Public Advertiser* to address "the Senate of GREAT BRITAIN." Praising the heroes of the abolitionist movement, he encouraged the legislators to do the right thing:

> May Heaven make you what you should be, the dispensers of light, liberty and science to the uttermost parts of the earth; then will be glory to God on the highest – on earth peace and goodwill to man: – Glory, honour, peace, &c. to every soul of man that worketh good; to the Britons first (because to them the Gospel is preached) and also to the nations: To that truly immortal and illustrious advocate of our liberty, Granville Sharp, Esq., the philanthropist and justly Reverend James Ramsay, and

the much to be honoured body of gentlemen called *Friends*, who have exerted every endeavour to break the accursed yoke of Slavery, and ease
the heavy burthens of the oppressed Negroes. . . . May the fear of the
Lord prolong their days, and cause their memory to be blessed, and may
their numbers be increased, and their expectations filled with gladness,
for commiserating the poor Africans, who are counted as beasts of
burthen by base-minded men. (334–35)

Although the letter is signed "AETHIOPIANUS," we know that
Equiano was the author and that in it he intended to speak for all black
Britons. The same letter appeared on 21 February in the *Morning Post, and
Daily Advertiser*, signed "Gustavus Vasa, for the Ethiopians."[54]

When the Privy Council's Board of Trade began to gather evidence,
Equiano offered to testify before it. Turned down, he wrote a letter as "Gustavus Vassa, late Commissary for the African Settlement," to Lord Hawkesbury on 13 March. He also published a slightly revised version of the same
letter in the *London Advertiser* on 31 March (335–36). Forgoing the biblical
diction and allusions as well as the appeals to feelings found in some of his
earlier public letters, Equiano offers Hawkesbury a logical argument implicitly based on Adam Smith's principles of economics. "A commercial Intercourse with Africa," he says, would open "an inexhaustible Source of Wealth
to the manufacturing Interest of Great Britain; and to all which the Slave
Trade is a physical Obstruction." The case for "a free Trade" with Africa,
which would lead to the "Abolition of . . . diabolical Slavery," was more compelling now than ever before because, "if I am not misinformed, the manufacturing Interest is equal, if not superior to the landed Interest as to Value."
Through commerce, "Civilization" turned the "Aborigines of Britain" into consumers. Civilization would do the same for Africans: "A SYSTEM of commerce once established in Africa, the Demand for Manufactories will most
rapidly augment, as the native Inhabitants will sensibly adopt our Fashions,
Manner, Customs, &c. &c." As a trade in goods replaced a trade in people,
"in proportion to the Civilization, so will be the Consumption of British
Manufactures." Equiano included another slightly modified version of his
letter to Hawkesbury in his autobiography the next year, thus widening his
audience for a third time.

While Equiano was trying to influence the Board of Trade, he also went
over their heads by sending a "petition on behalf of my African brethren" to
Queen Charlotte on 21 March, asking her to intercede with King George III
in their favor:

To the QUEEN's *Most Excellent Majesty.*

MADAM,

YOUR Majesty's well known benevolence and humanity embolden me to approach your royal presence, trusting that the obscurity of my situation will not prevent your Majesty from attending to the sufferings for which I plead.

Yet I do not solicit your royal pity for my own distress: my sufferings, although numerous, are in a measure forgotten. I supplicate your Majesty's compassion for millions of my African countrymen, who groan under the lash of tyranny in the West Indies.

The oppression and cruelty exercised to the unhappy negroes there, have at length reached the British legislature, and they are now deliberating on its redress; even several persons of property in slaves in the West Indies, have petitioned parliament against its continuance, sensible that it is as impolitic as it is unjust and what is inhuman must ever be unwise.

Your majesty's reign has hitherto been distinguished by private acts of benevolence and bounty; surely the more extended the misery is, the greater claim it has to your Majesty's compassion, and the greater must be your Majesty's pleasure in administering to its relief.

I presume, therefore, gracious Queen, to implore your interposition with your royal consort, in favour of the wretched Africans; that, by your Majesty's benevolent influence, a period may now be put to their misery; and that they may be raised from the condition of brutes, to which they are at present degraded, to the rights and situation of men,[55] and be admitted to partake of the blessings of your Majesty's happy government; so shall your Majesty enjoy the heart-felt pleasure of procuring happiness to millions, and be rewarded in the grateful prayers of themselves, and of their posterity.

And may the all-bountiful Creator shower on your Majesty, and the Royal Family, every blessing that this world can afford, and every fulness of joy which divine revelation has promised us in the next.

I am your Majesty's most dutiful and devoted servant to command,

GUSTAVUS VASSA,

The oppressed Ethiopian.

No. 53, Baldwin's-Gardens. (231–32)

In 1783 Benezet had petitioned the queen on the same subject.

Equiano followed the legislative progress of Dolben's regulation bill in person and in print. On 19 June 1788, the day after the House of Commons passed the bill, the *Public Advertiser* published a letter from "Gustavus Vassa, the African," "to the Honourable and Worthy Members of the BRITISH SENATE" (339–40). As "one of the oppressed natives of Africa" he was writing "to offer you the warmest thanks of a heart glowing with gratitude for your late humane interference on the behalf of my injured countrymen." He had been willing to testify against the slave trade but found that his testimony was not needed: "While I attended your debate on the Bill for the relief of my countrymen, now depending before you, my heart burned within me, and glowed with gratitude to those who supported the cause of humanity. I could have wished for an opportunity of recounting to you not only my own sufferings, which, though numerous, have been nearly forgotten, but those of which I have been a witness for many years, that they might have influenced your decision; but I thank God, your humanity anticipated my wishes, and rendered such recital unnecessary." He was already anticipating further victories "the next year": "Our cries have at length reached your ears, and I trust you are already in some measure convinced that the Slave Trade is as impolitic as inhuman, and as such must ever be unwise." If he is able "to return to my estate in Elese" in Africa, he will host the legislators who supported the bill and erect an altar to Ramsay and Clarkson (he specifically thanks three of his future subscribers: Dolben, Samuel Whitbread, and George Pitt). As "the African" he had finally settled on a public identity he would maintain for the rest of his life.

When Lord Sidney opposed Dolben's bill in the House of Lords, "Gustavus Vassa, the African," responded to him in the *Public Advertiser* on 28 June: "Having been present last Wednesday [25 June] at the debate on the Slave Bill, now depending in the House of Lords, I with much surprize heard your Lordship combat the very principle of the Bill, and assert that it was founded in mistaken humanity. At the first, such assertion would appear rather paradoxical. If imposing a restraint on the cruelties practised towards wretches who never injured us, be mistaken humanity, what are the proper channels through which it ought to be directed?" Sidney had called for deferring any discussion of the slave trade until the next session of Parliament, adding that he believed enslaved Africans benefited from being taken from a land of barbarism to the allegedly better conditions they found in the West Indies. In support of his belief he cited information he received from Captain Thompson about the failure of the Sierra Leone settlement and the desire some of the settlers expressed to leave Africa and return to the West Indies. After again justifying his own behavior in the resettlement project, Equiano pointed out that the project failed because the poorly supplied settlers reached Sierra Leona, just at the commencement of the rains – At that season of the year, it is impossible to cultivate the lands; their provisions therefore were exhausted before they could derive benefit from agriculture. – And it is not surprising that many, especially the Lascars, whose constitutions are very tender, and who had been cooped up in a ship from October to June, and accommodated in the manner I have mentioned, should be so wasted by their confinement as not long to survive it. – As for the native Africans who remained, there was no object for their industry; and surely, my Lord, they shewed a much less indulgent spirit in going to the West-Indies than staying at Sierra Leona to starve.

He repeated his offer to testify in person before Parliament: "The above facts and many more instances of oppression and injustices, not only relative to the expedition to Sierra Leona, but to the Slave Trade in general, I could incontrovertibly establish, if at any time it should be judged necessary to call upon me for that purpose" (341–43).

On 15 July, five days after Dolben's bill became law, the *Morning Chronicle, and London Advertiser* published three letters signed by Gustavus Vassa and several other "persons of colour" (343–45). They were addressed to Dolben, Pitt, and Charles James Fox, who in the spirit of bipartisanship had "cooperated with the minister [Pitt], and . . . nobly considered the rights of humanity as a common cause" (345).

Equiano's participation in the abolition debate did not go unremarked in 1788. By March he had already become a well-enough-known commentator that when a correspondent to the *Gentleman's Magazine* counseled moderation to abolitionists, he hid his identity behind the pseudonym "Gustavus." He was presumably trying to appropriate Equiano's authority and credibility to support a position Equiano himself did not hold. On 5 July, during the debate in the Lords over Dolben's bill, the *Times* offered its readers an image of Equiano as a man with a sardonic sense of humor rarely displayed in his writings: "GUSTAVUS VASA, the black, who has personally attended all the discussions on the Slave Trade in both Houses of Parliament, was asked what became of the prisoners taken in the African wars, who were not sold to the European Merchants? He replied, 'That they made of them *Sable Soup*, and *Black Bouille*!'"

Equiano's prominence also caused his name to be invoked in a yearlong debate among pseudonymous correspondents in the *Morning Chronicle, and London Advertiser* over the alleged inferiority of Africans. The debate began on 5 February 1788 when "Civis," citing the philosopher David Hume and the historian Edward Gibbon, among others, asserted that the enslavement of blacks was justified because Africans were below Europeans on the chain of being. "Civis" also makes pseudoscientific claims for racial inferiority based on alleged differences in head shape and size and the location of calf muscles. He situates blacks on the chain "between the Monkeys and the Whites," likening them to "the Ourang Outang." Consequently, he says, "African Blacks" are mentally and culturally inferior to whites. In comments that echo those Thomas Jefferson had made four years earlier in his *Notes on the State of Virginia*, "Civis" specifically denigrates Ignatius Sancho: "I have seen his letters, and feel no hesitation to declare, there does not appear to me any mark of genius, any taste, any correctness of thought or expression throughout the whole book; it is a languid, lifeless production, and had a White man been the author, I will venture to say, it would not have been known out of the bookseller's shop."[56]

Several opponents challenged "Civis," including "Christian" on 11 July. If the chain of being exists as "Civis" describes it, "Christian" argues,

> supposing a superior and inferior race, there must be a line drawn between the lowest of the higher, and the highest of the lower. Therefore, if they be superior and inferior races, there must be a distinction between the lowest white man and highest Negro, in their intellects, and the degree of their capacity for moral improvement. Now I am far from thinking Civis is one of the lowest of the white race; I dare say he is a very respectable person. Yet from any thing that has appeared under his name, I should not fear to have a black correspondent of yours, Gustavus Vasa, pitted against him, and the publick left to determine which of the two has the best claim to humanity.

To bolster his case "Christian" quoted Ramsay.

"Civis" fired back at his critics – "Benezet, jun.," "Humanitas," "Matth. Goodenough," and "Christian" – on 19 August. Of "Christian," who he mistakenly assumes is Ramsay, "Civis" says, "I will neither envy nor interrupt this gentleman in the enjoyment of all the amusement and instruction he can derive from the performances of Mr. Ramsay and Gustavus Vasa. . . . If I were even to allow some share of merit to Gustavus Vasa, Ignatius Sancho, &c. it would not prove equality more, than a pig having been taught to fetch a card, letters, &c. would show it not to be a pig, but some other animal. As to the "Christian's" wish to be pitted against the former of these blacks, I can only assure him, I am neither apprehensive nor ambitious of meeting him or his friend; and should I decline the contest, it would be from emotions of a very opposite nature from fear."

The direct attack on Ramsay and his friend Equiano and the mistaken identification brought Ramsay into the fight on 11 September. Calling himself "George Fox," the name of the founder of the Society of Friends, Ramsay mocks the way "Civis" treated Equiano: "Poor Vasa, in shape of a pig, is made to bring up the rear." But he has no doubt that Equiano can fend for himself in a match with "Civis." Even the skeptic Gibbon, he suggests, would rule in Equiano's favor: "You are hurt at being proposed to be pitted against Gustavus Vasa. There was a time, when his ancestors would have been equally hurt by the suggestion of being pitted against an European savage. Now 'as you are a Christian,' . . . without imitating your sneering manner, or meaning to express the least contempt for your abilities, which I sincerely respect, I propose that the point of inferiority may be determined by the decision of your 'favorite Gibbon' from your or Vasa's most sensible account of your religion."[57]

Equiano chose not to involve himself directly in the verbal duel with "Civis" in the *Morning Chronicle, and London Advertiser* during the last half of 1788. His public correspondents in that period were the politicians voting on abolition. Equiano was already prominent in the movement to abolish the transatlantic African slave trade in the fall of 1788 as the opening of the new session of Parliament was approaching. Ramsay wanted Equiano to become even more involved in the abolition movement than he had been. In a letter dated 6 September 1788 Ramsay suggested that Equiano greet every returning member of Parliament with a written address protesting against the slave trade. We do not know if Equiano acted upon his suggestion.[58] As the legislative struggle was about to be renewed in the upcoming session of Parliament, he was privately preparing to reveal a much more formidable rhetorical weapon in support of the cause.

Chapter Twelve

MAKING
A LIFE

Equiano followed with great interest the rapid development of the abolition movement during 1788. He did what he could in person and print to help it succeed. He recognized that the secular conversion narratives of former slave owners, slave-ship surgeons, and slave-ship captains moved the public toward the abolitionist position. He saw that effective witnesses to the cruelty of the slave trade could influence legislators. And he certainly noticed how large the market was for information about the trade. Most important of all, he understood that what the abolitionist cause needed now and what readers desired was exactly what he had positioned himself to give them – the story told from the victim's point of view.

Equiano had spent years developing contacts with abolitionists through his friendship with Ramsay, his association with Sharp, and his involvement with the project to resettle the black poor in Africa. He had spent recent months defending his integrity, establishing himself as a public figure participating in the debate over abolition, and honing an African identity. He had learned the art of self-promotion and the usefulness of making the right enemies. His success had earned him the attacks by "Civis," whose comments, despite his bad intentions, only increased interest in the life of his African opponent. The attention "Civis" gave Equiano acknowledged his prominence as the leading black abolitionist. Arguments over the literary abilities and achievements of people of African descent and hence their suitability for enslavement indicated that a black voice needed to be heard. Equiano's status in the black community meant that it should be his.

He may have already begun working on his autobiography when he announced in February 1788 that he might soon "enumerate even my own sufferings in the West Indies, which perhaps I may one day offer to the public, [though] the disgusting catalogue would be almost too great for belief." By November he was soliciting buyers for his forthcoming book. The handwritten note he sent Josiah Wedgwood on a printed solicitation indicates that they were already on fairly familiar terms: "Worthy Sir &c. this my Dutiful Respect to you I Pray you to Pardon this freedom I have taken in beging your favour, or the apperence of your Name amongst others of my Worthy friends. – & you will much oblige your Huml. Servt. to Command. Gustavus Vassa The African" (345–47).[1] His solicitation proposal was the first known time that Gustavus Vassa publicly identified himself as Olaudah Equiano. The proposal merits full quotation because it shows how fully conceived Equiano's book and marketing strategy were some five months before *The Interesting Narrative* appeared in print:

London, November, 1788.

TO THE NOBILITY, GENTRY, AND OTHERS.

PROPOSALS

For publishing by Subscription

THE INTERESTING

NARRATIVE

OF THE

LIFE

OF

Mr. *Olaudah Equiano,*

OR

Gustavus Vasa,

THE AFRICAN.

WRITTEN BY HIMSELF:

Who most respectfully solicits the Favour of the Public.

The Narrative contains the following Articles:

The Author's Observations on his Country, and the different Nations in Africa; with an Account of their Manners and Customs, Religion, Marriages, Agriculture, Buildings, &c. – His Birth – The Manner how he and his Sister were kidnapped, and of their accidentally meeting again in Africa – His Astonishment at sight of the Sea, the Vessel, White Men, Men on Horseback, and the various Objects he beheld on his first Arrival in England; particularly a Fall of Snow – An Account of Five Years Transactions in the Wars, under Admiral Boscawen, &c. from 1757 to the Peace in December 1762 – Of his being immediately after sent into Slavery, in the West Indies – Of the Treatment, and cruel Scenes of punishing the Negroes – The manner of obtaining his Freedom – The verification of Five remarkable Dreams, or Visions; particularly in being shipwrecked in 1767, and picking up Eleven miserable Men at Sea in 1774, &c. – The wonderful Manner of his Conversion to the Faith of CHRIST JESUS, and his Attempt to convert an Indian Prince – Various Actions at Sea and Land, from 1777 to the present Time, &c. &c.

CONDITIONS.

I. This Work shall be neatly printed on a good Paper, in a Duodecimo, or Pocket Size, and comprized in two handsome Volumes.

II. Price to Subscribers Seven Shillings bound, or Six Shillings unbound; one half to be paid at subscribing, and the other on the delivery of the Books, which will be very early in Spring.

III. A few Copies will be printed on Fine Paper, at a moderate advance of Price. It is therefore requested, that those Ladies and Gentlemen who may choose to have paper of that quality, will please to signify the same at subscribing.

IV. In Volume I, will be given an elegant Frontispiece of the Author's Portrait.

SUBSCRIPTIONS *are taken in by the following Booksellers:*

Mr. [John] Murray, Fleet-Street; Mess. [James] Robson and [William] Clark[e], Bond-Street; Mr. [Lockyer] Davis, opposite Gray's Inn, Holborn; Messrs. [John] Shepperson and [Thomas] Reynolds, Oxford-Street; Mr. [James] Lackington, Chiswell-Street; Mr. [David] Mathews, Strand; Mr. [David or John] Murray, Prince's Street, Soho; Mr. Taylor and Co. South Arch, Royal Exchange; Mr. Thomson, Little Pultney-Street, Golden Square; Mr. [William] Harrison, No. 154, Borough; Mr. Hallo- well, Cockhill, Ratcliff; Mr. [William?] Button, Newington Causeway; Mr. Burton, over the Brook, Chatham; and by the Booksellers in Dover, Sandwich, Exeter, Portsmouth, and Plymouth.

First-time authors trying to get a book into print during the eighteenth century faced as many obstacles as first-time writers in the twenty-first cen- tury do. Equiano published his book by advertising it publicly and selling it openly through booksellers. During the eighteenth century the term *bookseller* was used to describe publishers as well as wholesale dealers and retail sellers of books, whose functions often overlapped in practice. But to have a book to sell an author needed to acquire funding to enable him or her to produce it. No one involved in the book trade was normally keen to invest in an un- known author's first attempt at publication, especially if the author wanted to keep his or her copyright rather than sell it. If aspiring authors had sufficient means, they could, of course, risk investing in themselves. If not, they had to find other sources of venture capital.

A traditional way of getting the required capital was to sell the proposed book by subscription, convincing buyers to commit in advance of publica- tion to purchase copies of the book when it appeared. Booksellers would ef- fectively act as the aspiring author's agents in accepting subscriptions, probably receiving a commission for doing so. Subscribers typically were promised the book for a lower price than the one asked for retail sales. With a list of subscribers as proof of a guaranteed market, the novice sought a bookseller-publisher who would produce the book, paying the costs of pub- lication plus a small sum to the author for its copyright. If his or her book proved to have a market beyond its subscribers, the self-published author could negotiate a premium price for the copyright. With the sale of the copy- right, the author also sold any right to profits, or royalties, from any future sales of the book. Just as important, by giving up his copyright, an author lost control of the content as well as production of his text. The author would no longer have the legal power to revise his own text in subsequent editions, nor would he have the authority to choose what, if any, illustrations or other sup- plementary materials his published book might include.

First-time authors in England had published by subscription since the early seventeenth century, but by the end of the eighteenth the practice had become very uncommon because it was so susceptible to abuse. Too many would-be buyers had been disappointed by people who never produced the promised books. Publication by subscription was liable to far greater abuse if either the author or bookseller required payment in advance from sub-scribers. They rarely did so.[2] Writing in a letter in 1775 of subscription by ad-vance payment, the bookseller John Murray noted, "That mode (which formerly was fashionable) is so much disliked now that the bare attempt is suf-ficient to throw discredit upon the performance."[3] Of the 1,063 works Murray is known to have produced between 1768 and 1795, *The Interesting Narrative* was one of only about 25 he published by subscription.[4] If authors were able to get subscribers to pay at least part of their book's price in advance, they subsequently paid the production costs, found bookseller-agents to distribute the work, and normally sold their copyright. Unlike the vast majority of late-eighteenth-century authors, Equiano required partial payment in advance from his subscribers, no doubt to cover his living and production costs. Even more unusually, Equiano chose not to sell his copyright, even after his book proved as popular as he could have hoped.

Subscription may have been the only source of financial support avail-able to Equiano for the publication of his autobiography. The publishers and retailers he approached about acting as his agents by taking in subscriptions for his narrative and distributing it wholesale would have been understand-ably reluctant to risk investing more directly in a relatively inexperienced au-thor. He was probably unable to benefit directly from SEAST's production and distribution network. Despite the ideological and personal ties he had to the abolition movement and the compelling argument his book makes against the slave trade, a subsidy from SEAST was probably unattainable. Equiano had publicly expressed animosity toward SEAST's treasurer and banker, Samuel Hoare, and he reiterated his charges against him in his *Inter-esting Narrative.*

Equiano may not have looked for other financial sources besides subscrip-tion. Even though he had never published a book, his newspaper writings had made him known to his potential audience. Once his book was published, he chose not to sell his copyright cheaply to a bookseller-publisher. He was confi-dent enough in the sales of his autobiography to gamble on self-publication rather than forgo future profits. At least three of his bookseller-agents, James Lackington, Thomas Burton, and John Parsons, shared his confidence. They each subscribed for six copies, undoubtedly expecting to be able to sell the books they had received as payment for acting as Equiano's agents. Another bookseller, Charles Dilly, subscribed for two copies, though he was not one of Equiano's agents. Equiano's 311 original subscribers included many others involved in the book trade: John Abraham, John Almon, Thomas Bellamy, Thomas Bensley, Thomas Bentley, Thomas Dickie, Robert Huntley, William Justins, William Massey, Walter Rowe, John Simco, John Wheble, and Charles Wood. A "Mr. W. Button" was perhaps the bookseller-agent William Button.

Even for subscribers receiving the book at a discount, at seven shillings bound (six unbound) Equiano's *Interesting Narrative* was rather expensive for "a duodecimo, or pocket size . . . in two handsome volumes." John Murray usually charged six shillings for equivalent two-volume books.[5] Subscribers could buy a deluxe copy of Equiano's autobiography for an unspecified higher price. The pocketbook format, commonly used for novels, memoirs, and other works aimed at a relatively wide audience, was both fashionable and frequently profitable during the last quarter of the eighteenth century.[6] Equiano's use of "the Booksellers in Dover, Sandwich, Exeter, Portsmouth, and Plymouth" shows that he and they anticipated publishing success throughout southern England, especially in areas where the author had naval and personal affiliations.

Equiano's detailed description of his forthcoming book in his subscription proposal and its list of specific distributors indicate that he was well on his way to producing his autobiography "very early in Spring" 1789 as promised, while the House of Commons would be considering the slave trade again. The momentum against the slave trade had been building all summer in anticipation of the next session. At the direction of the London Abolition Committee of SEAST, Clarkson was gathering evidence throughout the southwestern ports, and Woods published in the *Morning Chronicle* copies of acts outlawing the slave trade in Massachusetts and Rhode Island. The Privy Council resumed its investigation of the trade in November 1788. But, as an advertisement in the 29 April 1789 issue of the *Morning Star* tells us, Equiano first offered his book for public sale from his own address and through various booksellers around the beginning of May, in late rather than early spring. Why the delay in publication?

The answer probably lies in an illness far more significant than the one that forced Wilberforce to postpone introducing a slave-trade bill during the preceding session. In November 1788 King George III slipped into an apparently irreversible state of madness, recently attributed to a chemical imbalance called porphyria.[7] The king's affliction caused a constitutional dilemma, and the Regency Crisis, as it became known, dominated public attention. Debates among the politicians about how to react properly and politically to the king's sudden illness quickly superseded the public argument over the slave trade. Like his Hanoverian forebears, the present Prince of Wales was constantly at loggerheads with his reigning father. Consequently, the parliamentary opponents of William Pitt's ministry gravitated to the prince. Opposition politicians understandably thought themselves on the verge of taking power, either on the death of George III or in the event of the creation of a regency, with the Prince of Wales ruling as the de facto monarch. No one doubted that a regency would mean the immediate end of the Pitt administration. Hence, Pitt did all he could to maintain his majority in the House of Commons in hopes of George III's full recovery. Both sides had difficult hands to play. The Prince of Wales and his followers could not afford to appear to be too eager for the king to die or be declared permanently incapacitated. Pitt and his supporters, on the other hand, could not risk appearing to place their own political careers ahead of concern for the national good by trying to hang on to power. The longer the king's illness continued, the greater the difficulty Pitt had in keeping his men from shifting political allegiance and thus in forestalling the passage of a Regency Bill. Many people seeking either power or patronage understandably tried to maintain or establish relationships with both Pitt and the Prince of Wales. The crisis lasted until the king's sudden and unexpected full recovery was announced on 10 March 1789.

A man with his eye ever on the market, Equiano made sure to keep his name before the public as the king's illness ended and his own book was about to be published. By either astounding coincidence or astute design, Equiano's autobiography appeared when national attention could return to the slave-trade debate and just as the evidence and testimony taken in the House of Commons and the Privy Council Board of Trade during the preceding session were being published. On 14 February 1789, as "Gustavus Vassa, the African," Equiano published a letter addressed "to the Committee for the Abolition of the Slave Trade at Plymouth" in the *Public Advertiser* thanking the local abolition society for having sent "the Rev. Mr. Clarkson, a worthy friend of mine, . . . a plate representing the form in which Negroes are stowed on board the Guinea ships." The plate was a print of the slave ship *Brookes.* Equiano was bringing national attention to an image designed in December 1788 and published in January 1789 by the Plymouth Abolition Committee of SEAST. Equiano wished that "this year" may "bear [the] record of acts worthy of a British Senate" and that the Plymouth committee may "have the satisfaction of seeing the completion of the work you have so humanely assisted us in" (347). As Clarkson later recalled, "this print seemed to make an instantaneous impression of horror upon all who saw it, and . . . it was therefore very instrumental, in consequence of the wide circulation given it, in serving the cause of the injured Africans."[8] The London Abolition Committee of SEAST directed Phillips to publish seventeen hundred copies of a more developed image of the *Brookes* as a single-sheet copper engraving for the high end of the market as well as seven thousand copies of the slave ship from a wood-engraved impression for the low end as Equiano's autobiography was about to appear. Earlier in the same week that he published his book "Olaudah Equiano, or Gustavus Vassa," joined eight others of African descent in addressing a 25 April 1789 letter in *The Diary; or Woodfall's Register* "to Mr. William Dickson, formerly Private Secretary to the Hon. Edward Hay, Governor of the Island of Barbadoes." Using both his Equiano and Vassa identities publicly for the first time, Equiano praised the man who called for the "literary performance" from an African that he was about to deliver. *The Interesting Narrative* became available less than a month before Wilberforce made his much-anticipated speech of 12 May in the House of Commons against the transatlantic African slave trade.

Equiano was so confident about the investment he had made in the story of his life that he registered his copyright with the Stationers' Company. By the end of the eighteenth century many authors and publishers chose not to register their books with the company to avoid the expense of depositing the nine copies of a book required for registration. Equiano, however, decided to take the financial risk to protect his copyright. On 24 March 1789 he registered the 530-page, two-volume first edition of his *Interesting Narrative* with the company at Stationers' Hall as the "Property of Author," declaring his figurative as well as real ownership of his self. The printer of Equiano's first edition is not certainly known, though he may have been the Thomas Wilkins identified in the imprint to the second edition of *The Interesting Narrative* (December 1789): "LONDON: printed and sold for the AUTHOR, by T. WILKINS, No. 23, Aldermanbury." The second edition is the only one of the nine that Equiano published that identifies a printer.

The 29 April 1789 advertisement in the *Morning Star* shows that Equiano had made additional marketing decisions since the previous November. Some of his distributors differ from those through whom he solicited his subscription copies as well as from those listed on the title page of the book itself. For

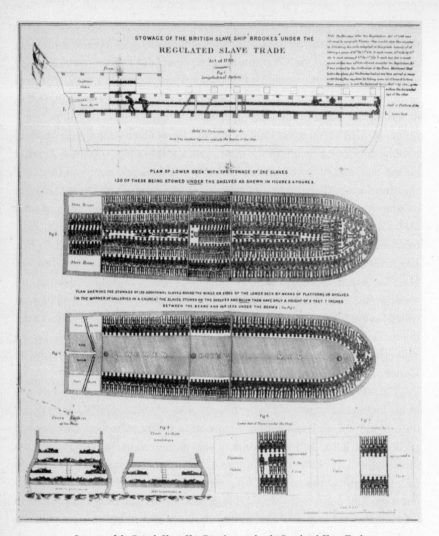

Stowage of the British Slave Ship Brookes *under the Regulated Slave Trade.*
This illustration of an overcrowded slave ship immediately became one of the most powerful representations of the abuses of the slave trade. First published by the Plymouth committee of the Society for Effecting the Abolition of the Slave Trade in 1788, the image was quickly adapted and distributed on both sides of the Atlantic by the London committee.

(Library of Congress)

example, the name of the bookseller Humanitas Jackson first appeared on the finished volume. Since Jackson operated a circulating library as well as a press at his Oxford Street shop, the presence of his name indicates another way Equiano found to distribute his book. Comparison of the subscription proposal and the initial advertisement shows that sometime after the initial solicitation he decided to add a frontispiece for the second volume of the auto-biography. Subscribers paid a discounted price of seven shillings for a bound copy (six unbound), while the public at large paid seven shillings for an un-bound copy. The advertisement in the *Morning Star* further indicates that Equiano exercised independent control over the production and distribution of his book. The short-lived antiministerial *Morning Star* had been created in 1789 to subvert the ministerial *Star*. Equiano's bookseller-agent John Murray was one of the *Star*'s proprietors.[9]

In revising the advertisement by including the subscription solicitation, Equiano made several stylistic and factual corrections, the latter probably re-flecting the evolution of his book from plan to product. Perhaps hoping to ap-peal to as wide an audience as possible and to emphasize the extent to which the work is a spiritual autobiography, neither the proposal nor the news-paper advertisement describes *The Interesting Narrative* as in part a petition against the slave trade. Nor does either the proposal or the advertisement mention that the book is also a defense of Equiano's role in the projected set-tlement of Sierra Leone. Potential buyers familiar with Equiano's letters pub-lished in London newspapers during 1787 and 1788, however, would have known of his opposition to the slave trade as well as his participation in the resettlement plan. Thus they would not have been surprised to find him say in his opening address "to the Lords Spiritual and Temporal, and the Com-mons of the Parliament of Great Britain" that "the chief design of [the book] is to excite in your august assemblies a sense of compassion for the miseries which the Slave Trade has entailed on my unfortunate countrymen" (7). In the first edition Equiano closes this opening address with "Union-Street, Mary-le-bone, March 24, 1789." He had obviously made enough money on prepublication sales of his book to be able to afford to move to a better sec-tion of greater London than the Baldwin's Gardens, Holborn, address from which he wrote his public letters in 1788. He had also expanded his distribu-tion network since the time of his initial proposal. Now the book "may be had of all the Booksellers in Town and Country."

Many elements in the book itself, not least the two illustrations, further demonstrate Equiano's genius for marketing and self-representation. Retention of his copyright meant that he exercised control over the selection of the visual images in his autobiography. His proposal promised potential subscribers "an elegant Frontispiece of the Author's Portrait." Indeed, this "elegant Frontispiece" is mentioned as the last of the "Conditions," as if to emphasize the value it adds to the book's worth. But it also adds value to Equiano's character and visually demonstrates his claim to *gentle* status because it is "elegant" in subject as well as in execution.[10] We see an African man dressed as an English *gentleman*, a figure who visually combines the written identities of both Olaudah Equiano and Gustavus Vassa revealed in print beneath the frontispiece as well as on the title page opposite it. The Bible in his hand is open to Acts 4:12, illustrating his literacy and his piety. The frontispiece is "Published March 1, 1789 by G. Vassa." All the evidence we have, such as Equiano's registering his book in his own name at Stationers' Hall and marketing it himself, suggests that he chose the artists to create and reproduce his likeness. The frontispiece was painted ("pinx[i]t") by the miniaturist William Denton, about whom very little is known beyond the fact that he exhibited portraits at the Royal Academy from 1792 to 1795. Denton's painting was reproduced in stipple and line engraving by Daniel Orme at the beginning of what was to become a distinguished career as a miniaturist portrait painter. Orme exhibited at the Royal Academy between 1797 and 1801 and was appointed engraver to George III.

To appreciate the possible significance of Equiano's frontispiece we need to consider the tradition of visual representations of people of African descent in Britain, most of whom had lower social status than Equiano when he published his autobiography. By calling himself in his opening paragraph "a private and obscure individual, and a stranger too" (31) Equiano invokes the concept of the stranger in a strange land familiar in verbal and visual satires. Typically, the stranger casts either a naive and innocent or a knowing and critical eye on the follies or sins around him. Eighteenth-century visual satirists increasingly employed the image of the obvious outsider to comment on English behavior. In Hogarth's 1762 engraving *Credulity, Superstition and Fanaticism: A Medley* a smiling Turk looks on bemused at the enthusiastic antics of the Methodist preacher and his congregation of miscreants. The Turk stands outside the window, whose bars make the meetinghouse with its inhabitants appear to be a lunatic asylum. Although he is emphatically neither a Christian nor an Englishman, the Turk is clearly the only truly sane and positive image in the print. In many other prints a black servant observes and mocks the actions of the whites, thus serving as the

Olaudah Equiano;
or
GUSTAVUS VASSA,
the African?

Publish'd March 1789 by G. Vassa

Frontispiece from the first edition of volume 1 of Olaudah Equiano's
Interesting Narrative (London, 1789). The portrait was painted by
William Denton and reproduced as an engraving by Daniel Orme.
(The John Carter Brown Library at Brown University)

moral norm within the visual text and morally equivalent to the viewer outside the text.

By the middle of the eighteenth century even pretenders to high social status were able to own or employ black slaves or servants. In the second plate of Hogarth's series *A Harlot's Progress* (1732) an exotically dressed black boy attends a young harlot and her older "keeper." The boy's dress is a fanciful combination of African and Asian Indian attire, reflecting the fact that in the eighteenth century, as is still the case today, the British frequently referred to both Africans and East Indians as black. Although the boy is physically placed at the margin of the design, his facial expression locates him at the moral center of the print. He looks with surprise, if not shock, at the collapsing table and breaking china, symbols of the disasters that lie ahead for the keeper and his newly acquired whore at the middle of the design. Like the harlot, the boy is one of the possessions in the room, but, from his position at the margin of the print and as an African at the margin of British society, he serves to help direct the external viewer's judgment of the other characters in the scene. As a stranger in a strange land he recognizes what goes unnoticed by those to whom the immoral is so familiar that it appears natural.

The Rabbits, published anonymously in 1792, complexly expresses the often complicated and frequently ambivalent representations and misrepresentations of blacks in eighteenth-century Britain. The print reflects the intersections of race, social status or class, and sexuality in many eighteenth-century popular prints. It shows a respectably dressed African British vendor trying to sell his wares to a fashionable young white woman living in a better section of London. Behind the woman an equally well dressed white man indicates by his facial expression and the finger he holds to his nose that the proffered rabbit has passed its sell-by date. The standing whites are physically as well as sartorially and socially superior to the black who kneels before their doorway, and the white woman, identified as "Miss" in the lines beneath the design, expresses her skepticism about the freshness of the rabbit meat: " – O la how it smells – sure its not fresh." Verbally identifying him as "Mungo" and having him speak imaginary black dialect comically diminishes the street vendor. But the black salesman not only has the last word but also asserts the possibility of a surprisingly bold sexual familiarity with "Miss": "Be gar, Misse, dat no fair – If Blacke Man take you by Leg so – you smell too." The black's witty superiority effectively challenges and undercuts the social superiority of the whites. The name "Mungo" invokes the stereotype of the comic black from Isaac Bickerstaffe's play *The Padlock*

Harlot's Progress, plate 2 (1732), by William Hogarth. Note the black boy in Oriental dress on the viewer's right. As an African at the margin of British society, he helps direct the external viewer's judgment of the other characters in the scene.

(1768), a loose dramatization of a short story by Cervantes. In the character of the slave Mungo, Charles Dibdin introduced to the stage both blackface comedy and the stereotype of the lazy, credulous, unreliable, yet witty black servant who has become all too familiar since. We should note, however, that the common people, white or black, were normally treated in the popular prints as comic figures. Who is the butt of the comedy in *The Rabbits?*

Further complicating the viewer's response to *The Rabbits* is its apparent visual allusion to by far the most familiar contemporaneous image of the black man at the end of the eighteenth century, the kneeling African slave encircled by the inscription "Am I Not a Man and a Brother?" Does the pose of the black vendor in *The Rabbits* simply recall that of the imploring, passive slave seeking mercy from an unseen white potential liberator located somewhere above him but beyond the visual range of Wedgwood's design? Is the

The Rabbits (1792). Note how the unknown artist has adapted the design
of the kneeling slave in *Am I Not a Man and a Brother* to create an image
of a verbally and economically assertive black figure.

similarity of the poses merely accidental or coincidental? Or is the similarity intentional, invoking Wedgwood's design rather than just recalling it? If it is intentional, then the assertive expression on the vendor's face in *The Rabbits* replaces the pathetic one on the cameo and visually reflects the verbal assertiveness found in the vendor's subscribed voice. The black salesman holds up the rabbits as if to substitute them for the unbroken chain of enslavement in Wedgwood's design. Commerce has replaced slavery in the economic relationship between blacks and whites.

Although many of the depictions of African Britons during the eighteenth century were in comic contexts, white Britons had numerous fictional and historical visual reminders that not all blacks were slaves or even servants, that not all slaves were black, that some blacks were socially superior to many whites, and that slavery was considered an inappropriate condition for at least some blacks. One of the best fictional examples is the Charles Grignion print after a painting by John James Barralet that appeared as the frontispiece to a 1776 edition of Thomas Southerne's play *Oroonoko*. Adapted in 1696 from Aphra Behn's prose romance *Oroonoko, or the History of the Royal Slave*, which had been published in 1688, Southerne's play was performed repeatedly during the following century. Southerne has made Behn's enslaved *African* heroine, Imoinda, the enslaved *white* wife of Oroonoko. As the costumes they wear in the frontispiece suggest, Imoinda and Oroonoko should *own* slaves, not *be* them. The pathos of the play is not caused by the institution of slavery but, rather, by the inappropriate enslavement of those who should, by right of birth, be at the top of the social order.

The concept of the African too inherently noble to be enslaved was not restricted to fictional accounts. In two separate historical cases during the first half of the eighteenth century Africans who were thought to have been wrongfully enslaved were ransomed into freedom when their situations became publicly known. Job Ben Solomon and William Ansah Sessarakoo were enslaved in Africa and taken, respectively, to Maryland and the West Indies. When their fates became known in London, the Royal Africa Company redeemed Ben Solomon, and the British government bought Sessarakoo's freedom. Both men, who had been slave owners in their native lands, were repatriated to Africa. An illustration in the June 1750 issue of the *Gentleman's Magazine* reflects the belief that Ben Solomon (on the left), who wrote down the Koran in Arabic from memory while in England in 1734, was considered too well educated to be enslaved. Sessarakoo (on the right), a prince in Africa, was thought too well born and well bred to be a slave. The

Job Son of Solliman and William Ansah Sessarakoo. These portraits, published in *Gentleman's Magazine* in 1750, present two enslaved Africans who, because of their "noble" births, were freed in London and repatriated to Africa.
(By permission of the Folger Shakespeare Library)

book Ben Solomon wears around his neck is presumably either his transcription of the Koran or the Arabic translation of the New Testament he was given while in England. And, like the Bible in Equiano's frontispiece, the book in the engraving of Ben Solomon indicates his literacy. In 1749 the *Gentleman's Magazine* had reported that the newly freed Prince Sessarakoo was a man of feeling so moved by a performance of Southerne's *Oroonoko* in Covent Garden that he had to leave at the end of the fourth act.

The position of blacks in eighteenth-century Britain – strangers in a strange land – was neither a simple nor a uniform one. The images of some of the thousands of African Britons, more often depicted as agents rather than subjects of commentary during this period, were frequently at least ambivalent and often positive. But rarely were the eighteenth-century British representations of blacks merely negative, as they would so unfortunately and frequently become in nineteenth-century American popular art. When Equiano published his *Interesting Narrative* in 1789, he was closer in social status to Job Ben Solomon and William Ansah Sessarakoo than to the black figures in eighteenth-century visual satires. But, being a "stranger," as he calls himself (31), like the servants in the visual satires, he can observe white Britons from a privileged moral position.

To appreciate the significance of Equiano's "elegant Frontispiece" we need to compare his portrait to the earlier published frontispiece portraits of presently or formerly enslaved Africans. Phillis Wheatley's portrait appears in her *Poems on Various Subjects, Religious and Moral* (London, 1773). Ignatius Sancho's portrait appears in *Letters of the Late Ignatius Sancho, an African*, published two years after his death.[11] The image of Wheatley was added to her book at the suggestion of her patron, the Countess of Huntingdon. It may have been engraved after a painting by Scipio Moorhead, the subject of her poem "To S.M. a Young *African* Painter, on Seeing his Works." The frontispiece displays the aspiring poet very modestly dressed as a domestic servant or slave, depicted in a contemplative pose. Her social status clearly inferior to that of most of her likely readers, she stares upward to the viewer's left, as if hoping for inspiration for the pen she holds. The book on the table before her may be intended to represent her own poems as well as to indicate that her literacy enables her to have been influenced by earlier writers. The revolutionary implications of a frontispiece depicting a black woman capable of writing poetry notwithstanding, the artistic quality of Wheatley's frontispiece is as modest as her social status.

Sancho's frontispiece, on the other hand, vies with Equiano's in elegance of subject and execution. Francesco Bartolozzi engraved it in 1781, the year after Sancho's death, from a painting of the then-valet to the Duke of Montagu hastily done by Thomas Gainsborough in an hour and forty minutes at Bath on 29 November 1768. Sancho is very well dressed. As befits the servant of a nobleman, his attire enhances the status of his master more than his own. His pose, with his hand in his waistcoat, is the traditional expression of a reserved English gentleman.[12] At best, however, Sancho appears as a gentleman's gentleman. As was conventional in visual depictions of servants, neither Sancho nor Wheatley directly engages the gaze of the viewer, as does Equiano, the only one of the three who had any control over his visual representation. For the first time in a book by a writer of African descent, the author Equiano asserts the equality of his free social status with that of his viewers and readers. Represented as a gentleman in his own right, he looks directly at them. As their moral equal, if not superior, he guides his readers to a passage in Acts 4 telling them that spiritual salvation comes through faith alone.

Unlike the frontispieces to the works of Wheatley and Sancho, Equiano's frontispiece clearly bears a thematic relationship to the text that follows. It is

Frontispiece from Phillis Wheatley's *Poems on Various Subjects, Religious and Moral* (London, 1773). The image of Wheatley was added to her book at the suggestion of her patron, the Countess of Huntingdon, and may have been engraved after a painting by Scipio Moorhead, the subject of her poem "To S. M. a Young *African* Painter, on Seeing his Works." (Library of Congress)

both the first and last illustration of the trope of the "talking book" that the author uses to emphasize the significance of literacy and acculturation in his autobiography.[13] From the reader's perspective, the frontispiece introduces the trope. From the perspective of the narrator's life, it marks the culmination of his development of the trope. Within the written text the trope first appears

Frontispiece from Ignatius Sancho's *Letters of the Late Ignatius Sancho,*
an African (London, 1782). Francesco Bartolozzi engraved the
portrait from a painting of the then-valet to the Duke of Montagu
hastily produced by Thomas Gainsborough.
(Library of Congress)

when the child Equiano observes his master and comrade reading (see chapter 4). Later in *The Interesting Narrative*, having learned to read, the now-free adult Equiano demonstrates his mastery not only of books but of *the* Book – the Bible. Faced with unruly, drunken Indians in Central America, he "thought of a strategem to appease the riot" (see chapter 9). As the frontispiece illustrates, the fully acculturated African British author of *The Interesting Narrative* now intends to use his rhetorical magic to make the Bible as well as his own text speak to his readers.

Whether Equiano himself suggested the design of his frontispiece portrait or approved one chosen by the academically trained Denton, one of its precursors was the oval portrait Rembrandt etched in 1646 of the Dutch

Reformed Church preacher Jan Cornelisz Sylvius.[14] Given Denton's training, he was probably aware of Rembrandt's image, if only through copies. The design of Rembrandt's portrait of Sylvius is arguably more assertive than Denton's. Sylvius's right hand casts a shadow as it extends beyond the frame to beckon the viewer toward the unidentified passage in the book, presumably the Bible, marked by his left hand. The more direct eye contact made by the well-dressed black man Equiano with his predominantly white viewers and the clearer direction he gives them to a specific passage in the Bible render the content of Denton's portrait at least as assertive as Rembrandt's design. Denied ordination by the bishop of London in 1779, Equiano used his *Interesting Narrative* to address a far larger congregation than he would have found in Africa. His image in the frontispiece anticipates and acknowledges the spiritual authority he asserts verbally in his autobiography: "O, ye nominal Christians! might not an African ask you, learned you this from your God? who says unto you, Do unto all men as you would men should do unto you?" (61).

Even closer visual anticipations of Equiano's frontispiece can be found in the portraits of the author included in Jacobus Elisa Johannes Capitein's *Dissertation*, published in Latin in Leyden, Holland, in 1742.[15] Although no evidence has been found that either Denton or Equiano was familiar with them, the images of Capitein suggest that Equiano's portrait is part of an iconographic tradition. It appears to conflate the design, contents, and gestures of the earlier portraits of Capitein: the oval frame, the direct gaze at the viewer, the hand extending the Bible toward the viewer, and the finger directing the viewer to a particular biblical passage. Capitein was an ordained clergyman in the Dutch Reformed Church and is depicted in his religious dress. Equiano, shown in fashionable secular clothing, is represented as a Protestant lay preacher, also directing his readers to the truth and the way.

Sometime after November 1788 Equiano decided to add a frontispiece to the second volume. The subscription proposal does not promise one. The print of *Bahama Banks*, "a Plate shewing the manner the Author was shipwrecked in 1767," is after a painting by Samuel Atkins, who in 1789 had already begun to establish his reputation as a marine painter. His work was exhibited at the Royal Academy in 1787–88 and from 1791 to 1796 and 1804 to 1808. Readers of *The Interesting Narrative* would soon discover the significance of the second frontispiece. It illustrates an incident in which Equiano, the natural leader of men, saved his white companions after a shipwreck. Equiano's selection of such talented artists as Denton, Orme, and Atkins, who, like Equiano himself, were at or near the beginning of their careers, re-

Jan Cornelis Sylvius, Preacher (1646), etching (27.9 cm. x 18.5 cm.),
by Rembrandt Harmensz van Rijn (Leyden, 1606–69, Amsterdam).
Photo by Allan Macintyre. This portrait of a Dutch Reformed
Church preacher was a likely precursor to Equiano's
frontispiece, with its appeal to religious authority.
(Courtesy of the Fogg Art Museum, Harvard University
Art Museums, Gift of William Gray from the collection of Francis
Calley Gray. © 2005 President and Fellows of Harvard College.)

Frontispiece from Jacobus Elisa Johannes Capitein's *Dissertation*
(Leyden, 1742). This portrait of a Dutch Reformed Church preacher
shows that Equiano's frontispiece was part of an iconographic
tradition involving religious figures. (Andover-Harvard Theological
Library, Harvard University Divinity School)

flects his business acumen as well as his artistic taste. Although engravers
were frequently paid in kind with copies of the book they illustrated, Atkins
and Denton may have donated their talents to what they considered a worthy cause whose anticipated success would enhance their own reputations as
well as that of the author. They are listed among the initial subscribers to *The
Interesting Narrative.*

Equiano's readers confronted his dual identity as soon as they opened
his book. The initial frontispiece presents an indisputably African body in
European dress, and the title page offers us "Olaudah Equiano, or Gustavus
Vassa, the African." To call him consistently by either the one name or the
other is to oversimplify his identity. Equiano periodically reminds readers of

his narrative that he exists on the boundary between African and British identities: "From the various scenes I had beheld on ship-board, I soon grew a stranger to terror of every kind, and was in that respect, at least, almost an Englishman." Several lines later he adds, "I now not only felt myself quite easy with these new countrymen, but relished their society and manners. I no longer looked upon them as spirits, but as men superior to us; and therefore I had the stronger desire to resemble them; to imbibe their spirit, and imitate their manners; I therefore embraced every occasion of improvement; and every new thing that I observed I treasured up in my memory" (77–78).

Using the name Equiano rather than Vassa, as I and most contemporary scholars and critics do, is to go against the author's own practice. Moreover, as the phrase "the African" reminds us, the author was very aware that his readers would assess him not just as an individual but as the representative of his race, as a type as well as a person. He was the first Anglophone writer of African descent to use the definite article to refer to himself: James Ukaw-saw Gronniosaw was "an African Prince," Wheatley simply "a Negro Servant," Sancho "an African," John Marrant "a Black," and Cugoano "a Native of Africa."[16]

Equiano's consciousness of being both African and British is reflected in his decision to entitle his autobiography *The Interesting Narrative*, a title apparently not used before 1789.[17] As Samuel Johnson's *Dictionary of the English Language* (1755) reminds us, *to interest* meant "to affect; to move; to touch with passion; to gain the affections; as, this is an *interesting story*." It also meant "to concern; to affect; to give share in." As a noun, *interest* meant "concern; advantage; good." Equiano intended his narrative to be received as "interesting" in all these ways, as the close of the first paragraph of his autobiography demonstrates. Assuming the pose of the humble author writing at the behest of his friends, he tells his readers,

> If, then, the following narrative does not appear sufficiently *interesting* to engage general attention, let my motive be some excuse for its publication. I am not so foolishly vain as to expect from it either immortality or literary reputation. If it affords any satisfaction to my numerous friends, at whose request it has been written, or in the smallest degree promotes the *interest* of humanity, the ends for which it was undertaken will be fully attained, and every wish of my heart gratified. Let it therefore be remembered that, in wishing to avoid censure, I do not aspire to praise. (31–32, emphasis added)

Equiano's narrative is interesting because his audience could sympathize or even empathize with his life. Sharing at least part of his cultural identity, they recognized much of his life as emblematic of the human condition. But his narrative is at the same time interesting in the more familiar modern sense of arousing curiosity and fascination because of the ways in which Equiano differs from his readers. He is at once Gustavus Vassa and Olaudah Equiano.

Purchasers of Equiano's *Interesting Narrative* familiar with the earlier published works of Wheatley, Sancho, and other Anglophone African writers probably noticed how distinctively Equiano identified and authorized himself on his title page. With the exception of Cugoano, the author of *The Interesting Narrative* was the first writer of African descent to present his work as self-authored and self-authorized, proudly announcing on the title page that it had been "Written by Himself." The phrase "written by himself" appears in more than a thousand eighteenth-century titles of fiction and nonfiction, almost always of works attributed to authors whose presumed levels of education and social status were likely to make readers suspect their authenticity.[18] A familiar example is Daniel Defoe's *Robinson Crusoe* (1719), a fictional text to which Equiano's was compared early in the nineteenth century. Black authors faced greater suspicion than others. Cugoano and Equiano were unusual in publishing their works without any of the authenticating documentation or mediation by white authorities that prefaces the works of Wheatley, Sancho, and other eighteenth-century black writers. The white voices reassured readers that the claim of authorship was valid and implied that the black authors had been supervised before publication. Wheatley's case represents the extreme. Having failed to find a publisher in Boston, in part because of doubts about her ability to have written her poems, she went to London to have her book published with the aid of the Countess of Huntingdon. Her *Poems on Various Subjects* was prefaced by a statement from her owner and an "attestation" signed by Boston worthies to assure readers that her literary achievement was authentic.

Equiano's equivalent attestation is the list of the names of subscribers with which he prefaces every edition of his *Interesting Narrative*. From the first edition of 1789 on, every edition identifies more subscribers than the preceding one. Equiano was an atypical author who combined faith in his work with business acumen. Never selling his copyright to a publisher-bookseller after his book was a proven financial success, he continued to seek subscribers for subsequent editions. By the ninth edition (1794) the original 311 subscribers (for a total of 350 copies) had increased to 894, with lists of English, Irish, and

Henry 56/2

THE

INTERESTING NARRATIVE

OF

THE LIFE

OF

OLAUDAH EQUIANO,

OR

GUSTAVUS VASSA,

THE AFRICAN.

WRITTEN BY HIMSELF.

VOL I.

Behold, God is my salvation; I will trust and not be afraid, for the Lord Jehovah is my strength and my song; he also is become my salvation.
And in that day shall ye say, Praise the Lord, call upon his name, declare his doings among the people. Isaiah xii. 2, 4.

LONDON:

Printed for and sold by the AUTHOR, No. 10, Union-Street, Middlesex Hospital;

Sold also by Mr. Johnson, St. Paul's Church-Yard; Mr. Murray, Fleet-Street; Messrs. Robson and Clark, Bond-Street; Mr. Davis, opposite Gray's Inn, Holborn; Messrs. Shepperson and Reynolds, and Mr. Jackson, Oxford-Street; Mr. Lackington, Chiswell-Street; Mr. Mathews, Strand; Mr. Murray, Prince's-Street, Soho; Mess. Taylor and Co. South Arch, Royal Exchange; Mr. Button, Newington-Causeway; Mr. Parsons, Paternoster-Row; and may be had of all the Booksellers in Town and Country.

[Entered at Stationer's Hall.]

Title page from the first edition of Olaudah Equiano's *Interesting Narrative* (London, 1789). With the exception of Quobna Ottobah Cugoano, Equiano was the first writer of African descent to present his work as self-authored and self-authorized.

(The John Carter Brown Library at Brown University)

Scottish buyers. But the number of Equiano's subscribers for all of the nine editions he published was much higher than the 894 names listed on his final edition. Although most of them do not appear on the final list, the names of 1,132 new subscribers, many for multiple copies, appear initially on the lists for the editions between the first and the ninth: 89 new names in the second edition (London, 24 December 1789), 22 in the third (London, 30 October 1790), 221 in the fourth (Dublin, 20 May 1791), 163 in the fifth (Edinburgh, June 1792), 269 in the sixth (London, 30 December 1792), 76 in the seventh (London, August 1793), 251 in the eighth (Norwich, March 1794), and 41 in the ninth (London, 1794).[19] The total number of subscribers was even higher. Equiano had many subscribers and buyers – 61 in Birmingham alone in 1790, for example – whose names never appeared in any of the published editions.

The significance of many of Equiano's subscribers changed over time. In spring 1789 Equiano was already known to many of his potential readers. Under his legal name Gustavus Vassa he had been publishing book reviews and what we might now call "opinion pieces" in London newspapers for more than a year before he published his autobiography. Some of his subscribers, however, who would go on to achieve legal, literary, or political fame or infamy in the years following the French Revolution of 14 July 1789, were not yet well known in April 1789, or at least not known as they would be after the Revolution. One such example is "Miss J. Baillie," the last listed and least significant subscribing member of the Baillie family, preceded on the subscription list by her at the time far more famous brother, Matthew Baillie, the physician, her mother, Dorothea, and her older sister, Agnes. But once Joanna Baillie began her career in 1790 as a published dramatist and poet, in subsequent editions of Equiano's autobiography her name increasingly became the most significant name in the family. Joanna, Dorothea, and Agnes Baillie were among the 11 percent of Equiano's original subscribers who were women.

A subscriber whose significance changed even more than Joanna Baillie's in the wake of the French Revolution was George Walne, a tailor living obscurely on Buckingham Street in April 1789. But in January 1792 he, along with his brother-in-law Thomas Hardy and Robert Boyd, organized the London Corresponding Society (LCS). The LCS was intended to create a nationwide means of promoting reform through persuasion, petitions, and publications. Hardy himself subscribed to the second edition of Equiano's *Interesting Narrative*, published in December 1789. Equiano was living with Hardy and his wife in 1792 when the LCS was being formed and even recruited members for the organization while he was conducting his own book tours outside London. On 12 May 1794 Thomas Hardy was arrested on a charge of seditious activities on behalf of the LCS, indicted on 6 October, and tried and acquitted from 25 October to 5 November. Subsequent events may make Equiano appear to have been more politically radical than he actually was. Equiano's original 1789 subscription list reflects the generally nonpartisan and nondenominational makeup of the early opposition to the African slave trade. Parliamentary success in a moral cause seemed imminent, and opposition to the transatlantic trade did not require one to be opposed to the institution of slavery itself as well.

A second London edition of *The Interesting Narrative* appeared at the end of 1789, suggesting that the first edition was probably the standard run of five hundred copies, including subscriptions. As a good man of business Equiano probably limited his risk of having many unsold books left from a first printing, but once the popularity of his work was clear, he increased the number of copies for the second and subsequent editions.[20] Because publication by subscription, with its attendant lists, was itself traditionally a form of self-promotion, the lists must be approached with some caution and skepticism. Authors, publishers, and booksellers all clearly had a motive for inflating the number and status of the names of subscribers, but the increasing number and repetition of names prefacing the multiple editions of Equiano's narrative render them more credible, and thus more valuable, to the historian than they would be had they appeared in only one edition of the author's work.

Clearly, a growing number of people wanted to be publicly associated with *The Interesting Narrative* and its author. Equiano's subscription lists demonstrate how skilled he was at what we now call networking, developing a constellation of influential and powerful contacts through often overlapping categories of individuals connected to one another in smaller groupings. At the top of Equiano's lists, literally and politically, is the Prince of Wales, an especially significant name during the fall of 1788 and the spring of 1789, when George III's lapse into madness appeared to make a regency under the prince's rule inevitable. Equiano had access to the Prince of Wales's patronage through others on the initial subscription list. Through his employer, Richard Cosway, the Prince of Wales's official painter, Cugoano had frequent direct contact with the prince. Through either the prince himself, Cosway, or Cugoano Equiano could have developed his connections to the prince's brother, the Duke of York, as well as to other members of the prince's official household who also subscribed.[21] They included Thomas Atwood, carver and gilder to the Prince of Wales, Henry Seymour Conway, Master of the Robes and Privy Purse, Walter Lewis, Messenger to the Treasury, and John Phillips, Esq., the prince's surgeon. On 5 March 1782 Phillips had married Frances Crewe, the editor of Sancho's letters. Lord Rawdon, grandson of the Countess of Huntingdon, was one of the prince's most intimate advisors. Of the fifteen members of Parliament who subscribed to the first edition of Equiano's narrative, Sir Gilbert Elliot, Edward Lovedon Lovedon, Sir Herbert Mackworth, James Martin, and William Windham supported the prince's claims to a regency.

But whether wisely hedging his bets on the course of the king's illness or simply reflecting the contemporaneous nonpartisan nature of the anti-slave-trade movement, Equiano also sought his original subscribers from among the politically powerful opponents of the prince's premature claim to rule. Among the subscribing members of Parliament supporting William Pitt during the Regency Crisis were Francis John Brown, Sir William Dolben, Sir Richard Hill, Sir Charles Middleton, Paul Le Mesurier, George Pitt, George Rose, Thomas Steele, Henry Thornton, and Samuel Whitbread. Rose and Steele were joint secretaries of the Treasury. Rose managed the Secret Service account that subsidized the pro-Pitt newspapers.

The newspaper printers and publishers on Equiano's list also reflected the bipartisan nature of his subscribers. Although he published letters in the ministerial newspapers the *Public Advertiser*, the *Morning Chronicle*, and the *Diary*, his original subscribers included John Almon, the proprietor of the opposition paper the *General Advertiser*, and William Justins, printer and publisher of the opposition paper the *Argus*. Almon in particular had long been active in opposition politics, initially in association with John Wilkes during the early years of George III's reign. In 1786 he had been convicted of libeling Pitt and fined £150; in 1789 he was convicted of libeling the king and eventually imprisoned for fourteen months in 1792–93.

Equiano's credibility and stature were enhanced by the presence of the names of members of the royal family, the aristocracy, and other socially and politically prominent figures such as men well known in trade and the arts, like Cosway and Wedgwood. Elizabeth Montagu and Hannah More, the leading bluestocking writers, were among Equiano's original subscribers. Furthermore, the names on his subscription list linked him to the larger movement against the slave trade. The bishop of London, Rowland Hill, Thomas Clarkson, Thomas Cooper, William Dickson, James Ramsay, Granville Sharp, John Wesley, and others on the list represented a range of

Anglican, Dissenting, and secular voices who had already attacked the invidious practice, in print or from the pulpit.

Moreover, the lists connected Equiano explicitly and implicitly with the African British writers of the preceding fifteen years: Cugoano's name appears, as do those of Gronniosaw and Wheatley by association with their patron, the Countess of Huntingdon, and Marrant by association with his editor, the Reverend William Aldridge. Equiano certainly knew of Wheatley and had read at least some of her poems in Clarkson's *Essay*. Cugoano mentions Gronniosaw and Marrant in his *Thoughts and Sentiments* (1787). Gronniosaw's *A Narrative of the Most Remarkable Particulars in the Life of James Albert Ukawsaw Gronniosaw, an African Prince, As Related by Himself* (1772) was published at least ten times in Britain and America before Equiano first published his autobiography. Marrant's *A Narrative of the Lord's Wonderful Dealings with John Marrant, a Black, (Now Going to Preach the Gospel in Nova-Scotia) Born in New-York, in North-America* (1785) went through at least fifteen London printings before 1790. Both texts were dictated to and revised by white amanuenses. The late Ignatius Sancho appears via his son William. The inclusion on the original subscription list of "William, the Son of Ignatius Sancho," clearly demonstrates that Equiano wanted to associate himself with earlier black writers. Since William was only thirteen years old in March 1789, his name obviously appears only because it enables Equiano to invoke his father's. A recognized tradition of African British authors had been established by the time Equiano published his autobiography, with new writers aware of the work of their predecessors. An African British canon was being created by the commentators, who argued about the most representative authors and works. The publishing success of his predecessors gave Equiano cause for believing that a market already existed for the autobiography of a black entrepreneur.

Equiano's subscription lists also play a structural role in *The Interesting Narrative*, which is presented as a petition, one of the hundreds submitted to Parliament between 1789 and 1792. They contained thousands of names of people asking the members to outlaw the slave trade. A petition to the Houses of Parliament that immediately follows the list of Equiano's subscribers formally frames the narrative, and the book virtually closes with an appeal to Queen Charlotte. By placement and implication, the subscribers are Equiano's copetitioners. Although, like most of his subscribers, he was not qualified to vote, he thus declares himself a loyal member of the larger British polity, which can still effect change within the walls of Westminster.

He effectively aligns himself politically with the subscribing members of Parliament who opposed the trade.

When the one-volume third edition was published, Equiano registered it at Stationers' Hall on 30 October 1790, depositing another required nine copies with the company. The primary reason for moving from two volumes to one was probably economic: the latter sold for four shillings instead of seven, a very important consideration as the market for books and other luxury items declined in the shrinking national economy of the 1790s. The six subsequent editions were all single volumes: Dublin (1791), Edinburgh (1792), two London editions (1793), Norwich (1794), and London again (1794).

Equiano's publication of several editions outside of London anticipated the nineteenth-century growth of the provincial press. For later editions Equiano also conducted eighteenth-century versions of the modern book promotion tour throughout England, Ireland, and Scotland, speaking out against the slave trade while selling his book. As one of his few extant manuscript letters attests, he was a very successful salesman. He told his correspondent in February 1792 that he "sold 1900 copies of my narrative" during eight and a half months in Ireland. During the eighteenth century selling five hundred copies of a book meant relative success, and a thousand copies indicated a best seller. Individual buyers purchased up to one hundred copies of *The Interesting Narrative*, no doubt for resale or free distribution. Readers outside of London also had access to Equiano's autobiography through circulating libraries. In Newcastle, for example, *The Interesting Narrative* was one of the 5,416 books that subscribers to R. Fisher's Circulating Library could borrow in 1791 for an annual fee of twelve shillings.[22]

Demand for his narrative was so great that Equiano decided to raise the price for his ninth edition to five shillings. *The Interesting Narrative* also found an international market during Equiano's lifetime. Unauthorized translations appeared in Holland (1790), Germany (1792), and Russia (1794). An unauthorized reprint of his second edition (1789) was also published in the United States (1791).[23] Although he could not, of course, do anything to stop them or profit directly from them, Equiano cleverly found a way to use these unauthorized reprintings to further advertise the appeal of his book. In a passage added to his fifth (1792) and subsequent editions of *The Interesting Narrative* Equiano acknowledged the international piracies that he knew about: "Soon after[,] I returned to London [in 1791], where I found persons of note from Holland and Germany, who requested me to go there; and I was glad to hear that an edition of my Narrative had been printed in both places, also in New York" (235).

By acting as his own publisher Equiano kept much of the profit margin for himself. Consequently, we can roughly estimate how much money he made on the sales of his narrative. According to Samuel Johnson's calculations in 1776, the total profit margin on a book was about 30 percent of the retail price, the other 70 percent being the cost of production, including payment to the author for copyright. The total profit margin covered the costs and profits of the wholesaler and retailer, approximately 12.5 and 17.5 percent, respectively.[24] But complicating the calculation of Equiano's profits after his subscription proposal was his increasing control of the distribution of *The Interesting Narrative* and thus of his own profit by reducing in subsequent editions the number of bookseller-agents with whom he probably shared the profit margin. Equiano's initial proposal names thirteen bookseller-agents, the first edition twelve, the second eight, the third seven, the fourth one, the fifth one, the sixth two, and the seventh, eighth, and ninth each zero. If we assume, conservatively, that Equiano took half of the total profit margin of the first edition, he would have earned about one shilling on every seven-shilling book sold, approximately twenty-five pounds, if we assume only five hundred copies in the initial printing.[25] Sharing his margin with one third fewer bookseller-agents for the second edition, Equiano probably made at least forty pounds on it, substantially more if the number of copies printed increased, which is very likely, given the success of the first edition. On each copy of the four-shilling, one-volume third edition he might have made over one shilling, with the total number of sales more than compensating for the loss in price per unit. By 1790 he was having at least two thousand copies printed. The sale of more than nineteen hundred copies of the fourth edition at four shillings may have earned him over £120.[26] Similar profits may be assumed for each of the fifth, sixth, seventh, and eighth editions. And at five shillings retail for his last edition, with no sharing booksellers, he could have anticipated a profit of one and a half shillings per book. Equiano could easily have garnered more than a thousand pounds in total gross profits from the nine editions of his *Interesting Narrative*.

Equiano's gamble on investing in the publication of the story of his life, whether that gamble was initially voluntary or forced upon him, obviously paid off. Unlike the vast majority of his fellow eighteenth-century authors, he retained his copyright even after it proved to have a high market value. By doing so and acting as his own publisher and principal distributor he made himself a relatively wealthy man. But the motivation for his behavior may have been as much psychological as financial. Far more than other authors, the formerly enslaved Equiano was aware of the consequences of losing control over one's own physical self and legal identity. That heightened awareness may help explain why he was so resistant to relinquishing control over the verbal and visual representations of his free self. He had spent too much time and effort in establishing an identity to allow anyone else to claim ownership of it.

Chapter Thirteen

THE ART OF THE BOOK

Equiano's *Interesting Narrative* is a remarkable achievement. It is very difficult, if not impossible, to classify in terms of its genre. Among other things, it is a spiritual autobiography, captivity narrative, travel book, adventure tale, slave narrative, rags-to-riches saga, economic treatise, apologia, testimony, and possibly even historical fiction. Equiano's own descriptions of his autobiography's contents accurately reflect his book's heterogeneous nature as well as his desire to appeal to as wide an audience as possible. Some of his book's generic components are less noticed today than they would have been in the eighteenth century. For example, few readers now recognize the degree to which his autobiography is an apologia, or formal defense of his conduct and motives, particularly in regard to the Sierra Leone resettlement project. Rather than seeing *The Interesting Narrative* as a relatively late example of a spiritual autobiography, most twenty-first-century readers approach it as the progenitor of later, more secular African American slave narratives. Historically and generically,

Equiano's autobiography lies between earlier seventeenth- and eighteenth-century captivity narratives, most by European whites abducted into alien cultures, and the nineteenth-century North American slave narrative epitomized by *Narrative of the Life of Frederick Douglass, an American Slave. Written by Himself* (1845).[1] The earliest commentators on *The Interesting Narrative* considered the book a life, a history, or memoirs, indicating that eighteenth-century readers most likely received it as an example of history writing, which included autobiography (memoirs), biography, and the treatment of the manners, customs, and activities of people below the rank of statesmen and military heroes. But whether we approach Equiano's *Interesting Narrative* as a spiritual autobiography, a history, or an anticipation of later slave narratives, we cannot fail to recognize that the author had designs upon his audience when he wrote it. A careful consideration of the content, organization, and argument of Equiano's book demonstrates that his designs were personal as well as political and that the personal and political were intimately connected.

"Olaudah Equiano, or Gustavus Vassa," begins his autobiography by representing himself as having a conventionally humble rhetorical ethos, or character. In his address "to the Lords spiritual and Temporal, and the Commons of the Parliament of Great Britain" he describes himself as "an unlettered [lacking formal education] African" whose book is "wholly devoid of literary merit." He is explicit about his motivation and purpose in publishing his *Interesting Narrative.* "Actuated by the hope of becoming an instrument towards the relief of his suffering countrymen," his "chief design . . . is to excite in your august assemblies [the House of Lords and the House of Commons] a sense of compassion for the miseries which the Slave Trade has entailed on my unfortunate countrymen." Careful to avoid sounding too strident, he flatters his readers by emphasizing that his own enslavement has been a fortunate fall: "By the horrors of that trade I was first torn away from all the tender connexions that were dear to my heart; but these, through the mysterious ways of Providence, I ought to regard as infinitely more than compensated by the introduction I have thence obtained to the knowledge of the Christian religion, and of a nation which, by its liberal sentiments, its humanity, the glorious freedom of its government, and its proficiency in arts and sciences, has exalted the dignity of human nature." He "trust[s] that *such a man*, pleading in *such a cause*, will be acquitted of boldness and presumption" (7, emphasis in original).

Throughout his narrative Equiano retains the ethos established in his dedication. The opening paragraph of the story of his life reveals how aware he was of his readers' likely assumptions about the motives behind autobiographical writings:

> I BELIEVE it is difficult for those who publish their own memoirs to escape the imputation of vanity; nor is this the only disadvantage under which they labour; it is also their misfortune, that whatever is uncommon is rarely, if ever, believed; and what is obvious we are apt to turn from with disgust, and to charge the writer with impertinence. People generally think those memoirs only worthy to be read or remembered which abound in great or striking events; those, in short, which in a high degree excite either admiration or pity: all others they consign to contempt and oblivion. It is, therefore, I confess, not a little hazardous, in a private and obscure individual, and a stranger too, thus to solicit the indulgent attention of the public; especially when I own I offer here the history of neither a saint, a hero, nor a tyrant. I believe there are a few events in my life which have not happened to many; it is true the incidents of it are numerous; and, did I consider myself an European, I might say my sufferings were great; but, when I compare my lot with that of most of my countrymen, I regard myself as a *particular favourite of Heaven,* and acknowledge the mercies of Providence in every occurrence of my life. If, then, the following narrative does not appear sufficiently interesting to engage general attention, let my motive be some excuse for its publication. I am not so foolishly vain as to expect from it either immortality or literary reputation. If it affords any satisfaction to my numerous friends, at whose request it has been written, or in the smallest degree promotes the interest of humanity, the ends for which it was undertaken will be fully attained, and every wish of my heart gratified. Let it therefore be remembered that, in wishing to avoid censure, I do not aspire to praise. (31–32, emphasis in original)

Twice Equiano refers to his book as memoirs and once as a history. During the eighteenth century the latter was a more respected genre of history writing than the former, which, in practice, was prone to self-praise, as Hugh Blair warns in his *Lectures on Rhetoric and Belles Lettres* (1783).[2] Especially in the first two chapters of his *Interesting Narrative,* Equiano apparently wants to combine the intimacy of memoir writing with the authority of history writing. He desires "to escape the imputation of vanity" by publishing an autobiography whose lessons have universal application because "there are few events in my life which have not happened to many" (31). The "history of neither a saint, a hero, nor a tyrant" was increasingly seen in the seventeenth and eighteenth centuries as the proper subject for autobiography, biography, the novel, and history. In his *Rambler* 60 (13 October 1750) Samuel Johnson tells us why:

> Our passions are therefore more strongly moved, in proportion as we can more readily adopt the pains or pleasures proposed to our minds, by recognising them as once our own, or considering them as naturally incident to our state of life. It is not easy for the most artful writer to give us an interest in happiness or misery, which we think ourselves never likely to feel, and with which we have never yet been made acquainted. Histories of the downfall of kingdoms, and revolutions of empires, are read with great tranquillity; the imperial tragedy pleases common auditors only by its pomp of ornament, and grandeur of ideas; and the man whose faculties have been engrossed by business, and whose heart never fluttered but at the rise or fall of stocks, wonders how the attention can be seized, or the affections agitated by a tale of love. (3:319)

Eighteenth-century readers came to believe that the most instructive works of history included the private lives and thoughts – the memoirs – of "private and obscure" people with whom they could sympathize and whom they thus could more easily imitate:

> The lives and actions of illustrious warriors and statesmen have ever been esteemed worthy the attention of the public: but this age has been the first to enter the more private walks of life, to contemplate merit in the shades, and to admire the more silent virtues. Dazzled with the glare of military talents, or caught in the intricacies of state politics; the world seldom condescended to look upon literary accomplishments even of the highest order; but wholly disdained the study of common life, and those characters which it would be of the most general use to be acquainted with, because they lie most open to imitation.[3]

The growing concern with economic and social subjects, especially the development of customs or manners in distant times and places, together with the traditional emphasis on military and political history, led to the eighteenth-century development of philosophical history. Philosophical history, exemplified in the historical works of David Hume, William Robertson, and Edward Gibbon, combined historical narrative and didactic commentary. Blair writes:

I cannot conclude the subject of History without taking notice of a very great improvement which has, of late years, begun to be introduced into Historical Composition; I mean a more particular attention than was formerly given to laws, customs, commerce, religion, literature, and every other thing that tends to show the spirit and genius of nations. It is now understood to be the business of an able Historian to exhibit manners, as well as facts and events; and assuredly, whatever displays the state and life of mankind, in different periods, and illustrates the progress of the human mind, is more useful and interesting than the detail of sieges and battles.[4]

Edmund Burke's comment to Robertson after reading his *History of America* (1778) is indicative of the enthusiastic response the new subject matter of history evoked:

The part which I read with the greatest pleasure is the discussion on the manners and characters of the inhabitants of that new world. I have always thought with you, that we possess, at this time, very great advantages towards the knowledge of human nature. We need no longer go to history to have it in all its periods and stages. History, from its comparative youth, is but a poor instructor. When the Egyptians called the Greeks children in antiquities, we may call them children; and so we may call all those nations which were able to trace the progress of society only within their own limits. But now the great map of mankind is unraveled at once, and there is no state or gradation of barbarism, and no mode of refinement, which we have not, at the same instant, under our view. . . . You have employed philosophy to judge of manners, and from manners you have drawn new resources for philosophy.[5]

Fundamental to Burke's notion of the significance of historical writing is the belief in uniformitarianism he shared with the vast majority of his contemporaries. The idea that human nature is everywhere and at all times essentially the same is the logical extension of the orthodox monogenist belief that all humans are direct descendants of Adam and Eve. Customs (or manners) change and vary. Human nature does not. One of the most important aspects of shared human nature was thought to be a naturally good moral sense that responded instinctively to the feelings (sentiments) of others. The moral sense could be refined or corrupted. Transcending the divisions of time, space, and status, these shared sentiments enabled the skilled author to render the distant near, the past present, and the exotic familiar through the power of sympathy. He or she could transform "human life into an inter-esting spectacle" through the "relations" of history and the "fictions" of po-etry.[6] A growing interest in literature of temporally, geographically, and socially exotic origins resulted in James Macpherson's Ossianic forgeries of ancient Gaelic epics (1762) as well as in the poems of the African British Phillis Wheatley (1773), the Scot Robert Burns (1786), and the milkwoman Ann Yearsley (1785). Distance, whether of space, time, status, or ethnicity, could be made proximate by appealing to the reader's feelings. In saying "did I consider myself an European, I might say my sufferings were great" (31), Equiano anticipated that most members of his audience would at least entertain the argument that beneath the apparent physical difference be-tween them and himself lay an essential sameness of shared sentiment and humanity.

The greatest challenge Equiano faced as an author was demonstrating that while he wrote with an authoritative African voice, he also was as British as his readers. He needed to show that exotic Africans and familiar Britons were equally human. He had to locate Africans, particularly Igbos, on Burke's "great map of mankind" for his readers. Compared to the publicly available information about some other West African ethnic groups and po-litical states in the eighteenth century, very little was known in Britain about either Igbo culture or Benin, even though almost one quarter of the enslaved Africans sent to North America came from the Bights of Benin and Biafra. And what little other information existed came through white intermediaries or observers. For example, in 1788 James Penny, a merchant who had spent eighteen years in the slave trade until 1784, testified before the House of Commons that he could speak only at secondhand about "the interior Part of the Country from whence the Bulk of the Slaves are received, and which is of vast Extent, called Ebo."[7]

Contemporary scholars value Equiano's "unique first-hand account of eighteenth-century Igboland" so highly because so little other direct informa-tion about the mid-eighteenth-century Igbo exists.[8] But this same absence of evidence gave Equiano the opportunity for invention he needed if he was born in South Carolina rather than Africa. Equiano uses his autobiography to practice nation formation as well as self-creation. His British readers were more sympathetic to the familiar idea of a state centrally organized by na-tionality, culture, economics, and religion than they would have been to the eighteenth-century reality of autonomous villages in Igboland. "No sense of pan-Igbo identity" existed before the nineteenth century.[9] During the era of the slave trade Africans living in the area of present-day Nigeria distinguished between Olu and Igbo, riverain and inland: "Olu meant riverain or riverain-derived, slave-dealing, kingdom-associated peoples; igbo meant upland, slave-providing, kingship-lacking populations."[10] Claiming or reclaiming an Igbo identity in the eighteenth century was by definition an act of invention because *Igbo*, roughly translated as *outsider*, was a term Europeans and coastal Africans often used pejoratively to cover a range of peoples living farther inland in West Africa. James Grainger, for example, conflated the coastal Ibibios, who filed their teeth, with inland Igbos, who did not. Alexander Falconbridge, an abolitionist, also confused the two groups, testifying in 1788 that "the Ebo Negroes have their Teeth filed like a Saw."[11] During the later colonial period the peoples in Africa who were earlier called Igbo by others and who shared a common language increasingly came to identify themselves as Igbo. Equiano was a pioneer in the forging of an Igbo national identity.

To be sure, an argument has been made that an Igbo national identity was developing during the eighteenth century, but even if such an identity had been established by the time Equiano was writing, it was not the primary identity a native West African would likely have claimed, except possibly to outsiders.[12] During the eighteenth century the now more familiar national sense of Igbo was the result of the involuntary African diaspora: "A sense of pan-Igbo identity came only when its people left Igboland – an experience first imposed by the slave trade."[13] Whites used the term *Eboe*, or *Igbo*, in the diasporan sense throughout the eighteenth century. Bryan Edwards's comment that "all the Negroes imported from these vast and unexplored regions [the Bights of Benin and Biafra] . . . are called in the West Indies *Eboes*" is telling in this respect.[14] Similarly, Edwards speaks of the "frank and fearless temper of the Koromantyn Negroes," using a diasporan term – Koromantyn – that Europeans created to refer to any slaves taken from Africa through the slave factory located at Cormantin, on the coast of present-day Ghana, no matter what their ethnic identities might have been. Like the terms *Guinea* and *Koromantyn*, *Eboe* was a geographical and supraethnic concept Europeans created that elided the significant cultural differences among various ethnic groups in West Africa.

Equiano indicates his own uneasiness, or at least uncertainty, about the term *Eboe* in several ways. Only the first edition of *The Interesting Narrative* includes the words "called Eboe" in the sentence "This kingdom is divided into many provinces or districts: in one of the most remote and fertile of which, called Eboe, I was born, in the year 1745, in a charming fruitful vale, named Essaka." Perhaps on second thought Equiano acknowledged that no such place actually existed. Similarly, attempts by modern scholars to locate "Essaka" have been unsuccessful, though of course the name may have changed.[15] Scholars also disagree about which side of the Niger River his native village was located on.[16] Equiano oddly seems to see Benin and Eboe as separate places, even though he elsewhere tells us that the latter is in the former. The fact that Benin was located west of the Niger River and Igboland largely east may explain the inconsistency. He uses Eboe once to mean "outsider": "*Oye-Eboe*, which term signifies red men living at a distance" (37).

The eighteenth-century account of Igbo culture closest in length to Equiano's is the very brief Moravian *Lebenslauf* (spiritual autobiography) Ofodobendo Wooma dictated in German in 1746. Born in "Ibo land" around 1729, Wooma was kidnapped into slavery about eight years later and renamed Andrew the Moor. Significantly, Andrew the Moor locates "Ibo land, in the unknown part of Africa." Unfortunately, Equiano's and Andrew the Moor's accounts of Igboland have so little in common that one cannot be used to corroborate the other. We have no evidence that Equiano knew of Andrew, whose German *Lebenslauf* was completed after his death in 1779. It was not translated into English and published until 1988.[17]

Nor was Equiano likely to have read the references to Igbos in the text radically abridged from the manuscript of the Moravian missionary Christian Georg Andreas Oldendorp and published in 1777 as *Geschichte der Mission der evangelischen Brȧder auf den caraibischen Inseln S. Thomas, S. Croix und S. Jan* [*History of the Mission of the Evangelical Brethren on the Caribbean Islands of St. Thomas, St. Croix, and St. John*]. With the exception of the scarification "reserved for notables," there appears to be no significant overlap between Equiano's account and that published under Oldendorp's name. Oldendorp's references to African cannibalism and human sacrifice by the Igbo are certainly absent from Equiano's story, though not surprisingly so.[18]

Equiano speaks with the voice of an Igbo protonationalist proud of his homeland, no doubt aware that if he could rehabilitate the reputation of the Igbo in particular, he would rehabilitate the reputation of Africans in general. To talk of Igbo nationalism in the eighteenth century is anachronistic because "populations like those in the hinterland of the Bight of Biafra . . . neither possessed centralized political institutions nor were in the process of developing them."[19] Equiano must have known that most earlier and contemporaneous commentators disagreed with his positive assessment of the peoples

Europeans called Igbos, the slaves least desired by planters in the British colonies.[20] As one historian points out, "No Chesapeake planter is known to have expressed a preference for laborers originating in the Bight of Biafra, and indeed Ibo . . . slaves were held in particularly low esteem in much of the Caribbean and in South Carolina."[21]

Further complicating the lack of information about the Igbo in Africa was the assumption that the behavior of enslaved people of African descent in the West Indies represented native African culture. At midcentury Grainger noted in *The Sugar-Cane. A Poem* (1764) that the "teeth-fil'd Ibbos or *Ebboes*, as they are more commonly called, are a numerous nation. Many of them have their teeth filed, and blackened in an extraordinary manner. They make good slaves when bought young; but are, in general, foul feeders, many of them greedily devouring the raw guts of fowls: They also feed on dead mules and horses; whose carcases, therefore, should be buried deep, that the Negroes may not come at them. But the surest way is to burn them; otherwise they will be apt, privily, to kill those useful animals, in order to feast on them."[22] And in *An Essay on the More Common West-India Diseases . . . To which Are Added, Some Hints on the Management . . . of Negroes* (1764) Grainger remarks, "In the Ibbo country, the women chiefly work; they, therefore, are to be preferred to the men of the same country at a negroe sale."[23] Similarly, Edward Long gives us in *The History of Jamaica . . . in Three Volumes* (1774) a very negative picture of the Igbo in Africa based on his observations in the West Indies: "The Ebo men are lazy, and averse to every laborious employment; the women performing almost all the work in their own country; these men are sullen, and often make away with themselves, rather than submit to any drudgery: the Ebo women labour well, but are subject to obstructions of the *menstrua*, often attended with sterility, and incurable."[24] Equiano's praise of Igbo women and his emphasis on the sanctity of marriage contrast sharply with proslavery assertions of African sexual promiscuity. Such promiscuity allegedly accounted for the low birthrate among slaves that necessitated the slave trade. Grainger, for example, claims that "black women are not so prolific as the white inhabitants, because they are less chaste."[25]

Bryan Edwards, in *The History, Civil and Commercial, of the British Colonies in the West Indies. In Two Volumes* (1793), also offers the image of the Igbo that helps account for why planters often refused to buy them as slaves:

All the Negroes imported from these vast and unexplored regions [the Bights of Benin and Biafra] . . . are called in the West Indies *Eboes*, and in general they appear to be the lowest and most wretched of all the nations of Africa. In complexion they are much yellower than the Gold Coast and Whidah Negroes; but it is a sickly hue, and their eyes appear as if suffused with bile, even when they are in perfect health. I cannot help observing too, that the conformation of the face, in a great majority of them, very much resembles that of the baboon. . . .

The great objection to the Eboe as slaves, is their constitutional timidity, and despondency of mind; which are so great as to occasion them very frequently to seek, in a voluntary death, a refuge from their own melancholy reflections. They require therefore the gentlest and mildest treatment to reconcile them to their situation; but if their confidence be once obtained, they manifest as great fidelity, affection, and gratitude, as can reasonably be expected from men in a state of slavery. The females of this nation are better labourers than the men, probably from having been more hardly treated in Africa.

The depression of spirits which these people seem to be under, on their first arrival in the West Indies, gives them an air of softness and submission, which forms a striking contrast to the frank and fearless temper of the Koromantyn Negroes. Nevertheless, the Eboes are in fact more truly savage than any nation of the Gold Coast; inasmuch as many tribes among them . . . have been, without doubt, accustomed to the shocking practice of feeding on human flesh. . . .

Of the religious opinions and modes of worship of the Eboes, we know but little; except that . . . they pay adoration to certain reptiles, of which the guana (a species of lizard) is in the highest estimation. They universally practice circumcision.[26]

Scholars who overemphasize the few times Equiano uses the term *Eboe* often ignore the way he organizes his account of Africa. He moves from recollections about "Eboe" specifically to comments about Africans in general, and he closes his first chapter with a series of rhetorical questions that forces his readers to draw uniformitarian conclusions from the evidence he has presented. Despite claiming to describe distinctively Igbo manners, he conflates accounts of various African ethnic groups to construct a kind of pan-African identity, a sort of essential African. For example, he cites John Matthews's proslavery *A Voyage to the River Sierra-Leone* (1788) in support of his own story.[27] If we see Equiano as intentionally moving outward in chapter 1 from an Igbo identity to an African identity, we should not be surprised to find that his apparently unique account of a particular African people echoes earlier works. Equiano's own footnotes citing works by James Field Stanfield, Anthony Benezet, and John Matthews, among others, indicate that he depended on secondary sources for at least some of his information about Africa to supplement "the imperfect sketch my memory has furnished me with" (43). Certainly, he is more fastidious than many eighteenth-century writers about citing sources, as one would expect from a history writer, though he is understandably not as careful as current scholarly standards would require. Later readers have assumed that Equiano's footnotes serve to verify the accounts he cites, and he certainly uses his notes to demonstrate his familiarity with the debate over the slave trade and his intention to participate in that debate.

A closer look at some of the details of African life Equiano mentions but does not footnote reveals that very similar information was available elsewhere. For example, in the opening sentence of his description of Africa – "that part of Africa, known by the name of Guinea, to which the trade for slaves is carried on, extends along the coast above 3400 miles" (32) – Equiano paraphrases without acknowledgment a passage in Benezet's *Some Historical Account of Guinea*: "That part of Africa from which the Negroes are sold to be carried into slavery, commonly known by the name of Guinea, extends along the coast three or four thousand miles."[28] In other places Equiano cites Benezet as his authority for general comments beyond his own personal experience about the punishments for adultery and the means for procuring slaves in Africa. William Smith, Thomas Astley, and Michel Adanson anticipated much of Equiano's African story, as did John Wesley in *Thoughts upon Slavery*. Smith and Astley, for example, had earlier described similar African religious beliefs and customs, and both had also likened them to the faith and practices of Judaism.

Many of Equiano's predecessors were themselves heavily dependent on the accounts of others. Benezet's books were essentially digests of earlier writings, many of which were themselves digests of even earlier accounts of Africa. Benezet's digests differed significantly from earlier such compilations because he very selectively included only examples and evidence favorable to the antislavery cause. Equiano found in earlier works accounts of African, albeit not always specifically Igbo, social and military practices very like the ones he ascribes to his homeland. He tells us, for example, that if a chief who starts a war is "vanquished, and he falls into the hands of the enemy, he is put to death: for, as he has been known to foment their quarrels, it is thought dangerous to let him survive, and no ransom can save him, though all other prisoners may be redeemed" (39). Equiano had read the description of a very similar practice reported earlier by William Bosman and quoted by Benezet: "If the person who occasioned the beginning of the war be taken, they will not easily admit him to ransom, though his weight in gold be offered, for fear he should in future form some new design against their repose."[29] When Equiano could, he used positive accounts of Africa by others to support his own argument. In the last two editions of his autobiography, both published in 1794, Equiano underscores his rather idyllic depiction of his homeland by quoting from letter 4 of James Field Stanfield's *Observations on a Voyage to the Coast of Africa* (1788): "I never saw a happier race of people than those of the kingdom of Benin, seated in ease and plenty, the Slave Trade, and its unavoidable bad effects excepted; every thing bore the appearance of friendship, tranquillity, and primitive independence."[30]

Like Benezet, Equiano often carefully chose his evidence from earlier ambivalent and even hostile descriptions of Africa and Africans. His description of "Eboe" architecture and the enclosed groups of masters' houses and slave quarters that "frequently present the appearance of a village" (36) is quite similar to Mathews's description of the dwelling arrangements in Sierra Leone.[31] Equiano elsewhere cites Matthews as a corroborating authority, even though he and Matthews were writing about quite different and geographically widely separated ethnic groups:

> I recollect an instance or two, which I hope it will not be deemed impertinent here to insert, as it may serve as a kind of specimen of the rest, and is still used by the negroes in the West Indies. A young woman had been poisoned, but it was not known by whom; the doctors ordered the corpse to be taken up by some persons, and carried to the grave. As soon as the bearers had raised it on their shoulders, they seemed seized with some sudden impulse, and ran to and fro', unable to stop themselves.[32] At last, after having passed through a number of thorns and prickly bushes unhurt, the corpse fell from them close to a house, and defaced it in the fall; and the owner being taken up, he immediately confessed the poisoning. (42–43)

A lieutenant in the royal navy, Matthews had been one of the principal witnesses testifying in Parliament in 1788 in favor of the African slave trade, and his *Voyage to the River Sierra-Leone* argued for the continuation of the trade as well. By citing him Equiano in effect cleverly compels him to testify for the opposition.

Sources for even some of the erroneous or dubious information Equiano includes about his homeland can be found in contemporaneous writings. For example, his erroneous claim that cotton grows wild in Africa is one his original subscriber Carl Bernhard Wadstrom also makes in *Observations on the Slave Trade and a Description of Some Part of the Coast of Guinea during a Voyage Made in 1787, and 1788, in Company with Doctor A. Sparrman and Captain Arrehenius* (1789). And Equiano's improbable statement that "even our women are warriors, and march boldly out to fight along with the men" (39) may have been influenced by Astley.[33] Later in his autobiography Equiano says that he encountered warrior women everywhere he went in Africa: "Both the males and females, as with us, were . . . trained in the arts of war" (55).[34]

Equiano's eclectic comments about Benin may also have been indebted to information found in William Smith's *A New Voyage to Guinea* (1744), either directly or through Benezet. Benin, Smith says, "is the most potent Kingdom of *Guinea*, and more nearly resembles an *European* Monarchy" than any other, and "as to Religion, they believe there is a God, the efficient Cause of all Things." "The Inhabitants are generally very good-natur'd and exceedingly civil and courteous." "Pregnant and menstruous Women," Smith writes, "they abstain from, and circumcise both Male and Female."[35] Smith, as well as Bosman and Benezet, all mention the absence of beggars and idleness Equiano notes.[36] Smith, too, likens social customs in Benin to those "practised by the Patriarchs of the *Old Testament*."[37]

Smith and Equiano both use comparative cultural anthropology in part to render unfamiliar African practices comprehensible to their European audiences. Equiano renders the alien familiar through the analogy he draws between eighteenth-century Africans and ancient Hebrews. But for Equiano the Bible serves as more than simply a standard of cultural comparison. For him it was a mnemonic device so powerful that we should question the extent to which it may have affected his memory through the power of suggestion. He tells us that just before he was sold into West Indian slavery at the end of 1762 a fellow seaman taught him "to read in the Bible, explaining many passages . . . which I did not comprehend." He was "wonderfully surprised to see the laws and rules of my country written almost exactly there: a circumstance which I believe tended to impress our manners and customs more deeply on my memory" (92).

Equiano's story of his life in Africa differs from the rest of his autobiography in the amount and specificity of detail it contains and in the way it is told. For example, he recalls the names of neither his parents nor any of his siblings, not even his beloved sister. Such an erasure of specific identities is more appropriate for a diasporan author of African descent than for one of African birth. Equiano's post-Africa account of his life, on the other hand, is extremely detailed. There he gives dates, places, and names almost without fail, as one would expect a diasporan writer to do. Much of the lack of specificity in his first chapter may derive from the calculated innocence he uses to represent a past that can now be reconstructed only with the help of others. In recalling "Eboe" he alternates between using the first-person *we* and the third-person *they*. The effect of doing so gives readers the impression of someone who has neither quite lost his identification with a former African culture nor fully embraced the European one in which he now finds himself. Similarly, his alternating use of present and past tenses to describe life in "Eboe" demonstrates just how present the past remains in his memory. He generally uses the first-person voice and past tense to refer to events that he says he experienced or observed and the third person and present tense to refer to Igbo practices that he has learned about from others. Equiano gives us the point of view both of the innocent boy who lived in Africa and of the experienced man who tells his story.

Equiano's African chapter also differs from his later ones in being more overtly rhetorical. More directly here than elsewhere he states the inferences and conclusions he wants his readers to draw from the events he recounts and the actions he wants them to take. In particular, he seeks to convince his English readers that they are fundamentally more like than unlike "their sable brethren" (45) because he wants to expand further his categories of identification. Having moved from Igbo to African, he next situates Africans in the larger category of human, just as one might talk about English people as also being Europeans, who in turn are as much humans as are Africans. Jews and Judaism are the biological and cultural bridges he uses to close the gap between Africans and Europeans. "Eboan Africans" and Old Testament Hebrews were necessarily unaware of the truth of Christian revelation, Africans because of geographical isolation and Hebrews because of historical distance. Equiano does not compare Africans culturally to eighteenth-century Jews, isolated and treated as aliens by their Christian neighbors, because they had the opportunity to embrace Christianity but refused to do so. In the face of the small but increasingly influential number of polygenists, who argued that God created various types of humans at different times, Equiano uses his description of "Eboe" to support the orthodox Christian monogenetic belief that all humans descended directly from Adam and Eve.[38] By elaborating his

analogy between Africans and Old Testament Jews he both makes his mono-
genistic point and implies that Africans are fully prepared for Christian revelation:

> I cannot forbear suggesting what has long struck me very forcibly,
> namely, the strong analogy which even by this sketch, imperfect as it is,
> appears to prevail in the manners and customs of my countrymen, and
> those of the Jews, before they reached the Land of Promise, and particu-
> larly the patriarchs, while they were yet in that pastoral state which is de-
> scribed in Genesis – an analogy, which alone would induce me to think
> that the one people had sprung from the other.[39] . . . Like the Israelites in
> their primitive state, our government was conducted by our chiefs, our
> judges, our wise men, and elders; and the head of a family with us en-
> joyed a similar authority over his household with that which is ascribed to
> Abraham and the other patriarchs. The law of retaliation [lex talionis, the
> law of an eye for an eye and a tooth for a tooth] obtained almost univer-
> sally with us as with them: and even their religion appeared to have shed
> upon us a ray of its glory, though broken and spent in its passage, or
> eclipsed by the cloud with which time, tradition, and ignorance might
> have enveloped it: for we had our circumcision (a rule I believe peculiar
> to that people): we had also our sacrifices and burnt-offerings, our wash-
> ings and purifications, on the same occasions as they had. (44)

For Equiano and many of his contemporaries the cultural differences between Africans and Europeans were more significant than the "elastic" conception of complexion during the period.[40] "As to the difference of colour
between the Eboan Africans and the modern Jews," Equiano defers to the
opinions of "men of both genius and learning" because the subject "is far
above my strength" (44). In particular, he cites Thomas Clarkson and John
Mitchel on the environmental causes of the difference in complexion. He no
doubt enjoyed calling Dr. Mitchel's comments to the attention of anyone
who believed in the superiority of whiteness or in polygenesis:

> The white people, who look on themselves as the primitive race of man,
> from a certain superiority of worth, either supposed or assumed, seem to
> have the least pretention to it of any, either from history or philosophy; for
> they seem to have degenerated more from the primitive and original com-
> plexion, in *Noah* and his sons, than even the *Indians* and negroes; and that
> to the worst extreme, the most delicate, tender, and sickly. . . .

. . . [W]e do not affirm, that either Blacks or Whites were originally descended from one another, but that both were descended from people of an intermediate tawny colour; whose posterity became more and more tawny, i.e. black, in the southern regions, and less so, or white, in the northern climes: whilst those who remained in the middle regions, where the first men resided, continued of their primitive tawny complexions; which we see confirmed by matter of fact, in all the different people in the world.[41]

Equiano notes that Spaniards living in the "torrid zone" of America become as dark as Native Americans and that Portuguese intermarrying with Africans nonetheless remain Portuguese. He hopes that examples of how climate affects complexion will "remove the prejudice that some conceive against the natives of Africa on account of their colour. Surely the minds of the Spaniards did not change with their complexions! Are there not causes enough to which the apparent inferiority of an African may be ascribed, without limiting the goodness of God, and supposing he forbore to stamp understanding on certainly his own image, because 'carved in ebony?'" (45). The inferiority is apparent, not real, because complexion is superficial.

Not even the most fervent eighteenth-century opponent of slavery contended that Africans were the cultural equals of Europeans, of whom the most advanced, in the eyes of the English, were, of course, themselves. But like the ancient Hebrews, Africans are as fully human as Europeans, though at different stages of social and economic development. Their "apparent inferiority" is due only to their "situation." By using the analogy between Jews and Africans to invoke stadial theory, which held that human societies progressed from the stage of hunting and gathering (e.g., Native Americans), to herding (Scottish Highlanders), to agriculture (classical Greeks and Romans, Old Testament Hebrews), to commercial exchange, Equiano places Africans just one step below civilized Europeans. Thus, they are closer to becoming equivalent to modern Englishmen than some Britons are. This argument becomes overt in the concluding paragraph of chapter 1, where implications of Equiano's expanding categories from Igbo to African to human are spelled out: "Let the polished and haughty European recollect that *his* ancestors were once, like the Africans, uncivilized, and even barbarous. Did Nature make *them* inferior to their sons? and should *they too* have been made slaves? Every rational mind answers, No. Let such reflections as these melt the pride of their superiority into sympathy for the wants and miseries of their sable brethren, and compel them to acknowledge, that understanding is not confined to feature or colour."

Equiano conflates passages he adapts from Acts 17:26 and Isaiah 55:8 to close his opening chapter: "If, when they look round the world, they feel exultation, let it be tempered with benevolence to others, and gratitude to God, 'who hath made of one blood all nations of men for to dwell on all the face of the earth; and whose wisdom is not our wisdom, neither are our ways his ways'" (45). He subtly acknowledges his debt to Benezet by quoting the same words of Saint Paul he used the year before as the epigraph to *Some Historical Account of Guinea*. And by appropriating and combining texts from the Old and New Testaments he embodies the African enlightened by Christian revelation that his account of Hebraic "Eboe" anticipates.

A confused memory of childhood events recounted some forty years later may explain the discrepancy between the ages Equiano records in his *Interesting Narrative* and the external documentary evidence, the problematic nature of his account of Africa, and his uncertainty about the name and location of his native village. This explanation, however, seems unlikely given the extraordinary accuracy of his memory for details when they can be checked against the historical record. The discrepancy was more likely rhetorically motivated: Equiano no doubt recognized that the younger he was thought to have been when he left Africa, the less credible his memories of his homeland would be. External evidence proves that he was significantly younger than he says he was when he first entered exclusively English-speaking environments. He was too young to have experienced or observed many of the events and customs in Africa he describes and probably too young to have recalled others.

If, as his baptismal and naval records say, Equiano was "a Black born in Carolina" rather than in Africa, he probably would still have first spoken "no language but that of Africa," as he later claimed (5). During the first half of the eighteenth century, due to the low rate of acculturation of slaves born in Low-Country South Carolina, an African or Creole language was likely to have been a slave's first language.[42] Older Igbos forcibly removed from Africa to America and/or England may have shared their memories of their homeland with him. Given the unpopularity of Igbos, particularly among South Carolina planters, an Igbo-descended slave born there might well have been brought to Virginia for sale.[43]

Modern scholars rightly point out that of the surviving brief eighteenth-century descriptions of the kingdom of Benin Equiano's account of Igboland is the most fully developed. Equiano's description is certainly the most complete eighteenth-century ethnography of "Eboe" we have from a person of African descent and the only one not mediated by a white translator or transcriber. But critics and scholars have increasingly come to recognize that his account's apparent uniqueness does not guarantee its authenticity.[44] Almost all the information about the Igbo he gives us can also be found in contemporaneous sources, many of which we know he was familiar with. The data unique to his account are often either false, such as the spontaneous growth of cotton and the use of women warriors, or unverifiable precisely because of their uniqueness. The evidence in Equiano's description of Africa alone does not prove that he had been born and raised there. Furthermore, external baptismal and naval records contradict his account. Hence, reasonable doubt inclines me to believe that Equiano's accounts of Africa and the Middle Passage were imaginary rather than real. But we must keep in mind that reasonable doubt is not the same as conclusive proof. We will probably never know the truth about Equiano's birth and upbringing.

Acts of appropriation and the combination of sources, imagination, and memory characterize the account Gustavus Vassa gives us of Olaudah Equiano's Africa. The evidence that Gustavus Vassa invented the African birth of Olaudah Equiano is indecisive, but a compelling circumstantial case for self-invention can be made based on what we now know about the evolution of his reclamation of an African identity, the timing and context of the publication of his autobiography, his manipulation of dates, his reliance on secondary sources, and his rhetorical shaping of an African past. The opening chapters of *The Interesting Narrative* remain a classic example of cultural memory if not history.[45] Whether he was born an Igbo in Africa or raised as an Igbo in South Carolina, Gustavus Vassa re-created himself as the spokesman for a nation not yet born on a continent still largely unknown during the eighteenth century. He anticipated by more than a century the Igbo nationalist and pan-African movements of the twentieth century. He did so to supply the abolitionist cause with the much-needed African voice Thomas Clarkson wanted of someone who had apparently "really been there."

Personal as well as political motives lay behind Equiano's reclamation of an African identity. The author's dual identity – revealed or assumed – enabled him to imply that what draws him to Englishness is not so much an urge for assimilation as it is a desire for recuperation, a desire best understood within a frame of status rather than race. What the "almost English" Equiano seeks is restoration to the social status in Africa allegedly stolen from him when he was kidnapped into slavery. Although he was enslaved, he was never a slave in the sense of accepting that condition as his appropriate social status. In his eyes slavery was inappropriate because of his birth and subsequent behavior. From the beginning of his enslavement he resisted the "social death" an enslaved person suffered when he accepted the new status of *slave* imposed upon him.[46] Equiano wishes us to believe that he is not an egocentric social climber. He is, he suggests, returning socially to the status denied him but never rejected by him, the status lost in Africa equivalent to that of *gentleman* in Europe.[47] By the time of *The Interesting Narrative*'s publication, a claim of high-born African status had long been a convention in fictional and factual narratives recounted by and about former slaves, such as Aphra Behn's *Oroonoko*.[48]

The social significance to an English-speaking audience of Equiano's placing himself in the category of Embrenché was clear. Several decades later John Adams noted,

> [Em]Breeché, in the Heebo [Igbo] language, signifies *gentleman*, or the eldest son of one, and who is not allowed in his own country any menial office. He inherits, at his father's death, all his slaves, and has the absolute control over the wives and children which he has left behind him. Before attaining the age of manhood, his forehead is scarified, and the skin brought down from the hair to the eye-brows, so as to form a line of indurated skin from one temple to the other. This peculiar mark is distinctive of his rank, the ordinary mark of the Heebo being formed by numerous perpendicular incisions on each temple, as if the operation of cupping had been often performed.[49]

In the cultures of both Igboland and Britain, a gentleman was ideally someone who did not have to work for a living, someone who had the leisure and disinterest required of a judge and legislator, and someone who lived by codes of honor, propriety, and decorum. Furthermore, in Britain, a gentleman's income was ideally derived from the ownership of land. In an age and in cultures that respected the concepts of social hierarchy and the significance of one's inherited place in that hierarchy, Equiano stresses in his description of Africa the social status he should hold. Like the fictional Oroonoko a century earlier, to Equiano the idea of an enslaved Embrenché is as oxymoronic as the idea of Oroonoko, "the royal slave." He assumes that many of his readers will agree. Since both Equiano and Oroonoko came from slave-owning societies and families, the primary problem in both cases is not the fact of the existence of slavery as an institution; rather, it is what we might call the status dissonance of the enslavement of those born to a higher order of society.

Equiano's African culture, in which heredity had determined his status, was violently disrupted by the external force of the slave trade, conducted by a European culture in which internal economic forces were disrupting the tradition of inherited status. In Europe and the Americas these forces increasingly challenged the hereditary basis for social rank with a meritocratic one. In his dictionary Samuel Johnson offers two definitions of the word "gentleman": first, "a man of birth; a man of extraction, though not noble"; second, "a man raised above the vulgar by his character or post." Historically, a gentleman was someone entitled to bear arms. He was expected to act honorably and honestly, and his word was, consequently, his bond. In effect, Equiano's status claim was also a credibility claim. John Gabriel Stedman, a professional soldier and Equiano's contemporary, expected his readers to recall the hereditary, meritocratic, and historical senses of the term *gentleman* when he wrote in the first paragraph of the 1790 manuscript version of his *Narrative of a Five Years Expedition against the Revolted Negroes of Surinam in Guiana on the Wild Coast of South-America* (1796), "then let Truth, Simple Truth alone be my Apology – more so since in the Army & Navy ought ever to be met with the Fewest Compliments but the greatest sincerity – this Stamps the Gentleman."[50]

Equiano's *Interesting Narrative* demonstrates repeatedly that he, too, saw himself as a professional warrior deserving the rank of gentleman by both descent and desert. At a number of points in his autobiography he plays upon the difference between the roles of birth and behavior in contemporaneous definitions of a gentleman. For example, while on the island of Jamaica in 1772 the now-free Equiano sold goods to "one Mr. Smith, at Port Morant," one of many whites who cheated him: "When I demanded payment from him, he was each time going to beat me, and threatened that he would put me in gaol. One time he would say I was going to set his house on fire; at another he would swear I was going to run away with his slaves. I was astonished at this usage from *a person who was in the situation of a gentleman*, but I had no alternative, and was therefore obliged to submit" (172, emphasis added). Long-standing as well as more recent ironic uses of "gentleman" enabled Equiano to treat the status of "Mr. Smith" sarcastically. For example, in *The Beggar's Opera* (1728) John Gay exploits the irony of calling highwaymen "gentlemen of the road," and Stedman repeatedly refers to his despised commanding officer as "the Old Gentleman," a common name for the devil. The debate over the slave trade and slavery during the last two decades of the eighteenth century frequently led opponents of the trade and the institution to emphasize the ironic gap between the status claims and the inhumane behavior of the slave traders and owners. Even Stedman, though more ambivalent than Equiano about the trade and slavery, speaks ironically of members of the planter class in Surinam as "West India Nabobs" and "this fine Gentleman."[51]

Equiano's claim to gentle birth was not recognized outside of Africa. He took full advantage of the opportunities British society gave him to "raise himself above the vulgar by his character or post," to elevate himself over those like Mr. Smith in Jamaica whose vulgar behavior erased their claim to be gentlemen by birth. Service in the Royal Navy appealed to Equiano because it was necessarily more meritocratic than most occupations. Competence mattered more than complexion, behavior more than birth. On the personal level, Equiano's belief in the honor of a true gentleman may help explain why he chose to buy his freedom from Robert King rather than avail himself of several chances to emancipate himself by escape. He and King had an agreement that he could purchase his freedom, and he expected each side to live up to his part of the bargain.

Once free, several experiences demonstrated Equiano's right to claim gentility by both character and post. He was so proud of his conduct and recognized status as honorary captain in the West Indies that he chose the shipwreck to be the subject for the frontispiece, *Bahama Banks*, to the second volume in the first edition of his *Interesting Narrative*. In 1767 both whites and blacks recognized Equiano as being almost white: "Before I left Georgia, a black woman who had a child lying dead, being very tenacious of church burial service, and not able to get any white person to perform it, applied to me for that purpose. . . . I . . . therefore complied with her entreaties, and at last consented to act the parson for the first time in my life. As she was much respected, there was a great company both of white and black people at the grave. I then accordingly assumed my new vocation, and performed the funeral ceremony to the satisfaction of all present" (160). And during the voyage at the end of 1775 to establish a plantation in Central America the Mosquito Indian prince considered Equiano a white man and superior to the others. The post that raised Equiano the highest above the vulgar and the one whose loss prompted his most spirited self-defense was, of course, that of "Commissary on the part of the Government." But his loss within a few months of this exalted position clearly did not diminish his conviction that he deserved the status of gentleman. The letters and petitions he cited and included in his narrative render it in part an expanded apologia of self-justification.

Equiano's apologia for his conduct during the Sierra Leone resettlement project reinforced the image he projected of a black British patriot. Calling attention to one's loyalty to Britain was conventional in the works by almost all the African British writers. Gronniosaw and Marrant do so by speaking of their military service in the British army and navy, and Sancho does so by his comments on the conduct of the war against the North American colonists. Williams and Wheatley wrote poems praising, respectively, the governor of Jamaica and the king of Great Britain. None of his predecessors asserts his or her identity as a Briton more fully than Equiano. African by birth, he is British by acculturation and choice. He could, of course, never be English, in the ethnic sense in which that word was used during the period, as his wife was English. But he adopts the cultural, political, religious, and social values that enable him to be accepted as British. Yet he always retains the perspective of an African who has been deracinated and thus has the advantage of knowing his adopted British culture from both the inside and the outside, a perspective that W. E. B. Du Bois calls the double consciousness of the black person in a predominantly white society.

Equiano's encounter with a black boy on the Isle of Wight during the 1750s indicates to the reader, if not to Equiano either at the time of the event or at the time of recalling it, that he may not have been fully comfortable in his position on the border between African and European identities. Although he calls the encounter "a trifling incident," it is a telling example of how quickly he had become acculturated into his new self and at the same time readily defined by others as still African. Confronted by the black boy, in effect his own mirror image, he at first turned away but then embraced his African side. At the beginning of chapter 8, referring to the Western Hemisphere, Equiano remarks, "I began to think of leaving this part of the world, of which I had been long tired, and of returning to England, where my heart had always been." Later in the same chapter the behavior of whites in Georgia forcefully reminds him that he may never be able to fully adopt a British identity.

But a question the prince of the Mosquito Indians asks in chapter 11 subtly reminds the author (although he does not seem to notice) and his readers just how far Equiano has come in the process of his British acculturation: "At last he asked me, 'How comes it that *all the white men on board*, who can read and write, observe the sun, and know all things, yet swear, lie, and get drunk, *only excepting yourself*?'" (my emphasis). In the eyes of another non-European who has encountered the Old World, Equiano appears to be morally whiter than whites. Like Moses in the book of Exodus, Equiano often finds himself a stranger in a strange land, but so too is the Indian, and though Equiano employs this perspective throughout *The Interesting Narrative*, it is for once turned on him, with significant but understated effect. Like the Indian, when Equiano uses this perspective, it enables him to comment ironically on the behavior, especially the religious behavior, of those fellow Britons who falsely and foolishly suppose themselves his superiors. He can, at times, directly assume the stance of the satirist, who traditionally views his own or another society from a vantage point on the margin of or from outside that society. He does so, for example, in the last five editions of his autobiography, when he appropriates the voice and words of the great Roman satirist Juvenal in his address "To the Reader."

The way *The Interesting Narrative* is told also reflects the double vision of someone with a dual identity speaking both from within and from outside his society. Equiano addresses his audience from two positions at once. On a narrative level he speaks of past events both as he experienced them at the time and as he reinterprets them from the perspective of the time in which he is recalling them. Thus he can write from the perspective of an innocent African boy terrified by his first sight of white men as well as interpret the religious significance of past events he failed to note at the time but now fully recognizes.

A dual perspective is inherent in retrospective autobiography and even more pronounced in a spiritual autobiography, the most obviously dominant generic influence on *The Interesting Narrative*. Protestant spiritual autobiographies, which include John Bunyan's nonfiction *Grace Abounding to the Chief of Sinners* (1666) and Daniel Defoe's fictional *Robinson Crusoe* (1719), typically recount a life that follows a pattern of sin, repentance, spiritual backsliding, and a new birth through true faith. Consequently, the protagonist is normally offered as an Everyman figure, neither extraordinarily good nor bad. As Equiano says at the opening of the first chapter, "I own I offer here the history of neither a saint, a hero, nor a tyrant" (though his decision to use the name of Gustavus Vassa, the Swedish patriot king who overthrew a tyrannical usurper, certainly gives him a heroic cast). Equiano uses the conventions of the genre, particularly the metaphor of being enslaved to sin, to contrast temporal and spiritual slavery. Although he buys his freedom halfway through the book (and almost halfway through his life), he is literally and spiritually still a slave, albeit his own, until he surrenders himself to Christ and thus gains true, spiritual freedom.

The genre of the spiritual autobiography assumes that the spiritual life of an individual Christian, no matter how minutely detailed and seemingly

326 ■ CHAPTER THIRTEEN

singular his or her temporal existence, reflects the paradigm of progress any true believer repeats. This implicit invocation of the paradigm the author and his overwhelmingly Christian audience shared serves as the most powerful argument in *The Interesting Narrative* for their common humanity. Equiano couples it with a secular argument based on the philosophical premise that the human heart, uncorrupted by bad nurturing, has naturally benevolent feelings for others because it can empathize with their sufferings. Consequently, people of feeling, or sentiment, will share the sufferings of others and, by so doing, demonstrate their shared humanity, a humanity that supporters of slavery and the trade denied to people of African descent.

More subtly, Equiano offers the transformation of his own attitude toward the transatlantic slave trade and the varieties of eighteenth-century slavery as a model for the moral progress of his readers as individuals and of the society he now shares with them. By claiming personal experience and observation, Equiano becomes an expert on the institution of slavery as well as on the effects of the African slave trade. Rhetorically, Equiano had the advantage over most whites of having experienced both sides of slavery. He tells us he was born into a slave-owning class before he was enslaved, and he was a slave driver in Central America after he regained his freedom. Initially, slavery was simply one of the many levels that constitute the apparently healthy social order in which Equiano found himself near the top. But, like an infectious disease, the European slave trade with Africa had gradually spread farther inland until it destroyed the tranquility of even Equiano's homeland. The closer his successive African owners were to the European source of the infection, the more inhumane they became. The corruption of the transatlantic slave trade, he discovered, contaminated everyone. But only long after he reaches Old England, the land of liberty, "where [his] heart had always been," does he come to see that the trade must be abolished because it cannot be ameliorated.

In the little worlds of the ships of the British Royal Navy and the merchant marine Equiano offers us a vision of what seems to be an almost utopian, microcosmic alternative to the slavery-infested greater world. The demands of the seafaring life permitted him to transcend the barriers imposed by race, forcing even whites to acknowledge that he merited the position, if not the rank itself, of a ship's captain. He experienced a world in which artificially imposed racial limitations would have destroyed everyone, white and black. But, perhaps because he does not want to distance himself too far from his audience, by the end of *The Interesting Narrative*, like most of his readers, he has not quite reached the position of absolutely rejecting slavery itself. Readers can reasonably extrapolate from the progress he has made that the next logical step is such total rejection. If he can carry his audience as far as he has come in his autobiography, he will bring them a great way toward his probable ultimate goal. Unlike Cugoano in his jeremiad-like *Thoughts and Sentiments* or Equiano himself in some of his letters to the newspapers, Equiano rarely engages in lengthy lamentations and exhortations in his narrative. He tries not to lecture to his readers. He teaches by example, inviting readers to emulate him.

Conciliatory as he is in the main, Equiano does not refrain from intimating a more combative side. Throughout *The Interesting Narrative* he is willing and able to resist whites in childhood boxing matches or when mistreated by them as an adult. This willingness to resist is almost always limited, however, to threat and is not carried into action, probably lest he alienate his overwhelmingly white readership. He was certainly not reluctant to affront some of his white audience directly. He knew that his inclusion in the fifth and later editions of the news of his marriage to a white woman would appall racist readers like James Tobin, Gordon Turnbull, and "Civis."

To antagonists like "Civis," who denied that people of African descent were capable of writing literature, publication of *The Interesting Narrative* was itself an act of resistance and aggression. Equiano knew that the most effective way to respond to "Civis's" charge that he was incapable of doing more than "fetch a card, letters, &c." was to write a book. Writing his narrative gave Equiano an opportunity to display his learning by citing, quoting, and appropriating the Bible as well as works by Homer, Sir John Denham, John Milton, Alexander Pope, Thomas Day, William Cowper, and many other literary and religious writers. Moreover, he included his own original poetry to remind his readers that they had never "heard of poems written by a monkey . . . or by an oran-outang."

Sometimes Equiano's intimations of resistance are quite subtle, as when he quotes John Milton, one of the most esteemed icons of his shared British culture, at the end of chapter 5.[52] By quoting lines spoken in *Paradise Lost* by Beelzebub, one of Satan's followers, Equiano appropriates a voice of alienation and resistance from within the very culture he is demonstrating that he has assimilated. He similarly used Shakespeare in later editions. From 1792 on, in his initial address to the reader in all the editions that include the announcement of his marriage to a white woman, Equiano appropriates Othello's words. Surely he had bigots like Tobin, Turnbull, and "Civis" in mind when he invoked the image of Britain's most famous literary instance of intermarriage in the tragic figure of African sexuality and power. Even the most venerated icon of British culture, the King James Version of the Bible, became a means of self-expression. At first glance the image of the author in the frontispiece to *The Interesting Narrative* seems to be a representation of humble fidelity to the text of the sacred book, but as we discover at the end of his "Miscellaneous Verses," which conclude chapter 10, Equiano appropriates Acts 4:12 by paraphrasing the original in his own words, an interactive relationship with the sacred text that may have been influenced by Cugoano's example.

Equiano's rhetorical ethos depended upon his credibility as someone who could legitimately claim both African and British identities. Equiano's acknowledged reliance on the descriptions of his homeland by secondary sources like Anthony Benezet renders his own account at once both remotely familiar and familiarly remote. Like his use of the Judaic analogy, his traditional description of Africa keeps the foreign from being too alien. As a native-born African his authority comes from personal experience, experience apparently confirmed by the authority of European commentators. Equiano's own later measured and fairly objective and circumstantial descriptions of places remote from both Europe and Africa suggest that his descriptions and evaluations of Africa, America, the West Indies, and England are reliable. Equiano places his original African culture within a Judeo-Christian context, both by a kind of comparative anthropological drawing of analogies between Judaic and African traditions as well as by invoking the authority of biblical scholarship. By doing so he implies that his own personal progress from pre-Christian to Christian can be paralleled by the potential development of Africa from its present spiritual condition to that of a fully Christian culture, a progress that would be as natural and preordained on a societal level as his has demonstrably already been on an individual level. Later in *The Interesting Narrative*, when his book briefly becomes an economic treatise, he explicitly argues that Africa too can be brought into the European commercial world, as he has been. Spiritual, cultural, and economic progress are intertwined on the public as well as the personal levels.

Equiano's ethos depended as well on the success of his claim to an African British social status, also first revealed or assumed in 1789. He subtly and rather quickly offers himself to his audience as the definition of a true gentleman, "almost an Englishman" (77). He is a hero indeed worthy of his namesake, the sixteenth-century Swedish nobleman who saved his people from Danish tyranny. Cleverly, he challenges the assumption that the differences between blacks and whites only attest to the inferiority of people of African descent. He begins the story of his life by telling his readers that he is made of sterner stuff than they: "Did I consider myself an European, I might say my sufferings were great" (31). He calls for a union between Britain and Africa to be brought about through "economic intercourse" (234) and conversion of both Africans and Britons to the true faith and opposition to the slave trade. From the fifth edition of his narrative on he mentions his marriage in April 1792 to the white Englishwoman Susanna Cullen to demonstrate that the story of his own life anticipates on the personal level the bicultural union he calls for between nations.

By the time that Equiano's readers reach his autobiography's conclusion, surely very few of them fail to recognize the irony of the conventionally modest pose he briefly reassumes: "I am far from the vanity of thinking there is any merit in this Narrative; I hope censure will be suspended, when it is considered that it was written by one who was as unwilling as unable to adorn the plainness of truth by the colouring of imagination." He more candidly notes, "My life and fortune have been extremely chequered, and my adventures various" though "considerably abridged." Looking backward from his postconversion perspective, he believes that "almost every event of my life made an impression on my mind, and influenced my conduct. I early accustomed myself to look at the hand of God in the minutest occurrence, and to learn from it a lesson of morality and religion; and in this light every circumstance I have related was to me of importance." Equiano closes by using the voice of the preacher addressing his congregation, like the figure depicted in his frontispiece. To emphasize his own spiritual authority and that of his book he conflates the voices of the Old Testament prophet Micah and the New Testament evangelist Saint Paul: "What makes any event important, unless by it's observation we become better and wiser, and learn 'to do justly, to love mercy, and to walk humbly before God!' To those who are possessed of this spirit, there is scarcely any book or incident so trifling that does not afford some profit, while to others the experience of ages seems of no use; and even to pour out to them the treasures of wisdom is throwing the jewels of instruction away."[53]

Chapter Fourteen

A SELF-MADE MAN

The reception the public and reviewers gave *The Interesting Narrative* and its author proved that Equiano had certainly not thrown his "jewels of instruction away." He quickly took advantage of additional ways to distribute those "jewels." Interest in abolition led to many public debates on the topic. Debating societies gave authors the opportunity for the eighteenth-century equivalent of twenty-first-century promotional appearances on television. Some of the societies were restricted by gender. For example, on 7 April 1788 the *Morning Chronicle* advertised the forthcoming debate by "La Belle Assemblee" of women on the subject "Ought not those Ladies, whose husbands are Peers and Members of Parliament, to exert their influence over them, to obtain an Abolition of the Slave Trade." Other groups, such as the Coach-Makers Hall Society for Free Debate, included both men and women in their audiences. The debating societies gave the disenfranchised at least an indirect political voice. The *Daily Advertiser* informed its readers on 9 May 1789 that "the celebrated Olaudah Equiano, or Gustavus Vassa, who has lately published his memoirs," would speak at an upcoming event. Equiano was probably "the African Prince" who unsuccessfully sought to participate in a 1 May 1789 debate at the Westminster Forum. The *Times* reported, "We are sorry to refuse the request of the African prince, but reading his Narrative from the Chair would be unprecedented; however, he shall, if he wishes, certainly be heard on the subject." Equiano very quickly became the first person of African descent people thought of when they imagined a black speaker. On 14 May 1789 the *Diary; or Woodfall's Register* described a crowded debate at Coach-Makers Hall on the question "Would not the Abolition of the Slave Trade be yielding to the principles of mistaken humanity, and highly injurious to the interest of this country?" The newspaper reported, "One gentleman only opposed the Abolition, which he did in a speech of great fluency and strength of reasoning. He was replied to by an African, (not Gustavus Vassa) who discovered much strong natural sense, and spoke with wonderful facility."

Combined with the celebrity Equiano had worked so hard to achieve, the presence of publishers on his subscription list guaranteed that book reviewers would not ignore his autobiography. The reviews, though mixed, were generally favorable. They give us a sense of the variety of ways Equiano's contemporaneous readers approached *The Interesting Narrative*. The first and most extensive review appeared in the May issue of the *Analytical Review*, published by Equiano's subscriber and distributor, the reform-minded Joseph Johnson. The reviewer was the soon-to-become-famous Mary Wollstonecraft. Given her philosophical and anthropological interests, Wollstonecraft understandably emphasizes the importance of the African identity Equiano claimed. She is completely uninterested in *The Interesting Narrative* as a spiritual autobiography:

> The life of an African, written by himself, is certainly a curiosity, as it has been a favourite philosophic whim to degrade the numerous nations, on whom the sun-beams more directly dart, below the common level of humanity, and hastily to conclude that nature, by making them inferior to the rest of the human race, designed to stamp them with a mark of slavery. How they are shaded down, from the fresh colour of northern rustics, to the sable hue seen on the African sands, is not our task to inquire, nor do we intend to draw a parallel between the abilities of a negro and

European mechanic; we shall only observe, that if these volumes do not exhibit extraordinary intellectual powers, sufficient to wipe off the stigma, yet the activity and ingenuity, which conspicuously appear in the character of Gustavus, place him on a par with the general mass of men, who fill the subordinate stations in a more civilized society than that which he was thrown into at his birth.

The first volume contains, with a variety of other matter, a short description of the manners of his native country, an account of his family, his being kidnapped with his sister, his journey to the sea coast, and terror when carried on shipboard. Many anecdotes are simply told, relative to the treatment of male and female slaves, on the voyage, and in the West Indies, which makes the blood turn its course; and the whole account of his unwearied endeavours to obtain his freedom, is very interesting. The narrative should have closed when he once more became his own master. The latter part of the second volume appears flat; and he is entangled in many, comparatively speaking, insignificant cares, which almost efface the lively impression made by the miseries of the slave. The long account of his religious sentiments and conversion to methodism, is rather tiresome.

Throughout, a kind of contradiction is apparent: many childish stories and puerile remarks, do not agree with some more solid reflections, which occur in the first pages. In the style also we observed a striking contrast: a few well written periods do not smoothly unite with the general tenor of the language.

Richard Gough appropriated Wollstonecraft's judgments and phrasing, giving them a more negative emphasis, in his rather dismissive treatment of *The Interesting Narrative*. His review appeared in the June 1789 issue of the *Gentleman's Magazine*, a periodical inclined toward the proslavery cause:

> Among other contrivances (and perhaps one of the most innocent) to interest the national humanity in favour of the Negro slaves, one of them here writes his own history, as formerly another of them [Sancho] published his correspondence. . . . These memoirs, written in a very unequal style, place the writer on a par with the general mass of men in the subordinate stations of civilized society, and prove that there is no general rule without an exception. The first volume treats of the manners of his countrymen, and his own adventures till he obtained his freedom; the

trivial

second, from that period to the present, is uninteresting; and his conversion to methodism oversets the whole.

The *Monthly Review* printed a far more sympathetic and balanced comment on Equiano's book in its June issue. The anonymous writer noted the ethos of its author, the timeliness of its publication, and the significance of its subscription list. But though he does not share Wollstonecraft's and Gough's hostility to the book's religious content, his assessment is not completely positive. His praise for Equiano's writing is stronger than Wollstonecraft's, though still faint. And he directly raises the question of whether Equiano could have written his autobiography by himself. His review is as much an evaluation of Equiano's character as it is of his book:

> WE entertain no doubt of the authenticity of this very intelligent African's story; though it is not improbable that some English writer has assisted him in the compilement, or, at least, the correction of his book; for it is sufficiently well-written. The Narrative wears an honest face; and we have conceived a good opinion of the man, from the artless manner in which he has detailed the variety of adventures and vicissitudes which have fallen to his lot. His publication appears very seasonable, at a time when negro-slavery is the subject of public investigation; and it seems calculated to increase the odium that has been excited against the West-India planters, on account of the cruelties that some are said to have exercised on their slaves, many instances of which are here detailed.
>
> The sable author of this volume appears to be a very sensible man; and he is, surely, not the less worthy of credit from being a convert to Christianity. He is a Methodist, and has filled many pages towards the end of his work, with accounts of his dreams, visions, and divine influences; but all this, supposing him [not] to have been under any delusive influence, only serves to convince us that he is guided by principle, and that he is not one of those poor converts, who, having undergone the ceremony of baptism, have remained content with that portion only of the christian religion; instances of which are said to be almost innumerable in America and the West Indies.
>
> GUSTAVUS VASSA appears to possess a very different character; and, therefore, we heartily wish success to his publication, which we are glad to see has been encouraged by a very respectable subscription.

Equiano's favorite review was the last published. It appeared anonymously in the July 1789 issue of The *General Magazine and Impartial Review*, created and edited by Thomas Bellamy. Bellamy, another one of Equiano's subscribers, also wrote an ameliorationist play, *The Benevolent Planters*, in 1789. Bellamy's reviewer sees *The Interesting Narrative* primarily as a contribution to the abolitionist cause frequently espoused in the magazine:

> This is "a round unvarnished tale" of the chequered adventures of an African, who early in life, was torn from his native country, by those savage dealers in a traffic disgraceful to humanity, and which has fixed a stain on the legislature of Britain.[1] The Narrative appears to be written with much truth and simplicity. The Author's account of the manners of the natives of his own province (Eboe) is interesting and pleasing; and the reader, unless, perchance he is either a West-India planter, or Liverpool merchant, will find his humanity often severely wounded by the shameless barbarity practised towards the author's hapless countrymen in all our colonies: if he feels, as he ought, the oppressed and the oppressors will equally excite his pity and indignation. That so unjust, so iniquitous a commerce may be abolished, is our ardent wish; and we heartily join in our author's prayer, "That the God of Heaven may inspire the hearts of our Representatives in Parliament, with peculiar benevolence on that important day when so interesting a question is to be discussed; when thousands, in consequence of their determination, are to look for happiness or misery!"

Equiano thought so highly of this review that he used it to promote his book, much as modern-day publishers reprint testimonials from famous people or influential sources as blurbs on the back covers of books. He included an abridged version of the review in every edition from 1790 on. It was one of the first of many blurbs he would append to subsequent editions of his book. Among the great advantages Equiano gained by maintaining his copyright was retaining control of the text of *The Interesting Narrative*, the story of his life. He also controlled the paratext of his autobiography, the supplements to the text such as prefatory comments, the subscription list(s), and footnotes. Authors who sold their copyrights to publishers typically relinquished their right to influence the content of the text and paratext. They consequently gave up their power to control any changes made in future editions of their work. Equiano's biographers and editors can speak with some confidence about his intentions in his evolving text and paratext because we know that Equiano maintained control of every revision in all the editions he published of *The Interesting Narrative*. Equiano's *Narrative*, like his life itself, continued to be a work in progress.

Equiano did not restrict his attempts to promote himself and his autobiography to appearances at debating societies or through book reviews. Once the session of Parliament ended on 23 June, he quickly took more active advantage of the network of associations he had been developing throughout his life. The prospects for abolition looked very promising in 1789. During the king's illness SEAST had continued to work with William Wilberforce and the Earl of Stanhope on their strategies for identifying allies and introducing the subject in the House of Commons and the House of Lords. SEAST also had Clarkson give copies of the print of the slave ship *Brookes* to every member of Parliament. After the king's recovery was announced in March and several weeks after Pitt presented the Privy Council report to the House of Commons in April, in mid-May Wilberforce delivered twelve propositions in support of abolition. Pitt, Burke, and Fox all spoke in support of the propositions, which SEAST distributed and newspapers reprinted. In the summer of 1789 Equiano commenced his first book-promotion tour with a 9 July letter of introduction from Thomas Clarkson to his fellow SEAST member, the Reverend Thomas Jones, master of Trinity College, Cambridge University:

> Dear Sir
>
> I take the Liberty of introducing to your Notice Gustavus Vassa, the Bearer, a very honest, ingenious, and industrious African, who wishes to visit Cambridge. He takes with him a few Histories containing his own Life written by himself, of which he means to dispose to defray his Journey. Would you be so good as to recommend the Sale of a few and you will confer a Favour on your already obliged and obedt Servt
>
> Thomas Clarkson

Clarkson's letter was certainly the appropriate recommendation for Equiano to take with him. For the last couple of years Clarkson had been traveling throughout England gathering evidence against the slave trade. For the next several years Equiano would literally and figuratively travel in Clarkson's footsteps throughout Britain, bearing witness against the trade.

In 1789 Equiano was not simply traveling to Cambridge hoping to sell copies of his book to pay for his expenses. He was also seeking subscribers among its ten thousand residents for the second edition of his autobiography, which was ready for publication at the end of 1789. Equiano was developing new networks as well as expanding old ones. His new subscribers represented the highest levels of the political and ecclesiastical establishments in London and Cambridgeshire: the Duke of Cumberland; the Countess of Harrington; the bishop of Chester; the Duke of Queensberry; Edward Burch, the king's engraver for medals and seals; William Pickett, Lord Mayor of London; and the Reverend Peter Peckard, master of Magdalen College, Cambridge University. Amidst their eminent names are those of the future political radical Thomas Hardy and the tantalizingly obscure Mrs. Hogflesh. Peckard, John Audley, and Edward Ind were all members of SEAST. Audley and Ind, Cambridge gentry, later became the coexecutors of Equiano's will. Peckard was also an abolitionist author. His pamphlet *Am I Not a Man and a Brother?* had been published in 1788. Another abolitionist writer, the Reverend Elhanan Winchester, had published *A Sermon against the Slave Trade* in 1787 and subsequently offered SEAST one hundred sermons he had preached against slavery while he was living in Virginia between 1774 and 1787. Equiano's naval connections were represented by the appearance on the subscription list of Adm. George Balfour, under whom he had served forty years earlier, along with Adm. Robert Roddam and Capt. James Norman. Ninian Jeffreys, a master in the Royal Navy, testified in both the Privy Council and the House of Commons in favor of abolition. As a self-publishing author Equiano made sure to expand the number of booksellers he knew. At least four more subscribed to his second edition. Subscribers like the bookseller James Matthews and the Reverend Winchester, who each bought six copies of *The Interesting Narrative*, extended Equiano's networks even further than he could have on his own.

Equiano tried a third and final time to be sent to Africa, probably sometime between the summer of 1789, when he was gathering subscribers for his second edition, and the following summer, when he was collecting them for his third. His name, along with Cugoano's name and the names of eight others, appears on an undated list of volunteers to go to Africa under the sponsorship of the Association for Promoting the Discovery of the Interior Parts of Africa. Sir Joseph Banks and others founded the African Association, as it was more commonly known, in London on 9 June 1788. Its primary purpose was to collect biological and anthropological information about the continent. Many of the association's members, at least fifteen of whom were among Equiano's original subscribers, were also strongly interested in whatever economic opportunities the exploration of Africa might reveal.[2] Although the list of volunteers is undated, it must have been made after midsummer 1789, when Lord Rawdon and Banks first met one of the people on the list, a Mr. Morgan.[3] Equiano was most likely to have volunteered to go to Africa before the financial success of his book became obvious in 1790, after which he was almost constantly on the road promoting it in England, Ireland, and Scotland.

Equiano was back in London in time for the resumption of the abolition arguments in Parliament during the 1789–90 session. The previous session had ended on an optimistic note for the abolitionist cause, but signs of problems to come had already appeared. When Wilberforce had tried on 21 May 1789 to get the House to consider his propositions, opponents of abolition forced him to back down by insisting that the Privy Council investigation was not sufficient for House action. The House's own hearings on abolition had barely begun when the session ended in June 1789. Wilberforce finally convinced his fellow members in January 1790 to continue the investigation of the slave trade by a Select Committee rather than the more cumbersome Committee of the Whole. But the investigation had not ended in June 1790, when the current session closed and King George dissolved Parliament in preparation for elections. Equiano and Clarkson immediately went on the road again. SEAST sent Clarkson on 29 July to seek more evidence in northern England and Scotland. Equiano went to the Midlands on his own to seek support for the abolitionist cause and sales for his book.

By mid-June Equiano was in Birmingham, one of the earliest centers of opposition to the slave trade. With about seventy-four thousand people, Birmingham was England's third or fourth largest city. On 14 June *Aris's Birmingham Gazette* carried an advertisement, dated 24 December 1789, for "the second, and corrected edition" of *The Interesting Narrative.* The advertisement basically reproduces the description Equiano used in his subscription proposal of his book's contents, format, and price. He told potential buyers: "From the Reception this Work has met with, from above Seven Hundred Persons of all Denominations – the Author humbly Thanks his numerous Friends for past Favours; and as a new Edition is now out, he most respectfully solicits the Favour and Encouragement of the candid and unprejudiced Friends of the Africans."

Equiano's advertisement tells us a good deal about his marketing strategy and the eighteenth-century provincial book trade. Buyers could purchase the book in Birmingham either directly from the author at the shop of the large-scale grocer William Bliss or from the printers and booksellers Thomas Pearson, Myles Swinney, and Edward Piercy. It was also available through the printer J. W. Piercy in nearby Coventry, a city of sixteen thousand. Bliss would buy twelve copies of Equiano's next edition, published in December 1790. Pearson was the printer of *Aris's Birmingham Gazette*. Swinney was the printer and publisher of the rival newspaper, the *Birmingham and Stafford Chronicle*. Equiano clearly wanted to cover all the local printing, publishing, and bookselling venues. He sold his book through local members of the bookselling trade. He no doubt traveled with a wagonload of mostly the less expensive unbound copies of his book, which local printers could then bind for buyers. In the provincial market he asked only six shillings for an unbound copy. He charged buyers in Birmingham only "4s. 6d. if six Copies are taken." In London he had asked seven shillings a copy.

Equiano was a very active and successful salesman. He spent at least two weeks in Birmingham networking, selling his book, and adding another bookseller to his list of local distributors. The 28 June issue of *Aris's Birmingham Gazette* published his letter addressed "to the printer of the *Birmingham Gazette*," acknowledging the "great marks of Kindness" he had received "from the under-mentioned gentlemen of this Town, who have subscribed to my Narrative." The list of sixty-one leading businessmen, manufacturers, and clergymen of various political and religious persuasions includes at least twenty-three SEAST members. Among the latter were the industrialist Matthew Boulton and the politically and religiously controversial Reverend Dr. Joseph Priestly. Boulton and Priestley, along with Wedgwood and Samuel Galton, were among Equiano's subscribers who belonged to Birmingham's Lunar Society, so-called because it met on the Monday nearest each full moon, when its amateur scientists and experimenters had enough natural light to find their way home following an evening of conviviality, conversation, and consultation. In retrospect, the Lunar Society's businessmen, industrialists, and inventors are seen as significant contributors to the Industrial Revolution that was just beginning at the end of the eighteenth century. Mostly from humble origins, many of the self-described "Lunatics" were self-made men like Equiano himself. The presence of so many of the society's members among Equiano's subscribers suggests that he may have attended one of their meetings while he was in Birmingham.

Priestley was the most prominent example of the so-called rational Dissenters, who joined Quakers and evangelicals (in and out of the Church of

England) to form the religious opposition to the slave trade. Quakers and evangelicals emphasized the spiritual and emotional aspects of Protestant belief. On the other hand, the rational dissenters, who evolved into Unitarians, emphasized the human nature of Jesus and the ethical implications of trying to emulate his life. Equiano's distributor Joseph Johnson had published Priestley's sermon against the slave trade in 1788.[4] Little more than a year after Equiano's visit Priestley's support for religious toleration and political reform and his sympathetic response to the French Revolution made him the principal target of the notorious Birmingham riots of 14 July 1791, which destroyed his home and the meetinghouse where he preached. Priestley felt compelled to flee the city, first to the outskirts of London and eventually to the United States.

Equiano closed his public letter to his Birmingham subscribers by re-asserting his claim to the status of a gentleman by birth: "I beg you to suffer me, thus publicly to express my grateful Acknowledgments to them for their Favours, and for the Fellow-feeling they have discovered for my very poor and much oppressed Countrymen; these Acts of Kindness and Hospitality, have filled me with a longing Desire to see these worthy Friends on my own Estate in Africa, when the richest Produce of it should be devoted to their Entertainment; they should there partake of the luxuriant Pine-apples, and the well flavoured virgin Palm-wine; and to heighten the Bliss I would burn a certain Kind of Tree, that would afford us a Light as clear and brilliant as the Virtues of my Guests." He signed himself "Gustavus Vasa, the African," the only name and identity he continued to use privately and publicly for the rest of his life.

From Birmingham he went north to England's second largest city, Manchester, with eighty-thousand residents, and then southeast to Sheffield, with its thirty-five thousand people. Both cities were rapidly growing industrial centers with strong local SEAST committees. On 20 July 1790 the *Manchester Mercury, & Harrop's General Advertiser* ran the same advertisement Equiano had used in Birmingham. One of his two new distributors was James Harrop, the printer of the newspaper and a member of SEAST. Equiano was in Sheffield a few weeks later, running the same advertisement in the *Sheffield Register, Yorkshire, Derbyshire, & Nottinghamshire Universal Advertiser* on 20 August 1790. Again he used the newspaper's printer as his distributor. He stayed with the Reverend Mr. Thomas Bryant, another SEAST member, selling more books from his home.

Equiano's transatlantic reputation was being established by others while he was traveling around England. The international book trade brought his autobiography and the magazine reviews of it to the attention of an American audience. In 1790 Charles Crawford informed his readers in Philadelphia that "Olaudah Equiano, or, Gustavus Vassa, the African, is a man of talents, as appears by the narrative of his life, which was written by himself, and published in London, in 1789. The friends of humanity by encouraging the sale of his work, might make him some recompence for the injuries which he has received from mankind."[5]

Equiano returned to London in the fall of 1790, in time for the opening of the newly elected House of Commons. There he lived with Thomas Hardy, a shoemaker, and his wife, Lydia, at "No. 4 Taylor's Buildings, St. Martin's-Lane," while he prepared the "corrected and enlarged" third edition of his *Interesting Narrative*. On 1 December the *Times* advertised the latest edition as being "in one handsome Volume, Twelves, on good paper, price Four Shillings, sewed." Quite a bargain compared to the seven shillings Equiano originally asked for unbound copies! The new edition was enlarged primarily by the addition of four items to the prefatory paratext. Equiano included the July 1789 review from the *General Magazine* as well as three letters of introduction and recommendation from Reverend Peckard of Cambridge, Thomas Walker of Manchester, and six eminent residents of Sheffield. Peckard's letter "to the Chairmen of the Committees for the Abolition of the Slave Trade" is typical of the letters Equiano carried from one place to another:

Gentlemen,

I take the liberty, as being joined with you in the same laudable endeavours to support the cause of humanity in the abolition of the Slave Trade, to recommend the bearer of this note, GUSTAVUS VASSA, an African; and to beg the favour of your assistance to him in the sale of his book.

For the next two years Equiano had great need of such letters of introduction. He spent much of 1791 and 1792 on the road in England, Ireland, and Scotland. He obviously believed that he could make a greater contribution to the abolitionist cause and his own financial situation if he spent his time traveling rather than continuing to watch the deliberations in Parliament. He welcomed free publicity whenever he could get it. In February 1791 he stopped in Derby, a town of eleven thousand. On 10 February the *Derby Mercury* printed a poem entitled "On Slavery and the Slave Trade" opposite a report about the ongoing debate in the House of Commons over abolition. The editor of the newspaper appended a comment to the poem:

> Affecting as the above lively description of the sorrows of Slavery is, we would refer our readers to the Narrative of the Life of Gustavus Vassa, the African, (written by himself) who arrived in Derby a few days since, for a striking picture of the situation of the poor Negro, torn from the most tender ties of Friendship and Affection; suffering under the accumulated afflictions of Tyranny and Barbarity; and at length rejoicing in the blessings of Liberty, which he has finely, yet artlessly portrayed – This Narrative is another very strong evidence of the good mental powers of the natives of Africa, and leaves not the most distant room to doubt that they would, with European cultivation, exhibit equal instances of Ability and Humanity – And the proceedings of the British Senate, (see the opposite page) give the most flattering hopes, that this unnatural traffic will not long disgrace the British name.

By the end of March 1791 he had also visited the twenty-five thousand people in Nottingham and the twelve thousand in Halifax.

A man as active as Equiano inevitably made both friends and opponents on his bookselling tours. On 29 March 1791 Susannah Atkinson left a letter with her husband, Law, for her "much valued Friend" Equiano to read on his return from Halifax. She was going from her home near Huddersfield to Manchester. She expressed her gratitude to Equiano for a gift only the closest of friends would have offered: "I thank you for your picture – believe me we shall value it much – we will have it Framed – and hung with our own Family who are doing now [a family portrait is being painted or framed at the same time] – I hope you *may* see it – it wont be done the next time you come – but hope you will see it the time *after* next." But Mrs. Atkinson wrote mainly to console Equiano for some mistreatment he had received:

> I am sorry to hear you are low – suffer yourself not to be hurt with triffles [trifles] since you must in this transitory and deceitful World meet with many unpleasing changes – I was sorry we should be so unfortunate as to recommend you to any who should in the least slight you – which seem'd to be the case at Elland – but I sincerely hope you have since experienced that friendship and civility from those you have been with – which has amply made up for the treatment you there received – but you have a

friend above who can afford you more *real* comfort than Mortals here can give – not but friends are a Blessing – and afford that comfort – which I hope you will *never* want – but it is I believe absolutely necessary that we should meet with rebuffs – otherwise our Affections would be wholly placed *here* – which would in the end prove our destruction – but I ought to check my pen, as you have seen more of the World than me – and must of course know how to place a proper dependence on both God and Man. (354–55)

The Atkinsons were as ardent friends to the abolitionist cause as they were to one of its best-known proponents. Law Atkinson subscribed for one hundred copies of Equiano's *Interesting Narrative*, no doubt to be distributed among Huddersfield's seven thousand residents.

Equiano's sales were too good for him to remain "low" for very long, and he was very hopeful about the cause he saw himself and his book as serving. On 19 April the *Leeds Mercury* printed a letter from Equiano addressed to its printer and, through him, the fifty-three thousand people of Leeds. Equiano's letter followed the notice of a subscription drive to support the London Abolition Society. He was personally grateful for the "particular marks of kindness from Mr. Law Atkinson and Family, of Huddersfield, and many Gentlemen and Ladies, &c., of and near this town, who have purchased my genuine and interesting Narrative." But he was most thankful as the representative of his fellow Africans:

I beg to offer them my warmest thanks; and also to the friends of humanity here, on behalf of my much oppressed countrymen, whose case calls aloud for redress – May this year bear record of acts worthy of a British Senate, and you have a satisfaction of seeing the completion of the work you have so humanely assisted in: – 'Tis now the duty of everyone, who is a friend to religion and humanity, to assist the different Committees engaged in this pious work. Those who can feel for the distresses of their own countrymen, will also commiserate the case of the poor Africans. Since that it does not often fall to the lot of individuals to contribute to so important a moral and religious duty, as that of putting an end to a practice, which may, without exaggeration, be stiled one of the greatest evils now existing on the earth, it may be hoped, that each one will now use his utmost endeavours for that purpose. The Wise Man saith – "Righteousness exalteth a nation, but sin is a reproach to any people."

Permit me, dear friends, on behalf of myself and countrymen, to offer
you the warmest effusions of a heart replete with gratitude.

The juxtaposition in the *Leeds Mercury* of the subscription notice and
Equiano's letter renders the latter an additional call for subscribers to the
abolition cause. As Equiano no doubt knew, his letter appeared on the eve of
the vote in the House of Commons on Wilberforce's bill to abolish the
African slave trade to the West Indies. Wilberforce presented his bill as soon
as the Select Committee on the Slave Trade released its long-awaited report.
Unfortunately, as Equiano probably also knew, the release of the report and
the vote on the bill came only days after external events on the other side of
the world delivered a crippling blow to the abolitionist cause. News of the
successful slave revolt in the French colony of Saint Domingue, modern-day
Haiti, had reached Britain by the beginning of April. Proponents of slavery
contended that any further discussion of abolition would encourage more rebellions throughout the West Indies. Clarkson later recalled that the effect
the Haitian revolution had on the abolitionist cause was immediate: "Many
looked upon the abolitionists as monsters. They became also terrified themselves. The idea with these was, that unless the discussion on this subject was
terminated, all would be lost. Thus, under a combination of effects arising
from the publication of the Rights of Man, the rise and progress of the French
revolution, and the insurrections of the Negroes in the different islands, no
one of which events had any thing to do with the abolition of the Slave-trade,
the current was turned against us."[6]
Concern in Britain about the direction and implications of the French
Revolution had been growing for some time. When the Revolution began on
14 July 1789 with the fall of the Bastille, most Britons welcomed the events in
France as the onset of the overdue reformation of the French monarchy, government, and economy that would enable the French to become almost as
free and productive as themselves. In his *Reflections on the Revolution in France*,
published in November 1790, Edmund Burke was one of the first in Britain
to raise the alarm about what lay ahead for the French and their neighbors.
Most readers initially dismissed as alarmist his argument that the radical
equalitarianism promoted by supporters of the Revolution would threaten
the political and social stability of both France and Britain. France itself, he
predicted, would devolve into anarchy, which would in turn be replaced by
a military dictatorship. By 1791 calls in London from radicals like Thomas
Paine in his *Rights of Man* (1791, 1792) for the redistribution of wealth and

power, combined with the colonial slave revolts, made Burke appear to an increasing number of people to be clairvoyant. The horrors of the assassination of King Louis XVI in 1793, the subsequent Terror in France, and the rise of Napoleon at the end of the decade established Burke's image as a prophet. When Wilberforce brought in his abolition bill in April 1791 amidst the news of the Saint Domingue revolt, he was doomed to failure. The bill was defeated by a vote of 88 to 163.

We do not know exactly how Equiano reacted to the defeat. But his actions, like those of SEAST, indicate that he saw it as a temporary setback that required redoubled effort on behalf of the abolitionist cause. He went from Leeds north to York, a city of sixteen thousand. He advertised his book on 22 April in the *York Chronicle* on the same page as an account of the recent debate in the Commons. Perhaps assuming that his reputation preceded him, Equiano began to use a more concise advertisement, dispensing with the lengthy description of the contents of his autobiography and counting on the opening paragraph from the review in the *General Magazine* to introduce himself to potential buyers. In York Equiano relied on the overlapping Quaker and SEAST networks to promote his book. He stayed with a subscriber, the Quaker SEAST member William Tuke, a substantial retail merchant and tea dealer, and he distributed his book through the Quaker printer Robert Spence.

In May Equiano went to Ireland, where he would spend nearly nine months among its 4.5 million people. By the end of May he had collected enough new subscribers to justify publication of a "Fourth Edition, Enlarged" of *The Interesting Narrative* in Dublin, a city of 240,000 people. He now included separate English and Irish subscription lists and advertised it in the 31 May–2 June 1791 issue of the *Freeman's Journal.* Equiano's Irish connections and subscribers were at least as bipartisan as those he found in England. In Dublin he used two principal distributors. William Sleater, a subscriber, was the publisher of the *Dublin Chronicle* and printer for the Protestant Irish Parliament. Peter Byrne, on the other hand, was a successful Roman Catholic bookseller and printer who supported the Irish nationalist opposition, Catholic emancipation, and parliamentary reform. He published the *Universal Magazine*, which sympathetically covered the progress of the French Revolution. He also later published the political pamphlets of the Irish radical Wolfe Tone and became printer to the Catholic Committee and to the United Irishmen.

After several months in Dublin Equiano went to Belfast, Ireland's second-largest city.[7] With a population of more than eighteen thousand people, Belfast had recently replaced Dublin as the leader in exports of Irish linens. Equiano advertised the Dublin edition of his book on 20 December in the *Belfast News-Letter*. In Belfast he befriended his subscriber and distributor Samuel Neilson, whose politics were so radical that his ally Tone called him "the Jacobin" after the most extreme faction of the revolutionaries in France. The son of a Presbyterian minister, Neilson was a successful woolen draper. While Equiano was in Ireland, Neilson helped inaugurate the nationalist Belfast Irish Society, which pushed for reform of the Irish Parliament. During the same period he also became a founder and the editor of the Irish nationalist newspaper the *Northern Star*. Like Tone, Neilson supported reform, Roman Catholic emancipation, and independence for Ireland. The printer and proprietor of the *Northern Star* were arrested in 1792 on charges of seditious libel. Neilson was arrested on the same charges four years later.

Equiano was associating with people who were increasingly becoming politically controversial. Although he may not have known it, one of the shadiest characters he befriended in Ireland was Thomas Atwood Digges, who wrote him a letter of introduction on Christmas Day, 1791, to take with him to the town of Carrickfergus:[8]

> The bearer of this, Mr. GUSTAVUS VASSA, an enlightened African, of good sense, agreeable manners, and of an excellent character, and who comes well recommended to this place, and noticed by the first people here, goes to-morrow for your town, for the purpose of vending some books, written by himself, which is a Narrative of his own Life and Sufferings, with some account of his native country and its inhabitants. He was torn from his relatives and country (by the more savage white men of England) at an early period in life; and during his residence in England, at which time I have seen him, during my agency for the American prisoners, with Sir William Dolben, Mr. Granville Sharp, Mr. Wilkes, and many other distinguished characters; he supported an irreproachable character, and was a principal instrument in bringing about the motion for the repeal of the Slave-Act. I beg leave to introduce him to your notice and civility; and if you can spare the time, your introduction of him personally to your neighbours may be of essential benefit to him.

Equiano sailed from Ireland to Scotland at the end of January 1792 and was back in London by February. International fame greeted him. "Soon after" his return he "found persons of note from Holland and Germany, who requested me to go there; and I was glad to hear that an edition of my Narrative had been printed in both places, also in New York" (235). He had also achieved national fame. His name had enough cultural capital to be worth claiming or invoking by writers who assumed their readers knew who he was. In *The Baviad, a Paraphrastic Imitation of the First Satire of Persius* the satirist William Gifford invoked Equiano to mock the insipid love poetry of Robert Merry:

> What the ladies may say to such a swain [Merry], I know not; but certainly he is prone to run wild, die, &c. &c. Such indeed is the combustible nature of this gentleman, that he takes fire at every female signature in the papers; and I remember that when Olaudo Equiano (who, for a black, is not ill-featured) tried his hand at a soft sonnet, and by mistake subscribed it Olauda, Mr. Merry fell so desperately in love with him, and "yelled out such syllables of dolour" in consequence of it, that "the pitiful-hearted" negro was frightened at the mischief he had done, and transmitted in all haste the following correction to the editor – "For Olauda, please to read Olaudo, the black MAN."[9]

While Equiano was in London, on 15 March the *Glasgow Courier* published an antislavery response from the pseudonymous "Gustavus" to the equally pseudonymous "Columbus," who had earlier published a proslavery column in the newspaper. Identifying himself as belonging "to that unhappy race of men, who have been the object of this barbarous traffic," "Gustavus" uses many of Equiano's arguments to refute Columbus's claim that on "the chain of mutual dependence . . . Africans were intended to be Slaves." "Gustavus" goes on to dismiss the idea that slave owners must be compensated, should his "unfortunate countrymen" be emancipated. Equiano appeared in a far more lighthearted context in the *Shrewsbury Chronicle* on 23 March. The pseudonymous "Oroonoko" reported a dialogue he overheard in a London coffee-house between Sambo, a free negro, and "Mr. Ratoon, a rich Planter." Sambo tells Ratoon, "Politicks, Massa, me no understand politicks, but dis me know, dat black man no fool. You no read de writing of Ignatius Sancho, Gustavus Vada, and de Poems of a black Woman in Virginia?" To which Ratoon replies, "Writings, the Devil take their writings, instead of wielding a pen, they ought to have been with a hoe in the field." Despite the misspelling of Vassa's name and confusion about Phillis Wheatley's home, the fictional dialogue demonstrates that Equiano's place in the tradition of English-speaking writers of African descent was recognized even in the provinces.

In London Equiano was living again with Thomas and Lydia Hardy at No. 4 Taylor's Buildings. From there he sent a letter dated 27 February 1792 to the Reverend Mr. George Walker in Nottingham, thanking him for the hospitality he and his family had shown him on his way back from Scotland to London. Equiano had known Walker since at least 17 January 1791, the date of a letter of recommendation signed by Walker and nine other Nottingham residents that Equiano appended to his *Interesting Narrative* from the fifth edition on. Although nominally a Presbyterian, Walker was a rational dissenter in practice, like his friend Priestley. Like many of Equiano's subscribers and correspondents, Walker had reformist and radical connections. He was a business associate of Maj. John Cartwright, one of the founders of the Society for Constitutional Information decades earlier. Among Walker's cosigners of the January 1791 letter was Francis Wakefield, brother of Gilbert Wakefield, whose radical pamphlet addressed to the bishop of Llandaff would lead to the arrest of his publisher, Joseph Johnson, in 1798.[10]

Equiano is exuberant in his 1792 letter to Walker. He had many reasons for being so. Walker had subscribed for twenty copies of the fourth edition of *The Interesting Narrative.* Equiano informed Walker that he had sold nineteen hundred copies of his book during his just-concluded trip to Ireland. Equiano took particular pride in having done as much good for the abolitionist cause as he had done for himself: "I Trust that my going about has been of much use to the Cause of the abolition of the accu[r]sed Slave Trade – a Gentleman of the Committee the Revd. Dr. Baker has said that I am more use to the Cause than half the People in the Country – I wish to God, I could be so. A noble Earl of Stanhope has Lately Consulted me twice about a Bill which his Ld.ship now mean[s] to bring in to the House to allow the sable People in the wt Indias the Rights of taking an oath against any White Person – I hope it may Pass, tis high time – & will be of much use. – may the Lord Bless all the friends of Humanity" (358).

Equiano was also writing to Walker to invite him to his wedding to an Englishwoman: "I now mean as it seem Pleasing to my Good God! – to leave London in about 8 – or, 10 Days more, & take me a Wife – (one Miss Cullen –) of Soham in Cambridge shire. . . . I will be Glad to see you at my Wedg" (358). Equiano probably first met the now-thirty-year-old Susanna Cullen on his bookselling tour in Cambridgeshire in 1789. She subscribed to the third edition of his autobiography. As Equiano's will shows, Susanna's parents,

James and Ann, were people of moderate means, a respectable family for a former slave to marry into. He was a very worthy son-in-law, well enough known to have his 7 April provincial marriage announced in the London press. The 19–21 April 1792 issue of the *General Evening Post*, for example, reported, "Gustavus Vassa (Equiano Olaudah), the African, well known in England as the champion and advocate for procuring a suppression of the Slave Trade, was married at Soham, in Cambridgeshire to Miss Cullen daughter of Mr. Cullen of Ely, in the same County, in the presence of a vast number of people assembled on the occasion."

For Equiano, April 1792 was the kindest month, politically as well as personally. A few days before his wedding he attended "the debate in the house of Commons on the Slave Trade, April the 2d and 3d" (235). Like most of the listeners in the gallery, to be sure of a place he probably arrived before noon on the 2nd, though Wilberforce did not speak until 6:00 P.M., and he probably stayed until the House rose at 7:00 A.M. the following morning. SEAST and its allies in Parliament had been very busy since the defeat of the abolition bill in 1791. SEAST had Phillips print and distribute throughout Britain thousands of copies of *An Abstract of the Evidence Delivered before a Select Committee of the House of Commons in the Years 1790 and 1791*. He was also ordered to republish and distribute William Bell Crafton's *A Short Sketch of the Evidence Delivered before a Committee of the House of Commons for the Abolition of the Slave Trade*.[11] Clarkson had successfully encouraged the public to boycott sugar from the West Indies. The House of Commons had been flooded with 519 petitions in favor of abolition. The abolitionists had done everything possible to set the stage for the debate in early April. Both Pitt and his political adversary Fox spoke in favor of Wilberforce's bill to abolish the trade at some time in the future. Accepting Henry Dundas's amendment that the abolition be gradual, the House approved the bill by a vote of 230 to 85 and sent it on to the House of Lords for consideration. Equiano could hardly have asked for more.

He had anticipated the outcome of the vote. Even the prospect of marriage barely distracted him from promoting the cause and his book. He assured Walker before his wedding that "when I have given her about 8 or 10 Days Comfort, I mean Directly to go to Scotland – and sell my 5th. Editions." His optimism was understandable. He could not have known that events would prove the vote the high-water mark of the surge in abolitionist success in Parliament before the end of the century rather than the turning point he and most observers thought it to be.

He had no reason to doubt that he would have a profitable tour of Scotland, with its population of almost 1.5 million. Two years earlier SEAST had sent Clarkson there to gather evidence. At the beginning of 1792, to mobilize support for the abolitionist cause, SEAST had sent William Dickson to Scotland, where he found opposition to the slave trade much stronger and more widespread than either he or SEAST had anticipated. Equiano changed his mind about leaving Susanna behind in England. He and his bride reached Scotland by 10 April. They went first to Paisley, a city of twenty-five thousand people in western Scotland, and from there to Glasgow, with seventy-five thousand people the second-largest city in Scotland. They reached Edinburgh, a city of eighty-three thousand, by early May. As his advertisements in the *Glasgow Advertiser and Evening Intelligencer* on 27 April and in the *Caledonian Mercury* on 21 May show, Equiano was still selling copies of his fourth (Dublin) edition.

As usual during his book tours, Equiano also engaged in political activity. He wrote to his London landlord, Hardy, on 28 May that four days earlier he "was in the General assembley of the Church of Scotland, now Convened, & they agreed unanimously on a petition, or an address to the House of Lords to abolish the Slave Trade" (362). He thanked the members of the assembly publicly in the 26 May issue of the *Edinburgh Evening Courant*: "PERMIT me, one of the oppressed natives of Africa, to offer you the warmest thanks of a heart glowing with gratitude on the unanimous decision of your debate of this day – It filled me with love towards you. It is no doubt the indispensable duty of every man, who is a friend to religion and humanity, to give his testimony against that iniquitous branch of commerce the slave trade. It does not often fall to the lot of individuals to contribute to so important a moral and religious duty, as that of putting an end to a practice which may, without exaggeration, be stiled one of the greatest evils now existing on the earth" (361).

Some of Equiano's political activities on the road were more private and increasingly more risky.[12] He wrote Hardy, "My best Respect to my fellow members of your society. I hope they do yet increase. I do not hear in this place that there is any such societys – I think Mr. Alexr. Mathews in Glasgow told me that there was (or is) some there" (361). During his book promotion tours in the provinces Equiano recruited or, at least, identified potential fellow members for the London Corresponding Society (LCS), a radical working-class organization. Hardy had helped create the LCS on 25 January 1792 to develop a nationwide network of correspondents promoting the expansion of the electorate. Hardy was the society's first secretary. Equiano had brought to Hardy's attention the Reverend Mr. Thomas Bryant, with whom he had stayed in Sheffield in 1790.[13] Hardy later described his subsequent letter to Bryant as "the first correspondence of the Society."[14] Hardy's letter indicates how closely he and, presumably, Equiano associated opposition to the slave trade with calls for more radical political reformation. He used language familiar from the French Revolution and Paine's writings: "I hope you will pardon that freedom which I take in troubling you with the following sentiments; nothing but the importance of the business could have induced me to address one who is an entire stranger to me, except *only* by report. Hearing from my friend, Gustavus Vassa, the African, who is now writing memoirs of his life in my house, that you are a zealous friend to the abolition of that cursed traffic, the Slave Trade, I infer, from that circumstance, *that you are a zealous friend to freedom on the broad basis of the RIGHTS OF MAN*. I am fully persuaded that there is no man, who is, from principle, an advocate for the liberty of the black man, but will zealously support the rights of the white man, and *vice versa*."[15] On 2 April 1792, in its first public pronouncement, the LCS made the radical claim that all men possessed "unalienable Rights of Resistance to Oppression."[16]

Equiano had more personal reasons for writing to Hardy as well. He asked him to buy him a copy of the April 1792 issue of the *Gentleman's Magazine*, which included a notice of Equiano's marriage. He also hoped that Hardy could help him recover a piece of jewelry he had left behind: "Pray ask Mr. & Mrs. Peters who Lodged in the next Room to me, if they have found a Little Round Gold Breast Buckel, or broach, sett in, or with fine stones – if they have, I will pay them well for it. – & if they have found it pray write to me on that account Directly" (362). Unfortunately, there was nothing Hardy could do to help him regain the £232 he had lent to someone months earlier: "I hope the good Lord will enable me to hear & to profit, & to hold out to the end – & keep me from all such Rascals as I have met with in London – Mr. Lewis wrote me a Letter within 12 Days after I Left you & acquaintd. me of that villain who owed me above 200£ – Dying on the 17th. of April – & that is all the Comfort I got from him since – & now I am again obliged to slave on more than before if possible – as I have a Wife" (362).[17]

Equiano's unnamed debtor was not the worst of the "Rascals" he had left behind in London. By the time he went to Scotland he had become well enough known throughout Great Britain that even his private life had become a matter of public interest. On 30 May, for example, the *Gazetteer and*

New Daily Advertiser reported his activities to its readers in London: "GUS-TAVUS VASA, with his *white* wife, is at Edinburgh, where he has published a letter of thanks to the General Assembly of the Church of Scotland, for their just and humane interference upon the question of the SLAVE TRADE" (emphasis in the original). If the *Gazetteer* was trying to stir up racial animosity by emphasizing Susanna Vassa's complexion, no evidence suggests that it succeeded. Equiano discovered, however, that celebrity came with a price. He informed Hardy, "Sir, I am sorry to tell you that some Rascal or Rascals have asserted in the news parpers viz. Oracle of the 25th. of april, & the Star. 27th. – that I am a native of a Danish Island, Santa Cruz, in the Wt. Indias. The assertion has hurted the sale of my Books – I have now the aforesaid Oracle & will be much obliged to you to get me the Star, & take care of it till you see or hear from me" (361–62).

While Equiano was out of town two London newspapers, the *Oracle* and the *Star*, questioned his true identity. The *Oracle* reported that "there is no absurdity, however gross, but popular credulity has a throat wide enough to swallow it. It is a fact that the Public may depend on, that *Gustavus Vassa*, who has publicly asserted that he was kidnapped in Africa, never was upon that Continent, but was born and bred up in the Danish Island of Santa Cruz, in the West Indies [now Saint Croix in the U.S. Virgin Islands]. *Ex hoc uno disce omnes* [that one fact tells all]. What, we will ask any man of plain understanding, must that cause be, which can lean for support on falsehoods as audaciously propagated as they are easily detected?" The newspaper went on to impugn the motives of the leading abolitionists and, by implication, Equiano's as well: "Modern Patriotism, which wantons so much in sentiment, is *really* founded rather in private interested views, than in a regard for the Public Weal. The conduct of the friends to the Abolition is a proof of the justice of this remark. It is a fact, of which, perhaps, the People are not apprized, but which it well becomes them to know, that WILBERFORCE and the THORNTONS are concerned in settling the Island of Bulam in Sugar Plantations; of course their interests clash with those of the present Planters and hence their clamour against the Slave Trade."

Following the destruction of the Granville Town settlement at the end of 1789, Parliament incorporated the Sierra Leone Company, a private commercial organization, in 1791 to establish a second settlement on the ruins of the first. Freetown was established in February 1792 by the few survivors of Granville Town and more than a thousand African Britons resettled from Nova Scotia. Henry Thornton was chairman of the Sierra Leone Company's court of directors. As agent for the company, Thomas Clarkson's brother, John, recruited the settlers from Nova Scotia. He became governor of the new settlement. Both Thornton and John Clarkson were among Equiano's original subscribers. Many of Equiano's subscribers were also shareholders in the Sierra Leone Company. Neither Wilberforce, Thornton, nor Clarkson participated in the short-lived scheme of the Bulama Island Association to set up an agricultural colony off the coast of western Africa, which the West Indian planters rightly saw as a potential commercial threat to their own interests.

Two days after the attack in the *Oracle*, the *Star* reported that "the Negroe, called GUSTAVUS VASA, who has published an history of his life, and gives so admirable an account of the laws, religion, and natural productions of the interior parts of Africa; and in which he relates his having been kidnapped in his infancy, is neither more nor less, than a native of the Danish island of Santa Cruz." Suddenly both sides of the author's binomial African British identity had been challenged and his sincerity as an abolitionist questioned. The need to publish the new edition of *The Interesting Narrative*, which Equiano had been working on since before he left London for Scotland, was now urgent. He had it ready by the third week of August, when he advertised it in the *Aberdeen Journal* on the 20th.

Equiano recognized the issues at stake in the challenge the *Oracle* and the *Star* had made to his identity, credibility, and motives. He prefaced the fifth and subsequent editions of his narrative with a letter addressed "to the Reader," in which he counterattacked the "invidious falsehood [that] appeared in the Oracle . . . with a view to hurt my character, and to discredit and prevent the sale of my Narrative" (5). Typically, he was as concerned for his pocketbook as he was for his integrity. Sales depended upon his authority, which derived from his African British identity. In a footnote to the word *character* he takes a confrontational position toward his assailants by appropriating the words of Shakespeare's Othello:

> Speak of me as I am,
> Nothing extenuate, nor set down aught
> In malice.

And in another footnote he responds to his attackers with the words of the great Roman satirist Juvenal:

> I may now justly say,
> There is a lust in man no charm can tame,

Of loudly publishing his neighbour's shame;
On eagles' wings immortal scandals fly,
But virtuous actions are but born and die.

The new address "to the Reader" suggests that his primary audience had shifted since 1789 from the members of Parliament to the public at large. In the previous four editions his address to the members of Parliament had opened his paratext. From the fifth edition on the new address and two letters on the question of Equiano's character precede the address to Parliament. The first of the new letters is from the publisher of the *Star*, explaining that he had innocently reprinted the offending passage from the *Oracle*. He admits that he may have been wrong to have done so: "As to G[ustavus].V[assa]. I know nothing about him. After examining the paragraph in the Oracle which immediately follows the one in question, I am inclined to believe that the one respecting G.V. may have been fabricated by some of the advocates for continuing the Slave Trade, for the purpose of weakening the force of the evidence brought against that trade; for, I believe, if they could, they would stifle the evidence altogether" (6). The second new letter is from the Reverend Mr. John Baker, a prominent member of SEAST who demanded an apology on Equiano's behalf from the publisher of the *Oracle*. He advises Equiano, "I think it is not worth while to go to the expence of a law-suit, especially if a proper apology is made. . . . [C]an any man that reads your Narrative believe that you are not a native of Africa? I see therefore no good reason for not printing a fifth edition, on account of a scandalous paragraph in a newspaper" (6–7).

To further defend his character Equiano also identified six of his subscribers as "those numerous and respectable persons of character who knew me when I first arrived in England, and could speak no language but that of Africa" (5). "My friend Mrs. Baynes, formerly Miss Guerin," was the former Mary Guerin, the younger sister of Maynard and Elizabeth Martha Guerin (238). Equiano does not mention that Mrs. Baynes had been present when he was baptized in 1759 as having been "born in Carolina." Others knew him from their days together with the Royal Navy: John Hill, Captain Gallia, and Admirals Affleck and Balfour. The last witness, "Mrs. Shaw," was "Captain Pascal's daughter." Pascal himself had died in 1787. The prefatory paratext to the new edition also added Equiano's letter of introduction from Thomas Atwood Digges and the notice of *The Interesting Narrative* that had appeared in the June 1789 issue of the *Monthly Review*. Equiano demonstrated his self-assuredness by including the reviewer's comment that "it is not improbable that some English writer has assisted him in the compilement, or, at least, the correction of his book; for it is sufficiently well-written." A writer less secure in his own achievement would have deleted that passage. With the addition of new prefatory letters and references attesting to his character and credibility, the apologia began to replace the petition as *The Interesting Narrative*'s generic frame.

Equiano revised his subscription lists and text as carefully as he did his prefatory letters and notes. To his lists of English and Irish subscribers he added a list of Scottish subscribers, but what he removed is as significant as what he added. In the face of rising concern about the possible destabilizing effects of abolition, the names of Hardy and Walne, founders of the LCS, and of Cugoano, who had encouraged slave resistance, disappeared from the fifth and later editions. The new items of defensive self-promotion Equiano placed at the front of his book were balanced by the celebratory penultimate paragraph and footnotes he added to its conclusion, in which he calls attention to his recent marriage and to the international reception of his autobiography. In light of his marriage he scrupulously revised an earlier passage in his text in which he had announced his desire to meet available young women. From beginning to end, the fifth edition of *The Interesting Narrative* demonstrates that Equiano took as much care in how he represented his life as in how he lived it.

Having visited Aberdeen, Dundee, and Perth during the summer of 1792, Equiano headed back to England, reaching Newcastle around the beginning of September.[18] There he advertised his autobiography on 15 September in the *Newcastle Chronicle, or, Weekly Advertiser, and Register of News, Commerce, and Entertainment.* At least some of his twenty-eight thousand potential buyers in Newcastle were already familiar with his narrative because it was available to them through a local circulating library. Perhaps because he did not have to work as hard as elsewhere to make himself known, he had the leisure to go "90 fathoms down St. Anthony's Colliery, at Newcastle, under the river Tyne, some hundreds of yards on the Durham side" (305). Equiano stopped at Durham in October on his way south, reaching Hull, a city of thirty thousand people, in November. By the time he returned to London at the end of the year he had collected enough new subscribers to justify a sixth edition, with a separate list of Hull subscribers. It appeared in January 1793, adding two new prefatory letters of introduction from subscribers in Durham and Hull attesting to his character and veracity.

While Equiano and his wife were successfully touring Scotland and northeastern England, the abolitionist cause was suffering setbacks. The

House of Lords had taken up Wilberforce's bill in May, but consideration of it was so deliberate that no action had occurred before the session ended. By the next session, however, a series of domestic and foreign events had led to a growing public perception that the movement to abolish the slave trade was associated with dangerous political and social radicalism at home and abroad. Some of the most vocal opponents of the trade, such as Paine and the LCS, called for very significant reforms modeled on what was happening in France. France was beginning to demonstrate an aggressive willingness to export its revolutionary principles, declaring war on the Hapsburg Empire in April 1792. France became more aggressively revolutionary at home as well. King Louis XVI of France was executed on 21 January 1793. On 1 February France declared war on Britain and Holland. When the Earl of Abingdon opposed abolition on 11 April 1793, he deplored correspondence between the London Abolition Committee of SEAST and French abolitionists. He asked, "What does the abolition of the slave trade mean more or less in effect than liberty and equality?"[19] Revolutionary France abolished slavery the following year. Although Wilberforce reintroduced his abolition bill each year from 1793 to 1796, it never again garnered enough votes to get out of the House of Commons.

Despite the growing resistance in Britain to calls for reform of any kind, Equiano did not stay off the road for long. When he returned from his Scottish tour, he and Susanna used Soham as their home base. In the summer of 1793 Equiano headed west to sell the story of his life. In June he stopped at Longnor to visit the Anglican reverend Joseph Plymley, who was the very active representative of SEAST in Shropshire, but Equiano missed him because he "was engaged & indefatigable in his parochial visitation," according to his sister Katherine. A friend of Clarkson, Plymley had met Equiano during his trip to London to attend the debate in the House of Commons in April 1792 and "had then purchased of him the memoires of his life written by himself." But, as Katherine Plymley recorded in her diary, Reverend Plymley had doubts about the usefulness of Equiano's bookselling tours to the abolitionist cause: "I believe [Equiano's] business at this time was to get introduced wherever he could & to dispose of them – my brother was rather concerned at his going through the country for this purpose, as he feared it would only tend to increase the difficulty of getting subscriptions when he wanted, for carrying on the business of the abolition. The luke-warm would be too apt to think if, this be the case, & we are to have Negroes come about in this way, it will, be very troublesome; my brother thought there was something not quite right about him or he would have been at Sierra Leone." Despite her brother's reservations, she adds, "Be that as it may, had my Brother been at home, he would have done all he could for him, & did endeavour to see him afterwards in Shrewsbury but he was gone."[20] Plymley did subsequently write letters of recommendation for Equiano's visit to Bridgenorth. Katherine mentions that in addition to selling his book Equiano also distributed "little pamphlets against the use of sugar." He charmed her young niece and nephew when he dined at her brother's, "though they had never been accustomed to blacks," inviting them to go to Africa with him. He gave her nephew one of the pamphlets and an autographed copy of his narrative.

From Shropshire Equiano went south to Tewkesbury. There he used his Quaker contacts to sell his book. He arrived with a letter of introduction from the glover Stanley Pumphrey to his fellow abolitionist writer William Bell Crafton. Equiano had met Pumphrey in Worcester. Like Crafton, Pumphrey was a Quaker subscriber to *The Interesting Narrative.* In his 1 July 1793 letter of thanks to Pumphrey Equiano adopted the Quaker practice of using the second-person familiar voice – thee and thou – to address his correspondent:

> Dr. friends &c. / This with my best Respts. Hope thou are well – & got the 7 Books I sent to thee on Friday Last if the parcel did not come, pray write to me – Directly by the return of the Post – & Direct to me at Mr. John Mountains – Grocer – Gloucester – & if thou have Recd. the above – I think there is no need of Writing – I am exceeding much obliged to thee for thy very kind Letter to the friends here, they have been very kind to me in going about with me – & by Saturday night we had sold (or engaged) 53 Books which is all Delivered to Day. I go from here to morrow for Gloucester – & are much obliged to thee for all favours & also to those friends here which thou made mention of. & they went with me to several of their neighbours – may my God ever hear my Prayers & reward you all for every Kindness to me & the Sable People –[21]

After his visit to Gloucester, where he advertised his narrative in the *Gloucester Journal* on 15 July, Equiano returned briefly to London. While there he decided to take a risky gamble. All of his bookselling tours during the previous four years had been to places where abolitionist sentiment was strong and the local economic ties to the slave trade were relatively weak. He had encountered some resistance and doubts about his message and the messenger, but they were disappointing rather than dangerous. Now, when concern about the wisdom of abolition in a revolutionary age was widespread, he decided to go to Bristol. With sixty-four thousand people, Bristol was England's fifth largest city and one of the centers of proslavery support. Clarkson had needed a bodyguard when he visited the slave-trading ports to gather evidence a few years earlier, before abolition had become nationally controversial. Twenty years later Clarkson recalled his fear at the prospect of going to Bristol: "I began now to tremble, for the first time, at the arduous task I had undertaken, of attempting to subvert one of the branches of the commerce of the great place which was then before me. I began to think of the host of people I should have to encounter in it. I anticipated much persecution in it also; and I questioned whether I should even get out of it alive."[22] If a white man supported directly by the abolition organization in London was endangered in 1788, what might a black man on his own face in 1793?

Equiano was not naive about the prospect before him. As he was about to leave for Bristol, he wrote to Wedgwood telling him of his plans and reminding Wedgwood of an offer of protection he had once made. As an experienced seaman Equiano was liable to being pressed into the Royal Navy during the current war with France. At nearly fifty years old his age would normally protect him, but his eligibility gave his proslavery opponents a legal pretext for physically removing him from the abolitionist cause. Wedgwood had offered to use his influence with Philip Stephens, M.P. for Sandwich, on Equiano's behalf. Stephens was first secretary to the Lords of the Admiralty and first secretary in the Marine Department:

Dr. & Worthy Sir, &c.
I am with great respects – hope you are Well.
Dr. Sir I hope you do remember that you did once tell me, if that I was to be molested by the press gang to Write to Mr. Phillip Steven – at the Admiralty – I will now take it a great favour to inform me, if I may act so in Case I am molested – I mean next Week to be in Bristol where I have some of my narrative engaged – & I am very apt to think I must have enemys there – on the account of my Publick spirit to put an end to Slavery – or reather in being active to have the Slave Trade Abolished. Dr. Sir, I leave London on friday the 23d. inst. therefore will take it a particular favour if you will be kind enough as to Direct to me few Lines at the post office – till Calld. for – Bristol.

Wedgwood did not reply until 19 September because he had been out of town when Equiano's letter arrived. Hoping he was not too late to be of help and signing himself "your friend and servant," Wedgwood advised Equiano to contact Wedgwood's nephew and personal secretary, Thomas Byerley, in his own absence. Fortunately, Equiano did not need Wedgwood's intervention. By the time he received Wedgwood's letter he had returned to London, having stopped at the town of Devizes on the way. In London he published the seventh edition of his autobiography, adding a list of Bristol subscribers.

He was on his next tour by early February 1794. He spent at least the next four months selling his autobiography in the southeastern English counties of Suffolk, Norfolk, and Essex before returning to London. Understandably, he spent much of this tour in Norwich. With nearly forty thousand inhabitants, it was by far the largest town in Norfolk. A century earlier Norwich had been the second most populous city in England, but it had recently been superseded by Birmingham, Bristol, and Manchester. Norwich was still one of the major manufacturing centers in the country and especially sensitive to any disruptions to trade with Europe.[23] Located on the east coast of England, its inhabitants had little direct investment in the transatlantic slave trade. Unlike the larger city of Manchester, which had no direct representation in the House of Commons, Norwich had one of the widest franchises in Britain. All of its freemen could vote, whether resident or not, and since Norwich was also ranked as a county, any man owning a freehold property worth at least forty shillings was also eligible to vote.

By the time of Equiano's visit many opponents of the French Revolution considered Norwich a "Jacobin city," using the name of the most radical group of the French revolutionaries to imply that most of the city's residents were disloyal to the British monarchy. Like the rest of Britain, Norwich was remarkable for the number of clubs and societies it had. Norwich had approximately forty clubs and societies with some four thousand members. It was unusual, however, in having such a high percentage of associations whose members came from the lower levels of society and in having so many that called for economic, political, and social reform.[24] While staying in the nearby Norfolk hamlet of Aylsham in late November 1792, the novelist and diarist Frances Burney wrote to a friend back in London, "I am truly amazed, & half alarmed, to find this County filled with little Revolution Societies which transmit their *notions of things* to the larger Committees at Norwich, which communicate the whole to the Reformists in London. I am told there is scarce a Village in Norfolk free from these meetings."[25] The Norwich Revolution Society (NRS) established an association with the LCS in April 1792. Not surprisingly, the president and secretary of the NRS subscribed to

Equiano's Norwich edition, as did seven of the nine members of the NRS nominated to join the LCS.

The national government was understandably concerned about the political atmosphere in Norwich. In March 1793 the United Political Societies of Norwich wrote to London supporting universal suffrage and annual elections, asking for the sense of the people and whether a petition to Parliament, an address to the king, or a convention would be most effective. The LCS chose the most threatening method of holding a convention.[26] Seditious handbills were posted in Norwich in the fall of 1793. Despite the arrest in December 1793 of the leaders of the convention in Edinburgh, the Norwich political societies published the Declarations and Resolutions of the United Constitutional Societies of Norwich, dated 16 January 1794. They commended the convention leaders and condemned the unconstitutional actions of the magistrates of Edinburgh. They further claimed that various acts of Parliament had invaded their rights under the Glorious Revolution settlement of 1688 by controlling grain exports, running up the national debt, limiting the franchise to men of property, and extending the tenure of members of the House of Commons from annual to seven-year terms.

We know more about the political inclinations of Equiano's Norwich subscribers than about his other provincial subscribers because he was in the city only a few months before a special election for the House of Commons. The ballot was not secret. Eighteenth-century polling records identify voters and the candidates they chose. One of Norwich's two members, William Windham, an original subscriber in 1789 to Equiano's narrative, had to stand for reelection in July 1794 because Pitt had appointed him to his cabinet as secretary at war. Like most Britons, Windham initially greeted the French Revolution with enthusiasm. But, influenced by Burke's *Reflections*, Windham turned against the Revolution sooner than many of his countrymen and much earlier than the vast majority of his constituents. Consequently, a reform candidate, James Mingay, contested Windham's reelection. Windham won by a vote of 1,236 to 770, a very respectable showing for his challenger.

Equiano went to Norwich intending to publish his eighth edition there. He advertised on 22 February in both William Stevenson's *Norfolk Chronicle* and Richard Bacon and his son-in-law William Yarrington's *Norwich Mercury* that the eighth edition "enlarged . . . was already in the press" and would "be published, ready to be delivered on the 12th of March next." Buyers were told that, "as it is intended to publish a List of Subscribers, the Author would be happy to have the names of such friends as mean to subscribe by the 6th of March at farthest." Since Stevenson, who had been a close friend and correspondent of Sancho, was the only distributor of *The Interesting Narrative* other than Equiano, he was probably the printer of the Norwich edition. The eighth edition was delivered as promised, and its reception prompted a thank-you note in both newspapers on 15 March. Equiano addressed it "to the Inhabitants of this City and its Environs, and also of Bury St. Edmund."

Equiano had very carefully laid the groundwork for the reception he and his book received in Norwich. If his behavior there was representative of his activities elsewhere during his book tours, he quickly developed personal relationships in the places he visited that went well beyond the more formal national networks of Quaker, SEAST, and LCS contacts that gained him initial entry into local communities. He was, in his contemporary Samuel Johnson's terms, a very "clubbable" man, someone who relished social engagement.On 13 February, more than a week before he announced the forthcoming publication of his eighth edition, Equiano attended a meeting of the Tusculan School, a Norwich debating society.[27] The debates were open to "visitors," women as well as men, who could vote on the outcomes of the debates and speak at the meetings. On 15 November 1793 Catherine Buck, daughter of William Buck of Bury and future wife of Thomas Clarkson, attended the debate on the question, "Ought Dramatic Performances to be Encouraged?" with another young woman. Unfortunately, "the Female Visitors declined giving their opinions." On 19 December she and a Miss Jarrold attended the Tusculan School meeting to hear the debate on the question "What is the foundation of the moral virtues?" Their reaction was not recorded. Catherine Buck, her father, and Miss Jarrold all subscribed to Equiano's Norwich edition.

On Equiano's visit to the Tusculan School on Thursday, 13 February, he was one of three observers, who all voted. The minutes report that on the question "Is Courage natural or acquired? . . . the discussion proved very animated and interesting. The Society has reason to regret that sufficient minutes were not taken. The opinion was unanimous in the end that Courage is acquired and not natural." On Friday, 7 March, Equiano was one of four visitors attending the debate on the question "Has the Government of a Country a right in any Circumstances to compel its citizens to arm?" One of the visitors, Hudson Gurney, "in a very animated and impressive language denied the right. 'If I lived under a despotic Government,' said he, 'and the tyrant issued his requisition commanding me to go into the field against the generous people who were hastening to free my Country, I would arm, I would enter the field but it should be to point the bayonet against the tyrant's heart!'" Equiano voted with the more moderate majority, 5 to 3, that the government had such a right. Gurney, as well as most of the others involved in the debates Equiano attended, subscribed to the Norwich edition. Equiano's association with the members of the Tusculan School may have continued beyond his stay in Norwich. The school debates evolved into the *Cabinet. By a Society of Gentlemen*, a biweekly periodical published in Norwich between October 1794 and September 1795. Its issues were subsequently collected and published in three volumes simultaneously in Norwich and London in late 1795. The author of the antiwar essay entitled "Mischievous Effects of War" used the pseudonym "Othello," which suggests that the writer was of African descent. Equiano may have been "Othello."[28] Of the twenty known contributors to the *Cabinet*, all publishing pseudonymously, thirteen subscribed to Equiano's Norwich edition.

Like the subscribers to all previous editions of *The Interesting Narrative*, the subscribers to the eighth edition represented the full range of occupations, politics, and religions in Norwich and the surrounding villages. Windham's supporters signed up next to Mingay's voters. Equiano spent at least part of the summer of 1794 traveling through the counties northeast of London gathering subscribers from Lynn and Wisbech, Clarkson's hometown, for his ninth edition. But, perhaps recognizing that a subscription list acceptable in "Jacobin" Norwich might be controversial elsewhere, when Equiano published his last edition in London later in 1794, the names of many of Mingay's supporters had disappeared. Most notably absent from the ninth edition were the names of the surgeon Edward Rigby and the Baptist minister Mark Wilks, the most ardent defenders of the French Revolution and the LCS.

Even while Equiano was collecting more subscribers for what was to be the last edition he published of *The Interesting Narrative*, he continued to revise his autobiography to better serve the abolitionist cause. For example, he added to the ninth edition a substantial footnote intended to appeal to both his readers' emotions and their economic self-interest:

In the ship Trusty, lately for the new settlement of Sierra Leona, in Africa, were 1300 pairs of shoes (an article hitherto scarcely known to be exported to that country) with several others equally new, as articles of export. – Thus will it not become the interest as well as the duty of every artificer, mechanic, and tradesman, publicly to enter their protest

against this traffic of the human species? What a striking – what a beautiful contrast is here presented to view, when compared with the cargo of a
slave-ship! Every feeling heart indeed sensibly participates of the joy,
and with a degree of rapture reads barrels of *flour* instead of *gunpowder –
biscuits and bread* instead of *horsebeans – implements of husbandry* instead of
guns for destruction, rapine, and murder – and various articles of *usefulness*
are the pleasing substitutes for the *torturing thumb-screw* and the *galling
chain*, &.

Why was the ninth edition the last Equiano published? The arrest in
May 1794 of Hardy and others on the capital charge of high treason had a
chilling effect on supporters of reform. The letter that Equiano wrote to
Hardy from Edinburgh on 28 May 1792 was among the papers seized when
Hardy was arrested. The arrests of Hardy and others culminated a series of
government moves, such as the suspension of habeas corpus in May 1794, to
identify and suppress seditious and treasonous behavior during the war with
France.[29] Even though Hardy's trial for high treason, like those of his fellow
radical reformers John Horne Tooke and John Thelwall, ended in acquittal in
November 1794, the government's willingness to prosecute may have dis-
couraged the publication of radical or reformist sentiments in general and
perhaps helps explain Equiano's apparent public silence after 1794. Equiano's
concern for his own safety would be understandable in light of the government's desire to suppress the voices of those who espoused social and political reforms. He was known to have many connections with the reformers. In
December 1797, apparently unaware that Equiano had died almost nine months
earlier, the government-sponsored *Anti-Jacobin; or, Weekly Examiner* satirically
included "OLAUDAH EQUIANO, the African" at a fictional "Meeting of the
Friends of Freedom."

One could argue, however, that the arrests and acquittals in 1794 an-
gered and emboldened other writers. Between the times of the arrests and
the trial, for example, the *Morning Post and Fashionable World* published
critical comments on the government's actions as well as several appeals
from the LCS for aid for those charged and their families. On 5 September
the *Morning Post* claimed that "Mrs Hardy, who died on Wednesday sennight
last, [and who] was considerably advanced in a state of pregnancy, at the
time her husband was apprehended," was one of the "Victims of the Suspension of the HABEAS CORPUS ACT." Following Hardy's trial and acquittal
the newspaper carried an advertisement placed by the LCS on 5 December

for a new weekly periodical called the *Politician*, and on 18 December the *Morning Post* advertised the second volume of Thomas Spence's very radical *Pig's Meat, or Lessons for the People, alias (according to Burke) the Swinish Multitude.*

Equiano's public silence after his ninth edition was likely due to a combination of the current political climate, the success of his bookselling tours, and the demands of his growing family responsibilities. Unfortunately, we know very little about Equiano's family life beyond what public documents tell us. Between his bookselling tours he may have gone back to Soham for the 16 October 1793 birth of his first child, Ann Mary (Maria) Vassa. On the other hand, her baptism may have been delayed until 30 January 1794 because he had not returned in time for her birth. In either case, Equiano did not stay around for very long. His second daughter, Joanna, was born on 11 April 1795.[30] The publication of four editions of *The Interesting Narrative* in 1793 and 1794 indicated a continuing market for his autobiography, but the subscription lists in the ninth edition also show that his successful tours had taken him to almost every city in England with more than twenty thousand people as well as to all the major urban centers in Ireland and Scotland. Further tours in the British Isles would have been only marginally more profitable. After the publication of the last edition of his autobiography Equiano no longer needed to work.

The sales of his book gave Equiano enough money to be able to live the life of a gentleman. Even before his marriage brought him status and property ties, he had significant disposable income. As early as February 1792 he was able to lend someone the sizeable sum of £232, roughly equivalent in 2005 currency to about £18,000, or nearly $35,000. More significantly, he could afford to lose the money when the unidentified borrower defaulted on the loan.[31] By the end of 1794 Equiano was financially secure enough to reciprocate the favor of subscription. "Gustavus Vassa, *a native of Africa*," subscribed to Carl Bernhard Wadstrom's *An Essay on Colonization particularly applied to the West Coast of Africa*, published in November 1794.[32] Wadstrom had been one of Equiano's original subscribers in 1789. Equiano's well-earned sense of achievement was soon interrupted, however.

On 20 February 1796 the Saturday weekly the *Cambridge Chronicle and Journal* reported, "On Tuesday died at Soham, after a long illness, which she supported with Christian fortitude, Mrs. Susannah Vassa, the wife of Gustavus Vassa the African." Knowing that her death was coming, "Susanna the wife of Gustavus Vassa of Soham in the County of Cambridge Gentleman" wrote her will on 12 December 1795.[33] Her will is a testament to her piety and practicality. She was no less a predestinarian than Equiano himself. "Sincerely penitent and heartily sorry for my Sins," Susanna committed her "Soul into the Hands of Almighty God in whom and by whose Mercy I trust and assuredly believe to be saved." Convinced of her own spiritual future, she sought to secure the material future of her husband and daughters. She left everything to Equiano. Her older sister, Mary Cullen, had already willed to Susanna "all her Right Title and Interest of and in all that pasture Ground with the appurtenances situate lying and being in Sutton in the Isle of Ely and County of Cambridge," which Mary expected to inherit upon the future death of their mother, Ann Cullen. In turn, Susanna willed her anticipated inheritance to her husband, should her mother and sister die before him. The two acres of pastureland would not have rendered Equiano a landed gentleman, however. They were copyhold rather than freehold, meaning that rather than belonging to the tenant free and clear of anyone else's claim upon it, the land's tenure was taken for the tenant's lifetime and that of his immediate heirs but could be reclaimed by the lord of the manor at the time of renewal. Susanna never imagined that her mother would live until 1820, long after Susanna's own death and that of her husband and after the transportation of her sister to Australia on a charge of shoplifting.[34]

Soon after Susanna's death Equiano moved from Soham back to London, leaving his infant daughters in the care of others while he tried to make provisions for their futures. The results are found in his will, his last known piece of writing and thus apparently his last act of verbal self-fashioning. By the time of his death Equiano had become probably the wealthiest Briton of African descent living in England. During the eighteenth century an annual income of forty pounds was sufficient to support a family of four modestly in London, and a gentleman could live well on three hundred pounds per annum. The vast majority of Equiano's fellow Britons did not have enough wealth to justify making a will. He was one of the very few eighteenth-century African Britons in this position.[35] He felt entitled to proclaim himself "Gustavus Vassa of Addle Street Aldermanbury in the City of London Gentleman." In the event of his death his executors, "my Friends John Audley and Edward Ind both of Cambridge Esquires," both early subscribers, were to provide for "the Board Maintenance and Education" of his daughters until they reached the age of twenty-one. They would then inherit the "Estate and property I have dearly earned by the sweat of my Brow in some of the most remote and adverse Corners of the whole world" (373–75). His daughters were not to forget how much he had deserved the financial success he had achieved. In the codicil of his will he bequeathed to them the acres of land he would inherit if he outlived his mother-in-law, along with "sundry Household Goods and Furniture wearing apparel and printed Books," several annuities totaling nearly two hundred pounds, and "three hundred pounds at present undisposed of." He also left them "three hundred pounds secured to me by an Assignment of the lease of Plasterers Hall situate in Addle Street N. 25 in the City of London."[36]

Equiano was living in Plasterers' Hall when he drew up his will on 28 May 1796. It belonged to the Plasterers' Company, one of the City of London livery companies. The company had been chartered in 1501, and its original hall was destroyed in the Great Fire of 1666. Sir Christopher Wren designed the replacement hall, which was built in 1669. Fire destroyed it in 1882. The company used the hall as a source of rental income, leasing it to others, who in turn subleased its rooms to various occupants. Equiano must have subleased the hall from William Rolfe, a goldsmith who had signed a twenty-one-year lease for the hall and several nearby houses on 5 October 1790.[37] Equiano in turn subleased the hall to someone else. A 1 September 1796 advertisement in the *Times* for the lease of the hall gives a detailed description of it and its potential for generating income:

> Very desirable, roomy, convenient, substantial BRICK-BUILT PREM-
> ISES, called PLASTERERS HALL, very advantageously situated in
> Addle-street, leading from Aldermanbury to Wood-street, Cheapside, con-
> taining numerous convenient apartments, a spacious Hall, upwards of 40
> feet in length, with a Music Gallery, a large yard, a store cellar, capable of
> holding 100 butts, and a fore-court, enclosed with folding gates. The
> Premises are particularly suitable for many businesses requiring room.
> The Hall is let off for occasional purposes, and also the Store Cellar, at
> rents amounting to 63£ per annum; held for an unexpired term of 15
> years at a moderate rate.

Although Equiano maintained his lease on the Plasterers' Hall until he died, he moved from the hall in the City of London to the county of Middlesex sometime after 16 June 1796. He probably left the hall around September 1796, when the lease was advertised.[38] By 22 October he was living on "John Street, Tottenham Court Road in the County of Middlesex."[39] And by the time of his death, he was living on Paddington Street, Middlesex.

Equiano's will demonstrates the sincerity of his religious beliefs and his continued interest in Africa. Should both his children die before they

366 ■ CHAPTER FOURTEEN

reached the age of twenty-one, he bequeathed half his "Estate and Effects thereof . . . to the Treasurer and Directors of the Sierra Leona Company for the Use and benefit of the School established by the said Company at Sierra Leona." Equiano bequeathed the other half of his "Estate and Effects thereof" to the interdenominational "Society instituted at the Spa Fields Chapel . . . for sending Missionaries to preach the Gospel in Foreign parts." This society later became the London Missionary Society. Denied the chance to go to Africa himself, Equiano never wavered in his economic and spiritual commitments to his ancestral homeland.

Equiano did not long survive his wife. Bordered on both sides by cemeteries, Paddington Street was a grimly appropriate place to end one's life. The only eyewitness account we have of Equiano's last days comes, fittingly, from Granville Sharp, his ally in the fight for abolition of the slave trade. Sharp later wrote to his niece, "He was a sober, honest man, and I went to see him when he lay upon his deathbed, and had lost his voice so that he could only whisper." Equiano died on 31 March 1797, attended by his nurse, Mrs. Edwards. Although his death was reported in the London and national press, his burial site is unknown.[40] Equiano's oldest daughter, Ann Mary, died on 21 July 1797, just six months after him.[41] In 1816 Equiano's surviving daughter, Joanna, received £950 from her father's estate on her twenty-first birthday. Her inheritance was worth roughly £80,000, or about $160,000 in today's currency.[42] Among her father's personal effects was a silver watch, perhaps one of those inscribed "for strict attention to duty with H.M.S. Racehorse. North Pole Expedition" that had been given to the members of the crews serving under Phipps in 1773.[43] Equiano achieved the fame and wealth he sought and deserved. Some of his wealth came to him through his marriage. Much of it, however, came from his success as a self-made man who took advantage of the opportunities he found during a life of varied adventures, obstacles, and ultimate personal triumph.

A genius at self-representation and self-promotion, Equiano defied convention by writing his autobiography and then publishing, marketing, and distributing it himself. He became the first successful professional writer of African descent in the English-speaking world. By retaining the copyright to his book he maintained control over his "round unvarnished tale" and could make changes in every one of the nine editions he published of his autobiography.

Equiano also defied convention by marrying a white Englishwoman and making sure that his racist opponents knew that he had done so by announc-

A SELF-MADE MAN ■ 367

ing his wedding in every edition of his autobiography from 1792 on. Mentioning his marriage was probably intended to serve a larger purpose as well: "If any incident in this little work should appear uninteresting and trifling . . . , I can only say . . . that almost every event of my life made an impression on my mind. . . . I early accustomed myself to look at the hand of God in the minutest occurrence, and to learn from it a lesson of morality and religion; and in this light every circumstance I have related was to me of importance" (236). Equiano's marriage to Susanna Cullen anticipated the commercial union he advocated between Africa and Europe.

Through a combination of natural ability, accident, and determination Equiano seized every opportunity to rise from the legal status of being an object to be sold by others to become an international celebrity, the story of whose life became his own most valuable possession. Once Equiano was free from enslavement his every action reflected his repudiation of the constraints bondage had imposed on him. As if to flaunt his liberty he traveled the world virtually at will, recognizing the sea as a bridge rather than a barrier between continents and people. His freedom gave him the chance to move socially, economically, religiously, and politically as well as geographically. Having known what the loss of liberty entailed, once free he took as much control of his life as he could, even revising the events in it to make a profit in a just cause. He became the exemplary "Atlantic creole."

Print allowed Equiano to resurrect not only himself publicly from the "social death" enslavement had imposed on him but also the millions of other diasporan Africans he represented. By combining his own experiences with those of others he encountered in his travels around the Atlantic he refashioned himself as *the* African. Rejected in his attempts to be sent by Europeans to Africa as a missionary or diplomat, through *The Interesting Narrative* Equiano made himself into an African missionary and diplomat to a European audience. In the re-creation of his own life he forged a compelling story of spiritual and moral conversion to serve as a model to be imitated by his readers.

Unfortunately, Equiano did not live to see the abolition of the slave trade he had done so much to accomplish. The political triumph of the abolitionist cause in 1807 came ten years too late for him to celebrate. It might not have come that soon, however, had he not contributed to the cause by so skillfully and creatively fashioning the story of his life "to put a speedy end to a traffic both cruel and unjust" (5). He gave the abolitionist cause the African voice it needed. The role he played in the last mission of his life earned him the right to claim an African name that "signifies vicissitude, or fortunate also; one favoured, and having a loud voice and well spoken." That role also entitled him to accept the name of a European liberator of his people ironically given him in slavery. He had made himself a true "citizen of the world."

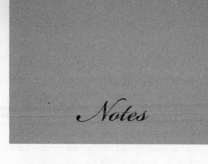
Notes

PREFACE

Documents in the Public Record Office (PRO) in Kew are identified by their class codes and piece numbers. Class codes are cited as follows: ADM (Admiralty), CO (Colonial Office), PC (Privy Council Office), PRIS (King's Bench Prison), PROB (Prerogative Court of Canterbury), RG (General Register Office), T (Treasury), and TS (Treasury Solicitor).

1. All quotations from Equiano's works, including *The Interesting Narrative*, book reviews, letters to individuals and periodicals, and his will, are taken from Equiano, *The Interesting Narrative*, and are cited by page number parenthetically within the text.

2. Berlin, "From Creole to African," 254. I have substituted "Anglophone African" for Berlin's "African-American" because his characterization of the "Atlantic creole" can be applied to many English-speaking people of African descent on both sides of the Atlantic during the seventeenth and eighteenth centuries. Berlin uses the term *creole* to refer to a person of mixed cultures and languages. During the eighteenth century, a Creole was someone of African or European descent who had been born in the Americas.

3. See my "Questioning the Identity."

4. Walvin, *An African's Life*, xiv.

5. Hochschild, *Bury the Chains*, 372.

6. Appiah, *In My Father's House*, 191. I have adapted and applied to Equiano words that Appiah uses to describe the significance of his late father's life: "Only something so particular as a single life – as my father's life, encapsulated in the complex pattern of social and personal relations around his coffin – could capture the multiplicity of our lives in a postcolonial world."

7. Quoted in ibid., 177.

ONE. EQUIANO'S AFRICA

1. The term *autobiography*, meaning the account of one's own life, was very rarely used in the eighteenth century. Such writings were usually called *memoirs* or *histories* and were included under the broader term *biography*, which we now reserve for accounts of someone else's life. I use *autobiography* and *biography* in their modern senses.

2. Representative examples of fictional black voices can be found in volumes 4–6 in Kitson and Lee, eds., *Slavery, Abolition and Emancipation.*

3. Clarkson, *An Essay*, 117–18.

4. Cugoano, *Thoughts and Sentiments*, 15.

5. Lambert, ed., *House of Commons Sessional Papers*, 69:98–99. The "Letter from Gustavus Vassa, late Commissary for the African Settlement, to the Right Honourable Lord Hawkesbury" is item 14 of the "Detached Pieces of Evidence Relating to the Trade to Africa generally."

6. See, for example, Bosman, *A New and Accurate Description*; Barbot, *A Description*; Phillips, *A Journal*; Bluett, *Some Memoirs*; Snelgrave, *A New Account*; Atkins, *A Voyage*; Smith, *A New Voyage*; and Adanson, *A Voyage.*

7. Examples include Churchill and Churchill, *A Collection*; Harris, *A Complete Collection*; Astley, *A New General Collection*; and *The Universal History.*

8. Stanhope, *The Letters*, 2:503.

9. Adanson, *A Voyage*, 54.

10. Benezet, *A Short Account*; Benezet, *A Caution and Warning*; Benezet, *Some Historical Account*, appeared first in Philadelphia in 1771 and was revised and republished in London in 1784. In 1788, four years after Benezet's death, the Society for Effecting the Abolition of the Slave Trade published an expanded edition of *Some Historical Account* in London.

11. Edwards, "Introduction," xviii.

12. Achebe, *Morning Yet on Creation Day*, 50, 79.

13. See my "Questioning the Identity."

14. Edwards cites G. I. Jones and Chinua Achebe on possible equivalents and meanings of the name *Equiano* ("Introduction," xx–xxi).

15. Ibid., xviii.

16. Equiano's note in editions 1–9 reads: "When I was in Smyrna [under the dominion of Turkey] I have frequently seen the Greeks dance after this manner."

17. "The word for year, 'Ah-affoe,' is clearly the modern Ibo word *afo*; and though his word for 'calculators or yearly men,' recorded as 'Ah-affoe-way-cah,' does not exist in modern Ibo, in addition to 'affoe' it contains the word *ka*, one meaning of which is 'to fix a date' (i.e. for festivals)" (Edwards, "Introduction," xviii).

18. Chambers, "The Significance."

19. Equiano's note in editions 1–9 reads: "See Benezet's account of Africa throughout."

20. Peel, *Devout Breathings.*

TWO. THE MIDDLE PASSAGE

1. Ramsay, *An Inquiry*, 16. The earliest example the *Oxford English Dictionary Online* gives of *middle passage* in relation to the transatlantic slave trade is from Clarkson, *An Essay.*

2. The best brief and scholarly up-to-date history of the trade is Klein, *The Atlantic Slave Trade.*

3. Rawley observes, "In the assessment of the mortality incurred by Africans in their forced migration from one continent to another the preembarkation and postembarkation deaths before they were sold into American slavery should be noted" (*The Transatlantic Slave Trade*, 305). Klein and others agree: "The voyage was only one part of the movement from a slave's capture to acclimatization in the Americas; and the total mortality rates were a multiple of the deaths [during the voyage]" ("Transoceanic Mortality," 97).

4. Segal, *Islam's Black Slaves*, 55–57.

5. Eltis, "The Volume and Structure," par. 32.

6. Richardson, "The British Empire," 462.

7. Craton, *Sinews of Empire*, 4.

8. See Rozbicki, "To Save Them from Themselves."

9. For an account of Sessarakoo see Sypher, "The African Prince in London." For Diallo see Grant, *The Fortunate Slave.*

10. See Wood, *The Origins*, 7.

11. Patterson, *Slavery and Social Death.*

12. Jones, "Olaudah Equiano," 68.

13. Ibid.

14. Wesley, *Thoughts upon Slavery*, 16.

15. James Ramsay Papers, MSS BRIT EMP. S.2. Ramsay's comment is undated, but internal evidence and context suggest a 1788 date of composition.

16. Klein, *The Atlantic Slave Trade*, 155–56. Andrew the Moor says that he also passed through a number of African masters before he was sold to Europeans on the coast.

17. See Nwokeji, "African Conceptions," 49.

18. I am indebted to David Richardson for sharing with me information from the Du Bois Institute data set of slave-trade statistics (PRO, CO 28/30 dd 61–dd 76), which enabled me to identify the *Ogden* as the most probable vessel bearing Equiano from the Bight of Biafra to Barbados by comparing the Du Bois data with those found in Minchinton, King, and Waite, eds., *Virginia Slave-Trade Statistics*, 155, and with the information Equiano gives us about his arrival in Virginia. The 1754 voyage of the *Ogden* has identity number 90473 in the Du Bois database. For the period 1714 to 1779 the Du Bois Institute data set includes 95 percent of the voyages originating in Britain.

19. Behrendt calculates that "African traders transported three times as many slaves to Biafran coastal markets after the yam harvest as during the planting season" ("Markets," 185).

20. African fear of European cannibalism is reported, for example, in Barbot, *A Description*, 2:639; and Long, *The History of Jamaica*, 2:397. See also Pierson, *Black Legacy*, 5–14.

21. Foremast: the term *ship* was "particularly applied to a vessel furnished with three masts, each of which is composed of a lower mast, top mast, and top-gallant mast, with the usual machinery thereto belonging. The mast . . . placed at the middle of the ship's length, is called the main-mast, . . . that which is placed in the fore-part, the fore-mast, . . . and that which is towards the stern [the rear] is termed the mizen-mast" (Falconer, *An Universal Dictionary*).

22. Edwards, *The History*, 2:69–71.

23. Quoted in Behrendt, "Markets," 200.

24. Klein et al., "Transoceanic Mortality," 101.

25. The second *Ogden* voyage has identity number 90474 in the Du Bois database.

26. Falconbridge, *An Account*, 34. Falconbridge's *Account* was written at the behest of the Society for Effecting the Abolition of the Slave Trade, which printed and distributed six thousand copies of it.

27. The sloop *Nancy*, built in Virginia in 1753, which may have brought Equiano to Virginia from Barbados, was not the same slave-trading sloop *Nancy*, built in Massachusetts Bay in 1762, on which Vassa, then owned by Robert King, sailed under the command of Thomas Farmer in 1766 (Donnan, *Documents*, 4:620). I gained access to some of the relevant Public Record Office (Kew) records through the Virginia Colonial Records Project Database at the Library of Virginia.

28. Behrendt, "Markets," 196.

29. Gomez, *Exchanging*, 115. On the acculturation of Africans in Virginia see Kulikoff, *Tobacco and Slaves*; Chambers, "He Is an African."

THREE. AT SEA

1. PRO, ADM 1/2290.

2. PRO, ADM 3/62.

3. PRO, ADM 7/87.

4. Achebe notes, "In taking the colourful name of Gustavus Vassa the African, Equiano no doubt sought to bring to his cause the magic and success of the Swedish patriot who led his people to freedom" (*Morning Yet on Creation Day*, 80).

5. Oliver, "William Borlase's Contribution," 309. I thank Joanna Mattingly, assistant curator at the Cornwall Maritime Museum, for bringing Oliver's article to my attention.

6. My discussion of conditions in the eighteenth-century Royal Navy is indebted to Colledge, *Ships of the Royal Navy*; Lavery, *The Ship of the Line*; Rodger, *The Wooden World*; Lavery, *The Arming and Fitting*; Gardiner, ed., *The Line of Battle*; Hepper, *British Warship Losses*.

7. Spavens, *The Narrative*, 68–69.

8. Rawley, *The Transatlantic Slave Trade*, 292.

9. [Oglethorpe], *The Sailors Advocate*, 4. A manuscript note in the British Library copy of the seventh edition attributes *The Sailors Advocate* to "General Oglethorpe," the philanthropist James Edward Oglethorpe, who outlawed slavery in the colony he founded in Georgia in 1735, and the addition to the preface to "G.S." (Granville Sharp).

10. PRO, ADM 1/932.

11. Rodger, *The Wooden World*, 344.

12. Cremer, *Ramblin' Jack*, 43.

13. For the causes, course, and consequences of the Seven Years' War see Anderson, *Crucible of War*.

14. PRO, ADM 36/6367.

15. PRO, ADM 36/6365.

16. PRO, ADM 36/5743.

17. PRO, ADM 36/62530.

18. Donovan, *Slaves in Cape Breton*, notes that Equiano's account of the death and scalping of the Mi'kmaq chief is corroborated in Gen. James Wolfe to Lord George Germain, Louisbourg, 1 July 1758, Germain Papers, as well as in the Journals of James Thompson Sr., 1758–1883 [*sic*], reel M-2312, vol. 1.

19. Spavens, *The Narrative*, 55.

20. PRO, ADM 32/5.

21. Spavens, *The Narrative*, 69.

22. PRO, ADM 32/5.

FOUR. FREEDOM DENIED

1. Rodger, *The Wooden World*, 160.

2. Ibid., 11.

3. Mole: "a name given in the Mediterranean to a long pier, or artificial bulwark of masonry, extending obliquely across the entrance of a harbour, in order to break the force of the sea from the vessels which are anchored within" (Falconer, *An Universal Dictionary*).

4. Wrigley, "A Simple Model."

5. Boswell, *Life of Johnson*, 859 (20 September 1777).

6. Edwards points out in his introduction that other black writers used the motif of the talking book. Equiano appears to be paraphrasing a similar account by a fellow Afro-Briton of a talking book found in Gronniosaw: "And when first I saw [my master] read, I was never so surprized in my life, as when I saw the book talk to my master, for I thought it did, as I observed him to look upon it, and move his lips. – I wished it would do so to me. As soon as my master had done reading, I followed him

to the place where he took the book, being mightily delighted with it, and when no-body saw me, I opened it and put my ears down close upon it, in great hopes that it would say something to me; but was very sorry, and greatly disappointed when I found it would not speak, this thought immediately presented itself to me, that every body and every thing despised me because I was black" (*A Narrative*, 16–17). Related examples of the motif appear in Marrant, *A Narrative*, 27; Cugoano, *Thoughts and Sentiments*, 80 (Cugoano's unacknowledged source for the anecdote is Robertson, *The History of America*, 2:175); Jea, *The Life*, 33. The literary and ideological significance of the motif of the talking book is most fully treated in Gates, "Introduction."

7. Lavery, ed., *Shipboard Life*, 43.

8. PRO, ADM 32/5.

9. Boswell, *Life of Johnson*, 686 (18 March 1776).

10. PRO, ADM 36/6755, 6756.

11. Boswell, *Life of Johnson*, 248 (1759).

12. Patton, *Strictures*, quoted in Lavery, ed., *Shipboard Life*, 622.

13. Wiecek, "*Somerset*," 94.

14. Collier, *An Essay*, 74.

15. Blackstone, *Commentaries*, vol. 1, chap. 1. At the behest of Lord Mansfield, his mentor and patron, Blackstone revised this passage in the second and subsequent editions. The second (1766) and third (1768) editions read: "A slave or a Negro, the moment he lands in England, falls under the protection of the laws, and so far becomes a freeman; though the master's right to his service may probably still continue." In the fourth (1770) and later editions, "probably" reads "possibly."

16. PRO, ADM 1/927.

17. Patton, *Strictures*, 10–14, quoted in Lavery, ed., *Shipboard Life*, 622–25.

FIVE. BEARING WITNESS

1. Turley, *The Culture*, 9.

2. Soderlund, *Quakers and Slavery*; Nash and Soderlund, *Freedom by Degrees*.

3. Equiano's note in editions 1–9 reads: "Mr. Dubury, and many others in Montserrat."

4. Estwick, *Considerations*, 79n, only in the second and subsequent editions. Estwick was referring specifically to the free black Jamaican poet Francis Williams. See my "Who Was Francis Williams?"

5. Equiano's note in editions 1–9 reads: "These pisterines are of the value of a shilling." The following phrase, "a day," was added in the eighth and ninth editions.

6. Clarkson, *An Essay*, 135.

7. Liber D: book or register D. The use of authenticating documentation, including correspondence, became a hallmark of eighteenth-century autobiographical and bi-

ographical writings, both fictional and nonfictional. The technique is epitomized in Boswell's *Life of Johnson*.

8. Equiano is probably trying to sound unbiased by using examples from the geographical and racial extremes of humankind, commonly thought to be neither Negroes nor Caucasians. With the term *Samiade* he seems to conflate the Sami people, also known as Lapps, and the Nentsy, also known as Samoyeds. See Vaughan, *The Arctic*, 13–16. On Equiano's use of "Samiade" see Goldsmith: "The first distinct race of men is found round the polar regions. The Laplanders, the Esquimaux Indians, the Samoeid Tartars, the inhabitants of Nova Zembla, the Borandians, the Greenlanders, and the natives of Kamskatka, may be considered as one peculiar race of people, all greatly resembling each other in their stature, their complexion, their customs, and their ignorance. . . . These nations not only resemble each other in their deformity, their dwarfishness, the colour of their hair and eyes, but they have all, in a great measure, the same inclinations, and the same manners, being all equally rude, superstitious, and stupid" (*An History*, 2:214). On the image of the Hottentot see Merians, *Envisioning the Worst*. See also Maxwel: "The *Hottentots* . . . are a race of men distinct both from *Negroes* and *European Whites*; for their hair is woolly, short and frizzled; their noses flat, and lips thick; but their skin is naturally as white as ours. . . . Mr. *Maxwel* takes them to be the most lazy, and ignorant part of mankind" ("An Account," 60, 61). Equiano might better have followed the advice Benezet offers in *Some Historical Account* (the 1788 edition): "But nothing shews more clearly how unsafe it is to form a judgment of distant people from the accounts given of them by travellers, who have taken but a transient view of things, than the case of the Hottentots, . . . those several nations of Negroes who inhabit the most southern part of Africa: *these people* are represented by several authors, who appear to have very much copied their relations one from the other, as so savage and barbarous as to have little of human, but the shape: but these accounts are strongly contradicted by others, particularly Peter Kolben [1675–1726], who has given a circumstantial relation of the disposition and manners of those people. He was a man of learning, sent from the court of Prussia solely to make astronomical observations there; and having no interest in the slavery of the Negroes, had not the same inducement as most other relators had, to misrepresent the natives of Africa"(85).

9. Milton, *Paradise Lost*, 1:26, in *Complete Poems*.

10. Equiano may have been consciously anticipating the ironic distinction William Blake makes in *The Marriage of Heaven and Hell* between the oppressively rational nature of institutionalized religion – so-called Christianity – and the liberating emotional vitality of true faith – "the Devil's party." Such a distinction helps explain why Equiano almost always uses the term *Christian* ironically to refer to slave owners in his account of his enslavement in the West Indies.

11. Equiano's footnote in editions 8 and 9 reads: "See the Observations on a Guinea Voyage, in a series of letters to the Rev. T. Clarkson, by James Field, Stanfield, in 1788, p. 21, 22. – 'The subjects of the king of Benin, at Gatoe, where I was, had

their markets regular and well stocked; they teemed with luxuries unknown to the Europeans."

12. Adapted from Beelzebub's speech in Milton, *Paradise Lost*, 2:332–40. According to Matthew 12:24, Beelzebub is "the prince of the devils."

SIX. FREEDOM OF A SORT

1. Falconer, *An Universal Dictionary*.

2. Dutch Creole: a person of Dutch descent born in the Western Hemisphere. Interestingly, Equiano does not classify him as white.

3. Davis, *The Rise of the English Shipping Industry*, 133–34.

SEVEN. TOWARD THE NORTH POLE

1. Phipps, *A Voyage*, 218.

2. *Annual Register* (1772), 98.

3. Davis, *The Rise of the English Shipping Industry*, 138.

4. Since the time of the Crusades, when many of the European invaders originated from what is now France, the Turks used the terms *Frank* and *Christian* interchangeably.

5. Walvin, *Fruits of Empire*, 124.

6. Burnard and Morgan, "The Dynamics."

7. Vaughan, *The Arctic*, 145.

8. Engel, *Mémoires*.

9. Williams, *The British Search*, 163–65. The Phipps expedition receives brief mentions in Vaughan, *The Arctic*; Savours, *The Search*; and Williams, *Voyages of Delusion*.

10. Phipps, *A Voyage*, 10.

11. It first appeared in Markham, ed., *Northward Ho!* 81–228. Floyd does not mention Vassa/Equiano, nor does he comment on the presence of blacks among the crew members.

12. Anonymous, *The Journal*, xxvi.

13. Ibid., xxvi–xxviii.

14. Banks, *The Letters*, 42.

15. Phipps, *A Voyage*, 20. Phipps received the orders, dated 25 May, on 26 May.

16. Ibid., 20 (27 May).

17. Ibid., 10.

18. Nelson, "Lord Nelson's Memoir," 1:4.

19. PRO, ADM 36/7567.

20. Anonymous, *The Journal*, 29.

21. Floyd, "Journal," 175, in Markham, ed., *Northward Ho!* 81–228.

22. PRO, ADM 33/675. Equiano appears as "Feston" and as "Weston" in PRO, ADM 36/7490.

23. Equiano's data on the apparatus agree with those found in Phipps's account, which includes an illustration and explanation of Doctor Irving's invention. The "Logg Book Commencing April the 19th 1773 ending 13 October 1773" kept by John Crane, master of the *Racehorse*, notes that on Sunday, 20 June, the vessel received "from Dr. Irwin's Still twenty four Galls. fresh water."

24. Anonymous, *The Journal*, 54.

25. Phipps, *A Voyage*, 230.

26. Ibid., 31 (29 June).

27. Spitsbergen, not, as Equiano misremembers, Greenland, which was much farther west (174).

28. Phipps, *A Voyage*, 35 (4 July).

29. Ibid., 35–36.

30. Anonymous, *The Journal*, 41; Phipps, *A Voyage*, 41 (10 July).

31. Equiano's words (174) are taken from Phipps, *A Voyage*, 42 (11 July).

32. The "anecdote recollected by Admiral Lutwidge" is found in Nelson, "Lord Nelson's Memoir," 1:12.

33. "Some of our people . . . they dispersed": compare Phipps, *A Voyage*, 57–58 (29 July). Harrison first identified Nelson as the leader of the rescue in *Life*. Harrison's version of the incident, which does not mention Equiano, gained widespread currency when Southey repeated it in his popular *Life of Nelson*. Sugden, in his carefully researched *Nelson*, argues persuasively that Harrison's identification is unlikely (72).

34. "We had generally . . . uncommon scene": compare Phipps, *A Voyage*, 31 (29 June).

35. Floyd, "Journal," 199.

36. Nelson, "Lord Nelson's Memoir," 4.

37. Although Phipps says almost nothing about the reactions of the crew to their predicament and escape, the account in the *Journal*, 85–86, anticipates Equiano's.

38. Phipps, *A Voyage*, 74.

39. Anonymous, *The Journal*, 92.

40. Phipps, *A Voyage*, 74–75.

41. Booms: "Certain long poles run out from different places in the ship to extend the bottoms of particular sails." Chuck or chock: "A sort of wedge used to confine a cask or other weighty body, in a certain place, and to prevent it from fetching way when the ship is in motion" (Falconer, *An Universal Dictionary*).

42. Phipps's captain's log books, "Journal of the proceeding of His Majesty's Sloop Racehorse The Hon.ble Captn. Constantine John Phipps Commencing April the 19th 1773 Ending October the 13th 1773" and "A Journal of the Proceedings of His Majesty's Sloop Racehorse The Hon.ble Conste. John Phipps Commander between the 19th of April and 13th of October 1773" (PRO, ADM 51/757 and 52/1416)

do not mention the near-disaster Equiano records. Nor does John Crane's master's "Logg" (PRO, ADM 52/1416), which also covers the 19 April–13 October 1773 period.

43. *Regulations and Instructions.*

44. Anonymous, *The Journal*, 101, 102.

45. Phipps, *A Voyage*, 76.

EIGHT. BORN AGAIN

1. Boswell, *Life of Johnson*, 327 (31 July 1763).

2. Since the Turks were conventionally seen as brutal infidels, comparing hypocritical or false Christians unfavorably to them was a common rhetorical ploy used by satirists. For an example see Hogarth's *Credulity*, where the smiling Turk is clearly a more sane and positive figure than the lunatic Methodists he observes.

3. Equiano could not have heard George Whitefield in Philadelphia in either 1766 or 1767, as he says he did. Whitefield did not leave Great Britain between 7 July 1765 and 16 September 1768. Equiano must have heard Whitefield on Sunday, 10 February 1765, in Savannah, Georgia. The weekly newspaper the *Georgia Gazette* (14 and 21 February) reported that Whitefield was in the town on the 9th. The sloop *Prudence*, on which Equiano served under Thomas Farmer, was in port between the 7th and the 16th.

4. The writings of Hammon, Liele, Marrant, George, and King are reproduced in Carretta, ed., *Unchained Voices*.

5. Compare Sharp's opinion in *A Representation*: "It were better for the English nation, that these American dominions had never existed, or even that they should have been sunk into the sea, than that the kingdom of Great Britain, should be loaded with the horrid guilt of tolerating such abominable wickedness!" (73).

6. Wesley, *Thoughts upon Slavery*, 16–17, 18, 39, 31, 36, 45, 40–41, 42–43.

7. Smith, *State of the Gaols*, 26.

NINE. SEEKING A MISSION

1. Adapted from "The Spiritual Victory," no. 312, in Toplady, *Psalms and Hymns*.

2. "Appendix to the Chronicle," *Annual Register* (1777), 258.

3. The best brief account of the "Musquito" Amerindians during the eighteenth century is Rogers, "Caribbean Borderland." Also useful is Dawson, "William Pitt's Settlement."

4. On the concept of marchlands see Bailyn, *The Peopling*, 112–13.

5. Bryan Edwards, letters of 10 November 1773, in *The Parliamentary Register*, 6:333. Much of my information about the Mosquito Coast in the 1770s comes from Alexan-

der Blair's petition to the House of Commons on behalf of himself and Dr. Irving, along with its supporting documentation, seeking restitution for the Spanish seizure of the *Morning Star* (*The Parliamentary Register*, 6:303–37).

6. Jefferys, *The West India Atlas*, 11.

7. Bryan Edwards, quoted in *The Parliamentary Register*, 6:334.

8. Helms, "Of Kings and Contexts."

9. Editions 1–4 read "to be baptized." The revision, though grammatically clumsy, is more consistent with the sense of the rest of the sentence: to baptize the Indians without teaching them Christian theology and morality was indeed to practice mock religion.

10. Purver, *A New and Literal Translation*, 1:47.

11. *The Parliamentary Register*, 6:303–37.

12. PRO, ADM 36/9078. Yorke had gone directly from the Arctic expedition to the *Squirrel*.

13. To distinguish between the Gustavus Vassa of the *Morning Post* letters and the Gustavus Vassa/Olaudah Equiano of *The Interesting Narrative* I refer to the former in quotation marks. The *Morning Post* letters are reproduced in my "Possible Gustavus Vassa/Olaudah Equiano Attributions."

14. On the American Revolution and its impact on Britain see Conway, *The War*, and Conway, *The British Isles*.

15. Sancho's letters to the *Morning Post* are reproduced in my "Three West Indian Writers." See also Sancho, *Letters*.

16. Sancho, *Letters*, 191.

17. Carretta, "Three West Indian Writers," 77.

18. I thank Linda Coleman, Joan Radner, and Steven Rutledge for advice on Equiano's use of the Irish language and classical references.

19. For an argument that one of the purposes Equiano had in writing *The Interesting Narrative* was to claim the status of gentleman see my "Defining a Gentleman."

20. Morse to Lord Townsend, 12 August 1782, PRO, CO 267/20; quoted in Gray, *A History*, 244.

21. Lambert, ed., *House of Commons Sessional Papers*, "Detached Pieces of Evidence relating to the Trade to Africa generally," no. 3, in 69:78–79.

22. Ibid., 69:79.

23. See Patterson, *The Other Armada*; Tracy, *Navies*, 118–55; Baugh, "Why Did Britain Lose Command"; Herbert, "Coxheath Camp."

24. Sancho to Roger Rush, in Sancho, *Letters*, 176.

25. Sancho to Mrs. Cocksedge, 25 August 1779, in Sancho, *Letters*, 169. For a discussion of contemporaneous literary, especially dramatic, references to the invasion scare see Jones, "Sheridan."

26. The 5 August 1786 issue of the *Public Advertiser* reports that the *Harmony* reached Gravesend on 3 August.

TEN. THE BLACK POOR

1. For a thorough and balanced account of the black poor and the settlement of Sierra Leone, to which I am much indebted, see Braidwood, *Black Poor*.

2. Hoare, *Memoirs of Granville Sharp*, 263.

3. Kulikoff, "Uprooted Peoples," 144.

4. Fielding, *Extracts*, 143–45. John was the half brother of the novelists Henry (1707–54) and Sarah (1710–68) Fielding. Sarah collaborated with Jane Collier on the satiric novel *The Cry: A New Dramatic Fable* (1754). John, although totally or almost totally blind, was the leading magistrate in Middlesex and well known for his efforts to enforce the laws vigorously and to organize a local London police force. The mob burned down his house during the Gordon Riots of 1780. The mob also burned down Mansfield's house, destroying his library and many of his papers.

5. Estwick, *Considerations*, 41.

6. On the significance of the Mansfield decision and the arguments over its interpretation since its rendering see Wiecek, "*Somerset*"; Cotter, "The Somerset Case." Wiecek argues that *Somerset* abolished slavery in England de facto if not de jure; Cotter's argument that *Somerset* abolished it de jure as well as de facto has been challenged by Paley, "After *Somerset*." For an account of North American newspaper reports of the Mansfield ruling see Bradley, *Slavery*, 66–80.

7. Quoted in Wiecek, "*Somerset*," 86.

8. [Long], *Candid Reflections*, 56. Long incorrectly conflates the English and Scottish legal systems when he uses the term *Great Britain*.

9. On the effects of Mansfield's ruling see, in addition to Wiecek and Cotter, Drescher, *Capitalism and Antislavery*, 25–49.

10. Edmund Burke, *Letter to the Sheriffs of Bristol*, in Burke, *The Writings and Speeches*, 3:297.

11. Hutchinson, *The Diary and Letters*, 2:276–77.

12. Sancho to John Ireland, in Sancho, *Letters*, 164.

13. Hoare, *Memoirs of Granville Sharp*, 333.

14. Cugoano, *Thoughts and Sentiments*, 115–16. Cugoano's writings are cited hereafter parenthetically in the text.

15. Granville Sharp to Jemima Sharp, 27 February 1811, Granville Sharp Papers.

16. Introduction, sec. 4 ("Of the COUNTRIES Subject to the LAWS of ENGLAND"), 1:107.

17. *The Speech of Edmund Burke Esq; on Moving His Resolutions for Conciliation with the Colonies, March 22, 1775*, in Burke, *The Writings and Speeches*, 3:123.

18. Johnson, *Taxation No Tyranny*, 454.

19. Day, *Fragment*, 24, 34. Although the letter is dated 1776, Day did not publish it until after the American Revolution ended. Day's poem *The Dying Negro*, coauthored with Thomas Bicknell, appeared in 1773. Day's novel, *The History of Sandford and Mer-*

ton, a Work Intended for the Use of Children, appeared in three installments (1783, 1786, and 1789).

20. George Washington to Richard Henry Lee, 26 December 1775, in Washington, *The Writings*, 4:187.

21. Quarles, "The Revolutionary War." See also Quarles, *The Negro*; Frey, *Water from the Rock*.

22. Belinda's petition, Banneker's letter, and George's account are reproduced in Carretta, ed., *Unchained Voices*, 142–44.

23. After carefully reviewing the contemporaneous and contemporary estimates of the eighteenth-century black population in England, Meyers says that "a figure persistently of at least 5,000 seems highly likely" (*Reconstructing the Black Past*, 31).

24. Drescher, *Capitalism and Antislavery*, 25–49.

25. Lorimer, "Black Slaves."

26. [Long], *Candid Reflections*, 48.

27. For the writings of Hammon, Gronniosaw, and Marrant see Carretta, ed., *Unchained Voices*, 20–25, 32–58, 110–33.

28. See Visram, *Asians in Britain*, 14–33.

29. On the black loyalists who went to Canada see Wilson, *The Loyal Blacks*; Walker, *The Black Loyalists*. Cahill, "The Black Loyalist Myth," argues that the blacks were motivated by a desire for self-emancipation, not loyalism. Walker responds in the same issue (88–105).

30. Smeathman also read his findings to the Royal Society on 15 February 1781, and they were published in *Philosophical Transactions of the Royal Society of London* the same year.

31. Although it is dated 1 August 1783, Sharp's *Memorandum* may not have been published before it appeared several years later as tract no. 3 in the second edition of his *An Account of the Constitutional English Polity of Congregational Courts* (London, 1786).

32. Smeathman, *Plan*, 16–17.

33. A doglegged street connecting Lombard and Gracechurch Streets, Whitehart Court was often called White Heart (or Hart) Yard, Gracechurch Street, during the eighteenth century.

34. First published by Benezet in Philadelphia in 1766 under the title *A Caution and Warning* and retitled for the 1767 London edition, this antislavery tract was printed in 1784 and 1785 editions by the Quakers' printer, James Phillips. See Minutes of Meeting for Sufferings, 25 February 1785, and Minutes of the Committee on the Slave Trade, 14 and 20 March 1784.

35. According to the copy in John Kemp's Commonplace Book, 1786, MS Box X3/2, this letter was "presented by Gustavus Vassa and Seven others the 21st Octr. 1785."

36. See Shyllon, *James Ramsay*.

37. Cugoano, *Thoughts and Sentiments*, 106.

38. Copies of Equiano's muster lists for the *Atlantic, Belisarius,* and *Vernon* transport ships are in PRO, T 1/643 (no. 487). The settlers were not exclusively black and included mixed-race couples. His lists total 459 people: 344 blacks (290 men, 43 women, 11 children) and 115 whites (31 men, 75 women, 9 children). The muster numbers continued to rise and fall because people who left, were expelled, or died before the voyage were often replaced by others.

39. PRO, T 1/643/681 and 29/58, 279, cited in Braidwood, *Black Poor,* 150.

40. PRO, T 1/643.

41. Hoare, *Memoirs of Granville Sharp,* 313.

42. Braidwood, *Black Poor,* 149–58, carefully weighs and interprets the evidence.

43. Ibid., 157.

44. See, for example, comments by Norton, "The Fate"; Shyllon, *Black Slaves.*

45. Compare Cugoano, *Thoughts and Sentiments,* 104–6.

46. PRO, T 1/645/968, Navy Commissioners to Steele, 26 April 1787, "Account of Expences incurred in sending the Black Poor to Sierra Leona"; PRO, T 29/60, 29 July 1789; PRO, T 1/638, "An Alphabetical List of the Black People who have received the Bounty from Government."

47. See, for example, Asiegbu, *Slavery,* 4; Norton, "The Fate," 409; Walvin, *Black and White,* 148; Shyllon, *Black Slaves,* x; Davis, *The Problem of Slavery in the Age of Revolution,* 495; Fryer, *Staying Power,* 195; Ramdin, *The Making,* 17; Latimer, "Black Resistance."

48. See, for example, Barker, *The African Link;* Drescher, *Capitalism and Antislavery,* 60–61; Braidwood, *Black Poor,* 63–107.

49. PRO, T 1/646/1295.

50. James Ramsay Papers, MSS BRIT EMP. S.2. Ramsay's comment is undated, but internal evidence and context suggest a 1788 date of composition.

51. PRO, T 1/645/968, Navy Commissioners to Steele.

ELEVEN. TURNING AGAINST THE SLAVE TRADE

1. Hoare, *Memoirs of Granville Sharp,* 236.

2. Rawley, *The Transatlantic Slave Trade,* 298–99.

3. Philmore, *Two Dialogues on the Man-Trade,* 17.

4. Benezet to Joseph Phipps and John Fothergill, 28 May 1763, Spriggs MSS 156/56, and Benezet to Fothergill, 28 April 1773, Gibson MSS 1:27. The two Benezet letters are also quoted in Jennings, *Business,* 22. *Business* is the most detailed and reliable account of the roles the four Quaker businessmen – George Harrison, Samuel Hoare, James Phillips, and Joseph Wood – played in the abolition movement. A good recent general history of the Society of Friends is Walvin, *The Quakers.*

5. Colley, *Britons,* 352.

6. The publications on both sides are identified in Hogg, *The African Slave Trade*, item nos. 1758–80.

7. Wesley, *Thoughts upon Slavery*, 43.

8. Sharp, *A Representation*, 51.

9. [Dillwyn and Lloyd], *The Case*, 37 (27 August 1784).

10. Quoted in Jennings, *Business*, 23.

11. Adam Hochschild, private correspondence, 4 September 2004.

12. Woods, *Thoughts*, 9–10.

13. Ibid., 23–24.

14. Thompson-Clarkson MSS 2:9 (6 July 1784).

15. Clarkson, *History*, 1:125–26.

16. Smith, *A Letter*, 45.

17. Ramsay, *An Essay*, 4, 18–19.

18. Ibid., 63, 64, 66.

19. Ibid., 198.

20. Ibid., 231.

21. See my "Who Was Francis Williams?"

22. Ramsay, *An Essay*, 204.

23. Clarkson, *An Essay*, xiv.

24. Publication of the *Essay* initiated a dialogue between Ramsay, whose writings on slavery were all published by James Phillips, and Tobin, who identified himself after the first edition of his *Cursory Remarks*: Ramsay, *A Reply*; Tobin, *A Short Rejoinder*; Ramsay, *A Letter*; Tobin, *A Farewel Address*; Ramsay, *Objections*.

25. Tobin, *Cursory Remarks*, 6.

26. Ibid., 33, 34.

27. Ibid., 116–18.

28. Turnbull, *An Apology*.

29. Ibid., 45.

30. Ibid., 34.

31. Ibid., 34–35.

32. Ibid., 45, 53.

33. Ramsay, *Objections*, 6–8.

34. Smith, *The Wealth of Nations*, bk. 1, chap. 8; bk. 3, chap. 2; bk. 4, chap. 7.

35. Turnbull, *An Apology*, 63–64.

36. Ibid., 59.

37. Ibid., 64.

38. Clarkson, *History*, 1:207–9.

39. Clarkson, *Essay*, xvii.

40. Ibid., xiv, xv.

41. Ibid., 122, Clarkson's emphasis.

42. Additional Manuscripts 21,254, 22 May 1787.

43. Clarkson, *History*, 1:288.

44. Ibid., 1:286.

45. Hoare and Hoare, *Memoirs of Samuel Hoare*, 39.

46. Additional Manuscripts 21,254, 5 July and 27 August 1787.

47. See Oldfield, *Popular Politics*.

48. See Brewer, McKendrick, and Plumb, *The Birth of a Consumer Society*; Brewer and Porter, eds., *Consumption*; Jennings, "Joseph Woods."

49. See Logerfo, "Sir William Dolben."

50. Cobbett, ed., *The Parliamentary History*, 27, cols. 580 ff.

51. Ramsay, *A Letter*, 23.

52. Cugoano, *Thoughts and Sentiments*, 18, had earlier likened "the Cursory Remarker" to Demetrius, the silversmith who made shrines for Diana. On Demetrius see Acts 19:23–41.

53. For a fuller discussion of the context and significance of Harris's argument and responses to it other than Equiano's see Davis, *The Problem of Slavery in the Age of Revolution*, 541–51.

54. Equiano adapted part of this letter for inclusion in *The Interesting Narrative*, 233.

55. Editions 1–5 read "freemen." Perhaps in response to the emphasis during the French Revolution on the universal rights of man, Equiano's revision is intended to suggest that no distinction between free and unfree men should exist: all should be free if they are men.

56. "Ignatius Sancho has approached nearer [than Phillis Wheatley] to merit in composition; yet his letters do more honour to the heart than to the head. They breathe the purest effusions of friendship and general philanthropy, and show how great a degree of the latter may be compounded with strong religious zeal. He is often happy in the turn of his compliments, and his stile is easy and familiar, except when he affects a Shandean fabrication of words. But his imagination is wild and extravagant, escapes incessantly from every restraint of reason and taste, and, in the course of its vagaries, leaves a tract of thought as incoherent and eccentric, as is the course of a meteor through the sky. His subjects should often have led him to a process of sober reasoning: yet we find him always substituting sentiment for demonstration. Upon the whole, though we admit him to the first place among those of his own colour who have presented themselves to the public judgment, yet when we compare him with the writers of the race among whom he lived, and particularly with the epistolary class, in which he has taken his own stand, we are compelled to enroll him at the bottom of the column" (Jefferson, *Notes*, 140–41).

57. "George Fox" can be identified as Ramsay because the draft of the letter exists among Ramsay's papers in the Rhodes House Library, Oxford University. With the draft is Ramsay's undated description of Equiano, probably written in 1788: "Gustavus Vasa, is a well known instance of what improvement a Negroe is capable. He was kidnapped when about 11 years old perhaps above 1000 miles in land. He con-

tinued a slave for many years till he by his industry bought out his own freedom. He has learned to read and write; and in vindication of the rights of his colour has not been afraid to contend in Argument with men of high rank, and acuteness of parts. But the extent of his abilities appeared very clearly, when Government resolved to return the Negroes lately to Africa. Those to whom the management of the expedition was committed, dreaded so much his influence over his countrymen, that they contrived to procure an order for his being sent ashore. In particular, his knowledge of the Scriptures is truly surprising, and shows that he could study and really understand them" (James Ramsay Papers, MSS BRIT EMP. S.2).

58. Thompson-Clarkson MSS 3/156. The unknown correspondent may have been the Reverend John Baker, one of Equiano's original subscribers.

TWELVE. MAKING A LIFE

1. Dr. Mark Jones found the subscription proposal among the Josiah Wedgwood Papers in the Keele University Library Special Collections and very kindly brought it to my attention. Wedgwood was one of Equiano's original subscribers.

2. Green notes the relative rarity of asking for advance payment from subscribers ("The Publishing History," 363).

3. John Murray to William Boutcher, 30 December 1775, quoted in Zachs, *The First John Murray*, 69. Zachs notes that Murray reiterates his opinion of publication by subscription in a letter to John Imison, 27 August 1784.

4. Murray is the first bookseller-agent listed in Equiano's subscription proposal. He was one of Equiano's principal distributors. Equiano may have been drawn to Murray because he published the monthly *Political Magazine and Parliamentary, Naval, Military and Literary Journal* (London, 1788–91), which presented both sides of the slave-trade debate.

5. My comment on the relative expense of Equiano's *Narrative* is based on comparison to comparable duodecimos published by Murray from 1788 to 1790: see entries 628, 632, 653, 655, 677, 687, 698, 699, 706, 721, 726, 746, 768, 777, 785, 795 in Zachs, *The First John Murray*, "A Checklist of Murray Publications, 1768–1795."

6. Raven, *Judging New Wealth*, 52.

7. See Macalpine and Hunter, *George III*.

8. Clarkson, *History*, 2:111.

9. For the complex relationship between the two newspapers see Werkmeister, *The London Daily Press*, 219–316.

10. For a fuller discussion of how and why Equiano represents himself as a gentleman see my "Defining a Gentleman."

11. Wheatley's *Poems* had been published in England and America at least four times by 1789. Her poetry, though not Wheatley herself, was known to Sancho, who

calls her a "Genius in bondage" in a letter dated 27 January 1778 (Sancho, *Letters*, 111–12). Sancho's *Letters* went through four editions before Equiano's first edition.

12. Meyer, "Re-dressing Classical Statuary."

13. Neither Paul Edwards nor Henry Louis Gates, Jr., cites either the Central American incident or the frontispiece as an example of the "motif of the talking book" in Equiano's *Narrative.*

14. Hinterding, Luijten, and Royalton-Kisch, *Rembrandt the Printmaker*, 223–27.

15. The portraits are reproduced in Capitein, *The Agony of Asar*, 44, 48.

16. The first edition of Gronniosaw's *Narrative* and the fourth edition of Marrant's *Narrative* are reproduced in Carretta, ed., *Unchained Voices*, 110–33.

17. According to the *Eighteenth-Century Short Title Catalogue* (*ESTC*).

18. The ongoing *ESTC* identifies 1,110 titles of fiction and nonfiction as "Written by Himself." Another 135 titles claim to be "Written by Herself."

19. The dates given parenthetically are those found in Equiano's various prefatory comments.

20. Green estimates that the size of the first edition was 750 copies ("The Publishing History," 364–65). At least 1,900 copies of the fourth (1791) edition were produced.

21. The name of the Duke of Cumberland, another brother of the Prince of Wales, first appears on the subscription list heading the second edition of *The Interesting Narrative.* Although the name of a third brother, the Duke of Gloucester, appears on none of Equiano's nine subscription lists, the first list includes the names of the duke's mistress, Lady Almiria Carpenter, and George Fallowdown, one of the Pages of the Presence in the duke's establishment.

22. *A Catalogue of R. Fisher's Circulating Library.* "The Life of Olaudah Equiano, or Gustavus Vasa the African" is included among the "Lives. Octavo."

23. Green, "The Publishing History," 367–73, and Ito, "Olaudah Equiano," discuss the New York edition.

24. Johnson to Nathan Wetherell, 12 March 1776, in Johnson, *The Letters*, 2:304–8; Feather, *The Provincial Book Trade*, 53–59.

25. Green, assuming that the first edition printed 750 copies and that Equiano received a quite generous three shillings per copy, estimates that he earned about a hundred pounds from the first edition alone ("The Publishing History," 364–65).

26. I assume that at least two thousand copies of the fourth edition were printed because Equiano had sold nineteen hundred copies of it by 27 February 1792. The fifth edition was printed several months later: its address to the members of Parliament is dated June 1792.

THIRTEEN. THE ART OF THE BOOK

1. Examples of the European captivity narrative include Rowlandson's often-republished *The Soveraignty and Goodness of God*, Kingdon's *Redeemed Slaves*, and Aubin's fictional *The Noble Slaves*. Eighteenth-century captivity narratives had also been written or recorded by people of African descent: Hammon's *Narrative*, Gronniosaw's *Narrative*, and Marrant's *Narrative*.

2. For an insightful treatment of history writing during Equiano's lifetime see Phillips, *Society and Sentiment*.

3. Thomas Martyn's life of his father, John Martyn (*Dissertations*, i).

4. Blair, *Lectures*, 288.

5. Burke to Robertson, 9 June 1777, in *Correspondence*.

6. Ferguson, *Essay*, 36.

7. Penny quoted in Lambert, ed., *House of Commons Sessional Papers*, 69:19. Penny had made five voyages to Bonny on the Bight of Biafra.

8. Isichei, *A History*, 21. Thornton notes that "almost all we know about the [Igbo] region in the eighteenth century comes from the testimony of Olaudah Equiano, an Igbo who was enslaved as a youth around 1755" (*Africa and Africans*, 310). The fullest treatment of Equiano's claim to an Igbo identity is Byrd, "Eboe, Country."

9. Isichei, *A History*, 19.

10. Henderson, *The King in Every Man*, 41.

11. Alexander Falconbridge quoted in Lambert, ed., *House of Commons Sessional Papers*, 69:48.

12. The most thorough treatment of the effects the transatlantic slave trade had on the conception and development of African identities during the early modern period is Thornton, *Africa and Africans*. On the absence of a pan-Igbo identity in Africa during the eighteenth century see Koelle, *Polyglotta Africana*, 7–8; Chambers, "My Own Nation"; Gomez, *Exchanging Our Country Marks*, 125–26; Northrup, "Igbo and Myth Igbo"; Chambers, "Ethnicity"; Chambers, "The Significance."

13. Isichei, *A History*, 20.

14. Edwards, *The History*, 2:69.

15. Achebe says, "Equiano was an Ibo, I believe from the village of Iseke in the Orlu division of Eastern Nigeria" (*Morning Yet on Creation Day*, 59). Arguments supporting the accuracy of Equiano's memory of Africa appear in Acholonu, "The Home"; and Edwards and Shaw, "The Invisible *Chi*." Acholonu, *The Igbo Roots*, identifies "Essaka" as modern-day Isseke near Ihiala, Nigeria, and claims she has found Equiano's direct descendants. But since her argument requires us to believe that her sources lived to be more than 150 years old, her methodology is suspect.

16. Edwards suggests east of the Niger ("Introduction," xix–xx); see also Jones, "Olaudah Equiano," 61.

17. Thorp notes that "the phrase 'the unknown part of' seems to be a marginal addition" ("Chattel with a Soul," 447).

18. A translation into English of Oldendorp's abridged manuscript published in 1777 is Oldendorp, *History of the Mission*. The complete German manuscript of Oldendorp's text has been published as *Historie der caribischen Inseln*. I thank John Thornton for providing me with an English translation of the section on Igbos in the German manuscript.

19. Northrup, "Igbo and Myth Igbo," 15.

20. Morgan, *Slave Counterpoint*, 62–67; Behrendt, "Markets," 196.

21. Walsh, "The Chesapeake Slave Trade," 153.

22. Grainger, *The Sugar-Cane*, 2:75.

23. Grainger, *An Essay*, 7.

24. [Long], *The History*, 2:403–4.

25. Grainger, *An Essay*, 14.

26. Edwards, *The History*, 2:69–71. Other negative eighteenth-century characterizations of the Igbo include Beckford, *Remarks*, and McNeill, *Observations*, 24–25.

27. Matthews, *A Voyage*.

28. Benezet, *Some Historical Account* (1784 ed.), 5.

29. Ibid., 92.

30. Stanfield, *Observations*, 241.

31. Matthews, *A Voyage*, 113.

32. Equiano's note in editions 1–9, inserted after the word "some," reads, "See also Lieut. Matthew's Voyage, p. 123."

33. Astley, *A New General Collection*, 502.

34. Jones remarks on the improbability of Equiano's having seen women warriors ("Olaudah Equiano," 66).

35. Smith, *A New Voyage to Guinea*, 233–34, 237, 228, 233.

36. Ibid., 230; Bosman, *A New and Accurate Description*, 409; Benezet, *Some Historical Account* (1784 ed.), 33.

37. Smith, *A New Voyage to Guinea*, 244.

38. The most significant polygenicist at the time was Edward Long, whose atypical eighteenth-century arguments in his *History of Jamaica* anticipate dominant nineteenth-century pseudoscientific racism.

39. Equiano's note in editions 6–9 reads: "See 1 Chron. 1. 33. Also John Brown's [A] Dictionary of the [Holy] Bible [Edinburgh, 1788] on the same verse." Equiano's comparison of Africans to Jews reflects the widespread belief among both supporters and opponents of the slave trade that the descendants of Noah's son Ham settled Africa and much of Asia. The two sides disputed whether these descendants of Ham were, like him, cursed for his having mocked Noah. If so, they were doomed to be "most wicked and miserable, and few of them have hitherto enjoyed the light of the gospel" (Brown, *A Dictionary*, 2:573). Since Brown's *Dictionary* is arranged topically

and does not annotate particular verses, Equiano is probably thinking here (and again in chapter 11, when he cites Brown) of Henry, *An Exposition*, the eighth edition (Edinburgh, 1772) of which he bought in London on 2 May 1777. Equiano certainly knew the discussions of the subject found in Sharp, *The Just Limitation*, Clarkson, *Essay*, and Cugoano, *Thoughts and Sentiments*.

40. Wheeler, *The Complexion of Race*, 4.

41. Mitchel, "Causes of the Different Colours," a paper read at meetings of the Royal Society from 3 May to 14 June 1744; see 10:947, 948. Cited in Clarkson, *Essay*, 205. See also Braude, "The Sons of Noah."

42. Morgan, *Slave Counterpoint*, 465.

43. Gomez calculates that during the period 1733–1807 only about 2 percent of South Carolina's Africans originated from the Bight of Biafra, as contrasted with Virginia, which imported more than 40 percent of its slaves from that region during the same period (*Exchanging Our Country Marks*, 114–22).

44. Ogude argues that because an eleven-year-old child was very unlikely to have the almost total recall Equiano claims, "Equiano relied less on the memory of his experience and more on other sources" ("Facts into Fiction," 32) in his account of Africa. In his "No Roots Here" Ogude also denies that linguistic evidence supports Equiano's account. Despite Ogude's skepticism about Equiano's veracity, he does not question Equiano's fundamental identity as an African. Jones finds Equiano's account of his "home and travels in Nigeria . . . disappointingly brief and confused." He believes that "the little he can remember of his travels is naturally muddled and incoherent" because Equiano "was only eleven years old when he was kidnapped" (Jones, "Olaudah Equiano," 61, 69). In her review of Paul Edwards, *The Life of Olaudah Equiano*, and Catherine Obianju Acholonu, *The Igbo Roots of Olaudah Equiano*, Isichei remarks of Equiano's description of Africa, "I have come to believe that it is a palimpsest, and that though he was indeed an Igbo (though even this has been questioned) he fused his own recollections with details obtained from other Igbo into a single version" (165). Eze considers "Equiano's Igbo past [to be] mostly a reconstruction of European or Colonial American travel narratives, most obviously, Anthony Benezet's *Some Historical Account of Guinea*" ("Self-Encounters," 33, 50n22).

45. Nora, "Between Memory and History"; Austen, "The Slave Trade."

46. Patterson, *Slavery and Social Death*.

47. Equiano's proper place in literary history has not yet been widely recognized. For example, even the Equiano scholar Angelo Costanzo wrongly "places [Vassa's] work in the secular autobiographical tradition established by Benjamin Franklin" ("Introduction," 1019). Mascuch, *Origins*, overlooks Equiano as a contender for status as the first self-published autobiographer who advertised and distributed the story of his life. Mascuch bestows that recognition on James Lackington, one of the booksellers through whom Equiano sold *The Interesting Narrative* two years before Lackington published his own autobiography in 1791.

48. Other examples are Bluett, *Some Memoirs*, Gronniosaw, *A Narrative*, and the brief autobiographical comments by Equiano's binomial friend and sometime collaborator Quobna Ottobah Cugoano (John Stuart) in his *Thoughts and Sentiments*.

49. Adams, *Sketches*, 41–42, emphasis added.

50. Stedman, *Narrative*, 27.

51. Ibid., 363, 364.

52. Equiano alters slightly lines from Milton, *Paradise Lost*, 2:332–40:

> No peace is given
> To us enslav'd, but custody severe;
> And stripes and arbitrary punishment
> Inflicted – What peace can we return?
> But to our power, hostility and hate;
> Untam'd reluctance, and revenge, tho' slow,
> Yet ever plotting how the conqueror least
> May reap his conquest, and may least rejoice
> In doing what we most in suff'ring feel.

53. Micah 6:8: "[The Lord] hath shewed thee, O man, what is good; and what doeth the Lord require of thee, but to do justly, and to love mercy, and to walk humbly with thy God?" (King James Bible, 1611). Cf. John Wesley's 1755 version of Colossians 2:3–4: "Both the Father and Christ, in whom are hid the treasures of wisdom and knowledge. 4. And this I say, that no man may beguile you with inticing words."

FOURTEEN. A SELF-MADE MAN

1. See Othello's speech: "Yet, by your gracious patience, I will a round unvarnished tale deliver of my whole course of love" (Shakespeare, *Othello* 1.3.89).

2. Subscribers to Equiano's first (1789) edition who were also members of the African Association include Henry Seymour Conway, G. Noel Edwards, the Earl of Gainsborough, Lord Hawke, Sir Charles Middleton, James Martin, Paul Le Mesurier, the Duke of Northumberland, Lord Rawdon, Lieutenant General Rainsford, William Smith, John Symmons, Henry Thornton, the Earl of Warwick, and Samuel Whitbread. In addition, the spouses of Equiano's subscribers the Earl of Ailesbury and the Duchess of Buccleugh were members. Wedgwood had been affiliated with the association since its inception but did not actually join until the early 1790s.

3. Lord Rawdon to Banks, 14 June 1789, Papers of Sir Joseph Banks (Series 72.139); Banks to Lord Rawdon, 15 July 1789, Papers of Sir Joseph Banks (Series 73.028).

4. Priestley, *A Sermon*.

5. Crawford, *Observations*, 29. The 125-page 1790 edition was a much-expanded version of the 21-page first edition, printed and sold by Joseph Crukshank in Philadelphia in 1784. Crawford's 1790 edition also quotes part of the letter to Sir William Dol-

ben cosigned by Gustavus Vassa, Cugoano, and others of African descent published in the 15 July 1788 issue of the *Morning Chronicle* (113).

6. Clarkson, *History*, 2:212.

7. See Rodgers, "Equiano in Belfast."

8. See my "A New Letter."

9. Gifford, *The Baviad*, 38–39. Gifford's first quotation in this passage is from William Shakespeare, *Macbeth* 4.3; the second is from Betterton, *King Henry IV*. I have not found the sonnet by Equiano Gifford mentions.

10. I thank Paul Magnuson for privately conveyed information on Walker's religious beliefs and political connections.

11. [Society for Effecting the Abolition of the Slave Trade], *An Abstract*; Crafton, *A Short Sketch*.

12. Equiano's letter to Hardy survives because it was one of the documents the government seized when Hardy was arrested on 12 May 1794. Hardy was tried and acquitted on 5 November 1794 on a charge of high treason for his role in the London Corresponding Society.

13. See the letter from Hardy to Bryant dated 8 March 1792, Additional Manuscripts 27,811 ("Original Letter Book of the London Corresponding Society"), fols. 4v–5r.

14. [Hardy], *Memoir*, 14.

15. Additional Manuscripts 27,811, fols. 4v–5r.

16. Quoted in Jennings, *Business*, 74.

17. In his 27 February 1792 letter from London to the Reverend Mr. George Walker, Equiano was more specific about the size of the loan: "I have been in the uttermost hurry ever since I have being in this wickd. Town. – & I only came now to save if I can, £232, I lent to man, who [is] now Dying" (358).

18. Aberdeen had a population of twenty-seven thousand and Dundee twenty-six thousand.

19. Quoted in Jennings, *Business*, 80.

20. Katherine Plymley reports Equiano's 20 June visit in her diary, 19 May–17 August 1793, 1066/17.

21. Worcestershire Record Office, Ref. 705:938, BA 8720/1/ii/8.

22. Clarkson, *History*, 1:293–94.

23. Jewson, *The Jacobin City*.

24. Clark, *British Clubs*.

25. Burney, *The Journals*, 1:259.

26. PRO, TS 24/1/5.

27. "List of Members of the Tusculan School," in "MS Minutes Book of the Norwich Tusculan School, 27 Sept. 1793–2 May 1794."

28. "Mischievous Effects of War" is reproduced in my "Possible Gustavus Vassa/ Olaudah Equiano Attributions," 136–39.

29. For the treason trials of Hardy and the others see Barrell, *Imagining the King's Death*.

392 ■ NOTES TO CHAPTER FOURTEEN

30. She was baptized in Soham on 29 April 1795.

31. Equiano mentions the loan in his 27 February 1792 letter to the Reverend George Walker (358) and the death of the borrower before it was repaid in his 28 May 1792 letter to Thomas Hardy (362).

32. I thank David Worrall for bringing Equiano's subscription to my attention.

33. John Audley Papers, 132B/4.

34. See John Audley's July 1816 notes on the codicil of Vassa's will, John Audley Papers, 132B/16.

35. At least one other African Briton, John Scipio, in 1760 had a will in which he left three hundred pounds in cash legacies alone. See Chater, "Where There's a Will." I thank Arthur Torrington for bringing Chater's work to my attention.

36. Not all of Equiano's investments were sound. In 1796 he lent his clothier and neighbor, John Douglas Abercrombie, about three hundred pounds, which were never repaid.

37. Plasterers' Company Records, MS 6135/2.

38. The *Times* advertised the lease on 1, 3, 8, and 22 September 1796. On 2, 11, and 17 January 1798, more than nine months after Equiano's death, his executors advertised the resale of the lease in the *Times*.

39. John Audley Papers, 132B/9.

40. Sharp to his niece Jemima, 27 February 1811, Granville Sharp Papers. Equiano's nurse is identified in Audley's notes on Equiano's will (John Audley Papers, 132B/16). The *Morning Herald*, Tuesday, 4 April 1797, reported, "DIED . . . On Friday morning, in Paddington-street, Mr Gustavus Vason, aged fifty-two years." The *Morning Post and Fashionable World*, Friday, 14 April, noted, "DIED . . . A few days ago, Mr. Gustavus Vassa, the African, well known to the public for the interesting narrative of his life, supposed to be written by himself." The *Gentleman's Magazine* (April) recorded the death of "Gustavus Vassa, the African." The *European Magazine* 31 (April): 294, reported, "In Paddington-street, Mr. Gustavus Vassa, aged 52 years, author of an interesting 'Narrative of his Life.'" The American press noted his passing as well. On 9 August 1797 the *Massachusetts Spy: or, the Worcester Gazette* listed his death first among its obituaries: "In London, Mr. Gustavus Vasa, an African, known to the public, by his interesting narrative of his own life." Three days later the *Providence Gazette and Country Journal* closed its list of deaths with "In London, GUSTAVUS VASA, the celebrated African." The record of Equiano's burial may have disappeared because German bombing during World War II destroyed the parish records of St. Alban's, Wood Street, one of the churches closest to Plasterers' Hall. The hall remained Equiano's primary address even after he moved to Middlesex. Joanna Vassa refers to "Gustavus Vassa of Addle Street Aldermanbury in the city of London Gentleman" in her 8 April 1816 acknowledgment to John Audley, surviving executor of her father's will, of receipt of her inheritance (John Audley Papers, 132B/17).

41. Although her burial place is not known, her death is commemorated by an inscription on the exterior wall of St. Andrew's Church, Chesterton, Cambridge:

Near this Place lies Interred
ANNA MARIA VASSA
Daughter of Gustavus Vassa the African
She died July 21 1797

Should simple village rhymes attract thine eye,
Stranger, as thoughtfully thou pasest by,
Know that there lies beside this humble stone
A child of colour haply not thine own.
Her father born of Afric's sun-burnt race,
Torn from his native fields, ah, foul disgrace;
Through various toils, at length to Britain came
Espouse'd, so Heaven ordain'd, an English dame,
And follow'd Christ; their hope two infants dear.
But one, a hapless Orphan, slumbers here.
To bury her the village children came,
And dropp'd choice flowers, and lisp'd her early fame:
And some that lov'd her most as if unblest
Bedew'd with tears the white wreath on their breast:
But she is gone and dwells in that abode
Where some of every clime shall joy in God.

St. Andrew's has recently established a tradition of having local children annually celebrate her life beneath the plaque.

42. In 1821 Joanna Vassa married the Reverend Henry Bromley, a Congregationalist minister. She was buried 16 March 1857 in Abney Park Cemetery, apparently with no surviving children. No children were living with Joanna and Henry Bromley when the 1841 census was taken while they were residing in Clavering, Essex. Joanna's gravestone notes that she was the daughter of "Gustavus Vassa the African," indicating that Equiano's fame continued into the second half of the nineteenth century and that Joanna's husband, who died in 1878, was publicly proud of his late wife's African British heritage. The General Record Office Certificae of Joanna Vassa Bromley's death in the Family Records' Centre (London) tells us that she was living at 21 Benyon Terrace, Buckingham Road, Hackney, when she died on 10 March 1857. Her cause of death is given as "Uterine Disease unknown Subacute Peritonitis." Henry Bromley's 1879 obituary mentions his marriage to "Miss Joanna Vassa, a daughter of the then well-known, and well-remembered, Gustavus Vassa, the African" (*The Congregational Year Book, 1879* [London: Hodder and Stoughton, 1879]).

43. John Audley Papers, 132B/16. Nelson's watch commemorating the Arctic expedition is in the National Maritime Museum, Greenwich, England.

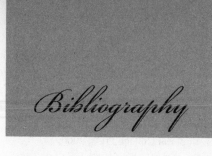

PUBLISHED SOURCES

An Abstract of the Evidence Delivered before a Select Committee of the House of Commons in the Years 1790 and 1791; on the Part of the Petitioners for the Abolition of the Slave-trade. London, 1791.

Achebe, Chinua. *Morning Yet on Creation Day: Essays.* London: Heinemann, 1975.

Acholonu, Catherine Obianju. "The Home of Olaudah Equiano – A Linguistic and Anthropological Search." *Journal of Commonwealth Literature* 22 (1987).

——. *The Igbo Roots of Olaudah Equiano.* Owerri, Nigeria: Ata Publications, 1989.

Adams, John. *Sketches Taken during Ten Voyages to Africa, Between the Years 1786 and 1800.* London, 1822.

Adanson, Michael. *A Voyage to Senegal.* London, 1759.

Alleine, Joseph. *An Alarme to Unconverted Sinners.* London, 1673.

Anderson, Fred. *Crucible of War: The Seven Years' War and the Fate of Empire in British North America, 1754–1766.* New York: Vintage, 2001.

Andrew, Donna T. *London Debating Societies, 1776–1799.* London: London Record Society, 1994.

Anstey, Roger, and P. E. H. Hair, eds. *Liverpool, the African Slave Trade, and Abolition: Essays to Illustrate Current Knowledge and Research.* Liverpool: Historic Society of Lancashire and Cheshire, 1976.

An Answer to the Reverend James Ramsay's Essay. Basseterre in St. Christopher, 1784.

Appiah, Kwame Anthony. *In My Father's House: Africa in the Philosophy of Culture.* New York: Oxford University Press, 1992.

Asiegbu, Johnson U. *Slavery and the Politics of Liberation, 1787–1861: A Study of Liberated African Emigration and British Antislavery Policy.* Harlow, U.K.: Longmans, 1969.

Astley, Thomas. *A New General Collection of Voyages and Travels.* 4 vols. London, 1743–47.

Atkins, John. *A Voyage to Guinea, Brasil, and the West Indies.* London, 1735; 2nd ed., 1737.

Aubin, Penelope. *The Noble Slaves.* Dublin, 1736.

Austen, Ralph A. "The Slave Trade as History and Memory: Confrontations of Slaving Voyage Documents and Communal Traditions." *William and Mary Quarterly* (2001).

Bailyn, Bernard. *The Peopling of British North America.* New York: Knopf, 1986.

Banks, Sir Joseph. *The Letters of Sir Joseph Banks: A Selection, 1768–1820.* Edited by Neil Chambers. London: Imperial College Press, 2000.

Barbot, John. *A Description of the Coasts of North and South Guinea.* In *Barbot on Guinea: The Writings of Jean Barbot on West Africa 1678–1712,* edited by P. E. H. Hair, Adam Jones, and Robin Law. 2 vols. London: Hakluyt Society, 1992.

Barker, Anthony J. *The African Link: British Attitudes to the Negro in the Era of the Atlantic Slave Trade, 1550–1807.* London: Frank Cass, 1978.

Barrell, John. *Imagining the King's Death: Figurative Treason, Fantasies of Regicide, 1793–1796.* Oxford: Oxford University Press, 2000.

Baugh, Daniel A. "Why Did Britain Lose Command of the Sea during the War for America?" In Black and Woodfine, *The British Navy.*

Beckford, William, Jr. *Remarks upon the Situation of Negroes in Jamaica, Impartially Made from a local Experience of nearly thirteen Years in that Island, by William Beckford, jun.* London, 1788.

Behn, Aphra. *Oroonoko, or the Royal Slave.* London, 1688.

Behrendt, Stephen D. "The Annual Volume and Regional Distribution of the British Slave Trade, 1780–1807." *Journal of African History* 38 (1997).

———. "Crew Mortality in the Atlantic Slave Trade." *Slavery and Abolition* 18 (1997).

———. "Markets, Transaction Cycles, and Profits: Merchant Decision Making in the British Slave Trade." *William and Mary Quarterly* 58 (2001).

Bellamy, Thomas. *The Benevolent Planters.* London, 1789.

Benezet, Anthony. *A Caution and Warning to Great Britain and her Colonies in a Short Representation of the Calamitous State of the Enslaved Negroes in the British Dominions. Collected from various Authors, and Submitted to the serious Consideration of all, more especially of those in Power.* Philadelphia, 1766.

———. *Observations on the Inslaving, Importing and Purchasing of Negroes. With some Advice thereon Extracted from the Yearly Meeting Epistles of London for the Present Year.* Germantown, Pa., 1759.

———. *A Short Account of that Part of Africa, Inhabited by the Negroes. With Respect to the Fertility of the Country; the good Disposition of many of the Natives, and the Manner by which the Slave Trade Is Carried on. Extracted from several Authors, in Order to Shew the Iniquity of that Trade, and the Falsity of the Arguments usually Advanced in its Vindication. With a Quotation from George Wallis's System of the Laws, &c. and a large Extract from a Pamphlet lately Published in London on the Subject of the Slave Trade.* Philadelphia, 1762.

———. *Some Historical Account of Guinea, Its Situation, Produce, and the General Disposition of Its Inhabitants. With an Inquiry into the Rise and Progress of the Slave Trade, Its Nature, and Lamentable Effects. Also a Re-publication of the Sentiments of several authors of Note, on this Interesting Subject; particularly an Extract of a Treatise, by Granville Sharp.* Philadelphia, 1771; rev. and republished, London, 1784, 1788.

Berlin, Ira. "From Creole to African: Atlantic Creoles and the Origins of African-American Society in Mainland North America." *William and Mary Quarterly* 33 (1996).

———. *Many Thousands Gone: The First Two Centuries of Slavery in North America.* Cambridge, Mass.: Harvard University Press, 1998.

Berlin, Ira, and Ronald Hoffman, eds. *Slavery and Freedom in the Age of the American Revolution.* Charlottesville: University of Virginia Press, 1983.

Betterton, Thomas. *King Henry IV, with the Humours of Sir John Falstaff. A Tragi-Comedy.* London, 1700.

Bickerstaffe, Isaac. *The Padlock.* London, 1768.

Black, Eugene. *The Association: British Extraparliamentary Political Organization, 1769–1793.* Cambridge, Mass.: Harvard University Press, 1963.

Black, Jeremy, and Philip Woodfine, eds. *The British Navy and the Use of Naval Power in the Eighteenth Century.* Leicester: Leicester University Press, 1988.

Blackburn, Robin. *The Overthrow of Colonial Slavery, 1776–1848.* London: Verso, 1988.

Blackstone, William. *Commentaries on the Laws of England.* 4 vols. London, 1765–69.

Blair, Hugh. *Lectures on Rhetoric and Belles Lettres.* Edinburgh, 1783. 2 vols. Edited by H. F. Harding. Carbondale: University of Southern Illinois Press, 1965.

Blake, William. *The Complete Illuminated Books.* Introduction by David Bindman. New York: Thames and Hudson, 2001.

Bluett, Thomas. *Some Memoirs of the Life of Job, Son of Solomon, the High Priest of Boonda in Africa.* London, 1734.

Board of Trade. *Report of the Lords of the Committee of Council Appointed for the Consideration of all Matters relating to Trade and Foreign Plantations.* London, 1789.

Bosman, William. *A New and Accurate Description of the Coast of Guinea.* London, 1705; 2nd ed., 1721.

Boswell, James. *Life of Johnson.* London, 1791. Edited by R. W. Chapman, revised by J. D. Fleeman, introduction by Pat Rogers. New York: Oxford University Press, 1980.

Bradley, Ian. "James Ramsay and the Slave Trade." *History Today* 22 (1972).

Bradley, Patricia. *Slavery, Propaganda, and the American Revolution.* Jackson: University Press of Mississippi, 1998.

Braidwood, Stephen J. *Black Poor and White Philanthropists: London's Blacks and the Foundation of the Sierra Leone Settlement 1786–1791.* Liverpool: Liverpool University Press, 1994.

Braude, Benjamin. "The Sons of Noah and the Construction of Ethnic and Geographical Identities in the Medieval and Early-Modern Periods." *William and Mary Quarterly*, 3rd ser., 54 (1997).

Brewer, John, Neil McKendrick, and J. H. Plumb. *The Birth of a Consumer Society: The Commercialization of Eighteenth-Century England.* Bloomington: Indiana University Press, 1982.

Brewer, John, and Roy Porter, eds. *Consumption and the World of Goods.* London: Routledge, 1993.

Brooke, Henry. *Gustavus Vasa, the Deliverer of his Country.* London, 1739.

Brown, Christopher L. "Empire without Slaves: British Concepts of Emancipation in the Age of the American Revolution." *William and Mary Quarterly*, 3rd ser., 61 (1999).

Brown, John. *A Dictionary of the Holy Bible.* Edinburgh, 1788.

Bunyan, John. *Grace Abounding to the Chief of Sinners.* London, 1666.

Burke, Edmund. *The Correspondence of Edmund Burke.* Edited by Thomas W. Copeland. 10 vols. Cambridge: Cambridge University Press, 1958–78.

———. *Reflections on the Revolution in France.* London, 1790. Edited by L. G. Mitchell. New York: Oxford University Press, 1993.

———. *The Writings and Speeches of Edmund Burke.* Vol. 3. Edited by Warren M. Elofson and John A. Woods. Oxford: Clarendon Press, 1996.

Burnard, Trevor, and Kenneth Morgan. "The Dynamics of the Slave Trade and Slave Purchasing Patterns in Jamaica, 1655–1788." *William and Mary Quarterly* 58 (2001).

Burney, Frances. *The Journals and Letters of Fanny Burney (Madame D'Arblay).* 12 vols. Edited by Joyce Hemlow. Oxford: Clarendon Press, 1972–84.

Burton, Ann M. "British Evangelicals, Economic Warfare and the Abolition of the Atlantic Slave Trade, 1794–1810." *Anglican and Episcopal History* 65 (1996).

Byrd, Alexander. "Eboe, Country, Nation and Gustavus Vassa's *Interesting Narrative.*" *William and Mary Quarterly* 63 (2006).

The Cabinet. By a Society of Gentlemen. Norwich and London, 1795.

Cahill, Barry. "The Black Loyalist Myth in Atlantic Canada." *Acadiensis* 29 (1999).

Capitein, Jacobus Elisa Johannes. *The Agony of Asar: A Thesis on Slavery by the Former Slave, Jacobus Elisa Johannes Capitein, 1717–1747.* Translated and edited by Grant Parker. Princeton, N.J.: Markus Wiener Publishers, 2001.

Carretta, Vincent. "Defining a Gentleman: The Status of Olaudah Equiano or Gustavus Vassa." *Language Sciences* 22 (2000).

———. "A New Letter by Gustavus Vassa/Olaudah Equiano?" *Early American Literature* 39 (2004).

———. "Possible Gustavus Vassa/Olaudah Equiano Attributions." In Griffin, *The Faces of Anonymity.*

———. "Questioning the Identity of Olaudah Equiano, or Gustavus Vassa, the African." In Nussbaum, *The Global Eighteenth Century.*

——. "Three West Indian Writers of the 1780s Revisited and Revised." *Research in African Literatures* 29 (1998).

——, ed. *Unchained Voices: An Anthology of Black Authors in the English-Speaking World of the Eighteenth Century.* Lexington: University Press of Kentucky, 1997; rev. ed., 2004.

——. "Who Was Francis Williams?" *Early American Literature* 38 (2003).

A Catalogue of R. Fisher's Circulating Library, in the High-Bridge, Newcastle. Comprising a Selection of the Best Authors on History, Biography, Divinity, Philosophy, Husbandry, Aerostation, Chemistry; and a Choice Collection of Voyages and Travels, Novels and Romances, Poems and Plays, in the English and French Languages: with a Great Variety of Pamphlets on the Most Interesting Subjects. Which are Lent to be Read, at Twelve Shillings a Year, Three Shillings a Quarter. All New Books and Pamphlets on Interesting or Entertaining Subjects, Will Be Added to the Library as soon as Published. Newcastle upon Tyne, 1791.

Cateau, Heather, and S. H. H. Carrington, eds. *Capitalism and Slavery Fifty Years Later: Eric Eustace Williams – A Reassessment of the Man and His Work.* New York: Peter Lang, 2000.

Chambers, Douglas B. "Ethnicity in the Diaspora: The Slave Trade and the Creation of African 'Nations' in the Americas." *Slavery and Abolition* 22 (2001).

——. "'He Is an African, but Speaks Plain': Historical Creolization in Eighteenth-Century Virginia." In Jalloh and Maizlish, *The African Diaspora.*

——. "'My Own Nation': Igbo Exiles in the Diaspora." *Slavery & Abolition* 18 (1997).

——. "The Significance of the Igbo in the Bight of Biafra Slave-Trade: A Rejoinder to Northrup's 'Myth Igbo.'" *Slavery and Abolition* 23 (2002).

Chater, Kathy. "Where There's a Will." *History Today* 50, no. 4 (2000).

Churchill, Awnsham, and John Churchill. *A Collection of Voyages and Travels.* 4 vols. London, 1704; 6 vols., 1732; 8 vols., 1745, 1752.

Cobbett, William, ed. *The Parliamentary History of England.* London, 1816.

Clark, Peter. *British Clubs and Societies 1580–1800: The Origins of an Associational World.* Oxford: Clarendon Press, 2000.

Clarke, James Stainer, and John M'Arthur. *The Life of Admiral Lord Nelson.* 2 vols. London, 1809.

Clarkson, John. *Clarkson's Mission to America, 1791–1792.* Edited by Charles Bruce Ferguson. Halifax: Public Archives of Nova Scotia, 1971.

Clarkson, Thomas. *An Essay on the Slavery and Commerce of the Human Species, Particularly the African, Translated from a Latin Dissertation, which Was Honoured with the First Prize in the University of Cambridge, for the Year 1785, with Additions.* London, 1786.

——. *History of the Abolition of the Slave Trade.* 2 vols. London, 1808.

Cobbett, William, ed. *The Parliamentary History of England, from the Earliest Period to the Year 1803.* London: T. C. Hansard, 1806–20.

Colledge, J. J. *Ships of the Royal Navy: The Complete Record of All Fighting Ships of the Royal Navy from the Fifteenth Century to the Present.* London: Greenhill Books, 1969.

Colley, Linda. *Britons: Forging the Nation 1707–1837.* New Haven, Conn.: Yale University Press, 1992.

——. *Captives.* New York: Pantheon, 2002.

Collier, Jane. *An Essay on the Art of Ingeniously Tormenting; With Proper Rules for the Exercise of that Pleasant Art.* London, 1753.

Collier, Jane, and Sarah Fielding. *The Cry: A New Dramatic Fable.* London, 1754.

Conway, Stephen. *The British Isles and the War of American Independence.* Oxford: Oxford University Press, 2000.

——. *The War of American Independence 1775–1783.* London: Edward Arnold, 1995.

Costanzo, Angelo. "Introduction to Olaudah Equiano." In Lauter, *The Heath Anthology of American Literature.*

Cotter, William R. "The Somerset Case and the Abolition of Slavery in England." *History* 79 (1994).

Crafton, William Bell. *A Short Sketch of the Evidence Delivered before a Committee of the House of Commons for the Abolition of the Slave Trade: To which Is Added, A Recommendation of the Subject to the Serious Attention of People in General.* Tewkesbury, 1791.

Craton, Michael. *Sinews of Empire: A Short History of British Slavery.* Garden City, N.Y.: Anchor Press, 1974.

Crawford, Charles. *Observations upon Negro-Slavery. A New Edition.* Philadelphia, 1790.

Cremer, John. *Ramblin' Jack: The Journal of Captain John Cremer 1700–1774.* Transcribed by R. Reynell Bellamy. London: Jonathan Cape, 1936.

Cugoano, Quobna Ottobah. *Thoughts and Sentiments on the Evil of Slavery.* London, 1791. Edited by Vincent Carretta. New York: Penguin, 1999.

Curtin, Philip D., ed. *Africa Remembered: Narratives by West Africans from the Era of the Slave Trade.* Madison: University of Wisconsin Press, 1967.

Dabydeen, David. *Hogarth's Blacks: Images of Blacks in Eighteenth-Century English Art.* Athens: University of Georgia Press, 1987.

Daunton, Martin, and Rick Halpern, eds. *Empire and Others: British Encounters with Indigenous Peoples, 1600–1850.* Philadelphia: University of Pennsylvania Press, 1999.

Davis, David Brion. *The Problem of Slavery in the Age of Revolution, 1770–1823.* Ithaca, N.Y.: Cornell University Press, 1975.

——. *The Problem of Slavery in Western Culture.* Ithaca, N.Y.: Cornell University Press, 1966.

——. *Slavery and Human Progress.* New York: Oxford University Press, 1984.

Davis, Ralph. *The Rise of the English Shipping Industry in the Seventeenth and Eighteenth Centuries.* London: Macmillan, 1962.

Dawson, Frank Griffith. "William Pitt's Settlement at Black River on the Mosquito Shore: A Challenge to Spain in Central America, 1732–87." *Hispanic American Historical Review* 63 (1983).

Day, Thomas. *Fragment of an Original Letter on the Slavery of the Negroes.* London, 1784.

———. *The History of Sandford and Merton, A Work Intended for the Use of Children.* London, 1783, 1786, 1789.

Day, Thomas, and Thomas Bicknell. *The Dying Negro.* London, 1773.

Defoe, Daniel. *Robinson Crusoe.* London, 1719.

Dickson, William. *Letters on Slavery, to which are added, Addresses to the Whites, and to the Free Negroes of Barbadoes; and Accounts of some Negroes eminent for their Virtues and Abilities.* London, 1789.

[Dillwyn, William, and John Lloyd]. *The Case of our Fellow Creatures, the Oppressed Africans, Respectfully Recommended to the Serious Consideration of the Legislature of Great Britain by the People Called Quakers.* London, 1783.

Donnan, Elizabeth. *Documents Illustrative of the History of the Slave Trade to America.* 4 vols. Washington, D.C.: Carnegie Institution, 1930–35.

Donovan, Kenneth. *Slaves in Cape Breton, 1713–1815.* Lincoln: University of Nebraska Press, forthcoming.

Douglass, Frederick. *Narrative of the Life of Frederick Douglass, an American Slave. Written by Himself.* Boston, 1845.

Drescher, Seymour. *Capitalism and Antislavery: British Mobilization in Comparative Perspective.* London: Macmillan, 1986.

———. *Econocide: British Slavery in the Era of Abolition.* Pittsburgh: University of Pittsburgh Press, 1977.

———. *From Slavery to Freedom: Comparative Studies in the Rise and Fall of Atlantic Slavery.* New York: New York University Press, 1999.

———. "The Historical Context of British Abolition." In *Abolition and Its Aftermath: The Historical Context, 1790–1916.* London: Frank Cass, 1985.

———. "Manumission in a Society without Slave Law: Eighteenth-Century England." *Slavery and Abolition* 10 (1989).

———. "Whose Abolition? Popular Pressure and the Ending of the British Slave Trade." *Past and Present* 143 (1994).

Dresser, Madge. *Slavery Obscured: The Social History of the Slave Trade in an English Provincial Port.* London: Continuum, 2001.

Edwards, Bryan. *The History, Civil and Commercial, of the British Colonies in the West Indies. In Two Volumes.* London, 1793.

Edwards, Paul. "Introduction." In *The Life of Olaudah Equiano. Or Gustavus Vassa, the African.* London: Dawsons of Pall Mall, 1969.

Edwards, Paul, and Rosalind Shaw. "The Invisible *Chi* in Equiano's *Interesting Narrative.*" *Journal of Religion in Africa* 19 (1989).

Edwards, Paul, and James Walvin. *Black Personalities in the Era of the Slave Trade.* Baton Rouge: Louisiana State University Press, 1983.

The Eighteenth-Century Short Title Catalogue (ESTC).

Eltis, David. "The Volume and Structure of the Transatlantic Slave Trade: A Reassessment." *William and Mary Quarterly* 58 (2001). Online at http://www.historycoopera tive.org/journals/wm/58.1/eltis.html. Accessed 19 February 2004.

Engel, Samuel. *Mémoires et Observations Géographiques et Critiques sur la Situation des Pays Septentrionaux de l'Asie et l'Amérique.* Lausanne, 1765.

Ennis, Daniel James. *Enter the Press-Gang: Naval Impressment in Eighteenth-Century Literature.* Newark: University of Delaware Press, 2002.

Equiano, Olaudah. *The Interesting Narrative and Other Writings.* Edited by Vincent Carretta. New York: Penguin Putnam, 1995; 2nd ed., 2003.

Estwick, Samuel. *Considerations on the Negroe Cause Commonly So Called, Addressed to the Right Honourable Lord Mansfield, Lord Chief Justice of the Court of King's Bench, &c. By a West Indian.* London, 1772; 2nd ed., 1773.

Extracts from the Minutes and Advices of the Yearly Meeting of Friends Held in London, from its first Institution. London, 1783.

Eze, Katherine Faull. "Self-Encounters: Two Eighteenth-Century African Memoirs from Moravian Bethlehem." In McBride, Hopkins, and Blackshire-Belay, *Crosscurrents.*

Falconbridge, Alexander. *An Account of the Slave Trade on the Coast of Africa.* London, 1788.

Falconer, William. *An Universal Dictionary of the Marine.* London, 1769; rev. ed., 1784.

Farrer, Katherine Eufemia, ed. *Correspondence of Josiah Wedgwood, 1781–1794.* London: Women's Printing Society, 1906.

Feather, John. *The Provincial Book Trade in Eighteenth-Century England.* Cambridge: Cambridge University Press, 1985.

Ferguson, Adam. *Essay on the History of Civil Society.* London, 1767.

Ferguson, Moira. *Subject to Others: British Women Writers and Colonial Slavery, 1670–1834.* New York: Routledge, 1992.

Fielding, Sir John. *Extracts from Such of the Laws, as Particularly Relate to the Peace and Good Order of this Metropolis.* London, 1768.

Fladeland, Betty. *Men and Brothers: Anglo-American Antislavery Cooperation.* Urbana: University of Illinois Press, 1972.

Fox, John. *The Acts and Monuments of the Church, or Book of Martyrs.* London, 1563.

Fox, William. *An Address to the People of Great-Britain, on the Propriety of Abstaining from West-India Sugar and Rum.* London, 1791.

Frey, Sylvia R. *Water from the Rock: Black Resistance in a Revolutionary Age.* Princeton, N.J.: Princeton University Press, 1991.

Fryer, Peter. *Staying Power: The History of Black People in Britain.* London: Pluto Press, 1984.

Fyfe, Christopher. *A History of Sierra Leone.* London: Oxford University Press, 1963.

Gardiner, Robert, ed. *The Line of Battle: The Sailing Warship 1650–1840.* London: Conway Maritime Press, 1992.

Gates, Henry Louis, Jr. "Introduction: The Talking Book." In Gates and Andrews, *Pioneers of the Black Atlantic.*

Gates, Henry Louis, Jr., and William L. Andrews, eds. *Pioneers of the Black Atlantic: Five Slave Narratives from the Enlightenment 1772–1815.* Washington, D.C.: Civitas, 1998.

Gay, John. *The Beggar's Opera.* London, 1728.

Gerzina, Gretchen. *Black London: Life before Emancipation.* New Brunswick, N.J.: Rutgers University Press, 1995.

Gifford, William. *The Baviad, a Paraphrastic Imitation of the First Satire of Persius.* London, 1791.

Gifford, Zerbanoo. *Thomas Clarkson and the Campaign against Slavery.* London: Antislavery International, 1996.

Gilroy, Paul. *The Black Atlantic: Modernity and Double Consciousness.* London: Verso, 1993.

Goldsmith, Oliver. *The Deserted Village.* London, 1770.

———. *An History of the Earth, and Animated Nature.* London, 1774.

Gomez, Michael A. *Exchanging Our Country Marks: The Transformation of African Identities in the Colonial and Antebellum South.* Chapel Hill: University of North Carolina Press, 1998.

Goodwin, Albert. *The Friends of Liberty: The English Democratic Movement in the Age of the French Revolution.* Cambridge, Mass.: Harvard University Press, 1979.

Graham, Jenny. *The Nation, the Law and the King: Reform Politics in England, 1789–1799.* 2 vols. Lanham, Md.: University Press of America, 2000.

Grainger, James. *An Essay on the More Common West-India Diseases. . . . To which Are Added, Some Hints on the Management . . . of Negroes.* London, 1764.

———. *The Sugar-Cane. A Poem.* London, 1764.

Grant, Douglas. *The Fortunate Slave: An Illustration of African Slavery in the Early Eighteenth Century.* London: Oxford University Press, 1968.

Gray, J. M. *A History of the Gambia.* 1940; reprint, New York: Frank Cass, 1966.

Green, James. "The Publishing History of Olaudah Equiano's *Interesting Narrative.*" *Slavery and Abolition* 16 (1995).

Griffin, Robert J., ed. *The Faces of Anonymity: Anonymous and Pseudonymous Publication from the Sixteenth to the Twentieth Century.* New York: Palgrave Macmillan, 2003.

Gronniosaw, James Albert Ukawsaw. *A Narrative of the Most Remarkable Particulars in the Life of James Albert Ukawsaw Gronniosaw, an African Prince, As Related by Himself.* Bath, 1772. In Carretta, *Unchained Voices.*

Gundara, Jagdish S., and Ian Duffield, eds. *Essays on the History of Blacks in Britain, from Roman Times to the Mid-twentieth Century.* Brookfield, Vt.: Avebury, 1992.

Hancock, David. *Citizens of the World: London Merchants and the Integration of the British Atlantic Community, 1735–1785.* Cambridge: Cambridge University Press, 1995.

Hanway, Jonas. *The Seaman's Faithful Companion.* London, 1763.

[Hardy, Thomas]. *Memoir of Thomas Hardy, Founder of, and Secretary to, the London Corresponding Society, for Diffusing Useful Political Knowledge among the People of Great Britain & Ireland, and for Promoting Parliamentary Reform, from its Establishment, in Jan. 1792, until his Arrest, on a False Charge of High Treason, on the 12th of May, 1794. Written by Himself.* London: James Ridgway, 1832.

Harlow, Laurence. *The Conversion of an Indian.* London, 1774.

Harris, John. *A Complete Collection of Voyages and Travels.* 2 vols. London, 1705; rev. and enlarged, 2 vols., 1744–48.

Harris, Raymund. *Scriptural Researches on the Licitness of the Slave-Trade, Shewing its Conformity with the Principles of Natural and Revealed Religion, Delineated in the Sacred Writings of the Word of God.* London, 1788.

Harrison, James. *Life of the Rt Honourable Horatio, Lord Viscount Nelson.* 2 vols. London, 1806.

Hecht, J. Jean. *Continental and Colonial Servants in Eighteenth Century England.* Smith College Studies in History, vol. 40, 1954.

Helms, Mary W. "Of Kings and Contexts: Ethnohistorical Interpretations of Miskito Political Structure and Function." *American Ethnologist* 13 (1986).

Henderson, Richard N. *The King in Every Man: Evolutionary Trends in Onitsha Society and Culture.* New Haven, Conn.: Yale University Press, 1972.

Henry, Matthew. *An Exposition of the Old Testament, in Four Volumes.* London, 1710; 8th ed., Edinburgh, 1772.

Hepper, David J. *British Warship Losses in the Age of Sail 1650–1859.* Rotherfield: Jean Boudriot, 1994.

Herbert, Charles. "Coxheath Camp, 1778–1779." *Journal of the Society for Army Historical Research* 45 (1967).

Heward, Edmund. *Lord Mansfield: A Biography of William Murray 1st Earl of Mansfield 1705–1793, Lord Chief Justice for 32 Years.* London: Barry Rose, 1979.

Hinterding, Erik, Ger Luijten, and Martin Royalton-Kisch. *Rembrandt the Printmaker.* London: British Museum Press, 2000.

Hoare, Prince. *Memoirs of Granville Sharp, Esq.* London, 1820.

Hoare, Sarah, and Hannah Hoare. *Memoirs of Samuel Hoare.* London: Headly Brothers, 1911.

Hochschild, Adam. *Bury the Chains: Prophets and Rebels in the Fight to Free an Empire's Slaves.* Boston: Houghton Mifflin, 2005.

Hogarth, William. *Credulity, Superstition, and Fanaticism. A Medley.* London, 1762.

———. *The Harlot's Progress.* Plate 2. London, 1732.

Hogg, Peter C. *The African Slave Trade and Its Suppression: A Classified and Annotated Bibliography of Books, Pamphlets and Periodical Articles.* London: Frank Cass, 1973.

Honour, Hugh. *The Image of the Black in Western Art.* Vol. 4, *From the American Revolution to World War I. Part I: Slaves and Liberators.* Cambridge, Mass.: Harvard University Press, 1989.

Howell, Colin, and Richard J. Twomey, eds. *Jack Tar in History: Essays in the History of Maritime Life and Labor.* Fredericton, N.B.: Acadiensis Press, 1991.

Hutchinson, Thomas. *The Diary and Letters of His Excellency Thomas Hutchinson, Esq.* Edited by Peter Orlando Hutchinson. Boston, 1886.

Isichei, Elizabeth. *A History of the Igbo People.* New York: St. Martin's Press, 1976.

——. Review of Paul Edwards, *The Life of Olaudah Equiano,* and Catherine Obianju Acholonu, *The Igbo Roots of Olaudah Equiano. Journal of African History* 33 (1992).

Ito, Akiyo. "Olaudah Equiano and the New York Artisans: The First American Edition of *The Interesting Narrative of the Life of Olaudah Equiano, or Gustavus Vassa, the African." Early American Literature* 32 (1997).

Jalloh, Alusine, and Stephen E. Maizlish, eds. *The African Diaspora.* College Station: Texas A&M University Press, 1996.

Jea, John. *The Life, History, and Unparalleled Sufferings of John Jea, The African Preacher. Compiled and Written by Himself.* Portsea, 1812? In Gates and Andrews, *Pioneers of the Black Atlantic.*

Jefferson, Thomas. *Notes on the State of Virginia.* Edited by William Peden. Chapel Hill: University of North Carolina Press, 1982.

Jefferys, Thomas. *The West India Atlas.* London, 1794.

Jennings, Judith. *The Business of Abolishing the British Slave Trade, 1783–1807.* London: Frank Cass, 1997.

——. "Joseph Woods, Merchant and Philosopher, and the Making of the British Anti-Slave Trade Ethic." *Slavery and Abolition* (1993).

Jewson, C. B. *The Jacobin City: A Portrait of Norwich in Its Reaction to the French Revolution 1788–1802.* Glasgow: Blackie & Son, 1975.

Johnson, Samuel. *Dictionary of the English Language.* London, 1755.

——. *Taxation No Tyranny.* In *Samuel Johnson: Political Writings.* Vol. 10 of *The Yale Edition of the Works of Samuel Johnson,* edited by Donald J. Greene. New Haven, Conn.: Yale University Press, 1977.

Jones, G. I. "Olaudah Equiano of the Niger Ibo." In Curtin, *Africa Remembered.*

Jones, Robert W. "Sheridan and the Theatre of Patriotism: Staging Dissent during the War for America." *Eighteenth-Century Life* 26 (2002).

Jordan, Winthrop D. *White over Black: American Attitudes toward the Negro, 1550–1812.* Chapel Hill: University of North Carolina Press, 1968.

The Journal of a Voyage Undertaken by Order of His Present Majesty, for Making Discoveries towards the North Pole, by the Hon. Commodore Phipps, and Captain Lutwidge, in His Majesty's Sloops Racehorse and Carcase. To which is prefixed, An Account of the several Voyages undertaken for the Discovery of a North-East Passage to China and Japan. London, 1774.

Kaufmann, Chaim D., and Robert A. Pape. "Explaining Costly International Moral Action: Britain's Sixty-Year Campaign against the Atlantic Slave Trade." *International Organization* 53 (1999).

Kemp, Peter. *The British Sailor: A Social History of the Lower Deck.* London: J. M. Dent, 1970.

Kingdon, John. *Redeemed Slaves.* Bristol, 1780?

Kitson, Peter J., and Debbie Lee, eds. *Slavery, Abolition and Emancipation: Writings in the British Romantic Period.* 8 vols. London: Pickering & Chatto, 1999.

Klein, Herbert S. *The Atlantic Slave Trade.* Cambridge: Cambridge University Press, 1999.

Klein, Herbert S., Stanley L. Engerman, Robin Haines, and Ralph Shlomowitz. "Transoceanic Mortality: The Slave Trade in Comparative Perspective." *William and Mary Quarterly* 58 (2001).

Koelle, Sigismund W. *Polyglotta Africana.* London: Church Missionary House, 1854.

Kulikoff, Allan. *Tobacco and Slaves: The Development of Southern Cultures in the Chesapeake, 1680–1800.* Chapel Hill: University of North Carolina Press, 1986.

——. "Uprooted Peoples: Black Migrants in the Age of the American Revolution 1790–1820." In Berlin and Hoffman, *Slavery and Freedom.*

Lamb, D. P. "Volume and Tonnage of the Liverpool Slave Trade, 1772–1807." In Anstey and Hair, *Liverpool, the African Slave Trade, and Abolition.*

Lambert, Sheila, ed. *House of Commons Sessional Papers of the Eighteenth Century.* Wilmington, Del.: Scholarly Resources, 1975.

Landau, Norma, ed. *Law, Crime and English Society, 1660–1830.* Cambridge: Cambridge University Press, 2002.

Lascelles, E. C. P. *Granville Sharp and the Freedom of Slaves in England.* London: Humphrey Milford/Oxford University Press, 1928.

Lasky, Melvin J. "The Recantation of Henry Redhead Yorke: A Forgotten English Ideologist." *Encounter* 41 (1973).

Latimer, Douglas A. "Black Resistance to Slavery and Racism in Eighteenth-Century England." In Gundara and Duffield, *Essays on the History of Blacks in Britain.*

Lauter, Paul, ed. *The Heath Anthology of American Literature.* 3rd ed. Boston: Houghton Mifflin, 1998.

Lavery, Brian. *The Arming and Fitting of English Ships of War 1600–1815.* London: Conway Maritime Press, 1987.

——, ed. *Shipboard Life and Organisation, 1731–1815.* Aldershot: Ashgate, 1998.

——. *The Ship of the Line.* 2 vols. London: Conway Maritime Press, 1984.

Linebaugh, Peter, and Marcus Rediker. *The Many-Headed Hydra: Sailors, Slaves, Commoners, and the Hidden History of the Revolutionary Atlantic.* Boston: Beacon Press, 2000.

Logerfo, James W. "Sir William Dolben and 'The Cause of Humanity': The Passage of the Slave Trade Regulation Act of 1788." *Eighteenth-Century Studies* 6 (1973).

[Long, Edward]. A Planter. *Candid Reflections upon the Judgement Lately Awarded by the Court of King's Bench, in Westminster-Hall, On What Is Commonly Called The Negroe-Cause.* London, 1772.

——. *The History of Jamaica . . . in Three Volumes.* London, 1774.

Lorimer, Douglas A. "Black Resistance to Slavery and Racism in Eighteenth-Century England." In Gundara and Duffield, *Essays on the History of Blacks in Britain.*

——. "Black Slaves and English Liberty: A Re-examination of Racial Slavery in England." *Immigrants and Minorities* 3 (1984).

Macalpine, Ida, and Richard Hunter. *George III and the Mad Business.* London: Allen Lane, 1969.

Markham, Albert H., ed. *Northward Ho!* London: Macmillan, 1879.

Marrant, John. *A Narrative of the Lord's Wonderful Dealings with John Marrant, a Black, (Now Going to Preach the Gospel in Nova-Scotia) Born in New-York, in North-America.* 2nd ed., London, 1785. In Carretta, *Unchained Voices.*

Marshall, P. J., ed. *The Eighteenth Century.* Vol. 2 of *The Oxford History of the British Empire.* Oxford: Oxford University Press, 1998.

Martyn, John. *Dissertations upon the Aeneids.* Edited by Thomas Martyn. London, 1770.

Mascuch, Michael. *Origins of the Individualist Self: Autobiography and Self-Identity in England, 1591–1791.* Cambridge: Polity Press, 1997.

Matthews, John. *A Voyage to the River Sierra-Leone, on the Coast of Africa; Containing an Account of the Trade and Productions of the Country, and of the Civil and Religious Customs and Manners of the People; in a Series of Letters to a Friend in England. By John Matthews, Lieutenant in the Royal Navy; During his Residence in that Country in the Years 1785, 1786, and 1787.* London, 1788.

Maxwel, John. "An Account of the Cape of Good Hope; by Mr. John Maxwell. Philosophical Transaction No. 310, p. 2423." In *Memoirs of the Royal Society; or, a New Abridgment of the Philosophical Transactions. . . . By Mr. [Benjamin] Baddam.* 3rd ed., London, 1745.

McBride, David, LeRoy Hopkins, and C. Aisha Blackshire-Belay, eds. *Crosscurrents: African Americans, Africa, and Germany in the Modern World.* Columbia, S.C.: Camden House, 1998.

McNeill, Hector. *Observations on the Treatment of the Negroes, in the Island of Jamaica, Including some Account of their Temper and Character, with Remarks on the Importation of Slaves from the Coast of Africa. In a letter to a Physician in England, from Hector McNeill.* London: Printed for G. G. J. and J. Robinson and J. Gore, Liverpool, [1788].

Merians, Linda E. *Envisioning the Worst: Representations of "Hottentots" in Early-Modern England.* Newark: University of Delaware Press, 2001.

Meyer, Arline. "Re-dressing Classical Statuary: The Eighteenth-Century 'Hand-in-Waistcoat' Portrait." *Art Bulletin* 77 (1995).

Meyers, Norma. *Reconstructing the Black Past: Blacks in Britain c. 1780–1830.* London: Frank Cass, 1996.

Midgley, Clare. *Women against Slavery: The British Campaigns, 1780–1870.* London: Routledge, 1992.

Miller, Joseph C., ed. *Slavery and Slaving in World History: A Bibliography.* 2 vols. Armonk, N.Y.: M. E. Sharp, 1999.

Milton, John. *Complete Poems and Major Prose.* Edited by Merritt Y. Hughes. Indianapolis: Hackett, 2003.

Minchinton, Walter, Celia King, and Peter Waite, eds. *Virginia Slave-Trade Statistics 1698–1775.* Richmond: Virginia State Library, 1984.

Mitchel, John. "Causes of the Different Colours of Persons in Different Climates." In *The Philosophical Transactions (From the Year 1743 to the Year 1750) Abridged and Disposed under General Heads. . . . By John Martyn,* vol. 10. London, 1756.

Mitchell, Austin. "The Association Movement of 1792–3." *Historical Journal* 4 (1961).

Morgan, Philip D. "The Black Experience in the British Empire." In Marshall, *The Eighteenth Century.*

———. *Slave Counterpoint: Black Culture in the Eighteenth-Century Chesapeake & Lowcountry.* Chapel Hill: University of North Carolina Press, 1998.

Myers, Norma. *Reconstructing the Black Past: Blacks in Britain, 1780–1830.* London: Frank Cass, 1996.

Nash, Gary B., and Jean R. Soderlund. *Freedom by Degrees: Emancipation in Pennsylvania and Its Aftermath.* New York: Oxford University Press, 1991.

Nelson, Horatio. "Lord Nelson's Memoir of His Services." In *The Life of Admiral Lord Nelson,* edited by James Stainer Clarke and John M'Arthur. 2 vols. London, 1809.

Newton, John. *Thoughts on the African Slave Trade.* London, 1788.

Nichols, Robert Boucher. *A Letter to the Treasurer of the Society Instituted for the Purpose of Effecting the Abolition of the Slave Trade.* London, 1787.

Nora, Pierre. "Between Memory and History: Les Lieux de Mámoire." *Representations* 26 (1989).

Northrup, David. "Igbo and Myth Igbo: Culture and Ethnicity in the Atlantic World, 1600–1815." *Slavery and Abolition* 21 (2000).

Norton, Mary Beth. "The Fate of Some Black Loyalists of the American Revolution." *Journal of Negro History* 58 (1973).

Nussbaum, Felicity, ed. *The Global Eighteenth Century.* Baltimore, Md.: Johns Hopkins University Press, 2003.

Nwokeji, G. Ugo. "African Conceptions of Gender and the Slave Trade." *William and Mary Quarterly* 58 (2001).

[Oglethorpe, James Edward?]. *The Sailors Advocate. First Printed in 1727–8. To which is now Prefixed, Some Strictures, Drawn from the Statutes and Records, Relating to the Pre-*

tended Right of Taking away Men by Force under the Name of Pressing Seamen. The Seventh Edition. London, 1777.

Ogude, S. E. "Facts into Fiction: Equiano's *Narrative* Reconsidered." *Research in African Literatures* 13 (1982).

———. "No Roots Here: On the Igbo Roots of Olaudah Equiano." *Review of English and Literary Studies* 5 (1989).

Oldendorp, Christian Georg Andreas. *Historie der caribischen Inseln Sanct Thomas, Sanct Crux und Sanct Jan, insbesondere der dasigen Neger und der Mission der evangelischen Brüder unter denselben.* Edited by Gudrun Meier, Stephan Palmié, and Horst Ulbricht. Dresden: Staatliches Museum für Völkerkunde, 2000.

———. *History of the Mission of the Evangelical Brethren on the Caribbean Islands of St. Thomas, St. Croix, and St. John.* Edited by Johann Jakob Bossard. Translated by Arnold R. Highfield and Vladimir Barac. Ann Arbor: Karoma Publishers, 1987.

Oldfield, J. R. *Popular Politics and British Antislavery: The Mobilization of Public Opinion against the Slave Trade, 1787–1807.* Manchester: Manchester University Press, 1995.

Oldham, James. "New Light on Mansfield and Slavery." *Journal of British Studies* 27 (1988).

Oliver, J. "William Borlase's Contribution to Eighteenth-Century Meteorology and Climatology." *Annals of Science* 25 (1969).

Paine, Thomas. *The Rights of Man.* London, 1791, 1792.

Paley, Ruth. "After *Somerset*: Mansfield, Slavery and the Law in England, 1772–1830." In Landau, *Law, Crime and English Society.*

The Parliamentary Register; or History of the Proceeding and Debates of the House of Commons; Containing an Account of the Most Interesting Speeches and Motions; Accurate Copies of the Most Remarkable Letters and Papers; of the Most Material Evidence, Petitions, &. Laid before and Offered to the House, during the Third Session of the Fourteenth Parliament of Great Britain. London, 1777.

Patterson, A. Temple. *The Other Armada: The Franco-Spanish Attempt to Invade Britain in 1779.* Manchester: Manchester University Press, 1960.

Patterson, Orlando. *Slavery and Social Death: A Comparative Study.* Cambridge, Mass.: Harvard University Press, 1982.

Patton, Philip. *Strictures on Naval Discipline and the Conduct of a Ship of War, Intended to Produce a Uniformity of Opinion among Sea Officers.* London: National Maritime Museum, ca. 1807.

Peckard, Peter. *Am I Not a Man and a Brother?* London, 1788.

Peel, Joshua. *Devout Breathings of the Soul to God, in Hymns and Spiritual Songs, in Two Parts. Composed by Joshua Peel, Preacher of the Gospel; on a Variety of Serious and Interesting Subjects, Relative to his own Experience and Enlarged Desire for the Glory of God, and the Salvation of all Men, which he now Publishes, Hoping they Will be of real Use for the Benefit of the true Church of God of every Denomination.* York: Printed for the Author by Wilson, Spence, & Mawman, 1793.

Phillips, Mark Salber. *Society and Sentiment: Genres of Historical Writing in Britain, 1740–1820.* Princeton, N.J.: Princeton University Press, 2000.

Phillips, Thomas. *A Journal of a Voyage Made . . . along the Coast of Guiney to Whidaw.* London, 1732.

Philmore, J. *Two Dialogues on the Man-Trade.* London, 1760.

Phipps, Constantine John. *A Voyage towards the North Pole: Undertaken by His Majesty's Command, 1773.* London, 1774.

Pierson, William D. *Black Legacy: America's Hidden Heritage.* Amherst: University of Massachusetts Press, 1993.

[Pitt, William]. *The Speech of the Right Honourable William Pitt, on a Motion for the Abolition of the Slave Trade in the House of Commons, on Monday the Second of April, 1792.* London, 1792.

Porter, Dale H. *The Abolition of the Slave Trade in England, 1784–1807.* Hamden, Conn.: Archon Books, 1970.

Porteus, Beilby. *A Sermon Preached before the Incorporated Society for the Propagation of the Gospel in Foreign Parts; at the Anniversary Meeting in the Parish Church of St. Mary-le-Bow, on Friday, February 21, 1783.* London, 1783.

Pratt, Samuel Jackson. *Humanity, or the Rights of Nature, a Poem; in Two Books. By the Author of Sympathy.* London, 1788.

Priestley, Joseph. *A Sermon on the Subject of the Slave Trade; Delivered to a Society of Protestant Dissenters, at the New Meeting, in Birmingham: and Published at their Request.* Birmingham, 1788.

Purver, Anthony. *A New and Literal Translation of All the Books of the Old and New Testaments; with Notes Explanatory. . . .* London, 1764.

Quarles, Benjamin. *The Negro in the American Revolution.* Chapel Hill: University of North Carolina Press, 1961.

———. "The Revolutionary War as a Black Declaration of Independence." In Berlin and Hoffman, *Slavery and Freedom.*

The Rabbits. London, 1792.

Ramdin, Ron. *The Making of the Black Working Class in Britain.* Brookfield, Vt.: Gower, 1987.

Ramsay, James. *An Essay on the Treatment and Conversion of African Slaves in the British Sugar Colonies.* London, 1784.

———. *An Inquiry into the Effects of Putting a Stop to the African Slave Trade, and of Granting Liberty to the Slaves in the British Sugar Colonies. By the Author of the Essay on the Treatment and Conversion of African Slaves in the British Sugar Colonies.* London, 1784.

———. *A Letter to James Tobin, Esq. Late Member of His Majesty's Council in the Island of Nevis.* London, 1787.

———. *Objections to the Abolition of the Slave Trade, with Answers. To Which Are Prefixed, Strictures on a Late Publication, Intitled, "Considerations on the Emancipation of Negroes, and the Abolition of the Slave Trade, by a West India Planter."* London, 1788.

———. *A Reply to the Personal Invectives and Objections Contained in Two Answers, Published by Certain Anonymous Persons, to An Essay on the Treatment and Conversion of African Slaves, in the British Colonies.* London, 1785.

Raven, James. *Judging New Wealth: Popular Publishing and Responses to Commerce in England, 1750–1800.* Oxford: Clarendon Press, 1992.

Rawley, James A. *The Transatlantic Slave Trade: A History.* New York: W. W. Norton, 1981.

Reader, John. *Africa: A Biography of the Continent.* New York: Knopf, 1998.

Rees, Alan M. "Pitt and the Achievement of Abolition." *Journal of Negro History* 39 (1954).

Regulations and Instructions Relating to His Majesty's Service at Sea. London, 1731; 5th ed., 1745; 8th ed., 1756, with *Additional Regulations and Instructions.*

Remarks on a Pamphlet, Written by the Reverend James Ramsay, M.A.: Under the Title of Thoughts on the Slavery of the Negroes, in the American Colonies. London, 1784.

Richardson, David. "The British Empire and the Atlantic Slave Trade, 1660–1807." In Marshall, *The Eighteenth Century.*

Robertson, William. *The History of America.* 2nd ed. London, 1778.

Rodger, N. A. M. Introduction to William Spavens. *The Narrative of William Spavens A Chatham Pensioner.* London: Chatham Publishing, 1998.

———. *The Wooden World: An Anatomy of the Georgian Navy.* London: William Collins, 1986.

Rodgers, Nini. "Equiano in Belfast: A Study of the Antislavery Ethos in a Northern Town." *Slavery and Abolition* 18 (1997).

Rogers, Nicholas. "Caribbean Borderland: Empire, Ethnicity, and the Exotic on the Mosquito Coast." *Eighteenth-Century Life* 26 (2002).

———. "Impressment and the Law in Eighteenth-Century Britain." In Landau, *Law, Crime and English Society.*

Rowlandson, Mary. *The Sovereignty and Goodness of God, Together with the Faithfulness of His Promises Displayed; Being a Narrative of the Captivity and Restauration of Mrs. Mary Rowlandson.* Cambridge, Mass., 1682.

Rozbicki, Michal J. "To Save Them from Themselves: Proposals to Enslave the British Poor, 1698–1755." *Slavery and Abolition* 22 (2001).

Sancho, Ignatius. *Letters of the Late Ignatius Sancho, an African.* London, 1782. Edited by Vincent Carretta. New York: Penguin Putnam, 1998.

Savours, Ann. *The Search for the Northwest Passage.* London: Chatham Publishing, 1999.

Segal, Ronald. *Islam's Black Slaves: The Other Black Diaspora.* New York: Farrar, Straus and Giroux, 2001.

Shakespeare, William. *The Riverside Shakespeare.* Edited by G. Blakemore Evans. Boston: Houghton Mifflin, 1997.

Sharp, Granville. *Free English Territory in Africa.* London, 1790.

———. *The Just Limitation of Slavery.* London, 1776.

——. *Memorandum on a Late Proposal for a New Settlement to Be Made on the Coast of Africa; Recommending to the Author of that Proposal, several Alterations in his Plan, and more especially the Adoption of the ancient Mode of Government by Tithings (or Decenaries) and Hundreds, as being the most useful and effectual Mode of Government for all Nations and Countries.* In *An Account of the Constitutional English Polity of Congregational Courts.* 2nd ed. London, 1786.

——. *A Representation of the Injustice and Dangerous Tendency of Tolerating Slavery; or of Admitting the Least Claim of Private Property in the Persons of Men, in England.* London, 1769.

——. *A Short Sketch of Temporary Regulations (Until Better Shall Be Proposed) for the Intended Settlement on the Grain Coast of Africa, near Sierra Leona.* London, 1786.

Shyllon, Folarin O. *Black Slaves in Britain.* London: Institute of Race Relations/ Oxford University Press, 1974.

——. *James Ramsay: The Unknown Abolitionist.* Edinburgh: Canongate, 1977.

——. "Olaudah Equiano: Nigerian Abolitionist and First National Leader of Africans in Britain." *Journal of African Studies* 4 (1977).

Sloane, Sir Hans. *Voyage to the Islands of Medera, Barbados, Nieves. S. Christopher's and Jamaica. . . .* London, 1707.

Smeathman, Henry. *Plan of a Settlement to Be Made near Sierra Leona, on the Grain Coast of Africa. Intended more particularly for the Service and Happy Establishment of Blacks and People of Colour, to Be Shipped as Freemen under the Direction of the Committee for Relieving the Black Poor, and under the Protection of the British Government. By Henry Smeathman, Esq. Who Resided in that Country near Four Years.* London, 1786.

——. *Some Account of the Termites, which are Found in Africa and other hot Climates.* London, 1781.

Smith, Adam. *An Inquiry into the Nature and Causes of the Wealth of Nations. . . .* London, 1776.

Smith, John Samuel. *A Letter from J. S. Smith to the Revd. Mr. Hill on the State of the Negroe Slaves. To which Is Added an Introduction, and Remarks on free Negroes, &c. By the Editor.* Edited by James Ramsay. London: James Phillips, 1786.

Smith, William. *A New Voyage to Guinea.* London, 1744; 2nd ed., 1745.

——. *State of the Gaols in London, Westminster, and Borough of Southwark. . . .* London, 1776.

Snelgrave, William. *A New Account of Some Parts of Guinea and the Slave Trade.* London, 1734; 2nd ed., 1754.

[Society for Effecting the Abolition of the Slave Trade]. *An Abstract of the Evidence Delivered Before a Select Committee of the House of Commons in the Years 1790 and 1791, on the Part of the Petitioners for the Abolition of the Slave Trade.* London, 1791.

Soderlund, Jean R. *Quakers and Slavery: A Divided Society.* Princeton, N.J.: Princeton University Press, 1985.

Southerne, Thomas. *Oroonoko.* London, 1695.

Southey, Robert. *Life of Nelson.* London, 1813.

Spavens, William. *The Narrative of William Spavens A Chatham Pensioner.* Louth: R. Sheardown, 1796; reprint, London: Chatham Publishing, 1998.

Stanfield, James Field. *Observations on a Voyage to the Coast of Africa, in a Series of Letters to Thomas Clarkson, by James Field Stanfield, Formerly a Mariner in the African Trade.* London, 1788.

Stanhope, Philip Dormer, Earl of Chesterfield. *The Letters of Philip Dormer Stanhope, 4th Earl of Chesterfield.* 6 vols. Edited by Bonamy Dobrée. London: Eyre & Spottiswoode, 1932.

Stedman, John Gabriel. *Narrative of a Five Years Expedition against the Revolted Negroes of Surinam.* London, 1796. Edited by Richard Price and Sally Price. Baltimore, Md.: Johns Hopkins University Press, 1988.

Sugden, John. *Nelson: A Dream of Glory.* London: Jonathan Cape, 2004.

Sussman, Charlotte. "Women and the Politics of Sugar, 1792." *Representations* 48 (1994).

Sypher, Wylie. "The African Prince in London." *Journal of the History of Ideas* 2 (1941).

———. *Guinea's Captive Kings: British Antislavery Literature of the XVIIIth Century.* Chapel Hill, N.C., 1942; reprint, New York: Octagon Books, 1969.

Thale, Mary. "London Debating Societies in the 1790s." *Historical Journal* 32 (1989).

Thornton, John. *Africa and Africans in the Making of the Atlantic World, 1400–1800.* Cambridge: Cambridge University Press, 1992; rev. ed., 1998.

Thorp, Daniel B. "Chattel with a Soul: The Autobiography of a Moravian Slave." *Pennsylvania Magazine of History & Biography* 112 (1988).

Tobin, James. *Cursory Remarks upon the Reverend Mr. Ramsay's Essay on the Treatment and Conversion of African Slaves in the Sugar Colonies. By a Friend to the West-India Colonies, and their Inhabitants.* London, 1785.

———. *A Farewel Address to the Rev. Mr. James Ramsay: From James Tobin, Esq. To Which Is Added a Letter from the Society for Propagating the Gospel, to Mr. Anthony Benezet of Philadelphia: and also a Translation of the French King's Declaration Relating to the Situation of Negroes, &c. in his European Dominions.* London, 1788.

———. *A Short Rejoinder to the Reverend Mr. Ramsay's Reply: With a Word or Two on Some Other Publications of the Same Tendency.* London, 1787.

Toplady, Augustus Montague. *Psalms and Hymns for Public and Private Worship. Collected (for the Most Part), and Published, by Augustus Toplady.* London, 1776.

Tracy, Nicholas. *Navies, Deterrence, and American Independence: Britain and Sea Power in the 1760s and 1770s.* Vancouver: University of British Columbia Press, 1988.

Turley, David. *The Culture of English Antislavery, 1780–1860.* London: Routledge, 1991.

Turnbull, Gordon. *An Apology for Negro Slavery: Or, the West-India Planters Vindicated from the Charge of Inhumanity. By the Author of Letters to a Young Planter.* London, 1786.

The Universal History. 65 vols. London, 1747–60.

Vaughan, Richard. *The Arctic: A History.* Gloucestershire: Alan Sutton, 1994.

Visram, Rozina. *Asians in Britain: 400 Years of History.* London: Pluto Press, 2002.

Wadstrom, Carl Bernhard. *An Essay on Colonization particularly applied to the West Coast of Africa with some free Thoughts on Cultivation and Commerce.* 2 vols. London, 1794.

———. *Observations on the Slave Trade and a Description of Some Part of the Coast of Guinea during a Voyage Made in 1787, and 1788, in Company with Doctor A. Sparrman and Captain Arrehenius.* London, 1789.

Walker, James W. St. G. *The Black Loyalists: The Search for a Promised Land in Nova Scotia and Sierra Leone, 1783–1870.* New York: Africana, 1976.

Walsh, Lorena S. "The Chesapeake Slave Trade: Regional Patterns, African Origins, and Some Implications." *William and Mary Quarterly* 58 (2001).

Walvin, James. *An African's Life: The Life and Times of Olaudah Equiano, 1745–1797.* London: Cassell, 1998.

———. *Black and White: The Negro and English Society 1555–1945.* London: Penguin, 1973.

———. *Fruits of Empire: Exotic Produce and British Taste, 1660–1800.* New York: New York University Press, 1997.

———. "The Impact of Slavery on British Radical Politics, 1787–1838." *Annals of the New York Academy of Sciences* 292 (1977).

———. *The Quakers: Money and Morals.* London: John Murray, 1997.

Ward, J. R. "The British West Indies, 1748–1815." In Marshall, *The Eighteenth Century.*

Washington, George. *The Writings of George Washington from the Original Manuscript Sources, 1745–1799.* 39 vols. Edited by John C. Fitzpatrick and David Matteson. Washington, D.C.: Government Printing Office, 1931–44.

Werkmeister, Lucyle. *The London Daily Press 1772–1792.* Lincoln: University of Nebraska Press, 1963.

Wesley, John. *Thoughts upon Slavery.* London, 1774.

Wheatley, Phillis. *Complete Writings.* Edited by Vincent Carretta. New York: Penguin Putnam, 2001.

Wheeler, Roxann. *The Complexion of Race: Categories of Difference in Eighteenth-Century British Culture.* Philadelphia: University of Pennsylvania Press, 2000.

Wiecek, William M. "*Somerset:* Lord Mansfield and the Legitimacy of Slavery in the Anglo-American World." *University of Chicago Law Review* 42 (1974).

Williams, Eric. *Capitalism and Slavery.* Chapel Hill: University of North Carolina Press, 1944.

Williams, Glyndwr. *The British Search for the Northwest Passage in the Eighteenth Century.* London: Longmans, 1962.

———. *Voyages of Delusion: The Northwest Passage in the Age of Reason.* London: HarperCollins, 2002.

Wilson, Ellen Gibson. *John Clarkson and the African Adventure.* London: Macmillan, 1980.

———. *The Loyal Blacks.* New York: Putnam's Sons, 1976.

———. *Thomas Clarkson: A Biography*. London: Macmillan, 1989.

Wilson, Thomas. *An Essay towards an Instruction for the Indians; Explaining the Most Essential Doctrines of Christianity. Which May Be of Use to Such Christians, as Have not well Considered the Meaning of the Religion they Profess; or, Who Profess to Know GOD, but in Works Do Deny Him. In Several Short and Plain Dialogues.* . . . London, 1740.

Winchester, Elhanan. *A Sermon against the Slave Trade*. London, 1787.

Wise, Steven M. *Though the Heavens May Fall: The Landmark Trial that Led to the End of Human Slavery*. Cambridge, Mass.: Da Capo Press, 2005.

Wood, Betty. *The Origins of American Slavery*. New York: Hill and Wang, 1997.

Wood, Marcus. *Blind Memory: Visual Representations of Slavery in England and America, 1780–1865*. New York: Routledge, 2000.

Woods, Joseph. *Thoughts on the Slavery of the Negroes*. London, 1784.

Woodward, Josiah. *The Seaman's Monitor, or Advice to Sea-Faring Men*. London, 1700.

Wooma, Ofodobendo (Andrew the Moor). "Lebenslauf." In Daniel B. Thorp. "Chattel with a Soul: The Autobiography of a Moravian Slave." *Pennsylvania Magazine of History & Biography* 112 (1988).

Wrigley, E. A. "A Simple Model of London's Importance in Changing English Society and Economy, 1650–1750." In *People, Cities and Wealth: The Transformation of Traditional Society*, by E. A. Wrigley. Oxford: Oxford University Press, 1987.

Zachs, William. *The First John Murray and the Late Eighteenth-Century Book Trade*. Oxford: Oxford University Press, 1998.

NEWSPAPERS AND PERIODICALS

Aberdeen Journal. 1792.

Analytical Review. 1789.

Annual Register. 1772, 1777.

Anti-Jacobin; or, Weekly Examiner. 1797.

Argus. 1789.

Aris's Birmingham Gazette. 1790.

Arminian Magazine. 1778–91.

Belfast News-Letter. 1791.

Birmingham and Stafford Chronicle. 1790.

Boston Gazette. 1772.

Caledonian Mercury. 1792.

Cambridge Chronicle and Journal. 1796.

Daily Advertiser. 1789.

Derby Mercury. 1791.

Diary; or Woodfall's Register. 1789.

Dublin Chronicle. 1791.

Edinburgh Evening Courant. 1792.

European Magazine. 1797.

Freeman's Journal (Dublin). 1791.

Gazeteer and New Daily Advertiser. 1792.

General Advertiser. 1789.

General Evening Post. 1792.

General Magazine and Impartial Review. 1789.

Gentleman's Magazine. 1750–1800.

Georgia Gazette. 1765.

Glasgow Advertiser and Evening Intelligencer. 1792.

Glasgow Courier. 1792.

Gloucester Journal. 1793.

Leeds Mercury. 1791.

London Advertiser. 1788.

London Chronicle. 1774–90.

Manchester Mercury, & Harrop's General Advertiser. 1790.

Massachusetts Spy: or, the Worcester Gazette. 1797.

Methodist Magazine (London). 1791.

Monthly Review. 1789.

Morning Chronicle, and London Advertiser. 1772–1800.

Morning Herald. 1786–97.

Morning Post, and Daily Advertiser. 1776–90.

Morning Post and Fashionable World. 1794.

Morning Star. 1789.

Newcastle Chronicle, or, Weekly Advertiser, and Register of News, Commerce, and Entertainment. 1792.

Norfolk Chronicle. 1794.

Northern Star (Belfast). 1791.

Norwich Mercury. 1794.

Oracle. 1792.

Pennsylvania Packet. 1774.

Political Magazine and Parliamentary, Naval, Military and Literary Journal. 1788–91.

Providence Gazette and Country Journal. 1797.

Public Advertiser. 1772–97.

Rambler. 1750.

Scots Magazine. 1772.

Sheffield Register, Yorkshire, Derbyshire, & Nottinghamshire Universal Advertiser. 1790.

Shrewsbury Chronicle. 1792.

Star. 1792.

Times (London). 1788–98.

Universal Magazine. 1791.

Virginia Gazette. 1752–55.
York Chronicle. 1791.

ARCHIVAL SOURCES

Additional Manuscripts, Francis Place Collection, British Library
John Audley Papers, Cambridgeshire Record Office
Banks Collection (A1:10), California State Library, Sutro Branch
Sir Joseph Banks Papers, 1786–92, Natural History Museum, London
Papers of Sir Joseph Banks (Series 73.028, 72.139), State Library of New South Wales
Binyon, Spriggs, and Other Worcester Family Papers, Worcestershire Record Office
Dickson, William. "Diary of a Visit to Scotland, 5th January–19th March 1792 on Behalf of the Committee for the Abolition of the Slave Trade," Library of the Society of Friends House, London
George Germain Papers, part of Brig. Gen. Jeffrey Amherst Papers, William Clements Library, Ann Arbor, Michigan
Gibson MSS, Library of the Society of Friends House, London
John Kemp's Commonplace Book, 1786, Library of the Society of Friends House, London
"Minute Book of the Committee of the Society for Effecting the Abolition of the Slave Trade," British Library
Minutes of Meeting for Sufferings, Library of the Society of Friends House, London
Minutes of the Committee on the Slave Trade, Library of the Society of Friends House, London
"MS Minutes Book of the Norwich Tusculan School, 27 Sept. 1793–2 May 1794," Norfolk Public Record Office
Plasterers' Company Records, Guildhall Library
Katherine Plymley Diary, Shropshire Record Office
Public Record Office (PRO), Kew, England
Admiralty (ADM)
Colonial Office (CO)
General Register Office (RG)
King's Bench Prison (PRIS)
Prerogative Court of Canterbury (PROB)
Privy Council Office (PC)
Treasury (T)
Treasury Solicitor (TS)
James Ramsay Papers, MSS BRIT EMP. S.2, Rhodes House Library, Oxford University
Granville Sharp Papers, Gloucestershire Record Office

Spriggs MSS, Library of the Society of Friends House, London
Thompson-Clarkson MSS, Library of the Society of Friends House, London
Journals of James Thompson Sr., 1758–1883 [*sic*], Archives nationales du Québec
Virginia Colonial Records Project Database, Library of Virginia
Josiah Wedgwood Papers, Keele University Library Special Collections

Equiano, Olaudah (*continued*)
of, with Europeans, 31; as freeman, 113–15,
131–33; and hiatus of two years, 192–93;
hopes and plans of, for freedom, 70, 82,
84, 86, 89, 103–6, 109–10; and Igbo
language, 10; illnesses of, 76–77, 108–9;
intends to build an altar in Elese to
Ramsay and Sharp, 266; languages of, 10,
47, 80; letters of introduction for, 335, 340,
345; meets Granville Sharp, 211; moves
from Soham to London, 364; opinion of,
on Pascal's mistresses, 91; opinions of, on
worldwide slavery, 115, 185, 237;
ordination application of, denied, 198–99;
political associations of, 345, 349;
purchases freedom from King, 113–15;
racist antagonists of, 327; reputation of,
after *Interesting Narrative*, 355; and rescue of
shipwrecked sailors, 179, 290, 323; returns
to London, 135–37, 142, 161–62, 165,
192–93, 202; Royal Navy service of, under
Pascal, 45–91; sale of, as slave, 25–26, 36,
37–38, 85–86, 95, 319; during Seven Years'
War, xi, 45, 53–70; in Shropshire, 201; at
siege of Belle-Île-en-Mer, 68–70; and
Sierra Leone resettlement project, 210,
224–30, 232–35; social relations of,
altered, 122–24; social status of, at sea, 53,
63, 68, 71–74, 323, 326; as stranger, 195;
subleases Plasterers' Hall rooms, 365;
subscribes to Wadstrom's work, 363; and
threat of impressment, 50–51, 357; Turkey
as possible home of, xiii, 164; as venture
capitalist in West Indies, 102–3, 111–12,
121, 126; victimization of, by confidence
man, 112–13; vindication of, by friends,
235; volunteers to go to Africa, 197–200,
336–37, 390n2; wealth of, 363–65; in West
Indies, 153, 190–91; will of, 336, 364–66,
392n38; *Zong* atrocity brought to Sharp's
attention by, 237–38. See also *Interesting
Narrative, The* (Equiano)
–birthplace/birth date of: according to
baptismal and naval records, xiv, 2, 8, 81,

319; according to *Interesting Narrative*, xi, 7,
319; as Africa, xi, 4, 197, 256–57, 263, 266;
disputed, xi, xvi, 319–20, 350–53; as Santa
Cruz (West Indies), 351–52; as South
Carolina, xiv, 2, 8, 81, 148, 319
–education of, 77–79, 80–82, 96–98, 105; as
able seaman, 121; in commodity
computation, 136–37; as hairdresser, 136;
and interest in Catholic education, 179
–employment of: as able seaman, 126–29,
133, 148; as clerk, 97–98; as domestic
servant, 193, 200, 210; as hairdresser, 137,
161; as Mosquito Shore plantation
manager, 184; as "powder monkey,"
65–66; as press-gang member, 51; with
Sierra Leone resettlement project, 223–26,
229–35; as steward/purser, 67–68, 210
–family of: Ann Mary (Maria; daughter),
363, 365–66, 392n41; Joanna (daughter),
xii, 363, 365–66, 392n40, 393n42;
children, xii, 217; parents, 8–10, 28–29;
sister, 17, 28–30, 73; unidentified in
Interesting Narrative, 315–16. *See also* Vassa,
Susanna Cullen (wife of Equiano)
–friendships of: with Baker, Dick, 45–46,
51–52, 73; with Baynes, Mrs. (Mary
Guerin), 353; with Bryant, 350; with
Farmer, 102–3, 105–6, 109, 112–14,
124–26; with Guerin family, 80–81; with
Hardys, 296–97, 336, 340, 347, 349–50;
with Irving, 137, 145, 148–50, 161, 179–80,
185, 192; and letters of introduction, 335,
340, 345, 354–56; and networking
opportunities, 297, 336, 340, 344, 360;
with Pascal, 4, 38, 52, 71–73, 84–90, 136;
as politically controversial, 345–47; with
Smith, George, 173; as substitute family
figures, 4, 45, 52, 71–73, 82, 86–90, 103,
121, 125–26; with Walker, George, 347
–identity of: as African, 320–21; as Atlantic
creole, xiii–xiv, xix, 367; dual, 292–93; as
Guinean, 3; as Igbo, 319; questioned by
media, 351; and race and ethnicity,
72, 74

Equiano, Olaudah (*continued*)
  Preston, 45–46; *Racehorse*, 144; *Roebuck*,
  45–55; *Royal George*, 59–60; *Savage*, 45–46,
  147; *Speedwell*, 132–33
—as slave: in Africa, 17–30; of Campbell,
  37–38; of Doran, 92–95; of King, Robert,
  95–114; on Middle Passage, 30–37; of
  Pascal, 39–72; of Whitwell, 53, 59
—voyages of: Arctic and northwest passage
  quest, 142–60; Barcelona, 49; Cádiz, 173,
  176, 179; Canada, 62–63; Canary Islands,
  61; Europe and Turkey, 137–40; Georgia,
  108–9, 112, 131–32; Gibraltar, 74; Guernsey,
  46, 72; Montserrat, 3, 92–103; New
  Providence, 13, 129–30; Philadelphia, 111,
  201; West Indies, 112, 121, 126, 140–42
Essay on Colonization, An (Wadstrom), 363
*Essay on the Slavery and Commerce of the Human
  Species, An* (Clarkson, Thomas), 3, 6, 33,
  253
*Essay on the Treatment and Conversion of African
  Slaves* (Ramsay), 244
Essay towards an Instruction for the Indians, An
  (Wilson), 81
Estwick, Samuel, 206
Ethiopian Regiment, 215
ethnography, of Igboland, 8–11
Europeans: as corrupting native peoples, 27,
  186; feared as cannibals, 31–32, 35, 43; as
  inhumane slave owners, 29
Evans, John, 55
*Extracts from the Minutes and Advices of the
  Yearly Meeting of Friends Held in London*, 241

Falconbridge, Alexander, 33, 36, 253,
  309
Farmer, Thomas, 101–26; death of, 124–25;
  friendship of, with Equiano, 101–6, 109,
  112–14, 121–26; as man of feeling, 116; as
  slave-ship commander, 101–2, 372n27;
  victimized by confidence man, 112–13
Fielding, Henry, 183
Fielding, Sir John, 88, 203–4, 380n4
Finnie, John Austin, 212

Fisher, R., 301
Floyd, Thomas, 144, 153, 158, 376n11
Fort Louisbourg, 40
Fothergill, John, 221–22, 239–40
Fox, Charles James, 255, 335, 348
Fox, George, 269, 384n57
Fox, Henry, 54, 58
Fox, John, 182
France: abolishes slave trade, 355; declares
  war on Britain and Holland, 355; defeats
  Britain, 54–55; and King George's
  War/War of Austrian Succession, 39–40;
  revolution of, and effect on abolitionist
  movement, 344; and Seven Years' War, xi,
  45, 53–70
Franklin, Benjamin, xiii, 193, 206
Fraser, Patrick, 223, 230, 234
Frederick the Great (Prussia), 21
freedom: by flight, 206–9, 380n6 (*see also*
  Mansfield decision); as precarious for
  Negroes, 119–20, 122–24, 237; purchased
  by Equiano, 113–15, 119–21
French and Indian War (Seven Years' War),
  xi, 45, 53–70

Gainsborough, Thomas, 287
Galgacus (Calgacus), 194–95
Gallia, Captain, 353
Galton, Samuel, 338
Gastelu, Captain, 185
Gates, Henry Louis, Jr., xiii
Gates, Horatio, 194
Gay, John, 322
gentlemen: as defined by Johnson, 322; and
  social dissonance, 321–23; social status of,
  at sea, 53, 63, 67, 71–74, 323
George (Mosquito prince), 182–83
George, David, 168, 216
George II, King (Britain), 54, 58–59, 68
George III, King (Britain): ascension of, 68;
  dissolves Parliament, 337; and Leicester
  House faction, 58; and Macnamara case,
  199; madness of, 275–76; and North Pole
  expedition, 143; orders Privy Council

investigation of slave trade, 2, 255, 263; and slave trade, 214, 240, 264

Georgia, 108, 131–32

Gibbon, Edward, 268, 269, 306

Gifford, William, 346

Goldsmith, Oliver, 14

Gough, Richard, 332

Grace Abounding to the Chief of Sinners (Bunyon), 325

Grainger, James, 309, 311

Green, Mr. (Methodist preacher), 72

Gregson, William, 238

Grignion, Charles, 285

Gronniosaw, James Albert Ukawsaw, 168, 217, 293, 299, 300, 324

Guerin siblings (Elizabeth Martha, Mary, Maynard), 80–81, 135–36, 353

Gurney, Hudson, 360–61

Gustavus Vasa, the Deliverer of His Country (Brooke), 41–42

Guthrie, Mr. (tailor), 198

Hackwood, William, 254

Hallowell, Mr. (bookseller), 273

Hamer, John, 133

Hammon, Briton, 217

Hammon, Jupiter, 168

Hanway, Jonas: heads Sierra Leone resettlement project, 223; *The Seaman's Faithful Companion,* 91

Hardy, Sir Charles, 200

Hardy, Lydia, 296, 340, 347, 349, 390n12; dies in pregnancy, 362

Hardy, Thomas: as cofounder of LCS, 296–97, 336; deleted from subscriber list, 354; and letter from Equiano, 350, 391n12; lodges Equiano, 340, 347, 350; tried for and acquitted of high treason, 362, 391n12

Hargrave, Francis, 206, 210

Harlot's Progress, A (Hogarth), 282

Harlow, Laurence, 171

Harmensen, Jacob (Jacobus Arminius), 166

Harrington, Countess of (Louisa Stanhope), 336

Harris, Raymund (Don Raymundo Hormaza), 253, 261

Harrison, John, 150

Harrison, William, 273

Harrop, James, 339

Hastings, Selina. *See* Huntingdon, Countess of (Selina Hastings)

Hawke, Sir Edward, 63, 65

Hawkesbury, Lord (Charles Jenkinson), 4, 255, 264

Hay, Edward, 277

Hay, George, 84

Henley, Robert, 85

Hill, John, 353

Hill, Patrick, 82

Hill, Sir Richard, 298

Hill, Rowland, 298

historiography: and autobiography, xvi–xvii, xviii, 115–16; and philosophical history, 306–7; and reliability of British Royal Navy records, 47; and research value of *Interesting Narrative,* 297, 308–9

History of the Mission (Oldendorp), 310

Hoare, Samuel, Jr., 220, 224, 243, 253; anti-slave-trade work of, 241; Equiano's animosity toward, 229–30, 234, 274; joins SEAST and London Abolition Committee, 251–52

Hochschild, Adam, xvi, 242

Hodgson, Robert, 180

Hodgson, Studholme, 68

Hogarth, William, 167, 217; and "stranger" motif, 282

Hogarth, William, works of: *Credulity, Superstition and Fanaticism,* 167–69, 280; *A Harlot's Progress,* 282

Hogflesh, Mrs. (subscriber), 336

Holburne, Francis, 51, 87–88

Homer, 327

Hopkins, Martin, 201

Hormaza, Don Raymondo (Raymund Harris), 253, 261

Pius VIII (pope), 178

Plan of a Settlement (Smeathman), 222

Plasmyah, Captain, 187

Plasterers' Hall, 365, 392n40

Plymley, Joseph, 355–56

Plymley, Katherine, 355

Plymouth Abolition Committee, 276

Poems on Various Subjects (Wheatley), 287

Poland, 21

polygenism, 244–45, 316–18

Pope, Alexander, 327

Porteus, Beilby (bishop of London), 243–44, 245, 263, 298

Pratt, Samuel Jackson, 263

Priestly, Joseph, 338–39, 347

Pumphrey, Stanley, 356

Purver, Anthony, 184

Quakers (Society of Friends): and abolition in America, 239; antislavery views of, 96, 241; Equiano's view of, 111, 162, 224–25; and lobby of Parliament against slave trade, 254; overview of, 95–96, 162–64; and Philadelphia school for blacks, 224; and poor relief in England, 220; support of, for resettlement project, 225

Quaque, Philip, 198–99

Queen (Quin), Daniel, 82, 84, 89

Queensberry, fourth Duke of (William Douglas), 336

Rabbits, The, 282–85

race: blacks as inferior, 23, 244–47; color of, affected by climate, 317–18; distinctiveness of, 21, 23, 375n8; versus ethnicity, 183; as justification for slavery, 23, 244–46; not a factor in seafaring, 72, 74–75, 126–31, 133, 147–48

Ramsay, James, 27, 243–51, 258–59, 263, 266, 268–69, 298; and accusations against Equiano, 234; advocate of, for West Indian slaves, 225; coins "Middle Passage" term, 17–18; as former slave owner, 245; as George Fox, 269, 384n57; praise of, for

Equiano, 384n57; praise of, for Sharp, 244; and Ramsay-Tobin pamphlet war, 245–47, 383n24; and Tobin, 260–61

Ramsey, James, works of: *Essay on the Treatment and Conversion of African Slaves*, 244; *An Inquiry into the Effects*, 247

Rawdon, Lord (Francis Rawdon-Hastings), 298, 337

Read, Mr. (Savannah merchant), 122–23

Reflections on the Revolution in France (Edmund Burke), 343

Regency Crisis, 276, 298

Regulations and Instructions, 81, 158

Remarks on a Pamphlet, 245

rendezvous houses, and impressment, 50

Representation of the Injustice, A (Sharp), 205

resettlement movement, in England, 219–35

Reynolds, Thomas, 273

Richardson, David, 371n18

Rigby, Edward, 361

Rights of Man (Paine), 343

Rivers, Baron (George Pitt), 200

Robertson, William (captain), 140

Robertson, William (historian), 306–7

Robinson, Thomas, 142

Robinson Crusoe (Defoe), 294, 325

Robson, James, 272

Roddam, Robert, 336

Rolfe, William, 365

Romaine, William, 168, 175

Roman Catholicism, 178–79, 182–83

Rose, George, 220, 223, 235, 298

Rowe, Walter, 275

Rowson, Susanna Haswell, 21

Royal Africa Company, 285

Sailors Advocate, The, 50, 372n9

Saint Croix, Chevalier de, 68

Samaide/Samoeid people, 116, 170, 375n8

Sancho, Ignatius, 193–96, 200, 209, 299; as Africanus, 193; as British patriot, 324; condemns American slavery, 215; denigrated by "Civis," 268; denigrated by Tobin, 246; lauded by Clarkson, 251;

Wakefield, Gilbert, 347

Wales, Prince of (Frederick), 68

Wales, Prince of (George), 216, 276, 297–98

Walker, George, 347, 348

Walker, James, 34

Walker, Thomas, 252, 340

Wallace, Thomas, 198–99

Wallis, Richard, 37

Walne, George, 297, 354

Walpole, Sir Robert, 41

Walvin, James, xii, xiv

War of Jenkins' Ear, 39

War of the Austrian Succession, 39–40

Washington, George, 24, 203, 215

Watson, Alexander, 37

Watt, David, 140

Wealth of Nations, The (Smith, Adam), 248

Wedgwood, Josiah, 338; and "Am I Not a
Man or Brother" seal, 253–54, 283, 285;
Equiano appeals to, for protection, 357; as
Interesting Narrative subscriber, 271, 385n1

Wells, Richard, 213

Welsh, Molly, 22

Wesley, Charles, 165

Wesley, John, 27, 165–70, 242, 298, 313; on
abolitionist movement, 240; *Thoughts upon
Slavery*, 169, 253

West, Benjamin, 63

West Indies, 93–134 passim, 140–42, 180–192
passim; colonial slaveholdings in, 19, 33,
94; and cultural practices of slaves, 141;
Equiano's enslavement in, 92–102; and
French colonies ceded to Britain, 94;
miscegenation laws in, 119; and
Montserrat's social climate, 93–94, 119–20;
slave revolts in, 141; slavery practices in,
140–41

Wheatley, Phillis, 168, 287, 294, 294, 299,
308, 324, 346–47; lauded by Clarkson,
251; portrait of, 287

Wheatley, Phillis, works of: "On Being
Brought from Africa to America," 170;
Poems on Various Subjects, 287; "To His
Excellency General Washington," 215

Wheble, John, 275

Whitbread, Samuel, 266, 298

Whitefield, George, 165–69

Whitwell, Matthew, 53

Wilberforce, William, 220, 251, 255, 277;
impugned in newspapers, 351; and slave
trade bill before House of Commons, 335,
337, 343, 348, 355

Wilkes, John, 298, 345

Wilkins, Thomas, 277

Wilks, Mark, 361

Willett, John, 201

Williams, Francis, 245, 324

Williams, James, 67

Wilson, Thomas, 81

Winchester, Elhanan, 336

Windham, William, 298, 359

Wolfe, James, 61, 63

Wollstonecraft, Mary, 331–33

Wood, Charles, 275

Woods, Joseph, 241–43, 245, 251, 253;
Thoughts on the Slavery of the Negroes,
242–43

Woodward, Josiah, 91

Wooma, Ofodobendo (Andrew the Moor),
310

Yarrington, William, 359

Yearsley, Ann, 308

York, Duke of (Frederick), 297

Yorke, Sir Philip, 85

Yorke, Richard, 147–48, 192

Yorke-Talbot opinion on slavery, 85,
205

Zong, 237–38, 246